THE CAMBRIDGE COMPANION TO
MODERN AMERICAN CULTURE

The Cambridge Companion to Modern American Culture offers a comprehensive, authoritative, and accessible overview of the cultural themes and intellectual issues that drive the dominant culture of the twentieth century. This companion explores the social, political, and economic forces that have made America what it is today. It shows how these contexts impact upon twentieth-century American literature, cinema, and art. An international team of contributors examines the special contribution of African Americans and of immigrant communities to the variety and vibrancy of modern America. The essays range from art to politics, popular culture to sport, immigration and race to religion and war. Varied, extensive and challenging, this Companion is essential reading for students and teachers of American studies around the world. It is the most accessible and useful introduction available to a exciting range of topics in modern American culture.

CHRISTOPHER BIGSBY is Professor of American Studies at the University of East Anglia. He has published some thirty books on British and American literature and is also a novelist and broadcaster.

THE CAMBRIDGE
COMPANION TO
MODERN
AMERICAN CULTURE

EDITED BY
CHRISTOPHER BIGSBY

CAMBRIDGE UNIVERSITY PRESS
Cambridge, New York, Melbourne, Madrid, Cape Town, Singapore, São Paulo

Cambridge University Press
The Edinburgh Building, Cambridge CB2 2RU, UK

Published in the United States of America by Cambridge University Press, New York

www.cambridge.org
Information on this title: www.cambridge.org/9780521601092

© Cambridge University Press 2006

First published 2006

Printed in the United Kingdom at the University Press, Cambridge

A catalogue record for this publication is available from the British Library

Library of Congress Cataloguing in Publication data

Bigsby, C. W. E.
The Cambridge Companion to Modern American Culture / Christopher Bigsby.
p. cm.
Includes bibliographical references and index.
ISBN-13: 978-0-521-84132-0
ISBN-10: 0-521-84132-1
ISBN-13: 978-0-521-60109-2 (pbk.)
ISBN-10: 0-521-60109-60 (pbk.)
1. United States – Civilization – 20th century. 2. United
States – Intellectual life – 20th century. 3. United States – Social
conditions – 20th century. 4. Popular culture – United States – History – 20th
century. 5. United States – Study and teaching. I. Title.
E169.1.B54 2006
973.9 – dc22
2006010014

ISBN-13 978-0-521-84132-0 hardback
ISBN-10 0-521-84132-1 hardback
ISBN-13 978-0-521-60109-2 paperback
ISBN-10 0-521-60109-6 paperback

CONTENTS

CONTENTS

CONTENTS

CONTRIBUTORS

CHRISTOPHER BIGSBY is Professor of American Studies at the University of East Anglia and Director of the Arthur Miller Centre for American Studies.

WILLIAM BROOKS is Professor of Music at the University of York.

PAUL BUHLE is Professor of American Civilization, Brown University, Rhode Island.

NATHALIE CARON is Associate Professor in the department of British and American Studies at the University of Paris 10 – Nanterre.

ROGER DANIELS is Charles Phelps Taft Professor Emeritus of the University of Cincinatti.

EMORY ELLIOTT is Professor of English at the University of California, Riverside.

JOHN HELLMANN is Professor of English at Ohio State University at Lima.

GODFREY HODGSON is Director of the Reuter Foundation Programme for Journalists, University of Oxford.

ERIC HOMBERGER is Professor of American Studies at the University of East Anglia.

NICOLÁS KANELLOS is Professor of Hispanic Literature at the University of Houston.

RICHARD H. KING is Professor of American Intellectual History at Nottingham University.

S.J. KLEINBERG is Professor of American Studies at Brunel University.

JAMES KYUNG-JIN LEE is Professor of English and Asian American Studies and Associate Director of the Centre for Asian American Studies at the University of Texas, Austin.

WALTER METZ is Associate Professor of Media and Theatre Arts at Montana State University, Bozeman.

BRENDA MURPHY is Professor of English at the University of Connecticut, Storrs.

ROBERT MCRUER is Professor of English at George Washington University, Washington, D. C.

KENNETH P. O'BRIEN is Professor of History at the State University of New York at Brockport.

PAUL OLIVER was Associate Head of School of Architecture at Oxford Brooks University, 1978–1988.

WADE CLARK ROOF is Professor of Religion and Society and Director of the Walter H. Capps Center for the Study of Ethics, Religion, and Public Life at the University of California, Santa Barbara.

WERNER SOLLORS is the Henry B. and Anne M. Cabot Professor of English Literature and Professor of African American and American Studies at Harvard University.

STEPHEN J. WHITFIELD is the Max Richter Professor of American Civilization at Brandeis University, Massachusetts.

HUGH WILFORD teaches in the Department of History, Sheffield University.

PETER W. WILLIAMS is Professor of Religion and American Studies at Miami University.

TIM WOODS is Professor of Literature at the University of Wales, Aberystwyth.

1900	William McKinley elected for a second term. One-dollar Brownie camera on sale.
1901	McKinley assassinated, Theodore Roosevelt assumes the Presidency.
1903	Panama grants canal rights to the United States. Henry Ford sells first Model A for 850 dollars. Boston beats Pittsburgh in the first Baseball World Series. Wright Brothers aircraft makes twelve-second flight. W. E. B. DuBois writes *The Souls of Black Folk*.
1904	Theodore Roosevelt re-elected. Steerage fare from Europe to America 10 dollars.
1905	W. E. B. DuBois participates in the Niagara Movement. William Benjamin Smith writes *The Color Line*.
1906	San Francisco School Board segregates Asian schoolchildren. San Francisco earthquake.
1908	Race riots in Springfield, Illinois. William Howard Taft elected. First Ford Model T produced.
1909	Robert Edwin Peary reaches North Pole.
1910	NAACP founded.
1911	Standard Oil broken up.
1912	Woodrow Wilson elected. Sinking of Titanic.
1913	Sixteenth Amendments allows income tax.
1914	First World War begins in Europe. Panama Canal opens.
1915	*Birth of a Nation* released. Death of Booker T. Washington. Sinking of the Lusitania.
1916	Wilson re-elected.
1917	United States enters First World War. Russian Revolution begins.
1918	Wilson's fourteen-points peace plan.

1919	May Day Bombing and the Red Scare. Eighteenth Amendment authorizes prohibition of alcohol.
1920	Majority of Americans now live in cities. Nineteenth Amendment gives votes to women. Warren G. Harding elected.
1921	Sacco and Vanzetti convicted of murder.
1922	Sinclair Lewis's *Babbitt* published.
1923	Calvin Coolidge assumes the Presidency following the death of Harding. Supreme Court rules on Adkins v. Childrens' Hospital. W. G. Cash writes *The Mind of the South*.
1924	Gershwin's *Rhapsody in Blue* released.
1925	Calvin Coolidge declares that "the business of America is business."
1926	Ernest Hemingway publishes *The Sun Also Rises*.
1927	Lindbergh flies Atlantic.
1929	Young Plan reduces German reparations. Wall Street crashes and Great Depression begins.
1930	US population 122 million. Grant Wood paints *American Gothic*.
1931	Scottsboro Boys case in Alabama. Empire State Building opens.
1932	Franklyn Delano Roosevelt elected. New Deal initiated.
1933	Agricultural Adjustment Act. National Industrial Recovery Act (N.I.R.A.). Tennessee Valley Authority. United States recognizes USSR.
1934	Huey P. Long starts Share Our Wealth Society. Bonnie and Clyde killed.
1935	The "Dust Bowl." Huey Long assassinated. N.I.R.A ruled unconstitutional.
1936	F. Roosevelt re-elected. Agricultural Adjustment Act ruled unconstitutional. Failure of Roosevelt's "Court Packing" plan to increase size of Supreme Court.
1937	Hindenburg explodes.
1939	Outbreak of Second World War. New York World's Fair. John Steinbeck publishes *The Grapes of Wrath*.
1940	F. Roosevelt re-elected. Ernest Hemingway publishes *For Whom the Bell Tolls*.
1941	Pearl Harbour. United States joins Second World War. Lend-Lease Act. Executive Order 8802 prevents racial discrimination in defense industry.

1942	Internment of Japanese Americans. Manhattan Project to develop atom bomb begins. Congress of Racial Equality. Battle of Midway founded.
1943	Race riots in more than forty-five cities. Rodgers and Hammerstein's *Oklahoma*.
1944	D-Day landings. Gunnar Myrdal writes *An American Dilemma*. F. Roosevelt wins fourth term.
1945	Death of F. Roosevelt. Harry S. Truman becomes President. Atom bombs dropped at Hiroshima and Nagasaki. UN Charter signed.
1946	George Kennan's "Long Telegram," an analysis of the Soviet Union. Churchill delivers "Iron Curtain" speech. G. I. Bill passed. Baby boom begins. Dr. Spock's *Baby and Child Care* published. Truman establishes President's Committee on Civil Rights.
1947	Establishment of Truman Doctrine, which promises support for countries threatened by communism. Marshall Plan established to rebuild European economies. HUAC hearings, including the "Hollywood 10." Construction begins on mass-produced "Levittowns." Jackie Robinson breaks baseball's color line. Chuck Yeager breaks sound barrier.
1948	The United States recognizes Israel. Berlin airlift. Executive orders desegregate armed forces and federal government.
1949	NATO founded. Russia explodes first Soviet A-bomb. Truman re-elected. Mao Tse Tung wins power in China. Arthur Miller stages *Death of a Salesman*.
1950	Korean War begins. Senator Joseph McCarthy makes first accusations.
1951	Truman dismisses General MacArthur.
1952	Hydrogen bomb tested. Dwight D. Eisenhower elected.
1953	Korean War ends. Death of Stalin. Julius and Ethel Rosenberg executed for espionage. *Playboy* magazine launched.
1954	Supreme Court rules on Brown v. Board of Education. Army–McCarthy hearings begin. Senate condemns McCarthy.
1955	Warsaw Pact established. G. L. Mehta – Indian Ambassador – refused service in restaurant. Rise of White Citizens' Councils. Montgomery bus boycott.

1956   Uprising crushed in Hungary. Launch of Interstate system. Suez crisis. Eisenhower re-elected. First appearance of Elvis Presley. *Invasion of the Bodysnatchers* released in cinemas.

1957   Sputnik launched. Martin Luther King elected leader of Southern Christian Leadership Conference. Little Rock crisis as Governor Orval Faubus attempts to prevent the desegregation of Central High School. Civil Rights Act.

1958   NASA created. US troops deployed to Lebanon.

1959   Castro comes to power in Cuba.

1960   Greensboro sit-ins. John F. Kennedy elected. Student Non-Violent Coordinating Committee created. Birth-control pill becomes available. Freedom rides.

1961   Bay of Pigs invasion of Cuba.

1962   Cuban missile crisis. Port Huron statement of Students for a Democratic Society. John Glenn orbits Earth in Friendship Seven.

1963   Kennedy assassinated. Lyndon Johnson becomes President. March on Washington for Jobs and Freedom.

1964   China explodes first A-bomb. Civil Rights Act. Gulf of Tonkin resolution following a supposed attack on the American destroyer *Maddox* by Vietnamese forces. Johnson elected. First American appearance of the Beatles.

1965   Johnson sets out plan for "Great Society." Watts Riot Voting Rights Act. Operation Rolling Thunder and troop escalation in Vietnam. Malcolm X assassinated.

1966   Black Power and Black Panthers appear. National Organization for Women established. Fulbright hearings on Vietnam.

1967   Summer of Love in Haight-Ashbury, San Francisco. Race riots in Newark, Detroit, and over 125 other cities.

1968   Tet Offensive. Martin Luther King assassinated. Robert Kennedy assassinated. Antiwar protests. Richard Nixon elected.

1969   Woodstock festival. Apollo 11 lands on Moon. Indian occupation of Alcatraz. Nixon administration begins affirmative action plan. My Lai massacre.

1970   Invasion of Cambodia. Kent State and Jackson State shootings.

1971   Pentagon Papers.

1972	Nixon visits China and Soviet Union. Watergate break-in.
1973	Paris agreement ends US involvement in Vietnam. Supreme Court rules on *Roe v. Wade*, permitting abortion. Vice-President Spiro Agnew resigns, Gerald M. Ford becomes Vice-President.
1974	Nixon resigns, Ford becomes President.
1975	Unemployment hits 8.5 percent. Indian Self-Determination and Education Assistance Act. Last Americans leave Saigon.
1976	Jimmy Carter elected.
1977	Elvis Presley dies.
1978	Supreme Court rules on *Regents of the University of California v. Bakke*: fixed racial quotas declared unconstitutional. Proposition 13 places cap on property taxes in California.
1979	Three Mile Island disaster at nuclear power plant. Camp David accords between Israel and Egypt. American hostages taken in Iran. Soviet invasion of Afghanistan.
1980	Ronald Reagan elected. Iranian hostages released.
1981	AIDS first noted in US. Interest rates rise to 21.5 percent. "Reaganomics" approved by Congress.
1982	Unemployment reaches 10 percent – highest since Great Depression. Ratification of ERA fails.
1983	Strategic Defense Initiative proposes a missile defense system. US Marines killed in Lebanon. United States invades Grenada.
1984	American aid to Contras in Nicaragua. Economic recovery. Reagan re-elected. Mikhail Gorbachev begins reform.
1986	Iran–Contra scandal (in which the proceeds of arms sold to Iran were used to finance the right-wing Contra guerillas in Nicaragua). Space shuttle Challenger explodes.
1987	Palestinian Intifada begins.
1988	George Bush Sr. elected.
1989	Berlin Wall falls. United States invades Panama.
1990	Collapse of communist regimes. Iraq invades Kuwait.
1991	Gulf War begins. USSR dissolves. Pan-American World Airways ceases flying.

1992	Riots in Los Angeles after verdict in Rodney King trial. Troops sent to Somalia. William Jefferson Clinton elected.
1993	Congress approves North American Free Trade Agreement. US Marines killed in Somalia, United States withdraws.
1994	Republicans claim majorities in House and Senate. Genocide begins in Rwanda. United States intervenes in Haiti.
1995	Oklahoma City bombing.
1996	Welfare Reform bill. Clinton re-elected.
1998	House votes to impeach Clinton.
1999	Senate acquits Clinton. NATO airstrikes in Kosovo. Anti-globalization protests at World Trade Organization meeting in Seattle.
2000	Longest economic expansion in nation's history. Supreme Court rules in favour of George W. Bush in disputed election.
2001	September 11 attacks on the twin towers of the World Trade Center in New York and on the Pentagon. Patriot Act. Enron scandal. United States intervenes in Afghanistan, Taliban regime falls.
2003	United States invades Iraq.
2004	George W. Bush re-elected.
2005	Retirement of Sandra Day O'Connor, first female Supreme Court Justice. Death of Chief Justice Rehnquist. New Orleans flooded as a result of Hurricane Katrina. Continuing occupation of Iraq.

I

CHRISTOPHER BIGSBY

Introduction:
What, then, is the American?

Every year, on March 22, Riverside, Iowa, celebrates an event that has not yet happened and never will. It is the place and date designated for the birth of Captain James Tiberius Kirk, Captain of the Star Ship Enterprise. America has so successfully colonized the future that it has mastered the art of prospective nostalgia. Its natural tense is the future perfect. It looks forward to a time when something will have happened. It is a place, too, where fact and fiction, myth and reality dance a curious gavotte. It is a society born out of its own imaginings.

There are those who believe they can remember alternative past lives. The science fiction writer Philip K. Dick claimed to remember a different present life. In his case it may have had something to do with amphetamines, but in fact we do inhabit different and parallel presents. The 1920s constituted the jazz age, except for those who tapped their feet to different rhythms. The 1960s were about drugs and rock and roll, except for the majority for whom they were not. Thoreau once wrote of his wriggling his toes in the mud of Walden Pond in search of the rock beneath. The search for a secure foundation is understandable but cannot always be satisfied. Nineteenth-century American writers dealt in symbols for a reason. Unlike the metaphor, the symbol suggested a field of meaning, an ambiguity which in the end perhaps could more truthfully capture a world in flux, desperate for clear definitions yet aware that in stasis lay a denial of, rather than a route to, meaning in a society wedded to the idea of possibility, always coming into being and never fixed.

Herman Melville's *Moby Dick* begins in a curious way. A late consumptive usher to a grammar school offers an etymology and a sub-sub librarian supplies a series of abstracts which together identify what is described as a "veritable gospel cetology," a seemingly comprehensive account of whales, their types, weight, size, reproductive habits. Detail after detail is offered as if thereby to reveal an undeniable truth. It is a mock taxonomy or, as Melville suggests, "a glancing bird's eye view." For what follows is a novel with the ultimate in floating signifiers, the great white whale that is Moby Dick, a screen onto which the characters project their own meanings in a novel in which identity is problematic. Even the narrator coyly refuses to define who he might be, offering instead a name which identifies him with an ancestor of twelve tribes but a name which also means "outcast." "Call me Ishmael," he suggests, as if mocking the desire for a true self and this in a novel about the wish to pin down, harpoon a singular meaning.[1] Here is Melville's allegory for the similar desire to stabilize America, identify what it might be and thereby define its citizens.

James Fenimore Cooper, another chonicler of an emerging country, created a protagonist who at one moment was the prosaic Natty Bumppo, then Long Rife, Leatherstocking, Hawkeye. Only the British soldiers in those novels, which track back near to the beginning of the American experience, were manifestly who they seemed. The American was legion. At the same time Nathaniel Hawthorne was creating his own fable of an ambiguous identity in *The Scarlet Letter*, in which the letter A, inscribed on the breast of Hester Prynne, offered as a definition by those intent to insist upon a singular meaning, is transformed by experience, this being the gift offered by a culture in which transformation is the essence. Call me Chillingworth, says her cold-hearted husband, implying that a name is no more than a convenience, as she suggests to her fearful lover that he could change his name and so liberate himself from his own past, liberation from the past being a national imperative.

At one moment America was to be self-evident fact; at another its virtue lay in its resolute refusal of definition. For Henry Steal Commager, writing in 1950, "Over a period of two and a half centuries, marked by such adventures as few other people had known, Americans had created an American character and formulated an American philosophy." However, "that character all but eludes description and that philosophy definition" even if "both were unmistakable."[2]

This was the existential space where existence preceded essence and yet essence was in a curious way assumed. No one knew what America would become and yet everyone assumed they knew it for what it was. America was a blank sheet on which her identity was yet to be inscribed. It was also a new Eden, undefined, yet one whose parameters were known because delineated in myth. It was simultaneously what it was and what it would become. It was the future and the past in the same moment.

To travel west was to travel back in time toward a primitive encounter with nature and to travel forward into a new land of possibility. The writers knew early that the essence of the country lay in a resistance to definition, hence their preference for symbols rather than metaphor. It was a kaleidoscope of shifting possibilities. At the same time the root meaning of the word "symbol" is "thrown together", so that there is the potential for this centripetal urge to terraform a country, improvise it into being, and improvisation has always been an American virtue and necessity. The ache to be clear about national identity and destiny was clear in encomiums to what did not in truth yet exist but along with this went a perception that this was a culture endlessly wedded to becoming, that being its special gift to the world, charged with a kinetic energy you could feel from across the oceans of the world but which could never discharge completely or it would lose its force.

In 2004, Bruce Springsteen, in explaining his reluctant decision to involve himself in that year's presidential election, remarked that in the aftermath of 9/11 "I felt the country's unity." He could not, though, "remember anything quite like it." Nor did the feeling last. The election, he suggested, was essentially about "who we are, what we stand for," though what that "who" and "what" might be was clearly no more evident to him than to those who had sung America a century and a half before, a Walt Whitman, say, who celebrated heterogeneity in what was offered as a national epic in which the narrative voice was an I that contained multitudes. "Why is it," Springsteen asked,

> that the wealthiest nation in the world finds it so hard to keep its promise and faith with its weakest citizens? Why do we continue to find it so difficult to see beyond the veil of race? How do we conduct ourselves during difficult times without killing the things we hold dear? Why does the fulfilment of our promise as a people always seem to be just within grasp yet for ever out of reach?

He may have been "Born in the USA" but the question remained, what is this thing, the USA?[3] That question has echoed down the corridors of American consciousness.

At 8.46 a.m. on September 11, 2001, a Boeing 767 American Airlines plane flying from Boston to Los Angeles, carrying eighty-one passengers and eleven crew, crashed into the North Tower of the World Trade Center in Manhattan. Seventeen minutes later, another 767, a United Airlines flight carrying fifty-six passengers and nine crew, also en route from Boston to Los Angeles, crashed into the South Tower. At 10.05 the South Tower collapsed, followed, twenty-three minutes later, by the North. In just one hour and forty-two minutes, 2,752 people died.

Those who had begun their day with a hurried kiss of farewell, thinking of no more than what they must do and their destinations, found this to be their last day on earth, never knowing why this should be so or that this was, indeed, their fate. After the sudden shock of flame, smoke drifted across the water, papers blew through streets rimed with dust, words unwriting themselves in the artificial night. People stood, unbelieving and yet not altogether unprepared. Figures began to fall, dwarfed by the scale of the buildings, as men and women chose to take their own lives rather than have them taken by fire, until the towers themselves fell inwards and down as if consuming themselves. It was, as many remarked, like a dream or a movie and this is why a unique event seemed to stir a sense of déjà vu. For the fact is that the towers had fallen before.

They had fallen in movies, in *Armageddon* and *Independence Day*. The visual rhyme was so precise and disturbing as to prompt the question of whether the terrorists had been filmgoers before they were killers of men and women. New York was the site of apocalypse on film long before it was in fact. The Manhattan skyline, symbol of modernity, had always carried the promise and threat of the future. The city experience itself, with its raw energy and reckless violence, its opportunities and corruptions, had always been viewed ambiguously. And for those who wished not only to challenge America's power but modernity itself, what better way to bring the country low, using nothing more advanced than box cutters and America's technology turned against itself. In the luna dust which swathed the broken buildings and streets, cell phones rang their jaunty tunes, never to be answered. Cars in station car parks stood abandoned, accumulating fines never to be paid. Individuals came forward to recount final calls from the doomed aircraft, love declared in the face of human dereliction. The twenty-first century, it seemed, was to be recursive. In the course of a hundred and two minutes, something had ended.

The Twin Towers were no more casually chosen than perhaps was the date. September 11 was the anniversary of the British mandate in Palestine and of George Bush Senior's proclamation of a "New World Order," just as the Bali nightclub bombing and the attack on the USS *Cole* took place on the anniversary of the opening of the Camp David peace talks between Egypt and Israel. In Washington, the Pentagon came under attack while almost certainly the White House was another target. Under assault were symbols of America's economic, military, and political supremacy. Those who launched the assault, far from seeing America as the new paradigm, rejected the very idea of its global primacy and in particular the presence in the Middle East (and especially in Saudi Arabia) of military units, which they saw as bridgeheads into Arab territory, and the export of cultural values, which they saw as at odds with their own. There were few at the time, however, inclined to look for rational explanations of a seemingly irrational action. Indeed, the very attempt to do so seemed akin to believing that there could be a justification for the unthinkable. The response was less analytical than visceral.

America's primary response was bewilderment. What cause could be served by mass murder? Why would America, which saw itself as carrying the torch of freedom, as a model for the world, custodian of the future, be targeted in this way? Flags flew from every building, house, car, truck. Church services were held. New heroes were identified and celebrated. Money was raised. For a brief while the world offered sympathy and shared in the agony. But the question was, where was the enemy and how might it be brought low?

Americans were so many trauma victims. They had been injured but the full pain had yet to register. People wandered the streets, covered in grey dust, like living statues, survivors of Pompeii. Soon, trucks began to make their way through the streets, gathering up the rubble of broken lives along with the concrete and steel, the smashed computers, memories wiped, screens broken or blank. Yet behind this, often unspoken, because at such a moment some things may not be spoken, there were other questions, questions about national purpose and identity, the fate of the Great Experiment.

Many had expected the millennium to precipitate apocalypse, to mark the passing of the American Century. In the end the gestation of disaster lasted nearly a full nine months longer but when it came it went far further than the fear that computers would reset their internal clocks to 1900, though America's future has always tended to be seen in terms of its past, with references to a dream first dreamed centuries ago and to a frontier closed for more than a hundred years. Suddenly, the future seemed occluded, cataracted over with pain. America's most intelligent television drama, *The West Wing*, scrapped its season premiere. Its stars stepped out of character to solicit funds for those who had suffered before staging a fictional debate between White House staffers and a group of high school students on a visit whose first question is "why is everybody trying to kill us?" Its determinedly liberal scriptwriter tried his best to explain, warned against intolerance, but the effect, though worthy, was inert. Later, 24, a taut adventure series, envisaged a group of Americans hiding behind supposed terrorists in order to provoke a Middle East war. The evidence is fraudulent. The war is stopped. Except that it was not. A real war was launched on Iraq before the series had finished shooting. Creators of fiction tried desperately to insist on complexity. Devisers of national policy settled for something altogether simpler.

Who are we, many asked, that others should seek our lives? What is this America that they believe they know well enough to wish its end? And such questions had the force they did because they were questions which had been asked before.

Since this was a country that had long believed itself the trailblazer, the pathfinder, the pioneer of modernity, why were there those who not merely refused to follow the yellow brick road to paradise but instead chose death, their own no less than that of their victims, as a route to a paradise which owed nothing to freedom of speech and assembly, to liberal democracy or material prosperity? Beneath the confident recommitment to familiar principles, the announcement of a new Pax Americana, to be enforced by the military might of the world's only superpower, was a series of troubling questions, questions whose answers would have taken them back, if that were a direction Americans liked to go. What is America? Who are Americans? What is this culture they have forged? What is the future toward which they march? And what of those who march to a different drummer? This book is hardly designed to answer those questions but in looking back over a hundred or so years it does attempt to explore some aspects of a country and its culture which are a central fact of the modern experience.

Writing in 1782, just six years after the establishment of the new Republic, Hector St. John de Crevecoeur asked a question that has hardly lost its cogency with the centuries: "What, then, is the American, this new man?" He offered an answer. "He is an American," he explained,

> who, leaving behind him all his ancient prejudices and manners, receives new ones from the new mode of life he has embraced, the new government he obeys, and the new rank he holds. He becomes an American by being received in the broad lap of our great Alma Mater. Here individuals of all nations are melted into a new race of men whose labours and posterity will one day cause great changes in the world. Americans are the western pilgrims who are carrying along with them that great mass of arts, sciences, vigour, and industry which began long since in the East; they will finish the great circle.[4]

What he offered, however, was largely a process not an identity, a destiny rather than a description. His confidence in that destiny, though, was shared half a century later by another French observer.

Writing in 1835, Alexis de Tocqueville was entirely convinced that, "whatever they do, the Americans of the United States will turn into one of the greatest nations of the world . . . One day wealth, power, and glory cannot fail to be theirs." Admittedly, he was not right about everything. He insisted, for example, that lawyers formed "the only enlightened class not distrusted by the people."[5] For the most part, though, he was an excellent analyst and fair prophet. He predicted that by 1935, 100 years later, there would be 100 million Americans living in 40 states and that one day the figure would reach 150 million sharing the same religion and language. In fact the twentieth century began with a population of 72,212,168, which rose by the year 2000 to 281,421,906 (the population not only growing in numbers but weight, gaining ten pounds each during the 1990s, causing airlines to use an additional 350 million gallons of fuel releasing an additional 3.8 million tons of carbon dioxide into the atmosphere), while in 1935 there were 48 states and a population of 127,250,272. He was not, then, so far off. Nor was he wrong about the religion and (until the late twentieth century) the language. For him, slavery aside, the restless and threatening power of the majority aside, the new country's insufferably high opinion of itself aside, the fact that the President seemed to place re-election higher in his priorities than public service aside, America was a good news story. At a time when its myths were still in the making, he was ready to acknowledge the substance behind those myths. America was, indeed, he insisted, about freedom and opportunity and he celebrated the new country.

What is a culture? It is, as the dictionary (*Chambers*) helpfully tells us, "the total of the inherited ideas, beliefs, values, and knowledge, which constitute the shared bases of social action, the total range of activities and ideas of a group of people with shared traditions, which are transmitted and reinforced by members of the group." All of which makes the idea of capturing it in a single volume a touch presumptuous. More simply, it is "a particular civilization at a particular period." It is also, though, in a more restricted sense, "the artistic and social pursuits, expression, and tastes valued by a society or class as in the arts, manners, dress, etc."

What is the modern? The same dictionary (*Chambers*) insists it is the historical period beginning with the Middle Ages, which would make Chaucer our contemporary and the Black Death headline news. More plausibly, it dates from those Enlightenment values which characterized eighteenth-century England and France and which made their way into American thought, indeed most conspicuously into the American Constitution. In that sense, the modern experience is coterminous with the American experience. Such values stressed the politics of liberty, on a personal and social level, and in America, certainly, religious tolerance (though scarcely in the original Puritan settlement) and a certain moral strenuousness, neither tolerance nor religion coming high on the list in revolutionary France. It is not hard to see how this gave birth to classic nineteenth-century liberalism, to a practical stress on the self-made man, on private charity, and, indeed, to an emphasis on capitalism, whose excesses would eventually be contained by a social ethic which was itself a product of the Enlightenment.

Such a definition of the modern, however, would in effect call for a history of America and that is not what follows. For the purposes of this study, then, I have chosen to define the modern more narrowly, focusing on the twentieth century while taking both a broad and a narrow definition of culture. This, in other words, is an attempt to explore what once used to be called American civilization. It is an effort to understand America and its cultural products. It is not a book about modernism, though that was one expression of a self-conscious modernity, but about the modern, and for much of the twentieth century America was seen as the embodiment of that, so much so that for some the two became confused to the point that what was often described as Americanization was in truth modernity, whose wave first broke on the American shore. This is a study which moves us from a time when America was regarded as marginal to the political, economic, and artistic world to a moment, a few years into the twenty-first century, when it had become the only superpower, when its cultural products were ubiquitous and when it had invaded the consciousness of virtually everyone on the planet.

Quite the most contentious aspect of the title of this book, though, lies in that word "American," not simply because it seems to arrogate to a single country the name of a continent but because its very identity has always been the subject of debate and because to Janice Radway – the President-elect of the American Studies Association, speaking in 1998 – the word seemed to homogenize what was in effect a series of groups previously disempowered and ignored by such a seemingly singular designation. To Daniel Bell, in *The End of Ideology*, America is a cluster of meanings and to ask what its secret might be "is to pose a metaphysical question whose purpose is either ideological or mythopoeic." The emergence in the postwar world of something called American studies was, to his mind, simply an attempt to prove to the rest of the world "that America has a culture too,"[6] itself an observation that betokens the self-doubt which he seems to be attacking.

In fact, American studies had its roots before the war and displayed, at least originally, a confident conviction that America could be located through a study of its history, literature, and values even if its originators, in the late 1930s, saw a contradiction between capitalism and the principles on which the country had been founded. In other words, here was an academic movement which still believed that the culture could be explained to itself but whose members were simultaneously in contention with its then current direction. This was how communism could be seen as twentieth-century Americanism, the slogan which a young Leo Marx (author of *The Machine in the Garden*, 1964, and later to be Chair of the American Studies

Association) saw on the huge banner above a meeting of the Communist Party USA in the Boston Garden, in 1939, a meeting addressed by Earl Browder, Chairman of the Party. And Marx was a regular attender of Party meetings just as was a historian, Daniel Boorstin, later to become the Librarian of Congress. Others, such as Henry Nash Smith (*Virgin Land: The American West as Myth and Symbol*, 1950) and Daniel Aaron (*Writers on the Left*, 1974), were also of the Left. F. O. Matthiessen (*American Renaissance*, 1941) was a socialist. Their confidence in ideology would falter but not their belief in the academic project to which they were wedded. They believed there was a definable America to be addressed. By 1998, however, things had changed. Janice Radway proposed that the word "American" should be struck from the American Studies Association's title because it implied an homogeneity that could no longer be sustained. Her America had dissolved into subgroups which had no desire to be thought of as such. America had been a kind of surrogate mother and the time had come to acknowledge that the offspring had no necessary organic connection but were, like Gatsby, their own Platonic creations.

It is not, it should be said, how most outsiders saw America. From a distance it was not difference which first struck observers. Just as in 1969 the planet had been viewed for the first time from space, whole and entire, so from elsewhere America seemed entirely defined and definable, and sometimes threateningly so.

America is a country built on contradictions. Imperial in origin, it has remained such ever since, yet seldom if ever confesses as much. It is a secular state suffused with religion, a puritan culture in love with pornography (all expensive hotels will have a Gideon Bible – 112 of which were placed in them every minute in 2004) and pornographic movies, the one free, the other being discretely labeled on hotel checks so as to keep a guilty secret. Fifty percent of hotel guests pay for pornographic films while, in 2004, Godfrey Hodgson tells us, 11,000 "adult films" were released. America gave the world *Playboy* magazine, its first "Playmate" featuring Marilyn Monroe. America pioneered the topless and bottomless bar (there is even a plaque celebrating the latter) even as, if statistics mean anything, those watching in-house porn, purchasing "adult magazines" and, increasingly, visiting pornographic websites, dutifully go to church on a Sunday, no doubt to repent of such actions. Indeed, the *Atlanta Journal-Constitution*'s "Faith and Values" section (itself evidence of the religious orientation of its readers) brought news of "The Christian Porn Site" (www.xxxChurch.com) which offered advice to Christians trying to resist pornography. It marketed an online programme called "30 days to purity" and software that could notify a partner whenever a porn site has been visited.[7] It was, seemingly, an uphill task. In 2004 one software management company had 16 million adult web pages on its database, raising the question of what the word "adult" might mean.

America celebrates the individual yet its citizens are, as Sinclair Lewis observed, always joining clubs, cults, goodfellow societies, teams (though Godfrey Hodgson notes that in the last decade of the twentieth century this process would seemingly decline, marking a withdrawal from communalism) while, as de Toqueville noted, there is a constant risk of a tyranny of the majority ("If ever freedom is lost in America, blame will have to be laid at the door of the omnipotence of the majority.")[8] The standardization against which Lewis had warned in *Babbitt* remains as evident in the twenty-first century in everything from food and coffee through hotels and stores to clothes and television programmes. The salesman with prostate problems who visits the lavatory (never called such of course) in the middle of the night in a Holiday Inn need never open his eyes. The bathroom and the toilet will always be reliably in the same place.

In its films America is drawn to apocalypse provided it is followed by redemption. It weds violence to sentimentality, invincibility to vulnerability. America celebrates the family while for every two marriages there is one divorce. Ronald Reagan reaffirmed the iconic status of the family, despite his own dysfunctional one. America is presented as a City on the Hill, a model for good practice (with First Amendment rights and due process) while abandoning such good practice when under pressure (the internment of Japanese Americans in World War II; the witchhunts of the 1950s; the Patriot Act of the twenty-first century). It is a country with its eyes set on the future but whose utopia is Eden, to be located in a mythic past. All men, it declares, are created equal, even as the gap between the rich and the poor or, indeed, the middle class, grows ever wider (Godfrey Hodgson points out that between 1989 and 1997 the share of wealth owned by the top 1 percent of American households grew from 37.4 percent to 39.1 percent while the total share in the national wealth of the middle fifth of American families fell from 4.8 percent to 4.4 percent).[9] According to the United States Census Bureau, in 2003, 35.9 million Americans (roughly the equivalent of the population of California) were living below the poverty line, representing 12.5 percent of the population, up from 11.3 percent in 2000. Its national dream speaks of the move from poverty to wealth yet as Hodgson has pointed out, in 1994 the United States had the highest poverty rate of sixteen developed countries and the second lowest rate of escape from poverty.[10]

It has the best and the worst health care in the world, depending on income and location, though in 1999 the infant mortality rate was higher than that of the United Kingdom, Belgium, Italy, France, Ireland, Denmark, New Zealand, Canada, and a dozen other countries[11] while World Health Organization figures released in June 2000 placed the United States twenty-fourth in terms of life expectancy in a list of 191 countries, once again falling behind several European countries, Japan, and Canada.[12] In 2003, 45 million Americans lacked health insurance, representing 15.6 percent of the population, an increase of 6.3 million in four years. Pro life advocates murder doctors to indicate their commitment to that life. America places children at the center of its concern and sanctions the sale of weapons which kill them in high school shootings, drive-by murders, and suicides. The death of 58,000 Americans ended the Vietnam War. The death of getting on for 3,000 in the Twin Towers traumatized the nation on September 11, 2001, as had the deaths of 6,000 who died on September 17, 1862 in the Battle of Antietam/Sharpsburg in the Civil War. Every year, though, 30,000 Americans die of gunshots, 18,000 of those suicides, those for whom the pursuit of happiness proved too much to bear. In 2002, 442,880 victims of violent crimes stated that they had faced an offender with a firearm, while 67 percent of the 16,204 murders committed involved a firearm. For a country so desperate to be at peace with itself, violence is a fact of daily life, which is perhaps scarcely surprising when 48 percent of voters in the 2000 election were gun owners, believing that the possession of deadly weapons is a birthright sanctioned by a constitutional amendment which speaks of the need for a well-regulated militia as if the British might at any moment send scarlet-coated soldiers marching towards Concord.

A country anxious above all to celebrate freedom imprisons a greater proportion of its citizens than any other democracy (702 per 100,000 in 2001, according to the Bureau of Statistics, compared with a European average of 88 per 100,000. The figure for France was 91). A disproportionate number of these were black (10.4 percent of African Americans were in prison in 2002, compared with 1.2 percent of whites and 2.4 percent of Hispanics; 46 percent of prisoners were African American), while unlike other democracies it enforced capital punishment by gun, rope, or lethal injection (between 1976 and 2004, according to the Death Penalty Information Center in Washington, 732 have died by injection, 151 by electrocution, 11 by gas, 3 by hanging and 2 by firing squad).

America is undeniably a shape-shifting culture which for all its assurance and power has never ceased to explore and question its own coherence, not least when it insists that coherence to be self-evident. The indivisible country celebrated in the oath of allegiance is the country in which John Brown once set out to "purge this land with blood" and in which, today, difference is a talismanic slogan for some and the source of a deepening anxiety for others.

America is always in the making. Like Arthur Miller's Willy Loman, it is always "kind of temporary," tearing its buildings down to construct new ones, consigning history to the garbage can as if its true function were as harbinger, the trailing edge of tomorrow. Godfrey Hodgson has reminded us that the motto of Microsoft is "Attack the Future," and certainly no other society is so invested in the future as if it contained a meaning which, Godot-like, would one day reveal itself and retrospectively flood the present with true significance. The names of two of Eugene O'Neill's characters in *The Iceman Cometh* are Harry Hope and Jimmy Tomorrow. They are ironic names because these two fear the future. They are betrayers of the dream in dreaming of their yesterdays. The culture does not. President Clinton never tired of telling people that he came from a small town called Hope. A slogan of the Democratic National Convention in 2004 declared "Hope is on the way," as if a concept that involved a deferred realization was itself to be deferred. It was not that good times were on the way but that the possibility of good times was on the way. Perhaps for a puritan society happiness itself smacks a little too much of hedonism. The pursuit of happiness implies that a certain rigorous commitment will be needed before the birth of delight. Americans are, on the whole, not susceptible to the idea that hope might be the source of an absurdist irony. It was, after all, the last element in Pandora's box and for Beckett, heir to a post-Holocaust world, an essential component of a bone-deep irony which left the individual profoundly vulnerable, always looking for a revealed purpose denied by the blank face of a cold universe. Such ideas, the wasteland sensibility of the modernists aside, could never take root in a society born out of imagined possibilities.

Alternately retreating behind its own borders, as if it had no need of the world, and reaching out, consciously or otherwise, to mold the world to its own image, it is the modern, admired and detested, the pointman, vulnerable as pointmen are, determinedly avant-garde in the arts if not in the soul, in love with technology even while treasuring the idea of simpler times and forms. It is inventing the world we will all inhabit and hence is an unavoidable fact. It is deeply admired by many and profoundly disliked by others. It bears the marks of the past it affects to despise while its belief in a transformed future offers hope to those who despair of the change for which they hunger.

Daniel Bell draws attention to the ambiguous encomium offered by Max Lerner in his oddly named *America as a Civilization*. The American, he insists, is the double figure in Marlowe of Tamerlane and Dr. Faustus, the one sweeping like a foot-loose barbarian across the plains to overleap the barriers of early civilization, the other breaking the taboos against knowledge and experience, even at the cost of his soul . . . Thus the great themes of the Renaissance and Reformation are fulfilled in the American as the archetypal modern man – the discovery of new areas, the charting of skies, the lure of power, the realization of self in works, the magic of science, the consciousness of the individual, the sense of the unity of history.[13]

So, the American is the very epitome of the modern, prepared, moreover, to risk his soul to lead us into the future, some ultimate synthesis of historic process if contemptuous of that process as mere precursor to this hybrid figure who will surely be spared Faustus's fate because his is a disinterested endeavor.

In *Foreign Policy* magazine in 2004, an extract from Samuel Huntington's *Who Are We?* was entitled, "José, Can You See?" The joke turned on the fact that Huntington was warning against the United States losing its identity as immigration, legal and illegal, from Latin America, Cuba, Puerto Rico, the Dominican Republic, and, most spectacularly, Mexico, spread the Spanish language and culture. In 2003, for the first time since the 1850s, a majority of newborn children in California were Hispanic, with José indeed becoming the most popular boy's name in both California and Texas, supplanting Michael. A society rooted in the English language, in supposed Protestant virtues, in the English legal system, was suddenly confronted with those who apparently saw no necessity for and no virtue in blending in, or acquiring fluency in the dominant language. In the 1990s, 25 percent of legal immigrants were Mexican. In 2000, Huntington pointed out, 27.6 percent of the foreign-born population were from Mexico. Meanwhile, illegal immigration from south of the border was running at an estimated 105,000 to 350,000, the very imprecision of the estimates suggesting the impossibility of patrolling the southern border (in *The Day After Tomorrow*, in a self-consciously ironic reversal, Americans flee south across the Rio Grande in the face of climatic disaster, allowed in on condition that all Latin American debt is canceled). America was no longer multicultural; it was, Huntington insisted, "two peoples with two cultures (Anglo and Hispanic) and two languages (English and Spanish)."[14] What America was witnessing was a reconquest of territories previously lost to Mexico in the wars of 1835–6 and 1846–8. African Americans no longer constituted the largest minority. In 2005 Antonio Villaraigosa became Mayor of Los Angeles, America's second largest city. He was the first Latino mayor since Cristolbal Aguilar in the early 1870s when the city hardly existed. In 2000, Hispanics represented 46.5 percent of Los Angeles residents, two-thirds of

Miami's and 12 percent of the US population. For Huntington that raised the question: what is the American?

But does the essence of America not lie in the fact that it is an immigrant nation? Not according to Huntington. He insists that it is in essence a settler culture and that large-scale immigration has only been an intermittent feature of American life. As he has argued,

> Immigration did not become significant in absolute and relative terms until the 1830s, declined in the 1850s, increased dramatically in the 1880s, declined in the 1890s, became very high in the decade and a half before World War I, declined drastically after passage of the 1924 immigration act, and stayed low until the 1965 immigration act generated a massive new wave.[15]

The figures do not quite match up. In fact it was the 1840s before immigration became truly significant. It did not decline in the 1850s and though it declined in the 1890s there were still more than three and a half million immigrants, nearly a million more than in any previous decade except the 1880s. It did decline after the 1924 Act but the 1920s still saw over four million enter the country.[16] Huntington further argues that since the percentage of foreign-born averaged only just over 10 percent of the population, to describe America as a nation of immigrants is "to stretch a partial truth into a misleading falsehood, and to ignore the central fact of America's beginning as a society of settlers."[17]

In this view the template for American institutions and values was effectively established by the initial settlers while later immigrants essentially accommodated to it. That in itself seems a partial truth. The fact that at any one time 10 percent of the population were born outside the country is a striking fact, the society they join not being a constant but adjusting to those who brought something other than settler values. The percentage of Jews in the population, for example, is small at little over 2 percent. Their impact on the culture, its arts, its politics, its science is considerable. Enlightenment values did not arrive in a flat pack in the seventeenth century, once erected to remain intact and unchanging. The children of Jewish immigrants helped to define American culture, indeed in many respects became cultural arbiters, ready to embrace European modernism because Europe was not remote to their minds. For the same reason, perhaps, American opened itself to Freud as few other cultures did. It was Jews who infiltrated and shaped the language. Indeed, Huntington's chief worry lies precisely in the power of immigrants to redefine the culture so long as we are thinking of those who speak Spanish. Today slightly more than one third of Americans are of Hispanic, African American, East Asian, or South Asian descent.

The truth is that America can scarcely be understood unless it be acknowledged that its motor has been fueled by immigration. Though at first the immigrants clung to old ways, they were encouraged to sweep the tracks behind them, see history as something to be transcended. They reset their cultural clocks, saw different stars pass overhead. For many there was a new language to be mastered. They had a dream and that dream became formularized, but the society to which they wedded their destiny was not implacable. It took the impress of those who arrived, subtly adjusting to them as they were required to adjust to it.

But transitions as radical as this can be painful. Godfrey Hodgson reminds us that fully one-third of immigrants to America, over a century and a half, have turned around and left, finding something other than the advertised paradise. Only 5 percent of Jews, however, took this course, despite a fierce anti-Semitism which excluded them from jobs, hotels, and, on occasion (as in the case of Leo Franks, a Jew falsely accused of murder in 1913 and the subject of David Mamet's novel *The Old Religion*), life itself. It depends, it seems, on the nature of the alternative. For those who stayed, acculturation, assimilation was the goal, if also the source, on occasion, of a residual guilt. Fiercely held beliefs were liable to be modified. Young people married out of the tribe. The generational gap potentially became a gap of something more than experience. David Mamet would accuse himself of neglecting a faith once carried across the ocean only to be too readily traded in for secular achievement and acceptance. He set himself to reinhabit beliefs seemingly surrendered for a future bright with unexamined possibilities. It was not an unfamiliar dilemma, especially when what was surrendered was something more than a familiar topography, mores dictated by tradition: a faith.

The new immigrants were offered a series of myths to embrace, no matter how alien to their own experience or how at odds with historical fact. They were given mantras to chant. A flag was placed in their hands to wave in the face of doubt. Those who chose America were assured that they were chosen along with the country whose fate they now readily embraced as their own. And this new country created a sense of shock and awe.

Not the least startling thing to the immigrant was the sheer size of the country they entered, a country which did indeed stretch from sea to shining sea. John Locke observed that "in the beginning the whole world was America." The poet Charles Olson also spoke of the centrality of SPACE, explaining that he wrote the word large because "it comes large there." As Gertrude Stein remarked, the truth of so much of America was that there was no there there. There was, she insisted, more space where nobody is than where somebody is and this was what made America what it was. In his 2005 novel *Villages* John Updike preferred a different formulation: "There are fewer somewheres in America, and more and more anywheres, strung out along numbered roads."[18]

Beyond the question of size, then, was the more important fact of space, and space explained something of the attitude toward the individual, the locality, power, other countries. The distance between San Francisco and Washington is twice as great as that between London and Minsk (2,437 miles versus 1,164). Why should anyone trust a government quite so far away and what could they have in common? As de Tocqueville observed, "in America, centralization is not at all popular and there is no better way of flattering the majority than by rising up against the so-called encroachments of central government."[19] Today, even Washington insiders have to rehearse familiar arguments against big government, asking to be sent back to the very place they affect to despise, simulating suspicion of the very forces they embody.

Other countries seem and are further away, except Canada, which few Americans treat seriously and Mexico, which 50 percent of US high school students failed to locate on a map, as they did the Pacific, on the face of it difficult to miss. Only a tiny proportion of Americans possess passports, though there is an argument as to the percentage (ranging from 7 percent to 25 percent). The sheer size and variety of America makes it seem to many sufficient unto itself. The rest of the world appears always slightly out of focus. Yet still the definition of America and Americans remains problematic.

America, as de Tocqueville recognized, is a fiction. "The Union," he observed, "is an idealized nation which exists, as it were, only in men's imagination."[20] His point, to be sure, was that the Union was, as he called it, "a work of art" while the individual states had an immediate reality, being closer to the individual. Nonetheless, it is hardly stretching his point to suggest that the America invoked by politicians or embraced by its citizens is a proposition, or series of propositions, themselves always under pressure. Why else, after all, require schoolchildren to pledge allegiance to the flag ("of the United States" they were reminded when it was discovered that many immigrant children still carried an image of quite other flags in their minds)? Why else "under God" (a phrase added in 1954 during the Cold War), except for fear of the politics of secularism? E Pluribus Unum, declares the Great Seal and the small change jangling in the pocket of those to whom Latin is a mystery, and why but for a sense of trepidation about a society that could so easily fracture along the fault lines of race, language, national origin? What is the American?

In 1996, J. Dionne Jr., of the *Washington Post*, published a book entitled *They Only Look Dead* whose subtitle was *Why Progressives Will Dominate the Next Political Era*. It was a little premature. In the 2000 election, George W. Bush was elected, though admittedly under controversial circumstances, the result depending on the outcome of the Florida election where voting machines proved fallible. The final result was delayed for five weeks, with the possibility of ninety-eight year-old Senator Strom Thurman becoming President by default, enough to have resolved any electoral difficulties one would have hoped. Al Gore won the popular vote but, following a five to four ruling by the Supreme Court, Bush was declared the winner by four votes in the electoral college. The result reflected a divided nation in which the Senate was split 50:50 for the first time since 1880.

America was not, though, simply divided between Republicans and Democrats. It was also geographically and racially divided. As Robert Singh has explained of the 2000 election: "favouring the Republicans, there exists a Republican 'L-shaped' sector that comprises the South, the Plains and Mountain states, and Alaska; against this is a Democratic, bicoastal and industrial heartland sector that now includes the Northeast and industrial Midwest, the Pacific Coast and Hawaii,"[21] though, after the 2004 election, the industrial Midwest drifted away from the Democrats. Ninety percent of African Americans voted for Gore, 9 percent for Bush. Sixty-two percent of Latinos voted for Gore, 35 percent for Bush.

In fact, as the new century arrived the races seemed more divided than ever. In a list of the top ten television programs favored by African Americans and whites, only one was common to both lists (a crime series called *CSI*). Two famous trials had split the country along racial lines: that of O. J. Simpson, charged with the murder of his wife in 1995, and the Los Angeles police officers charged with the beating of Rodney King, an unemployed black man caught speeding in 1991. Two of George W. Bush's most prominent cabinet members may have been African American but this barely seemed to impact on the racial situation. When the African American playwright August Wilson (who died in 2005) set out, in a series of plays, to tell the story of the black American in the twentieth century, it proved a story which barely intersected with that of white America, though those plays made their way to Broadway, where audiences were mixed but predominantly white. In 1993, an African American won the Nobel Prize for literature: Toni Morrison. In one of her novels, *Beloved*, she returned to slavery, reclaiming an experience simultaneously distant and close. In the course of the twentieth century, nine American authors became Nobel laureates. One was raised in China, one was born in Canada, and one in Poland. What is the American?

Today, America's cars no longer burn mostly American oil and Americans burn much of the world's supply (a US aircraft carrier carries one million gallons of fuel. There were five in the Gulf in 2003). As a consequence, foreign policies and domestic attitudes of necessity begin to change to accommodate that fact. Americans could no longer draw a circle around themselves and retreat into that space. An American is liable to own a car, television, computer, telephone made in Japan, wear shoes and clothes made in a low-wage Third World country, fly an American flag made in China, speak to a call centre in India, eat Mexican or Vietnamese food, see British plays on Broadway, watch television programs transmitted by a company owned by an Australian who has taken American citizenship for commercial reasons (Rupert Murdoch's New Corp owns 20th Century Fox, Fox broadcasting, HarperCollins, William Morrow, the *New York Post* and the LA Dodgers, and has partial ownership of the *New York Times*: the German-based Bertelsmann owns Bantam Doubleday, Dell, Knopf and has partial ownership of Barnes and Noble and Napster). A major Hollywood studio was owned by the Sony Corporation. At one time the British owned Brooks Brothers, Howard Johnsons, and Smith and Wesson, the company that made the gun that won the West. Indeed, with a massive national debt a significant proportion of the national economy is effectively owned by other countries. Is the question of who owns America entirely distinct from what America is? In an age of global corporations does it even control its own destiny?

Yet globalization has meant the spread of international capitalism, a system enforced by the terms and conditions of IMF loans and World Bank policies in which America is the driving force. In that sense, the world is becoming America, if we mean by that that it is accommodating itself to the system propounded by America. Barriers to the spread of American products have been tumbling, but do those products carry American values any more than the products moving the other way carry the seeds of alien cultures? Do the British know that when they breakfast on Kellogg's cornflakes, followed by Heinz baked beans with a dollop of ketchup and a glass of orange juice they are swallowing the products of American industry and, if so, that they are swallowing cultural values along with them, any more than they did when they drank Dutch gin with Swiss tonic and a slice of lemon from the West Indies? If there is a tendency in the modern world for tastes to be homogenized we also learn to take what we wish from the international smorgasbord, discovering in that process freedom of a kind, albeit a freedom which does slowly redefine who and what we might be. A marketplace is a marketplace. Trade changes patterns of consumption and patterns of consumption define a lifestyle which may become a life.

The twenty-first century may or may not be American but for many around the world America remains a lure, the epitome of the modern, futurity embodied. That it continues to seem so confident of its righteousness, how-ever, is the source of an irritation sometimes deepening to antagonism. Such an assertive virtue, however, may conceal uncertainties which make such brash claims necessary. Certainly de Tocqueville suspected as much.

Americans, he wrote in the second volume of *Democracy in America* in 1840,

> seem irritated by the slightest criticism and appear greedy for praise. The flimsiest compliment pleases them and the most fulsome rarely manages to satisfy them; they plague you constantly to make you praise them and, if you show yourself reluctant, they praise themselves. Doubting their own worth, they could be said to need a constant illustration of it before their eyes . . . A more intrusive and garrulous patriotism would be hard to imagine. It wearies even those who respect it.[22]

He had made essentially the same point in the first volume, five years earlier. Evidently, Americans had not relented in the intervening period.

Nor have they since. Few leaders feel the need to reassure their citizens, with quite the vigor and regularity of American presidents, that they are good, the envy of the world, paradigms and paragons. In his State of the Union Address in 1984, in the context of American supremacy in space, Ronald Reagan declared, "We are the first. We are the best, and we are so because we are free." "Faith, family, work, neighborhood, freedom and peace," he explained, "are not just words. They are expressions of what America means, definitions of what makes us good and loving people," quite as if such adjectives were unique to, and definitions of, one country. How, he asked,

> can we not believe in the goodness and greatness of Americans? How can we not do what is right and needed to preserve this last, best hope of man on earth? . . . We are a powerful force for good . . . We will carry on the traditions of a good and worthy people who have brought light where there was darkness.[23]

In 2001, in the aftermath of 9/11, George W. Bush declared, "I'm amazed that there's such misunderstanding of what our country is about that people hate us. I am – like most Americans, I just can't believe it because I know how good we are."[24] In a poll of the parents of schoolchildren conducted in 1998, 91 percent of whites and 92 percent of Hispanics agreed with the statement that "The U.S. is a better country than most other countries in the world."[25] By contrast, when the European edition of *Time* magazine com-missioned a poll which asked which country constituted the greatest danger to the world the results were: North Korea 6.7 percent; Iraq 6.3 percent; the United States 86.9 percent.[26]

It is not surprising that following the September 11 attack, 80 percent of Americans claimed to be deploying the flag, but George Bush Sr. had campaigned for the presidency at a flag factory a decade earlier and the American habit of flying the flag is one of the more striking features of American life. Clearly, a public declaration is being made. The question is to whom and why? Arthur Miller's characters are forever shouting out their names but they do so not out of confidence but out of fear that their lives lack the coherence and meaning for which they yearn. Those confident of their identities do not spend their lives reaffirming them. What, then, are we to make of a country that does?

George Bush Sr., in his Thanksgiving Day Address in 1992, explained that "America has become a model of freedom and justice to the world – as our pilgrim ancestors envisioned, a shining city upon a hill."[27] The rest of the world, it seemed, was mired in eternal night, waiting to be redeemed by the bright light of America's self-evident virtue. A decade later, his son approved the use of assassination as an agent of public policy, sanctioned the denial of due process, domestically and abroad, while his Secretary of Defense declared the irrelevance of the Geneva Convention and individual American troops tortured and abused the citizens of a country whose liberation had been used to justify invasion (an August 2002 memo prepared by the Justice Department's Official Legal Counsel for the White House argued that torture was permissible provided it fell short of the pain associated with organ failure or death).[28] George W. Bush's State of the Union address in 2005 invoked the words "free" or "freedom" twenty-four times, even as librarians across the country were required to turn informers, providing the names of borrowers and the titles of the books they borrowed.

In 2003 General Boykin announced of the Muslim Bin Laden that, "I knew that my God was bigger than his. I knew that my God was a real God and his was an idol." At an Evangelical meeting he declared that in the war in Iraq the United States was a "Christian nation battling Satan." He preached that "Satan wants to destroy this nation, he wants to destroy us as a nation, and he wants to destroy us as a Christian army," declaring that "George Bush was not elected by the majority of the voters in the United States," which was true enough, but adding, "He was anointed by God."[29] That, he assumed, rather ended the argument. Somehow a twenty-first-century American had argued his way back to believing in the divine right of rulers. In 2005, George W. Bush seemed to suggest that the invasion of Afghanistan and Iraq had been divine suggestions, if not instruction.

In 2003, 92 percent of Americans declared their belief in God, the percentage of those claiming church membership was in the mid-1960s, while 57 percent believed that atheists should not be allowed to teach in schools or universities.[30] George W. Bush's statement that he was launching a "crusade" against Muslim terrorists, no doubt meant innocently enough, caused a collective shudder around the world for those aware of the history of the Christian crusades, but Americans have always had a particular relationship with history, and, indeed, with religion.

America has been something of a spiritual shopping center, with customized faiths catering for a heterogeneous population. For a country ostensibly rooted in Enlightenment values, a fascination with the irrational has always been a defining characteristic, as if belief has a validity of its own independent of its focus. It has certainly set about the business of inventing its own religions, from Mormonism to Scientology, itself perhaps fittingly invented by a science fiction writer and beloved of Hollywood stars who have already negotiated riches on this earth and now wish to open negotiations on the next.

The Seventh Day Adventists had their origin in the Millerites, who had looked for the return of Christ in 1844. His failure to oblige was called "The Great Disappointment." In the 1930s a group called the Davidian Seventh-Day Adventists split away, this time picking 1959 for Christ's return. This further disappointment led to another split and the forming of the Branch Davidians, one of whose followers changed his name to David Koresh and, on February 28, 1993, their compound, in Waco, Texas, was attacked by the ATF (Bureau of Alcohol, Tobacco, Firearms and Explosives) leaving eighty-six people dead. This, in turn, along with a similar assault on white supremacists at Ruby Ridge, Idaho, the previous year (in fact a small family group), was instrumental in provoking the militia movement which flourished in the 1990s, a loosely knit anti-government, conspiracy-oriented group which saw the federal government as an enemy. Though not part of that movement, Timothy McVeigh seemed to share some of their sentiments when, in 1995, he detonated a bomb outside the Alfred P. Murrah federal building in Oklahoma City, killing 186 people, the largest death toll in any internal terrorist attack. The last days seemed to have arrived. Americans were consuming their own.

In 2002, 59 percent of Americans believed that the apocalyptic prophesies of the Book of Revelations would come true[31] and 39 percent believed in the literal truth of the Bible. The end, it seemed, might be nigh, the moment when the chosen and the damned would be separated. Among the bestsellers of the new century were *The Purpose Driven Lifestyle* (total sales to date, 20 million), written by Rick Warren, head of one of America's five largest mega-churches and at the heart of a global religious network, and the *Left Behind* series (sales to date 17 million), which explores the fate of those caught on the wrong side in the great separation following the return of

Christ, 39 percent of Americans presumably being secure since they described themselves as born again. And if there were chosen individuals, then there was also a chosen nation which had come into existence to offer itself as a beacon of something more than freedom. Evangelical Christians constituted 40 percent of the total voters in the 2000 presidential elections, the vast majority of whom (84 percent)[32] voted for a man who declared himself to be born again, on a secular level the promise America had always offered its citizens.

In his Nomination acceptance speech, in 1988, George Bush had announced "America as the leader – a unique nation with a special role in the world." Nor was it enough that the twentieth century had, indeed, been the American Century. For President Bush, "now we will go on to a new century, and what country's name will it wear? I say it will be another American century."[33] In 1997 a group of neoconservatives launched the "Project for the New American Century," an organization designed to "promote American global leadership . . . to shape a new century favorable to American principles and interests." In other words, it was no longer enough for America to offer an example; the world had to be reshaped to enable America to flourish. The history of the twentieth century, its proponents announced, "should have taught us to embrace the cause of American leadership."[34]

What form would that world leadership take? Plainly not financial. At the end of the century the United States contributed a smaller amount of aid as a proportion of its gross national product than any other developed country.[35] This, though, was not the brand of leadership on offer. The Project for a New American Century focused on the need for military expansion to underwrite the spread of American values. It was an organization which proved immensely influential with the new President who carried America forward from the twentieth to the twenty-first century, a number of its members serving in key roles in the new administration, such as the Vice-President, Dick Cheney, Secretary of Defense, Donald Rumsfeld, and the *éminence grise*, Paul Wolfowitz.[36]

When, on February 17, 1941, Henry Luce declared the reality of the American Century he was merely registering the logic that had placed power and, it has to be said, responsibility, in American hands; the Project for the New American Century, by contrast, was a conscious effort to ensure that America remained the dominant culture, with Israel as a democratic bridgehead into an oil-rich Middle East (without support for Israel "a significant portion of the world's supply of oil will be put at risk,"[37] its proponents warned). It thus fully supported what it declared the "first war of the twenty-first century," the Gulf War, in which Iraqi aggression was met on the battlefield. The word "first" would seem to imply an acknowledgment of others to come, which in turn meant that a modern American society would need to shape itself to the demands of a new world, as the new world would need to shape itself to the demands of America.

The authors of a paper entitled "Rebuilding America's Defenses" declared that the "United States is the world's only superpower, combining pre-eminent military power, global technological leadership, and the world's largest economy. At the present moment," the paper declared, "the United States faces no global rival. America's grand strategy should aim to preserve and extend this advantageous position as far into the future as possible," by preparing to "fight and decisively win multiple, simultaneous major theatre wars."[38] A new military service was to be created, called US Space Forces, to take command of outer space. The Pax Americana was to be enforced from above because, as the National Defense Panel had agreed, "Unrestricted use of space has become a major strategic interest of the United States." The old Air Force slogan, "global reach, global power" was now to have a new significance. At a time when "Air Force aircraft can attack any target on earth with great accuracy and virtual impunity," American air power, the paper declared, "has become a metaphor for as well as the literal manifestation of American military pre-eminence."[39]

Yet if America was not ready to sustain global peace who was? Somewhere in the course of the twentieth century responsibility had passed from the old empires to the new. The amount the United States has spent on defense since the Second World War is equivalent to $2.6 million a year since the birth of Christ. The combined annual defense budgets of North Korea, Iran, Iraq, Cuba, Lybia, and Syria are less than half the cost of one Nimitz-class aircraft carrier.[40] This time, however, there was little interest in the acquisition of territory. There was, to be sure, a determination to acquire natural resources without which a modern society could not hope to operate, but these were to be secured less by conquest than by establishing and maintaining a world order in which they could be protected. That America was to bear the burden seemed its destiny and what better country, after all, could bear such responsibility? All it required was that others acknowledge that destiny and those qualities which made it necessary.

De Tocqueville had declared,

> [there is] nothing more irksome in the conduct of life than the irritable patriotism Americans have. The foreigner would be very willing to praise much in their country but would like to be allowed a few criticisms; that is exactly what he is refused. So, America is a land of freedom where the foreigner, to avoid offending anyone, must not speak freely about either

individuals, or the state, or the governed, or the government, or public or private undertakings, indeed about anything he encounters except perhaps climate and the soil both of which, however, some Americans are apt to defend as if they had helped to create them.

For fifty years, he observed, Americans had been told that "they form the only religious, enlightened, and free nation . . . They possess, therefore, an inordinate opinion of themselves and are not far from believing that they form a species apart from the rest of humanity."[41]

He was not wrong. America was the innocence against which the guilt of the world was to be defined, a nation, it seemed, especially blessed of God. As President Reagan declared, "America was founded by people who believed that God was their rock of safety. He is ours. I recognize we must be cautious in claiming that God is on our side. But I think it's alright to keep asking if we are on his side." For George Bush there was a clear connection between American freedoms and what he called the nation's Judeo-Christian moral heritage. And if so, then why should religion not permeate the life of a country only ostensibly secular. As President Reagan asked the members of Congress, "If you can begin your day with a member of the clergy standing right here to lead you in prayer, then why can't freedom to acknowledge God be enjoyed again by children in every classroom across this land?"[42] After all, it was argued, and not simply by American presidents with a constituency to address, America past and present was rooted in Christian values.

In 2004, nearly 170 years after Tocqueville, Samuel P. Huntington published a book still asking *Who Are We?* as if that were indeed a question to be asked by every generation of Americans, indeed by every American born again to a new day rising. "It is morning in America," declared Ronald Reagan. It is always morning in America. In 2004, Senator John Kerry insisted "the sun is rising" in America. Huntington's book was subtitled *The Challenges to America's National Identity*, and as that implied it expressed some alarm at a threat to an identity that was in fact far from settled and coherent. American culture, American values, the very notion of what constituted an American were, he suggested, at risk. Even the common heritage of the English language and Protestant faith were no longer secure. The new century, it seemed to him, promised an indivisible nation divided. Somewhere America was cracking apart and the fault line, aptly enough, ran through California (and Florida, Texas, New Mexico).

Huntington called for Americans to "recommit themselves to the Anglo-Protestant culture, traditions, and values that for three and a half centuries have been embraced by Americans of all races, ethnicity and religion and that have been the source of their liberty, unity, power, prosperity, and moral leadership as a force for good in the world."[43] America is largely Protestant. It is, however, no longer so resolutely Anglo, and there is the source of his concern. It is only necessary to recommit (itself a word with religious overtones) because of the risk of cultural backsliding, because the assumed clarity of the national culture is no longer so evident.

In 2000 immigration to the United States was up from 646,568 in 1999 to 849,807. The top five countries of origin were Mexico (173,919), the People's Republic of China (45,652), the Philippines (42,474), India (42,046), and Vietnam (26,747). The primary destinations were California, New York, Florida, Texas, New Jersey, and Illinois, those heading there constituting 66 percent of legal immigrants in 2000. In 1900, 84.9 percent of immigrants had come from Europe, 12.6 percent from Asia and 1.3 percent from Latin America. In 2000 the figures were 15 percent, 26 percent and 51 percent respectively. In 1900 the foreign-born represented 13.6 percent of the population. In 2000 the figure was 10.4 percent. The total foreign-born in 1900 was 10.3 million. In 2000 it was 28.4 million.

Huntington noted, in particular, the dramatic rise in immigration from Hispanic countries, especially Mexico and Cuba, which seemingly threatened the Anglo-Protestant values he regarded as definitional. Suddenly, there were those who showed no inclination to relinquish old loyalties or the language in which those loyalties were expressed. As a result, a number of states (Florida, Arizona, Colorado, California) moved to enact legislation to establish English as the official language. In 2000, he noted, 47 million Americans spoke a non-English language at home, 21.1 million speaking Spanish. Staring into the future, he saw a country that would be 25 percent Hispanic a decade before mid-century, a change that he suspected would not be entirely peaceful and which, anyway, would threaten the very identity of the country such people had opted to embrace. "Would America," he asked, "be the America it is today if in the seventeenth and eighteenth centuries it had been settled not by British Protestants but by French, Spanish, or Portugese Catholics? The answer," he insisted, "is no. It would not be America; it would be Quebec, Montreal, Brazil."[44]

According to Huntington, the Anglo-Protestant culture of the founding settlers remained the bedrock of US identity until the last decades of the twentieth century, despite a history of immigration. He saw trouble ahead, drawing parallels with Bosnia and suggesting that perceived loss of power and status by any group was liable to provoke a backlash. There is, Huntington insisted, "no Americano dream. There is only the American dream created by an Anglo-Protestant society. Mexican Americans will share in that dream and in that society only if they dream in English."[45]

His book quickly came under fierce assault. His assumptions about language acquisition were challenged (in 2002 a Pew Hispanic Center poll of third generation US Latinos found that 78 percent said English was their primary language[46]) as was what seemed to some his seeming failure to make adequate distinction between the different ethnic, national, and economic backgrounds of those he homogenized as Hispanic. Perhaps predictably, a newspaper commentator in Miami called for national protests against both him and his publisher. To Huntington himself, however, he was doing no more than register a sense of crisis. Modern American culture was under threat. Identity was insecure. How, after all, could it lead if it had no coherent sense of itself? Meanwhile, 57 percent of immigrant Muslims and 32 percent of American-born Muslims in 2000 indicated that they would prefer to leave America and live in a Muslim country. The cultural glue was beginning to fail.

But America is an unfinished story. If its end were implicit in its beginning, it would lose its allure. The idea of America and its reality are not coterminous. That space, indeed, has generated the energy that has driven much of America's endeavor and a fair proportion of its literature. It is only seemingly a single story, a grand narrative. It is, indeed, a fiction, or more truly a series of fictions whose pattern changes with every shake of a hand which 92 percent of Americans believe to be cosmic, but which may also be the dream of a man or woman who speaks Spanish and is even now moving from room to room in a Howard Johnson hotel, placing chocolate kisses on a pure white pillow.

There is an argument to be made that America is essentially a postmodern culture, a world of stories within stories, quotations within quotations, a culture which recapitulates the past as aesthetic gesture rather than lived experience. Perhaps, indeed, an immigrant culture is bound to be postmodern, simultaneously inventing a master story of new beginnings, and infiltrating old stories, old myths, old values no longer operative except as quotations. America thus becomes a fiction, a proposition to which all are asked to subscribe. But Willa Cather's Ántonia eventually refused incorporation within the language of her new country, reverting to that which she had carried across the ocean.

In 1900, the presidential campaign cost $5 million and was the most expensive in history. In 2004, the cost was a billion dollars. Both candidates in 2004 were millionaires, as were their running mates. In 2005, the Mayor of New York was a billionaire who thought nothing of spending $50 million to be re-elected. Was this a golden age or a second gilded age? On chartered jets the presidential hopefuls flew across the country like stones skipping across a lake, splish-splashing generalities and dentally perfect smiles at citizens who were flattered to think that even for a second or two they had plugged into global power. President Johnson used to give lessons in how to disengage his hand from those who thought their own hold on power should last longer than the magnesium flash of a camera.

Such physical presence, though, is now offered to few. Most have to settle for television ads as subtle as a scream, a virtual world of billowing flags, short-sleeved endeavor, rictus smiles. This is American democracy in action, culminating in the fake orgasm of the Convention in which has-beens and wannabes sing the praises of the chosen one and balloons float down as from the hand of a beneficent god, albeit one wholly lacking in taste or plausibility. At such moments America presents itself as divided only by party politics but united in its sense of itself. Indeed, in an essentially un-ideological political system, in a European sense, in which both parties are capable of containing a full spectrum of opinion, the distinction between the parties can seem difficult to detect in what John Updike has called a conservative country built upon radicalism.

In 2004, it was rather easier as President Bush's conservatism was challenged by Senator John Kerry's liberalism. There were, indeed, real differences on domestic policy. They were divided on moral issues to do with abortion and homosexuality, Bush's born-again agenda being proposed as public policy. At a time of war such debates seemed to many beside the point as the country faced the threat of terrorism, the attack on Iraq having bred a new nest of terrorists. Neither man, in the end, could do anything but insist on his virtues as a war leader, one who had evaded service in Vietnam and who now paraded his military decisiveness, the other who had served then turned against that war but now wished to insist on the credentials established in that conflict. Both asserted that they were patriots, sharing essentially the same dream, offering hope, an expansive future, faith in the family and America's destiny to lead the world. Care was taken to ensure that the full range of America's ethnic diversity would be caught on camera as equal care was taken to insist on the irrelevance of difference, except in so far as Bush sacrificed gays and freedom of choice for women for the Evangelical vote and Kerry alienated religious conservatives to maintain his liberal base. Both made a bid for the black and Hispanic votes. Both blessed America, one nation, indivisible, with liberty and justice for all, the envy of the world, taking on the burden of moral leadership because moral destiny was a fate first acknowledged four centuries before. Meanwhile, behind the scenes, thousands of lawyers stood by to challenge the legitimacy of the vote, the bizarre conclusion to the 2000 elections leaving many unconvinced of the exemplary nature of the American democratic system even then being offered to others as a political and even moral paradigm.

In the end the lawyers went back to their daily litigations as the election was resolved in favor of a man who had successfully represented himself as a war leader.

Yet the divisions were real. 63 percent of the poor (earning less than $10,000 per annum) voted Democrat; 36 percent Republican. For those earning over $200,000 the figures were 37 percent/62 percent. Eighty-nine percent of African Americans voted Democrat; 11 percent voted Republican. Asians split 59/42, Latinos 55/45, Whites 42/57. 77 percent of gays voted Democrat; 23 percent Republican. Forty-one percent of gun-owners favored the Democrats and 61 percent the Republicans. Thirty-five percent of those attending church more than weekly chose the Democrats while 63 percent opted for the Republicans. The east coast, west coast, and upper Midwest voted Democrat; the Midwest, West and South voted Republican.[47] The single most important issue, voters told exit pollsters, was "moral values," with the economy and terrorism close behind. Modern America, it seemed, was returning to its roots, remaking itself in the image of its own past. Nonetheless, the reliability of exit polls aside, the 22 percent who listed moral values as the most important issue were only two percentage points more numerous than those who cited the economy. More significantly, they constituted a smaller percentage than in the two previous elections, in which 35 percent and 40 percent respectively had placed moral issues first. The percentage of Evangelical Protestants in the electorate seems to have remained the same. The percentage voting Republican increased as did the percentage of Catholics voting the same way.[48]

One final irony lay in the fact that with marriage and family values a key issue, the divorce rate in John Kerry's Massachusetts, at 2.4 per 1,000 inhabitants, was considerably lower than in George Bush's Texas, where the figure was 4.1. Indeed, the highest divorce rate is to be found in the Republican-voting South and the lowest in the Democratic-voting Northeast, while 23 percent of married born-again Christians have been twice divorced, or more. Meanwhile, teenage births in Texas ran at twice those of Massachusetts while abortion in the United States runs at three times the rate of supposedly liberal Holland.[49]

In New York especially, the past is used up; the new embraced. Yesterday's cold-water walk-up is gentrified. Where the poor once stared out from Brooklyn Heights, by the century's end the rich vied for an apartment that looked out across the water to Ellis Island and on to a Europe whose irrelevance was declared a century ago by those who had traveled steerage and stepped into what only seemed the future. America continues to change. In parts of Brooklyn, one immigrant group replaces another, a shifting spectrum of immigrant life. Ghetto gives way to neighborhood, church to synagogue to mosque; keplach is replaced by borscht which in turn is replaced by tortilla, each in turn homogenized to meet the general taste. The future beckons, a future never to be realized because always provisional. The rhetoric of American exceptionalism, its sometimes arrogant assertions of superiority, its too casual dismissal of the interests, indeed the virtues of other peoples, their systems, their ways of being, may repel, but the reality of its freedoms are as compelling in the twenty-first century as they were to Crevecoeur and de Tocqueville as, centuries before, they watched a nation begin the process of inventing itself.

The irony is that while for most Americans the city is the one shared, if un-communal, experience it is not what is meant by those who celebrate America. Not even the suburbs, with their Sunday-mown front lawns and a newspaper tossed by a boy on a bicycle dreaming of one day playing in the state university's football team. In some way the America they propose is out there beyond the Susquehana, somewhere beyond St. Joseph, where the wagons once began their journey across a continent in the search of gold, confusing it with a search for happiness. It is in the heartland, daily less populated as farms are sold and barn doors left to swing in the wind as the early twenty-first-century population move towards the West and South, by-passing such mythic sites. There, where the eye can focus ten miles off, and see the face of God in a salmon-pink sky, is the Platonic paradigm.

The fallen towers of New York are fifteen hundred miles away. Grain silos take the place of skyscrapers. Dirt roads cut across railroad tracks and Main Street has no more than a dozen stores taking as their model something seen in a 1950s movie. The restaurant has an array of guns on the wall and there are flags put up long ago and never taken down because no one sees a reason to do so. These are places that exist in reality but exist still more in the mind because they are untainted by the modern, because they reach back for something feared lost elsewhere. Here a man says something and has to stand by it because he will be here tomorrow and the day beyond. He buys things for their utility not their looks. Generations of his family are buried just out of town and if many have left to go to the city, disappearing into the millions who represent America's future, here there is a past and here are values handed down. This is a place in which, in the words of Lanford Wilson's play *Book of Days,* "the smell of smoke from burning leaves lies in the air in the fall for days."[50]

This is the America schoolchildren pledge allegiance to, not the America manufactured by politicians to justify their power, not the America of winner take all, of my country right or wrong, or even of liberty and justice for all. Not America the envy of the world, the Pax Americana. Even those who have never been there occasionally hear the wind that blows across open country rather than the electronic music that rasps in their ears. There is, they know, another America, the America that should be and somewhere is. It is not the modern, because the modern is about noise and change and distraction and the future. The modern may be what they embrace, what they are certain they want above all, but it is the other America that pulls them, an America which exists outside of time. This is the happiness they are sure lies somewhere ahead, the happiness they pursue but in truth never possess, not least because it lies behind them in the trackless land they once took for possibility.

And if it is not in the small towns of the Midwest, perhaps it is in the villages of Pennsylvania and New England, those places celebrated by John Updike, who was raised in one and who lives in another but for whom their force as metaphor has long since outstripped their true force as paradigm. "It is a mad thing to be alive," he insists, villages "exist to moderate this madness – to protect us from the darkness without and the darkness within."[51] It is the America of myth, the America F. Scott Fitzgerald identifies in the concluding paragraphs of *The Great Gatsby*:

> He had come a long way . . . and his dream must have seemed so close that he could hardly fail to grasp it. He did not know that it was already behind him, somewhere back in that vast obscurity beyond the city, where the dark fields of the republic rolled on under the night. Gatsby believed in the green light, the orgastic future that year by year recedes before us. It eluded us then, but that's no matter – tomorrow we will run faster, stretch out our arms further . . . And one fine morning – So we beat on, boats against the current, born back ceaselessly into the past.[52]

And what of those who centuries before had watched as the first white men rode up from the southwest, paddled their canoes down from the north in search of beaver or cut the line of the horizon to the west as they came in search of spiritual grace or material wealth? By the end of the twentieth century, they seemed to have discovered a stake in American society previously denied them, as they established casinos. In 2006, though, Jack Abramoff, a Washington lobbyist who had liberally bribed leading American politicians, was revealed to have received $82 million from two tribes fighting over gambling rights. In emails, he called them "monkeys" and "morons," happy, it seemed, to continue a tradition of defrauding those who sought access to the culture that had so casually displaced them.

By 1997, they had shrunk to 0.9 percent of the population. 2.3 million Native Americans, Inuit, and Aleuts were alive to see the century's end but half of that number were below the age of twenty-seven and estimates saw their numbers doubling by 2050. These, too, after all, are Americans who look backwards as well as forwards, who, at least in myth, recall an innocence undone by time and the restless drive toward modernity. What, then, is the American?

NOTES

1. Herman Melville, *Moby Dick*, New York, 1950, p. xxiii.
2. Henry Steel Commager, *The American Mind: An Interpretation of American Thought and Character Since the 1880s* (New Haven: Yale University Press, 1950), p. 3.
3. Bruce Springsteen, "The Stakes Are Too High to Sit This One Out," *The Guardian*, August 6, 2004, p. 26.
4. J. Hector St. John de Crevecoeur, *Letters from an American Farmer and Sketches of 18th Century America* (Harmondsworth: Penguin, 1981), p. 70.
5. Alexis de Tocqueville, *Democracy in America and Two Essays on America*, trans. Gerald E. Bevan (London: Penguin, 2003), pp. 451, 314.
6. Daniel Bell, *The End of Ideology: On the Exhaustion of Political Ideas in the Fifties*, revised ed. (New York: The Free Press, 1965), p. 101.
7. "Anti-Porn Crusade Targets Christian's 'Secret,'" *The Atlanta Journal-Constitution*, "Faith and Values," November 13, 2004, p. 1.
8. De Tocqueville, *Democracy*, p. 304.
9. Godfrey Hodgson, *More Equal Than Others: America from Nixon to the New Century* (Princeton: Princeton University Press, 2004), p. 91.
10. *Ibid.*, p. 94.
11. http://www.photius.com/wfb1999./rankings/infant_mortality_0.html
12. http//www.who.int/infopr2000-life.html
13. Bell, *The End of Ideology*, p. 98.
14. Samuel Huntington, "José, Can You See?", *Foreign Policy* (March–April 2004), p. 32.
15. *Ibid.*, p. 46.
16. *U.S. Statistical Year Book, 1990* (Washington DC: Government Printing Office, 1990).
17. Huntington, "José, Can you See?", p. 46.
18. John Locke, *Two Treatises of Government*, ed. Peter Laslett (Cambridge: Cambridge University Press, 1988), Treatise II, para. 49; John Updike, *Villages* (London: Hamish Hamilton, 2005), p. 309.
19. De Tocqueville, *Democracy*, p. 451.
20. *Ibid.*, p. 193.
21. Robert Singh, ed., *American Politics and Society Today* (Cambridge: Polity Press, 2002), p. 40.
22. De Tocqueville, *Democracy*, p. 710.
23. http://reagan2020.com/speeches/state_of_the_union_1984.asp
24. White House Press Conference, October 11, 2001.
25. Samuel P. Huntington, *Who Are We? The Challenges to American Identity* (New York: Simon and Schuster, 2004), p. 275.
26. Rory Bremner, John Bird, and John Fortune, *You Are Here* (London: Weidenfeld and Nicolson, 2004), p. 166.

27. bushlibrary.tamu.edu/research/papers 1992/toc 9111/.
28. Michael R. Gordon, "The Army and Torture: What the Rule Book Says," *International Herald Tribune*, June 18, 2004, p. 2.
29. Sidney Blumenthal, The *Guardian*, May 20, 2004, p. 26.
30. Huntington, *Who Are We?*, pp. 86–8.
31. *Ibid.*, p. 344.
32. *Ibid.*, p. 342.
33. http:///www.geocities.com/rickmatlik/nomahbush88.htm
34. www.newamericancentury.org.
35. Hodgson, *More Equal Than Others*, p. 273.
36. www.newamericancentury.org.
37. *Ibid.*
38. *Rebuilding America's Defenses: Strategy, Forces and Resources for a New Century*, www.newamericancentury.org
39. *Ibid.*
40. Bremner, Bird, and Fortune, *You Are Here*, p. 109.
41. De Tocqueville, *Democracy*, pp. 277, 440.
42. Ronald Reagan, 1984 State of the Union addresses, www.presidency.ucsb.edu/sou.php.
43. Huntington, *Who Are We?*, p. xvii.
44. *Ibid.*, pp. 319, 59.
45. *Ibid.*, p. 256.
46. Malcolm Beith, "Latinos and Lucre," *Newsweek*, November 22, 2004, p. 52.
47. *New York Times, CNN* exit polls, The *Guardian*, November 4, 2004, p. 3.
48. "The Triumph of the Religious Right," *The Economist*, November 13–19, 2004, p. 29.
49. Andrew Sullivan, "Where the Bible Belt are Sinful and the Liberals Pure," The *Sunday Times*, November 28, 2004, p. 15
50. Lanford Wilson, *Book of Days* (New York: Grove Press, 2000), p. 2.
51. Updike, *Villages*, p. 321.
52. F. Scott Fitzgerald, *The Great Gatsby* (Harmondsworth: Penguin, 1950), p. 88.

2

GODFREY HODGSON

The American century

It was Henry Luce, the founder of *Time*, who in a signed editorial in his own magazine made popular the phrase "the American Century." The century was then already more than two-fifths over. It was 1941, and the Japanese had not yet attacked Pearl Harbor. The argument rumbled on whether the United States should enter the war on the side of Britain against Japanese militarism and German and Italian fascism, as President Franklin Delano Roosevelt privately thought inevitable, or should remain neutral, as a majority of both Congress and public opinion still preferred.

Luce wrote of the American Century not out of triumphalist nationalism but as a prophet calling on his countrymen to take up a burden in the spirit of Christian sacrifice. America should save Britain, Luce said, but, more than that, "we must undertake now to be the Good Samaritan of the entire world." He saw his country as destined to lift mankind "from the level of the beasts to what the Psalmist called a little lower than the angels."[1] The history of the rest of the American century can be seen as a commentary on the extent to which Luce's countrymen lived up to his vision, at home and abroad.

A few days after the century ended, President Clinton in a millennial State of the Union address, drew up his own balance sheet for the century. He spoke as if it was obvious that what Henry Luce dreamed of had come true. "We are fortunate to be alive at this moment in history," he began, to applause from the senators and congressmen, some of whom had only weeks earlier been trying to impeach him. "Never before has our nation enjoyed, at once, so much prosperity and social progress with so little internal crisis and so few external threats. Never before have we had such a blessed opportunity . . . to build the more perfect union of our founders' dreams."[2]

Within weeks, prosperity had been threatened by the sharpest break in the stock market since 1929. Within months external threats of a sinister new kind had shattered New York and Washington. Clinton called on the country to pursue ideals of social progress that would have been familiar to Franklin Roosevelt. But influential voices were calling for a "new American century" that had less to do with social progress at home and more to say about hegemony abroad. "Does the United States have the resolve," a group of conservative and "neoconservative" intellectuals asked, "to shape a new century favorable to American principles and interests?"[3]

The history of the twentieth century, in so far as the United States is concerned, can be seen in two ways. Objectively, it is a success story: the narrative of growing prosperity at home and steadily growing American power and influence abroad. Subjectively, it is a story of constant internal disagreement over such questions as the proper role of government in American society, over the meaning of equality between individuals, races, classes, and sexes, and over America's responsibilities towards the rest of the world. Twentieth-century America was at once stubbornly conservative and obsessed with change, instinctively libertarian and often punitive, secular and religious, egalitarian and yet increasingly unequal, confident and – as the century went on – frequently self-doubting. It was also constantly torn between an impulse to withdraw from a morally dubious world beyond the oceans, and a desire to extend the American way to as much of that world as possible.

It was on the whole a very open society, in the literal sense that it was largely defined by immigration. In 1900 there were 76 million Americans. By the end of the century that had almost quadrupled, to just under 300 million. The rate of economic growth slowed somewhat, from 2 percent a year in the first decade to less than 1 percent at its end. Where in the early nineteenth century American population growth had been maintained by exceptionally high rates of natural increase, in the twentieth century it was largely driven by immigration.

In the first twenty years of the century, immigration was high, mainly from southern and eastern Europe. In the first decade, 8.7 million immigrants arrived, representing a remarkable 10.4 percent of the population. Over the whole sixty years from before the Civil War to the end of World War I, the foreign-born hovered between 13 and 15 percent of the population. Many old-stock Americans felt it was too much. Immigration restrictions were imposed, aimed at allowing in few immigrants who were not of north European ancestry. Then came the Great Depression and World War II. Immigration sank to a trickle: half a million immigrants in the 1930s. Only after the relaxation of immigration controls by the Kennedy and Johnson administrations began to have their effect did a new great flood of immigrants enter the United States, a total of more than 30 million in the last third of the twentieth century.[4]

This time they were very different people. Up to the 1960s the great majority of immigrants (not counting slaves, those involuntary immigrants) came from Europe; fewer than one in six of the Second Great Migration of the late twentieth century were Europeans. Just over half of them were born in Latin America (half of those in Mexico), and almost exactly a quarter in Asia. Where in 1970 only 5 percent of the population were Hispanic and a mere 1 percent Asian, a widely accepted estimate is that by the middle of the twenty-first century barely half of the population will be of European descent. More than a quarter will be "Hispanic," 8 percent Asian, and 14 percent African American.[5]

In 1900 the American economy and therefore American society were already changing rapidly. After the Civil War, undeterred by sharp recessions in 1873 and 1893, the economy grew rapidly. Manufacturing industry exploded. First textiles and food-processing boomed, then coal to fuel the railroads, iron and steel to build them, machine-building of all kinds, and at the turn of the century the electrical and chemical industries, and a myriad specialist businesses, from retailing, advertising, insurance, banking, printing, and entertainment. At the very beginning of the century, the Spindletop gusher in Texas inaugurated decades of abundant supplies of petroleum and natural gas. No wonder one of the most influential historians wrote a book called *People of Plenty*.[6]

Until the twentieth century, American exports were overwhelmingly agricultural: over 70 percent in each of the three decades from 1870 to 1900. World War I, with German and British industry absorbed with war production, and Britain, France, and (until the Revolution) Russia desperate to buy American food, munitions, and metals, was a decisive opportunity for American manufacturing. It was also the moment, with the City of London stretched to the limits of its credit to pay for American goods and to lend to the Allies, when Wall Street replaced London as the financial capital of the world.

These economic changes altered *where* and *how* Americans lived. In 1900 two-thirds of all Americans, about 50 million, lived in rural settlements, either on the farm or in small towns. In 2000 urban and suburban settlements housed more than 200 million. First it was the great cities that swelled. Railroads concentrate, automobiles disperse. Millions of Americans moved from the farm to the city. Millions both of poor whites and African Americans moved north to Washington and New York, Chicago and Detroit. By the 1920s the urban population had passed the rural population in numbers.

Well-to-do people had long chosen to live in the suburbs. But after World War II, automobile ownership made possible a new kind of commuting. Developers and builders, helped by cheap loans and federal subsidies, built more modest suburbs, and the federal government funded up to 90 percent of highway costs. The freeway, the supermarket, and the suburban mall, reinforced by zoning and tax regimes, gave strong incentives to move out of town.[7] In the 1960s and 1970s, these long-established trends were reinforced by "white flight." Even after the black migration from the Deep South, only 16 percent of the city was black.[8] By the end of the century, African Americans made up over three-quarters of the population, which itself had shrunk from over two million. The black population of the most important metropolitan cities – New York, Boston, Chicago, Los Angeles – grew from under 10 percent to 25 percent, and even higher percentages.

The effects were complex, but dramatic. Crime grew, at least until the 1990s. Racial tension flared sporadically. In spite of the efforts of the Johnson administration, and of countless reform mayors across the country, many of them black, middle-class whites largely abandoned the public school systems. New York, Chicago, Los Angeles, Detroit, Cleveland, Atlanta, and Washington all elected black mayors from time to time.

The suburbs, too, changed as they became the typical American habitat. Much of the turmoil of the Progressive Era in the early twentieth century, said the great historian Richard Hofstadter, could be explained by the fact that America was born in the country but moved to town. Some of the tensions and frustrations of late twentieth-century America can be put down to the fact that by the end of the century more than half the population had moved on out to the suburbs, where great material comfort and convenience are sometimes purchased at the cost of loneliness, isolation, and even a sense of alienation.

In the twentieth century, the United States was reluctant to fight wars, but did very well out of them when it did. World War I was a bonanza for American industry even before the United States entered the war. The Wilson administration only decided reluctantly to fight when the intercepted Zimmermann telegram revealed that imperial Germany planned to reward Mexico for joining the war on Germany's side with American territory.[9] President Wilson arrived at the Paris peace conference as the arbiter of the world. All the other great powers had either collapsed, like the German, Austro-Hungarian, Russian, and Ottoman empires, or were much impoverished and diminished, like Britain and France. The United States stepped back from a leading role in the League of Nations because of

Wilson's failure to meet the objections of Henry Cabot Lodge and his supporters in the Senate.[10]

That led to a decade when the American economy prospered exceedingly, while American politics stagnated and American society entered a conservative phase. The twenties has been remembered as the Jazz Age, the decade of the Charleston and the Martini glass: it was also the decade of the second Ku Klux Klan, the Scopes trial, isolationism, business domination, and heavy dark furniture.

The American economy was badly damaged by the Great Depression. But when war came again, once again the territory and industry of the United States were untouched. The economy was revived again by war orders before Pearl Harbor and by the prodigious effort to build American military power between 1942 and 1945. When the conflict ended American industry, with for a time no competitors, enjoyed monopoly profits.

The immediate postwar years were a time not just of great prosperity but of wealth more equitably distributed than at any time since the United States first began to industrialize after the Civil War. With strong government controls and a major role for government in investment, development, and research, it was a social democratic boom. For the first time, millions of Americans bought their own homes. Developers like William J. Levitt put decent suburban homes within reach of the many. Millions, helped by the GI bill, now went to college. Unions collaborated with corporate management.[11] Unemployment was low, real wages grew rapidly, and there was massive investment in housing, industrial plant, and transport. This was the age of the "liberal consensus": conservatives, more or less reluctantly, accepted the domestic welfare state, while liberals – admittedly with significant exceptions on the Left – accepted the anti-communist foreign policy of the Right.

Once it became apparent that Stalin was not the benign "Uncle Joe" of wartime propaganda, the United States was committed to maintaining a state of military preparedness unprecedented in peace time. The Cold War that ensued transformed American society in many ways for the rest of the century.

It created a "military-industrial complex" and what came to be known as the "national security state." This was perhaps necessary, given the real danger from the Soviet Union in an age of nuclear weapons. But it was also something quite alien to the American tradition, hitherto – in spite of the Mexican war, the Civil War, Indian wars, and Caribbean interventions – profoundly civilian. In 1947 the National Security Act reorganized the federal government. It set up the National Security Council and provided the President with a National Security Adviser, soon to become one of the most powerful officials in the federal government. It merged the army air corps and the naval air service into a United States air force, put the air force, the army, and the navy under a new Department of Defense, and created a Central Intelligence Agency. In 1950, a presidential document, NSC68, placed the government in effect on a war footing and led in a brief period to a fourfold increase in defense expenditure.

Much legislation, including the vast interstate highway program, was justified on grounds of national security. The atomic weapons program, the Cold War, and the expansion of the military permanently altered the balance between the separated powers – in favor of the executive branch. Paranoia about the threat from domestic communism began to shift the centre of gravity of political debate to the Right.

Abroad, the United States built up a network of alliances, treaties, and more than 700 military bases in almost every country outside the sphere of Soviet control. With the larger states of Western Europe, more or less correct diplomatic relations veiled the asymmetry between American power and allied dependence. In developing countries, many of them former colonies emancipated from European domination in large part as a result of American pressure, American ambassadors, in fortress-like embassies, browbeat weak sovereign governments like nineteenth-century European proconsuls.

After the Chinese revolution of 1949, the United States faced not one but two communist potential superpowers, as well as a whole string of East European and Asian "satellites." American policy, proposed by the Russian expert George F. Kennan and interpreted by the "Wise Men" of the foreign policy "Establishment" (Henry Stimson, Dean Acheson, John J. McCloy, and their heirs such as the Bundy brothers) sought to "contain" Soviet and Chinese power, by diplomacy, by nuclear deterrence, and by force only as a last resort.[12] After 1949 Moscow abandoned any intention of a frontal attempt at adding Western Europe to the Soviet empire. Instead, the Soviet leadership sought to isolate the West from markets and sources of raw materials by supporting nationalist and revolutionary movements.

The United States became involved in counterinsurgency operations which often meant supporting authoritarian regimes that were profoundly alien to American traditions of respect for human rights and the rule of law. The culmination of these trends towards unacknowledged imperialism was the war in Vietnam. In the spring of 1965 President Johnson ordered a decisive escalation of American commitment to supporting the government of South Vietnam. North Vietnam, which was supporting a national communist guerrilla war in the South, was bombed, and American troops in the theatre were increased from the 16,000 "advisers" discreetly deployed by President Kennedy to over 500,000, backed by massive air and naval power, in 1968. Yet it gradually became apparent that a great power that does not win a war, loses it.

The Vietnam War had a complex effect on American society. Many came to feel that the war was morally unjustified. Another, probably larger, segment of public opinion, asked what purpose it served. By the hinge election year of 1968, these very different bodies of opinion, combined, had become a majority. Popular support for the war dwindled. In that year, President Johnson withdrew from running for a second term.

President Nixon, elected as a result of Johnson's abdication, adopted a complicated strategy that amounted to a partially concealed retreat from the war. He and his adviser, Henry Kissinger, devised a strategy for limiting the great damage the war was doing to American society at home and to the reputation of America abroad. They initiated diplomatic contacts with both Russia and China, hoping to persuade them to rein in the Vietnamese communists. They reduced American military presence, claiming that they would rely on air war. To no avail: in 1975 Americans watched with distress as their last forces withdrew, unable to protect those Vietnamese who had supported them from the vengeance of the victors. Publicly and painfully, the greatest power on earth had lost its first war.

African Americans in the South, and to a lesser extent elsewhere in America, enjoyed less than full freedom. Segregated residentially and socially, they were denied civil rights and in the Deep South the vote. Their separate system of education was far from equal. The problem went far beyond the specific injustices suffered by black Americans. In states with almost one-third of the US population, the defense of segregation maintained a flagrantly undemocratic pyramid of power. At the base, police officers, often brutally, kept African Americans in a subordinate role. Too often the courts denied justice to black people. And at the apex of the system a dozen states were virtually one party polities. Political power was a monopoly enjoyed by conservative Democrats devoted to protecting the South's "way of life." A quarter of the United States Senate and 100 members of the House constituted a bloc of conservative Democrats. Far beyond the racial question, this southern domination of national politics affected everything from foreign affairs to budgetary and social policy. Southern senators and congressmen benefited from a "seniority system" that did not begin to crack until the middle 1970s.[13]

In the late 1930s a small group of African American lawyers dared to drive the first wedge into this formidable structure of repressive power. Tactically they chose to campaign for desegregation in education, first in law schools, then in universities generally, and finally in secondary schools. After a long campaign they won a great victory in 1954. In the famous case of *Brown v. the School Board of Topeka, Kansas* the Supreme Court held that separate education was intrinsically unequal.[14]

Even after the *Brown* decision the Deep South was determined to resist. Change came from activist groups. The Southern Christian Leadership Conference was led by Dr. Martin Luther King Jr., educated son of a respected Atlanta preacher. King had absorbed the ideals and techniques of M. K. Gandhi and the Indian nonviolent resistance movement against British rule. He began to lead demonstrations in one Deep South town after another, culminating in his campaign to desegregate Birmingham, Alabama, and in his great speech at the March on Washington in 1963. At the same time younger activists, less thoughtful than King, in the Congress for Racial Equality and the Student Non-Violent Coordinating Committee, began to work at registering black voters in the rural South.[15]

This put national Democratic politicians, torn between their northern labor union, liberal, and black voters and the serried ranks of the southern Democracy, under pressure. It was not until Lyndon Johnson became President (a Texan with conservative instincts but also with a deep commitment to justice for black people) that Congress passed a Civil Rights Act (1964) and a Voting Rights Act (1965).

This marked the end of the first phase of a revolution in the politics of race in America. Black people in the South achieved legal equality. Most southern whites, after the initial shock of desegregation, accepted legal equality more or less reluctantly, sometimes indeed with relief and even pride. But the political geography of the South was profoundly changed.

Many of the more conservative southerners, who had supported conservative Democrats, became Republicans. This process had incalculably important consequences for national politics. Stripped of most of the southern conservatives, and reinforced by millions of southern black voters, the national Democratic party moved sharply to the Left. The Republican party, on the other hand, once proud of its part in preserving the Union and emancipating the slaves, became more clearly identified as conservative.

One unanticipated consequence of the end of the one-party Democratic South was to change the ideological color of the national two-party system. Until the 1960s, if you had to explain to an intelligent foreigner what divided the two American parties, you would have had to refer to the great events of the 1860s: civil war, emancipation, and "Reconstruction." Now, after the great political victories of the Johnson administration, the parties were defined by the events of the 1960s.

The majority of white Americans, even in the South, found it hard to argue with the end of segregation by law. To achieve equality as a fact in the North was far harder. The North, too, was racially segregated, not by law, but by custom. Northern cities and their suburbs were in practice almost as sharply segregated in residential terms as the South, and residential segregation was reflected in schools. Efforts to change this by such court-approved devices as busing were bitterly resented. So were most forms of "affirmative action." White working-class families felt they were being asked to shoulder an unfair share of the burden of social and racial transformation. Efforts to use the power of the federal government for social purposes were more likely to make the government unpopular than to achieve its aims.

Starting as early as 1964, when the Republicans nominated Senator Barry Goldwater of Arizona as their candidate, only to hear him proclaim that "extremism in the defense of liberty is no crime," a new radical Right made itself felt in politics. This had many sources: in religious and moral feelings, in economic fears, and in an offended patriotism, brilliantly expressed by Ronald Reagan among many others, that sprang from the feeling that the security and the prestige of the United States had been put at risk.

By the middle 1970s, the United States was experiencing serious economic competition, first from western Europe, then from East Asia. For the first time, the United States was importing energy. After the Arab oil embargo of 1973 and the consequent price rise, Americans, sitting in gas lines, found themselves wondering whether the cheap energy that had fueled American prosperity would last for their children. The country experienced weak economic growth and high inflation.

Now corporate business determined to be master in its own house again. A new generation of managers aggressively challenged the unions, which lost members. The inflation of house prices took whole bands of modestly paid workers, for the first time, into higher tax brackets. Beginning in California in 1977 a tax rebellion spread across the country. Conservative intellectuals began to develop a whole series of new doctrines with appeal to groups of people for whom the old Republican conservatism meant nothing. One was the immensely popular, if fallacious, idea that "liberalism",[16] so far from being the ideology of the working man, was the philosophy of snobbish elites.

Monetarism, supply side economics, and other critiques of New Deal liberalism flourished. The axe was first laid to the roots of "Keynesian" orthodoxy by Milton Friedman in his presidential lecture to the American Economic Association as early as 1967. By the middle 1970s, as he prepared to make a serious run for the presidency, Ronald Reagan had recruited a powerful team of conservative economists to advise him.

A new breed of conservative intellectual impresarios sought to deprive the liberals of the virtual monopoly of influence they had enjoyed. An event of great resonance in this process was the founding in 1973 by a small group led by Irving Kristol of the journal *The Public Interest*. This, together with the group who provided the ideas for Senator Henry "Scoop" Jackson's unsuccessful campaign for the Democratic presidential nomination in 1976, which included Daniel Patrick Moynihan, Norman Podhoretz, and Richard Perle, was the first generation of what came to be called the "neoconservatives." At first, the group (admittedly a loose and indeed disparate one) was concerned with refuting what it saw as the un-American New Left thrown up by the antiwar civil rights movements. Only later did a second generation (including some of the sons of the first generation, notably Irving Kristol's son William Kristol) focus more on foreign policy issues.

Foreign policy was, however, one of the fields where the new conservatism first found a response. The Soviet leader, Leonid Brezhnev, enunciated the doctrine that bears his name, that the Soviet Union would always support those struggling for revolution. Soviet policymakers decided to take advantage of the Watergate crisis and of the Carter administration, often by supporting their ally, Cuba. The culmination of this newly aggressive Soviet policy in the developing world came with the invasion of Afghanistan at the end of 1979.

American conservatives were more concerned by the Nixon–Kissinger policy of détente with the Soviet Union in strategic matters. In the early 1970s the neoconservative group around Senator Jackson linked trade concessions to the Soviet Union with Soviet policy on emigration, especially of Jews. In 1976 a number of influential men formed a Committee on the Present Danger to alert the Washington community to the Soviet threat, and President Ford allowed his Director of Central Intelligence, George H. W. Bush, to set up a group of conservative figures, known as Team B, to criticize the CIA's official estimate of Soviet capabilities and intentions. The stage was being set for a new, more confrontational policy under Ronald Reagan.

Reagan's foreign policy was less simple than many expected when, in a speech to Evangelical ministers in 1983, he characterized the Soviet Union as an "evil empire."[17] By his second term, he could claim decisive success in dismantling the Soviet threat, though much of that happy outcome was due to the unexpectedly rapid disintegration of the Soviet economy. Reagan was intent from the start on successful negotiations with the Soviet Union, but did not believe that a conciliatory stance was the right approach. In the summer of 1983, however, he asked a disarmingly simple question about the conventional belief in "mutually assured deterrence." "Wouldn't it be better," he asked a national television audience, "to save lives than to avenge them?"[18]

Almost a quarter of a century later, SDI still does not work as a weapons system. But as a diplomatic offensive it was instantly successful. Mikhail Gorbachev, the new Soviet leader, who was attempting to save communism by a strategy of transparency and transformation (*glasnost* and *perestroika*), calculated that an attempt to match American technology would shake the Soviet economy to pieces. He was prepared to end the nuclear competition of the Cold War. Reagan had foreseen this. The supposed simpleton had read the realities of diplomatic conflict better than the experts.

The Gorbachev policy in the Soviet Union led to the collapse of communist regimes in eastern Europe, an event of immense resonance. Reagan's record in the peripheral battlefields was less impressive. He launched a number of military attacks, in Lebanon, Grenada, and Libya. He overestimated the threat from a Leftist government in Nicaragua, and allowed undisciplined staff to mount a clumsy operation to circumvent congressional prohibitions against supporting Right-wing guerrillas there. Yet by his inimitable combination of joviality and toughness, he evoked almost fanatical affection and persuaded a majority of Americans that it was "morning in America."

Lionel Trilling famously declared, in 1950, that liberalism is the only intellectual tradition in the United States. By the 1960s conservative journals and magazines were no longer confined to a ghetto. William F. Buckley and his *National Review* united libertarian and traditional conservatives under the banner of anti-communist nationalism. Editorial writers like Robert Bartley of the *Wall Street Journal* and columnists such as George F. Will in the *Washington Post*, demanded to be taken seriously even by their opponents.

Conservative activists took Democratic political professionals on at their own game. Direct mail fund-raisers like Richard Viguerie and conservative angels such as Joseph Coors of the Heritage Foundation and William Baroody Jr. of the American Enterprise Institute provided the money. From the 1970s, they established first beach-heads, then dominant political machines in many states, prosperous suburban counties, and cities.

The trend was reinforced by developments in the all-important news media.[19] National television arrived in the United States only in 1953, when the first "coast-to-coast hookup" was achieved. For the first few years, American television went through a springtime of innovation, then settled down to what was to be its continuing forte, earning immense profits by not overestimating the taste of the American audience. From the late 1950s until about 1980 both news and entertainment were dominated by the three national networks, CBS, NBC, and ABC. The country was divided into several hundred markets, almost all of which boasted a local station "affiliated" to each of the networks. Public broadcasting, introduced in 1967, with the Public Broadcasting System for television and National Public Radio, was limited to providing such material as was thought desirable, but from which the commercial networks could not make money.

By the 1960s, more than 80 percent of the population cited television, not radio or newspapers, as the primary source of their national and international news. All three networks were located in New York. They unconsciously imported into their presentation of the news a relatively liberal New York "take." In the 1960s and 1970s the technology, both of production and of distribution, changed fast. Eventually digital technology was to have even greater impact. There was a ready market for a new, higher quality cable television, introduced by pioneers like Ted Turner of Atlanta around 1980. By the early 1990s, cable was giving American viewers quality programming as well as choice. It cut sharply into the near-monopoly of the three networks. Their share of the national audience, once over 90 percent, fell to 60 percent and below. The influence of New York dwindled accordingly. CNN is based in Atlanta. Much cable production comes from Los Angeles. And when Rupert Murdoch's News International launched the Fox network from California, it was unapologetically patriotic, populist, and conservative.

The economy entered the twentieth century still heavily dependent on primary sectors: agriculture, mining, and forestry, though industry was already growing rapidly. In the second and third quarters of the century, manufacturing, using new technologies derived from chemistry and physics and the techniques of mass production and "scientific" management, became the dominant force in the American economy. At the beginning of the century farmers were still numerous, but the dominant unit was the "small town," admittedly an elastic concept that covered many kinds of settlements. When the century began great cities had already acquired the accoutrements of metropolitan life: great universities, public buildings to be compared with those of the great European cities, office buildings that far outstripped in efficiency, not to mention height, anything to be seen on the other side of the Atlantic, museums, symphony orchestras, sports arenas, mass transit systems. More typical than either the very rich or the very poor was a growing American middle class of clerks, industrial workers, and artisans of every kind, most of them living in realistic hope of achieving a decent standard of comfort and dignity.

Several European manufacturers were building cars before Ransom E. Olds built the first gasoline car in America in 1900. Thereafter the American automobile industry grew with astonishing speed. It also offered a kind of model for the development of other industries (radio, aviation, domestic appliances, television, computers) based on technical innovation and production engineering. Competing car manufacturers increasingly relied on marketing that exploited psychological insights as well as on design and commercial hyperbole.

Henry Ford made the first Model T in 1908.[20] By 1913 he was using moving assembly lines, progressively improved. In 1914 he introduced the five-dollar, eight-hour day for workers, and in 1916 US automobile production passed one million units for the first time. In 1917, the year when the United States entered World War I, 14.8 million cars and trucks were registered in the United States, and only 720,000 in the rest of the world. Manufacturing cars, mainly in and immediately around Detroit, became the centerpiece of a vast industrial complex involving steel, glass, and rubber manufacturers, body makers, and subcontractors making thousands of parts.

In the late nineteenth century, an industrial geography had been created between the coal of Pennsylvania and West Virginia and the iron ore of northern Minnesota, shipped by barge through the Sault canal, to the steel mills of Pittsburgh, to be used in the manufacture of steel rails, locomotives, and railroad cars. Now a new industrial empire grew up. It created a lobby in politics even more powerful than the railroads had been in the Gilded Age, involving the automobile, tyre, plastics industries, the truckers and the highway builders and the most powerful industrial lobby of all, the oil industry. The drive to put America on wheels, to build highways and develop ever more and more far-flung suburbs, was backed by growing real estate interests, and by the banking, insurance, and advertising industries.

Even more important was the impact of the automobile industry on American labor. Millions of workers left the farms of the Great Plains and the South to find work in the industrial Midwest. They included millions of African American workers from the Cotton Belt who poured north into Detroit, the South Side of Chicago, the Hough neighborhood in Cleveland, and such Great Lakes industrial cities as Akron, Gary, and Milwaukee. The migration created the preconditions for the racial and political conflicts of the 1960s.

The new consumer-based manufacturing of the 1920s to the 1950s saw the growth of a new "industrial" (as opposed to "craft") unionism. The United Auto Workers pioneered a cooperative unionism based on collective bargaining, elaborate contracts, and broad welfare packages. That won the loyalty of the industrial army that until the 1960s powered the politics of the New Deal and of the Roosevelt coalition in the Democratic party. For a time, the new labor movement encouraged a new, relatively liberal management and so the politics of consensus.

By the end of the century many different kinds of suburbs had developed. Some were major centers of employment as well as residential settlements. No longer were they all enviably opulent. There were black suburbs and white suburbs, and one notable change was that, where once immigrants had begun their life in America by crowding into city neighborhoods with their "landsmen," in the last quarter of the century immigrants headed straight for the suburbs. Diverse as the suburbs are, they share a characteristic that explains much about the political shift to the Right in the last third of the century. For William Schneider, the chief political commentator for CNN, the move to the suburbs suggested a preference for the private over the public. In 2000 and 2004, President George W. Bush reaped a substantial margin in suburban neighborhoods.

For a time after World War II, as after World War I, other industrial nations were too disrupted to compete with American productivity and efficiency. By 1960, though, the automobile and other engineering industries had revived in Europe. Then came the rise of Japan, and later the appearance of new industrial competitors, especially in Southeast Asia, taking advantage of their wage cost advantage to compete, first in third markets, and increasingly in the American market itself. By the end of the twentieth century, the once all-conquering American manufacturing industry was struggling to survive at home, let alone abroad, and American managements were forced to "outsource" manufacturing to countries many Americans had never heard of. To visit a suburban mall became a geography lesson, with American retailers displaying a profusion of high quality textiles, clothing, and appliances produced in such places as China, India, Central America, and even the Andaman Islands.

The decline of American manufacturing industry was concealed by the technological brilliance and wealth-creating capacity of government military, or as it was called "defense," expenditure. In his farewell address in January 1961, President Eisenhower, warned against what he called "the military-industrial complex":

> This conjunction of an immense military establishment and a large arms industry is new in the American experience. The total influence – economic, political, even spiritual – is felt in every city, every State house, every office of the Federal government. We recognize the imperative need for this development. Yet we must not fail to comprehend its grave implications.[21]

In the last third of the twentieth century, the economic geography and the social tone of America changed into a post-industrial pattern that was created in large part by the development of this military industrial complex. (The Internet, for example, developed largely out of the efforts of the Pentagon's Advanced Projects Research Agency.) This profoundly transformed what had once been a deeply civilian country. Tens of millions of American workers can enter the workplace only with name tags and electronic security clearance. By the end of the twentieth century, industry had become intimately tied into the military services. Military officers habitually left to take well-paid jobs in defense industries. Whole new industrial regions, in California and Texas, sprang up to serve the military.

Although around the millennium rash claims were made on behalf of the "new economy," in reality even the relatively brief period of prosperity in the late 1990s did not achieve the all-round success of the years immediately after World War II. Though there was respectable growth, unemployment was relatively low, and there was plenty of technological innovation, the most striking character of the late twentieth-century economy was not its prosperity but its changing nature. Where in mid-century the American economy was driven by manufacturing, now the financial sector was in the driving seat, and its demands were paramount. The values of bankers, brokers, accountants, consultants, and above all lawyers lorded it over those of researchers, scientists, engineers, or inventors. Management took back the control that had been partially lost to unions. Business, too, was remarkably successful in overcoming the unpopularity it had experienced in the Progressive and New Deal eras. Consumers uncritically accepted the authority of brands; many of them became walking billboards, every garment advertising some product or corporation.

Though unemployment never threatened to reach the levels it had reached in the Depression, employment was insecure. The late twentieth century was an age of corporate power. Yet even the corporate elite trod in fear of the stock market and its harsh, unpredictable judgments. The corporate scandals of the time perhaps owed as much to executive fear as to executive greed.

If American society, at the close of the twentieth century, was surprisingly militarized, another transformation struck many observers.[22] Society had also become "southernized." The new conservatism was unmistakably southern. It had many causes, as we have seen. But one of the fundamental causes of the conservative ascendancy was the shifting of the political ballast in the South as a result of the Civil Rights Movement and the enfranchisement of southern blacks. In the late twentieth century southerners dominated the political leadership in both parties, as the names of Jimmy Carter, Bill Clinton, and Al Gore, as well as George Herbert Walker Bush, George W. Bush, Newt Gingrich, Tom DeLay, Trent Lott, and many others remind us.

In the 1960s, it seemed that the South must inevitably become more like the North. Instead, in significant ways the whole country became more like the South. This was not only a matter of enthusiasm for country music and NASCAR racing. Where once the South had been seen as backward, by the 1970s it had become the Sun Belt, representing all that was dynamic in the economy and society, and contrasted with a declining Rust Belt in the Northeast and Midwest. The most prosperous industries congregated in southern California, Texas, Florida, now three of the four most populous states. The new American way of life was to be found in its purest form no longer in New York or Chicago, but in the sprawling metropolises of the Sun Belt and their suburbs, from Miami and Atlanta to Houston, Phoenix, and Los Angeles. "The southernization of American society," writes Michael Lind, "was visible in many realms, from civil rights, where political polarization along racial lines came to define national politics, to economics, where the age-old southern formula of tax cuts, deregulation, free trade and commodity exports came to define the national mainstream."[23]

Nowhere was this more clearly marked than in the role of a new, politicized religion that was quintessentially southern. The new conservatism was inseparable from evangelical Protestantism. Conservative Protestants, especially evangelicals and most of all the Southern Baptists, allied to conservative Catholics and conservative Jews, had acquired power and influence that their own congregations could scarcely have dreamed of at mid-century.

Suburbanized, militarized, "southernized" it might be, but their society at the end of the twentieth century continued to offer Americans practical as well as juridical freedom on a scale unmatched by any society in history. True, even by the end of the 1970s, many of the hopes of the 1960s for the emancipation of racial minorities and the equality of women had proved disappointing. The failure of the Equal Rights Amendment and the rise of the "pro-life" movement are evidence of the latter, and the revulsion against busing, affirmative action, and other measures by which liberal government ought to achieve racial equality, illustrate the former reaction. Yet both minorities and women were in a far stronger and freer state, in terms of both esteem and opportunities, at the end of the century than they had been at its midpoint. Even as the last barriers to advancement for African Americans and for women fell, symbolized by the appointment of Madeleine Albright, Colin Powell, and Condoleezza Rice successively as Secretary of State, so the statistical evidence ground slowly closer and closer to parity. Equality, however, was no longer elusive only for blacks and for women. Whether in terms of income, wealth, education, health care, or opportunity, Americans were getting less equal than they had been, and less equal than the citizens of other advanced democracies.[24]

The freedom of American life, however, as distinct from equality, was not primarily the product of political action. To some degree, it had always been inherent in the space and the resources of America. It was implied in the near-complete absence of feudal relations in American society from the beginning.[25] Freedom and opportunity have always been central to the American ideology. They have also been delivered by institutions of many kinds, and the number of those who could enjoy practical freedom and opportunity grew steadily over the course of the twentieth century. If internationally the twentieth century was the American century, internally it was the century of steadily expanding opportunity to enjoy freedoms that had once been the prerogative of the few.

Educational opportunity extended steadily. For the first half of the century the quality of public schools and of public universities improved. Immigrants from abroad, and internal migrants from poor regions, could receive an education that put them close to equality with those privileged by private education. In the last quarter of the century, to be sure, that process was slowed and in some places reversed. Public secondary schools, at least in the bigger cities, fell behind private schools and the best suburban public schools. Public universities, except for a dozen or so with substantial endowments, could not compete with the great private universities. But that was a worry for the future. The striking fact in the twentieth century was the contribution educational institutions made to opportunity of many kinds.

Less obvious, but even more pervasive, was the contribution of commercial energy and innovation, and especially that of the institutions of credit. Banks, mortgage lenders, credit card companies, and retailers made it possible for the ordinary citizen to travel, to buy homes, cars, appliances, many manufactured cheaply abroad, in a variety and profusion of ways unimagined in earlier generations.

The expansion of credit may have dangers for the future. Not only has the federal government, even in the hands of the Republican party, traditional guardian of monetary probity, lurched into unprecedented levels of deficit and debt. Individual Americans, too, have grown accustomed to owe their soul, not to the "company store," but to the credit card providers. By the end of the century many questioned how long foreign holders of the dollar will be content to hold dollar assets. That was a dramatic shift since the days when the dollar was the world's only "hard currency."

The "default" in American domestic politics has been business hegemony. Business and its spokesmen reigned in the 1920s and the 1950s and again in the closing years of the twentieth century. Every generation or so, however, business is perceived as having failed or overreached itself. Thus in the Progressive era it was seen as having usurped political power. In the Great

Depression it failed to provide prosperity. In the 1950s, as a succession of worried bestsellers warned, a Power Elite led by the Man in the Gray Flannel suit, the Organization Man and his Hidden Persuaders was felt to be trying to impose conformism. In the 1960s, business dominance was challenged by housewives, students, environmentalists, and sexual and racial minorities. By the 1980s, however, business ascendancy was back, reinforced by a new morality, a new nationalism, and a newly politicized religion. At the end of the century, American society was polarized between those who found the dominance of business chafing, and those – a narrow but decisive majority – who resented criticism of the status quo more than they wanted to criticize its limitations.

The American twentieth century divides rather neatly into three periods, separated by two ties of social and political crisis. The first third of the century, astride the triumph of World War I, was a time of buoyant optimism. Before the war, this took the form of Progressivism, itself a complex blend of nostalgia for the imagined simplicities of the agrarian past and ambition to build a juster and more efficient society. In the 1920s the emphasis was on social conservatism and economic expansion. Then, in 1929, came the Great Crash. Unemployment reached close to one-quarter of the workforce. Banks closed. Panic was only calmed by Franklin Roosevelt's bold action to preserve American capitalism and constitutional government.

The middle third of the century was a time of recovery, leading to triumphant success. The United States emerged from World War II not only the most powerful nation on earth, but also a fairer and more open social democracy than even the Progressives had contemplated. A "liberal consensus" brought conservatives and liberals together, as both agreed to restrain their ambition to impose their vision. Yet the Cold War subjected American society to strains that were not always fully understood. As a result, a second, more subtle time of troubles arrived at about the two-thirds mark of the century. The Civil Rights Movement and the Vietnam War combined to challenge all traditional forms of authority. During the five years from the assassination of President Kennedy in November 1963 to the election of President Nixon in November 1968, these strains ended the era of liberal consensus and social democracy and opened the way for a conservative ascendancy that was sealed by the election of Ronald Reagan in 1980.

The mood of 2000 hardly qualified as national contentment. But it did constitute a broad acceptance that American life, if not perfect, was better than any alternative. It was this, rather than any Lucean ambition to be the world's Good Samaritan, that inspired a growing belief that it would be the destiny of the United States, in spite of the incomprehension of an ungrateful world, to build a new American century.

NOTES

1. Henry R. Luce, editorial, *Time* magazine, February 1941.
2. William Jefferson Clinton, State of the Union message, January 27, 2000.
3. William Kristol and others, *Project for a New American Century*, www. newamericancentury.org.
4. Desmond King, *Making Americans: Immigration, Race and the Making of a Diverse Democracy* (Cambridge, MA: Harvard University Press, 2000).
5. James P. Smith and Barry Edmonston (eds.), *The New American Economics, Demographic and Fiscal Effects of Immigration* (Washington DC: National Academy Press, 1997).
6. David M. Potter, *People of Plenty, Economic Abundance and the American Character* (Chicago: University of Chicago Press, 1954).
7. On the problems of cities and the rise of the suburbs, see Jane Jacobs, *Death and Life of Great American Cities* (New York: Random House, 1961); Kenneth T. Jackson, *Crabgrass Frontier* (New York: Oxford University Press, 1985); Joel Garreau, *Edge City: Life on the New Frontier* (New York: Doubleday, 1991).
8. On the black migration, Nicholas Lemann, *The Promised Land: the Great Black Migration and How It Changed America* (New York: Knopf, 1991).
9. Barbara W. Tuchman, *The Zimmermann Telegram* (New York: Ballantine (Random House), 1958).
10. John Milton Cooper, Jr., *Breaking the Heart of the World* (Cambridge: Cambridge University Press, 2001).
11. Nelson Lichtenstein, *The Most Dangerous Man in Detroit: Walter Reuther and the Fate of American Labor* (New York: Basic Books, 1995); Nelson Lichtenstein, *State of the Union* (Princeton, NJ: Princeton University Press, 2001).
12. Walter Isaacson and Evan Thomas, *The Wise Men: Six Friends and the World They Made* (New York: Simon & Schuster, 1986).
13. On the lasting effect of the racial conflicts of the 1960s on the rise of conservatism, see Dan T. Carter, *The Politics of Rage: George Wallace, the Origins of the New Conservatism and the Transformation of American Politics* (New York: Simon & Schuster, 1995).
14. See C. Vann Woodward, *The Strange Career of Jim Crow* (New York: Oxford University Press, 1955).
15. On the civil rights revolution, there is a vast literature. Try Taylor Branch, *Parting the Waters: America in the King Years, 1954 to 1963* (New York: Simon & Schuster, 1988).
16. The word "liberalism," which had once described the free trade, *laissez-faire* ideas of businessmen, had become a euphemism for socialist or social democratic ideas.
17. Speech to National Association of Evangelicals, March 1983. See Gil Troy, *Morning in America: How Ronald Reagan Invented the 1980s* (Princeton, NJ: Princeton University Press, 2005), p. 241.
18. Address to the Nation on National Security by President Ronald Reagan, March 23, 1983.
19. A good introduction is Michael and Edwin Emery, *The Press and America* (Englewood Cliffs, NJ: Prentice Hall, 1992).

20. The following automobile statistics are taken from Richard A. Wright, *West of Laramie*, a history of the automobile written for the Antique Automobile Club of America and published on its website, aaca.org.
21. President Dwight D. Eisenhower, Farewell Address to the Nation, January 17, 1961.
22. For example, John Egerton, *The Americanization of Dixie; the Southernization of America* (New York: Harper's Magazine Press, 1973); Peter Applebome, *Dixie Rising: How the South Is Shaping American Values, Politics and Culture* (New York: Random House, 1996); Dan T. Carter, *The Politics of Rage: George Wallace, the Origins of the New Conservatism, and the Transformation of American Politics* (Baton Rouge: Louisiana State University Press, 1996); Godfrey Hodgson, *More Equal Than Others* (Princeton, NJ, Princeton University Press, 2004); Michael Lind, in Steve Fraser and Gary Gerstle (eds.) *Ruling America* (Cambridge, MA, Harvard University Press, 2005).
23. Lind in Fraser and Gerstle, *Ruling America*, p. 253.
24. See Lawrence Mishel, Jared Bernstein, and John Schmitt, *The State of Working America, 2000/2001*, Washington DC, Economic Policy Council (Ithaca, NY: Cornel University Press, 2001); Hodgson, *More Equal Than Others.*
25. Only near complete. Slavery notoriously imitated and indeed exceeded the power relations of feudal society, since rights were implicit in feudal societies, while slavery, at least in North America, denied all rights. And here and there a kind of feudalism lasted well into the nineteenth century. See Howard Zinn, *A People's History of the United States* (New York: HarperCollins, 1999), p. 212, for the 80,000 tenants of the van Rensselaer manor in the Hudson valley in the 1830s. Similar conditions have appeared in south Texas, northern New Mexico and elsewhere. But American institutions have never been feudal, and the feudal spirit has never reigned unchallenged in America.

FURTHER READING

Louis Auchincloss, *Theodore Roosevelt*, New York: Times Books, 2001.

Susan Brownmiller, *In Our Time: Memoir of a Revolution*, New York: Random House, 1999.

Lou Cannon, *President Reagan: The Role of a Lifetime*, New York: Public Affairs, 2000.

James Chace, *1912: Wilson, Roosevelt, Taft and Debs: The Election that Changed the World*, New York: Simon & Schuster, 2004.

David Greenberg, *Nixon's Shadow*, New York: Norton, 2003.

Stanley Karnow, *Vietnam*, New York: Viking, 1983.

David L. Lewis, *Martin Luther King: A Critical Biography*, New York: Praeger, 1970.

William A. Rusher, *The Rise of the Right*, New York: Morrow, 1983.

Arthur M. Schlesinger Jr., *The Age of Roosevelt, Vol.* II, *The Coming of the New Deal*, Boston: Houghton Mifflin, 1957.

C. Vann Woodward, *The Strange Career of Jim Crow*, New York: Oxford University Press, 1955.

3

RICHARD H. KING

The regions and regionalism

US history has been profoundly shaped by the existence of regions and regional consciousness, though the terms "sections" and "sectionalism" were more commonly used until the late nineteenth century. In its formative moments – the Continental Congress and the Constitutional Convention – the new republic was already divided along sectional lines that in turn marked out different economic, social, political, and security interests. Indeed, two of the defining "facts" about the United States of America – the existence of slavery and the presence of (so-called) "free land" in the West – made sectional politics inevitable. From them emerged the North–South and the East–West polarities in American politics and culture. Moreover, the three-sided contest among the Northeast, the South, and the West was one of the preconditions for the American Civil War (1861–5), with the South squared off against the North for control of the trans-Mississippi West. Without slavery there would have been no war, but had the peculiar institution been scattered evenly across the continent, it is hard to imagine that there could have been a sectional crisis.

Several other factors have worked to make regions crucially important in the history of the United States. First, that the United States was a *federal* republic was of great, if ambiguous, importance. On the one hand, the federal structure of the United States and the strong (largely southern) sense that the United States was a compact among states rather than a contract among individuals encouraged hostility to federal interference in the affairs of the separate states. Still, a growing consciousness that common interests united the slave states and the desire to create a free state majority by excluding slavery from the West clearly challenged individual state sovereignty as much as did the exercise of federal power. Furthermore, the Confederate States of America, it has sometimes been said, came to grief over the issue of states' rights. Thus, constitutional federalism could both encourage and stifle the emergence of sectional unity.

From this follows a second factor – the explicitly sectional rhetoric of the Civil War, in referring to the contending sides as the "North" and the "South." Race and labor systems, economic and political interests were of course extremely important, but the conflict that led to the war itself was couched in the language of political geography rather than race or class as such. More importantly, the Civil War itself played a major role in consolidating regional loyalties and thus creating a stronger South than had perhaps existed during the fighting itself. If the Confederacy was destroyed by the war as a political entity, the South as a region emerged with renewed, even heightened, historical-cultural identity after the war.

Yet a third factor in helping to consolidate regional divisions was the influence of romantic modes of thought in the first half of the nineteenth century.[1] Increasingly, writers, intellectuals, and politicians conceived of nations ("peoples" or "races") as possessing something like permanent qualities, which were more than the sum of individual preferences and behavior. Romanticism also made it easier to formulate notions of regional identity, since it suggested that shared cultural characteristics were more important than political boundaries and institutions in defining group identity. The New England version of American romanticism, transcendentalism, tended to spiritualize place and landscape. From that it was but a short step to the belief that there was an organic relationship between place and race, which produced the unified sensibility of the people (a *Volksgeist* or spirit). Out of this shared spirit, so this argument went, works of literature, art, and architecture, traditions of value and morality, and shared ways of doing and being would emerge.

Finally, the existence of a vast continent empty of Europeans meant two things. On the one hand, as historian Frederick Jackson Turner emphasized in his famous "The Significance of the Frontier in American History"(1893), the frontier experience helped create a national sense of democratic identity and the democratic institutions to accompany that new feeling. Yet Turner also emphasized the importance of sections/regions in the development of the United States. Undoubtedly, as historian Richard Hofstadter later noted, the emergence of sections seemed to contradict Turner's own thesis concerning the creation of a unified democratic ethos, but his sectional thesis struck a realistic note by emphasizing the way that sectional divisions were both inevitable (due to geographic and hence economic differences) and valuable in contributing to a sense of interdependence that helped cement the nation into one. If there is a single intellectual forebear of regionalism, it is the Wisconsin-born Turner.[2]

And yet, the process of turning "space" into "place," of transforming vast expanses of empty land into "somewhere," took time. For all the spread-eagle patriotism that white Americans often voiced, a continental nation, united by institutions, constitutions, and animating ideas rather than traditions and historical experience, remained something of an abstraction. Because the Civil War was an internal conflict, the creation of bonds of loyalty among white Americans through the shedding of blood against a common enemy was hardly possible. After the Civil War, the desperate attempt to re-establish national unity and a unified identity increasingly assumed a racialized form based on a common commitment to "whiteness."[3] What Lincoln referred to as the "mystic chords of union" came to be articulated in racial terms by the end of the century, though not without an admixture of political and moral universalism. Yet, if terms such as "multiculturalism" and "cultural difference" had existed circa 1900, they would have as likely referred to the uneasy co-existence of different regional cultures as to the co-presence of various racial, ethnic, and religious communities. One reassuring sign of restored national (white) unity to many Americans was the way southern (white) boys fought alongside northern (mostly white) boys in Cuba against the Spanish in 1898. In the long run, race may have functioned as the solvent of regional differences, but regional tensions and sectional rivalries still reflected the nation's most pressing concern – the creation of unified national identity.

Regionalism as ideology: 1918–1945

Several developments led to the emergence of an explicit ideology of regionalism, but one that rejected much of the tired position-taking derived from the Civil War experience (the southern evocation of "Lost Cause" versus the northern "waving of the bloody shirt"). Particularly important was the modernization of American society. As a cultural ideology, regionalism tended to have strong rural, small-town roots and suspected that the "real" America was being submerged by the threatening processes of urbanization and industrialization. Thus, in general, the concept of the "regional" was all but synonymous with the "rural," the "local," and the "folk" or "people."[4] By the 1920s, the cultural split in the United States was less one of North versus South than it was a rural, small-town versus an urban-industrial one. The second Ku Klux Klan (1915–25) was no longer an exclusively southern-based regional organization, but rather exerted strong – and open – political strength in the Midwest and Southwest. To the new urban cosmopolitans and the largely ethnic industrial working class, the regions seemed a breeding ground for disturbing phenomena such as the Klan and Prohibition, the Scopes Trial and Protestant fundamentalism, nativism and bigotry. One of the so-called Regionalist painters, Grant Wood, immortalized something of this crabbed, rural, and small-town sensibility in his painting *American Gothic*.

One might have expected that regionalism would justify itself with a *Voelkisch* ideology of racial and ethnic purity along the model of European racialized populism. Yet the intellectuals who contributed to the interwar ideology of regionalism, prominent among them Lewis Mumford, Howard Odum, B. A. Botkin, Marie Sandoz, and Benton MacKaye, avoided explicit racial and ethnic exclusivity or cultural chauvinism. Regionalism's most insightful historian, Robert Dorman, has suggested that, although region-alism tended to see modernization as a threat introduced by outside forces and emphasized "organic folk culture," it was by no means a monolithic movement. Several versions of "folk" culture, including "pioneer agrarian-republican communities, Indian tribal culture, and immigrant-born folk life" were articulated.[5] The racial exclusivity of the Vanderbilt Agrarians in Nashville, Tennessee, who issued their manifesto *I'll Take My Stand* in 1930, was an exception rather than the rule among the various regionalist movements in the South, the Midwest and Plains states (Nebraska was an active centre), the Southwest (focused on Hispanic and Native American populations), and New England. Indeed, the South generated two contrast-ing brands of regionalism – the conservative sectionalism of the Vanderbilt Agrarians and the progressive regionalism of sociologists and folklorists at the University of North Carolina, who emphasized the need to preserve the vanishing folk cultures and to develop the South economically through regional planning.[6]

Furthermore, though the regionalist movement broke no lances for the cause of racial justice, the new attention paid to African American culture in the "Negro" (or Harlem) Renaissance in the 1920s, the collecting of the music of black (and white) rural southerners in the 1930s, and efforts of New Deal agencies such as the Works Progress Administration (WPA) to preserve local and folk cultures were all informed by the same spirit that animated regionalism. Indeed, several of the publicists associated with the regionalist movements also worked for the New Deal. At its best, regional-ism was a version of cultural nationalism that defined "authentic" American folk culture in pluralist rather than monolithic terms.

In addition, many regionalist intellectuals shared a clear hostility to the emerging mass culture with radical groups such as the Frankfurt School of Social Research in exile and the emerging New York intellectuals.[7] They suspected that its function was to further the interests of monopoly and finance capitalism and to debase those folk cultures that still existed. And though regionalists had no more use for the communist term "masses" (they preferred "the people") than they did for "mass culture," regionalism was broadly a movement of the Left rather than the Right. It forged a cultural vision, an aesthetic and ultimately a politics of culture that sought to fight free of all the current "isms"– fascism, communism, corporate capitalism, and liberalism.

1930s regionalism was, then, part of an intellectual and cultural ground-swell to establish American culture "on native grounds," to use Alfred Kazin's resonant words. Thus a dialectic between America as a unified national culture and America as a "culture of cultures" was established. Though Malcolm Cowley spoke of an intellectual and artistic "exiles' return" from Europe after the stock market crash in 1929, the "rediscovery" of America had began already in the 1920s. Lewis Mumford, one of the architects of intellectual regionalism, was already announcing his ideas in the mid-1920s, while William Carlos Williams's *In the American Grain* appeared in 1925. One of the defining tensions in Vernon Lewis Parrington's unfinished *Main Currents in American Thought* (1927, 1930) was the dialectic of nation and region. While its title insisted on the reality of a national intellectual tradition, its first two volumes were subdivided into categories such as "The Mind of New England," "The Romance of the West," and "The Mind of the South." In other words, Parrington's pioneering work constructed a national intellectual tradition that was regionally articulated and organized. Harvard English Professor Perry Miller's powerful defense of seventeenth-century Puritanism against the onslaught of those who blamed America's cultural ills on the Puritans was named *The New England Mind* (1939). Yet Miller's colleague F. O. Matthiessen opted for a national cultural orientation when he named his masterwork, *American Renaissance* (1941), even though it might have more accurately, if less resonantly, been called *New England Renaissance*. Similarly, though Kazin's *On Native Grounds* (1942) located the origins of modern American writing in the realism on the way to becoming modernism of midwestern writers such as William Dean Howells, Theodore Dreiser, Sherwood Anderson, F. Scott Fitzgerald, and Ernest Hemingway, and though he paid considerable attention to the South's William Faulkner and the southern New Critics, his concern was with the emergence of a modern *American* literature, albeit one alienated from America itself. Thus, as World War II approached, regionalist orientation seemed to be giving way to national cultural consciousness.

If the shift in geographical focus between Miller and Matthiessen suggested the waning of a separate New England literary identity, the South hardly followed suit. W. J. Cash's *The Mind of the South* (1941) explained, but did not defend, the peculiar nature of southern identity rather than claiming that it was the "real" America. Although in agreement on little else, the Vanderbilt Agrarians concurred with Cash that the South was genuinely different, though they preferred to celebrate rather than condemn that difference. It was also becoming clear by the late 1930s, if not before, that the South was witnessing the emergence of an uncommon number of first-rate novelists, poets, journalists, and historians. While Robert Frost gradually assumed the mantle of an American rather than merely a New England poet, William Faulkner's work was suffused with an unmistakable "southernness." A high modernist in style and sensibility, Faulkner transformed the realism, the local color orientation, and the emphasis on dialect of literary regionalism into something unique in American writing. What made Faulkner, the Agrarians and other talented writers such as Eudora Welty and Katherine Ann Porter modernist-regionalists, as it were, was the way they, as southern writer Robert Penn Warren himself noted, tended to make the South a *theme* in rather than just the *setting* of their work. This distinction remains the best shorthand way to judge whether a writer (or any creative figure) is a regionalist in the modernist sense. Although few of Faulkner's contemporaries or successors were able to match the radical nature of his literary vision, the post-1930s literary tradition of the South demonstrated that a regionalist orientation, a grounding in place and locale, need not entail formal or aesthetic conservatism, even though it could mean that such a sophisticated regionalist sensibility lost its popular audience.

The only other artistic movements explicitly linked to the regionalist mood were the American Scene and Regionalist painters. Represented most famously by midwesterners such as Thomas Hart Benton (1889–1975), John Steuart Curry (1897–1946), and Grant Wood (1892–1942), these painters rejected the cosmopolitan iconography and high modernist style dominant in the contemporary art world. Expressing what one analyst calls their "romantic realism," they sought to forge an American artistic style from explicitly American themes and settings that would then speak to and for the "people."[8] By no means artistically untutored, Benton never confined himself exclusively to rural and small-town subjects or themes and never forgot that the American rural working class was black as well as white; but his most popular painting reveled in its sheer "Americanness." The underlying assumption was that through an immersion in the particularities of rural and small-town existence, the real America(n) could be recovered. Nor did Benton's painting, particularly the murals that became his metier, express a Conservative vision. (And, obviously, Wood's *American Gothic* was hardly a mindless celebration of the American farm family.) But in an era when Fascist monumentalism and Soviet Socialist Realism were bidding for mass attention in Europe, and when intellectuals such as

Mumford, Van Wyck Brooks, and Archibald MacLeish attacked the literary modernists for perpetuating a defeatist attitude and failure of nerve in the struggle against totalitarianism, the American Scene/Regionalist painters were suspected of peddling a kind of cultural chauvinism in the form of nostalgia by many modernist and politically radical critics.

Why regionalism in painting aroused more critical (though not popular) animosity than did southern literary regionalism is puzzling. It may have had to do with the fact that southern writing was, as mentioned, modernist in some of its basic impulses. New York intellectuals such as Delmore Schwartz and Alfred Kazin wrote with great appreciation of Faulkner, while Irving Howe's critical study of Faulkner in 1952 was the first serious, book-length treatment of the Mississippi writer. Yet the South never developed a strong tradition of either regionalist or modernist painting. Southerners who became influential on the national art scene in the 1950s – the Texan Robert Rauschenberg and South Carolina's Jasper Johns come to mind – disguised their southern roots in the cosmopolitan ambience of New York. It would be hard to maintain that their work was recognizably "southern." Thomas Hart Benton's most influential student, Jackson Pollock of Cody, Wyoming, led the post-1945 turn to abstraction and beyond. Pollock transformed the undeniable energy of Benton's style into the dynamism of his by now famous late 1940s drip paintings, while the commitment to figure, perspective, and recognizable setting disappeared. Like Benton, Pollock was influenced by Mexican mural painting as well as by Native American sand painting, but neither popular accessibility nor explicit political commitment was high among the priorities of the post-1945 New York painters. If there was any (indirect) echo of American values in their work, it lay in their independence and nonconformity, their refusal to place their art in any of the old niches or categories. Otherwise, American Scene painting settled back to become a minor, middlebrow genre after the war. Norman Rockwell and Grandma Moses were great popular successes but critical failures, while a hard to categorize painter such as Edward Hopper began to develop a considerable reputation all his own.

Interregnum: 1945–1975

No simple relationship exists between politics and culture, but America's emergence as a superpower and consumer society after World War II, and the effects of the Cold War on American life, helped to nationalize and, arguably, to homogenize American culture. Before the war, regionalism had been an influential intellectual and artistic movement; after the war, it survived mainly as an object of academic study and/or what Chapel Hill regionalist Rupert Vance referred to in a 1949 symposium as "a conceptual tool for research."[9] Louis Wirth's critique of regionalism in the same symposium enumerated some of the standard charges against regionalism: that it tended toward the "cultish"; that it was too much a "rural movement"; and that, as an analytical approach, it tended to be a "one factor explanation."[10] Symptomatic of the new postwar political climate was the failure of the Tennessee Valley Authority (TVA), a highly popular experiment in regional development, to be duplicated elsewhere around the country. To be sure, regional organizations in the South such as the Southern Regional Council and the Southern Regional Education Board played a role in regional development but they lacked the political or financial clout to play that role very decisively. Another strand of regionalism, particularly in its Western incarnations, contributed to the burgeoning environmentalist movement of the 1960s, while the folk music revival of the postwar years reflected a certain regionalist, grass-roots ideology. As a movement, however, regionalism was dead.

An important academic development in these years was the founding of an American Studies movement and the American Studies Association in 1951 devoted to its perpetuation. In his seminal book, *Virgin Land* (1950), Henry Nash Smith, who had earlier been identified with the regionalist movement in Texas, explored the representation of the West in nineteenth-century popular literature and William Taylor analyzed the antebellum intersectional battle between northern and southern cultural stereotypes in *Cavalier and Yankee* (1961). Yet, by and large, the wave of the future seemed to be the academic study of *American* identity, *American* exceptionalism, and the viability of the *American* liberal consensus on the world stage. Alexis de Tocqueville's nineteenth-century classic, *Democracy in America*, was also mined for its many insights into the American national character. Where Frederick Jackson Turner's focus had fallen upon the frontier as the shaping force in American national identity – and it was Turner the American nationalist rather than the midwestern sectionalist who was cited after 1945 – de Tocqueville warned his readers about the tyranny of the majority and saw the American impulse to form "secondary organizations" as a way of resisting what had come to be called "mass society" and "the tyranny of the majority" in the postwar years. A couple of decades earlier, someone might have thought to try to fit this into the regionalist ideology, but after 1945 it no longer seemed important to make the connections.

In racial matters, the trends were contradictory. A contemporary foreign analyst of American race relations, Sweden's Gunnar Myrdal, saw America's strength as lying in its commitment to an explicitly *national* set of values, organized around freedom and equality, what he named the "American Creed." Indeed, according to Myrdal, the function of the Creed was to discredit local and regional (which is to say southern) commitments to white supremacy. Internationally, a consensus had formed around the idea that all the human races were substantially equal to one another. Yet, in reaction to the 1954 *Brown v. Board of Education* decision outlawing school segregation, a politically charged southern regionalism devoted to the politics of racial division and white supremacy re-emerged with a vengeance. All the worst fears of regionalism's critics were realized. The racist and conservative potential of the doctrine of states' rights was brought home with full force; regionalism was discredited as a largely southern ideology of racial and political reaction.

After the war, American intellectual and literary life was centered largely in New York and dominated by a predominantly Jewish intellectual elite. Two new subgroupings joined the southerners as fresh voices in American writing. The first was an amazingly talented group of Jewish writers – Saul Bellow, Bernard Malamud, Arthur Miller, Philip Roth – whose work was thoroughly urban and cosmopolitan, a far cry from the regionalist tradition. The other group was a powerful duo of black writers, James Baldwin and Ralph Ellison, who sought to outstrip Richard Wright's now fading reputation. Though their themes and concerns were largely African American, they saw themselves as more than "just" black writers. In addition, their characters – and their fiction – sought to escape the black belt South of lynchings and sharecropping for the political radicalism, churches, and ghettos of northern cities. Not surprisingly, neither African American nor Jewish writers betrayed much nostalgia for their roots, respectively, in the US South or in Eastern Europe and Russia. Admittedly, it was more complicated with Ellison, who came to play a vital role in making use of the southern black vernacular "blues" culture; but neither he nor Baldwin seemed interested in returning to, or reproducing, the region that had produced them. As though to distance himself from the regionalist imperative, James Baldwin entitled one section of his powerful *The Fire Next Time* (1963) "Letter from a Region in My Mind." As a rule, Jewish and African American, but also Irish and Italian writers, intellectuals and popular entertainers were rarely considered regionalists, so identified was the regionalist idea with rural and small-town, largely Protestant America. Rather, their "place" was a distinctive sensibility and perhaps voice – in short, theirs was a consciousness grounded in a shared historical experience but without a strong claim on a specific place or landscape, except cities streets and ethnic neighborhoods.

As the 1960s unfolded, racial and ethnic particularism helped fill the vacuum left by the decline of regional consciousness. Race and ethnicity were increasingly seen as central, rather than marginal to, individual and group identity. Black Power groups applied the race concept to political matters, while the Black Arts movements insisted that race was the most important factor in determining cultural identity. It also became apparent by the end of the decade that the so-called melting pot hadn't done its job as European ethnic consciousness also made a comeback. The 1965 abolition of the Johnson–Reed Act of 1924 led to a steady influx of Hispanic/Latino/a population from Mexico, Central and South America; not to mention the Cubans who fled Castro's regime and settled in Miami and south Florida. The late 1960s also saw the growing political and cultural power of women as the second wave of feminism got underway. Finally, the gay rights movement become a public "fact" after the early 1970s.

What characterized these movements was that they were *group*-based rather than *place*-based movements. Group identity was increasingly a matter of consciousness and shared experience rather than anchored in place and location. Retrospectively, we can see that in 1998 when literary scholar Janice Radway rejected the idea that culture could be "conceived as a unitary, uniform thing, as the simple function of a fixed, isolated, and easily mapped territory" and instead affirmed the central role of "multiple, shifting imagined communities" in determining cultural identity, she was announcing a new trend but reflecting (on) a cultural development that had begun in the late 1960s.[11]

The varieties of contemporary regionalism

And yet several developments since the 1960s indicate that regionalism has not totally lost its power to compel interest and even belief. However much social and geographical mobility, the massive influx of new immigrants from Latin America, the Caribbean, and Asia, and the southward shift in demographic and economic power have scrambled traditional regional boundaries, Americans still want to discover (or create) some sort of connection between where and how they live. Several university-based regional studies centers began appearing in the mid-1970s, particularly in the South and the Midwest. The great publishing success of *The Encyclopaedia of Southern Culture* (1989), edited by William Ferris and Charles Reagan Wilson at the Center for the Study of Southern Culture at the University of Mississippi, tapped into a clear interest, both popular and scholarly, in American place and regional culture. The National Endowment of the Humanities (NEH), founded in 1965 and sometimes referred to as the second WPA, funded state-based projects that sought to nurture local and regional awareness. In Ferris's tenure as NEH chair during President

Clinton's second term, he proposed the establishment of regional humanities centers throughout the United States.[12] Indeed, though Radway's challenge to place-based cultural consciousness reflected a certain shift away
from the older regional consciousness, it was oversimplified as stated. It had
always been difficult, even impossible, to detach the bedrock regionalist
assumption about the centrality of place from race and ethnicity, religion,
class, or gender.

For instance, twentieth-century African American history illustrates the
complex and shifting relationship between race- and place-consciousness.
Historically, black American culture had its source in the places, experiences, and institutions of the South. Yet the peak period of regionalist
consciousness in the interwar years coincided with the period when African
Americans began the "great" migration from the South to the North and the
West and from rural to urban settings. Were blacks who lived/live in the
historic South "southerners"? Should one say "black Southerners" or
"southern blacks?" How long did African Americans have to live in
Chicago before their shared culture lost a specifically southern dimension?
Or did it ever? And what was/is the proper name for the cultural revival of
the 1920s – the "Negro" or the "Harlem" Renaissance? It is no secret that
there were strong regional tensions among the shock troops of the Civil
Rights Movement in the 1960s. Civil rights workers from the South tended
to be more religious and more committed to nonviolence as a vision as well
as strategy than their northern black counterparts. The persisting ideological
dichotomy between Malcolm X and Martin Luther King was, and is, a
function of regional as well as personal differences. The remarkable history
of African American music could also be explicated in either regional or
racial-cultural terms. By extension, the failure, for instance, of the blues and
jazz to find mass audience support among young African Americans since
the 1950s may reflect that fact that where and under what conditions
someone lives are, over the long haul, more important than skin color or
past group experience in shaping a response to certain cultural forms.

Similar questions arise about the white South, which shed some of its
negative reputation as the 1960s receded in time. The "new" South of
President Jimmy Carter of Georgia redefined itself apart from the disfiguring
racism and the commitment to segregation that had constituted much of the
region's modern political and cultural identity. Just a couple of years before
Carter was elected President in 1976, John Egerton's *The Americanization
of Dixie* (1974) added a new complexity to the question of regional self-
consciousness, for his thesis was that the South seemed increasingly to
resemble the rest of America. So much for southern distinctiveness. Yet his
subtitle – "The Southernization of America" – suggested something more

interesting, since he also claimed that the rest of the United States had embraced the cultural tastes and political preferences associated with the South. Among these were such phenomena as the growth of non-traditional Protestant churches, a clear shift to the right politically, persisting anxiety about race, crime, and declining family values, and a certain belligerence in foreign policy.

This diffusion rather than disappearance of regional differences was evident in one of the most interesting popular cultural developments of the 1970s – the spread of country music across the white nation. Significantly, folklorists and collectors in the interwar years had largely scorned country music, or at least were ambivalent about it as lacking authenticity. As it developed through Nashville's Grand Ole Opry, the pure mountain music of the Appalachian South, claimed the purists, had been corrupted by commercial interests and outsiders who came to laugh at the yokels. Of course, country music had once been known as "Country and Western" in the 1940s and 1950s, and Texas swing was one of its important components; Bakersfield, California was a centre of country music due to the immigration of "Okies" in the 1930s; and several Canadian country artists had successful music careers in Nashville. By the 1960s, however, the music found on the country charts was largely considered hillbilly, poor white, or redneck music and identified specifically as southern. Yet only a decade later, country music had not only spread across the nation but also garnered a new international audience. Ironically, it probably lost rather than gained in black listeners over the years, since the post-World War II generation of black popular artists had not grown up in the South listening to the Opry and other country radio stations as had many older black singers.

Another social and political variation on the southernization thesis has been the suggestion that a new region – the Sunbelt or Southern Rim – has emerged since the 1960s. The implication is that the traditional South and Southwest will have to be redefined and may in the process disappear in the forms we once knew them. Still, the possibility of a shared future is less effective than an actually shared past in creating regional solidarity. The South also remains a more coherent region "on the ground" than the West and thus will be harder to split apart. That said, the fact that every President since John Kennedy has come from a Sunbelt state must reflect something about the political and cultural importance of this emerging southern tier of states that spans the continent, a point to which I will return.

More recently, Tony Horwitz's *Confederates in the Attic* (1998) provides another confirmation of sorts of the Egerton thesis. Many of the Civil War re-enactors that Horwitz met in his travels to the various Civil War battlefields were not southerners at all, yet almost all of them wanted to "fight" as Confederates in the re-enacted battles around the South. (Needless to say the vast majority of re-enactors are white, whatever their regional origins.) This was not so much because they regretted the defeat of the Confederacy in the Civil War or that they wanted to revive slavery or segregation. Most re-enactors had little to do with mainstream politics and would have to be classified as gut-level libertarians and nothing more. Rather, to non-southerners the appeal of the Confederate cause and the states' rights ideology had more to do with their desire to be left alone, though such a desire for independence nearly always identified the federal government rather than large corporations as the enemy. Yet Horwitz notes that for some southerners "remembrance of the War had become a talisman against modernity, an emotional lever for their reactionary politics."[13] Very conservative, states' rights organizations such as the League of the South have grown up in the South in the last decade or so. Overall, the fact that the South and the Civil War still assume such talismanic status in American consciousness indicates that regional consciousness persists but is strangely diffuse and protean among white Americans as a kind of symbolic regionalism.

If the Egerton approach emphasizes the intermixing of regional values and traditions, but not their disappearance, there is another contemporary approach to post-1960s regionalism that focuses on the persistence of regional consciousness. It has been most shrewdly and influentially developed in the work of sociologist John Shelton Reed, who once taught at the University of North Carolina, the home of southern regionalism in the 1920s through the 1940s. Along with historian George Tindall, also a one-time faculty member at UNC, Reed has suggested that white southern identity should be treated as a form of ethnicity. Specifically, Reed found that southerners were more prone to resort to violence to solve disputes, were more committed to religious belief and observance, and placed a greater importance on place than most other Americans.[14] What he meant by southernness as ethnicity is captured in his claim that "It is less that Southerners are people who come from the South, for instance, than that the South is where Southerners come from." Put another way, being a Southerner – and by extension a Westerner or New Englander – is primarily a matter of "identification" rather than "location,"[15] of personal preference not place of residence. Thus, Reed in the 1970s clearly anticipated Radway at the turn of the twenty-first century. In both cases, place was replaced by self-identification as a way of defining cultural identity. Yet, Reed would also insist, I think, that place-consciousness remains at least as important as race, ethnicity, class, gender, or sexual preference in defining individual and group identity.

Clearly, the South still dominates most of the discussions of regionalist thinking among historians, social scientists, and journalists. For that reason, it is refreshing to encounter Robert D. Kaplan's recent *An Empire Wilderness* (1998), his account of a journey around the trans-Mississippi West. Kaplan's basic assumption is that the future of the United States will be worked out – or not – west rather than east of the Mississippi. Like other post-regionalist regionalists such as Joel Garreau, Kaplan is struck by the irrelevance of national boundaries in the Southwest and also in the Pacific Northwest. In addition, Kaplan, somewhat like William H. Whyte in the 1950s, is taken with the phenomena of suburbia. All over the West, he finds multinational, multicultural, micro-economies and social enclaves, what he calls "polycentric suburban pods," dotting the landscape. In particular, they seem to proliferate in southern California and along the West Coast, the area Garreau named "Ecotopia" in his *The Nine Nations of North America* nearly twenty years earlier.[16] (The best new candidate for regional status in contemporary America is California, a state, a region, a quasi-nation, and a mentality all rolled into one.) Still, everywhere Kaplan looks, he sees high-tech, multicultural affluence set cheek-to-jowl with low-end, third-world despair, and wonders about the ability of traditional American values to cope with this emerging bifurcated society. Writing in the same year as Kaplan, Horwitz expressed it thusly:

> In 1861, this was a regional dilemma which it wasn't any more. But socially and culturally, there were ample signs of separatism and disunion along class, race, ethnic and gender lines. The whole notion of a common people united by common principles – even a common language – seemed more open to question than at any period in my life time.[17]

Contemporary literary regionalists are also found in literature and cultural studies programs in the universities. They tend to see things in a less pessimistic light. For them, regionalism is the name for the oppositional voices to the centralizing tendencies of the national culture. Regionalism has been, notes one strong advocate, the "great comeback story of American literature" over the "past thirty or so years."[18] It is still centered in the university, but it has been politicized insofar as it encourages the obscure and marginalized literary voices that challenge the canonical texts of American literature and mainstream cultural values.

Overall, this new academic-based regionalism is organized around three basic assumptions. First, political and cultural boundaries no longer mirror one another, if they ever did. In fact, the new literary regionalism not only wants to ignore state boundaries within the United States, it imagines literary-cultural regionalism as ignoring national boundaries. As Jon Smith and Deborah Cohn write in introducing a new collection of essays on the circum-Caribbean South: "we define America hemispherically. . ."[19] Second, the prising apart of political and cultural boundaries is considered by many to be a form of political and cultural resistance. By thinking of America in trans-national and comparative rather than narrowly national terms, they hope that the power of the American *imperium* will somehow be diminished and the idea of American exceptionalism undermined. Third, the internal diversity of geographical regions receives much more emphasis than it did in interwar regionalism.[20] This is particularly apparent in the West, since at least three substantial ethnic "minorities" are found there – Latino/as, Native Americans, and Asians. Where the variety of regions re-enforced the national culture in older forms of regionalism, the variety of voices within, for instance, the West is now thought to enhance rather than threaten overall regional identity.

While much of this is intellectually and politically suggestive, it can also sound politically and historically naïve. If the history of regionalism teaches us anything, it is that there is no guarantee that regionalist and sectionalists will be politically progressive. The neo-Confederate libertarianism recorded by Tony Horwitz or the apolitical conservatism of the creative capitalists discovered by Robert Kaplan on his trips around the West is hardly likely to challenge trans-national capital or to encourage political insurgency at the grass-roots level. One can also think back to the antebellum period when the national political tradition opposed pro-slavery southern consciousness, as for instance in the 1840s and 1850s when the latter sought to annex parts of Mexico. Amy Kaplan has also recently identified another problem related to this one: "What I'm asking is how both to decenter the United States and analyze its centralized imperial power!"[21] Why, in other words, does paying attention to the American political and cultural empire strengthen it? Finally, it is also short-sighted to dismiss the relevance of national political boundaries in shaping regional consciousness. For instance, the Great Migration of black southerners beginning around World War I and lasting into the 1960s ran toward northern and western US cities rather than toward Havana or Bogota in search of a better future. Nor, in fact, did large numbers of black or white southerners try to go to Canada.

Overall, then, the two most important differences between pre-World War II and post-1960s regionalism are, first, that the old regionalism was much more committed to the importance of place and landscape in defining cultural consciousness, while the new regionalism emphasizes group or communal consciousness as prior to regional identification. Second, and even more important, the old regionalism generally saw the regional cultures in terms of the larger national cultural context and as contributing to the greater strength and richness of the national culture. By way of contrast, the new literary-academic regionalism is unconcerned with, or even opposed to, any strong idea of a national culture.

Finally, there are signs of a revival of literary regionalism from unexpected quarters. Arguably, there is something wrong with the concept of literary regionalism, if it cannot find a place for some of the strongest American literary sub-traditions and some of America's most important contemporary writers, especially African American and Jewish ones. This suggests that the notion of regionalism might be rethought to include the city and its extended environs as a kind of region, if we define region as a space which the author interrogates, criticizes, and defends as though it were a character in its own right. From this perspective, E. L. Doctorow's New York is such a "region," as is Saul Bellow's Chicago. Indeed, Philip Roth has recently confessed that when he began rereading modern American writers in the early 1990s, he discovered that: "The great American writers are regionalists. It's in the American grain. Think of Faulkner in Mississippi or Updike and the town in Pennsylvania he calls Brewer. . .What are these places like? Who lives there? What are the forces determining their lives?"[22] In coming "home" to Newark, New Jersey, Roth has renewed his voice and revitalized his vision. There is no better contemporary example of the enduring power of the literature of place as it intersects with communal consciousness than Roth's work.

Politics and regionalism

As we have seen, the politics of regionalism has played an important, at times crucial, role in American political history. While one set of contemporary observers stresses the interpenetration and overlapping of values and traditions from various parts of the country, others, such as Tony Horwitz and Robert Kaplan, worry out loud about whether Americans are any longer a common people. There are several things to be said about this particular cultural-political worry, besides the "fact" that America has rarely been a "common people" and, as Richard Rodriguez once observed, America's finest moments have rarely been during times of national unity or consensus. First, in the last few years, the debate between multiculturalists and those who yearned for a unitary American culture that raged in the late 1980s and early 1990s has diminished in intensity. What is striking about the conflicts that now divide Americans is the absence of a strong racial or ethnic dimension. For instance, as important as the issue of immigration from Mexico is, Americans are not mobilized against it in great numbers. Race and ethnicity are not the "hot-button" issues they once were. Whatever may divide the South, for instance, from the rest of the nation, it is not articulated in terms of, or fought out over, race. Not only is there no integration crisis, there is no busing controversy and even affirmative action has been an issue for the federal court system rather than fought out in the streets or on the political hustings. Nor, as the 2004 Presidential campaign seemed to demonstrate, are voters automatically galvanized by appeals to economic self-interest. It is not "just the economy, stupid," as Bill Clinton famously put it. What are the kinds of issues that divide Americans and, more to our theme, do they have anything to do with regional differences and regionalisms?

The most immediate answer is that the crucial issue for many voters in the 2004 Presidential election had to do with "moral values." By moral values most voters had in mind those values that strengthen the family, which explains why there was so much hostility to gay marriage and, indirectly, opposition to abortion in one form or another. In addition, issues such as gun control and prayer in the schools remain political rallying points for conservative voters. Essentially, moral values focus not on economic concerns or social status but the distribution, as it were, of symbolic moral capital. Significantly, most of those who advocate the politics of "moral values" assume that the term has to do with personal morality and "lifestyle" as defined by the largely Protestant religious right rather than with issues of economic or social justice, inequitable tax policies, or the absence of a medical care system to cover all Americans.

What the moral values debate harkens back to is journalist David Brooks's well-known "One Nation, Slightly Divisible" piece in *The Atlantic Monthly* in 2001. In that article, Brooks offered his by now well-known thesis that America was divided into two camps – a red and a blue sector. Brooks rightly saw that economic and class issues, so often emphasized by the liberals, were not the only story in explaining what divides Americans, but, in light of the 2000 election, he underestimated the cogency of the conservative argument that what crucially separates Americans are moral issues and cultural preferences of the type described above. Specifically, Brooks characterized this division as one between "red" America which is "traditional, religious, self-disciplined, and patriotic" and "blue" America which is "modern, secular, self-expressive, and discomfited by blatant displays of patriotism." At the time of writing, not long after the terrorist attacks of September 11, 2001, Brooks prematurely rejected the idea that America was divided into warring culture camps.[23]

Are there, then, any regional determinants to Brooks's red–blue division? One way to describe the divide is to place those who live in cities and older suburbs on one side and those who are concentrated in rural, small-town, and ex-urban America on the other. Red and blue are described electorally in terms of the blue West Coast, Middle-Atlantic and New England states plus the Rustbelt Great Lake states against the red South and Southwest (together encompassing the Sun Belt) plus the Louisiana Purchase, minus the Pacific Northwest. I would suggest that Brooks's red versus blue thesis is an updated version of John Egerton's "southernization of America" thesis as it has come to fruition. Note the mixed regional heritage of George Bush – New England grandparents, a home in west Texas, and strong hints of white "southernness." Overall, a generic "heartland" orientation predominates. It is also significant that a Country and Western band led off the celebrations at Bush headquarters on election night. It is highly doubtful that any such a band would have been engaged to play at a Kerry victory party had one been necessary.

The upshot is that in the early years of the twenty-first century, American regionalism and regional consciousness are no longer firmly grounded in place and space, though "southernness" has become the signifier of provincial America in its perpetual conflict with cosmopolitan America, a battle that has been waged since at least the 1920s. Despite George W. Bush's narrow but clear victory in 2004, the United States is not yet dominated enough by red America for its citizens to acknowledge that "We are all Southerners now." But the day may not be far off when that will be a possibility, the dream of some, the nightmare of others.

NOTES

1. Historian Michael O'Brien has in particular emphasized romanticism's role in the emergence of American national and sectional consciousness. See, in particular, *Rethinking the South: Essays in Intellectual History* (Baltimore, MD: Johns Hopkins University Press, 1988).
2. Frederick Jackson Turner, *Frontier and Section: Selected Essays of Frederick Jackson Turner* (Englewood Cliffs, NJ. : Prentice-Hall, Inc,1961); Richard Hofstadter, *The Progressive Historians: Turner, Beard and Parrington* (New York: Random House, 1968), pp. 99–103.
3. Grace Elizabeth Hale, *Making Whiteness: The Culture of Segregation in the South, 1890–1940* (New York: Vintage, 1999); and David Blight, *Race and Reunion: The Civil War in American Memory* (Cambridge, MA.: Belknap Press, 2000).
4. Robert L. Dorman, *Revolt of the Provinces: The Regionalist Movement in America, 1920–1945* (Chapel Hill: University of North Carolina Press, 1993) and Jerrold Hirsch, "Becoming History: The Interwar Regional Movement," *American Quarterly*, 49,1 (March 1997): 171–83.
5. Dorman, *Revolt of the Provinces*, p. 10.
6. Daniel J. Singal, *The War Within: From Victorian to Modernist Thought in the South* (Chapel Hill: University of North Carolina Press, 1982).
7. Dorman, *Revolt of the Provinces*, pp. 22–3, 292.

8. See Charles Hirschfield, "'Ash Can' Versus 'Modern' Art in America," *Western Humanities Review*, 10 (Autumn 1956): 353–73; and also Matthew Baigell, *A Concise History of American Painting and Sculpture*, rev. ed. (New York: HarperCollins, 1996), pp. 260–9.

9. Merrill Jensen (ed.), *Regionalism in America* (Madison: University of Wisconsin Press, 1952), p. 126.

10. *Ibid.*, p. 391.

11. Janice Radway, "'What's in a Name?'– Presidential Address to the American Studies Association, 20 November, 1998," *American Quarterly*, 51 (March 1999): 12.

12. William Ferris and Charles Reagan Wilson (eds.), *The Encyclopaedia of Southern Culture* (Chapel Hill: University of North Carolina Press, 1989).

13. Tony Horwitz, *Confederates in the Attic* (New York: Vintage, 1998), p. 386.

14. John Shelton Reed, *The Enduring South* (Chapel Hill: University of North Carolina Press, 1972).

15. John Shelton Reed, *One South: An Ethnic Approach to Regional Culture* (Baton Rouge and London: Louisiana State University Press, 1982), p. 13.

16. Robert D. Kaplan, *An Empire Wilderness: Travels into America's Future* (New York: Vintage, 1998), p. 42; Joel Garreau, *The Nine Nations of North America* (New York: Avon Books, 1982).

17. Horwitz, *Confederates in the Attic*, p. 386.

18. Stephanie Foote, "The Cultural Work of American Regionalism," in Charles L. Crow (ed.), *A Companion to the Regional Literatures of America* (Malden, MA and Oxford: Blackwell, 2003), p. 25.

19. Jon Smith and Deborah Cohn (eds.), "Introduction: Uncanny Hybridities," *Look Away: The US South in New World Studies* (Durham, NC and London: Duke University Press, 2004), p. 2.

20. Patricia Limerick, "The Realization of the American West," in Charles Reagan Wilson (ed.), *The New Regionalism* (Jackson: University Press of Mississippi, 1998), pp. 71–104.

21. Amy Kaplan, "'Violent Belongings and the Question of Empire Today' – Presidential Address to the American Studies Association, October 17, 2003," *American Quarterly*, 56,1 (March 2004): 1–18.

22. Philip Roth, Interview with Al Alvarez (Profile: "The long road home") *Guardian Review*, September 11, 2004, p. 23.

23. David Brooks, "One Nation, Slightly Divisible"(2001), *The Atlantic Online*, http://www.theatlantic.com/cgi-bin/send.cgi? page=http%3A//www.theatlantic.com/issues/2 p. 10.

FURTHER READING

Charles L. Crow (ed.), *A Companion to the Regional Literatures of America*, Malden, MA, and Oxford: Blackwell, 2003.

Robert L. Dorman, *Revolt of the Provinces: The Regionalist Movement in America, 1920–1945*, Chapel Hill, NC: UNC Press, 1993.

William Ferris and Charles Reagan Wilson (eds.), *The Encyclopaedia of Southern Culture*, Chapel Hill, NC: UNC Press, 1989.

Joel Garreau, *The Nine Nations of North America*, New York: Avon, 1982.

Tony Horwitz, *Confederates in the Attic*, New York: Vintage, 1998.

Merrill Jensen (ed.), *Regionalism in America*, Madison, WI: University of Wisconsin Press, 1952.

Robert D. Kaplan, *An Empire Wilderness: Travels into America's Future*, New York: Vintage, 1998.

Lewis Mumford, *The Golden Day*, Westport, CT: Greenwood Press, 1983.

John Shelton Reed, *The Enduring South*, Chapel Hill, NC: UNC Press, 1972.

Frederick Jackson Turner, *Frontier and Section: Selected Essays of Frederick Jackson Turner*, Englewood Cliffs, NJ: Prentice-Hall, Inc., 1961.

Charles Reagan Wilson (ed.), *The New Regionalism*, Jackson, MS: University Press of Mississippi, 1998.

4

ROGER DANIELS

Immigration to the United States in the twentieth century

A broad overview of immigration to America

Perhaps a million immigrants came to America between 1565 and 1800, about 20 million in the nineteenth century, and at least 55 million in the twentieth century. During the twentieth century, particularly after World War II, as American immigration laws and regulations became more complex, the phenomenon of illegal immigration became increasingly significant. The numbers above include some 10 million illegal twentieth-century immigrants.

Even these approximate numbers are, in a sense, illusory, as they seem to record a permanent move from one nation to another. Yet, from the earliest colonial times, many who came either returned or went somewhere else, and many of those came back again. Specialists estimate that perhaps one immigrant in three later left. Many of these, often called sojourners, always intended to return: but many who came as sojourners – usually to make money – actually stayed, while others, who came intending to remain, eventually left. Almost certainly the most reliable statistic about American immigration is the incidence of immigrants – that is persons who were born somewhere else – in the total population.

As Table 4.1 shows, the censuses from 1860 through 1920 report the incidence of foreign-born persons as close to 14 percent, one person in seven. Then began a half-century of decline: by 1970 only one person in twenty was an immigrant. By the end of the century the percentage had risen to 11 percent, one person in nine. The uneven pace of immigration in the twentieth century – more than half of all its immigrants came in just three decades – 1901–20 and 1991–2000 – was in part responsible for the largely foolish "furor" about immigration that erupted in its closing years. Historians call such anti-immigrant attitudes "nativism," defined by one scholar as "intense opposition to an internal minority on the ground of its foreign (i.e., 'un-American') connections."[1]

Table 4.1. *Foreign-born in the United States, 1850–2000*

Year	Number (in millions)	Percentage
1850	2.2	9.7%
1860	4.1	13.2%
1870	5.6	14.0%
1880	6.7	13.3%
1890	9.2	14.7%
1900	10.4	13.6%
1910	13.6	14.7%
1920	14.0	13.2%
1930	14.3	11.6%
1940	11.7	8.9%
1950	10.4	6.9%
1960	9.7	5.4%
1970	9.6	4.7%
1980	14.1	6.2%
1990	19.8	7.9%
2000	21.1	11.1%

Source: US Census data. A most useful analysis is in Campbell J. Gibson and Emily Lennon. "Historical Census Statistics on the Foreign-born Population of the United States:1850–1990," Population Division Working Paper No. 15, Washington: US Bureau of the Census, February, 1999.

By the middle of the twentieth century, if not before, most Americans had come to believe a variety of myths about their immigrant past. I have called three of them the myths of Plymouth Rock, the Statue of Liberty, and the Melting Pot. The first, much beloved by politicians, holds that most immigrants came for religious and/or political liberty; the second that most immigrants came desperately poor; while the third puts forth the assimilationist notion that ethnic differences quickly disappeared. Like most enduring myths, each of these has some relationship to reality. People have come to America seeking liberty; some have found the way to wealth from poverty; and while there has been a continuous genetic mixing of ethnic and racial groups in the New World, the vast majority of Americans can still describe their ethnic or racial backgrounds.

If these are myths when applied to the generality of immigrants, what are the realities? The motives that impel an individual to leave one way of life and exchange it for another are often complex, but, by and large, economic motives – the desire to improve one's position in life, to provide a better life for one's children – are the major causal factors.

From the beginning the vast majority of immigrants came – or were brought – to America to work. It follows, then, that immigrants were, disproportionably, of working age. Most were between their late teens and late thirties, and relatively few were either children or over forty. Given the nature of paid employment before the most recent decades, immigrants were predominantly male. Since 1950, for a variety of reasons there has been a slight female majority among legal immigrants to America.

The evolution of american immigration policy to 1917

For the first centuries of American history there was a vast continent to fill up, so the more the merrier. Interruptions of immigrant flows resulted chiefly from wars and unenforceable policies of European powers to halt or minimize emigration. Although the word "immigration" does not appear in the American Constitution, the founding fathers clearly favored it as is implied by the clauses that open all the offices under the Constitution, except President and Vice-President, to immigrants, and instruct Congress to "establish an uniform Rule of Naturalization." Thus, right from the beginning immigrants served in Congress, the cabinet, and the judiciary. In fact five of the thirty-eight signers of the original document (13 percent) were immigrants.

A broad pro-immigration consensus continued well into the nineteenth century. George Washington had declared that America would welcome "not only the opulent and respectable stranger, but the oppressed and persecuted of all nations and religions." Similarly, in 1841, the tenth President, John Tyler, invited "the people of other countries . . . to come and settle among us as members of our rapidly growing family."[1]

That consensus was cracked but not broken by the first anti-immigrant surge in American history, known as the Know Nothing Movement. Its members were particularly opposed to Catholics and wanted to amend the Constitution to limit office-holding to "native-born Protestant citizens." Although the movement elected many local officials in the mid-1850s it never managed to get any of its agenda adopted nationally. Some states did pass laws restricting immigration but the Supreme Court disallowed them in the *Passenger Cases* (1849) holding that: (1.) while the Constitution said nothing about immigration directly, it was a form of "foreign commerce" whose control the Constitution explicitly reserved to Congress; and (2.) Congress's jurisdiction was preemptive so that even in the absence of any federal legislation, state governments could not regulate immigration.

The first two successful American attempts to restrict immigration each involved race. The first affected only slaves, whom some refuse to consider as immigrants. In 1809, at Thomas Jefferson's urging, Congress outlawed the foreign slave trade, but did not interfere with either slavery or the buying and selling of slaves within the United States. Scholars estimate that, despite the law, some 50,000 slaves were imported into the United States before slavery was finally abolished in 1865. These were the first illegal immigrants.

The second restriction targeted Chinese laborers. Although a few Chinese had come to the United States in the 1780s, sustained Chinese immigration occurred first in the California Gold Rush. The Chinese were but a small portion of the quarter million migrants, foreign and domestic, who flocked to what had been a sparsely populated region. They performed all kinds of work in California and elsewhere in the West and, after a brief period of acceptance, began to be attacked by many whites, at first verbally and then with often fatal mob violence. That story cannot be told here, but if what happened to the Chinese in the United States had occurred in Russia it would have been called a pogrom.

Congress passed the 1882 Chinese Exclusion Act which barred the immigration of Chinese laborers but permitted the entry of merchants, their families, students, and "visitors for pleasure." It was the first law restricting the entrance of free immigrants, but a number of subsequent statutes enacted other kinds of restrictions. By the time the United States entered World War I in April 1917, seven categories of immigrants were barred: most Asians, certain criminals, people who failed to meet certain moral standards, those with various diseases, anarchists and other radicals who advocated the overthrow by force or violence of the government of the United States, illiterates, and paupers or persons likely to become a public charge. Despite these exclusions, immigration soared: by 1914 a million and more immigrants were entering every year, and few were excluded or deported. In 1914 only 33,000 were excluded and 4,600 deported.

The nature of early twentieth-century immigration

Between 1901 and 1914 13.2 million immigrants entered the United States, nearly a million a year. This level would not be reached again until the closing years of the century. But we must remember that in 1901–14 the nation's population was approaching the 100 million mark while in the 1986–2000 period it surpassed 250 million.

About 90 percent of those immigrants were Europeans but the sources within Europe were changing. Germans and British, who had long predominated, were only about one immigrant in seven in 1900–14 while most of the rest came from eastern and southern Europe, with people from Italy and the Russian and Austro-Hungarian Empires predominating.

The United States Immigration Commission, whose 1911 report would help shape immigration policy in the 1920s, popularized the terms "old" and "new" to stigmatize the latter groups in pejorative language: "The old immigration was essentially one of permanence. The new immigration is very largely one of individuals, a considerable portion of whom apparently have no intention of permanently changing their residence, their only purpose in coming to America being to temporarily take advantage of the greater wages paid by industrial labor in this country."[3]

These immigrants were primarily Roman Catholic, Jewish, or Greek Orthodox in religion. This, along with their strange tongues and odd-sounding names made them seen to most other Americans even more alien than, say, the Catholic Irish, or the German Catholics and Jews who had been the most numerous previous non-Protestant European immigrants.

These immigrants from eastern and southern Europe, like most other immigrants who arrived after the 1860s, settled in urban rather than rural or small-town America. The Census Bureau did not record an urban majority until 1920, and that was accomplished only by counting as "urban" any place containing 2,500 persons. Of the 54 million "urbanites," some 20 million lived in towns of 25,000 and less, so the nation was still dominated by persons who lived in small towns and rural areas. Only about a quarter of the 1920 population lived in cities of 100,000 and above, but nearly half of the immigrant population did.

Unlike most of their early nineteenth-century predecessors, the continental European emigrants of the early twentieth century had a wide range of possible destinations. The anthropologist William A. Douglass in his 1984 study, *Emigration in a South Italian Town*, lists the possibilities for a prospective Italian emigrant: "Stay in the village, move to the nearest city, seek work in Milan or Turin, emigrate to Germany or France, cross the Atlantic to Argentina or the United States, go alone, travel with spouse and children, help finance a brother's passage. . ."[4] While Americans tend to equate emigration from rural continental Europe with immigration overseas, the fact is that for every such European who crossed the Atlantic or the Mediterranean in search of work, nine moved to a European city.

To a greater or lesser degree the same factors applied to all Europeans, although most European emigrants to America were not among the poorest inhabitants of the nations they left. Although Jews had been coming to America since the 1600s, their small number as well as the pro-Hebraic orientation of many American Christians had made anti-Semitism a much less significant factor in early America than anywhere else in the Christian world. During the nineteenth-century heyday of German immigration to America a small but significant percentage were German-speaking Jews, most of whom had been affected by modernity. In 1880, when eastern European Jews were perhaps a sixth of American Jewry, there were perhaps 250,000 Jews in the United States. (American statistics, whether from the Census Bureau or the immigration authorities, do not specify religion, so estimating the numbers of religious groups is problematic.) By 1920 there were perhaps 4,000,000 Jews in America, where they comprised less than 4 percent of the population. Perhaps five-sixths were immigrants from eastern Europe or their children: most of the immigrant generation came with Yiddish (a German dialect written in the Hebrew alphabet) as their mother tongue and were little affected by most modern thought, although a significant minority were supporters of some form of socialism before they came.

Jewish immigrants were even more likely to be big city residents than their fellow immigrants and their concentration in New York City became most pronounced: in 1860 it is estimated that perhaps one-third of American Jews lived there; by 1920 the figure was perhaps 45 percent and more than a million Jews were crowded, along with hundreds of thousands of other mostly recent immigrants, in the few dozen blocks of Manhattan's Lower East Side, then one of the most densely inhabited districts on the planet.

There were other immigrants districts in New York and other large cities: "Little Italy" or a "Kleindeutschland," in other parts of Manhattan, Chicago's "Swedetown," or Cincinnati's "Over the Rhine" are representative of such ethnic enclaves. In some of the larger enclaves, such as the Italian districts of New York or Chicago, insiders understood that there was internal differentiation, so that Sicilians, for example, tended to cluster in certain blocks or tenement houses, while Neapolitans could be found in others. Such districts, like the ethnic churches, served as fortresses giving shelter to immigrant cultures against the alien world of old stock America. As long as one stayed within the fortress, it was not necessary to speak English, and the grocery stores stocked familiar foods, often made in America. Many of the first successful immigrant entrepreneurs began by catering to the dietary needs of the immigrant community.

It was necessary for most of them to leave their fortress enclaves to find work. Immigrants typically found niches within the larger economy. Italian men, for example, tended to do outdoor work, often seasonal. Just as in the nineteenth century it was chiefly Irish immigrants who had done most of the work on the nation's basic infrastructure, digging canals in the century's first half and, along with Chinese, laying rails in its second half, Italians built streets and roads, and dug tunnels in the early twentieth century. Although married immigrant women did not often work outside the home or small family business, immigrant girls and unmarried young women did work. The garment industry, often thought of as a Jewish industry, actually had a sizeable minority of Italian women workers. The more skilled jobs were largely filled by immigrant Jewish men, and most of the bosses were Jewish as well.

While Italians and Jews were concentrated in eastern cities, most Poles settled in interior northeastern cities and did heavy factory work. A Polish folksong telling the story of a worker returning to his family in Krakow after a three-year absence, appropriately begins: "When I journeyed from Amer'ca . . . And the foundry where I labored . . ."

Despite the fact that there was no Polish state at the time, Polish Americans displayed a fierce nationalism. While most immigrant groups created important ethno-cultural groups, and many influenced or tried to influence politics in the old country, only the chief Polish organization, The Polish National Alliance, claimed, on the eve of World War I, that Chicago-centered "Polonia" constituted the fourth province of their native land.

The outbreak of World War I, in August 1914, transformed American immigration. As noted previously, in the last year before the war, 1.2 million immigrants came; 1.1 million of them were Europeans. For 1915–19, see Table 4.2.

A little of the slack was made up by increased immigration from Canada and Mexico: the figures for Mexicans, however, do not include the 500,000 Mexicans brought in by the federal government as temporary workers in the first such program in American history. An indeterminable number of these workers simply stayed.

One might think that since immigration numbers had been so depressed during the war years a more relaxed attitude toward immigration might have resulted at war's end, but the reverse was true. The war years were marked by heightened ethnic tensions in the United States as the reactions to

Table 4.2. *Immigration 1915–19*

Year	All Immigrants	European Immigrants	Percent
1915	326,700	197,919	61
1916	298,826	145,699	49
1917	295,403	133,083	45
1918	110,618	31,063	28
1919	141,132	24,627	17

the war news by many members of European immigrant groups were shaped by homeland loyalties.

As immigration climbed – 430,000 in 1920, 800,000 in 1921 – largely chimerical fears of being swamped by immigrants and radicals caused Congress to reduce immigration drastically. The House of Representatives voted 296 to 42 to suspend all immigration for fourteen months; the more responsible Senate substituted an emergency one-year quota bill, based on a suggestion made by the 1911 Immigration Commission. Quotas for eligible immigrants from a particular nation would be based on a percentage of the foreign-born population from that nation present in the most recent census. The Senate bill proposed a 5 percent quota which would have produced about 600,000 quota spaces; the House cut this to 3 percent, which was thought to produce 360,000 quota spaces. Everyone knew, however, that many quota spaces, like most of those for Great Britain and the Scandinavian countries, would not be used.

Persons from the western Hemisphere could enter "without numerical restriction," that is outside the quota limits, as could close family members of persons already in the United States. The bill was vetoed by President Woodrow Wilson but was repassed and signed in early 1921 by President Warren G. Harding. The quota system, although modified, would endure until 1965. Even after that the revised system retained many of the features first introduced in 1921.

The 1921 law reduced immigration: in 1921–4 some 550,000 immigrants entered annually. Although this sliced prewar arrival numbers roughly in half, restrictionists made further cuts. The 1924 law reduced the quotas significantly in two ways, one straightforward, the other devious. It cut quota percentages from 3 to 2 percent and, instead of using the 1920 census went back to the 1890 census. These changes cut the total annual quota to 180,000. The quotas for Italy and Poland, for example, plummeted from 42,000 and 31,000 under the 1921 law to 4,000 and 6,000 after 1924 while the quotas for Britain, Ireland, Germany, and Scandinavia were expanded. The new law also stopped all immigration from Japan by barring the immigration of any person who was "ineligible for citizenship." Since the naturalization law limited acquired citizenship to "white persons" and "persons of African descent," Japanese were added to the other Asians who had previously been barred.

It is clear that a majority of Americans applauded the 1921–4 restrictions although immigration policy was one of the issues which bitterly divided Americans in the 1920s. John Higham's wonderful phrase, the "tribal twenties," strikes, I think, just the right note. If we think of the main "tribes" as teams, we can speak of four different contests going on simultaneously:

rural versus urban, dry versus wet, Protestant versus Catholic, and native stock versus immigrant stock. Many Americans were active in all four contests. Most immigrants, as we have seen, were urban and not Protestant. They also were "wet," that is opposed to the prohibition of all alcoholic beverages.

The onset of the Great Depression meant that economic concerns overrode other issues. By 1936 a majority of each of the eight tribes listed above could take part in Franklin D. Roosevelt's grand coalition. FDR, whose ancestors on both sides immigrated in the seventeenth century, believed some of the myths about immigration. As President he celebrated past and recent immigration, telling the conservative Daughters of the American Revolution in 1939 that: "Remember, remember always that all of us, and you and I especially, are descended from immigrants and revolutionists." But he, until the war years at least, seemed to subscribe to a stagnationist approach to both economic growth and immigration. As he put it in one of his 1932 campaign speeches: "We are not able to invite the immigrants from Europe to share our endless plenty."[5] Such an attitude, from the greatest leader of the party that spoke for immigrants, helps explain why the severe restrictionist mode dominated American thought about immigration for so long.

Historians have consistently overstated the effects of the quota system. Immigration from 1925 through 1930 averaged about 294,000 a year. After 1930, the Great Depression and the disruptions caused by World War II reduced immigration drastically so that the 1925–30 level of annual immigration was not reached until 1956. For the whole twenty-five year period, 1931–55, only 2.6 million immigrants entered, an average of about 106,000 annually. A comparable number of immigrants, 2.4 million, had arrived in just the last two years before World War I.

Although Roosevelt's New Deal, begun in the spring of 1933, changed almost every aspect of American public life, there was never a new deal for immigration, as previous quotations from Roosevelt suggest. That is not to say that had Herbert Hoover been re-elected immigration policy would have been the same. Hoover wanted immigration restricted even further, while the father of the New Deal was willing to stand pat.

Roosevelt's government treated resident aliens more generously than its predecessors. Deportations, which had risen steadily from 2,762 in 1920 to 19,865 in 1933, dropped to fewer than 9,000 the next year and stayed at about that level for the rest of the decade, and federal relief regulations insisted on the eligibility of resident aliens.

An entirely new problem arose stemming from the anti-Semitic policies of Nazi Germany. More than any other western leader in power in the early 1930s, Roosevelt understood the dangers that Hitler's policies created for the West. But he was President of a nation whose people were committed to a policy of non-intervention and in which discrimination against persons of color, Jews, and Catholics prevailed at varying levels of intensity. American immigration law made no distinction between refugees and other immigrants. It was not so much the quota system which kept out German Jewish refugees – until late 1938 (when Jewish stores, synagogues, and community buildings all over Germany were destroyed in an escalation of the persecution of the Jews which came to be known as *Kristallnacht*, the night of broken glass) there were unused German quota spaces – as the reluctance of many American consuls to issue visas to them.

Roosevelt publicly refused to support unpopular measures that would have saved more than the perhaps 250,000 Jewish refugees who managed, in one way or another, to get to the United States, but it took in more refugees in the period before the United States entered the war than the other western powers combined. However, many thousands of others could have been saved by a more resolute policy. But the claims made by some that a sizeable percentage of the millions of Jews of eastern Europe who perished in the Holocaust could have been saved by any conceivable American action is without foundation.

Franklin Roosevelt never wrote his memoirs so we cannot know how he would have defended his refugee policies, but we have a glimmer of what he might have said. The following quotation is from a note he wrote in 1941 to be printed in the 1938 volume of his public papers, putting forth arguments he never made to the American people during the crucial years of the prewar refugee crisis.

> For centuries this country has always been the traditional haven of refuge for countless victims of religious and political persecution in other lands. These immigrants have made outstanding contributions to American music, art, literature, business, finance, philanthropy, and many other phases of our cultural, political, industrial and commercial life.
>
> As this is written in June, 1941, it seems so tragically ironical to realize how many citizens of these various countries [which had been overly cautious in their attitude about receiving refugees] either are themselves now refugees, or pray for a chance to leave their native lands and seek some refuge from the cruel hand of the Nazi invader. Even the kings and queens and princes of some of them are now in the same position as these political and religious minorities were in 1938–knocking on the doors of other lands for admittance.[6]

When one compares his account with what the United States actually did and did not do in the months before war broke out in Europe, it is difficult not to believe that a guilty conscience lay behind his remarks, which would be easy to describe as hypocritical. It is hard to improve upon the judgment of Vice-President Walter Mondale in 1979 that the United States and other western nations of asylum "failed the test of civilization" by not responding appropriately to the refugee crisis of the 1930s.

The outbreak of World War II in September 1939 further reduced immigration from the Old World. Direct American involvement some twenty-seven months later reversed immigration priorities. An economy that had more than 10 percent of its workers unemployed became one in which the needs of war production plus the diversion of millions of workers to the armed forces produced labor shortages. One partial solution was, as in World War I, to recruit supposedly temporary workers from Mexico largely for southwestern agriculture, while eastern farmers were permitted to bring in workers from the West Indies, the Bahamas, Canada, and Newfoundland. Government data show nearly a quarter of a million agricultural workers – not reported as immigrants – brought in during the war years, three-quarters of them from Mexico. A separate program brought in 50,000 Mexicans to work on railroads. And a large but indeterminate number entered informally.

The Mexican workers, called *braceros*, from the Spanish *braccar*, (to wave one's arms), became a fixture and programs continuing their importation were maintained well into the 1960s. By 1964 government data reported the importation of 4.6 million temporary agricultural workers from Mexico and another 300,000 from the rest of the hemisphere. In these years southwestern agriculturalists became addicted to Mexican laborers and continued to depend on them after the program was brought to an end. Many *braceros* remained illegally in the United States and were often joined by family members. Others continued to come after the programs ended. Thus government policy abetted what became the major source of illegal immigration and created a problem which continued into the twenty-first century.

After 1939 national security concerns helped shape immigration policy. The crucial change was moving the immigration service from the Department of Labor, essentially a protective agency, to the Department of Justice, whose functions were prosecutorial. In addition, the Alien Registration Act of 1940 for the first time required all resident aliens – legal immigrants who had not become citizens – to register with the federal government and receive special identification cards.

Toward the end of 1943, in a gesture of support for an embattled ally, and after a careful campaign by a bipartisan elite pressure group, Congress, with the encouragement of President Roosevelt, not only repealed the fifteen statutes which had effected Chinese exclusion, but also enabled Chinese aliens to become naturalized citizens, and awarded Chinese people an annual immigration quota of 105 persons.

Roosevelt justified this dramatic change in American policy by reasons of state. As commander-in-chief he insisted that the legislation was "important in the cause of winning the war and of establishing a secure peace." Repeal would, he said, "correct a historic mistake and silence the distorted Japanese propaganda." He noted that the change would give the Chinese a "preferred status over certain other Oriental people" and predicted that it would also "be an earnest of our purpose to apply the policy of the good neighbor to our relations with other peoples."[7] Congress made Roosevelt a good prophet in 1946 when it passed separate bills making Filipinos and "natives of India" similarly eligible for naturalization and immigration.

Critics then and later argued that the bill was an "insult": they fail to see that just as the original adoption of Chinese Exclusion in 1882 was the hinge on which the immigration policy of the United States turned to an ever increasing restriction, its repeal was the hinge which began a process of removing many restrictions. In less than a decade all purely racial barriers to immigration were removed although much discrimination continued. The key – which Roosevelt never mentioned – was admissibility to naturalization which made it possible for newly naturalized Chinese men to bring in wives and caused a demographic revolution among Chinese Americans in the next few years, ending the community's status as a bachelor society.

In June 1944, Roosevelt took another small step by executive action which had momentous policy consequences by ordering "that approximately 1,000 refugees should be immediately brought from Italy to this country."[8] Three days later he informed Congress of what he had done, explaining that the refugees would be held in a camp in Oswego, New York and be returned to Europe after the war. His successor, President Harry S. Truman, just before Christmas 1945, ordered that they be allowed to remain. Although none of the public documents used the term "parole authority" this procedure was later authorized by Congress in 1952 under that name and was used by President Dwight D. Eisenhower and his successors to admit hundreds of thousands of refugees in the era of the Cold War and beyond.

Truman, in the same directive that allowed the Oswego refugees to stay, tried for the first time to do something about the condition of refugees in Europe who could not or did not want to return to their country of origin. There was a growing scandal about the general neglect and frequent mistreatment of Jewish and other "displaced persons" (DPs) by American military officials in Europe. Knowing that public opinion was against any change – a Gallup Poll in December 1945 showed that only 5 percent favored increasing European immigration, nearly a third said let in the same number, while 51 percent wanted fewer than before the war or none – he first tried to solve the problem within the existing quota system. The President ordered some minor rule changes, and estimated that this would bring in some 40,000 annually, but in all of 1946 only some 5,000 were actually admitted. At the beginning of 1947 he urged Congress to find ways in which the United States could fulfill its "responsibilities to these homeless and suffering refugees of all faiths."[9] This is the first time that an American President had spoken of American responsibility to take refugees: it would be recognized by all of his successors.

Truman's request set off a five-year battle over immigration policy similar to that waged in 1924, but with different results. He spoke of faiths, but American immigration law deals with nationalities. He did so to mask the fact that many – including both supporters and opponents of expanded refugee immigration – saw the refugee problem as a Jewish question. Polls showed Americans even more opposed to Jewish immigration than immigration in general: one reported more than four-fifths of those with opinions opposed any additional Jewish immigration.

In fact, Jews were but a minority of the remaining DPs – about a quarter of a million in late 1947 – and the vast majority of them wanted to go to Palestine, then a British mandate which would not accept them. The creation of the State of Israel in May 1948 meant that the struggle for DP admission, then under way, would culminate in the admission of fewer Jews than might have been the case otherwise. Partisans of a DP bill, in and out of Congress, strove for a measure allowing the entry of 100,000 DPs outside of the quota system in each of four years. In June 1948 Congress passed the first DP Act, admitting 250,000 persons in the next two years, and as that Act was expiring passed a second bill making the total authorized 415,000: some 410,000 DPs were actually admitted. Only about one in six were Jews; almost as many, about one in seven, were Christian Germans expelled from Czechoslovakia and other eastern European nations. Most of the rest were Stalin's victims, persons who had been displaced by the Soviet takeover of eastern Europe, particularly Poles and persons from the Baltic Republics of Estonia, Latvia, and Lithuania.

In 1952 Congress revised basic immigration law for the first time since 1924. Truman vetoed the Immigration and Nationality Act (INA) but Congress easily overrode it. The INA seemed to be a conservative reaffirmation of the 1924 Act. It reaffirmed the quota system, strengthened the authority of immigration officials, made a conviction for the possession of marijuana a bar to admission, and forbade "subversive" foreign intellectuals, such as Jean Paul Sartre, from even visiting the United States. Its major liberalization, the elimination of all racial bars to naturalization and the awarding of minimum quotas of 100 to every Asian nation, seemed to be vitiated by a provision limiting total Asian immigration to 2,000 persons annually. But during the thirteen years – 1953–65 – that the law was in effect 236,000 Asians legally immigrated to the United States, an average of more than 18,000 a year. Total immigration grew steadily. Why did these "unintended consequences" occur? Because of three little understood provisions in the INA that many members of Congress and commentators failed to grasp.

(1.) The relatively large Asian immigration was chiefly due to the fact that spouses and minor children of American citizens could enter "without numerical restriction," that is, outside the quotas. As had been the case with the Chinese after 1943, thousands of Asian males of other ethnicities long resident in the United States became citizens and either brought in previously inadmissible wives and children or went to Asia and brought home new wives. In addition, large numbers of Americans serving or working in Asia resulted in a growing number of interracial marriages, with Asian spouses brought to the United States.

(2.) Before 1953, immigration from the Americas, all of it non-quota, had been dominated by Canadians, most of whom were either Europeans or their descendants. During the INA years Latin Americans and Caribbeans comprised two-thirds of New World immigrants, some 1.25 million persons, or 32 percent of all immigrants. Congress did limit the immigration of persons coming from European colonies in the Caribbean by assigning them to the quotas of their European owners and limiting the numbers admitted to 100 from each colony. This affected mostly Jamaicans and Barbadians, who had been used to entering the United States as non-quota immigrants. Almost all of those affected were black. Some British scholars have argued that this change in American law greatly increased the number of post-1952 Caribbean migrants to Britain.[10]

(3.) Finally, even though the word "refugee" does not appear in the INA, an obscure provision – Section 212 (d)(5) – gave the President discretionary parole power to grant temporary admission to unlimited numbers of aliens. This meant, in practice, that a President could order the admission of specific groups of refugee aliens – Hungarians, Cubans, Tibetans, and Vietnamese – and Congress would later pass legislation regularizing that action. All told, more than 290,000 refugees were admitted outside the quotas under laws passed during the life of the INA.

What must be understood is that as the nature of the role that the United States sought to play in the world changed, so did its immigration policy. By the 1950s, when American foreign policy aspired to lead what its statesmen called the "free world," immigration policy that barred most of the world's peoples, as prewar American immigration policy had done, would have been a serious impediment.

The election of John F. Kennedy in 1960, who as a senator had voted to uphold Truman's veto of the INA, seemed to presage a change in American immigration policy. Yet Kennedy's thousand days saw no significant change in immigration law. Since his successor, Lyndon B. Johnson, had voted to override Truman's veto of the INA, immigration reformers were pessimistic. But President Johnson was not Senator Johnson, and after his landslide victory in 1964 he made the cause of immigration reform his own.

The Immigration Act of 1965, which Johnson ramrodded through Congress in 1965, marks, along with the Voting Rights Act and the Medicare/Medicaid legislation enacted in the same year, the highwater mark of late twentieth-century American liberalism. This was not immediately recognized. Johnson himself minimized the bill's significance. The President was not, most uncharacteristically, downplaying one of his achievements: he actually believed that this was the case because his "experts" had told him so. The law, technically an amendment to the INA, abolished the quota system and seemed to replace it with a annual ceiling of 170,000 immigrants from the eastern hemisphere plus 120,000 from the western hemisphere, for a presumed total of 290,000. This is the way that the *New York Times* and other media reported it.

But these caps were illusory because many persons could immigrate without numerical restriction. The new act expanded that category to include the parents of US citizens. The 1965 law also reserved 54 percent of the 290,000 enumerated slots for various relatives of US citizens – adult children and adult siblings – and another 20 percent for spouses and unmarried children of permanent resident aliens, i.e. unnaturalized immigrants. Thus the bulk of the 290,000 immigrants allowed under the cap – 74 percent – came as part of the concept of family reunification, and it was obviously to the advantage of immigrants who wanted to bring family members to the United States to become naturalized quickly, and unprecedented numbers began that process soon after arriving. Students of immigration call this process chain migration, as the immigrants follow one another as links in a chain. The remaining 26 percent of the allocated slots were divided as follows: 10 percent to professionals, scientists, and artists "of exceptional ability"; 10 percent to workers in occupations "for which labor is in short supply"; and 6 percent for refugees.

Johnson himself demonstrated the meaninglessness of the refugee cap – presumably 17,400 per year. The same day he signed the 1965 law he responded to a refugee crisis set off by Fidel Castro's Cuba by declaring "to the people of Cuba that those who seek refuge here in America will find it."[11]

Table 4.3. *Refugee Immigration since World War II*

Years	Total	Major Sources
1946–1950	213,347	Europe – 99%
1951–1960	492,371	Europe – 93%
1961–1970	212,843	Cuba – 62%; Europe – 26%
1971–1980	539,477	Cuba – 46%; Asia – 39%; Europe – 13%
1981–1990	1,013,620	Asia – 70%; Europe – 15%; Cuba – 11%
1991–2000	1,021,266	Europe – 42%; Asia – 34%; Cuba – 14%

Source: 2001 Statistical Yearbook of the Immigration and Naturalization Service, Washington, DC: GPO, 2003, pp. 111–121.

Within fifteen years 387,000 Cuban refugees arrived plus large numbers of other Cubans who came as regular immigrants. All told, between 1946 and 2000, more than 3.5 million persons were admitted as refugees.

Table 4.3 shows the growth and variety of refugee immigration. The European dominance in the 1940s and 1950s reflects the long aftermath of World War II. The Cuban dominance in the 1960s and early 1970s reflects the Castro revolution and the large Asian share since the 1970s reflects chiefly the consequences of the misbegotten American war in Vietnam. In 1980 Congress passed and President Jimmy Carter signed the final major liberalizing immigration statute of the twentieth century. It increased the supposed annual cap of 17,400 to 50,000, and recognized, for the first time, the right of asylum. Both Congress and the courts later expanded asylum to include persons fleeing China's one-child policy or women seeking to avoid genital mutilation. The law also provided an all but automatic process for anyone who achieved refugee or asylee status to become a "permanent resident" and eligible to begin the process of becoming an American citizen. The law also placed a cap of 5,000 asylees per year, as part of the 50,000 refugee cap. In the first twenty years of the law some 140,000 asylees achieved permanent resident status, some 40,000 above the putative cap.

The ink was hardly dry on the law when another Cuban refugee crisis was triggered by Castro's announcement that Cubans wanting to leave for the United States could do so as long as they left from the tiny fishing port of Mariel just 100 miles from Florida and provided their own transportation. For 162 days, from April 21 to September 25, 1980, boats plied back and forth. The United States Coast Guard which did picket duty reported that 124,776 men, women, and children made the trip successfully and that 27 persons were lost at sea, but it missed many of both the living and the dead. The new refugee policy was in ruins.

The Cold War imperative of taking all refugees from communism trumped the desire for an orderly refugee policy. After weeks of vacillation Carter, echoing Lyndon Johnson in 1965, announced that the United States would welcome all Cubans "with an open heart and open arms."[12] Then, after wildly exaggerated stories about the incidence of criminals and homosexuals released from Cuban jails and mental institutions among the refugees, the government again cracked down on boat owners, fining some and confiscating the vessels of others. The number of weekly arrivals fell from 17,000 to 700. The crisis ended on September 25 when, after 162 days, Castro closed the Mariel window. About 15,000 Cubans annually continued to arrive for the rest of the century.

But for other boat people, coming from Haiti, the rules were different. Although Haiti was ruled by a despotic government which ignored human rights, it was not a communist government, so Haitians, unlike Cubans, were turned back at sea when they attempted to flee what the US government insisted was merely economic misery and not the "well-founded fear of persecution" necessary for amnesty. Most of those Haitians who managed to get to the United States and apply for asylum, were not, like Cubans, all but automatically released on parole, but locked up, often in facilities notorious for ongoing mistreatment of inmates including sexual abuse of female prisoners by guards.

The fears generated among the public by the Mariel boatlift, exacerbated by lurid stories in the media, was another turning point in American attitudes toward immigration. Ronald W. Reagan, who became President while the often turbulent resettlement of Mariel refugees was still going on, warned the American people about the dangers of "feet people" fleeing turmoil in Central America pouring into the country as "boat people" from Vietnam, Cuba, and Haiti had done previously.

To be sure there had been some officially stimulated concern in the 1970s. Richard Nixon's chief immigration official had heightened public fears with repeated warnings about the dangers of uncontrolled immigration, and in 1978 Congress created the Select Commission on Immigration and Refugee Policy (SCIRP), the first such body since the Immigration Commission of 1909–11, with instructions to report in 1981. SCIRP, chaired by Father Theodore M. Hesburgh (b. 1917), the former President of the University of Notre Dame, recommended, in 1981, a broad package of changes. On the one hand, while suggesting a reduction in the level of immigration, it supported most of the reforms of the 1965 and 1980 laws, and proposed a broad amnesty so that illegal aliens who had been in the country for a long time could become citizens. On the other hand it proposed tighter border controls and in a typically American act of faith, urged the creation of a forgery-proof identity card.

The Immigration Reform and Control Act (IRCA) of 1986, designed to reduce immigration, was a compromise measure which satisfied few advocates of lower immigration. At the bill-signing ceremony, Reagan called it "the most comprehensive reform of our immigration laws since 1952," and predicted that it would "humanely regain control of our borders."[13]

IRCA actually expanded immigration. Its massive "legalization" for aliens who were illegally in the United States created an appetite for further "amnesties." Of the two most heralded "get tough" provisions, one was toothless and the other a kind of boomerang. The first, as summarized by the government, provided sanctions against employers who "knowingly" hired illegal aliens. The use of the word "knowingly" in a criminal statute showed that Congress had no intention of putting employers in jail. The second "get tough" provision provided increased policing of the border, which made it more onerous, but not at all impossible, for illegal migrants to enter the United States. This caused many migrants to abandon their customary circular pattern of migration – that is returning to Mexico at the end of a growing season – and remain permanently in the United States. The Border Patrol has reported millions of apprehensions, largely at or near the border, including multiple apprehensions of the same individuals, many of whom, eventually, manage to get across. And once agricultural workers get beyond the border zone their chances of being apprehended are minimal.

The legalization process under IRCA enrolled 3.1 million persons who admitted being in the United States illegally. Almost 70 percent of those in the program were Mexicans and 20 percent of the rest were from the New World, largely Central America. Since once legalized and naturalized the recipients could bring in other family members the potential increase in immigration was much larger.

The growing awareness of the failure of American immigration policies to control the border created increased public hostility to immigration. In 1977 a Gallup poll showed 42 percent wanted a decrease in immigration, but were outnumbered by those who either wanted more immigration, 37 percent, or no change, 7 percent. Polls taken in 1993 and 1995 showed a whopping 65 percent favoring a reduced level of immigration.

Congress showed its awareness of IRCA's failure in 1990 by appointing its second immigration commission in twelve years. Its chair, former Congressperson Barbara C. Jordan (1936–96), described the national mood correctly in 1994 as a "furor" rather than a discussion. As she spoke there were 150 separate immigration bills in Congress, some calling for a "moratorium" on all immigration. Despite much wind on Capitol Hill,

Table 4.4. *Legal Immigration in the Twentieth Century*

Years	Number (in millions)
1901–10	8.8
1911–20	5.7
1921–30	4.1
1931–40	.5
1941–50	1.0
1951–60	2.5
1961–70	3.3
1971–80	4.5
1981–90	7.3
1991–00	9.1
Total	46.8

Source: Immigration and Naturalization Service. 2000 *Statistical Yearbook of the Immigration and Naturalization Service.* (Washington: GPO, September 2002), Table 1, p. 15.

Congress failed to pass any legislation that would effectively reduce immigration levels which, as Table 4.4 shows, had risen in every decade since the 1930s. The pro- and anti-immigration forces in Congress were too well balanced for that. In fact pro-business forces had pushed through the controversial North American Free Trade Act (NAFTA) at the end of 1993 which greatly increased certain kinds of migration from both Canada and Mexico. But a Republican-dominated Congress, with the approval of centrist Democrat Bill Clinton, was able to pass a series of laws with tough-sounding titles, such as the Illegal Immigration Reform and Immigrant Responsibility Act (1996), which applied mean-spirited and fiscally insignificant "reforms" against legal resident aliens, aimed at excluding them from various benefits of the American welfare state.

But the most extreme example of the "furor" was the passage, by California's volatile electorate in 1994, of an anti-immigrant referendum, "Proposition 187 – Illegal Aliens." Almost 60 percent voted for it. "Prop 187," as it was called, made illegal immigrants ineligible for public social services or attendance at public schools of any kind, and required a whole host of local officials to report on their actions against immigrants to the California Attorney General. Its passage briefly rekindled the vigilante spirit of Gold Rush California, as persons who "looked like foreigners" met demands that they prove their citizenship or resident alien status before receiving medical treatment or filling a prescription. But within days of the

referendum a federal judge issued a preliminary injunction barring enforcement of many of the provisions of the new law which flew in the face of
recent US Supreme Court decisions, most notably a 1982 ruling which
declared the barring of the children of illegal immigrants from the public
schools unconstitutional. After five years of litigation the injunction became
permanent. All that remained of the heralded proposition were two provisions that criminalized the manufacture and/or use of false documents for
immigration purposes. Both had long been illegal under federal law.

In the short run, however, the electoral success inspired a spate of "copy
cat" legislation in many other states and, as noted, in Congress. But not all
states followed the California example. Most notable among those which
did not was Texas, whose Governor George W. Bush publicly denounced
Prop 187 and similar measures. As *The Economist* put it in 1996, Texas and
California represented "two states of mind" on the immigration issue.

Believing that Prop 187 reflected the national mood, both parties in 1996
adopted platform planks that spoke sternly about immigration. For those
who thought that emulating Prop 187 was a key to electoral success, the
1996 election provided a rude awakening. Not only did Bill Clinton – who
was less hostile to immigrants than his opponent – win a smashing victory,
despite well-founded doubts about his sexual behavior and veracity, but a
mobilized swell of Hispanic voters also boded ill for supporters of draco-
nian immigration legislation. Thus in six separate statutes passed in 1997
and 1998, Congress retreated from some of the more extreme provisions of
the immigration statutes it had passed in 1996. These rescissions signified
that the "furor" against immigration was over, at least for a time. Part of the
reason for the relatively rapid reversals was a sense, in the minds of many
swing segments of the voting population, that the key provisions of the
immigration statutes of the mid-nineties were simply unfair.

Nowhere was this more apparent than in California. In the 1998 elections
the Republicans lost all major and most minor state-wide offices by near
landslide proportions: the Democrat Gray Davis got 58 percent of the vote
while his Republican opponent, Dan Lungren, who as state Attorney General had led the defense of Prop 187, got just 38.4 percent. Even more
telling, not one initiative on immigration was among the twelve which
qualified for the ballot.

For the rest of the Clinton years immigration was further expanded by a
number of relatively minor statutes. The pro-immigration forces were
greatly bolstered in early 2000 when the Executive Council of the American
Federation of Labor/Congress of Industrial Organizations (AFL/CIO) announced its support for a blanket amnesty for illegal immigrants and an end
to most sanctions against employers who hired them. This reversed labor's

long-standing anti-immigrant policies and placed it and most business organizations on the same side.

It seemed clear as the century came to an end that the relatively heavy immigration levels of the previous decades would continue and that, with labor now supporting immigration, it would be immigration business as usual. How long that seeming stasis would last, no one could say. But it is worth noting that, even four years and counting after the trauma of the terrorist attacks of September 11, 2001, the rate of immigration was still near peak levels.

It was also clear by century's end that, just as the mass migrations of Europeans from the 1850s to the 1920s had brought a vast cultural transformation, similar changes were being wrought by the newcomers from Asia and Latin America who have dominated immigration since the late 1950s. And although the late twentieth century was more open to cultural change than was the late nineteenth, similar nativistic reactions, directed chiefly against Hispanic migrants and their descendants, occurred and were on the rise. By 2000 every eighth American was Hispanic, and, early in the twenty first century the Census Bureau reported that Hispanics outnumbered African Americans and had become the nation's largest group. Various aspects of Hispanic culture began to slip into the mainstream, nowhere more heavily than in popular music.

Hispanics, like most previous immigrant groups, were found chiefly in ethnic enclaves in large American cities and their use of Spanish set off the same negative reactions as had the use of German, Italian, Yiddish and other immigrant languages in earlier eras. Yet the Hispanic label imposed by the larger culture confused as much as it explained. Mexican Americans and Cuban Americans, to mention only the two largest groups, had very different cultures, were concentrated at opposite ends of the country, and had very different politics: Mexican Americans voted overwhelmingly for Democrats while Cuban Americans cast Republican ballots even more overwhelmingly. And although most Americans think of both groups as foreigners, growing majorities of each are native-born American citizens.

All of this fitted very nicely into the multiculturalism which had become the prevailing mode in the last two decades of the century. The descendants of the southern and eastern Europeans, whose grandparents had seemed so repugnant to the cultural gatekeepers of the first three decades of the century, had long since been culturally accepted, with Jews and Italians leading the way. Large numbers of Asian Americans, long confined to the lowest rungs on the American ladder of success, had made important breakthroughs, aided in part by their increased political clout when Hawaii became the fiftieth state in 1959.

NOTES

1. John Higham, *Strangers in the Land: Patterns of American Nativism, 1820–1925* (New Brunswick, NJ: Rutgers University Press, 1955), p. 4.
2. George Washington, "Address to the Members of the Volunteer Association of Ireland, December 2, 1783," in John C. Fitzpatrick (ed.), *The Writings of George Washington* (Washington DC: Government Printing Office, 1931), vol. XXVII, p.254; John Tyler, "Annual Message, 1841," in James D. Richardson (ed.), *Messages and Papers of the Presidents* (Washington DC: Bureau of National Literature and Art, 1903), vol. IV, p. 41.
3. United States Immigration Commission, Reports of the Immigration Commission (Washington DC: Government Printing Office, 1911), vol. I, p. 29.
4. William A. Douglass, *Emigration in a South Italian Town: An Anthropological History* (New Brunswick, NJ: Rutgers University Press, 1984), p. 84.
5. *The Public Papers and Addresses of Franklin D. Roosevelt*, comp. Samuel I. Roseman (New York: Random House, 1938, and Macmillan, 1941), vol. VII, pp. 258–60, vol. I, p. 750.
6. *The Public Papers and Addresses of Franklin D. Roosevelt*, ed. Samuel I. Roseman (New York: Macmillan, 1950), 1938 volume, pp. 170–1.
7. *Ibid.*, 1943 volume, pp. 427–8.
8. *Ibid.*, 1944, volume, pp. 163–5.
9. *Public Papers of the Presidents of the United States. Harry S. Truman, 1952–53* (Washington: Government Printing Office, 1966), p. 10.
10. See, e.g., Colin Holmes, *John Bull's Island: Immigration and British Society, 1871–1971* (Basingstoke: Macmillan, 1988), p. 221.
11. *Public Papers of the Presidents of the United States. Lyndon B. Johnson, 1965* (Washington: Government Printing Office, 1967), pp. 1039–40.
12. *Ibid.*
13. *Public Papers of the Presidents of the United States. Ronald W. Reagan, 1986* (Washington: Government Printing Office, 1989), p. 1521.

FURTHER READING

Roger Daniels, *Coming to America: A History of Race and Ethnicity in American Life*, 2nd ed., New York: HarperCollins, 2002.
  Guarding the Golden Door: American Immigration Policy and Immigrants since 1882, New York: Hill and Wang, 2004.
María Cristina García, *Havana USA: Cuban Exiles and Cuban Americans in South Florida, 1959–1994*, Berkeley: University of California Press, 1996.
Jeremy Hein, *From Vietnam, Laos, and Cambodia: A Refugee Experience in the United States*, New York: Twayne, 1995.
Alan Kraut, *Silent Travelers: Germs, Genes, and the "Immigrant Menace,"* New York: Basic Books, 1994.
David M. Reimers, *Still the Golden Door: The Third World Comes to America*, 2nd ed., New York: Columbia University Press, 1992.
George J. Sánchez, *Becoming Mexican American: Ethnicity, Culture and Identity in Chicano Los Angeles, 1900–1945*, New York: Oxford University Press, 1993.

Ronald Takaki, *Strangers from a Different Shore. A History of Asian Americans*, Boston: Little, Brown, 1989.

Stephan Thernstrom (ed.), *The Harvard Encyclopedia of American Ethnic Groups*, Cambridge, MA: Harvard University Press, 1980.

Rudolph J. Vecoli and Suzanne Sinke (eds.), *A Century of European Migrations*, Urbana University of Illinois Press, 1991.

To keep up with an expanding literature see the two English language journals which best cover immigration history, *The Journal of American Ethnic History* and *Immigrants & Minorities*.

5

PETER W. WILLIAMS

Religion in the United States in the twentieth century: 1900–1960

Two events which took place near the turn of the twentieth century are instructive places to begin to understand the dynamics of American religion: the World's Parliament of Religions in Chicago and the passage of the Eighteenth Amendment to the US Constitution. The former, which was held in conjunction with the World's Columbian Exposition in 1893, was the first time in US history that a conscious attempt was made to promote interreligious dialogue on a significant scale. Representatives of every conceivable tradition were invited by the organizers, who were themselves of the liberal wing of the itself liberal Unitarian movement, and a wide variety of spokespeople took advantage of the opportunity to explain to the American public exactly what their traditions taught. The event was not without controversy: Roman Catholic bishops, for example, were divided over the wisdom of participating, although the forward-looking Archbishop John Ireland of Minnesota decided that the risks of seeming to relativize his church were worth the opportunity of gaining a sympathetic hearing. In addition to the more general acknowledgment of religious pluralism in the nation, the Parliament resulted in the American public's having an opportunity to witness the diversity that already characterized the national religious scene as well as a chance to learn about heretofore exotic traditions such as Hinduism, which for the first time now began to reach an audience beyond the minute number of ethnic South Asians then resident in the country.

While the Parliament was taking place, another movement with particular implications for Chicago and other cities now being transformed by a vast influx of immigrants was Prohibition. Prohibition had its origins in the temperance movement of the early nineteenth century, a campaign to induce a voluntary "taking the pledge" to refrain from alcoholic beverages sponsored primarily by Protestant Evangelicals but also promoted by some Irish Catholics. Although this cause was overshadowed in mid-century by the slavery issue, it emerged again in the century's later decades in the context of the rapid expansion of American cities through the "new" immigration, primarily from southern and Eastern Europe. The shift of nomenclature from "temperance" to "prohibition" was indicative of a change of emphasis from voluntary abstention to a governmentally enforced ban on the production and distribution of intoxicating beverages. Prominent among the advocates for this now politicized cause were women, as evidenced in the role played by the Women's Christian Temperance Union, which was founded in Ohio in 1874.

Although both the intercontinental ecumenism of the World's Parliament and the neo-puritanical repressiveness of the Prohibitionists may seem to have been severely at odds with one another ideologically, both were seen at the time by their advocates as "progressive." For the twenty-first century observer, this characterization probably does not seem problematic when applied to the Parliament; however, Prohibition, which proved a proverbial train-wreck when actually enacted and enforced, has become virtually synonymous with social and religious retrogression. Actually, the motivation behind the passage of the Eighteenth Amendment in 1919 was ideologically complicated. It can be read as a *cri de coeur* of an older Protestant America, which was seeing its political power and moral authority eroded by the political bosses and urban gangsters who made use of the corner saloon as a means to deprive the immigrant laborer of his money, sobriety, self-respect, and independence. Not far behind lurked the Catholic priest, who seemed to be working hand-in-glove with the Irish politician and the German saloon-keeper. Prohibition could, on the one hand, be viewed as a campaign of intolerance against the mores of Catholics, Jews, and even Lutherans and Episcopalians, who viewed the moderate use of alcohol benignly or, on the other, a right-minded crusade against the evils of the saloon, the havoc which alcohol wreaked on the families of working men, and the errors of the immigrants' religious spokesmen, who, perhaps not surprisingly, viewed the movement as repression rather than reform.

World War I and the ensuing decade of the 1920s can be best read as a temporary victory for the forces of reform and homogenization, but also as a time in which forces corrosive of those goals were being nurtured. Prohibition was, after all, the law of the land, although the efforts of Elliott Ness and other federal agents to enforce it and to deal with the organized criminal syndicates which arose to defy it were, at best, very mixed. Intolerance of immigrants and their offspring was exemplified by, at one level, the arrest and deportation of many aliens by Attorney General Mitchell Palmer shortly after the Great War's conclusion, and, at another, by the reign of terror waged by the newly revived Ku Klux Klan not only against "uppity" Negroes – to use the polite language of the day – but against Catholics,

Jews, and immigrants as WELL. Immigration itself had come to a virtual standstill with the coming of the war, and a series of laws passed by Congress altered quotas to favor northwestern Europeans and to put a complete bar on Asians.

The watchword of "Americanization" for the declining number of newcomers was on the lips of, among many others, Henry Ford, who staged pageants in which his newly resocialized foreign-born workers would enter a "melting pot" clad in their Old World garb and emerge clothed as Americans. The ban on the teaching of German and other foreign languages which the war had brought about, as well as a deep suspicion of and even violent demonstrations against all things Teutonic, had a chilling effect on attempts of various national communities to maintain their cultures intact, and played into the hands of assimilation-minded Jewish and Catholic leaders who favored cultural homogenization and bureaucratic centralization for their flocks. Reform Judaism, pioneered by Isaac Mayer Wise and others during the previous century, represented a deliberate effort to strip from Jewish practice those customs, such as the wearing of the yarmulke, the segregation of the sexes during worship, and the observance of the Mosaic dietary codes, which they regarded as unjustified by modern rationality and which detracted from a focus on ethical behavior in harmony with the teachings of the Prophets. It was Reform that surged ahead of the ancient Orthodoxy and the even newer Conservatism that were its principal rivals among religiously minded Jews during these decades. The development of new institutions such as the "synagogue-center" – or, facetiously, the "*shul* [synagogue] with a pool" – further represented the inclination of both Reform and some of their more cautious Conservative counterparts to foster a Judaism which was in harmony with the gentile American culture amidst which they had often eagerly elected to live.

At the turn of the century, Roman Catholic leadership had been seriously divided among three groups: the progressives, such as St. Paul's Archbishop John Ireland, who regarded American culture and society as benign and preferable to European ecclesiastical tradition; traditionalists, also of predominantly Irish descent, who favored centralization of authority and deference to the wishes of the Pope and his advisors; and what might be called "ethnic particularists" – Catholic clergy and bishops of German, Polish, Lithuanian, and other central European origin. The latter argued that a weakening of the bond between institutional Catholicism and their own national traditions would seriously weaken the allegiance of Americans of similar stock who would be irresistibly tempted by the dominant, English-speaking, historically Protestant but increasingly secular dominant culture. Papal opposition to "Americanization" and broader social pressures toward assimilation effectively curtailed the abilities of the first and third factions to maintain their respective programs effectively, and a "ghetto" Catholicism – Irish-American dominated, English-speaking, institutionally expansionist, and dominated by clergy and especially bishops – emerged as the dominant force in American Catholicism from the World War I era to the 1960s. Catholic ambitions to exert social and political power, which had been achieved through organization and numbers in cities such as Boston and New York, however, ran into a seemingly insurmountable barrier in 1928, when the Irish-American "wet" Catholic governor of New York State, Al Smith, was soundly defeated by the Prohibitionist Republican Herbert Hoover in that year's Presidential contest.

It was also during this period that a major schism within America's Protestant churches was beginning to develop along fault lines that would remain unbridged even in the early twenty-first century. Beginning in the mid-nineteenth century, a battle over how the Bible was to be interpreted began to arise in the mutually reinforcing contexts of the emergence of German-based critical method and the publication in England of Charles Darwin's crucial *The Origin of Species* in 1861. The "higher" biblical criticism – also known as form or source criticism – that had begun to be taught in a number of influential American seminaries by the late nineteenth century was based on the supposition that, inspired though they may have been by the divine Word, the books of scripture nevertheless were the products of authorship by humans who were bound by the literary and intellectual conventions of their own era. Through this reasoning, the gospels were no longer seen as eyewitness accounts of the life and career of Jesus, but rather as composed by second-generation or later writers who utilized different combinations of oral and written sources from apostolic times. The Darwinian theory of organic evolution further undermined a literalist approach to the book of Genesis by casting doubt on the sequence of creation in that work's beginning, especially if the word "day" was to be interpreted as a twenty-four hour period.

The liberal theologians who had begun to dominate the faculties of the more prestigious seminaries, together with the ministers at many of the largest and most prestigious churches, were willing enough to embrace both evolution and biblical criticism as compatible with a Christian worldview in which the boundaries between the natural and supernatural realms were increasingly blurred, and in which advances in scientific thought were hailed for their potential benefits to human understanding and well-being rather than being condemned as threats to traditional faith. By the beginning of the twentieth century, a movement with which the term "Fundamentalist" was increasingly associated began to coalesce, especially within the highly contested struggles for leadership within the northern branches of the Baptist and Presbyterian churches. (Their southern counterparts, together with Methodists in that region, had split off prior to the Civil War over the slavery issue and maintained their own, conservative religious culture in the context of the South's prevailing cultural disposition.)

The gospel of Fundamentalism was formulated and spread in a variety of ways. Princeton Theological Seminary had by the late nineteenth century emerged as a bastion of defense of traditional biblical interpretation, with scholars there maintaining that the Bible was "inerrant in its original autographs" – that is, manuscripts which no longer existed. From 1907 to 1915, a pair of wealthy California brothers sponsored the publication and widespread distribution of a series of booklets entitled, collectively, *The Fundamentals*, which further laid the theological groundwork and provided a name for the movement that soon became known as "Fundamentalism." Its tenets were spread by revivalists, such as Billy Sunday; Bible schools, such as the Moody Bible Institute in Chicago, founded as a counter force to such liberal ecumenical divinity schools as those at Harvard and the University of Chicago; and urban ministers presiding over what would later be known as "megachurches," with thousands of members and the financial resources to own radio stations over which the Fundamentalist message could be broadcast widely.

Although Fundamentalism was predicated on a literal interpretation of the Bible, its adherents nevertheless claimed as essential some doctrines which others did not as readily find in that source. Foremost among these was "dispensational premillennialism," which originated in the teachings of the English clergyman John Nelson Darby in the 1840s and was disseminated widely in the United States in the twentieth century through the annotations in the Scofield Reference Bible, first published in 1909. Darby argued that the Bible could be divided into a number of ages, or dispensations, beginning with the creation of Adam and Eve in the Garden of Eden, each of which was characterized by a different covenantal relationship between God and humanity. The present age, which had come into existence after the time of Jesus on earth, was known as the "Church age," and was rapidly coming to a conclusion. Soon the events cryptically forecast in the apocalyptic book of "Revelation" would start to become fulfilled, beginning with the "Rapture," or bodily taking up into heaven, of those believers who were fully committed to Jesus' teaching. After this, the earth would come under control of the cosmic villain known as the Antichrist, and those believers who had been left behind after the Rapture but were unwilling to do the Antichrist's will would be horrifically persecuted. A final battle between the forces of the Antichrist and a newly returned Jesus would take place in the Middle East, after the successful conclusion of which the forces of good would live for a thousand years of peace and prosperity – the millennium – until the final vanquishing of the forces of evil by Jesus.

Although this millennial scenario would enjoy national attention at the end of the century, the more immediate focus in the 1920s was the teaching of evolution in the public schools, which had been formally banned by a number of state legislatures, including that of Tennessee. In 1925, the American Civil Liberties Union induced a high school biology teacher named John Scopes to let it be known publicly that he was defying the law by teaching evolution in his classes. The trial which ensued was one of the great "ballyhoo" events of a decade known for media sensationalism. Clarence Darrow, celebrity attorney and civil libertarian, defended Scopes, while William Jennings Bryan, former Secretary of State, populist spokesman, and erstwhile Democratic presidential candidate, volunteered his services to the prosecution as an expert on the Bible. Darrow repeatedly backed Bryan into the contradictions that resulted from his literalist interpretations, and Bryan died shortly afterwards. Scopes was convicted, but his conviction was reversed on a technicality, and the law remained on Tennessee's books until the 1950s.

Although the legal outcome of the Scopes trial was ambiguous, the nationally covered event proved a public relations disaster for the Fundamentalist cause. Battles within the northern denominations, especially the Baptists and Presbyterians, resulted in Fundamentalist losses, and the movement was largely relegated to the South until the Evangelical resurgence of the 1970s. In addition to the hard-core Fundamentalism which persisted especially in Baptist and Presbyterian camps – both, significantly, of Calvinist or Reformed origin – another species of Evangelicalism grew more quietly during these decades, generally set apart from controversies involving doctrine or public policy. Holiness was a movement which grew out of the Wesleyan tradition, specifically from John Wesley's teaching that it was possible to go beyond assurance of salvation, or "justification," to attain a spiritual "second blessing" known as "entire sanctification." Devotees of the Holiness persuasion, who relentlessly eschewed what they deemed "worldliness," grew restless during the nineteenth century as they saw their emphases downplayed by an increasingly middle-class Methodist community, and by the 1880s had begun to form separate denominations, such as the Church of God (Anderson, Indiana) and the Church of the Nazarene. By 1900, another movement, Pentecostalism, emerged out of the Holiness matrix, going beyond its origins by stressing the need for direct experience of the "gifts of the Holy Spirit," especially "glossolalia" – speaking in tongues – and faith-healing. Although interracial in some of its early manifestations, such as the long-running Azusa Street revival which began in Los Angeles in 1906, Pentecostalism soon routinized into denominational forms such as the Assemblies of God and the predominantly black Church of God in Christ. Although the movement flourished especially in the nation's southern and western regions, an occasional Pentecostal evangelist such as "Sister Aimee" Semple McPherson at her Angelus Temple in Los Angeles gained the national spotlight through a flamboyant style of evangelism.

Although the Social Gospel, a movement with origins in late nineteenth-century American liberal Protestantism, was among the religious movements eclipsed for some years by the First World War and the subsequent national glorification of business in the 1920s, the advent of the Depression in 1929 saw a revival of themes which had already been firmly planted. The most profound proponent of Social Gospel theology had been Walter Rauschenbusch, whose works such as *Christianity and the Social Crisis* (1907) and *A Theology for the Social Gospel* (1917) had been published in the wake of the bitter and sometimes violent labor disputes that had begun in the last decades of the previous century. Rauschenbusch, together with kindred spirits such as Washington Gladden of Columbus, Ohio, had succeeded in some measure in shifting the focus of Christian concern from the spiritual well-being of the individual to the elimination through Christian effort of the forces of evil which were pervasive in the social, economic, and political structures of American society. Although interdenominational agencies such as the Federal Council of Churches (founded 1908) had attempted to implement Social Gospel teachings through studying and mediating major strikes, the mood of the postwar years did not give their concerns much place amidst the "boosterism" that pervaded both an apparently vigorous business community as well as churchmen more concerned with numerical growth and innovative programming than social reform. More representative of the decade's ethos, perhaps, was Bruce Barton's bestselling *The Man Nobody Knows* of 1925, in which the advertising executive turned biblical scholar presented Jesus as the prototype of the American organizer and promoter.

During the Depression years, the themes of Social Christianity re-emerged from two very different quarters. Within the Protestant community, Reinhold Niebuhr combined the social concern of Rauschenbusch with a theological framework derived in considerable measure from the "crisis theology" formulated in postwar Europe by Swiss theologian Karl Barth and his contemporaries. This "Neo-Orthodoxy" rejected the tendency of the liberal Protestantism of the prewar years to downplay the impact of sinfulness on human nature, and instead found in classic theologians such as

Augustine, Luther, Calvin, and Kierkegaard what seemed in the context of the times a more realistic appraisal of the damage done to human prospects by the impact of Original Sin. The recovery of this earlier theology, however, was not accompanied, as it had been for the Fundamentalists, by an insistence on the rejection of contemporary approaches to biblical interpretation. Nor did it imply a turning away from worldly concerns such as social justice, which the advocates of dispensational premillennialism had branded as futile in a world which could not be redeemed until the second coming of Jesus. Niebuhr and his like-minded colleagues rather insisted that the Gospel necessitated a realistic concern for the application of Christian ethical principles to the political, social, and economic realms, as long as such concern was tempered with a suspicion of any claims to an easily achieved utopia. Niebuhr's "Christian realism" led him through a variety of political twists and turns, such as his repudiation of his earlier hopes for the Soviet Union after it declared its alliance with Nazi Germany in 1939.

Although relationships between American Catholics and other Christians were not particularly close, or even cordial, during these years, many Catholics shared with Protestants such as Reinhold Niebuhr a concern for issues of social justice, especially since most Catholics at the time were immigrants, or the children thereof, and belonged to the working class. The theological groundwork for Catholic social teaching had been laid by Pope Leo XIII, whose encyclical letter *Rerum Novarum* ("Of New Things") of 1891 had enunciated the theory of the "just wage." Elaborated in the United States in subsequent decades by social theologians such as Monsignor John A. Ryan of Catholic University, this teaching rejected the tenet of classic economic theory that employers were only obliged to pay workers what the market might bear. Rather, employees were entitled to a wage which was adequate for them to support themselves and their families at a level sufficient not simply to survive but to live with a modicum of dignity. The coincidence of these ideals with the secular New Deal of Franklin Roosevelt led to FDR's appointing of several Catholic clergy to positions of influence within his administration, as well as substantial numbers of Catholic and Jewish laymen to cabinet offices, judgeships, and other political offices from which they had previously been informally excluded.

Two other Catholics assumed prophetic roles on the social issues of the day during the 1930s in ways that pushed the boundaries of institutional church tolerance. Charles Coughlin, Detroit's "radio priest," utilized his suburban Royal Oak parish, the Shrine of the Little Flower, as a bully pulpit for a nationally distributed radio program in which he advocated a populist message urging strong governmental action against the financial interests which he held responsible for the nation's economic woes during the

Depression. Originally a supporter of the New Deal, Coughlin later turned against Roosevelt, supported a short-lived third party in the 1936 election, and then began to advocate a fascist-tinged position in which anti-Semitism played a prominent role. Coughlin was eventually silenced by his bishop, and withdrew from the public realm for the remainder of his career.

Dorothy Day, a Catholic convert who had lived a bohemian existence as a journalist in New York, took a very different direction from Coughlin in her confrontation with the widespread economic distress of the decade. Day founded the Catholic Worker movement, known for the tabloid of the same name which it produced, as well as the "houses of hospitality" which it maintained in many of the nation's largest cities. Day and her followers lived in these houses at a subsistence level with all of the urban needy they could accommodate. Although Day was repeatedly arrested for deliberate violations of the law, including protests against civil defense directives in the 1950s, she remained doctrinally orthodox and was never put under sanctions by the generally conservative archbishops in whose diocese she operated.

The next national trauma, World War II, had a profound if often indirect impact on the nation's religious communities, especially for those of a minority status. Although most denominations were careful to avoid the sometimes ill-considered enthusiasm they had exhibited during the century's earlier global conflict, most – except for traditionally peace-minded sects such as the Quakers and Mennonites – realized that neutrality in the midst of the radical evil represented by Nazism was untenable. The experience of millions of young men from almost every conceivable American ethnic background being thrown together into the appalling circumstances of combat went a considerable way toward breaking down the social taboos which had previously isolated minorities from the mainstream. The almost obligatory scene in war films in which a unit's roll call included names such as Cohen and Kowalski as well as Smith and Jones underlined the call of leaders for national unity. The notable exceptions were on racial rather than ethnic or religious grounds: African Americans were largely relegated to menial roles and, when allowed to engage in combat, did so under the supervision of white officers. Japanese Americans, when allowed out of west coast internment camps, were similarly segregated from the mainstream. Despite these unfortunate lapses, interreligious cooperation and self-sacrifice – such as that of the "four chaplains" who chose to perish with the USS *Dorchester* rather than see young sailors denied lifeboat space – became emblematic of a united people. The "Why We Fight" series directed by Frank Capra similarly stressed the importance of religion as part of the "American Way of Life" in its effort to educate the American public about the dangers of totalitarianism.

The alliance of the United States with the Soviet Union during the war – always an uneasy venture for most Americans – rapidly yielded to the "Cold War" after the final defeat of the Axis powers, and ushered in a new era in American consciousness. Although no single religious group had a monopoly on the promotion of a Cold War mentality or ideology, American Catholics assumed a certain prominence in the promotion of such a mindset. One reason was the rapid fall of many of the nations of eastern and central Europe, with large Catholic populations, under the thrall of communist regimes, with widespread persecution of such Catholic leaders as Hungary's Cardinal Jozef Mindzenty. Communism rapidly became associated for Americans with "godless atheism," a not entirely inaccurate label, and the subsequent rise of Wisconsin Senator Joseph McCarthy, a Catholic of Irish descent, helped associate a virulent anti-communist rhetoric with the American Catholic community. Although by no means all American Catholics supported McCarthy and the "ism" which he generated, his endorsement by highly visible Catholic leaders such as New York's Cardinal, Francis Spellman, made such support seem more pervasive than it actually was.

In addition to its oppression of religious institutions in the Soviet Union and allied Warsaw Pact nations, communism also inspired American fears through its rapid attainment of a potent nuclear arsenal thought by many as capable of unleashing a devastating third world war. This threat of virtually universal destruction was echoed in millenarian rhetoric by both Catholics and Protestants. In the case of the former, the appearances of the Virgin Mary, which had been alleged to have occurred to a group of Portuguese children at Fatima in 1917, gave rise in 1947 in the United States to an organization of devotees known as the "Blue Army," who promoted predictions of unparalleled supernatural and this-worldly suffering unless the Soviet Union was converted to Christianity and the world dedicated to the Virgin Mary. Much was made particularly of an unrevealed "third secret" thought to predict the end of the world, which was much later revealed by Pope John Paul II to consist of a considerably less dramatic message. This combination of apocalyptic prediction, Marian devotion, and anti-communism was also promoted in somewhat more sophisticated form by New York Bishop Fulton J. Sheen, whose television program *Life Is Worth Living*, broadcast between 1951 and 1957, helped expose Americans of a wide variety of backgrounds to an appealing statement of Catholic principles.

Sheen's Protestant counterpart in skilled media performance and apocalyptic rhetoric was the young Billy Graham, whose evangelistic campaign in Los Angeles in 1949 – bolstered greatly by William Randolph Hearst's legendary directive to his newspaper chain to "Puff Graham" – marked the beginnings of a career as a national Evangelical celebrity which would continue into the twenty-first century. Graham also became adept in using the new medium of television, and continued his "crusades" – large-scale revival meetings – in cities across the nation and eventually beyond. Graham's early Fundamentalism gradually morphed into a more moderate Evangelicalism, and a mutual courtship between himself and prominent politicians of both parties elevated him to the status of something resembling a chaplain to the nation. His somewhat uncritical association with Richard Nixon in the 1960s resulted in an embarrassing but ultimately minor setback to an unparalleled career, which helped bring Evangelicalism into a position of national respectability.

The 1950s was a decade subsequently celebrated for its "normalcy" and complacency, during which the adjustment of postwar Americans to a higher standard of living, frequently in the burgeoning suburbs, displaced more spiritual concerns. This characterization, which had a certain basis in reality, was not simply the result of critical retrospection from subsequent decades but was rooted in the social criticism of the time as well. The 1950s, in fact, were remarkable as a decade in which both theology and sociology escaped from the clutches of the academy and found a wide readership among literate Americans more widely. Henry Luce's *Time* magazine played some role in this by periodically featuring prominent theologians on its front page, such as Paul Tillich, a German refugee who taught at Harvard, Union Theological Seminary, and the University of Chicago, and expounded an interpretation of Christianity variously described as Neo-Orthodox and existentialist. Tillich's addressing issues of personal belief and cultural criticism in works such as *The Courage to Be* (1952) found a wide audience, as did Reinhold Niebuhr's ongoing critique of his age in works such as *The Irony of American History* (1952). By the early sixties, works such as Peter Berger's *The Noise of Solemn Assemblies* and Gibson Winter's *The Suburban Captivity of the Churches* (both 1961) would bring the "mainline" Protestant churches, now thriving in the suburbs, under fire for their complacency and lack of relevance to the social issues of the day.

A contemporary sociologist and theologian who offered one of the most influential appraisals of religion and American society during the fifties was Will Herberg, whose *Protestant, Catholic, Jew* of 1955 posited the "triple melting pot" theory. In this formulation, the United States, which until recently had been seen by many as a normatively Protestant society, had now reached a stage of assimilation in which Roman Catholic and Jewish religious identity were on a par with Protestantism in terms of social legitimacy. A corollary of this theory was that all three of these communities had by now accepted the essential "rightness" of the American order of things, and were able to function and even prosper in a society in which neither public favoritism nor persecution would define a religious community's status.

The Catholicism of the 1950s did support Herberg's thesis well enough. Large-scale immigration from Europe had ceased during the 1920s, and most Catholics in the United States were now native-born rather than immigrants. World War II had exerted a profound effect on the Catholic community, exposing Catholic service personnel to a wide variety of fellow citizens far different culturally from themselves. Upon their return, moreover, many availed themselves on the benefits of the "GI Bill" of 1944, which provided generous aid to veterans to pursue higher education and to obtain home mortgages at favorable terms. The result was an exodus of second- and third-generation Catholic Americans out of the ethnic and religious "ghettos" of the nation's large cities into the rapidly growing post-ethnic suburbs. Marriages within the Catholic community were increasingly made without regard to ethnic boundaries, although marriage outside the faith was still strongly discouraged. Catholic higher education was stimulated by the influx of veterans bringing government subsidies, and a new era of assimilated middle-class Catholic life rapidly began to displace the ethnic neighborhoods and working-class status of earlier generations.

Another way in which American Catholics were embracing American norms was at the intellectual level. Except through a few journals such as *Commonweal* and the *Catholic Worker*, previous generations of Catholics – again, mostly ethnic and working class in social composition – were neither encouraged nor likely to express dissent against official church teachings or policies. By the 1950s, a small group of Catholic intellectuals, such as the coterie of laity who expressed themselves in *Commonweal*, and clergy, primarily Jesuits, began to offer differing views on the issues which arose from the position of Catholics in a predominantly non-Catholic society. John Tracy Ellis, a priest who taught at the University of San Francisco, notably raised the question in public as to why Catholic intellectual life had attained so little visibility or distinction, in his *American Catholics and the Intellectual Life* of 1956. Similarly, the Jesuit John Courtney Murray, in his 1960 volume, *We Hold These Truths: Catholic Reflections on the American Proposition*, argued effectively that the American political system was in fact not only tolerable but actually positively good from the standpoint of Catholic ideals and interests, and played a significant role in shaping the "Declaration on Religious Freedom" that would issue from the Vatican II ecumenical council in 1965.

The most obvious and visible manifestation of acculturation among American Catholics, however, came in the political realm. John Fitzgerald Kennedy was born into the heart of Boston Irish Catholicdom, and had grandfathers on both side of his family who had been deeply involved in the robust ethnic politics that had reshaped that city, and many others, during the heyday of Irish-dominated urban machine politics. The wealth of Kennedy's father, Joseph, made it possible for him and his well-known brothers, Robert and Edward ("Teddy"), to attend Harvard and contemplate political careers that would transcend the parochial borders of eastern Massachusetts. In 1960, then-Senator John Kennedy became the first Roman Catholic since Al Smith in 1928 to receive the Democratic nomination for President of the United States. Unlike Smith, "JFK" actually won that office by the narrowest of margins, and achieved virtually mythic status after his assassination three years later. Although the question of whether Kennedy's Catholicism might put into question his ultimate loyalties as President was raised during his run for the presidency, he defused the issue so effectively during his campaign and brief tenure in office that it has never since been raised seriously for subsequent Catholics aspiring to high national office.

The American Jewish community had also become highly assimilated to middle-class American life during the decades after the cut-off of large-scale immigration in the 1920s. Isaac Mayer Wise, the indefatigable Bavarian-born rabbi who presided over Cincinnati's Plum Street Temple during the latter part of the nineteenth century, had thoroughly laid both the ideological and institutional groundwork for an assimilation-minded American version of Reform Judaism: The indigenous Conservative movement, which came together at the beginning of the twentieth century in the United States, was also harmonious with mainstream American life while maintaining a greater religious distinctiveness than Reform advocates preferred. Orthodoxy, which trailed the other two movements considerably in numerical terms, remained strong in the New York City area where ethnic enclaves were able to persist in relative isolation. The latter were bolstered by the arrival of Hasidim and other refugees from central and eastern Europe during and after World War II.

The major forces affecting twentieth-century American Judaism took place far from American shores. The Holocaust, which resulted in the deaths of some six million European Jews and the destruction of the cultures of ghetto and shtetl that they had nurtured for centuries, was obviously a shock to the collective system. Although some American Jews had worked to influence governmental policy during the war, residual anti-Semitism in the State Department and a general preoccupation of the Roosevelt administration with what seemed more crucial matters resulted in a general neglect until the liberation of the concentration camps at the war's end forced the public to confront the issue. One result of the shift in public opinion on the "Jewish question" was the establishing of Israel as an independent Jewish homeland by the United Nations in 1948, the culmination of a half-century of Zionist advocacy. Although a theological response to the Holocaust in the United States would not begin to take shape until the 1960s, the American Jewish community rallied to the support of the new nation of Israel, both financially and through a highly effective campaign of political advocacy which helped shape American foreign policy into the twenty-first century. Anti-Semitism, which had taken place more at the genteel than the crudely violent level in American life, was now largely discredited among the influential in society, and phenomena such as "Jewish quotas" in elite colleges and restrictive covenants in such exclusive neighborhoods as Detroit's Grosse Pointe began to collapse under legal challenges and the force of public opinion.

Herberg's paradigm of a "triple melting pot" still seems plausible, but for what it affirms rather than what it omits. Although Protestantism no longer exerted the normative role it once had, what Catholics and Jews had demonstrated by achieving social parity was that middle-class Euro-American culture was now the widely accepted standard of acceptability. Native Americans and their religions had sunk to a level of near-invisibility. Traditional religious practices had largely disappeared, except among a few peoples such as the Pueblo, who had managed to compartmentalize their traditional culture from the aspects of their life that required contact with the outside world. Many practiced some form of Christianity introduced by Catholic and Protestant missionaries during the previous century. The Ghost Dance, a militant pan-tribal movement of cultural resistance, had largely disappeared after the massacre at Wounded Knee in 1890. The most lasting of such new movements was the Peyote religion, which focused on the attainment of harmony between the individual and the cosmos through the ritual ingestion of hallucinogens, and which spread widely throughout the Western part of the nation. Mexican Americans, though numerous in the southwest, with some enclaves in the Great Lakes cities, were similarly invisible, marginalized through a combination of culture, economics, and, in the religious realm, incomprehension and indifference on the part of an Irish-American dominated Catholic hierarchy.

Religions outside the Jewish/Christian tradition were also highly inconspicuous until the 1960s, largely because of lack of numerical strength brought about by highly restrictive immigration legislation that would not be changed significantly until the 1960s. A number of Middle Eastern immigrants, including both Christians and Muslims, had settled in scattered regions of the Midwest earlier in the century. Dearborn, Michigan, the base of the vast Ford industrial empire, attracted many, beginning in the 1920s, who came in search of employment in the burgeoning auto industry and who remain the nucleus for one of the largest Arab American communities in the nation. Asian Americans could be found mainly along the west coast and in Hawaii, where they practiced Buddhism, including a Westernized form of the Pure Land strain, various forms and mixtures of traditional Chinese and Japanese popular religion, and both Protestant and Catholic Christianity. The perceived alien character of such peoples and their religions contributed to the movement to intern Japanese Americans during World War II.

More visible to the broader public were developments within the African American community, which had undergone a profound demographic transformation beginning with World War I, in which vast numbers of sharecroppers had left the South to seek employment in the factories of the great cities of the Northeast, Great Lakes, and west coast. The new communities which arose in New York, Detroit, Chicago, Los Angeles, and elsewhere fostered new forms of religious expression, as "Sanctified" (Holiness and Pentecostal) congregations appropriated empty urban storefronts for services conducted by preachers who felt called by the Holy Spirit and their congregations to the task of leading a highly expressive form of worship. Methodists and Baptists, already established in many of these cities and more middle class in culture, worshiped in more formal settings according to more decorous norms, and their clergy provided a cadre of political as well as spiritual leadership. The latter ranged from the Adam Clayton Powell dynasty in New York's Harlem, who provided congressional representation for the neighborhood, to the Martin Luther King succession in Atlanta, which produced, beginning in the 1950s, the most visible and effective leader of the Civil Rights Movement that would soon overturn completely the relations between white and black in America.

Beginning in the 1920s and 1930s, a variety of indigenous forms of African American religion began to arise in the black urban communities of the nation's northeastern quadrant. The Depression of the 1930s, which hit minorities especially hard, gave rise to charismatic figures such as Father Divine and "Sweet Daddy" Grace, who preached a combination of Christianity and their own distinctive teachings based on personal authority. Their appeal lay in part in the physical relief they offered the poor and unemployed, such as Father Divine's banquets given at his Long Island home. Of farther-reaching impact was the Nation of Islam, or black Muslims, which emerged in Detroit in the 1930s through the work of an itinerant silk salesman known as W. D. Fard (one of the several versions of his name). Although Fard soon disappeared under mysterious circumstances, his message was taken up by Elijah Muhammad (né Elijah Poole), who created a movement that rapidly spread to Chicago, Philadelphia, New York, Boston, and other cities. Although the movement's teachings bore only the most superficial relation to traditional Islam, its militant affirmation of the dignity of African Americans and their heritage and its insistence on a highly disciplined communal way of life appealed to many black Americans, especially as promulgated by the movement's charismatic spokesman, Malcolm X (né Malcolm Little.) During the 1960s, the Nation would provide a dramatic ideological challenge to the Christian-based message of Martin Luther King, Jr.

The course of American religious history during the first six decades of the twentieth century can be summarized under three main categories. First, American Protestantism, still numerically dominant when taken as a whole, was losing its once-unchallenged cultural authority and was dividing internally into irreconcilable camps based in part on willingness to come to terms with the broader culture, especially at the intellectual level. Second, religious minority communities of European origin were working their way into the American mainstream, although Catholics temporarily erected social and cultural barriers against what they still saw as a hostile Protestant/secular majority, and Jews were forced to reconsider their embrace of modernity and universalism after the trauma of the Holocaust. Finally, other minority communities whose origins lay outside Europe were still striving for sufficient self-consciousness and social strength to be able to assert their claims to acceptability – an assertion that had begun for African Americans in the 1950s and which would be taken up by others in the ensuing decades.

FURTHER READING

Sydney E. Ahlstrom, *A Religious History of the American People*, 2nd ed., New Haven, CT, and London: Yale University Press, 2004.

Richard Fox, *Reinhold Niebuhr: A Biography*, New York: Pantheon, 1985.

George Marsden, *Fundamentalism and American Culture: The Shaping of Twentieth Century Evangelicalism, 1870–1925*, New York: Oxford University Press, 1980.

Martin E. Marty, *Modern America Religion,Volume 1: The Irony of It All, 1893–1919*, Chicago: University of Chicago Press, 1987.

Modern American Religion, Volume 2: The Noise of Conflict, 1919–1941, Chicago: University of Chicago Press, 1991.

Modern American Religion, Volume 3: Under God, Indivisible, 1941–1960, Chicago: University of Chicago Press, 1996.

Charles R. Morris, *American Catholic: The Saints and Sinners Who Built America's Most Powerful Church*, New York: Times Books, 1997.

Jonathan Sarna, *American Judaism: A History*, New Haven: Yale University Press, 2004.

Grant Wacker, *Heaven Below: Early Pentecostals and American Culture*, Cambridge, MA.: Harvard University Press, 2001.

Peter W. Williams, *America's Religions: From Their Origins to the Twenty-First Century*, Urbana and Chicago: University of Illinois Press, 2002.

6

WADE CLARK ROOF AND NATHALIE CARON

Shifting boundaries: religion and the United States: 1960 to the present

Religion in the United States currently takes on a very visible – and in ways puzzling and disturbing – role in public life. In 2004, George W. Bush was re-elected President of the United States with strong support from evangelical Christians. His God-and-country rhetoric and support for government funding of faith communities signaled a worrisome alliance between political neoconservatives and evangelical Christianity and led to a blurring of boundaries between religion and government, despite an official legal separation of church and state. To critics, it looked, and looks, as if a national religion has been "institutionalized."

Recent developments have spurred secular reaction. One of the clearest signs of the reaction was the lawsuit brought to the Supreme Court in 2004 by Michael Newdow, an atheist who charged that the phrase "a nation under God" in the pledge of allegiance as it was recited in public schools violated the separation of church and state and was therefore unconstitutional. Though the court has not ruled on the substance of the case, it has spawned considerable controversy touching on what amounts to a sensitive and unresolved issue in American national identity.

In the eyes of the world, the United States is a highly religious country. It has always been so, from the time of the founding of the country when religion played a major role in binding a diversified people. Since then religion has flourished due to the non-establishment and free exercise clauses of the First Amendment, and also continuing waves of immigration. The 1965 Immigration Act, which facilitated immigration from Third World countries, has made the United States more pluralistic religiously and culturally by diversifying the Catholic population and by attracting more non-Judeo-Christian immigrants. Yet worries are now surfacing about this expanding pluralism, and especially about the growing presence of Latinos, most of whom are Mexicans. To opponents of pluralism, American Protestant culture and way of life seem to be in jeopardy. In the aftermath of September 11, 2001, for example, at a time when faith communities were brought together, Jerry Falwell and Pat Robertson warned the nation that the attacks had been the result of tolerance of non-Christian faiths and homosexuality.

Religion, of course, is not only a central issue in the United States. Globalization provides the larger context in which these domestic developments related to religion are occurring. In some instances they are a result of new challenges consequent upon immigration; in other instances they reflect a resurgence of militant religions. Followers of Islam, in particular, have chosen to re-examine their links to the West. On the other hand, globalization has resulted in greater relativism and secularization, thus inviting individuals to question traditional values and social norms, and to attempt to fill the gaps created by the erosion of religious authority. Nonetheless, the greater surprise is the vitality and force of traditional religions in many parts of the world. Old assumptions about modernization and modernity undermining religion are now being questioned; the secularization thesis, once widely accepted by western scholars as the dominant narrative pointing to religion's demise, is under considerable scrutiny, and in this context the United States poses an interesting case study.

It is a country where as Alan Wolfe writes, "Two hundred years after the brilliant writings of James Madison and Thomas Jefferson on the topic, Americans cannot make up their minds whether religion should be private, public, or some uneasy combination of the two."[1] The First Amendment established a "wall of separation" between church and state, legally assuring a distinction between the two. Americans expect religious bodies to express themselves in the public arena; it is a right which the "free exercise" clause of the First Amendment guarantees. There is also what commentators have called a "civil religion" – a set of widely held beliefs, symbols, prayers, and rituals such as those observed on July 4, Thanksgiving, and at presidential inaugurations – that gives the country a sense of shared history and purpose. Religion of this common-denominator sort permeates public life, creating a seemingly paradoxical situation. While this latter underscores the religious nature of the country, the First Amendment specifies a secular state. It might be said that the two guard against each other's excesses. As N. J. Demerath III observes: "we can indulge a symbolic civil religion, precisely because there is a substantive separation of church and state in important matters of government policy; at the same time, our separation is never a total rupture precisely because of the presence of overarching civil religious ceremonials."[2]

In actual practice, there is, in addition to church and state, a third powerful domain of influence – the public realm. By this latter, we refer not to the government but to the citizenry within a democracy who reflect upon the common good and deliberate together to advance it. This public realm overlaps with the church but incorporates not merely the religious – deeply committed or otherwise – but also those without religious faith. Popular mood and opinion, fluid, erratic, help shape life in a democracy. As Alexis de Tocqueville suggested, even religion bore the impress of that democracy holding sway "much less as a doctrine of revelation than as a commonly received opinion,"[3] and though he acknowledged a risk of the "tyranny of the majority," was aware of those checks within the democratic system intended to resist it. Whenever popular opinion drifts unduly in a sectarian religious or partisan political direction, and particularly if it threatens the rights of others, counterveiling forces come into play. People turn to the courts for legal redress or mobilize to bring about political change.

We are now living in a period of flux. There is considerable debate over religion's proper place within the public arena, shaped in no small part by the presidency of George W. Bush. The American people are divided, some deeply concerned about the particular mix of religion and politics that has emerged in recent years, others believing them to be compatible.[4] In this chapter, we examine in broad strokes the major cultural, religious, and political trends over the past half-century that have led to this present situation. We look at major shifts in boundaries defining the private and public aspects of religion – in its demographic makeup, its relation to the dominant culture, and its political alliances.

Religious demographics

No demographic over the past half-century is of greater symbolic consequence than the decline of the Protestant population. In 1950, Protestants accounted for roughly two-thirds of the American population, but today that figure hovers at 50 percent. In July 2004, the National Opinion Research Center at the University of Chicago announced that "after more than 200 years of history, the United States may soon no longer be a majority Protestant country . . . the percentage of the population that is Protestant has been falling and will likely fall below 50 percent by mid-decade and may be there already."[5] Although Protestants still wield considerable power politically and economically, and their imprint upon the culture is substantial, fundamentalists, the most conservative among them, have felt under siege for some time. Depending on how politically successful they are in the future, their awareness of this numerical decline may intensify fears of losing a cultural hegemony.

The Protestant landscape has greatly changed over the past half-century. Many members of the mainline traditions (particularly Presbyterians,

Methodists, Lutherans, United Church of Christ, Episcopalians) have shifted loyalties, considerable numbers to Evangelical Protestantism, some to other religions, and often to no religious affiliation. Mainline Protestants began losing members in the mid-1960s at a time when Evangelicalism was becoming more mobilized and visible. With a focus on conversion experience and personal faith in Jesus Christ, Evangelicalism appeals to many young Americans. Depending upon the poll, between 30 and 40 percent of Americans now are born-again Evangelicals – a constituency that is quite diverse, not necessarily culturally or politically conservative, and which includes fundamentalists, Pentecostals, charismatics, and neo-Evangelicals. The neo-Evangelicals see themselves as part of mainstream American culture and are more moderate in their views; fundamentalists, Pentecostals, and charismatics are more conservative and account for 20 to 30 percent of Evangelicals.

The non-affiliated sector has grown, but only gradually up until very recent times. Often called "Nones" in the polls, they made up only about 1 percent of the population during the Cold War and pro-religious years of the 1950s, increased to around 7 percent in the 1980s, and most recently to around 14 percent. It too is a very diverse constituency, including those who seldom or never attend religious services because they dislike organized religion, prefer to think of themselves as "spiritual but not religious," or are outright atheists (estimated at around 4 percent currently). Atheists are very much a minority – largely ignored and viewed unfavorably by the majority of Americans – yet their numbers are greater than for the Jewish population. Overall, the non-affiliated sector is increasingly important in that it is evidence of an expanding cultural and political cleavage in American life. Weekly church attendance – estimated now at 25 to 28 percent[6] – has declined over the past quarter-century, creating a "faith divide" between the religiously committed and those who are only nominally committed or who are religiously indifferent.

Of course, faith traditions other than Protestant, Catholic, or Jewish are diversifying the religious landscape. Diana Eck's well-received book *A New Religious America: How a Christian Nation Became the World's Most Religiously Diverse Nation*[7] captures this story. The United States has emerged as the world's most religiously diverse nation. In urban areas especially, the entrance of Muslims, perhaps the fastest growing community, plus significant numbers of Hispanics and African Americans converting to Islam, along with Buddhists, Hindus, Sikhs, and Asian Christians have broadened the meaning of a multireligious society. American religious pluralism is further enhanced by ethnic diversity within each faith tradition. In effect, the American scene is now the location of microcosms, especially of the Muslim, Catholic, and Buddhist worlds. The Muslim population is not more than 2 percent of the total population; Buddhists, Hindus, and Sikhs account for even less. Partly, their visibility and influence are a product of the fact that many of the post-1965 immigrants are well educated, computer savvy, and well networked, and thus capable of moving with ease into middle-class life. In many parts of the country, and especially in small towns and rural areas, however, Americans have yet to come to terms with the presence of these new faiths and cultures.

In spite of an increase in the number of non-Judeo-Christian faiths, the post-1965 migrations are actually making the country more, not less Christian. Latinos from South and Central America are largely Catholic, and immigrants from Asia tend to be more Christian than Buddhist. The latter bring indigenous styles of Christianity different from that which Christian missionaries from the United States carried to their countries a hundred and fifty years ago. Both Catholic and Protestant communities are becoming "less white," making it more difficult for Americans to think of Christianity as white and Euro-American in background. Put simply, the old image of the WASP – the White Anglo-Saxon Protestant – is gradually vanishing, which adds to the worries of many conservative Evangelical and fundamentalist Protestants.

The growing Latino presence creates still other worries. In 2000, over 16 million foreign-born in the United States were from Latin America, representing 52 percent of the total foreign-born population. With over 12 percent of the US population, Latinos are now the second largest separate constituency, more numerous than African Americans. Their public presence is accentuated by Spanish, their distinctive cultures, and the large proportion of them who work in the marginal sectors of the economy. About half of Latin American immigrants into the United States are from Mexico. Given the proximity of this large migrant stream to Mexico itself, its distinctiveness and continuity with home traditions are reinforced. The fact that the lands where the great majority of these immigrants settle in the Southwest were taken away from Mexico by the United States, adds to a borderland consciousness and mixed feelings. For conservative Anglo commentators like Samuel P. Huntington,[8] the trends raise a serious concern as well: Does the cultural shift taking place, that is, so huge a Mexican and Spanish-speaking population moving in at a time when the old Anglo-Protestant hegemony is eroding, not foretell an emerging bi-cultural society?

The American Catholic church is faced with having to absorb a growing number of Spanish-speaking Catholics – whose folk practices are often at odds with the norms of the church – and with the inevitable prospects of a

Latino majority within only a few decades. Catholic parishes in large cities offer masses in Spanish for the separate ethnic populations, trying to accommodate diversity among Latinos and to dissuade them from joining evangelical Protestant churches (about one out of four Latinos is Protestant). There is also an expanding religious and cultural gap between Euro-Americans and this new growing population. An earlier Catholic America was oriented to Europe; the new Catholic America is oriented to Latin America. The diversity within the Catholic community is also enhanced by growing numbers of Asians, Africans, and African Americans, all with distinctive heritages.

For the first time since the colonial era, the Jewish population is decreasing and now accounts for less than 2 percent of the total population. Its growth is limited because of low birth rates, a decline of Jewish immigration, fewer conversions, and a high level of interfaith marriage. But its public influence far exceeds its numbers. Compared with other religious groups, it is one of the most educated, highly professional constituencies. Religiously, it is very diverse, with Orthodox, Conservative, Reform and Reconstructionist communities. Actual ties to religious institutions are weaker than for most other groups because of interfaith marriages and historically high levels of agnosticism and atheism.

Taken as a whole, these demographic changes underscore just how dated and inappropriate are many of the older paradigms of American religion. Will Herberg's tripartite Protestant–Catholic–Jew model of the 1950s obviously no longer fits as the country becomes more multireligious.[9] The country is still predominately Christian, but ideological shifts within Protestantism, changing styles of Catholicism, the demographic decline of American Judaism, the many alternatives of an ever-increasing number of new religious movements, and an expanding non-religious sector all point to a new social context. A growing sense of religious and secular "others" poses difficult challenges for those who hold absolutist and exclusivist claims to truth.

New religious and spiritual expressions

Demographics tell us about numerical growth and decline of differing religions, but nothing about the cultural context in which they exist. Cultural settings are always thick and multilayered, and hence religion may express itself in many differing ways. Religion in the United States at present has two somewhat contradictory faces. It is deeply embedded in a struggle over values, beliefs, morality, and lifestyles, and at the same time its energies are directed inward to personal life, with attention to an enhanced subjectivity and a search for spiritual meaning. Yet the two realities co-exist, the first capturing religion's hard edge and the second its softer side.

The turn inward for greater spiritual depth became increasingly evident in the 1990s. A *US News and World Report* poll in 1994, for example, reported that 65 percent of Americans believed that religion was losing its influence in public life, yet almost equal numbers, 62 percent, claimed that the influence of religion was increasing in their personal lives.[10] This sharp contrast was striking. If, as many commentators argue, religion has to do with two major foci of concerns — personal meaning and social belonging — then clearly much energy revolves around the first of these today. Those born after World War II in the United States grew up in a culture of choice that had led to religious and spiritual options. New insight was presumed to offer the possibility of personal transformation and greater self-authenticity. A stress on individualism suggested that faith or spirituality were primarily matters of personal choice rather than cultural inheritances.

Nowhere is this quest culture more apparent than in the more moderate, culturally accommodating versions of neo-Evangelicalism. Over the past forty years a majority of the Evangelical Christian sector has moved in this softer direction, selectively absorbing aspects of mainstream culture, thereby transforming religion in content and style. In so doing, it has broken with an older, more fundamentalist and separatist religious conservatism. Neo-Evangelicals repackage the Gospel message and address contemporary life-situations using culturally current language. They draw off humanistic psychology, emphasizing a self in transformation: Journey and recovery narratives are particularly popular, describing, as they do, how Christians can deal positively with their personal needs and get closer to Jesus. Niche marketing techniques, fitting faith to the experiences of single moms, motor-cyclists for Jesus, children of divorced parents, and scores of other clearly defined groups, are adapted from secular culture.

The decade of the 1990s saw the rise of the "seeker church" at the hands of entrepreneurial neo-Evangelical leaders determined to reach a large, non-churched population. One such is the huge Saddleback Community Church in southern California, where Pastor Rick Warren reinvented church for those who found the traditional congregation boring and who knew little about Christian tradition. A secular person is one he describes as "skeptical, well-educated, a contemporary music fan, and self-satisfied, even smug."[11] His church offers innovative worship services with keyboards, electric guitars, and talented vocalists, as well as state-of-the-art technology to create a setting congenial to a consumption-oriented, post-Christian constituency. Like most other seeker churches, it is non-denominational, relies heavily on the lyrics and rhythm of contemporary music to set themes and entertain, and frames the message simply as a personal relationship with Christ. Once in the fold people are invited to grow spiritually and become committed. It proclaims itself as a "community" church so as to distance itself from old-style religious congregations; its architecture is more reminiscent of a mall, a sports or concert hall (complete with coffee bar, gymnasium, nursery, and school) than a traditional church; few religious symbols are displayed so as not to offend those who do not understand them; and people are encouraged to attend services in casual dress in a deliberate effort to appeal to an anti-church sentiment and make the thousands of people who attend their six services each week feel at home. Mega-churches offer dozens of small groups organized around age, marital status and family, and concerns and interests to address personal needs. Just how successful they are in creating a sustained sense of community is not altogether clear; but what is clear is that by virtue of their size they appeal to an American sensibility having to do with bigness and growth as good, if not a sign of God's approval.

Critics wonder if neo-Evangelicalism has sold out to contemporary culture. In his book aptly entitled *The Transformation of American Religion*, Alan Wolfe writes as follows:

> Talk of hell, damnation, and even sin has been replaced by a non-judgmental language of understanding and empathy. Gone are the arguments over doctrine and theology; if most believers cannot for the life of them recall what makes Luther different from Calvin, there is no need for the disputation and schism in which those reformers, as well as other religious leaders throughout the centuries, engaged. More Americans than ever proclaim themselves born again in Christ, but the lord to whom they turn rarely gets angry and frequently strengthens self-esteem. Traditional forms of worship, from reliance on organ music to the mysteries of the liturgy, have given way to audience participation and contemporary tastes.[12]

Elsewhere in his book Wolfe speaks of "salvation inflation," arguing that by making faith so easy to accept, by failing to address complexity, Evangelical Christians have watered down its significance. Yet for the society as a whole, as he notes, these adaptations can be viewed positively. Evangelical accommodation (as opposed to more fundamentalist separatism) "tames" God, so to speak. Monarchical and judgmental views of deity, so important historically in religious crusades and wars, are replaced by more friendly and supportive imageries, which bodes well for greater tolerance of other faiths, or even the lack of faith. Wolfe also points out that "Growth is the enemy of sectarianism,"[13] that is, because Evangelicalism is so preoccupied with framing the message in ways that will attract new believers, such converts are less likely to become religious fanatics. Adaptation to the secular culture, however, should not blind us to the fact that neo-Evangelical churches such as Saddleback do exercise considerable social control over their followers: they invite people to follow a clear direction in Christian living based on conservative biblical teachings and "family values," and paradoxically, while engaging the culture in recruiting, they appeal to people who feel that the world offers too much choice in moral and religious matters.

The success of Evangelicalism in reaching the mainstream culture is visibly evident: the popularity of televangelists as measured both by their influence and ability to raise huge sums of money for their programming; the rise of new genres of Christian music paralleling secular genres, such as "Christian Rock"; a flourishing publishing industry with astonishing book sales (for example, the *Left Behind* series of books on the Rapture to come and the awful plight of non-believers who will be left behind when Christ returns has sold 58 million copies); a Christian dieting movement embracing secular styles of femininity and redefining overeating as "sin"; jazzercise classes combined with moments of prayer accommodating a body and fitness culture; use of slides and Power Point presentations emphasizing image rather than print as a medium of communication; and espousal of a prosperity theology attractive to those who think, as many Americans do, that they are entitled to wealth and happiness.

To the many religious and spiritual options offered to Americans must be added what are called, somewhat inadequately, "new religious movements." Partly as a result of globalization and the high rate of immigration from the East, a large number of splinter groups as well as new indigenous movements have emerged over the last four decades. They have helped to extend the boundaries of what is regarded as acceptable religion. In effect, what forty years ago would have been thought of by most Americans as an "extraordinary" religion is now seen as "ordinary," or as one more option on the religious menu. Whether Pentecostal, communal, New Thought, spiritualist, New Age, neo-pagan, or rationalist, such movements are attractive as religious alternatives and fit well with a democratic-based culture. They extend options available to a public that is often loosely attached religiously, prone to switching faiths, picking and choosing what to believe and what not, allowing, as one commentator says, for "a former Christian, to turn a Deist looking into Wicca."[14]

Outside the churches, synagogues, temples, and mosques, the spiritual quest culture is sustained by a new and expanded cadre of spiritual suppliers.

A good example is the chain bookstore. At Borders, Barnes and Noble, and other such distributors, the old-style religious section has been replaced by a highly differentiated set of topical books categorized around such themes as angels, ancient wisdom, prophecy, goddess, mysticism, Buddhism, Bible, New Age, Sufi poetry, UFOs, and the like. They are marketed to an autonomous individual believing that he or she can best decide what is best spiritually. Many of the top selling books, such as those on angels, near-death experiences, and the invasion of aliens, explore themes catering to an audience caught, as Phyllis Tickle says, "somewhere between belief in and curiosity about such possibilities."[15] This description applies to many young Americans not sure of what to believe. Spiritual seeking is evident as well in the growing number of retreat centers with programs focused on personal concerns; in popular writers like Deepak Chopra and M. Scott Peck who address a wide range of issues like health, guilt, and self-esteem; in corporate consultants who help managers get work and spirituality into sync; and in medical schools that address questions about whether prayer and meditation can help in overcoming illness.

Given the decline of established religious authority generally, many Americans blend elements from various sources to create eclectic, highly personalized meaning systems. There is what is sometimes called a "mixing of codes." Sixty percent of baby boomers in the early 1990s, for example, said they preferred to "explore many different religious teachings rather than stick to a particular faith" and 43 percent affirmed that "all the great religions of the world are equally true and good." Twenty-eight percent of those surveyed in this same study, which includes sizable numbers of those born into mainline Protestant and Catholic families, reported belief in reincarnation.[16] That elements of belief combined together are logically inconsistent often seems not to matter. Modern life allows people to appropriate symbols, teachings, and practices from many times and places, often within the same church. Boundaries between religious traditions are blurred, as are those between many religious and secular systems of meaning. In a highly mobile society, the choice of a faith community also often depends on pragmatic considerations, such as location, style of worship, childcare facilities, social activities, pastor, or social services. Churches have always been social service providers, but more so since the 1980s when the Reagan administration began dismantling the state welfare system.

The Internet is no doubt playing a growing role in this "quiet revolution in religious sensibilities."[17] Almost all religious groups, large or small, have a presence in cyberspace, exposing people to a wide range of resources and activities on line. A recent survey reveals that 64 percent of Internet users say they have used the web for religious or spiritual purposes, such as forwarding spiritual email, sending greeting cards, reading religious news, downloading spiritual music, or making a prayer request.[18] The use of the web by religious groups, although to an extent revolutionary, is the logical extension of a mass communication strategy of Evangelicals in the revivals of the eighteenth and nineteenth centuries, and then later with radio ministries and televangelism. Yet in contrast with past use of advanced technology, the web gives peripheral groups a visibility and legitimacy they would not otherwise have. Today, the Internet amplifies, more than it creates, the development of new religious styles and new attitudes toward religious institutions by encouraging people to explore other faiths and express their faiths in a personal way.[19] Because it blurs the line between conviction and exploration, the Internet allows many spiritual seekers to experiment with and fashion their religious preferences "à la carte." Interestingly, however, the Internet users who most engage in religious online activities are connected to religious communities, which would seem to indicate that it is unlikely, at least for the time being, that the use of the Internet for religious purposes will supplant offline participation in religious activities.

Religious and cultural cleavage

Other boundary shifts of religion and culture are divisive and polarizing. Controversies over moral values and lifestyles tend to pull people in either a left-ward or right-ward direction. They generate pressures that cut across faith communities, reflecting new alignments of religion, culture, and politics. Conservative Protestants, for example, often have far more in common with traditional Catholics (including many Latinos) and Orthodox Jews than they do with liberal Protestants. Congregations themselves are often internally divided. Given that over 90 percent of Americans report believing in God, religious beliefs and values easily get drawn into controversial moral issues and often invoked passionately. Even college-educated American Muslims, much newer to the American scene and more self-contained within their community, are increasingly pulled into public discussion.[20]

Debate over values, morality, and lifestyles became more pronounced during the Reagan era of the 1980s. For televangelists and fundamentalist preachers, the issue was the gap between Judeo-Christian principles, on which the country and its way of life were founded, and misguided liberals, non-believers, left-leaning ideologues, and secular-humanists. This rhetoric increased in the years after the collapse of the Berlin Wall when reactionary Americans began to look for internal enemies in place of the communist threat. Patrick Buchanan brought the notion of moral warfare to the attention of the nation in his declaration of a "war for the nation's soul" at the

Republican National Convention in 1992. Of growing importance were divisions not grounded in economic class, race, or some other structural source of inequality, but instead in moral values and lifestyles. Partly because it is simplistic, the resulting rhetoric – "us" versus "them" – was useful in mobilizing moral and religious crusades, aimed particularly at a growing Evangelical audience concerned about traditional values and whose political involvement was on the rise.

In 1989, sociologist Robert Wuthnow described the situation as follows: "one finds general agreement in the following points: (a) the reality of the division between two opposing camps; (b) the predominance of 'fundamentalists,' 'evangelicals,' and 'religious conservatives' in one and the predominance of 'religious liberals,' 'humanists,' and 'secularists' in the other; and (c) the presence of deep hostility and misgiving between the two."[21] He cited survey data from as early as 1984 showing that even religious people in the country were split down the middle between these two camps: 43 percent of those surveyed claiming to be religious liberals and 41 percent religious conservatives. Two years later, James Davison Hunter went further, describing the situation as a "culture war," naming the two opposing camps as "orthodox" versus "progressives."[22] In his view the two constituencies differ primarily in their views of moral authority. The orthodox see authority as arising out of transcendent sources and emphasize the centrality of biblical text and divine revelation as opposed generally to scientifically and evolutionary explanations. Progressives, on the other hand, see authority as resting within society and underscore the arbitrary character of texts, teachings, and moral codes. Hunter saw the cleavage intensified by the growing number of religiously non-affiliated, free-thinking, and atheist constituencies who typically align themselves with progressives. These are the people – along with some religious liberals – who most express alarm about the intrusion of God-talk in the public arena. A small "Religious Left" now joins them, calling for greater attention on the part of the religiously faithful to social justice.

Progressives are concerned with how conservatives have co-opted God-talk in support of their pro-capitalist and national imperialistic views; they also point to the fact that religious language is just as adaptable to progressive causes, and thus subject to ideological construction. A good example is the German director Wim Wender's film, *Land of Plenty*, set in Los Angeles two years after the World Trade Center attacks, in which the leading woman character is an idealistic young missionary looking for her uncle, a Vietnam veteran. As a Christian, Wenders wanted to emphasize the compatibility of liberal ideas and Christian ideas. In spite of excellent reviews the film cannot find a buyer in the United States, indicating, as

Wenders put it, "that Christian ideas are so occupied by the right-wing that [buyers] don't know what to do with [the film]."[23]

Speaking of how conservatives use religious language, television commentator Bill Moyers writes:

> And they hijacked Jesus. The very Jesus who stood in Nazareth and proclaimed, "The Lord has anointed me to preach the good news to the poor." The very Jesus who told 5,000 hungry people that all of you will be fed, not just some of you. The very Jesus who . . . offered kindness to the prostitute and hospitality to the outcast, who raised the status of women and treated even the tax collector like a child of God . . . This Jesus has been hijacked and turned into a guardian of privilege instead of a champion of the dispossessed. Hijacked, he was made over into a militarist, hedonist, and lobbyist, sent prowling the halls of Congress in Guccis, seeking tax breaks and loopholes for the powerful, costly new weapon systems that don't work, and punitive public policies.[24]

This division within the culture is linked to old religious controversies from the early 1900s between the "fundamentalists" and the "modernists," but is now more visibly aligned with politics. It became more apparent as a backlash to the moral and political freedom of the 1960s and early 1970s, and has continued down to the present. Issues pertaining to women's reproductive rights, stem cell research, and, most recently, homosexuality have been at the center of the controversy. Family as an institution is a key concern. Progressives talk about "individual rights," and accept new types of families formed on the basis of choice; conservatives counter with the rhetoric of "family values," insist that marriage be restricted to heterosexual couples, and stress legitimate male authority in marriage and parental control over children, all judged to be in accord with biblical teachings. To an extent, the cleavage is exaggerated by the media, including televangelism, which has become an important means of popular persuasion especially for conservatives. Typically, the media portray issues in the most extreme version, and thus help to polarize public opinion. Important, too, are the many special-interest organizations selectively retrieving religious teachings and symbols suitable to their ideology. Both liberals and conservatives make use of mass marketing techniques and the Internet as a means of mobilizing large numbers of people around one or another moral perspective.

Of considerable importance in understanding the basis for this cleavage is the expansion of higher education since the 1950s. Large public universities have replaced small religious colleges as the major educational institutions. This expansion has placed greater emphasis on science and technology, their values and worldviews. It has also brought about greater attention to biblical criticism and the study of comparative religions, which in turn has encouraged greater relativism in matters of faith and ethics. Important too is the rise of the "knowledge class," those whose work involves the creation, distribution, and interpretation of symbolic knowledge in a modern, information-oriented society. These latter tend to look upon values, beliefs, and moral codes as themselves humanly constructed. They are thus less inclined to affirm them as absolute or universal. College-educated baby boomers born after World War II are still far less inclined to attend religious services and hold to literal biblical truths than a previous generation, and more likely to look upon all religions as differing paths to similar goals. Religious conservatives benefit from a backlash against the agnosticism and secularity of the highly educated and media elites; they exploit the moral relativism and lack of religious teachings in schools by offering absolute answers to life's big questions. At bottom is an irreconcilable conflict in truth-claims.

Talk of a "God-gap" emerged in the 2004 presidential election as pollsters and commentators recognized a radically realigned pattern of religion and politics. Based on survey studies prior to the election, it became evident that the best predictor of voting Republican was religious attendance, better than economic class, race, gender, or region. This current coalescence of churchgoing and Republican preference breaks significantly with earlier voting patterns. Until quite recently, both Republicans and Democrats drew upon a sizable social base that would describe itself as religious; both political parties appealed to civil religious values and symbols in their campaigns. But at a time when cultural values are more important than economic issues, political conservatives have as Bill Moyers says, "hijacked Jesus." This pattern runs against political loyalties as Americans have long expressed them. Working-class Americans, once inclined to vote Democratic for bread-and-butter reasons, are now likely to respond to concerns about values and lifestyles as much, if not more than, economic issues. Even Latinos, who on economic grounds would likely vote Democratic, are divided, many of them drawn to positions on moral and lifestyle issues championed by the Republicans. The same divide has emerged among African Americans, who are now being drawn to the Republicans as President Bush's party seeks their support by providing financial backing through faith-based initiatives. Some argue that the churches should accept federal funding while others point out that the government is simply trying to stifle black activism. A bulwark of support for Democrats in the days of Franklin Delano Roosevelt, the South is now almost solidly a Republican stronghold. Republicans are now seen as the party of God and country, Democrats as the party of liberal elites, humanists, and secularists, those uncomfortable with religious language.

Not to be overlooked, too, is the role of the Supreme Court in creating these new alliances. Prayer in public schools was ruled unconstitutional in 1962. This ruling rattled the Protestant establishment, which had long relied upon the schools to impose its prayers and ceremonies with little regard for people of other faiths or no faith. Then, in 1973, *Roe v. Wade* legalized abortion in the first trimester and made it negotiable in the second and third. It was this decision handed down by the highest court in the land that galvanized the country into intensely divided "pro-life" and "pro-choice" constituencies. Debates ever since have raged over basic moral and religious questions centered on the issue of when human life begins, the rights of the mother versus those of the fetus, and the role of the government in such private matters. Concern now arises out of the possibility that freedom of conscience is threatened by the Supreme Court and that the Bush administration might push to restrict possibilities for abortion in late-term pregnancies and appoint justices to the Supreme Court who may try to overturn the 1973 decision. In the past couple of years, battles have focused on issues that evoke strong moral and religious reaction such as marriage rights for gay couples and the "under God" clause in the American pledge of allegiance in the schools.

Two civil religions

In this contentious environment, fundamental myths, rituals, and symbols have all been drawn into the ideological debate. Historically, there has been an operative, yet somewhat amorphous, civil religion, or a set of generalized myths, symbols, and rituals by which Americans have interpreted their historical experience in relation to a transcendent power. Sociologist Robert Bellah argues that this civil religion is not reducible to worship of the state because, at its best, it has fostered a sense of mission to carry out God's will on earth and thus related the country to a power and purpose beyond itself. At its best, the God of the nation is broadly conceived, and belief in this Deity is reinforced by non-sectarian prayers and rituals. Although many early figures in American history were Deists, Judeo-Christian values solidified in the nineteenth and early twentieth centuries to create a civil religion drawing off biblical archetypes such as the Exodus, Promised Land, Chosen People, Sacrificial Death, and Rebirth.[25]

Judeo-Christian values as interpreted through the American experience gave rise to several distinctive myths: the myth of origin, or the view that America is a new beginning for humankind in relation to a divine order; the myth of innocence, implying that the nation is righteous, just, and superior in a world filled with demonic forces and shadowy figures seeking to destroy that which is good and right; the millennial myth of a Redeemer Nation, or the notion that the country was brought into being for the final fulfillment of God's work on earth, at home and abroad; and a primal myth, locating the nation's identity outside of ordinary time, that is, as a people suspended in the eternal present with unbounded possibilities and a glorious future. President Ronald Reagan articulated many of these themes, especially the latter in his State of the Union message in 1987 when he said, "The calendar can't measure America because we were meant to be an endless experiment in freedom, with no limit to our reaches, no boundaries to what we can do, no end point to our hopes."[26]

It is argued that there are "two civil religions" today, differing in their views of how best to relate religion and public life.[27] Conservatives privilege the myth of origin, and to a lesser extent the millennial myth, relating the nation to divine purposes: "One Nation Under God" is their rallying cry. In emphasizing the historic connection between the country and God, right-wing Evangelical and fundamentalist Christians lay claim not just to a religious foundation for the country but to themselves as the custodians of the American experiment. For them, faith in God mixes easily with free-dom, patriotism, strong military defense, capitalism, rejection of Darwin's theory of evolution, and the American Creed with its emphasis on freedom, individualism, democratic politics, and the work ethic. In its more strident version, as voiced by President George W. Bush, the Redeemer Nation must extend the freedom that God has granted this country; indeed, if it does not, it fails to live up to its responsibility of ridding the world of tyranny and oppression. Justifying the war on Iraq, President Bush said on November 6, 2003, the United States seeks "to promote liberty around the world because liberty is both the plan of Heaven for humanity, and the best hope for progress on earth."[28] Manifest Destiny as a theme underlies his comment although this doctrine is transformed in two important respects: one, rather than territorial expansion it includes resources such as oil, military bases, and economic markets; and two, freedom and prosperity, that is, the fruits of the market system, are seen as the gifts the American experiment has to offer the world.[29]

In contrast, liberals draw upon civil religious symbols not to emphasize the nation as a "Chosen People," but to focus attention on the responsibility to which it is called. "With Liberty and Justice for All" is their motto. A Redeemer Nation does not impose its ways upon the world out of self-righteousness or in the interest of imperialism, but rather uses its resources to help alleviate the world's problems. Human rights, international justice and cooperation, peace, scientific progress, the relief of hunger and AIDS, and the environment are all issues they champion. The compatibility of science and religion is emphasized as opposed to creationism. Civil religion in its more liberal version challenges the nation to live up to its moral and ethical ideals. President Clinton in fact on occasion drew upon this tradition in pointing to the responsibilities attending the role of the United States as a superpower on the international stage. In 1999, he said, "Because of the dramatic increase in our own prosperity and confidence in this, the longest peacetime economic expansion in our history, the United States has the opportunity and, I would argue, the solemn responsibility to shape a more peaceful, prosperous, democratic world in the twenty-first century."[30] Committed to social justice, liberals interpret this responsibility drawing upon biblical injunctions to feed the poor, to stand up to the arrogance of power, and to let justice roll down like waters.

Challenges facing American civil religion

Hence we are led to ask: Has American civil religion become captive to ideology, and thus lost its power as an overarching sacred canopy for the nation? Considerable evidence suggests this is the case. Deeply polarized, both sides – liberals and conservatives – now interpret civil faith through their own ideological lens. Conservatives especially blend religious symbols and beliefs with economic and political motives, religion becoming, as Bellah once said, a "cloak for petty interests and ugly passions."[31] While hardly new in American history, yet the melding of religion with political power and economic ideology now reaches mammoth proportions; as Susan Jacoby says, it now "goes far beyond the symbolic."[32] Political and civic leaders, as she also notes, often fail to speak out against Jesus-centered rhetoric in the public arena and violations of the separation of church and state under the Bush Administration for fear of being seen as irreligious. Because the majority of Americans approve of God-talk in the public arena and see it as blessing the nation, politicians know they cannot win elections if they do not engage in some public expression of faith, as John Kerry's change of tactics in the last weeks of the 2004 presidential campaign illustrates. At first holding the view that faith is a private matter, the Catholic Democratic candidate eventually recognized the need to appeal to religiously committed voters.

Yet the political use of God-talk has reached the point currently where many ordinary Americans are beginning to ask if such rhetoric has become empty, used, as it is, largely in an instrumental sense to advance particular interests. More so than usual patriotism is infused with religious rhetoric, as if good Americans cannot question the Iraqi War or proclaim themselves secularists. Some people question whether civil religion is morphing into religious nationalism. Hence many Americans, and not just civil libertarians, are now thinking seriously about the public religious order: Is the country Christian? Judeo-Christian? A Judeo-Christian-Islamic nation? Or more broadly a multireligious society? And what about secularists who are excluded from all these religious models?

Much debate at present centers around two religious visions – Christian America versus multireligious America. It is a spirited and unresolved debate because a majority of the country is Christian, yet at the same time the country is becoming more multireligious. Neither the religious nor the cultural dilemmas involved should be minimized. As Stephen Prothero writes,

> As a nation, Americans celebrate Christmas, not the Buddha's Birthday. And whatever religious diversity they enjoy is always being negotiated in what can only be described as a Christian context. In the United States, Buddhists are free to be Buddhists, but invariably they yank their traditions around to Christian norms and organizational forms – calling their temples "churches," voting for Zen masters, singing hymns such as "Onward Buddhist Soldiers," tending to the hungry and the homeless, and otherwise following their consciences wherever they might lead.[33]

But at the level of civil religious symbols pressures push in the more inclusive direction. Nowhere was this more apparent than in the aftermath of September 11, 2001. After that tragic event there were many services involving Muslims, Sikhs, Hindus, Native Americans, and others along with Protestants, Catholics, and Jews. However, the nation's official memorial service held at the National Cathedral in Washington, and thus the one of most public significance, did not succeed symbolically as well as it should. To the credit of the organizers, the service began as a tribute to a multifaith American society, but it ended with the stirring cadences of Julia Ward Howe's triumphal and crusading Battle Hymn of the Republic! Closing the service with this reaffirmation of the nation as Christian in this moment of crisis cast doubt on the extent of the nation's religious inclusiveness. If the civil religious heritage is to remain vital, sustaining a national identity that includes all the people, it must adapt. Symbols and teachings from other traditions must be incorporated without privileging one tradition over any other; a vision of a common humanity with universal standards must be honored in keeping with a country that welcomes people from around the globe. Admittedly, this is no small challenge given the American religious legacy.

At the global level, there are other challenges. Of all the shifting boundaries discussed in this chapter, especially troubling is the prospect that America and global capitalism are increasingly perceived as one and the same. The country is known abroad by its exports – its goods, gadgets, and God-talk, all seemingly bound up together under the label of "Made in the United States." This same perception is reinforced by President Bush when he speaks of freedom and democracy as God's gifts that the United States must carry to the world. The gifts – if that is what they are – are not likely to be carried to the world without political intervention or the cultivation of a consumption ethic in keeping with American economic interests, making for a volatile mix seemingly invisible to many neoconservatives at present. Civil religious ideas along with visions of global progress are not only extended through the development of new economic markets, they are conflated with transnational corporations identified with the United States. A striking example is that of a camera firm that underwrites an American July 4 celebration, elaborately stages the event with sounds and fireworks parading the latest of American technology, and video-streams it abroad as a Kodak moment.[34]

What are the risks of spreading a consumption ethic, wanting the latest and the best of everything, and promising it under the banner of something called the American Way of Life? Perhaps the greatest risk is that it might lead to higher expectations around the world than can be realized, and consequently, heightened anti-American feelings and isolationism. Moreover, the world might decide that what is being exported is really self-interested capitalism wrapped in the rhetoric of a divine mission. That is, the mix of God, money, and politics finally becomes transparent. Whatever authenticity the country's civil religious rhetoric might once had is then lost in the semiotic blur of confusing messages. David Chidester goes even further, raising the specter that America risks being viewed as a fake, with people in other countries coming to believe that neither the country nor its God will deliver on its promises.[35]

American civil religion now must adapt to a world where religion, politics, and economics are closely intertwined globally. Whether it can sustain a transcendent dimension with a capacity for calling the nation to live up to its ideals in this new environment remains to be seen. But civil religion will continue to evolve and take new shape. The country's heritage of ethnic and religious pluralism, combined with the legacy of separation of church and state guaranteeing the right to believe or not, is a foundation on which a broader vision of national unity perhaps can be built. A creative "positive pluralism" honoring differences and interfaith dialogue, as Diana Eck contends, is conceivable. Expanding non-Christian faiths will force the United States in time to adjust its legitimating myths. Pluralism as an ideology itself should gain favor, in which case that which unifies the country will look less like civil religion as we have known it, and more like a broadly construed constitutional or human rights culture recognizing religious – but also non-religious – sources for those rights. Should this happen, there may still be possibility of an inclusive and persuasive legitimating myth for the nation as it accommodates a global political and economic order.

NOTES

1. Alan Wolfe, "Judging the President," in E. J. Dionne Jr. and John J. Diiulio Jr. (eds.), *What's God Got To Do With the American Experiment?* (Washington DC: Brookings Institution Press, 2000), p. 90.
2. N. J. Demerath III, "Civil Society and Civil Religion as Mutually Dependent," in Michele Dillon (ed.), *Handbook of the Sociology of Religion* (Cambridge: Cambridge University Press, 2003), p. 355.
3. Alexis de Tocqueville, *Democracy in America*, vol. II (New York: Vintage Books, 1945), p. 12.
4. For an expression of this division in the wake of the 2004 presidential election, see Thomas L. Friedman, "Two Nations Under God," *New York Times*, November 4, 2004.
5. NORC website: http://www.norc.uchicago.edu/, July 2004.
6. There is considerable debate about churchgoing in the United States. Old estimates provided by Gallup of 40 percent attending weekly are exaggerated. See Mark Chaves and Laura Stephens, "Church Attendance in the United States," in Dillon, *Handbook of the Sociology of Religion*, pp. 85–95.
7. Diana Eck, *A New Religious America: How a Christian Nation Became the World's Most Religiously Diverse Nation* (San Francisco: Harper SanFrancisco, 2002).
8. Samuel P. Huntington, *Who Are We? The Challenges to America's National Identity* (New York: Simon & Schuster, 2004).
9. Will Herberg, *Protestant–Catholic–Jew* (Garden City, NY: Doubleday Anchor, 1960).
10. Eve Arnold-Magnum, "Spiritual America," *US News and World Report*, April 4, 1994, pp. 48–59.
11. Rob Walker, "Godly Synergy," *New York Times Magazine*, April 11, 2004, p. 24.
12. Alan Wolfe, *The Transformation of American Religion* (New York: Free Press, 2003), p. 3.
13. *Ibid.*, p. 256.
14. Yahoo.com/group/Deism, March 3, 2004.
15. Phyllis Tickle, *Rediscovering the Sacred: Spirituality in America* (New York: Crossroads, 1995), p. 35.
16. Wade Clark Roof, *A Generation of Seekers* (San Francisco: HarperSanFrancisco, 1993), pp. 63–88.
17. Lorne L. Dawson and Douglas E. Cowan (eds.), *Religion Online: Finding Faith on the Internet* (New York: Routledge, 2004), p. 3.
18. Pew Internet and American Life Project, "Faith Online," April 7, 2004.
19. Nathalie Caron, "La religion dans le cyberespace," in Isabelle Richet (ed.), *Religion, politique et societe aux Etats-Unis. Materiaux pour l'histoire de notre temps*, 75 (July September 2004): 17–27.

20. *Los Angeles Times*, January 18, 2003.
21. Robert Wuthnow, *The Struggle for America's Soul* (Grand Rapids, MI: Eerdmans Publishing Company, 1989), p. 22.
22. James Davison Hunter, *Culture Wars: The Struggle to Define America* (New York: Basic Books, 1991).
23. Wim Wenders's website: http://www.wim-wenders.com/ news_reel/2004/10-article.htm.September 2004.
24. Bill Moyers, "Democracy in the Balance," *Sojourners Magazine*, 33 (August 2004): 15.
25. Robert Bellah, "Civil Religion in America," *Daedalus*, 96 (1967): 1–21.
26. "Address before a Joint Session of Congress on the State of the Union," January 27, 1987, in *Public Papers of the Presidents of the United States: Ronald Reagan: 1987, vol. i, January 1 to July 3, 1987* (Washington DC: Government Printing Office, 1989), pp. 59–60.
27. Robert Wuthnow, *The Restructuring of American Religion* (Princeton: Princeton University Press, 1988), ch. 10.
28. Speech on November 6, 2003. Full texts of speeches of President George W. Bush can be found at http://www.whitehouse.gov/news/releases/
29. Robert A. Coles, "Manifest Destiny Adapted for 1990s War Discourse, Mission and Destiny Intertwined," *Sociology of Religion*, 63 (Winter 2002): 403–26.
30. *Weekly Compilation of Presidential Documents*, 35 (1–22): 1–242 (Washington DC: Government Printing Office, 1999).
31. Robert Bellah, "Civil Religion in America," p. 20.
32. Susan Jacoby, *Freethinkers: A History of American Secularism* (New York: Metropolitan Books, 2004), p. 356.
33. Stephen Prothero, *American Jesus: How the Son of God Became a National Icon* (New York: Farrar, Straus and Giroux, 2003), pp. 6–7.
34. David Chidester, *Authentic Fakes* (Berkeley: University of California Press, 2005).
35. Ibid.

FURTHER READING

Catherine L. Albanese, *America: Religions and Religion*, Belmont, CA: Wadsworth Publishing Company, 1999.
Robert N. Bellah, "Civil Religion in America," *Daedalus*, 96 (1967): 1–21.
E. J. Dionne, Jr. and John J. Diiulio, Jr. (eds.), *What's God Got To Do With The American Experiment?*, Washington DC: Brookings Institution Press, 2000.
Phillip E. Hammond, *With Liberty For All: Freedom of Religion in the United States*, Louisville: Westminster John Knox Press, 1998.
Phillip E. Hammond, David M. Machacek, and Eric M. Mazur, *Religion on Trial: How the Supreme Court Trends Threaten the Freedom of Conscience in America*, Walnut Creek, CA: Alta Mira Press, 2004.
William R. Hutchison, *Religious Pluralism in America: The Contentious History of a Founding Ideal*, New Haven: Yale University Press, 2003.
Martin E. Marty, *Righteous Empire: The Protestant Experience in America*, New York: Harper and Row, 1970.

R. Laurence Moore, *Religious Outsiders and the Making of Americans*, New York: Oxford University Press, 1986.

Stephen Prothero, *American Jesus: How the Son of God Became a National Icon*, New York: Farrar, Straus and Giroux, 2003.

Wade Clark Roof (ed.), *Contemporary American Religion*, New York: Macmillan, 2000.

Mark A. Shibley, *Resurgent Evangelicalism in the United States: Mapping Cultural Change Since 1970*, Columbia: University of South Carolina Press, 1996.

7

NICOLÁS KANELLOS

The Hispanic background of the United States

Those whom we call "Hispanics" or "Latinos" – terms deriving from "hispanoamericano" and "latinoamericano" – are United States residents with roots in Hispanic America. While "Latino" is often used interchangeably with "Hispanic," the nineteenth-century concept of "Latin America," from which "Latino" derives, broadly referred to the peoples emerging from Spain, Portugal, and France's colonies, whereas "Hispanoamérica" referred solely to the Spanish-speaking peoples formerly residing in the Spanish colonies. In common usage today, both terms refer to the US residents of diverse racial and historical backgrounds in the Spanish-speaking countries of the Americas, including the United States. The vast majority of them are of Mexican, Puerto Rican, or Cuban origin, and the presence of their ancestors in North America predates the arrival of English colonists. In fact, western civilization was introduced to North America and the lands that eventually would belong to the United States first by Hispanics. Many of the institutions and values that have become identified as "American" were really first introduced by Hispanic peoples – Spaniards, Hispanicized Africans and Amerindians, mestizos and mulattoes – during the exploration and settlement of these lands. Not only were advanced technologies, such as those essential to ranching, farming, and mining, introduced by the Hispanics but also all of the values and perspectives inherent in western intellectual culture. The Spanish and their mixed breed children continued to blend western culture with that of the indigenous peoples of the Americas and the peoples imported from Africa for five hundred years.

It was the Spanish-speaking peoples that first introduced and furthered European-style literacy and literate culture, not only in the hemisphere, but also in what would become the continental United States. The first introduction of a written European language into an area that would become the mainland United States was accomplished in Florida by Juan Ponce de León in 1513 with his travel diaries. From Ponce de León on, the history of literacy, books, and writing in what would become the United States was developed by Hispanics, many of whom ethnically were of Amerindian and African descent. Ponce de León's exploration marked the beginning of keeping civil, military, and ecclesiastical records that would eventually become commonplace in the Hispanic South and Southwest of what would become the United States. Written culture not only facilitated the keeping of the records of conquest and colonization, the maintaining of correspondence, planting the rudiments of commerce and standardizing social organization, but it also gave birth to the first written descriptions and studies of the fauna and flora of these lands new to the Europeans and mestizos. It made possible the writing of laws for their governance and commercial exploitation and for writing and maintaining a history – an official story and tradition – of Hispanic culture in these lands.

All of the institutions – schools, universities, libraries, state, county and municipal archives, the courts, and almost an infinity of others – that are common foundations of today's advanced social organization, science, and technology, and which so rely on literate culture, were first introduced by Hispanics to North America. The first schools in what would become the continental USA were established by 1600 in Spanish Catholic missions in what are today Florida, Georgia, and New Mexico. The first elementary school established in the Americas was opened in Santo Domingo in 1505 for the children of the Spaniards. From then on, elementary schools were included in convents, where children were taught reading, writing, arithmetic, and religion. Later, the mission system in the Americas functioned to instruct the children of Amerindians and mestizos. The first school in an area that would become part of the United States was established in 1513: the Escuela de Gramática (Grammar School) in Puerto Rico, which was opened at the Cathedral of San Juan by Bishop Alonso Manso.[1]

The first attempts at creating public schools in what would become the Southwest of the United States occurred in Texas and California. As elsewhere in the Spanish colonies, education was offered in the missions; it was not only important for the children of the settlers to learn to read, write, and master arithmetic, but the mission education system most importantly fostered the religious conversion and acculturation of the Amerindians, as well as their conversion into a laboring class that received food, clothes, and protection for their servitude.[2]

The building of the first European-style towns and cities, the first ports for commerce, the first European-bred livestock, the first ranching, the first mining, the first roads and highways, the first civil engineering, the introduction of other technologies from Europe should be credited to the Spaniards and their mixed blood descendants. Many important agricultural products were first introduced by Hispanics: wheat, cotton, wine grapes; the breeding and tending of livestock. The missions throughout the Southwest and South – as well as in all of New Spain – were the basis for a European-style social organization, the education of the natives, the creation of a self-supporting economic base through the development of local industry, the laying down of foundations that would eventually become a network of towns, cities, and commerce. Many areas in the South and southwestern United States still bear the Spanish names given by their founders, have their cities laid out in the grids created by those colonizers, have paved highways over the roads and paths blazed by these colonists, and even derive the region's livelihood from industries introduced or developed by the early Hispanics.

Hispanics established the bases for the agriculture and mining industries that would especially dominate the economies of the southwestern United States. By 1600, the Spanish settlers along the Rio Grande Valley had introduced the plow and beasts of burden to the Pueblo Indians and thus revolutionized agricultural technology that would endure for centuries in what would become the American Southwest. They also introduced irrigation and new craft techniques, such as those involved in carpentry and blacksmithing, and a new profit-driven economy.[3] In 1610, the first irrigation canals and irrigation systems north of the Rio Grande were built in Santa Fe, New Mexico, by Spanish, Indian, and mestizo colonizers. They dug two *acequias madres* (main ditches) on each side of the small river that passed through the center of the town they were establishing. The Spanish had strict codes and plans for the construction of irrigation systems for the towns they were founding in the arid Southwest; such systems were constructed often in advance of the building of the forts, houses, and churches. The undertaking was quite often massive, calling for the digging, dredging, transportation of materials, and feeding of humans and animals. This was the case in the founding of Albuquerque in 1706, San Antonio in 1731, and Los Angeles in 1781. The canals of San Antonio were so well planned, lined with stone and masonry as they were, that many of them are still functioning today.[4]

The foundation that was laid for farming and agriculture has resulted in California, Texas, and Florida being the largest producers of fruits and vegetables in the world.

The importance of the freight hauling business by mule and wagon train only subsided with the introduction of the railroads, and then some of these same entrepreneurs made the transition to hauling freight and people by wagon and stage coach to secondary and outlying communities. While Hispanics had followed trails blazed and used by Indians for centuries, they pioneered most of the techniques and opened most of the trails that would later be used for trade and communications during the territorial and early statehood periods. In fact, some of today's major highways run along those routes pioneered for trade by Hispanics and Mexicans.[5]

With the founding of Santa Fe, New Mexico, in 1610, many Spanish laws governing all facets of life were introduced to what would become the culture of the Southwest. Foremost among those laws were those concerning water and its management; many of these Spanish laws would pass into the legal codes of the United States, first through the Treaty of Guadalupe Hidalgo ending the Mexican War, then through the constitutions of the newly formed states in the Southwest. In the Spanish and Mexican judicial systems, the rights of the community weighed more heavily than those of the individual with respect to the precious resource of water in the arid Southwest. The water in Spanish and Mexican towns and cities was held in trust for the benefit of the entire community – a water right still codified today. Thus, the City of Los Angeles, which inherited these rights, was able to obtain a favorable ruling from the US Supreme Court over a water dispute with landowners of the San Fernando Valley. The court ruled that the city had prior claim to all waters originating within the watershed of the Los Angeles River; thus, the court asserted that "pueblo rights" took precedence over the common law rights of the landowners.[6]

At the time of establishing its republic and later when becoming a state of the union, Texas in particular held on to many laws from Hispanic tradition, especially those regarding family law, land, and property. In 1839, Texas adopted the first Homestead Law in an area that would become part of the United States; the principle of protecting certain pieces of personal property from creditors has its roots in Castilian practices that date to the thirteenth century and passed into Texas state law from the Hispano-Mexican legal codes. This made it possible for a debtor to protect the principle residence of the family from seizure by creditors; it also protected other basic items, such as clothing and implements of trade needed for the debtor to make a living.[7]

In 1840, the Texas legislature adopted the Hispano-Mexican system of a single court rather than continuing the dual court system (courts of law and courts of equity) of Anglo-American law. Under the Hispanic system, all issues could be considered simultaneously rather divided between two jurisdictions. Thus, the Republic of Texas became the first English-speaking country to adopt a permanent and full unitary system of justice. Also in 1840, the Texas legislature adopted from the Hispanic legal system the principle that a person must be sued in the locale in which he resides, for his convenience. These two principles passed into Texas state law.[8]

That same legislative session of the Republic of Texas adopted and subsequently passed on to the state legal code the Spanish legal concept of community property. Husband and wife were to share equally in the profits and fruits of their marriage. Under Anglo-American law, however, property belonged exclusively to the husband, and on the death of her spouse, the wife was protected only by a life-interest in one-third of the lands of her deceased spouse. The previously Hispanic provinces of Texas and Louisiana were the first to protect wives through common-law statutes. Today, community property law is prevalent in states that have an Hispanic heritage: Texas, Louisiana, New Mexico, Arizona, Nevada, and California. It has also been pointed out that even the right to file a joint income tax return derives from the Spanish principle.[9]

Numerous other principles of Spanish family law were incorporated into the legal code of Texas in 1841. They covered the rights of partners in marriage as well as the adoption of children. Included among these principles was the protection of the rights of parties in a common law relationship. Furthermore, children of such marriages, even if proven invalid later, were considered legitimate, and a fair division of the profits of marriage had to result. This legitimacy of such children is still part of Texas family law today.[10]

This very brief exposition of the Hispanic patrimony that is also part of the heritage of all of the peoples of the United States indicates the level and extent of cultural riches that the United States inherited when it expanded its southern and Western borders and when it broadened its sphere of political and economic interests to include the Caribbean, Mexico, and Central America. The cultural baggage brought with each Hispanic encompassed within the new borders or with each Hispanic immigrant is the product of centuries of development and, even before the United States was founded, had predetermined many fundamental aspects – be they economic, artistic, spiritual – of life as we know it today in the American Republic.

Hispanics in the twentieth century

Since the nineteenth century, three factors have determined the development of Hispanic peoples and their culture in the United States: their status as natives, immigrants, or exiles. A distinctive "native" culture has developed among Hispanics over the centuries, especially in the Southwest, where for generations they have been identified with the lands and history of the area. At the same time, since the abolition of slavery, US industry and agriculture have sought a low-cost replacement for the free labor on which southern agribusiness was developed; the answer from then on has been to import workers from the nearby Hispanic countries, principally Mexico, Puerto Rico, Cuba, and Central America. Both because of the proletarianization[11] of the southwesterners who were dispossessed of their lands and recruited for work in the mines, agricultural fields, and railroads, as well as because of the continued recruitment of menial laborers from south of the border, Hispanic culture in the United States has overwhelmingly developed working-class characteristics, from food ways to art, literature, and music. Nevertheless, throughout US history, educated and elite Hispanics have entered the United States as exiles, businesspeople, and professionals, and have often found themselves as a privileged minority assuming the leadership of the cultural institutions in the Hispanic communities they have adopted, where they have founded factories, theatre houses, and newspapers, for example, and tried to duplicate the elite lives they led before expulsion from or abandonment of their homelands. This was as true for the exiles from Spain and the Spanish Caribbean in the early nineteenth century as it was for the first wave of refugees from the Cuban Revolution of 1959.

From this diverse amalgamation – made more diverse when the race, national origin, and ethnicity of the individual Hispanics are also considered – there has arisen over the twentieth century an undeniable and irrepressible contribution to US society across many fields of endeavor, from sports to science. And while many of the accomplishments of individuals of Hispanic origin may, indeed, be attributed to their individual genius, as is certainly the case in the success of Hispanic nuclear physicists, for example, where there is no recognizable Hispanic tradition in the field, there are other arenas that have been fostered and cultivated in Hispanic culture for generations, if not centuries.

An example of Hispanic technology and artistry that has literally been an integral part of the construction of American culture is the use of ceramic tiles and the construction of domes and vaults. The history of ceramic tiles goes back centuries into the Arab and Asian roots of Spanish culture and extends throughout Spanish America; the design, manufacture, and application of ceramic tiles is ubiquitous in the Hispanic world today. Quite often Hispanic artisanry surrounds Americans without their realizing it. One of the most obvious examples relates to the construction of the New York subways in the late nineteenth century, where millions of people would travel day in and day out. Spanish immigrant Rafael Guastavino (1842–1908) was responsible for tiled vaults in subways as well as those in Grand Central Station, (the old) Penn Station, the Metropolitan Museum of Art, the Plaza and Biltmore Hotels, and the Cathedral of St. John the Divine, among many others. After having studied architecture and incorporated many of the traditional Mediterranean building technologies into his design and construction, Guastavino emigrated to the United States in 1881 and became one of the most recognized designers and builders of vaults, domes, and tiled surfaces, promoting their acoustics, elegance, and economy. By 1891, Guastavino's company had offices in New York, Boston, Providence, Chicago, and Milwaukee. After his death, Guastavino's sons continued the company and went on to build the domes for state capitals, universities, museums, and railroad stations, as well as the Supreme Court building and the Natural History Museum in Washington DC.[12]

Hispanic tradition in some sports goes back to the nineteenth century. Baseball was introduced to Cuba and Puerto Rico in the 1860s, when the game was just developing, and by 1871, the same year that the National Baseball Association was founded, there were already Hispanic players, such as Esteban Bellán, playing professional baseball in the United States.[13] While Bellán, a black Cuban, played on the Troy Haymakers at that time, by the turn of the century, racial segregation was imposed on professional baseball and no blacks were allowed to play. From then on, Hispanic participation in the sport was divided between the Negro leagues that developed and the white leagues, with Hispanic players who could "pass" as white allowed to participate on some teams until baseball was desegregated in 1947 with Brooklyn Dodger Jackie Robinson breaking the color line. Thus many of the spectacular contributions to the sport by Hispanics were made within the confines of the Negro Leagues. For example, pitcher José Méndez achieved a record of forty-four wins with only two losses in 1909 while playing for the Cuban Stars in the Negro Leagues. One of the best batters of all time, batting many consecutive seasons over .400, was Alejandro Oms, who played for the New York Cubans from 1921 to 1935. Shortly after the desegregation of baseball, however, Hispanic players gradually became ubiquitous and were responsible for some of the most longstanding achievements and records. For instance, Orestes (Minnie) Miñoso made the transition from the Negro Leagues into Major League baseball, breaking many records for stealing bases in 1951; by 1960, he led both leagues with hits: 184. By 1951, Hispanics such as Alfonso (Chico) Carrasquel were being selected for all-star teams, and in 1954 Roberto (Beto) Avila won the batting championship in the United States, batting .341, driving in 67 runs and scoring 112, including 15 home runs. In 1956, short stop Luis Aparicio became the first Hispanic player to be named Rookie of the Year; by 1970, he won more Golden Gloves as the best American short stop than any other player in the history of the game. Aparicio was inducted into the Hall of Fame in 1984; he still holds records for games played, assists, and double plays. Over the years, Hispanics have filled the record books with their fielding and batting prowess, repeatedly being named to all-star teams and receiving the ultimate recognition: a place in the Hall of Fame. Beginning with Roberto

Clemente in 1973, the list of Hispanic Hall of Famers is unending. And Hispanics have even ascended to and distinguished themselves in the coaching ranks – where also there had previously existed a color or ethnic barrier – with Al López being considered the seventh best coach in history and being named to the Hall of Fame in 1977.[14]

On the other hand, there have been accomplishments by Hispanics in many fields where there is no discernable Hispanic tradition. In sports, Rachel Elizondo McLish won the US Women's Bodybuilding Championship and Ms. Olympia in 1980; coach Tom Flores became the first Hispanic professional football coach in 1978 and eventually led the Oakland Raiders to two Super Bowl championships; golf counts two Hispanics in its Hall of Fame: Lee Treviño and Nancy López. Leadership by Hispanics has transformed two sports previously thought beyond Hispanic talent: ice skating and swimming. In 1996, Rudy Galindo became the first Hispanic to win the National Figure Skating championship; later that year he won a bronze medal in the Olympics.[15] In 1964, Donna De Varona won two Olympic gold medals in swimming; that same year she was named Most Outstanding Female Athlete in the World. In 1965, she became the youngest person (eighteen) and the first woman ever to be a sportscaster on network television. In 1991, she received the International Hall of Fame Gold Medallion as an inspiration for all swimmers.[16] Since the days of Richard Alonso "Pancho" González's US singles championships in 1948 and 1949, Hispanics have excelled in tennis. Rosemary Casals was rated nine times as number one in doubles by the US Lawn Tennis Association in the 1960s and 1970s. In 1970, she and her doubles partner Billi Jean King were principal founders of the Virginia Slims Invitational Women's Tournament. In 1990, Mary Joe Fernández became the highest ranked women's singles player and fourth in the world. She and her partner, Gigi Fernández (no relation) were ranked number one in doubles in the world in 1991. The two Fernándezes won the gold medal in the 1992 Olympics.[17] There are too many other sports achievements to list in such disparate sports as women's basketball, fencing, track and field, volleyball, wrestling, and boxing. In all, the face of sports has changed since Hispanics were allowed to participate and gain access to tennis courts, golf courses, and playing fields.

Many endeavors have been new for Hispanics within the United States, the challenges often involving breaking barriers of race and class and access to education. The physical sciences represent a field generally new to Hispanics; for the most part, the hard sciences are not distinguished in universities in Spanish-speaking countries, and in the United States high drop-out rates among Hispanics, low college enrollments, and economic barriers to attending graduate school have all worked against Hispanics distinguishing themselves in the disciplines of Newton and Einstein. Nevertheless, Hispanics have achieved great distinction, if not in number, at least in quality. For example, the Nobel-Prize winning (1968) physicist Luis Walter Alvarez is responsible for diverse, but highly influential contributions, from developing the triggering device for the first plutonium bomb during the Manhattan Project, in 1943, to being the first scientist to propose a credible theory for the disappearance of the dinosaurs, in 1980. Over the course of his life, Alvarez contributed to advances in physics, astrophysics, ophthalmic and television optics, geophysics, and air navigation.[18] Another example is Severo Ochoa's Nobel Prize-winning (1950) work in synthesizing RNA and DNA, work which made possible Watson and Crick's construction of the DNA model. Mario Molina's 1995 Nobel Prize in Chemistry was for identifying how chemicals deplete the ozone layer of the atmosphere, his discovery leading to the banning of certain chemical emissions throughout the world. But where a tradition has been lacking among Hispanics, new ones are forming. By 1996, there were enough Hispanic physicists to establish the National Society for Hispanic Physicists. That same year, President Bill Clinton appointed the first Hispanic member of the Nuclear Regulatory Commission: Nils J. Díaz, Professor and Director of the University of Florida Nuclear Space Power and Propulsion Institute.

In the world of business and commerce, there certainly has been precedence in the Hispanic world of a business know-how and tradition. However, within the confines of US segregation, inferior education for minorities, and institutional closed doors and glass ceilings limiting achievements in the corporate and private business worlds, individual Hispanic initiative has, nevertheless, achieved some success in corporate boardrooms and in creating outstandingly powerful businesses and industries. One need only remember the creation and total domination of the cigar manufacturing industry in Tampa, beginning in 1886, with the transfer of more than one hundred factories from Cuba to the Tampa swamps, and lasting past World War II until the decline of cigar smoking. After a century of laboring in factories and fields and an indomitable desire to move upward, some of today's largest corporations have been headed by Hispanics. In fact, the world's largest corporation, Coca-Cola Inc., was headed by Roberto C. Goizueta for more than two decades, beginning in 1981. Frank A. Lorenzo became the first Hispanic to head a major airline in 1980, when he became chairman and chief executive officer of Continental Airlines. In 1992, Goya Foods, headed by the Unanue family, became the largest Hispanic-owned company in the United States, its revenues rising to $453 million that year.[19] In 1995, Arthur C. Martínez became chief executive officer of the nation's largest merchandiser: Sears. Today there are Hispanic senior Vice-Presidents across the corporate world and Hispanics on boards. The ubiquity and success of Hispanics in business at every level is reflected in the numbers of Hispanic chambers of commerce in the nation and in the number of successful entrepreneurs. For example, in March 1996, *Hispanic Business* magazine published its first "Rich List" – it also publishes lists of the fastest growing Hispanic companies and the largest ones – documenting that there were at least eleven Hispanic entrepreneurs and corporate leaders whose net worth was more than $100 million. At the top of the list was Goizueta, followed by Joseph A. Unanue.

Labor

While the development of the United States as a culture, an economy, and a political power has much to do with the Hispanic background, the social and political patterns that were established by US government and business vis-à-vis the Hispanic world have greatly determined the evolution of Hispanic culture within US borders. On the one hand, the ideology of Manifest Destiny did much to justify United States expansion westward and southward and its grabbing of former Hispanic lands, with attendant displacement of Hispanic occupants and their gradual proletarianization in an effort to develop those lands and the resources they contained. On the other hand, US industrialization from the late nineteenth century on and its ever-increasing need for manpower led to the incorporation of workers via immigration from Mexico, Central America, and the Caribbean to operate the industrial machine and to perform as service workers. US political intervention in Latin America also pointed an unending stream of refugees to US shores. The economic and political decisions made by Washington DC, bending to the will of leading industrial and agribusiness interests, determined the character of the Hispanic population drawn to and nurtured within US borders from the late nineteenth century to the present. As a consequence, today more than 70 percent of Hispanics in the United States belong to the working class. This working-class background and identity accounts for many of the major contributions of Hispanics to US society, whether as laborers in the factories and fields, professional athletes, artists and entertainers, or as members of the armed forces.

From the late nineteenth century, Hispanic workers have struggled for a living wage, humane treatment, and health benefits. From Juan Gómez in 1883 leading cowboys in a strike in the Panhandle of Texas; to Lucy González Parsons's fifty years of organizing and publishing, beginning with the Haymarket Square riots of 1886; to Luisa Capetillo's organizing tobacco workers and pioneering feminism at the turn of the century in Puerto Rico, Tampa and

New York; to Santiago Yglesias Pantín establishing Puerto Rico's first labor union in 1899; to the cigar rollers in Tampa, striking in 1899, 1901, 1910, 1920, and 1931; the story of Hispanics in American labor is one of struggle against oppression and of blazing paths to new forms of activism. While Hispanic leadership in protecting the rights of miners in the Southwest and steelworkers in the Midwest can be charted as forging some of the essential rights and benefits for all workers in the United States, the longest and most protracted struggle for the human rights and working conditions of working people has been that of agricultural labor. Since the days of Juan Gómez, agriculture has not ceased to be manned by Hispanics, both natives and immigrants, and they have not as yet won the right to have representation, to negotiate, and to strike in most of the states of the Union. Thus the history of US agribusiness is also the history of the exploitation of Hispanic labor and the resistance by Hispanics to that exploitation, especially in the states that provide most fruits and vegetables to the world: California, Texas, and Florida.

Among the landmarks in labor history was the first strike won against the California agricultural industry, in Oxnard, led by the first farm worker union, the Japanese–Mexican Labor Association (JMLA) in 1903. Protesting unfair and racist labor practices by the contractors and the association of farmers and refiners of sugar beets, for the first time in history two distinct ethnic groups had banded together, overcoming linguistic and cultural barriers, to organize more than 90 percent of the workers in the industry and win a decent wage. Because of the success of the JMLA, other labor unions began to rethink their policy of not organizing non-white nor farm labor. In fact, it is widely believed that to this date most farm work is not unionized or protected by laws that exist in other industries because of racism and discrimination, not only among the growers, but also among the major US unions.[20]

The table grape industry, that would be embattled for decades, suffered its first strike in 1922, when a Mexican Independence Day celebration in Fresno turned into a union organizing effort. This initiative failed, but paved the way for later, more massive efforts, such as the effort in 1927 in southern California to organize and consolidate some twenty Mexican agricultural and industrial unions under the banner of the Confederación de Uniones Obreras Mexicanas (Federation of Mexican Worker Unions – CUOM). By May 1929, the federation had some three thousand members, organized in twenty locales. The first strike called by the union, in the Imperial Valley, was broken by arrests and deportations. Two years later, the union struck again by surprise, and the growers were forced to settle.[21] Perhaps one of the most famous events in Hispanic labor history was the El

Monte berry strike of 1933, the largest agricultural strike thus far. Led by the Mexican Farm Labor Union, an affiliate of the CUOM, the strike called for a minimum wage of twenty-five cents an hour. The strike spread from Los Angeles County to Orange County, and the union grew rapidly. Small increases in wages were won, and the union became the largest and most active agricultural union in California. In 1935, for instance, the union was responsible for six of the eighteen strikes in California agriculture and was also effective in winning concessions without striking. In 1936, it was a leader in establishing the Federation of Agricultural Workers Union of America. With the ravages of the Depression and surplus labor, as well as disputes with the AFL-CIO, the union waned by the late 1930s.[22]

Much more organizing and striking took place throughout the 1930s, extending to Arizona, New Mexico, and Texas. In 1933, Mexican and Mexican American workers in Texas organized one of the broadest unions in the history of Hispanic labor, the Asociación de Jornaleros (Journeymen's Association), which represented everything from hatmakers to agricultural workers; but the union's diversity was a problem as well as Texas Ranger harassment and the arrest of leaders in the onion fields of Laredo in 1934; the union died shortly thereafter.[23]

Another historic victory in Texas proved to be short-lived, when in 1938 Mexican and Mexican American workers struck the pecan shelling industry in San Antonio. After the industry announced a 15 percent wage cut, fully half of the workers in some 130 plants spontaneously walked out. A Mexican American pecan sheller, Emma Tenayuca, emerged as leader, who in addition to leading the workers with her fiery speeches also penned incisive essays on the condition of Mexican Americans. In the ensuing strife, tear gas was used against picketing strikers six times within the first two weeks of the strike and more than one thousand out of six thousand strikers were arrested, amid repeated violence against them. In March, the strike was settled through arbitration; the union was recognized, but there was a 7.5 percent decrease in wages. Nevertheless, in October, the Fair Labor Standards Act enforced a twenty-five cents per hour minimum wage, which became the stimulus for the industry to mechanize and eventually reduce its labor force drastically.[24] The same had happened to the Tampa cigar rollers, who also were replaced by machines after striking repeatedly.

Finally, in 1938 major labor unions began to open their doors to Hispanic minorities. In that year, Luisa Moreno, a Guatemalan immigrant who had been educated in US schools became the first Vice-President of the United Cannery, Agricultural, Packing, and Allied Workers of America (UCAPAWA). Moreno had broad experience in organizing Hispanics:

tobacco workers in Florida, factory workers in New York City, cotton pickers in Texas, and sugar beet workers in Colorado. Out of this experience, she developed an idea of organizing a national congress of Hispanic workers, which she was able to accomplish under the auspices of the Congress of Industrial Organizations (CIO) and with many other union organizers, especially women. The national Congress, El Congreso Nacional del Pueblo de Habla Hispana, was held in Los Angeles in April, 1939, bringing together for the first time in history Cubans and Spaniards from Florida, Puerto Ricans from New York, and Mexican Americans from the Southwest. The result of the convention and the organization of the Congress itself was that Spanish-speaking people in the United States began to realize that they constituted a national minority whose civil and labor rights were violated consistently across the country. Another important result of the convention was a highlighting of the role of Hispanic women, who had been leaders in organizing the Congress and the convention; not only were a high percentage of Hispanic women working outside of the home, but they were also leaders in the labor struggle.[25]

World War II led to the demise of the Congress, when the organization restricted its civil rights protests in order to support the war effort; it also lost numerous members to enlistment in the armed services. Although the organization attempted its revival after the war, McCarthyism and political persecution led to leaders, such as Moreno, going into voluntary exile rather than being grilled by the House Un-American Activities Committee or being deported.

After the war, an extensive Mexican guest worker program, instituted in 1939, was continued by Congress, after extensive agribusiness lobbying; the importation of workers undercut many efforts to unionize the resident agricultural workers. Nevertheless, union organizer Ernesto Galarza published an exposé of the abuses in this "Bracero Program," *Strangers in Our Fields* (1956), which spurred the AFL-CIO to begin supporting unionization of farm workers and bring about Congress's termination of the Bracero Program in 1964. The stage was now set for the most important farm labor movement in the history of the United States.[26]

Two trained community organizers, César Chávez and Dolores Huerta, founded the United Farmworkers Organizing Committee in Delano, California in 1962. With the Bracero Program defunct, in 1965 the fledgling union joined Filipino grape strikers and formed the United Farm Workers (UFW); through more than a decade of struggle it became the largest union of agricultural workers, creating national boycotts, court cases, and legislative action in California. From table grapes, the labor actions spread to lettuce and other crops and eventually won concessions and contracts on wages, working conditions, safe use of pesticides, and the right to unionize and strike. As a result, in 1975, the California legislature passed the California Labor Relations Act, which provided secret ballot union elections for farm workers. Over the years, Huerta became the most successful contract negotiator and lobbyist, and one of the most important fund raisers for the union. Chávez, on the other hand, employed pacifist tactics, hunger strikes, and spiritual crusades, and enlisted and received the support of national politicians, the Catholic Conference of Bishops, and, eventually, large scale organized labor.[27] When Chávez died in 1993, he was mourned as a national hero. In 1994, President Bill Clinton bestowed the United States Medal of Freedom upon him posthumously. Today the union is an affiliate of the AFL-CIO.

Leadership in many unions today is in the hands of Hispanics, as the percentage of Hispanics in labor increases and Hispanics learn to organize within the larger Anglo-American culture. In 1989, for example, Dennis Rivera was elected President of the 1199 National Health and Human Services Employee Union, which had a membership at that time of some 117,000 workers, primarily residing in New York and New Jersey. That same year, María Elena Durazo became the first woman to head a major union in the city of Los Angeles: the Hotel and Restaurant Employees Local 11, a union of some 13,000 that at that time had 70 percent Hispanic membership. In 1995, Linda Chávez Thompson became the highest-ranking Hispanic in the history of the CIO, when she assumed the position of Executive Vice-President of the combined AFL-CIO. She had served as national Vice-President and executive council member since 1993. Once again, the leadership of Hispanic women in labor has been significant.

Working-class culture

It is Hispanics' working-class culture that has most influenced the United States today in superficial, obvious ways, as well as through a deep transformation of the US worldview and sensibility. Hispanic popular culture at times seems to be everywhere, from the background music of innumerable television commercials to Mexican food, currently the most popular ethnic food, and salsa, the most popular condiment, to the transformation of pop music through Latin rhythms and the addition of Latin instruments, such as the congas, maracas, and other percussion instruments. Oscar de la Renta and Carolina Herrera have become famous fashion designers, Jennifer López the most sexy movie star, and Ricky Martin and Enrique Iglesias the heartthrobs of crooning. The sheer numbers of Hispanics residing in and immigrating to the United States augurs for an even greater transformation of the Protestant-Anglo-American identity of the country, with Hispanics forecast to become one quarter of the population by mid-century and a majority in the most populous and powerful states of California, Florida, Illinois, New York, and Texas. Hispanic demographics, buying power, political-party affiliation, linguistic preferences, bicultural identity – all have potential for transforming the identity of the United States in the world of tomorrow.

In the main, it has been Hispanic working-class tastes and traditions that have contributed the tortillas, chili peppers, rice, beans, and fried plantains to the American palate; the Afro-Caribbean music, arising first out of slavery and honed by the urban working class, to the American ear; the Hollywood stars, such as Jennifer López, Jimmy Smits, and Luis Valdez, all children of the barrios and fields, to the American imagination. In fact, it was the labor struggle in the California fields that launched the theatrical movement, led by Valdez, in 1965 that eventually would account for more than 150 grassroots theatrical groups from whom emerged two generations of playwrights, scriptwriters, actors, and directors who are now integrated in the Hollywood film industry, regional theatres, and Broadway. Valdez-influenced, ex-convict playwright Miguel Piñero was the first to go to Broadway in 1973 with his *Short Eyes*, followed in 1980 by Valdez himself, with *Zoot Suit*.

As noted at the outset of this chapter, the Hispanic roots of American civilization run deep and have accounted for much of what we call "American." Today, we are living in another period of great Hispanic cultural infusion into American society and identity. Today, it has been children of working-class immigrants who have best articulated this by merging the experience of their parents into the American novel, as has Pulitzer-Prize winner Oscar Hijuelos, MacArthur Fellow Sandra Cisneros and bestselling author Victor Villaseñor. Hispanics and their cultural contributions add to and transform the American Dream, unwilling as they are to renounce their Hispanic culture and their ties to the rest of the Spanish-speaking world. The waves of Hispanic immigration to the United States have been met at times with resistance from nativists who raise the specter of a "foreign" culture overwhelming the supposed Anglo base of American culture. Most nativists, from the nineteenth-century No-Nothing Party to respected intellectuals, such as Samuel Huntington, currently a professor at Harvard, decry the loss of a mythic "America" of racial purity, linguistic and cultural homogeneity. Their alarmism at times has resulted in racial persecution, exclusionary immigration laws, and wholesale deportations, but they have never been successful in fully closing the borders nor filtering out the diverse cultural infusions that have made the United States great. In fact, one of the major Hispanic contributions to American society in this era of globalization is the ability to commune with and serve as mediators with the rest of the hemisphere. This is especially significant in a country that has been officially isolationist and cultural imperialist. It is the Hispanics, it seems, who have the ability to understand other cultures, to see the United States from the double perspective of insider as well as outsider, to staunchly represent a working-class perspective in all of their art, literature, music, folkways, etc. They remember what it is to be the "foreigner," the Other, the citizen from the other side of the tracks, and in doing so they have the power to humanize and make more responsible the industrial-military machine that has become the United States.

NOTES

1. Jay P. Dolan and Allan Figueroa Deck, S.J., *Hispanic Catholic Culture in the United States* (Notre Dame: University of Notre Dame Press, 1994), p. 30.
2. Donald E. Chipman, *Spanish Texas, 1519–1822* (Austin: University of Texas Press, 1992), p. 256.
3. Bernard L. Fontana, *Entrada, The Legacy of Spain and Mexico in the United States* (Albuquerque: University of New Mexico Press, 1994), pp. 80–1.
4. Michael C. Meyer, *Water in the Hispanic Southwest: A Social and Legal History 1550–1850* (Tucson: University of Arizona Press, 1984), pp. 37–41.
5. Thomas E. Sheridan, *Los Tucsonenses: The Mexican Community in Tucson* (Tucson: University of Arizona Press, 1986), pp. 43–5.
6. Meyer, *Water in the Hispanic Southwest*, pp. 156–7.
7. Joseph McKnight, "Law Without Lawyers on the Hispano Mexican Frontier," *The West Texas Association Yearbook*, 64 (1990), p. 59; Chipman, *Spanish Texas*, pp. 253–4.
8. Chipman, *Spanish Texas*, pp. 250–1.
9. *Ibid.*, p. 253; McKnight, "Law Without Lawyers," p. 58.
10. Chipman, *Spanish Texas*, p. 252.
11. Tomás Almaguer, *Racial Fault Lines:The Historical Origins of White Supremacy in California* (Berkeley: University of California Press, 1994), pp. 183–203.
12. "Master Builders," *Humanities*, 16,3 (May/June 1995), pp. 29–30.
13. Nicolás Kanellos, ed., *The Hispanic American Almanac* (Detroit: Gale Research Inc., 1996), p. 699.
14. Nicolás Kanellos, *Hispanic Firsts: 500 Years of Extraordinary Achievement* (Detroit: Gale Research Inc., 1997), pp. 274–5; *The Hispanic American Almanac*, pp. 128, 231, 235–6, 529–30, 708.
15. "Edge of a Dream," *Time*, March 18, 1996.

16. Kanellos, *The Hispanic American Almanac*, p. 731.
17. Kanellos, *Hispanic Firsts*, pp. 298–301.
18. Joseph C. Tardiff and L. Mpho Mabunda, *Dictionary of Hispanic Biography* (Detroit: Gale Research Inc., 1996), pp. 38–40.
19. *Ibid.*, p. 907.
20. Almaguer, *Racial Fault Lines*, pp. 183–203.
21. Juan, Gómez-Quiñones, *Roots of Chicano Politics, 1600–1940* (Albuquerque: University of New Mexico Press, 1994), p. 381.
22. Sam Kushner, *Long Road to Delano: A Century of Farm Worker Struggle* (New York: International Publishers, 1975), pp. 68–76.
23. F. Arturo Rosales, *Chicano! The Mexican American Civil Rights Movement* (Houston: Arte Público Press, 1996), p. 121.
24. *Ibid.*, pp. 121–2.
25. *Ibid.*, pp. 123–4.
26. *Ibid.*, pp. 119–20.
27. *Ibid.*, pp. 170–3.

FURTHER READING

Tomás Almaguer, *Racial Fault Lines:The Historical Origins of White Supremacy in California*, Berkeley: University of California Press, 1994.

Arthur L. Campa, *Hispanic Culture in the Southwest*, Norman: University of Oklahoma Press, 1979.

Donald E. Chipman, *Spanish Texas, 1519–1822*, Austin: University of Texas Press, 1992.

Jay P. Dolan, and Allan Figueroa Deck, S J., *Hispanic Catholic Culture in the United States*, Notre Dame: University of Notre Dame Press, 1994.

Bernard L. Fontana, *Entrada: The Legacy of Spain and Mexico in the United States*, Albuquerque: University of New Mexico Press, 1994.

Ernesto Galarza, *Farm Workers and Agribusiness in California: 1947–1960*, Notre Dame: University of Notre Dame Press, 1977.

Juan Gómez-Quiñones, *Roots of Chicano Politics, 1600–1940*, Albuquerque: University of New Mexico Press, 1994.

Juan L. Gonzales, *Mexican and Mexican American Farm Workers: The California Agricultural Industry*, New York: Praeger, 1985.

Nicolás Kanellos, *Hispanic Firsts: 500 Years of Extraordinary Achievement*, Detroit: Gale Research Inc, 1997.

   Thirty Million Strong: Reclaiming the Hispanic Image in American Culture, Golden, CO: Fulcrum Publishing, 1998.

Nicolás, Kanellos, ed., *The Hispanic American Almanac*, Detroit: Gale Research Inc, 1996.

Nicolás Kanellos, and Claudio Esteva Fabregat, *Handbook of Hispanic Culture in the United States*, 4 vols., Houston: Arte Público Press, 1994–5.

Sam Kushner, *Long Road to Delano: A Century of Farm Worker Struggle*, New York: International Publishers, 1975.

Joseph McKnight, "Law Without Lawyers on the Hispano Mexican Frontier," *The West Texas Association Yearbook*, 64 (1990): 51–65.

Michael C. Meyer, *Water in the Hispanic Southwest: A Social and Legal History 1550–1850*, Tucson: University of Arizona Press, 1984.

F. Arturo Rosales, *Chicano! The Mexican American Civil Rights Movement*, Houston: Arte Público Press, 1996.

Thomas E. Sheridan, *Los Tucsonenses: The Mexican Community in Tucson*, Tucson: University of Arizona Press, 1986.

Joseph C. Tadiff and L. Mpho Mabunda, *Dictionary of Hispanic Biography*, Detroit: Gale Research Inc, 1996.

8

WERNER SOLLORS

African Americans since 1900

A new Negro for a new century

About half of the nearly ten million African Americans living in 1900 had been born during the slavery period, and while slavery had not yet receded into the distant past, it seemed important to the former slaves and their descendants to stress the distance they had traveled from that past. Only forty years earlier, the overwhelming majority of black Americans – more than 85 percent – had belonged to and could be bought and sold by white owners, a deep-seated contradiction in one of the world's oldest democracies with a founding document that declared that "all men are created equal." "Natally alienated" (to use Orlando Patterson's term), slaves were forced to perform unpaid labor, without any civil status that would guarantee them even such basic human rights as the right to marry, to raise their own children, or to learn how to read and write. Slavery was, and remained for a long time, a haunting and troubling memory, a scar of shame. Emancipation, which seemed like a rebirth from a state of social death, was indeed a "resurrection" from the tomb, as Frederick Douglass's famous slave narrative had represented his own transformation from the status of a slave to that of a self-freed man.

The titles of Booker T. Washington's *A New Negro for a New Century* (1900) and his autobiography *Up from Slavery* (1906) were also the slogans of the post-slavery era. Though W. E. B. Du Bois had many reasons to disagree with Washington, he shared the "up from slavery" mood and, in 1913, organized a gigantic pageant, *The Star of Ethiopia*, for the fiftieth anniversary celebration of the Emancipation from slavery. It was held in the New York Armory, the same building and year in which the Armory Show exposed a general American audience to modernist art. The mode was forward-looking, and at a time when an urbanizing and modernizing country seemed to love nostalgia in all forms from dialect poetry to folk cartoons, African Americans found it difficult to participate in a fake celebration of a simpler past that included an idealized memory of slavery complete with the stock evocation of contented black retainers and nursemaids happily ensconced in the family settings of the plantation tradition. The popular minstrel images may have suggested to many Americans a comic version of a happier past, but to many blacks these images ridiculed or trivialized what had been a painful experience. Du Bois was among many who opposed the caricaturing portraiture of blacks in the white press as " 'grinning' Negroes, 'happy' Negroes," or "Aunt Jemimas," and the "New Negro" movement spearheaded by Alain Locke defined itself in antithesis to the minstrel imagery of a "Sambo" past. For Locke, the days of "aunties," "uncles," and "mammies" were the days of the "old Negro" that the "New Negro" wished to leave behind. And though Locke had few sympathies for Marcus Garvey, the West Indian-born leader of the largest social movement among African Americans in the first half of the twentieth century (the Universal Negro Improvement Association), Garvey, too, proclaimed: "The Uncle Tom nigger has got to go, and his place must be taken by the new leader of the Negro race."[1]

What African Americans faced was not only an idealization of the slavery past by white Americans, but also a new and rapidly advancing system of racial segregation. Segregation curtailed more and more rights, relegated blacks to a second-class status, and created a parallel universe for them ("white separatism, black parallelism," as the historian Darlene Clark Hine put it). The concept of "separate but equal" – maintained in political journalism as well as by Supreme Court decisions like *Plessy v. Ferguson* (1896) – often meant an exclusion of former slaves and their descendants from ordinary citizens' rights and employment opportunities. It forced blacks, in fact, to inhabit a separate, inferior, and quite *un*equal world that became known under the name of the nineteenth-century minstrelsy act "Jim Crow." As the literary critic Jeffrey Ferguson stressed, racial separation was enacted not only concerning schools, parks, hospitals, means of transportation, residences, and marital relations, but also governing graveyards, mental institutions, homes for the elderly, special driving hours for blacks in automobiles, and separate black and white Bibles in some courts. The deepest fear stemmed from contact between black men and white women, and even the most fleeting forms of it could provoke the most violent reactions.

Washington, Du Bois, Locke, and Garvey had different notions of the direction in which blacks should be moving forward in the twentieth century: was it through industrial or higher education? Should they strive toward uplift and self-help in the here and now, while strategically accepting segregation? Should they develop a deeper historical consciousness and understanding of the African past, challenge absurd segregationist restrictions, and aim for full "social equality"? Should they adopt a "politics of respectability" or one of protest? Should African Americans embrace an aesthetic of black beauty or endorse the symbolic power of black pride and the slogan "Back to Africa"? Despite their different visions, the various leaders shared a sense of the importance of leaving the slavery past behind and of tackling the new obstacles to black freedom and equality that racial segregation presented.

Double-consciousness and race heroism

"The problem of the Twentieth Century is the problem of the color-line." This was the famous prophecy W. E. B. Du Bois pronounced upon several occasions around the turn from the nineteenth to the twentieth century, and he used this resonant phrasing twice in his epoch-making essay collection *The Souls of Black Folk*.[2] Trained as an undergraduate at Fisk and Harvard University, Du Bois (1868–1963) was the first African American to receive the Ph.D. degree from Harvard. He became a university professor at Atlanta, an activist in the civil rights organization the National Association for the Advancement of Colored People (which he helped found), an internationalist and participant in the Pan-Africanist movement, a path-breaking scholar in history and sociology as well as a prolific essayist and fiction writer. Addressing the question "How does it feel to be a problem?," Du Bois saw the "strange meaning of being black here in the dawning of the Twentieth Century" as carrying larger national and international significance. In his essay "Of Our Spiritual Strivings" (published in the *Atlantic Monthly* in 1897), Du Bois had described the American Negro at the crossroads, pondering the question, "what, after all, am I? Am I an American or am I a Negro? Can I be both?. . . Does my black blood place upon me any more obligation to assert my nationality than German, or Irish, or Italian blood would?" When he revised this essay for the opening of *The Souls of Black Folk*, Du Bois wrote what became, as Gerald Early argued, "one of the most famous quotations in American literature, and probably the most famous in all African American literature."[3]

> After the Egyptian and Indian, the Greek and Roman, the Teuton and Mongolian, the Negro is a sort of seventh son, born with a veil, and gifted with second-sight in this American world – a world which yields him no true self-consciousness, but only lets him see himself through the revelation of the other world. It is a peculiar sensation, this double-consciousness, this sense of always looking at one's self through the eyes of others, of measuring one's soul by the tape of a world that looks on in amused contempt and pity. One ever feels his two-ness – an American, a Negro; two souls, two thoughts, two

unreconciled strivings; two warring ideals in one dark body, whose dogged strength alone keeps it from being torn asunder.

The history of the American Negro is the history of this strife – this longing to attain self-conscious manhood, to merge his double self into a better and truer self.[4]

Du Bois viewed the black American minority – that characteristically was endowed with a double-consciousness by feeling both American and Negro – as part of a global struggle for racial equality in an age of intensifying racial conflict.

The black Americans' struggle to realize their American birthright – no matter whether it was questioned and challenged by Supreme Court decisions, Congressional actions, Presidential policies, or general white hostility and fear – had the quality of a myth-like heroic battle that demanded the fullest engagement of anyone whose voice could be heard. For Du Bois, the black "talented tenth" did, indeed, have a higher obligation to identify by their ancestry than did Irish or Italian Americans. Black writers and artists, historians and scientists, journalists and lawyers, entertainers and musicians, filmmakers and photographers, explorers and inventors as well as athletes were to speak for the whole black community and to act in ways that would make them a "credit to the race." Their accomplishments, prizes, and victories were to give a boost to black aspiration.

James Weldon Johnson, another NAACP activist who in 1900 wrote what became known as the "Negro National Anthem," embodied in his own life this black striving for excellence in order to advance the whole race. He worked as a teacher and principal in his segregated city of Jacksonville, Florida, took the Florida Bar examination, entered graduate school at Columbia with the intention of becoming a writer, worked in the election campaign for Theodore Roosevelt and then in the diplomatic service, served as Executive Secretary for the NAACP, published numerous books and did a voice recording of some of his poems, and taught at Fisk and New York University. He devoted much of his life to aid the struggle for civil rights, most specifically, to exert public pressure against the horrifying and widespread incidents of lynching and to help pass a federal lynching bill that, had it been ratified by both Houses, would have made easier the prosecution of participants in lynch mobs.

Between 1882 and 1951, 3,437 African Americans were lynched in the USA, in often gory rituals of which postcards and other macabre souvenirs were made. Only in 2005 did the US Senate pass an unusual voice-vote resolution, a public apology for the Senate's failure to enact such a bill at any time in the past. Johnson created an anti-hero protagonist in his novel about racial passing, *The Autobiography of an Ex-Colored Man* (1912), in which a talented and cosmopolitan ragtime pioneer, horrified at witnessing a lynching and humiliated at belonging to a race that could be treated in such a way, decides to go the path of least resistance, to pass for white, and to accumulate personal wealth. At the end of the novel, the first-person-singular narrator views himself as a "coward" and "deserter" and finds that, as "an ordinarily successful white man," he feels small and selfish when he compares himself to that small "band of colored men who are publicly fighting the cause of their race." He feels that even their opponents "know that these men have the eternal principles of right on their side, and they will be victors even though they should go down in defeat."[5] As an artist and "race man" loyal to his African American origins, he could have helped the cause along, but instead realizes at the end that in sacrificing his musical talent he has sold his "birthright for a mess of pottage."

The history of the race was often fleshed out in heroic biographies of race leaders and pioneers who were cast, or who cast themselves (in autobiographies with titles like *Along This Way* or *Yes, I Can*), as role models. The many "firsts" assumed a great importance for a sense of progress in which "black faces in high places" would symbolize an advance for all Negroes. For example, Booker T. Washington was celebrated as the first Negro to be invited to dine in the White House in 1901   and the fact that President Theodore Roosevelt's invitation was much vilified in the southern press only enhanced the racial significance of the event. The *Baltimore Sun*, for example, commented, under the front-page headline, "The Black Man to be Put on Top of the White Man," that this dangerous presidential weakening of racial barriers would lead to intermarriage and "mongrelization."

It was important that Maggie Walker was the first black woman to open a bank in 1903; that Madame C. J. Walker became the first African American millionairess in 1905 (on the basis of her hair straighteners, skin bleachers, and other cosmetics); that George Washington Buckner served as the first black minister to a foreign country from 1913–15; that in 1944 Harry McAlpin became the first black reporter with White House credentials; that in 1950, Ralph Bunche was the first African American to win the Nobel Peace Prize; that in 1966, Edward Brooke became the first black elected to the US Senate and Robert Weaver the first African American to hold a cabinet post; that in 1977, Patricia Harris was appointed as the first black woman to serve on a President's cabinet; that in 1990, Douglas Wilder was elected in Virginia as the first black governor in the twentieth century; and that in 1993, Toni Morrison became the first American-born writer of African descent to be awarded the Nobel Prize for Literature. Collections of life stories of race heroes like J. A. Rogers's *World's Greatest Men and Women of African Descent* (1931) became a popular genre.

The growing degree of general identification with such "firsts" is apparent in the case of Texas-born black boxer Jack Johnson, who defeated the white Canadian Tommy Burns in 1908 and became world champion. Johnson, who was scandalously married to a white woman, also beat the "great white hope" Jim Jeffries in 1910 and was then celebrated as a black hero. By contrast, Joe Louis's victory over Max Schmeling in 1938 marked the defeat of a foreign fascist by a hero of American democracy. This transformation of the figure of the black boxer from race hero to that of a representative American paralleled the cultural work of the New Negro, the Harlem Renaissance, that helped to demonstrate the modernity and Americanness of African American cultural actors.

Migration narrative and Harlem Renaissance

The interwar period witnessed a cultural flourishing in literature as well as in art and music that accompanied the Great Migration, the central theme of which the literary critic Farah Jasmine Griffin described as "the migration narrative" that swept an urbanizing black America.[6] It can be seen in the visual work of Jacob Lawrence and Aaron Douglas and heard in the urban blues of Bessie Smith and Billie Holiday as well as in the train-inspired rhythms of Count Basie's *Super Chief* or Duke Ellington's experimental "Daybreak Express." Harlem was the embodiment of all urban aspirations, the "race capital." In the twenties and thirties book titles called Harlem "Black Manhattan" or the "Negro Metropolis." It was the black capital city, the largest Negro community in the world, a magnet drawing migrants from everywhere. On several occasions Alain Locke, in his anthology *The New Negro* (1925), drew parallels between the New Negro's Harlem and "Palestine full of renascent Judaism"; in other words, Harlem was seen as the promised city, "the home of the Negro's 'Zionism.' The pulse of the world has begun to beat in Harlem."[7] This urban optimism was shared by many old-guard and "renaissance" intellectuals.

Thus, James Weldon Johnson believed that Harlem would "by-pass the patterns of race friction and violence established elsewhere and become, without doubt, the intellectual, the cultural and the financial center for Negroes of the United States, and would exert a vital influence upon all Negro peoples." And versatile though Johnson was in his own many careers, he strongly believed that it was on the field of Negro literature that the progress of the race depended. Thus he wrote programmatically in the preface to his pioneering *Book of American Negro Poetry* (1922):

A people may become great through many means, but there is only one measure by which its greatness is recognized and acknowledged. The final measure of the greatness of all peoples is the amount and standard of the literature and art they have produced . . . No people that has produced great literature and art has ever been looked upon by the world as distinctly inferior.

In Johnson's view, nothing would do more to change the "national mental attitude toward the race" and raise the Negro's status "than a demonstration of intellectual parity by the Negro through the production of literature and art."[8]

The New Negro literary flourishing was facilitated by the rise of new journals (foremost, the NAACP's *Crisis* and the Urban League's *Opportunity*) and defiant little magazines (*Fire!!* – of which only one issue was to appear), by the support of the older generation (Du Bois, Johnson), and by new sponsors who helped writers and artists financially (Mrs. Charlotte Osgood Mason) or helped open doors to publishers (Carl Van Vechten, who also photographed most of the members of the New Negro intellectual elite).

As the literary critic Robert A. Bone has emphasized, the literature of the Harlem Renaissance was produced by an extraordinarily well-educated set of writers. The Jamaica-born Claude McKay, whose poem "If We Must Die" (1919) has been viewed as beginning the Harlem Renaissance and whose novel *Home to Harlem* (1928) scandalously embodied the new urban spirit, attended Tuskegee and Kansas State. Jean Toomer dabbled in many fields at the universities of Wisconsin and Massachusetts, the American College of Physical Training in Chicago, New York University and the City College of New York before publishing his remarkable experimental work *Cane* (1923), a modernist mélange of poetry, prose, and drama set both in the rural South and the new urban centers; it is often considered the highest aesthetic achievement of the Renaissance. Sterling Brown, who became noted as a folk poet (*Southern Road*), as a pioneering critic of Negro drama and fiction, and as an exhaustive examiner of Negro stereotypes in white American literature, graduated from Williams and received an M.A. from Harvard. Zora Neale Hurston, who achieved fame not only as a Guggenheim and Rosenwald-fellowship-winning novelist of southern folk life (*Jonah's Gourd Vine* and the now most famous novel of the period, *Their Eyes Were Watching God*) but also as a folklore collector in Florida and Haiti (*Mules and Men* and *Tell My Horse*), had an undergraduate career at Howard and Barnard and also entered a Ph.D. program in anthropology at Columbia. The poet Countée Cullen, who published such collections as *Color* (1925), *Copper Sun* (1927), and *The Black Christ* (1929), held degrees from New York University and Harvard. The prolific Langston Hughes, whose many publications include poetry collections such as *The Weary Blues* (1926) and the short story collection *The Ways of White Folks* (1934), and whose *Mulatto* (1935) was the first play by an African American to run on Broadway, studied at but dropped out of Columbia University and later graduated at Lincoln University. Nella Larsen, who published the two color-line novels *Quicksand* and *Passing* in 1929, studied at Fisk, the University of Copenhagen, and the Lincoln School for Nursing. Arna Bontemps, who published *Black Thunder* (1934), the first black historical novel set in the slavery period, was an alumnus of Pacific Union College and the University of Chicago. Jessie Fauset, who authored such novels of manners as *There Is Confusion* (1924) and *Plum Bun* (1929), and who was also active as an editor and translator, graduated from Cornell University. And the philosopher Alain Locke, whose landmark anthology *The New Negro* (1925), illustrated by Winold Reiss and Aaron Douglas, gave the cultural movement its name, held a Harvard A.B. and Ph.D. and became in 1907 the first (and until 1963, the only) African American Rhodes scholar to go to Oxford. This catalogue is a testimony to the high esteem in which education was held in the interwar period. No wonder that more black literature was published between 1920 and 1940 than in the whole previous history. At the same time, if one remembers that only 1 percent of the black population had completed a college education in 1940, this list suggests the small segment from which Harlem Renaissance intellectuals were drawn.

In this illustrious group of intellectuals, George Schuyler and Richard Wright stand out as exceptions to the rule. George Schuyler dropped out from high school before becoming an always provocative journalist for the *Pittsburgh Courier*. Schuyler's raucously funny and politically completely incorrect novel *Black No More* (1931) questions the whole system of racial etiquette, makes fun of African American intellectuals from Du Bois to James Weldon Johnson, doubts that there is such a thing as a "Negro Problem," and may be the first text to use a version of the word "hiphop" ("The Incidence of Psittacosis among the Hiphopa Indians"). Richard Wright stands out as a lower-class, Mississippi-born, self-taught writer who only finished ninth grade. Wright's work helped to change the view of the city and gave greater urgency to the political struggles against segregation, while his short story collection *Uncle Tom's Children* (1938), novel *Native Son* (1940), and autobiography *Black Boy* (1945) marked the definite end of the "New Negro" period. *Native Son's* protagonist Bigger Thomas, the hardened young murderer who is unreachable by family members or minister, who proclaims, "what I killed for, I am," before he is taken to the electric chair, is a character unlike any in Harlem Renaissance literature.[9]

The rise of modernism as the dominant aesthetic to replace realism was perceived as a development that would help to combat the old stereotypes that were so prevalent in realist and local color writing and art. The *Messenger* motto, "I am an iconoclast: I smash the limbs of idols," was echoed by Alain Locke's dictum: "The Negro. . .has idols of the tribe to smash." Modernism also encouraged experiments in what Martha Nadell termed "interartistic" cooperation between writers and visual artists. Thus, Hurston worked with Miguel Covarrubias, Wright with Thomas Hart Benton and Edwin Rosskam's FSA photographs, and Langston Hughes with Jacob Lawrence. There were other collaborative ventures between literature and music; scenes in a club where black musicians play such as the one Johnson had portrayed in 1912 now became common in the literature of McKay, Hughes, or Toomer, as did attempts to replicate the sound of music in poetry or prose. One only has to think of Toomer's sentence, "The flute is a cat that ripples its fur against the deep-purring saxophone" or of Langston Hughes's "Dream Boogie" with the final lines, "Take it away!/ *Hey, pop! / Re-bop!/ Mop!/ Y-e-a-h!*"[10]

While the New Negro intellectuals were busy advocating and producing art that was deeply connected with racial themes, they also kept questioning the core issue of racial identification: Toomer was the Harlem Renaissance intellectual and mystic who presented the most thoroughgoing questioning of racial identity and could be called an early and quite utopian social constructionist. Thus he wrote emphatically: "There is only one pure race – and this is the *human* race. We all belong to it – and this is the most and the least that can be said of any of us with accuracy. For the rest, it is mere talk, mere labeling, merely a manner of speaking, merely a sociological, not a biological, thing." In his collection of aphorisms *Essentials* (1931) Toomer drew the consequences from such reflections and wrote about himself: "I am of no particular race. I am of the human race, a man at large in the human world, preparing a new race." Countée Cullen stated that while there were Negroes who wrote poetry there was no "Negro poetry," and Schuyler wrote an essay entitled "The Negro, Art Hokum" in which he provocatively argued that "Aside from his color, which ranges from very dark brown to pink, your American Negro is just plain American."[11] Langston Hughes responded with "The Negro Artist and the Racial Mountain," which was race-conscious and advocated the freedom of the artist from black and white expectations.

Many of the New Negro assertions seem to modify Du Bois's notion of double-consciousness, and Hurston's essay "How It Feels to Be Colored Me" (1928) is a case in point. As if arguing explicitly against Du Bois's question, "How does it feel to be a problem?" Hurston writes,

But I am not tragically colored. There is no great sorrow dammed up in my soul, nor lurking behind my eyes. I do not mind at all. I do not belong to the sobbing school of Negrohood who hold that nature somehow has given them a lowdown dirty deal and whose feelings are all hurt about it. Even in the helter-skelter skirmish that is my life, I have seen that the world is to the strong regardless of a little pigmentation more or less. No, I do not weep at the world – I am too busy sharpening my oyster knife.[12]

Hurston also commented upon the "forced grouping" of blacks that takes place in many social as well as intellectual encounters. She writes that when a black student couple goes on a New York subway and two scabby-looking Negroes enter the car, all other identities of the couple (college students on a date, theatregoers, etc.) get eclipsed by the category "Negro," and the silent comments in the white glances seem to be: "Only difference is some Negroes are better dressed" or "you are all colored aren't you?" She sighs, with another phrasing expressive of the increasing complexity of race heroism, "My skinfolks but not my kinfolks." Freedom from forced grouping also includes freedom from constant reminders of the slavery past: "Someone is always at my elbow reminding me that I am the granddaughter of slaves. It fails to register depression with me. Slavery is sixty years in the past. The operation was successful and the patient is doing well, thank you."[13] The New Negro was an impressive literary and cultural flourishing supported by an intelligentsia, but the fact that its excitement hardly touched the majority of black Americans is driven home by the sales figures of the book that is often regarded the best of this flourishing: Jean Toomer's *Cane* sold only 500 copies.

From the Depression toward civil rights

The Great Depression affected everyone and led to a cultural transformation in which the old, upbeat imagery of urban freedom gave way to settings of urban blight that can best be measured by the growing circulation of the term "ghetto," adapted from European Jewish history, to the black residential areas in cities. Marita Bonner had used the word "ghetto" in her essay "On Being Young – A Woman – and Colored" (1925) as a metaphor for forced grouping (finding oneself "entangled – enmeshed – pinioned in the seaweed of a Black Ghetto"), but also as the possible nucleus of community: "Cut off, flung together, shoved aside in a bundle because of color and with no more in common. Unless color is, after all, the real bond."[14]

Richard Wright's *Native Son* (1940) gave full expression to the new sense of city as a trap, of the ghetto as a form of imprisonment by invisible walls, of poor exploited blacks without any sense of any real bond. The migration rate had gone down in the Depression decade (only to accelerate again in the wartime 1940s), unemployment rates were high, leftist radicalism was brought to high visibility by the widespread protests against the wrongful imprisonment of the Scottsboro Boys, and the general struggle for unionization was on the increase. In the 1930s the pressures on the federal government intensified to address the issue of black civil rights on the highest level, to guarantee equal employment opportunities for blacks, and to support the growing efforts to end the legal basis of segregation. *Messenger* editor, antilynching campaigner, and head of the Pullman Porter union A. Philip Randolph formed the National Negro Congress and shaped a March on Washington movement, while the legal counsels of the NAACP, Charles Hamilton Houston and Thurgood Marshall, initiated carefully selected law suits that helped to undermine Jim Crow.

Scholarship by African Americans supported the political struggle for equality. Carter G. Woodson (Harvard Ph.D. 1912) introduced Negro History Week in 1926 to commemorate the second week of February with the birthdays of Frederick Douglass (1818) and of Abraham Lincoln (1809). Woodson had pioneered in history with such classic studies as *The Education of the Negro Prior to 1861* (1915) and *The History of the Negro Church* (1924), and with an early focus on the history of what in the United States is called "miscegenation" (interracial sexual, marital, and family relations). Benjamin Brawley's literary histories included *The Negro Genius* (1937), Eva B. Dykes (Harvard Ph.D. 1912) demonstrated the significance of the antislavery struggle for English Romantic literature in *The Negro in English Romantic Thought, or, A Study of Sympathy for the Oppressed* (1942), and the historian John Hope Franklin (Harvard Ph.D. 1947) offered a helpfully synthesizing textbook to complement American history textbooks, *From Slavery to Freedom* (1947). Charles H. Nichols and Dorothy Sterling undertook the first full-scale scholarly work on the slave narrative. Such scholarship had the effect of making visible the African American past, putting blacks into American history, rectifying omissions and neglect, and setting the record straight against then dominant scholarly opinion that undervalued the importance of blacks in America.

The social sciences were equally active and became particularly influential during and following World War II. Among the best-known black social scientists were Charles S. Johnson, Horace Cayton, St. Clair Drake, and E. Franklin Frazier. The military confrontation with the Axis Powers, and especially with Nazi Germany, which had put "race" at the center of its totalitarian universe, gave the development of scholarly thinking about race in a democratic context a new urgency and some new directions.

The single most important study of American race relations of the 1940s was Gunnar Myrdal's *An American Dilemma* (1944), produced with the support of the Carnegie Foundation and with contributions by the major black social scientists. Myrdal succeeded in portraying the American democratic creed as so universally shared that it could serve as the basis for changing the status quo of race relations because American racial etiquette was so obviously at variance with that creed. *An American Dilemma* embodied the wartime moment at which invoking national unity could be allied with a liberal call for fairly radical change and a sense of urgency that only grew in the 1950s, when, as NAACP leader Roy Wilkins predicted, Myrdal's book served as a bible for Americans concerned about racial injustice. Myrdal's theory of the damage caused by racism (and particularly the demonstrable damage to blacks) inspired other social scientists to attempt to change public policy. When Kenneth B. Clark testified in the 1951 *Briggs v. Elliott* case that the tested fact that black children preferred to play with white dolls showed that "segregation damaged the mental and emotional development of black children," the "state of South Carolina was unable to find a prominent social scientist who would testify in favor of segregation" (as historian Walter A. Jackson put it).[15] And in the 1954 *Brown v. Board* decision, Chief Justice Earl Warren famously cited Myrdal, Clark, E. Franklin Frazier, and other social scientists in support of the court's ruling.

The chronology of the mid-century shows a fast acceleration in the Civil Rights Movement from the years of World War II to the mid-1960s. In June 1941, President Roosevelt signed Executive Order 8802 which prohibited government contractors' employment discrimination on the basis of race, color, or national origin. It marked the beginning of the federal government's slow engagement in desegregation, in response to mounting black pressure and, during World War II and in the Cold War, international embarrassment. In the early war years, William G. Nunn's *Pittsburgh Courier* launched a "Double V" campaign – the victory over fascism abroad and over racism at home – that gained considerable momentum and drew on the participation of many intellectuals and of Hollywood. At the peak of the Cold War, the landmark decision *Brown v. Board of Education* in 1954 was followed by the most active and widely publicized period of struggle for civil rights, with Rosa Parks's refusal to sit in the back of a Montgomery bus in 1955, the ensuing bus boycott in 1956 in which Martin Luther King gained prominence, and the Eisenhower government's sending the National Guard to Little Rock, Arkansas in 1957 in order to support educational desegregation.

The 1960 lunch-counter sit-ins introduced an even more active phase of nonviolent protest that culminated on August 28, 1963 in the March on

Washington, in which 200,000 participants rallied around the Lincoln Memorial in the symbolic centennial year of Lincoln's Emancipation Proclamation and urged the Kennedy administration to take a more active role in passing a general Civil Rights Act. The high point of the rally was Martin Luther King's "I Have a Dream" speech with its Lincoln-inspired opening ("Five score years ago") and its explicit invocation of the Declaration of Independence, which he described as "a promissory note to which every American was to fall heir." King continued that this "note was a promise that all men would be guaranteed the inalienable rights of life, liberty, and the pursuit of happiness. It is obvious today that America has defaulted on this promissory note insofar as her citizens of color are concerned." He spoke of the "marvelous new militancy" of the Negro community. And he very much argued along the lines of Myrdal's *American Dilemma*: "I have a dream that one day this nation will rise up and live out the true meaning of its creed: 'We hold these truths to be self-evident: that all men are created equal.'" He ended on a hopeful note:

> When we let freedom ring, when we let it ring from every village and every hamlet, from every state and every city, we will be able to speed up that day when all of God's children, black men and white men, Jews and Gentiles, Protestants and Catholics, will be able to join hands and sing in the words of the old Negro spiritual, "Free at last! free at last! thank God Almighty, we are free at last!"[16]

This speech symbolized the changing mood of the country, and as non-violent protests continued with great intensity (Martin Luther King was imprisoned and wrote the famous letter from Birmingham Jail during his captivity), the Johnson Administration passed the Civil Rights Act in 1964. In 1967 in *Loving v. Virginia*, the Supreme Court struck down the still widespread prohibition of interracial marriage, and the system of legal segregation came to an end.

Although *Brown v. Board* and *Loving v. Virginia* do not seem to have inspired any major cultural productions, the movement to desegregate was accompanied by integrationist literature such as Lorraine Hansberry's play about residential integration, *A Raisin in the Sun* (1959), a Broadway success. Hansberry's heroine is also the first black character in search of her "identity" (a brand-new term for the sense of collective belonging that would become a buzzword in the subsequent decades, with 12,200,000 Google hits in 2005 for the "black identity" alone). There was, however, a perhaps stronger stream of voices questioning Myrdal, *Brown v. Board*, integration, and King's march on Washington.

Ralph Ellison's novel *Invisible Man* (1952) was a high point of American modernist literature and offered folk resilience as a source of strength – "I yam what I am," as his narrator puts it. Ellison argued against Myrdal's definition of the American Creed and the notion of black damage in a review of *American Dilemma* that remained unpublished until 1964. Ellison asked, "can a people (its faith in an idealized American Creed notwithstanding) live and develop for over three hundred years simply by *reacting? . . . why cannot Negroes have made a life upon the horns of the white man's dilemma?*" Ellison continued:

> Myrdal sees Negro culture and personality simply as the product of a "social pathology." Thus he assumes that "it is to the advantage of American Negroes as individuals and as a group to become assimilated into American culture, to acquire the traits held in esteem by the dominant white Americans." This, he admits, contains the value premise that "*here in America*, American culture is 'highest' in the pragmatic sense. . ." Which, aside from implying that Negro culture is not also American, assumes that Negroes should desire nothing better than what whites would consider highest. But in the "pragmatic sense" lynching and Hollywood, fadism and radio advertising are products of the "higher" culture, and the Negro might ask, "why, if my culture is pathological, must I exchange it for these?"[17]

James Baldwin, well known for his novel *Go Tell It on the Mountain* (1953) and his literary and political essays, supported the March on Washington from his Paris exile and participated in a town hall meeting with Gunnar Myrdal and Kenneth Clark (among others), in which he said that "there is much in that American pie that isn't worth eating"; he expressed hesitation about integration memorably when he asked in *The Fire Next Time* (1963): "Do I really want to be integrated into a burning house?"[18]

Questions concerning integration – or assimilation from a point of weakness – were raised with greater force in the 1960s, when Malcolm X's urban sarcasm became a countervoice to that of southern-based Martin Luther King. Thus Malcolm derided "the farce on Washington," and the very fact that Malcolm had given up his slave name "Little" and taken on the "X" instead made this Nation of Islam minister a symbol for a black resistance to assimilation, just when integration became a possibility. Poet-playwright-essayist LeRoi Jones who, inspired by Malcolm, changed his name to Amiri Baraka, followed in the same tracks and described integrating as if it were the same as catching an illness: "I ain't innarested in contracting your horrible ole disease."[19] In his essay "Tokenism: 300 Years for Five Cents" he also made fun of the catalogues of "first" Negroes and imagined the first Negro who pushed the button of an atomic bomb as part of that proud list.

The Vietnam War, the assassinations of the Kennedys, of Malcolm, of King, the urban riots and campus protests, and the revelations about the pervasive government surveillance of civil rights leaders changed the political climate, and the end of *de jure* segregation no longer made the headlines in the 1960s. Yet there did emerge another literary flourishing in the Black Arts Movement that C. W. Bigsby termed "second renaissance," and that the literary critic James Edward Smethurst has traced in its heterogeneous regional origins and analyzed in its relationship to the Black Power movement as well as with respect to the lasting imprint it has left on American culture. Jones/Baraka's own works were trendsetters: among them, *Dutchman* (1964), an absurdist one-act play about a deadly encounter between a white woman and a black man on the New York subway, and *Slave Ship* (1969), a ritual of domination extending from slavery times to the performance itself (at which black actors were sold off to newspaper critics in mock auctions). Other new dramatic voices were Adrienne Kennedy, whose experimental *Funnyhouse of a Negro* had preceded *Dutchman* and whose dramatic œuvre is still performed today, and Ed Bullins, whose large play cycles made him the theatrical hope of the 1960s and 1970s. Older poets like the Pulitzer-Prize-winning Gwendolyn Brooks, Robert Hayden, and Dudley Randall at times supported younger ones like Nikki Giovanni, Ted Joans, and Don L. Lee (who became Haki Madhubuti). New filmmakers emerged, among them Melvin Van Peebles, who managed to usher in a new period of black independent cinema with his French-produced *Story of a Three Day Pass* (1968) and his American *Sweet Sweetback's Baad Asssss Song* (1971).

Meanwhile, the number of black elected officials started growing, and the foundations for a new and expanded black middle class were laid. An important institutional change in the 1960s took place at the largest and most prestigious universities, which began to accept more black students than ever before; at one university more black students arrived in 1968 than had attended that university in its entire history. Afro-American Studies was established at major research universities (including Harvard in 1969) as the academic area through which "integration" was to take place in the academy as a whole.

Slavery began to take a more central stage in historical scholarship, a position it was to retain through the rest of the century, deepened by the many-sided contributions of historians like Nathan I. Huggins, Eugene D. Genovese, David Brion Davis, Herbert Gutman, Leon Litwack, and Lawrence Levine. In 2000, the database of Stephen Behrendt, David Richardson, and David Eltis determined that the total number of Africans transported to the Americas over the centuries was 11,569,000; the figure is based on records for 27,233 voyages by slavers. The narrative of slavery changed. The historian Herbert Gutman described the progression from "what was done for slaves" (the paternalistic approach), to "what was done to them" (the protest approach), and finally to "what was done by them" (the focus on black agency and subjectivity).

In belles-lettres, too, historical themes became much more apparent in numerous works that confronted the trauma of slavery – most famously in Toni Morrison's *Beloved* (1987), which returned to the nineteenth-century sentimental theme of the slave mother who kills her own child. But perhaps what galvanized the turn toward Afro-American history most was the unexpected success of Alex Haley's novel *Roots* (1976) and of the TV mini-series that followed it, which established the mini-series genre as a vehicle for bringing history back to life. Told in the familiar form of an American multigenerational family saga, *Roots* managed to connect the past (Africa and slavery) with the present (the bicentennial moment), and to create vivid character sketches in a shorthand fashion that readers and viewers could identify with. *Roots* thus displaced the most popular earlier white American fictional accounts of slavery in *Uncle Tom's Cabin*, *Birth of a Nation*, and *Gone with the Wind*. With its search for the symbolic ancestor Kunta Kinte, *Roots* also opened up a whole new genre of at times widely popular African American historical fiction, either set in the slavery period, or at a later time, or in the form of a modern quest into the legacy of the past and ancestry.

Post-black, neo-slave narratives, blackness for sale

Henry Louis Gates, Jr. has demonstrated how black writers have been "signifying," or have responded to each other and to white American writers as well as to intellectuals around the world. One of his examples is Ishmael Reed, whose poem "Dualism: in ralph ellison's invisible man" parodies not only Ellison's insight "that all life is divided and that only in division is there true health," but also Du Bois's double-consciousness. According to Gates, Reed tells us that double-consciousness is only a "rhetorical construct," and "not some preordained reality or thing." Among other contemporary black intellectuals who have addressed Du Bois's "double-consciousness" with detachment and skepticism are critic and writer Stanley Crouch, who sees in it a "muddle of ideas that purport to explicate an alienation between national and racial identity," and Afrocentric scholar Molefi Kete Asante, who claims, "I was never affected by the Du Boisian double-consciousness. I never felt 'two warring souls in one dark body' nor did I experience a conflict over my identity. Since I was a child I have always known that my heritage was not the same as that of whites." The religious historian C. Eric Lincoln thinks that "the critical question for most African Americans has nothing to do with double-consciousness... A more pertinent question than 'What am I?' is 'How can I be who I am and still hack it in America?'" Lincoln concludes:

> In the meantime, as more barriers deteriorate and the browning of America moves on inexorably to redefine the horizons which rim our perceptions of racial reality, one wonders if the notion of Du Boisian dubiety will finally become obsolete, or whether even now the software for the more precise calculation of *gens de couleur* and fragments of self-consciousness is being readied for the generation ahead.

Has Du Bois with his prophecy of the color line, his notion of double-consciousness, and his sense of the "strange meaning of being black here" become obsolete a century later?[20]

"What would America be like without the Negro?," African American writers from George Schuyler to Ralph Ellison and Douglas Turner Ward have asked, echoing W. E. B. Du Bois's earlier question, "Would America have been America without her Negro people?" The reasons may vary, but the answer inevitably has been: It would not be the country we know, as the African American presence has been central to the American experience. In 1900, this may not yet have been obvious; yet by the end of the twentieth century it seemed indisputable. Whereas the United States at the beginning of the twentieth century was an impressively active producer and exporter of racial stereotypes and of ideas inspired by racial segregation and eugenics, a century later US politicians typically criticize anything from Japanese department stores which use little black Sambo in their advertisements to Mexican stamps honoring caricatures which seem racist. While a century ago, it seemed more natural for white Americans to root for foreign white boxers, nowadays many, perhaps most national sports events are opened by blacks singing the national anthem. While the economic situation of the truly disadvantaged African Americans and their political representation remain very serious social issues, the varied and complex political presence of figures like Barack Obama, Colin Powell, Condoleezza Rice, Clarence Thomas, or Jesse Jackson has made a difference to the once more precise meaning of the slogan "black faces in high places."

The success of the Civil Rights Movement was partial but the changed racial climate seems to have freed black artists, writers, and cultural producers from continuing to play the role of race heroes. In *Being and Race* (1988) National Book Award-winner Charles Johnson polemicized against political sentimentalism and essentialist race Kitsch as

> a retreat from ambiguity, the complexity of Being occasioned by the conflict of interpretations, and a flight by the black artist from the agony of facing a universe silent as to its sense, where even black history (or all history) must be

seen as an ensemble of experiences and documents difficult to read, indeed, as an experience capable of inexhaustible readings.[21]

Charles Johnson's novel *Oxherding Tale* (1982) is a prototypical and outstanding "neo-slave narrative" as much as it is a mock-autobiography and a mock-historical novel in the tradition of the picaresque and of the comic novel, with a good inflection of western philosophy and eastern Buddhism. It represents the education of Andrew Hawkins (the son of a slave and the plantation mistress, whose birth comes as the result of a night when master and slave decide to switch places), who is trained by a transcendentalist tutor. The raucous first-person-singular novel includes an essay on the slave narrative as a genre as well as such found language as the word "bondsman." This anti-sentimental mode has affinities with the tradition from George Schuyler to Ishmael Reed, and it is a particularly strong tendency in contemporary art.

In 2000, Thelma Golden, who had become famous as the art curator for the Whitney Museum, where she staged the widely influential, politically inflected show entitled *Black Male* (1994), proclaimed, in planning her exhibition *Freestyle* at the Studio Museum in Harlem, the arrival of what she famously termed *Post-Black* (2001), a new and daring art by young contemporary African American artists untrammeled by political concerns of the past and by racial self-consciousness, an art that "steps beyond essentialist aesthetic notions of blackness."[22] What seemed to be the stereotypes to be fought and avoided a century ago can now be used and reshaped imaginatively in works of artists like Kara Walker or Robert Colescott and writers like Ishmael Reed or Suzan-Lori Parks – not to mention the globally disseminated racial representations in hiphop or "gangsta rap." The critic Glenda Carpio has examined how remarkably pervasive the historical memory of slavery now is in African American culture but how it may be employed not just without sentimentality but for explicitly humorous, satirical, and parodistic purposes. Exaggerated stereotypes – exactly the ones that would have made "Negro intellectuals" of an earlier period cringe – absurd incongruities, explicit and near-pornographic accounts, and shameless minstrelsy are among the strange aesthetic features of neo-slave narratives that would probably have constituted "racial blasphemy" in the eyes of the period of race heroism. Thus Michael Ray Charles employs Aunt Jemima and Sambo stereotypes from old posters, Fred Wilson has produced installations with plantation-themed figures, including salt and pepper shakers, ash trays and coin banks that are Negro caricatures, and DJ Spooky had the audacity to offer a "remix" of a largely intact version of D. W. Griffith's classic racist film *Birth of a Nation*.

A work of art that forms a fitting conclusion here is by the conceptual artist Keith Townsend Obadike, who in 2001 put up his blackness for sale on an eBay auction site: http://obadike.tripod.com/ebay.html. Ironically alluding to the legacy of slave auctions and to the racialism that makes "blackness" precisely a quality one cannot ever shed, and following the ordinary eBay conventions, Obadike gives potential buyers the following information: "Mr. Obadike's Blackness has been used primarily in the United States and its functionality outside of the US cannot be guaranteed. Buyer will receive a certificate of authenticity." Among the "Benefits" he lists: "This Blackness may be used for writing critical essays or scholarship about other blacks." "This Blackness may be used for making jokes about black people and/or laughing at black humor comfortably." "This Blackness may be used for accessing some affirmative action benefits. (Limited time offer. May already be prohibited in some areas.)" "This Blackness may be used for dating a black person without fear of public scrutiny." "This Blackness may be used for gaining access to exclusive, 'high risk' neighborhoods." "This Blackness may be used for securing the right to use the terms 'sista', 'brotha', or 'nigga' in reference to black people. (Be sure to have certificate of authenticity on hand when using option.)" "This Blackness may be used to augment the blackness of those already black, especially for purposes of playing 'blacker-than-thou'." The "Warnings" include: "The Seller does not recommend that this Blackness be used during legal proceedings of any sort." "The Seller does not recommend that this Blackness be used while seeking employment." "The Seller does not recommend that this Blackness be used while making intellectual claims." And "The Seller does not recommend that this Blackness be used while voting in the United States or Florida." Held in August 2001, Keith Obadike's "Blackness for Sale" was removed for inappropriateness by eBay after only four days. According to his website, there had been twelve bidders, and the highest bid was $152.50.

NOTES

1. W.E.B. Du Bois, "In Black," The Crisis (1920); quoted from Richard Barksdale and Keneth Kinnamon, *Black Writers of America: A Comprehensive Anthology* (New York: Macmillan, 1972, repr. n.d.), p. 382; Alain Locke, "The New Negro" (1925); quoted from Barksdale and Kinnamon, *Black Writers of America*, p. 576.
2. W.E.B. Du Bois, "The Forethought," *The Souls of Black Folk* (1903; repr. New York: Bantam Books, 1989), p. xxxi.
3. *Ibid.*, p. 1., first published under the title "Strivings of the Negro People," Atlantic Monthly (August 1897); Gerald Early, "Introduction," *Lure and Loathing: Essays on Race, Identity, and the Ambivalence of Assimilation* (New York: Allen Lane, The Penguin Press, 1993), p. xvii.
4. Du Bois, *The Souls of Black Folk*, pp. 2–3.

WERNER SOLLORS

5. James Weldon Johnson, *The Autobiography of an Ex-Colored Man* (1921; repr. New York: Penguin, 1990), p. 154.

6. The Great Migration from the South to the North gained momentum after World War I and, after a decline during the Great Depression, peaked in the decades from 1940 to 1970 when 4.5 million blacks went north. It created a new distribution of the black population, with a little over half remaining in the South, nearly a fifth each living in the northeast and the Midwest, and nearly a tenth in the West. Even those blacks who remained in or returned to the South, however, moved at a very high rate from rural to urban locations. Thus, whereas in 1890 four-fifths of the black population lived in rural areas and only one-fifth in urban areas, in 1910 more than a quarter (27 percent) lived in cities, and in 1940 nearly half (49 percent). By 2002 the original situation had more than reversed itself, for by then 87.5 percent of African Americans lived in metropolitan areas, and only 12.5 percent in non-metropolitan settings.

7. Alain Locke, ed. *The New Negro* (1925; repr. New York: Atheneum, 1970), pp. xv, 14.

8. *Ibid.*, p. 311; James Weldon Johnson, "Preface," *Book of American Negro Poetry* (New York: Harcourt, Brace and Company, 1922).

9. Richard Wright, *Native Son* (1940; repr. New York: Harper & Row, 1969), last chapter.

10. *Messenger* motto appeared on masthead of each journal issue; Alain Locke, "The New Negro" (1925); quoted from Barksdale and Kinnamon, *Black Writers of America*, p. 577; Jean Toomer, *Cane* (1923; repr. New York: Harper & Row, 1969), p. 149; Langston Hughes, "Dream Boogie," quoted from Barksdale and Kinnamon, *Black Writers of America*, p. 522.

11. Jean Toomer, "The Americans," in Frederik L. Rusch (ed.), *A Jean Toomer Reader: Selected Unpublished writings* (New York: Oxford University Press, 1993), p. 109; Jean Toomer, *Essentials* (1931; repr. Athens and London: University of Georgia Press, 1991), no. xxiv; George Schuyler, "The Negro-Art Hokum," in Henry Louis Gates, Jr. and Nellie Y. McKay (eds.), *The Norton Anthology of African American Literature* (New York: W. W. Norton, 1997), p. 1173.

12. Zora Neale Hurston, "How It Feels to Be Colored Me," in Alice Walker (ed.), *I Love Myself When I Am Laughing...: A Zora Neale Hurston Reader*, ed. Alice Walker (Old Westbury, NY: The Feminist Press, 1979), p. 153.

13. Zora Neale Hurston, "My People!" (1937), in *Dust Tracks on a Road: An Autobiography*, ed. Henry Louis Gates, Jr. (New York: Harper Perennial, 1991), pp. 214, 215; Hurston, "How it Feels to Be Colored Me," p. 153.

14. Marita Bonner, "On Being Young – A Woman – and Colored," in Gates and McKay, eds., *The Norton Anthology of African American Literature*, pp. 1206–7.

15. Walter A. Jackson, *Gunnar Myrdal and America's Conscience: Social Engineering and Racial Liberalism, 1938–1987* (Chapel Hill and London: University of North Carolina Press, 1990), p. 292.

16. Martin Luther King Jr., speech delivered as part of the "March on Washington for Jobs and Freedom," Lincoln Memorial, Washington DC, August 28, 1963. Reprinted as "I Have a Dream," in Melvin I. Urofsky (ed.), *Basic Readings in U. S. Democracy* (Washington: USIA, 1994), pp. 230–2.

17. Ralph Ellison, *The Collected Essays of Ralph Ellison*, ed. John F. Callahan (New York: Modern Library, 1995), p. 339.

18. James Baldwin, "Liberalism and the Negro: A Round-Table Discussion," *Commentary*, 37 (March 1964): 25–42; Baldwin, *The Fire Next Time* (Harmondsworth: Penguin Books, 1965), p. 81.

19. Amiri Baraka, *Home: Social Essays* (New York: Morrow, 1966), p. 65.

20. Ishmael Reed, cited by Henry Louis Gates, Jr., in *The Signifying Monkey: A Theory of Afro-American Literary Citicism* (New York: Oxford University Press, 1988); Early, ed., *Lure and Loathing*, pp. 83–4, 136.

21. Charles Johnson, *Being and Race: Black Writing Since 1970* (Bloomington: Indiana University Press, 1988), p. 20.

22. Thelma Golden, *Freestyle* (New York: Studio Museum in Harlem, 2001; Exhibition catalogue edited by Christine Y. Kim and Franklin Sirmans).

FURTHER READING

Thomas Cripps, *Slow Fade to Black: The Negro in American Film, 1900–1942*, New York: Oxford University Press, 1993.

  Making Movies Black: The Hollywood Message Movie from World War II to the Civil Rights Era, New York: Oxford University Press, 1993.

Henry Louis Gates, Jr. and Kwame Anthony Appiah (eds.), *Africana: The Encyclopedia of the African and African American Experience*, New York: Basic Civitas Books, 1999.

Henry Louis Gates, Jr. and Cornel West, *The African-American Century: How Black Americans Have Shaped Our Country*, New York and London: The Free Press, 2000.

Henry Louis Gates, Jr. and Evelyn Brooks Higginbotham (eds.), *African American Lives*, Oxford and New York: Oxford University Press, 2004.

Evelyn Brooks Higginbotham, (ed.), *The Harvard Guide to African-American History*, Cambridge, MA: Harvard University Press, 2001.

Robin D. G. Kelley and Earl Lewis, *To Make Our World Anew*, vol. II, *A History of African Americans from 1880*, Oxford and New York: Oxford University Press, 2000, 2005.

David Levering Lewis, *W. E. B. Du Bois*, vols. I and II, *Biography of a Race, 1868–1919 and The Fight for Equality and the American Century, 1919–1963*. New York: Henry Holt, 1993, 2000.

Gunnar Myrdal, *An American Dilemma: The Negro Problem and Modern Democracy*, New York and London: Harper & Brothers, 1944.

Jack Salzman, David Lionel Smith, and Cornel West (eds.), *Encyclopedia of African-American Culture and History*, New York: Macmillan, 1996.

US Department of Commerce, Bureau of the Census, The Social and Economic Status of the Black Population in the United States: An Historical View, 1790–1978. Current Population Reports, Special Studies, Series P-23, No. 80. Washington DC: Government Printing Office, 1979.

William Julius Wilson, *The Declining Significance of Race: Blacks and Changing American Institutions*, Chicago: University of Chicago Press, 1980.

9

JAMES KYUNG-JIN LEE

Asian Americans

As the rest of the nation, and indeed the world, prepared to commemorate the one-year anniversary of the September 11 terrorist attacks, a quieter remembrance was taking place in the halls of Asian American Studies programs around the United States. There was a special kind of grief at UCLA's Asian American Studies Center on September 6, 2002, when director Don T. Nakanishi issued a press release announcing the death of Yuji Ichioka on September 1. For more than three decades, Ichioka held the position of Senior Researcher at the Center; he taught the Center's first class shortly after its establishment in 1969. An award-winning author, he was effectively the creator of Asian America in the sense that, in 1968, while a young graduate student at the University of California at Berkeley, he coined the term "Asian American," and helped found the anti-Vietnam war, antiracist student group, the Asian American Political Alliance. The Asian students at San Francisco State College, who along with black, Chicana/o, Native, and leftist white students shut down the school for five months in a historic strike to call for, among many things, the establishment of a School of Ethnic Studies, might opt to identify themselves more as part of the "Third World Liberation Front" than a self-identified racial group,[1] but gradually "Asian American" became the accepted descriptive term.

1968, the year of the "days of rage" in Todd Gitlin's formulation, was pivotal in the development of US cultural politics and political culture. For Gitlin, it marked the beginning of the end of the New Left and its "years of hope," as groups such as Students for a Democratic Society (SDS) degenerated into the ultra-radical Weathermen; likewise, the southern-based civil rights movements led by avowedly nonviolent and mostly Christian-led groups, began to lose legitimacy to Black Power, particularly in poor, urban neighborhoods.[2] Two years earlier, Stokeley Carmichael replaced John Lewis as the head of the Student Nonviolent Coordinating Committee (SNCC), belying its name and effectively making armed resistance an option for the group in its struggle against white supremacy. But whereas Gitlin casts aspersions on the rise of this new militancy, others celebrate 1968 as a watershed moment in the development of historical self-consciousness among non-white peoples living in the United States, of which Asian Americans would be a part.[3] While most historians of this period regard the rise of radicalism as a major reason why the general US public shifted concretely and perhaps inexorably to the political Right, evidenced by Nixon's decisive victory for the "silent majority," the so-called "death" of the New Left took place coterminously with the birth of, among other things, "Asian America," created, debated, and nurtured in classrooms, activist meetings, social service agencies, poetry gatherings, and of course anti-Vietnam war rallies.

That Ichioka developed the term "Asian American" in the midst of protest against the United States' involvement in Vietnam throughout the 1960s is not simply historical coincidence. Something new was happening in the political air late in this decade that demanded new names, new formations, new values. One could argue that opposition to the war hit closer to home for Asian Americans than for other Americans; after all, this was a war fought in an Asian country, in fact one of the poorest, and as many Asian American soldiers returning from Vietnam later testified, it was like a brother fighting a brother.[4] Still, since the turn of the twentieth century, the United States has intervened militarily in Asia on at least three other occasions before Vietnam: the Philippine–American War that followed the United States' conflict with Spain, World War II with the United States fighting Japan in the aftermath of the Pearl Harbor attacks, and the US defense of South Korea against so-called communist "aggression" from the North.[5] In contrast to the 1960s, there were neither mass protests against US military involvement in Asia nor organized resistance to the war effort as would be the case with respect to Vietnam. People of Asian descent living in the United States did not share political convictions, let alone a sense of common interest, during these earlier international conflicts. Vietnam brought together former ethnic antagonists and while this coalition was never an easy one, it was a signal event not least because throughout the twentieth century one could otherwise offer little evidence of such panethnic solidarity.

The key to understanding the development of Asian America in 1968 is the conference at Bandung in 1955. When world leaders of newly decolonized nations from Africa and Asia gathered in Indonesia to further the strategy of "non-alignment" in the context of the US and Soviet scramble for world influence, they evidenced and prompted a sense of shared purpose, even if this solidarity was not always adhered to. Yet if the twenty-nine nations represented at Bandung would eventually fall victim to a de facto dependence on the former colonial powers (neo-colonialism), the official push to decolonization propelled by the chaos of World War II simultaneously brought new hopes for an expansion of social and political freedom as well as new anxieties and vulnerabilities. Bandung in 1955 led directly to the Non-aligned Movement of 1961, still in existence today. Despite the fact that China's invasion of India dashed any hope of the "Third World" forming a significant bloc against, in particular, western capitalist encroachment, the visual representation of non-white peoples joining together was as indelible as the tragedy of the political ineffectiveness of this movement for the next half-century.

The barest traces of cross-racial and panethnic solidarity emerge in John Okada's searing novel, *No-No Boy* (1957), about the aftermath of a post-World War II Seattle Japanese American community coming to terms with the collective trauma of the Internment.[6] Ichiro, the protagonist and representative "no-no boy" – those Japanese American men who refused both to serve in the US armed forces and pledge loyalty to the United States while they and their families remained incarcerated in the makeshift camps set up by the War Relocation Authority during the war – suffers a double dilemma: on the one hand, he is a victim of the ire of fellow Nisei (second-generation, US-born Japanese Americans) who view him as a "Jap" traitor to the community for refusing, unlike them, to fight for the United States; on the other, his pro-Japanese mother, convinced that Japan has won the war and that talk of US victory is mere propaganda, makes Ichiro's life miserable by celebrating the very decisions that turn him into a social pariah.

Beyond that, *No-No Boy* is the story of damaged masculinities: Ichiro's friend and sole confidant, Kenji, who suffers a debilitating wound and eventually dies, is a physical manifestation of Ichiro's emotional scars. Together, they form Okada's chiasmic mirroring of the social death that the Internment produced for Japanese Americans, those state-sanctioned vulnerabilities which left a residue of alienation, frustration, and despair pervading the community.[7] Only glimmers of hope penetrate the sad veil of truncated lives. The first such, which takes place at the end of *No-No Boy*, is a brief exchange between Ichiro and Rabbit, a black shoeshiner who, when realizing that Ichiro is a no-no boy, exclaims, "Good boy. If they had come for me, I would of told them where to shove their stinking uniform too."[8] Juxtaposed to the first scene of the story, in which some black men taunt Ichiro with cat-calls of "Jap-boy" and "Go back to Tokyo" at a bus depot, this later encounter with Rabbit briefly invites a new kind of social imagination such as that offered by Bandung, even if that was barely beginning to seep into the larger consciousness of US people of color.[9] In a more radical reading, this brief instance of solace through shared anger at injustices against Japanese Americans and blacks is that "insinuation of promise" that Ichiro begins to feel by the novel's end.

But another possibility that parallels this hope or "insinuation" undercuts *No-No Boy's* uneven presentation of "horizontal assimilation," and although posed as a social avenue, this second option limits and frames the vocabulary of legitimate postwar identity to one of assimilation along vertical, conventional lines.[10] In the middle of the novel, Emi, Ichiro's on-and-off girlfriend and the moral, albeit ineffectual, figure of the story suggests an emotional response to the protagonist's social and political alienation:

> This is a big country with a big heart. There's room here for all kinds of people . . . Make believe you're singing "The Star-Spangled Banner" and see the color guard march out on the stage and say the pledge of allegiance with all the other boys and girls. You'll get that feeling flooding into your chest and making you want to shout with glory. It might even make you feel like crying. That's how you've got to feel, so big that the bigness seems to want to bust out, and then you'll understand why it is that your mistake was no bigger than the mistake your country made.[11]

The key to alleviating racial injury, according to Emi, is to consent to a deeper "feeling" of belonging via Americanism. To acknowledge that the United States made a mistake in interning Japanese Americans and the no-no boy Ichiro in demonstrating "disloyalty" by refusing to fight, Emi suggests, is to facilitate a movement away from such a negative dialectic. But lurking beneath Emi's optimism is a more foundational narrative of terror that turns suggestion into imperative: "that's how you've got to feel." Okada's barely concealed satire in this passage masks a deeper pain at an often unspoken complicity with an Americanism which requires assent to white supremacy in order to survive.

This strain of Americanism, whose voluntary embrace by Asian Americans conceals a longer story of coercion, had its roots earlier in the century. After all, even the "disloyal" Ichiro is a *de jure* US citizen, since the Supreme Court decision of *Wong Kim Ark v. U.S.* in 1898 determined that persons born on soil under US sovereignty were guaranteed constitutional rights to citizenship. But for the generation of Asians residing in the United States earlier in the twentieth century, most of them immigrants, citizenship rights served as a sad site of racial struggle rather than a point from which to begin. The 1790 Naturalization Act, passed by Congress around the same time as the establishment of the Bill of Rights, laid bare the racial politics that would inhere in the struggle for citizenship, political and beyond, by determining that naturalized citizenship would only be granted to "free white persons." The Fourteenth Amendment, passed in the aftermath of the US Civil War, eight decades after this first naturalization law, extended citizenship rights to the nation's newly emancipated slaves, those of "African nativity." The promise of freedom and opportunity for African Americans that the post-Civil War amendments seemed to warrant, however, would be dashed by post-Reconstruction racial terror in the South and elsewhere, the development of segregation as a preferred mode of social organization, the ongoing disenfranchisement of black voters, and the economic pressures evidenced by the sharecropping systems.

But coterminous with the development of at least legal guarantees of citizenship rights to African Americans were corresponding ambiguities with regard to the United States's newest arrivals: Asians, first Chinese but later Japanese, Filipinos, Koreans, and South Asians. In the nineteenth century, the Chinese bore the brunt of exclusion and racist treatment. Cities like San Francisco passed ordinances that targeted, in practice if not in name, Chinese laundrymen. Federal exclusion laws aimed at the Chinese, from 1882 onward, paved the way for the exclusion of other groups: by 1917, the United States would bar entry to its shores to those from the "Asiatic" region; in 1924, the National Origins Act established a quota based on existing racial demographics in the United States, effectively shutting down immigration not only from Asia but also from then more obscure southern and eastern European regions.[12]

Immigration law targeting one group for exclusion could expand its parameters when expedient. Less certain, however, was the status of those already living in the United States. In 1922 and 1923, two men attempting to gain naturalized citizenship had their cases heard in the US Supreme Court. The first was a Japanese immigrant, Takao Ozawa, who spent much of his life in the United States accumulating all the necessary cultural signs of his "Americanness" before making his appeal in the courts. Schooled at both Berkeley High School and the University of California at Berkeley, Ozawa made English the primary language spoken at home, attended American churches, and sent his children to American schools. Unlike most other Issei at the time, he refused to register his children with the local Japanese consulate. This distancing from the Japanese American community was further enhanced, Ozawa's lawyers argued, by his disavowal of any relationship with other Asian groups.

Unlike the Chinese, whose communities, as a result of earlier exclusion laws which prevented the immigration of women, were mainly "bachelor," the Japanese enjoyed greater possibilities of assimilating into dominant US culture, with cohesive, nuclear families and greater cultural alignment with whites. "That he was well qualified by character and education for citizenship is conceded," began the Supreme Court decision. Ozawa's lawyers, indeed, took great pains to align him with the white world. In addition to evidence of his cultural assimilation, they noted that Ozawa's skin tone was lighter than, say, "swarthy" Europeans who had already attained citizenship under the auspices of Naturalization Acts from 1790 to 1906, which granted citizenship rights to "white persons." While the Fourteenth Amendment extended citizenship to persons of "African nativity," Ozawa's lawyers' case hinged around his proximity to his "white" status. The court, while acknowledging that Ozawa demonstrated the accouterments of citizenship, based its decision on the correspondence between whiteness and Caucasian identity. Although such correspondence did not entirely "dispose" of the problem of racial ambiguity, the connection was sufficient for the court to determine that "[Ozawa] . . . is clearly of a race which is not Caucasian and therefore belongs entirely outside the zone on the negative side."[13]

Less than six months later, Bhagat Singh Thind, an immigrant from India, tried to gain citizenship on the same grounds proscribed in the case of Ozawa's appeal. Like Ozawa, Thind attended the University of California at Berkeley and, when the United States entered the "Great War" in 1917, joined the Army and was honorably discharged in 1918. The conundrum of Thind's case centered on the question of whether, as a "high caste Hindu [sic] of full Indian blood" he was racially white. As in Ozawa's case, the court's decision turned on the ruling that, "If the applicant is a white person within the meaning of this section he is entitled to naturalization; otherwise not." Remarkably, Justice George Sutherland, himself an immigrant from England and a naturalized US citizen, and who wrote the opinion for both the Ozawa and Thind cases, followed the previous statement with the following: "The conclusion that the phrase 'white persons' and the word 'Caucasian' are synonymous does not end the matter." Thind's lawyers had argued that, as a high-caste Indian, he could trace linguistic, physical, and therefore racial lineage to "Aryan" ancestry, which would then align him with Europeans or "Caucasians." Thind's case added to this phenotypical claim to whiteness a different kind of disavowal from Ozawa's, but no less premised on white supremacist logic. As his lawyers suggested, "The high-caste Hindu regards the aboriginal Indian Mongoloid in the same manner as the American regards the Negro, speaking from a matrimonial standpoint." This claim of Thind's revulsion with respect to the "lower races," however, was not enough for the court, and Sutherland, in a striking reversal of racial logic, based the decision not to grant citizenship on racial "common sense":

What we now hold is that the words "free white persons" are words of common speech, to be interpreted in accordance with the understanding of the common man, synonymous with the word "Caucasian" only as that word is popularly understood. As so understood and used, whatever may be the speculations of the ethnologist, it does not include the body of people to whom the appellee belongs . . . It is very far from our thought to suggest the slightest question of racial superiority or inferiority. What we suggest is merely racial difference, and it is of such character and extent that the great body of our people instinctively recognize it and reject the thought of assimilation.[14]

These two unanimous decisions, that effectively prevented Asians from gaining citizenship for the next two decades, and which would only be modified piecemeal during and following World War II, had an immediate effect on communities, particularly on the west coast where the majority of Asians resided. Alien Land Laws passed in California, Oregon, and Washington, precluded "aliens ineligible for citizenship" from owning property; likewise the Cable Act of 1922 voided a white woman's citizenship if she were to marry such an "alien." More importantly, the Ozawa and Thind cases revealed the anxious, even agonizing, relationship, for Asian Americans, between culture and assimilation, rebellion and complicity, challenge to white supremacy and the tricky negotiations to reap racism's rewards.

Later, during World War II, Chinese and Korean Americans, for fear of being mistaken for Japanese, sought to distance themselves from a community utterly uprooted and displaced into the US heartland. Hisaye Yamamoto's postwar story "Wilshire Bus" (1950) chronicles a bus ride that her protagonist takes along a busy street, during which she witnesses a white man berating a Chinese couple and silently expresses relief that she was not targeted.[15] This moment of disavowal, however, provokes shame in Esther Kuriowa, a Nisei, who remembers that during the war a Korean man in Los Angeles wore a button that read "I Am Korean." Indeed, the fear of violence during the war was palpable: when Harry Kitano, one of the first professors in Asian American Studies, left the Topaz internment camp as a teenager in 1944, he took his trombone with him and played in all-white, segregated swing bands, but only after he officially registered his name with the local musicians union as "Harry Lee."

For Mike Masaoka, the twenty-five-year-old National Secretary of the Japanese American Citizens' League (JACL) – which became the de facto representative organization for Japanese Americans during Internment – loyalty meant sacrifice. In testimony to the US Senate in May 1941, he insisted on his pride at being an "American *citizen* of Japanese ancestry" (my emphasis). Later, in February 1942, as the Roosevelt administration made preparations for the mass incarceration of Japanese Americans, Masaoka spoke to a House Select Committee on National Defense Migration. The following exchange between Alabama Congressman John Sparkman and Masaoka indicates the extent of the sacrifices that Japanese Americans would be prepared to bear in order to brandish their Americanness:

REP. SPARKMAN: But in the event the evacuation is deemed necessary by those having charge of the defenses, as loyal Americans you are willing to prove your loyalty by cooperating?

MR. MASAOKA: Yes. I think it should be. . .

REP. SPARKMAN (INTERPOSING): Even at a sacrifice?

MR. MASAOKA: Oh, yes; definitely. I think that all of us are called upon to make sacrifices. I think that we will be called upon to make greater sacrifices than any others. But I think sincerely, if the military say "Move Out," we will be glad to move, because we recognize that even behind evacuation there is not just national security but also a thought as to our own welfare and security because we may be subject to mob violence and otherwise if we are permitted to remain.[16]

Mike Masaoka would never apologize for his active support of Internment as a sign of Japanese American loyalty, nor did he ever consider those men who resisted the draft, and were subsequently imprisoned at Tule Lake camp, equally "loyal" to their American consciences. He wanted them charged with sedition. Indeed, for the contemporary JACL, the divisions over *how* one demonstrated one's Americanness during World War II remain an area of sensitivity. When, recently, the national JACL leadership formally recognized the "no-no boys" as legitimately exercising their constitutional rights against mass injustice, a group of Japanese American veterans walked out of the meeting in protest. No wonder that, even in 1957, Okada's novel was so controversial that the 1,500 copies printed during *No-No Boy*'s first run never sold out.[17]

Thus, caught between a legacy of white supremacy enshrined in US legal narratives, and the pressure of Americanism which required a declaration of allegiance in the context of war, Asian Americans often felt compelled to engage in processes of dis-identification with one another as well as with other US people of color. Yet the first half of the twentieth century provides ghostly presences of the kind of alternative recognition that Bandung had proposed. Provisional and often unprogrammatic moments of cross-racial solidarity offered the traces of different possibilities than those proposed by the imperative of Americanism. In February 1903, 500 Japanese and 200 Mexican sugar beet workers in Oxnard, California formed the Japanese Mexican Labor Association (JMLA) and struck against the Oxnard brothers'

American Beet Sugar Company and their labor contractor, the Western Agricultural Contracting Company (WACC), itself headed by Japanese Inose Inosuke. After a month, violence erupted at the picket line on March 23, during which a Mexican worker was killed; this episode forced WACC to concede to the JMLA's demands for better pay and the abolition of an unfair subcontracting system. By this point, the union had grown to 1,200 workers, many of them emboldened into a militancy that outstripped the leaders' vision. Indeed, more significant than the strike itself was the aftermath. Following this initial victory, the secretary of the Mexican branch, J.M. Lizarras, applied for membership in the American Federation of Labor (AFL), the longtime national union that represented the vast majority of craft workers in the United States.

Impressed by the Oxnard victory, AFL president Samuel Gompers replied that he would indeed let the Mexican sugar beet workers join the AFL, provided that the "union must guarantee that it will under no circumstances accept membership of any Chinese or Japanese." Well known for his un-wavering belief in the "unassimilability" of Asians in the United States, Gompers in effect invited the Mexican workers to join the broader labor movement by sacrificing their Japanese compatriots. Lizarras's response is all the more remarkable, considering the convention of racial disidentifica-tion during the early twentieth century: "We are going to stand by men who stood by us in the long, hard fight ended in a victory over the enemy."[18] Decades later, Oxnard would continue to symbolize not so much US labor's consistent failure in overcoming its racist character, as one of the first moments that two racialized groups sought recognition and affirmation in and through one another, not for the approval of whites or through appeals to white supremacy.

Six years after the Oxnard strike, in 1909, Chinese–English writer Edith Eaton, whose pen name was Sui Sin Far, published an essay that served as a kind of episodic memoir. Titled "Leaves from the Mental Portfolio of an Eurasian," this story included moments during her childhood when she was targeted for being Chinese, as well as corresponding scenes of advocacy for Chinese people in the United States. In one vignette, situated in an unnamed Caribbean country (through her biography, we know that she is talking about Jamaica), Eaton relates her experience of meeting with white admin-istrators who instruct her that "It is not necessary to thank a black person [one of the servants of the household] for service." Eaton does not relate a response to this comment, but she does reflect on her particular set of social options that would either enable her to benefit from white privilege or identify in a different way. Confronting her seeming ability to look down upon the black "Ham people" (the pseudo-theological theory that blacks derived from the cursed son of Noah), Eaton, at least in her writing, asserts her difference and casts ironic light on her white hosts: "Occasionally an Englishman will warn me against the 'brown boys' of the island, little dreaming that I too am of the 'brown people' of the earth."[19] This passage exudes paradox: on the one hand, Eaton's ability to "hide" her "brown-ness" enables her passage into the rooms of white privilege and facilitates voluntary racial identification in a space that would otherwise read her as white; on the other hand, the claim to racial kinship with black Jamaicans works against the vertical assimilation that we see in the cases of Ozawa and Thind. For some contemporary readers, Eaton's claim of identification with black people smacks of social gospel sentimentalism. In 1909, how-ever, it was also a stance against scientific and religious understandings of racial purity and exclusion. Eaton's physiological biraciality and political allegiance to Chinese and blacks is testament to more fluid and alternative social choices that foreshadow the more coherent narratives of solidarity that would crystallize in the 1960s.[20]

At the end of "Leaves," Eaton relays the advice from some people to "trade" or benefit from her nationality, that is, to turn her Chinese cultural upbringing into commodity and generate money from being a "native" expert. It is a barely veiled critique of the career that her sister, Winifred Eaton, enjoyed into the 1920s. Adopting the pen name of Onoto Watanna, Winifred Eaton spent much of her career posing as a full-blooded Japanese, and wrote several successful romances in the early twentieth century. In contrast to Edith, Winifred Eaton's writing generated significant amounts of money, in part a consequence of the turn-of-the-century fascination with *japonisme*, concurrent with prevailing anti-Chinese sentiment in the United States. She has been long regarded as a figure of complicity, but scholars have recently turned attention to the extent to which Eaton's "Japanese romances" play on dominant racial ideologies by foregrounding the perfor-mativity of any racial identity. Certainly, her novel *The Heart of Hyacinth* (1903) highlights, as Dominika Ferens puts it, the "decoupling" of race and culture by featuring a white girl who, raised by a Japanese woman, believes herself to be wholly Japanese.[21] Challenging, at least provisionally, the idea that biology fixed race, which in turn produced distinct and discreet cultures or civilizations, Eaton's protagonist Hyacinth spends much of the novel clashing with the agents of her biological American father, who believe that she must return to the United States, where she rightfully belongs. As a romance written during the era of anti-miscegenation laws, Eaton's novel carefully resolves the social chaos produced by racial fluidity: Hyacinth marries her stepbrother Koma who, though Japanese by blood, is thor-oughly western in demeanor and appearance. The two remain in Japan, perhaps a conscious decision on Eaton's part to leave the biologically interracial couple in the fantasy of Japan as opposed to the harsh realities of interracial proscription in the United States. As an indictment of western assumptions of inherent cultural superiority and a coded treatise on culture against race, hybridity over purity, *The Heart of Hyacinth*'s claims are less strident than Edith Eaton's writings advocating Chinese American civil rights, but the novel's underlying move toward highlighting the fiction of racial identity through performance prefigures the current scholarly and creative interest in, to use the title of Lisa Lowe's now seminal essay, "heterogeneity, hybridity, and multiplicity."[22]

Whether in the movements that bring differentially racialized groups together in particular times and spaces, or in the creative narratives that expose the fictions of racial identity, the performance of Asian American-ness creates moments of crisis that suggest Raymond Williams's idea of "emergent" cultural practices. These new structures of feeling militate against more dominant, legible narratives of belonging and identity, and therein lies the tension that brought Asian Americans into the streets of US cities in the 1960s, marching against US imperialism by simultaneously claiming themselves as "Americans." But even these moments, with the glimmer of the new, are fettered by other contradictions that limit social imagination. At the height of rebellion in the late 1960s, despite the revolutionary showdown at the Stonewall Bar in New York that ushered in the gay and lesbian movement, the connections between the Asian American struggle against racism at home and abroad could not be made with gay liberation. Indeed, for many Asian American gays and lesbians active in antiwar, antiracist, community-based work, sexuality remained a limited political horizon, with their leftist comrades citing the Soviet and Maoist dictum that homosexuality signaled western, bourgeois decadence. Not-withstanding brief episodes in the 1970s during which some Asian Americans did speak out for Asian and gay liberation as corresponding struggles, as Dan Tsang has documented recently, the emergence of Asian American queer identity as legible, oppositional, and constitutive only received critical attention in the last two decades of the twentieth century.[23] Eric Wat, in his oral history of Asian American gay men and lesbians, points out that for many queer Asian Americans, the contradiction displayed by their col-leagues, who railed against racism while keeping intact and "natural" heterosexual privilege in both social practices and homophobic rhetoric, would render the liberationist ethos of the "Movement" partial at best, and at worst, a hypocritical failure.[24]

Asian American women, too, would suffer similar marginalization; like the queer Asian American struggle, feminism was often equated with and seen as a capitulation to white, bourgeois values. Asian American women were denounced as traitors if they aired the "dirty laundry" of sexism within the broader community, and like other US women of color, Asian American feminists bore the burden of what early Asian American scholars would refer to as the "double" or "triple jeopardy" of racial, gender, and class oppression. Intersectional identity and political formation would take longer than hoped.

Nowhere does the carving of Asian American culture as definitely masculine and straight emerge more forcefully than in the seminal essay "Fifty Years of Our Whole Voice," the introductory piece that accompanied one of the first anthologies of Asian American literature. The introduction to *Aiiieeeee! An Anthology of Asian American Writers* (1974) is a brash, unapologetic rejection of the conventional conceptions of Asian American identity and its attendant culture during this period. Challenging primarily the notion that Asian Americans suffered from a "dual identity" complex, which above all suggested for the editors an exclusivist notion of "Asian" cultures in conflict with "American" (read: white) values, the *Aiiieeeee!* editors lash out, first, at the legacy of white racism that Asian Americans have suffered historically, and then at their fellow Asian Americans who reinforce and transmit in their writing the "dual identity" thesis and, therefore, become emblems of "white racism's only success." After offering examples of Asian American writers who mirror "white standards" and those few exemplars who refuse, and through this negation form the possibility of an actual Asian American voice, the essay ends with what has become its most infamous statement on the confluence of language, culture, race, gender, and sexuality:

> Language is the medium of culture and the people's sensibility, including the style of manhood. Language coheres the people into a community by organizing and codifying the symbols of the people's common experience. Stunt the tongue and you have lopped off the culture and sensibility. On the simplest level, a man in any culture speaks for himself. Without a language of his own, he no longer is a man.[25]

Clearly influenced by the literary manifestos of the Black Arts movement some ten years earlier, "Fifty Years of Our Whole Voice" carries along with the radical claim for an alternative literary tradition, at once aesthetic and political, the assertion that the writing must also be manly. Notwithstanding the convention during this period of using "manhood" and "man" to represent the whole of a community, the castration metaphors that liken tongue with penis, phallus, and culture, link the "language" of culture to positions of masculinity. For the next quarter century, Frank Chin – one of the editors and a well-regarded writer in his own right – would crusade against "fake" Asian American writers and direct most of his anger at women. Perhaps unintentionally, the fact that the *Aiiieeeee!* editors, and Chin in particular, make this alignment between an oppositional Asian American culture and masculinity, and continue to disparage "feminine" works written primarily by women, has calcified the debate along gender lines.

Of course, Asian American feminists and others have responded forcefully, with essays and articles that assert that a feminist vision is not only compatible with Asian American identity, but brings greater, more critical insight to the question of culture, race, and power. So compelling have been the gender and queer studies critiques of Asian American culture that by the 1990s an analysis of any cultural work would be regarded as impoverished and partial if it did not see gender and sexuality as constitutive, not additive, to a study of race and culture. But this crucial development has come at a price. It has rendered the formative "movement" period in Asian American history, begun in 1968 and continued throughout the 1970s, "cultural nationalist," a term that implies a prejudice for masculinist, homophobic, and other narrow definitions of Asian American identity. Certainly, the underpinnings of the *Aiiieeeee!* introduction and Chin's continuation of a particular thread from that essay invite legitimate criticism. However, merely to dismiss them buries a more complex history.

First, the 1974 essay primarily attacked writers such as Jade Snow Wong and Daniel Okimoto, two writers who won mainstream acclaim by tacitly accepting a benign Americanism through which Asian Americans could enter that mainstream. Indeed, Wong's autobiography *Fifth Chinese Daughter* (1945) was so well regarded by US government officials that by 1953 it had been translated into numerous languages while the State Department sent her on a four-month tour of Asia to propagandize for America's treatment of its racial minorities. Likewise, Okimoto's autobiography *An American in Disguise* (1971), though sympathetic to the Civil Rights and even Black Power movements of the previous decade, claims an affinity between Japanese American and white American identity to the point that Okimoto, as narrator, "finds" himself by marrying a white woman by the end of the narrative. Chin and the other *Aiiieeeee!* writers were repelled by what they saw as an accommodation to mainstream values in the context of the struggles of other Asian Americans to highlight the contradictions between American claims to democracy and its imperial march through Asia.

Second, the idea of "cultural nationalism" belies the fragmentation of the Asian American demography, a historical phenomenon with which

Asian Americans continue to grapple today. In 1965, Congress passed and President Johnson enacted into law the most sweeping change in US immigration policy since the racially based 1924 National Origins Act. The Hart–Cellar Immigration and Naturalization Act rid itself of quotas based on nationality and proposed the selection of immigrants by employment preference and need, family reunification, and flight from communist countries. This immigration law has utterly transformed the landscape of the United States, especially with regard to its changing racial and ethnic composition, and coincided with the Civil Rights Act of 1964 and the Voting Rights Act of 1965, the two laws that capped the southern-based, Christian-led civil rights struggle of the 1950s and 1960s. It is in this context that the United States encountered a new cultural icon: formerly a national menace, the Asian in 1966 suddenly transmogrified into a model.

Two feature stories – one published in January in the *New York Times* and entitled "Success Story: Japanese-American Style," the other printed in December of the same year in *U.S. News and World Report*, called "Success Story of One Minority Group in the US" about Chinese Americans – proffered a new image of Asian Americans, who, in overcoming bitter racial discrimination, displayed social practices worthy of general American praise. Asian Americans, these articles suggested, with their low crime rates, high educational attainment, and, most importantly, little need for governmental welfare programs, were emerging as "model minorities," in stark contrast to the claims of racial injury and the need for state action from other communities of color. In fact, the second story on Chinese Americans makes the comparison explicit: "At a time when it is being proposed that hundreds of billions of dollars be spent to uplift Negroes and other minorities, the nation's 300,000 Chinese Americans are moving ahead on their own, with no help from anyone else."[26] A barely concealed swipe at President Johnson's "War on Poverty," the biggest expansion of social welfare since the New Deal, and a more muted attack on the growing influence of the Black Power movement, these articles set up a coherent political and social trajectory for Asian Americans.[27] This definitively aligned Asian Americans with the dominant social order, in contrast to the forces of rebellion and reform, and offered them a claim to full citizenship with the proviso that they disavow any kinship with the "other minorities."

It is this transformation of the Asian from national menace to ideal model that characterizes the ambivalent story of Asian Americans in the twentieth century. The "model minority" has re-emerged in the 1980s and 1990s, revised to appeal to an idea of multiculturalism that is no less damning of poor, "undeserving" blacks, especially in the wake of the Los Angeles uprisings of 1992, which will forever be visualized as a conflict between Korean storeowners "defending" their property and black and brown looters.[28] Asian American parents in San Francisco and some public figures have used the educational success of wealthy Asian American (and some educationally exceptional and materially poor) students to attack affirmative action and other redistributive programs in public services. In the twenty-first century, and particularly in the aftermath of the September 11 events in 2001, this Asian American neoconservatism has moved beyond domestic policy and into international affairs. Men such as Viet Dinh, former Assistant Attorney General of President George W. Bush's administration, helped coauthor the Patriot Act, a law that granted governmental agencies broad power to investigate, survey, and detain without due process. On the west coast, University of California law professor John Yoo has made the case that in the realm of international law in the age of terrorism, the United States is not subject to the United Nations-ratified Geneva Conventions. To this extent, Yoo asserts, there are cases in which torture can be legally sanctioned as a legitimate tool in the United States' war arsenal, and the indefinite detention of prisoners, now dubbed enemy combatants, upheld. The alignment of Asian American neoconservatives to the rightist drift in US political culture in the last two decades has won a substantial, if not universal, following within Asian American communities. Vietnamese Americans, for example, whose mostly refugee population suffered first hand the war that brought other Asian Americans to mass protest in the 1960s, are overwhelmingly supportive of conservative Republican candidates, the effects of the perceived correspondence between conservatism and anti-communism.[29]

Indeed, as some have suggested that the increasing Asian American presence in intellectual and popular culture will actually transform what it means to be "white" in twenty-first century America, the forces of capitalist globalization and the attendant transnationalism of both goods and people put greater pressure on the term Asian "American."[30] Intellectuals from the Indian subcontinent have engaged in vigorous debate amongst themselves and with other Asian American scholars and, armed with the powerful discourse of postcolonial theory, have turned to questions of diaspora and collective nostalgia as critical categories through which to explore community formation.[31] The emergence of South Asian American Studies has brought newfound attention to the complexity of Asian American belonging: for even as the South Asian presence has a century-long history since the arrival of mostly Punjabi Sikhs in California, this historiography has been largely and perhaps necessarily "forgotten" by more recent, professional, and wealthy South Asians from the post-1965 era.[32] Correspondingly, there are some communities categorized by the US Census Bureau as Asian American that remain virtually unorganized and out of mainstream sight except when criminalized: Cambodian Americans, for example, suffer unemployment rates in places like Long Beach, California, as high as 40 percent, and make their way into American consciousness through their popular demonization as gang members. In Hawaii, the myth of multiculturalism that has pervaded the islands because of its Asian majority has been dispelled by calls from Native Hawaiians who argue that "Asian Americans" constitute nothing less than the latest wave of colonial settlers to impose their power on the sovereign rights of its indigenous peoples.[33]

At a moment when Asian Americans have enjoyed visibility in ways unimaginable earlier in the twentieth century – cultural, social, economic – the political foundations that underwrote the term in 1968 have, then, been put into significant crisis. No longer, for example, are Asian American writers merely "ethnic" representatives; indeed, among the current crop of highly-touted *American* writers a significant number are of Asian descent. Chang-rae Lee's protagonist in the author's debut novel, *Native Speaker* (1995), does not suffer alienation from American culture, but rather struggles because his English is *too* perfect, his capacity to understand the nuances of America's contradictions too easy to coopt. Henry, Lee's narrator, is a self-conscious "model minority," a far cry from the Asian American figure Ichioka imagined in 1968, but in gaining a kind of aptitude that allows him safe travel across the social spectrum in New York City, Henry loses the language that is at once the privilege and cost of assimilation: "My ugly immigrant's truth . . . is that I have exploited my own, and those others who can be exploited . . . Here is all of my American education."[34]

For those who have enjoyed the social rewards that stemmed from the post-1965 transformations in the United States, it has never been easier to "belong," but the imperative remains. Jhumpa Lahiri's protagonist, in the final story of her Pulitzer Prize-winning *The Interpreter of Maladies* (1999), meditates on his life of immigration and settlement, from Bengal to Boston via London. The sheer ordinariness of his experience becomes itself an epic tale of continents coming together: "there are times when it is beyond my imagination." Also beyond his imagination, however, and perhaps necessarily so, are those working-class Bengalis he must leave behind in London.[35] Combine this specific literary forgetting with the larger contemporary class stratification of many Asian American communities – the extremely poor at one end and the very wealthy at the other – and much remains beyond the imagination of these newly minted Asian American paragons of American culture. It is perhaps for this reason that Vijay Prashad cleverly asks of Asian

Americans, in a rhetorical reversal of W. E. B. DuBois's query: "How does it feel to be a solution?"[36] The answer, of course, is not simple at all; there is, after all, complexity in complicity. So long branded America's "problem," it is thus not surprising that a willful forgetfulness by Asian Americans offers provisional, even if fraught, satisfaction.

While complicity and crisis have generated new complexities for Asian American culture, however, making definitions elusive, even impossible, the term continues to generate new meanings. Never before have so many Asian Americans pieced together the differential histories with other communities of color both through popular culture and in direct political action. Korean American activists in Los Angeles have attacked the exploitation of mostly Mexican and Central American workers by Korean-owned businesses, and have waged a decade-long campaign to advocate workers' rights. Earlier in the 1970s and 1980s, Japanese Americans rejected municipal plans to redevelop downtown areas by inviting Japanese corporate capital, in effect turning working-class residential neighborhoods into spaces attractive to out-of-town commerce and tourism, and tried to envision what a "Japanese American" community as an interracial space might mean.[37]

Cross-racial imaginations challenge and transform what it means to be Asian American. South Asian Americans "remix" hip-hop-infused bhangra dance parties into what one scholar has referred to as a "queer diaspora," transforming older internationalisms into a new, if unlikely, form of solidarity.[38] These alternative formations, at the very least, stand in clear contrast to the seemingly inexorable march of Asian Americans into the domain of neoconservative "whiteness." Indeed, within the short history of Asian American complicity and complexity there remains an Asian American culture, perhaps nothing more than a subcultural presence, which keeps alive the conviction that stirred Yuji Ichioka to think of calling himself something new and different.

NOTES

1. See Karen Umemoto, "'On Strike!' San Francisco State College Strike, 1968–9: The Role of Asian American Students," *Amerasia*, 15,1 (1989): 3–41.
2. Todd Gitlin, *The Sixties: Years of Hope, Days of Rage* (New York: Bantam, 1987).
3. Max Elbaum, *Revolution in the Air: Sixties Radicals Turn to Lenin, Mao, and Che* (New York: Verso, 2003); Glenn Omatsu, "The 'Four Prisons' and the Movements of Liberation: Asian American Activism from the 1960s to the 1990s," in Karing Aguilar-San Juan (ed.), *The State of Asian America: Activism and Resistance in the 1990s* (Boston: South End, 1994), pp. 19–69.

4. *Gidra*, a Los Angeles-based, Asian American "activist" newspaper, which ran from 1969 until 1974, ran several articles that exploited the contradiction of an Asian American soldier fighting Vietnamese, "fellow" Asians. It also culled testimony from veterans traumatized by their participation. See especially the May 1972 issue.

5. The most comprehensive account of the origins of the Korean conflict continues to be Bruce Cumings, *The Origins of the Korean War*, 2 vols. (Princeton, NJ: Princeton University Press, 1981, 1984).

6. John Okada, *No-No Boy* (Seattle: University of Washington Press, 1978).

7. This definition of racism, as the "state-sanctioned and/or extra-legal production of group differentiated vulnerabilities to hasten premature death," comes from Ruth Wilson Gilmore, "Race and Globalization," in R. J. Johnston, Peter J. Taylor, and Michael J. Watts (eds.), *Geographies of Social change* (Malden, MA: Blackwell, 2002), pp. 261–74.

8. Okada, *No-No Boy*, p. 238.

9. Numerous historical examples serve to heighten such cross-racial dreaming. Here are two: see George Lipsitz, "'Frantic to Join . . . the Japanese Army': Beyond the Black–White Binary," *The Possessive Investment in Whiteness: How White People Profit From Identity Politics* (Philadelphia: Temple University Press, 1998), pp. 184–210; Robin D. G. Kelley, "'Roaring From the East': Third World Dreaming," *Freedom Dreams: The Black Radical Imagination* (Boston: Beacon Press, 2003), pp. 60–109.

10. "Horizontal assimilation" is a term coined by Vijay Prashad in *Everybody Was Kung Fu Fighting: Afro-Asian Connections and the Myth of Cultural Purity* (Boston: Beacon Press, 2002).

11. Okada, *No-No Boy*, pp. 95–6.

12. Many of these historical documents have been compiled in Franklin Od (ed.), *The Columbia Documentary History of the Asian American Experience* (New York: Columbia University Press, 2002).

13. U.S. v. Takao Ozawa, 260 U.S. 178 (1922).

14. U.S. v. Bhagat Singh Thind, 261 U.S. 204 (1923).

15. Hisaye Yamamoto, *Seventeen Syllables and Other Stories*, rev. ed. (New Brunswick, NJ: Rutgers University Press, 2001), pp. 34–8.

16. *Hearings Before the Committee Investigating National Deleuse Migration*, Part 29, February 21 and 23, 1942 (Washington DC: Government Printing Office, 1942), pp. 11137–48.

17. And, thinking that the Japanese American community rejected his work, Okada never published his second novel. See Jinqi Ling, *Narrating Nationalisms: Ideology and Form in Asian American Literature* (New York: Oxford University Press, 1998), pp. 31–52.

18. Tomás Almagure, *Racial Fault Lines: The Historical Origins of White Supremacy in California* (Berkeley: University of Califoria Press, 1994), pp. 201–2.

19. Sui Sin Far (Edith Eaton), *Mrs. Spring Fragrance and Other Stories*, ed. Amy Ling and Annette White-Parks (Urbana, IL: University of Illinois Press, 1995), pp. 218–230.

20. For a compelling overview of the "Third World Left" *after* 1968, see Laura Pulido, "Race, Class, and Political Activism: Black, Chicana/o, and Japanese-American Leftists in Southern California, 1968–1978," *Antipode*, 34,4 (2002): 762–88.

21. Onoto Watanna (Winnifred Eaton), *The Heart of Hyacinth*, intro. Samini Namji (Seattle: University of Washington Press, 2000); Dominika Ferens, *Edith and Winnifred Eaton: Chinatown Missions and Japanese Romances* (Urbana, IL: University of Illinois Press, 2002).

22. Lisa Lowe, *Immigrant Acts* (Durham, NC: Duke University Press, 1996), pp. 60–83.

23. Daniel C. Tsang, "Slicing Silence: Asian Progressives Come Out," in Steve Louie and Glenn Omatsu (eds.), *Asian Americans: The Movement and the Moment* (Los Angeles: University of California Los Angeles Asian American Studies Center, 2001).

24. Eric C. Wat, *The Making of a Gay Asian Community: An Oral History of Pre-AIDS Los Angeles* (Lanham, MD: Rowman & Littlefield, 2002).

25. Chan, Jeffrey Paul, Frank Chin, Lawson Inada, and Shawn Wong, eds., *Aiiieeeee! An Anthology of Asian American Writers* (Washington DC: Howard University Press, 1974), p. 37.

26. *U.S. Newa & World Report*, December 26, 1966, pp 73–8. Reprinted in Min Hyoung Song and Jean Wu, eds., *Asian American Studies: A Reader* (New Brunswick, NJ: Rutgers University Press, (1999), pp 158–63.

27. For such an example, see Harry H. L. Kitano, *Japanese Americans: Evolution of a Subculture* (Englewood Cliffs, NJ:Prentice-Hall, 1975).

28. See Min Hyoung Song, *Strange Futures: Pessimism and the 1992 Los Angeles Riots* (Durham, NC: Duke University Press, 2005); Nancy Abelmann and John Lie, *Blue Dreams: Korean Americans and the Los Angeles Riots* (Cambridge, MA: Harvard University Press, 1995); Claire Jean Kim, *Bitter Fruit: The Politics of Black–Korean Conflict in New York City* (New Haven, CT: Yale University Press, 2000).

29. For a critical discussion of these issues, see Viet Thanh Nguyen, "What is the Political?: American Culture and the Example of Viet Nam," in Kent A. Ono (ed.), *Asian American Studies After Critical Mass* (Malden, MA: Blackwell, 2004).

30. See Susan Koshy, "Morphing Race Into Ethnicity: Asian Americans and Critical Transformations of Whiteness," *boundary* 2, 28,1 (2001): 153–94.

31. See Lavina Dhingra Shankar and Rajini Srikanth (eds.), *A Part, Yet Apart: South Asians in Asian America* (Philadelphia, PA: Temple University Press, 1998); Sunaina Marr Maira, *Desis In the House: Indian American Youth Culture in New York City* (Philadelphia, PA: Temple University Press, 2002).

32. Sandya Shukla, *India Abroad: Diasporic Cultures of Postwar America and England* (Princeton, NJ: Princeton University Press, 2003), p. 65.

33. See a special issue of *Amerasia Journal* titled "Whose Vision? Asian Settler Colonialism in Hawai'i," *Amerasia* 26,2 (2000).

34. Chang-rae Lee, *Native Speaker* (New York: Riverhead, 1995), pp. 319–20.

35. Jhumpa Lahiri, *The Interpreter of Maladies and Other Stories* (Boston: Houghton Mifflin, 1999), p. 198.

36. Vijay Prashad, *The Karma of Brown Folk* (Minneapolis: University of Minnesota Press, 1999), p. viii.

37. See Tram Nguyen, "Showdown in K-Town: KIWA Mounts a Multiracial Class Challenge in LA's Koreatown," *Colorlines*, 4,1 (April 30, 2001): 26–9; Mark Mano, "All Sides Agree the Evictions and Demolitions Will Continue: The Slow Death of Little Tokyo," *International Examiner*, 5,10 (November 30, 1978): 3f.

See also James Kyung-Jin Lee, *Urban Triage: Race and the Fictions of Multiculturalism* (Minneapolis: University of Minnesota Press), pp. 94–5, 204.
38. Gayatri Gopinath, *Impossible Desires: Queer Diasporas and South Asian Public Cultures* (Durham, NC: Duke University Press, 2005).

FURTHER READING

Kandice Chuh, *Imagine Otherwise: On Asian Americanist Critique*, Durham, NC: Duke University Press, 2003.

David L. Eng and Alice Y. Hom (eds.), *Q & A: Queer in Asian America*, Philadelphia: Temple University Press, 1998.

Yen Le Espiritu, *Asian American Panethnicity: Bridging Institutions and Identities*, Philadelphia: Temple University Press, 1991.

Robert Lee, *Orientals: Asian Americans in Popular Culture*, Philadelphia: Temple University Press, 2000.

Russell Leong (ed.), *Asian American Sexualities*, New York: Routledge, 1995.

Lisa Lowe, *Immigrant Acts: On Asian American Cultural Politics*, Durham, NC: Duke University Press, 1996.

Steve Louie and Glenn Omatsu (eds.), *Asian Americans: The Movement and the Moment*, Los Angeles: University of California Los Angeles Asian American Studies Center, 2001.

Viet Nguyen, *Race and Resistance: Literature and Politics of Asian America*, New York: Oxford University Press, 2002.

Gary Okihiro, *The Columbia Guide to Asian American History*, New York: Columbia University Press, 2001.

Kent A. Ono (ed.), *A Companion to Asian American Studies*, Malden, MA: Blackwell, 2004.

David Palumbio-Liu, *Asian/American: Historical Crossings of a Racial Frontier*, Stanford, CA: Stanford University Press, 1999.

John S. W. Park, *Elusive Citizenship: Immigration, Asian Americans, and the Paradox of Civil Rights*, New York: New York University Press, 2004.

Min Hyoung Song and Jean Wu (eds.), *Asian American Studies: A Reader*, New Brunswick, NJ: Rutgers University Press, 1999.

Min Zhou and James V. Gatewood (eds.), *Contemporary Asian America: A Multidisciplinary Reader*, New York: New York University Press, 1999.

10

S. J. KLEINBERG

Women in the twentieth century

American women's lives changed in many crucial respects over the course of the twentieth century. In 1900, domesticity framed most women's lives; few obtained education after the age of fourteen. Yet while almost all white women left the formal labor force after marriage, many African American women remained economically active throughout their adult lives. The vast majority of women married by the age of twenty-two or twenty-three, and stayed with their partner until he died. Divorce was a rarity. The average woman had four children. She typically survived the departure from home of her youngest child by only a handful of years, so living alone was a rarity. Many women participated in social and political events outside the home, even though only a small number could vote, mostly in local elections and some western states. Few women held public office, yet they worked effectively outside the political mainstream in various reform movements and voluntary activities.

By 2000, economic activity throughout adulthood has become the norm, with a shift in predominant occupations from domestic service and factory labor to paper-based employments in the professions and offices of the country. While domesticity still figures in the female experience, especially when children are young, few women remain outside the labor force entirely, and race and marital status have less affect on employment rates. Education levels have skyrocketed for women as well as men from every race and ethnic group. Almost all young women graduated from high school in 2000 and about half entered higher education. Over the course of the century, women went from being about one-fifth of all college graduates to over half, while the proportion of advanced degrees obtained by women increased from a handful to nearly two-fifths. Consequent upon these changes, the age of marriage rose, as did the proportion of women not marrying at all. Fertility levels fell (with the notable exception of the mid-twentieth century baby boom), as women obtained reliable birth control, notably the contraceptive pill in the 1960s. Abortions became legal across the nation in 1973, but remain highly controversial. A major shift occurred in the number of children brought up by a single parent, usually the mother, as divorce rates and levels of non-marital fertility rose sharply in the last quarter of the twentieth century.[1]

However, while the specifics of women's roles altered, the doubts and uncertainties over women's place in society continued. The debate over "women's place" surfaced repeatedly throughout the twentieth century at every social and political level. Suffrage did not resolve these issues, although women's participation in public affairs and office holding increased.[2] Through depression, war, and peace, each generation battled over discrepancies between the rhetoric and the reality of women's lives, about responsibility for family life and the extent and form of women's participation in matters outside the home.[3] Moreover, despite the efforts of many to ensure equality between women and men, the Equal Rights Amendment failed to obtain the requisite support at the state level to amend the Constitution. Gender, the social construction of biological roles, remained a powerful force shaping women's opportunities, despite all the modifications in women's activities inside and outside the home.[4]

This chapter traces women's changing roles and status through the complex events of the twentieth century, including long-term trends such as urbanization and immigration, shorter-term political events including wars and economic booms and busts, and various sociopolitical movements. It first examines women's lives in the Progressive Era. Next, it investigates the impact of the Great Depression and World War II on women. It then interrogates their "survival in the doldrums," the years in which American women supposedly returned to domesticity, although political activism in the civil rights and peace movements and rising levels of employment meant that women accomplished much in these years.[5] Finally, it turns to the Women's Liberation Movement, the demographic and educational changes of the last three decades of the twentieth century, looking at women's activities outside the home, the backlash against feminism, and the continued ambivalence about gender roles.

One of the chief attributes of American women's lives in the Progressive Era (1900–17), as in other times, was their diversity. United by their biology, but divided by class, race, ethnicity, place of birth, locale, education, religion, social values, and political beliefs, women, no less than men, constituted a varied group. Social constructions of biological roles influenced their lives, but so did a welter of other demographic, economic, and cultural factors. As always in a restless country, immigration and migration characterized women's experiences. They moved from southern and eastern Europe, Mexico, and Asia, searching for better opportunities or to escape persecution. The proportion of urban residents doubled between 1860 and 1900. Extreme mobility and diversity, hallmarks of the Progressive Era, led reformers to attempt to impose order upon the cities by using legislation to ensure conformity to dominant cultural values.[6]

Reformers emphasised education as a means of assimilating migrants and immigrants, which benefited many young women. Mandatory school attendance laws, passed in most northern and western states in the closing years of the nineteenth century (southern states passed similar laws in the 1910s and 1920s), applied to girls as well as boys. Working-class parents especially valued their sons' labor contributions (and higher wages) and withdrew them from school earlier than their daughters. By 1920, 17 percent of young women received a high school diploma, as did 29 percent in 1930, when 55 percent of all high school graduates were female. In 1900, 36 percent of American college students were female; by 1920, this figure reached 47 percent, its peak until the late twentieth century.[7]

Not all those in school were there voluntarily. A desire to assimilate Native Americans into mainstream US society resulted in the Bureau of Indian Affairs sending many young Native Americans to boarding schools a considerable distance from their reservations. These schools forbade their students to speak their native languages and made them wear conventional Anglo clothing. Removal from their own environment undermined maternal authority and Native American customs.[8]

In 1900, the Census recorded about 3 percent of married white women as holding jobs, compared with 26 percent of African American wives, additionally, many working-class and immigrant women contributed to their families' well-being by taking in boarders, washing, or sewing. By 1930, 12 percent of all wives were gainfully employed, with 10 percent of white and 33 percent of black women in the labor force, as were 9 percent of women from other races.[9] While white women's employment diversified in this era, economic activity remained overwhelmingly agricultural and service-oriented for women of color. Latinas had a broader range of employment opportunities than other women of color. Manufacturing establishments in the Southwest readily hired them, but few industrial employers gave jobs to African American women. The Chinese Exclusion Act (1882) and the Gentleman's Agreement with Japan (1907) meant that there were few Asian women in the United States in the early years of the twentieth century.[10]

The prevailing family wage ideology undermined the legitimacy of female economic activity even as employment increased, and a number of individual women and groups fought to place it on a more level footing. Most Americans believed that men should be paid a sufficiently large wage so that women and children did not have to work. However, few ordinary families could survive on one wage for very long. Unions such as the American Federation of Labor opposed women's employment as an attack on the family circle. Nevertheless, the AFL employed several women as general organizers, and favored equal pay for equal work, believing that employers would not hire women if they had to pay them fair wages. Given organized labor's ambivalence, it is not surprising that women comprised only 3 percent of all trade unionists in 1900.[11]

Labor union reluctance to recognize female ambitions and struggles led women to organize separate groups such as the Women's Trade Union League (WTUL). Formed in 1903, the Women's Trade Union League was a coalition of female middle-class reformers and working-class, frequently immigrant, laborers. Middle-class WTUL members agitated for improved working conditions through protective legislation. They used their contacts to publicize the strikers' cause and raised funds to sustain strikers.[12]

The immigrant labor force's shared culture facilitated walkouts. Ethnically based strikes occurred in the cigar, garment, textile, and shoe industries among Cuban cigar workers (Tampa), Mexican cannery workers (California), and textile and garments industries (New York and New England).[13] Clara Lemlich galvanized New York shirtwaist makers into striking in 1909 with an impassioned Jewish oath: "If I turn traitor to the cause I now pledge, may this hand wither from the arm I now raise."[14] Over 20,000 garment workers left their jobs, enduring great hardship, including frequent arrests. The strike ended after several months without the union recognition sought by the workers, although they did obtain better working conditions in some plants.[15]

Polish women working for the American Woolen Company in Lawrence, Massachusetts left their looms in protest over pay cuts in 1912. The company had lowered wages because a new state law reduced working hours for women and children. Joined by women from other ethnic groups these unskilled women relied upon community networks and support from the Industrial Workers of the World in a successful strike which coined the rallying cry, "give me bread, but give me roses, too." The WTUL supported the strikers, although the AFL did not.[16]

Reformers assumed that working women could not negotiate successfully with their employers. They urged state legislatures and city councils to pass protective legislation, effectively conceding that conventional forms of labor activism would not improve female employment status. The Supreme Court accepted that women had a different relationship to the state and the economy than men and required special protection from abusive employment relations. While the court rejected reformers' efforts to legislate improved wages, hours, and working conditions for all workers as an infringement of the right to contract one's labor freely, it decided in *Muller v. Oregon* (1908) that women, like children, constituted an exception to that right.[17]

Protective legislation only protected certain women. It completely ignored the physically arduous jobs done by women of color on farms or in kitchens, nor did it regulate the hours they worked cleaning offices or in other "non-industrial" employments. It did not control the speed of the machinery or curtail the need to work as fast as possible when faced with payment by the piece of work. The Triangle Shirtwaist Company exemplified the appalling working conditions endured by industrial workers. One of the targets of the 1909 garment workers' strike, the owners of this New York factory locked the exit doors so that workers could not take a break from their machines. In 1911, a fire broke out and 146 women burned or jumped to their deaths from the top floors of this factory building.[18]

Domestic servants organized sporadically across the South in an effort to improve wages and working conditions in household labor. These efforts sometimes achieved short-term gains, but the fragmented nature of domestic service and the willingness of employers to resort to the law to force their employees back to work undermined their efforts. During World War I, southern legislators and city council members applied the federal government's "work or fight" regulations to domestic servants. They arrested African American women as vagrants if they refused to work as servants. The National Association for the Advancement of Colored People protested this legislation vigorously, but the exploitation of black women continued unchecked in the South.[19]

In the early years of the twentieth century, urban women became important social activists in charity, municipal reform, and settlement house movements. Overlapping groups of social reformers promoted the Progressive reform agenda and in the process established new careers for women. Women such as Jane Addams, the founder of Hull House settlement, Florence Kelley, head of the National Consumers' League, and Julia Lathrop (first head of the Children's Bureau) established close bonds as settlement house residents. They worked to improve urban conditions and for women's suffrage. In innovative areas, including home economics and social work, these women and thousands like them, transferred many of women's traditional concerns into the public arena.[20]

Social reformers advocated aid to certain groups seen as disadvantaged in the marketplace, such as widows. Northern and western states passed widows' or mothers' pension legislation which publicly recognized motherhood and the jobs women did in the home as socially important. By paying mothers a small cash sum, reformers hoped to keep families intact, prevent child labor, and enable mothers to stay home. Pensions were mostly to white women (97 percent) and to widows (85 percent), only aiding a small fraction of those who needed help.[21]

Proponents of women's suffrage emphasized its utility to the reform agenda and made it less of a challenge to accepted gender conventions. The debate shifted away from women's natural rights to the good women could accomplish if they had the vote. They maintained that incorporating women's distinctive qualities into politics would enhance public well-being.[22] As Jane Addams expressed it, women deserved the vote because it would enable them to "discharge their duties" as housekeepers not just for their families but also for the nation. Because women cared for their homes and families, they needed a public voice to ensure that public officials heeded their concerns.[23] The expediency argument, as historian Aileen Kraditor labeled it, assumed gender differences.

When the battle for suffrage stalled in the first decade of the twentieth century, suffrage leaders such as Carrie Chapman Catt of the National American Woman Suffrage Association (NAWSA) maintained that giving immigrant and African American men the vote but denying it to genteel white women made them into "subjects." Some white suffragists argued for an educational qualification; others, especially in the African American community, supported universal suffrage. White suffragists rarely worked with African American women, who established their own organizations such as the Chicago-based Alpha Suffrage Club, led by Ida Wells-Barnett.

Suffrage opponents believed that the sexes had different interests, that suffrage would debase women, and that allowing women to vote would bring contention to the household. Suffrage opponents feared that if women got the vote they would use it to legislate temperance, higher wages for women, or an end to child labor. Bishops of the Roman Catholic Church, antagonized by the nativist tone of many suffrage proponents, worried that woman suffrage would harm the family.[24]

Alice Paul, who had observed the militancy of the English Women's Social and Political Union, urged direct action. The Congressional Union, later the Woman's Party, protested Woodrow Wilson's inauguration, picketed the White House, and embarrassed NAWSA leadership. During World War I, NAWSA lobbied the President and Congress to pass the suffrage amendment as a war measure. Congress responded to women's war work, at the front and on the home front, by voting to send the constitutional amendment to the states. Ratified in 1920, the Nineteenth Amendment permitted women to vote, but had less impact than expected. Women tended to vote as members of classes, races, ethnic and religious groups, not as a unified gender. Moreover, female activists needed to regroup after devoting so much of their energies to the single task of getting the vote. NAWSA became the League of Women Voters, dedicated to educating women for suffrage. The Woman's Party agitated for an Equal Rights Amendment, which many social reformers opposed for fear that it would unravel protective legislation.[25]

Other issues came to the fore. Margaret Sanger, a public health nurse in New York City, crusaded in the early decades of the century to make birth control available to poor women. She established a birth control clinic in Brooklyn, advertising for clients in English, Yiddish, and Italian. Arrested and convicted for her activities, she struggled against both legislation and the medical profession to disseminate contraceptive information widely, eventually achieving acceptance of the notion that women should be able to limit the size of their families.[26]

By the 1920s, single and married couples used contraception, principally diaphragms and condoms, obtained from doctors, drug stores, and by post. Only Massachusetts and Connecticut still made it illegal to provide birth control information to married couples.[27] Stimulated by the expanded employment opportunities brought, albeit briefly, by World War I, the development of the consumer society, and new technology such as automobiles, radio and cinema, the New Woman of the 1920s turned toward pleasure and a freer lifestyle. These women discarded their long skirts and corsets in favor of the flapper's short dress. They smoked cigarettes, went to nightclubs, and drank alcohol, despite Prohibition. They engaged in increased levels of premarital sexuality, and divorced unsatisfactory spouses more readily than previous generations.[28]

The advent of the Great Depression in 1929 ended the gaiety of the Jazz Age. People put their plans on hold until better times arrived. Marriage, birth, and divorce rates fell. The female employment profile shifted as the uncertain economic situation led more white wives to seek work. Despite widespread disapproval and government efforts to ban married women workers in the public sector, the proportion of employed married white women rose from 10 to 13 percent. In contrast, employment levels shrank from 43 to 38 percent among married African American women. The racial discrepancies in single women's employment were even greater. Unmarried white women's employment declined slightly (from 49 to 46 percent), but unmarried non-white women's employment plummeted from 52 to 42 percent.[29]

Several factors account for these shifts. Though urbanization meant more African Americans had access to education beyond elementary school (there were few high schools that accepted black pupils in the rural South), the Depression hit predominantly black occupations very hard. Agricultural employment tumbled, and employers either cut back on household help or replaced African American servants with white women "trading down" when they lost other jobs.[30] New Deal programs encouraged the movement of African Americans out of agriculture by paying crop subsidies to farm owners, who used the money to purchase machinery and reduce their reliance upon tenant farmers and sharecroppers. As a result, the proportion of African American women farm laborers decreased from 27 percent (1930) to 16 percent by 1940. Latina pecan shellers in Texas saw wages drop from $7 to $2 to $3 per week.[31]

Political and social activist Eleanor Roosevelt (ER) accompanied her husband Franklin (FDR) to the White House in 1933, bringing with her a coterie of politically committed women reformers. Joined by such astute operators as Molly Dewson, chair of the National Women's Committee of the Democratic Party, ER tried to obtain more federal positions for women at all governmental levels, from postmistresses to cabinet offices. She pressed for Frances Perkins's appointment as Secretary of Labor, making her the first female cabinet member. Other successes included Florence Allen to the Sixth Circuit of the US Court of Appeals. Mrs. Roosevelt urged her husband to appoint the African American educator and civil rights activist Mary McLeod Bethune to head the Division of Negro Affairs of the National Youth Administration. Some 4,000 women became postmistresses.[32]

Despite women's growing influence in the federal government, many New Deal policies reinforced socially conservative views of women's work inside and outside the home. The Public Works Administration, the Civil Works Administration, Federal Emergency Relief Administration, and Works Progress Administration (WPA), had limited openings for women. The National Recovery Administration accepted lower wages for women's work than men's jobs. White men constituted over 74 percent of those employed on WPA projects in 1938; African American men were 12 percent; white women 11 percent, but African American women were a mere 2 percent. Almost no other women of color gained public works employment.[33]

The Social Security Act of 1935 incorporated stereotyped gender roles into federal policy. It established national retirement benefits and unemployment compensation, primarily for white male industrial workers.[34] It excluded about half the working population, nearly three-fifths of all female workers, and more than nine-tenths of African Americans by not covering domestic servants, farm laborers, charity, or public employees.[35] The 1939 amendments rewarded non-employed wives' domestic focus, but undermined working women. A married woman who worked all her life and paid into the Social Security fund obtained no more pension than one who had never held a job outside the home.[36]

Aid to Dependent Children (ADC) and Old Age Assistance permitted states to establish their own eligibility criteria and establish stratagems to prevent people of color from receiving assistance. Initially, racial minorities were a smaller proportion of the ADC rolls than their numbers warranted, despite the greater poverty amongst these groups.[37] The 1939 amendments divided lone mothers into two categories, based on marital status. Widows whose late husbands' occupation had been covered by Social Security received more generous and uniform survivors' benefits. ADC, conditional upon meeting city or state eligibility criteria, paid lower benefits and could be withdrawn if one fell foul of either morality or financial strictures. Divorced, deserted, and never-married mothers remained segregated on ADC, with payments contingent upon social workers' investigation, a process that harked back to the mothers' pensions earlier in the century.[38]

The entrance of the United States into World War II relegated female policymakers to one side even in areas that affected women closely, at the same time that it gave women broader employment opportunities. Employers turned to women as a reserve labor force after the draft reduced the number of available men. By late 1942, women's share of vocational training programs and defense work increased. Government and private industry courted them with campaigns featuring Rosie the Riveter, an attractive middle-aged white woman who simultaneously wore cosmetics and had discernible muscles.[39] The need for labor induced the government to encourage women with domestic responsibilities to undertake employment. In 1940, 8 percent of mothers with young children had jobs outside the home; by 1944, this had increased to 13 percent, and in 1948, 20 percent were economically active. The number of employed women doubled during the war; many of these workers were older, married, and had previous employment experience.[40]

Women's salaries rose, although they rarely achieved pay parity with men. Some trade unions incorporated equal pay provisions into collective bargaining to prevent employers from using female labor to undercut men's wage rates. Unions frequently insisted on separate seniority ladders for women and men, with female seniority being only for the duration of the war.[41] This undermined women's position in industry and contributed to their postwar unemployment.

Armed forces chiefs accepted women's service in female auxiliary corps in order to free men to take up arms; nevertheless, gendered assumptions impeded efficient deployment. The services barred women from combat zones, weapons training, and many aspects of warfare. Married women could enlist, but not if they had children under the age of fourteen. Women could go no higher than Lieutenant Colonel or Commander, even in the nurses' corps.[42] Only 6 percent of the Women's Army Corps (WACs) were of African American heritage, who served in segregated units. The Marines refused to take women of color at all, and the Navy only accepted them when commanded to do so by President Roosevelt in 1944.[43] In 1948, President Harry Truman issued Executive Order 9981 desegregating the armed forces. The Navy and Army then accepted black women into their nurses' corps, integrating training and residential facilities in 1950.[44]

African American women increased their share of industrial employment from 6 to 18 percent during the war, achieving their biggest employment gains in heavy industrial settings such as shipbuilding and iron and steel mills. The proportion in agricultural employment halved (from 21 to 11 percent), while domestic service declined from 57 to 44 percent. Even though black women obtained industrial jobs, they still encountered prejudice from white co-workers, who sometimes refused to share toilet and canteen facilities. This resentment was strongest in the South, but less virulent in the West, where Mexican American women built upon earlier organizing experiences to improve pay and conditions. Latinas' share of white-collar employment increased, especially in clerical and sales work, while the proportion in service and agricultural work dropped sharply.[45]

Women's horizons changed during the war. Many worked for more money in a broader variety of jobs than previously and wished to keep their jobs. They combined employment with looking after their families, while being constantly reminded that their war service was a temporary expedient to bring the troops home faster. However, both government structures (the G. I. Bill promised veterans their old jobs back) and popular prejudices promoted a backlash against female economic activity and assertiveness. In 1942, Philip Wylie's bestselling diatribe, *A Generation of Vipers*, lambasted middle-aged, middle-class women as the source of social problems. He coined the derogatory term "momism" to describe a smothering love that prevented children from growing up. Sociologists, Freudian psychoanalysts, and politicians devalued women's contributions and made them a target of opprobrium by insisting that biology was destiny.[46]

The proportion of women workers declined after demobilization but rose from the 1950s onwards despite their exclusion from better-paid jobs. Women from all ethnic backgrounds swelled the ranks of white-collar workers (with whites predominating in these jobs). Women lost ground in some higher-level occupations: there were fewer female college professors in 1960 than at any time in the century.[47] The number of older women workers rose sharply and more mothers with young children worked. Women managed this increase in employment levels despite the postwar baby boom. In 1940, the average woman had two children; this rose to three by 1950. By

1960, families of three and four children were typical. Women also had their children more closely together, so that it was common to have four children within the space of six years.[48] The rising divorce rate also contributed to increased female employment. In the 1950s there were approximately 15 divorces for every 1,000 married women, a figure that more than doubled by 1977 and continued to climb through the end of the century.[49]

Manufacturers and women's magazines emphasized women's roles in the home and the technology that would facilitate homemaking. Most women's magazines also recognized female aspirations outside the home, in politics, and the workplace.[50] The *Ladies' Home Journal* published an extract from *The Feminine Mystique* in 1963 under the headline "Have American housewives traded brains for brooms?" Betty Friedan stated that ever since World War II, there had been an attempt "to get women back into the home by glorifying feminine fulfillment – woman's fulfillment as a wife and mother – as the sole aim and justification of woman's existence." This glorification was "responsible for the otherwise inexplicable distress of modern American women," a point around which women would organize later in the decade.[51]

Women's college education levels reached their nadir in 1950 when a mere three out of every ten undergraduates were women, as women married younger and former GIs displaced coeds on the nation's campuses. Their representation on the nation's campuses took decades to recover, only reaching 50 percent by 1980.[52] While women lost ground in higher education in the middle years of the century, high school attendance became common for both sexes and all races. In 1947 only 17 percent of non-white females were high school graduates compared with nearly half (48.5 percent) of white females. By 1964, half of all white females and two-fifths of all black women had completed high school. Mexican and Asian American women lagged behind in this regard, and Hispanic young people had especially low rates of college education.[53] As more blacks moved out of the South, they had access to the less discriminatory school systems of the North; those still in the South fought hard to attend better schools.[54]

Moving around the United States could be an eye-opening experience. When Hunter College (New York City) graduate Pauli Murray moved to Washington DC to attend Howard University Law School during World War II, she encountered racial segregation (as well as the sexist attitudes of her professors). Her response was to join other students in sitting in Washington restaurants to demand service.[55] A decade later, newspaper publisher Daisy Bates, President of the Arkansas NAACP, helped integrate the public schools of Little Rock.[56] Women played a vital role in the Civil Rights Movement, yet they rarely received credit as leaders. Rosa Parks, a college-educated seamstress and official of her local NAACP chapter, refused to give her seat on a Montgomery bus to a white man, sparking the Montgomery Bus Boycott in 1955. Although Rev. Martin Luther King, Jr. was the public leader of the movement, the initial organizing had been done by Jo Ann Robinson, who persuaded her students at Alabama State College to distribute leaflets advertising the boycott. Ella Baker, who set up the Southern Christian Leadership Conference's office in Atlanta, believed that her male colleagues were unlikely to accept a woman's leadership.[57]

As women participated in the student and antiwar movements of the 1960s, they experienced marginalization and mockery when they tried to assert themselves. Hispanic women had a history of union activism in the canneries and unions such as the Mine, Mill, and Smelter Workers and Neighborhood groups such as the Community Service Organization to enhanced civic and economic rights in the 1940s and 1950s.[58] In the early 1970s Latinas organized gatherings such as *La Conferencia de Mujeres Por La Raza* to focus on issues of race and gender.[59]

Although lacking a single issue such as the vote, women participated in myriad organizations including the American Association of University Women, the National Association of Colored Women, the League of Women Voters, and Business and Professional Women's Clubs from the 1920s onwards. They participated in ethnic, patriotic, and religious groups. Organizations such as Women Strike for Peace challenged contemporary politics in the 1950s by using suburban women's concerns over the safety of their children to call for nuclear disarmament. In the process, these mothers pushed female concerns into the political arena, even if they did not initially identify themselves as feminists.[60]

Legislation and political parties contributed to the emergence of the women's liberation movement and bridged the first and second waves of feminism. When President Kennedy established the Presidential Commission on the Status of Women, chaired by Eleanor Roosevelt, he paid his debt to the liberal women who had supported his presidential campaign. However, the most notable advance in women's quest for equal status came from an entirely unexpected source. In 1964, possibly in an attempt to wreck the bill, Representative Howard W. Smith (Democrat, Virginia) introduced an amendment to Title VII of the Civil Rights Act that would prohibit discrimination in hiring and promotion based on sex, as well as race, religion, and national origin. Smith opposed the Civil Rights Act, although he had supported the Equal Rights Amendment favored by the Woman's Party. Representative Martha Griffiths (Democrat, Michigan), a long-time supporter of feminism, lobbied vigorously to incorporate this provision. Other liberals opposed the addition of sex to the list of prohibited categories either because they believed this would hurt the bill's chances or because they feared it would undermine traditional family relationships. The passage of the bill gave women some legal protection for equality in employment.[61]

The subsequent unwillingness of the Equal Employment Opportunities Commission (EEOC) to take the gender provision seriously or to ban sex-segregated employment advertisements gave impetus to the formation of the National Organization for Women (NOW) in 1966 by Betty Friedan, Pauli Murray, United Auto Workers' Caroline Davis and Dorothy Haener, Aileen Hernandez, and a number of government officials. The organization lobbied strenuously to ensure that women were included in affirmative action plans. It wanted the EEOC to take action against gender-based employment discrimination. It also lobbied for reproductive rights, including the legalization of abortion, which previously lacked a unified or centralized pressure group.[62]

Responding to their equivocal status in the student, antiwar, and race-justice organizations, women on university campuses formed more militant organizations, usually on a local basis. The New York Radical Women, Boston Women's Health Collective, Redstockings, and the Chicago Women's Liberation Union sprang up in the late 1960s, responding to the political dynamics in their area. Activities included picketing the Miss America Pageant, publishing the pioneering women's health manual, *Our Bodies/Our Selves*, raising consciousness about the nature of women's oppression, and campaigning for an end to restrictive abortion legislation. Kate Millett's *Sexual Politics* (1970) examined the sexism of male authors and propounded a revolutionary approach to relationships, where the personal became political as feminists rejected the political and social hierarchies that infused society.[63]

As with the earlier women's movement, second-wave feminists debated how narrowly or broadly to define the issues for which they would work. Older women favored NOW, the Women's Equity Action League (which sought legal remedies to economic discrimination), or the Coalition of Labor Union Women, an organization that emerged from the labor union movement in 1974. Latina feminists gathered at the first National Chicana Conference in 1971 to consider the issues facing their community. The National Black Women's Organization formed in 1973 to address the specific concerns confronting African American women in their struggle against racism and sexism.[64] Some NOW members, notably Betty Friedan, resisted efforts to incorporate lesbian rights issues into the general women's movement. After the Stonewall Riot in 1969 (a police attack on a gay bar in New York City when homosexuals fought back), lesbians began to organize in significant numbers within the women's movement. This caused disquiet among some heterosexual women who feared that their presence would give impetus to the growing anti-feminist movement.[65]

In 1972, Congress passed the Equal Rights Amendment (ERA) which stated that "equality of rights under the law shall not be abridged by the United States or any state on the basis of sex." This sparked off anxieties about the role of women, the sanctity of family relationships, homosexuality, and reproductive rights. The growing radical right played on fears that the ERA would undermine traditional roles in the family and sought to block the passage of the ERA despite Congress's extension of the deadline for ratification to June 1982.[66] While state legislatures succumbed to anti-feminist rhetoric and pressure groups (the ERA never garnered the requisite number of states to amend the Constitution), a series of court cases extended employment rights. The courts ruled that firms could not pay women less than men because that was the so-called market rate; women could not be excluded from juries; they were entitled to unemployment benefits in the last three months of pregnancy; the drinking ages for both sexes should be the same; and that sexual harassment was a form of job discrimination. In what has come to be one of its most controversial decisions (*Roe v. Wade*, 1973) the Supreme Court ruled that abortion in the first trimester of pregnancy was a matter for a woman and her physician, although the state's interest increased as the pregnancy progressed. Anti-abortionists attempted to overturn that decision in a number of ways. The Hyde Amendment of 1976 refused federal Medicaid funding for abortions, making it much more difficult for poor women to terminate their pregnancies, but attempts to amend the Constitution to ban abortion have failed. In *Webster v. Reproductive Services* (1989) the Supreme Court sustained Missouri's very restrictive anti-abortion law which placed time limits on the performance of abortions. Yet, three years later, despite a conservative majority, the Court sustained the principles behind *Roe v. Wade*. Abortion continues to be a volatile issue in the United States and a key issue in Supreme Court nominees.[67]

The backlash against feminism, given fuel by the personal conservatism of Presidents George Bush, Sr. and Jr., and Ronald Reagan, attempted to reassert the centrality of women's role in the family as wives and mothers to their identity and status. Concerns about the ticking of the biological clock, the difficulty of finding a partner if one left it too late, and the "straitjacket of feminism" all contributed to attacks on feminism. The heightened biological determinism epitomized by books such as *Men Are From Mars, Women Are From Venus* blended with anxieties over non-marital fertility, high divorce rates, and increased number of female-headed households to attack women who did not know their place.[68]

Backlashers opposed the individualism of the women's liberation movement and the competition in the workplace, education, and political arenas that it engendered. They sought to end the availability of abortion and women's ability to control their own fertility without consulting their partner or their parents. Social conservatives also wished to decrease the role of the federal government in determining social policy, in part by limiting access to welfare.[69] Thus, the New Right supported President Clinton's Personal Responsibility and Opportunities at Work Reconciliation Act (PROWRA) in 1996. This act gave grants to states, with a time limit on help for needy families.[70]

Between 1970 and 2000 female labor force participation increased from 41 to 58 percent. There was little difference between black, white, and Asian women's employment rates, although Hispanic women were somewhat less likely to work outside the home. Marriage now had little impact on economic activity, and the proportion of working mothers continued to rise from less than half in 1975 to three-quarters by 2000. Even mothers of very young children took jobs; one-third worked in 1975 compared with over half in 2000, with little distinction between the races, except for Latina mothers, only 46 percent of whom worked outside the home.[71]

Nevertheless, segregation still characterizes the labor market. Women remain underrepresented in architecture, engineering, computer science, and the natural sciences. They dominate the ranks of teachers, nurses, dieticians, and physiotherapists, but not doctors or professors. They have made almost no inroads into construction or heavy industry. Racial disparities also remain; over one-third of all white women hold managerial and professional positions, compared with over one-fourth of blacks and less than one-fifth of Latinas.[72]

The pay gap has narrowed as the glass ceiling opened slightly to admit a few more women into higher paid posts. In 1979, working women earned 63 percent as much as men; by 2000 they averaged 76 percent of men's wages. In 2000, black and Hispanic women earned about 86 percent as much of men from their racial/ethnic groups compared with 76 percent for white women, a testimony to the generally higher remuneration of white men. Ten percent of Latinas, 12 percent of black, but only 5 percent of white women worked for poverty-level wages.[73]

Some, but not all women elected to public office have championed the cause of poor women. Yet while more women participate in politics at all levels, they have not achieved parity in elected or appointed offices. Representative Shirley Chisholm, (Democrat, Brooklyn) became the first African American woman to enter presidential primaries. Twelve years later, Walter Mondale selected Representative Geraldine Ferraro (Democrat, Brooklyn) as his Vice-Presidential running mate. Female politicians have been most successful at the state and local levels. They were 14 percent of the Senate and House of Representatives, 25 percent of statewide elected positions, and 22 percent of state legislatures in 2002. This is despite the formation of the National Women's Political Caucus in 1972 and the establishment of EMILY's list in 1985. EMILY (Early Money is Like Yeast) gives money to women to help them run for political office and has been credited with helping to elect three women as governors, forty-nine women to Congress, and six women to the Senate.[74]

Over the century, women's educational levels have risen, as has their participation in the labor force. However, they still have neither economic nor political parity with men. They strive to balance their lives at home and in the workplace, with little public support. Despite two feminist movements, much of women's legal protection depends upon the balance of the Supreme Court rather a constitutional amendment giving them equality before the law. Women are better educated, better paid, and better represented than ever before, but gender and race continue to shape their lives and life chances.

NOTES

1 Bureau of the Census, *Historical Statistics of the United States: Colonial Times to 1970*, part 1 (Washington DC: Government Printing Office, 1975); *Statistical Abstract of the United States* (Washington DC: Government Printing Office, 1992); Herbert S. Klein, *A Population History of the United States* (Cambridge: Cambridge University Press, 2004).

2. Kristi Andersen: *After Suffrage: Women in Partisan and Electoral Politics before the New Deal* (Chicago: University of Chicago Press, 1996).

3. Karen Anderson, *Changing Woman: A History of Racial Ethnic Women in Modern America* (New York: Oxford University Press, 1996); S. J. Kleinberg, *Women in the United States, 1830–1945* (New Brunswick, NJ: Rutgers University Press, 1999); Rochelle Gatlin, *American Women since 1945* (Basingstoke: Macmillan, 1987).

4. Alice Kessler-Harris, *In Pursuit of Equity: Women, Men and the Quest for Economic Citizenship in 20th Century America* (New York: Oxford University Press, 2001).

5. Leila Rupp and Verta Taylor, *Survival in the Doldrums: The American Women's Rights Movement, 1945 to the 1960s* (Columbus: Ohio State University Press, 1990).

6. Vicki L. Ruiz, *From Out of the Shadows: Mexican Women in Twentieth-Century America* (New York: Oxford University Press, 1998), 33–50, discusses Americanization programs.

7. Barbara Miller Solomon, *In the Company of Educated Women* (New Haven: Yale University Press, 1985).

8. Anderson, *Changing Woman*, pp. 45–51.
9. US Department of Commerce, Bureau of the Census, Fifteenth Census, 1930, *Population: General Report on Occupations*, vol. v, (Washington DC, Government Printing Office, 1933), p. 274.
10. Tera Hunter, *To 'Joy My Freedom: Southern Black Women's Lives and Labors after the Civil War* (Cambridge, MA: Harvard University Press, 1997); Vicki L. Ruiz, *Cannery Women, Cannery Lives: Mexican Women, Unionization, and the California Food Provision Industry 1930–1950* (Albuquerque: University of New Mexico Press, 1987).
11. Alice Kessler-Harris, *Out to Work: A History of Wage-Earning Women in the United States* (Oxford: Oxford University Press, 1982), pp. 153–6.
12. Diane Kirkby, *Alice Henry: The Power of Pen and Voice: The Life of an Australian-American Labor Reformer* (Cambridge: Cambridge University Press, 1991); Nancy Schrom Dye, *As Equals and As Sisters: Feminism, the Labor Movement and the Women's Trade Union League of New York* (Columbia: University of Missouri Press, 1980).
13. Nancy A. Hewitt, *Southern Discomfort: Women's Activism in Tampa, Florida, 1880s–1920s* (Urbana: University of Illinois Press, 2001); Robert Ingalls and Louis Perez, J., *Tampa Cigar Workers* (Gainesville: University of Florida Press, 2004); Ruiz, *Cannery Women*.
14. Louis Levine, *The Women's Garment Workers* (New York: B. W. Huebsch, 1924), p. 154.
15. Theresa S. Malkiel, *The Diary of a Shirtwaist Striker*, with an introductory essay by Francoise Basch (Ithaca, NY: ILR Press, 1990 [orig. 1910]).
16. Ardis Cameron, *Radicals of the Worst Sort: Laboring Women in Lawrence, Massachusetts, 1860–1912* (Urbana: University of Illinois Press, 1993).
17. Vivien Hart, *Bound by Our Constitution. Women, Workers, and the Minimum Wage* (Princeton: Princeton University Press, 1994).
18. Leon Stein, ed., *Out of the Sweatshop: The Struggle for Industrial Democracy* (New York: Quadrangle/New Times Book Company, 1977).
19. Hunter, *To 'Joy My Freedom*, pp. 227–9.
20. Robert Clarke, *Ellen Swallow: The Woman who Founded Ecology* (Chicago: Follett Publishing, 1973); Sheila M. Rothman, *Woman's Proper Place: A History of Changing Ideals and Practices, 1870 to the Present* (New York: Basic Books, 1978); Barbara Ehrenreich and Deirdre English, *For Her Own Good: 150 Years of Experts' Advice to Women* (New York: Doubleday, 1989).
21. S. J. Kleinberg, *Widows and Orphans First: The Family Economy and Social Welfare Policy, 1880–1939* (Urbana: University of Illinois Press, 2005); Theda Skocpol, *Protecting Soldiers and Mothers: The Political Origins of Social Policy in the United States* (Cambridge, MA: Harvard University Press, 1993); Robyn Muncy, *Creating a Female Dominion in American Reform, 1890–1935* (New York: Oxford University Press, 1991): Linda Gordon, "Black and White Visions of Welfare: Women's Welfare Activism, 1890–1945," *Journal of American History*, 78 (1991): 559–90.
22. Ross Evans Paulson, *Women's Suffrage and Prohibition: A Comparative Study of Equality and Social Control* (Chicago: Scott, Foreman, 1973); Jack S. Blacker, *"Give to the Winds Thy Fears": The Women's Temperance Crusade* (Westport, CN: Greenwood Press, 1985); Ruth Brigitte Anderson, *Women and*

Temperance: The Quest for Power and Liberty, 1873–1900 (Philadelphia: Temple University Press, 1981).

23. Jane Addams, "On Woman Suffrage," in Aileen S. Kraditor, *Up from the Pedestal* (Chicago: Quadrangle Books, 1968), pp. 282–3.

24. Angela Howard and Sasha Ranae Adams Tarrant (eds.), *Opposition to the Women's Movement in the United States, 1848–1929* (New York: Garland, 1997).

25. Christine Bolt, *The Women's Movements in the United States and Britain from the 1790s to the 1920s* (New York: Harvester Wheatsheaf, 1993), p. 262; Nancy Cott: *The Grounding of Modern Feminism* (New Haven: Yale University Press, 1987).

26. David Kennedy, *Birth Control in America: The Career of Margaret Sanger* (New Haven: Yale University Press, 1970); Carole R. McCann, *Birth Control Politics in the United States, 1916–1945* (Ithaca, NY: Cornell University Press, 1994).

27. Klein, *Population History*, pp. 158–9, 183–4; Beth Bailey, *From Front Porch to Back Seat: Courtship in Twentieth-Century America* (Baltimore: Johns Hopkins University Press, 1988); Robert and Helen Merrill Lynd, *Middletown: A Study of Contemporary American Culture* (New York: Harcourt, Brace, & World, 1956 [orig. 1929]); David Kennedy, *Birth Control in America: The Career of Margaret Sanger* (New Haven: Yale University Press, 1970). In 1965, the Supreme Court ruled in *Griswold v. Connecticut* that the right of privacy precluded state interference in couples' bedrooms and extended this right to single people in 1972.

28. Glenda Riley, *Divorce: An American Tradition* (Lincoln: University of Nebraska Press, 1991).

29. Bureau of the Census, Fifteenth Census of the US: 1930, *Occupational Statistics* (Washington DC: Government Printing Office, 1932); Bureau of the Census, Sixteenth Census of the US: 1940, *Population*, vol. III, *The Labor Force*, part I (Washington DC: Government Printing Office, 1943).

30. Brenda Clegg Gray, *Black Female Domestics During the Depression in New York City, 1930–1940* (New York: Garland, 1993).

31. Jacqueline Jones, *Labor of Love, Labor of Sorrow: Black Women, Work, and the Family from Slavery to the Present* (New York: Basic Books, 1985), pp. 200–2; Raymond Wolters, *Negroes and the Great Depression* (Westport, CN: Greenwood Press, 1970), pp. 21–56; Federal Emergency Relief Administration Bulletin no. 5054 in Women's Bureau papers, National Archives, RG 86, box 6; Julia Kirk Blackwelder, *Women of the Depression: Caste and Culture in San Antonio, 1929–1939* (College Station: Texas A & M Press, 1984).

32. Blanche Wiesen Cook, *Eleanor Roosevelt: The Defining Years, 1933–1938* (New York: Penguin Books, 1999).

33. Federal Works Agency, *Final Report on the WPA Program, 1935–1943* (Washington DC: Government Printing Office, 1947), p. 45.

34. Kessler-Harris, *In Pursuit of Equity*, discusses these points and the neglect of black women's labor.

35. E. Stina Lyon, "Race and the American Welfare State," *Ethnic and Racial Studies*, 24 (2001): 125–30; Edwin Witte, *The Development of the Social Security Act* (Madison: University of Wisconsin Press, 1963), p. 163.

36. Carole Haber and Brian Gratton, *Old Age and the Search for Security: An American Social History* (Bloomington: Indiana University Press, 1994), p. 85.

37. "Map of Approved Plans for Social Security," December 8, 1936, Children's Bureau Papers (National Archives) Box 546; Gunnar Myrdal, *An American Dilemma: The Negro Problem and Modern Democracy* (New York: Harper & Row, 1944), p. 359.

38. Kleinberg, *Widows and Orphans*; Alice Kessler-Harris, "Designing Women and Old Fools," in Linda Kerber, Alice Kessler-Harris, and Kathryn Kish Sklar eds., *U. S. History as Women's History: New Feminist Essays* (Chapel Hill: University of North Carolina Press, 1995).

39. Sherna Gluck, *Rosie the Riveter Revisited: Women, the War and Social Change* (Boston: Twayne, 1987); Maureen Honey, *Creating Rosie the Riveter: Class, Gender, and Propaganda during World War II* (Amherst: University of Massachusetts Press, 1984).

40. Women's Bureau, *1965 Handbook on Women Workers* (Washington DC: Government Printing Office, 1965), pp. 36–9.

41. William F. Chafe, *The American Woman: Her Changing Social, Economic, and Political Roles, 1920–1970* (New York: Oxford University Press, 1972), pp. 155–7.

42. Susan M. Hartmann, *The Home Front and Beyond: American Women in the 1940s* (Boston: Twayne Publishers, 1982); Karen Anderson, *Wartime Women: Sex Roles, Family Relations, and the Status of Women during World War II* (Westport, CN: Greenwood Press, 1981); D'Ann Campbell, *Women at War with America: Private Lives in a Patriotic Era* (Cambridge, MA: Harvard University Press, 1984).

43. Charity Adams Earley, *One Woman's Army: A Black Officer in the WAC* (College Station: Texas A & M Press, 1989); Jesse J. Johnson, *Black Women in the Armed Forces, 1942–1974* (Hampton, VA: Johnson, 1974).

44. Kathryn Sheldon, "Black Women in the Military," http://womensmemorial.org/Education/BBH1998.html#4.

45. Seymour L. Wolfbein, "Postwar Tends in Negro Employment," *Monthly Labor Review*, 65 (December 1947): 664; Karen Tucker Anderson, "Last Hired, First Fired: Black Women Workers during World War II," *Journal of American History*, 69 (June 1982): 82–97; Ruiz, *Cannery Workers*.

46. Philip Wylie, *A Generation of Vipers. Newly Annotated by the Author* (Marietta, GA: Larlin Corporation, 1978), ch. XI; Ferdinand Lundberg and Marynia F. Farnham, *Modern Woman: The Lost Sex* (New York: Harper and Brothers, 1947).

47. *1965 Handbook on Women Workers*, pp. 6, 18.

48. Richard Easterlin, *Population, Labor Force and Long Swings in Economic Growth: The American Experience* (New York: Columbia University Press, 1968).

49. Winifred D. Wandersee, *On the Move: American Women in the 1970s* (Boston: Twayne, 1988), p. 130.

50. Nancy A. Walker, *Women's Magazines, 1940–1960: Gender Roles and the Popular Press* (Boston: Bedford/St. Martin's Press, 1998), pp. 10–11.

51. *Ladies Home Journal*, 80, 1 (January–February, 1963): 24.

52. Mabel Newcomer, *A Century of Higher Education for American Women* (New York: Harper Brothers, 1959), p. 235, observed from her vantage point as Professor Emerita at Vassar College that in the 1950s there was not "general

acceptance of the idea that higher education is just as important for women as for men."

53. Abbott L. Ferriss, *Indicators of Trends in the Status of American Women* (New York: Russell Sage Foundation, 1971), pp. 302, 310; Women's Bureau, *1965 Handbook*, 15–18. Ruiz, *From Out of the Shadows*, pp. 103, 154.

54. J. Harvey Wilkinson III, *From Brown to Bakke* (New York: Oxford University Press, 1979).

55. Pauli Murray, *The Autobiography of a Black Activist, Feminist, Lawyer, Priest, and Poet* (Knoxville: University of Tennessee Press, 1989).

56. Daisy Bates, *The Long Shadow of Little Rock* (Fayetteville: University of Arkansas Press, 1987 [orig. 1962]).

57. Susan M. Hartmann, *From Margin to Mainstream: American Women and Politics since 1960* (New York: Alfred A. Knopf, 1989), p. 27.

58. Margaret Rose, "Gender and Civic Activism in Mexican Barrios in California: The Community Service Organization, 1947–1962," in Joanne Meyerowitz (ed.), *Not June Cleaver: Women and Gender in Postwar America* (Philadelphia: Temple University Press, 1994), pp. 177–200.

59. Ruiz, *From Out of the Shadows*, 108.

60. Amy Swerdlow, *Women Strike for Peace: Traditional Motherhood and Radical Politics in the 1960s* (Chicago: University of Chicago Press, 1993), pp. 237–8; Anna L. Harvey, *Votes without Leverage: Women in American Electoral Politics, 1920–1970* (Cambridge: Cambridge University Press, 1999).

61. Judith Hole and Ellen Levine, *Rebirth of Feminism* (New York: Quadrangle, 1971); Sara Evans, *Personal Politics: The Roots of Women's Liberation on the Civil Rights Movement and the New Left* (New York: Alfred A. Knopf, 1979).

62. Marcia Cohen, *The Sisterhood: The Inside Story of the Women's Movement and the Leaders Who Made it Happen* (New York: Fawcett Columbine, 1988).

63. Kate Millett, *Sexual Politics* (Garden City, NY: Doubleday, 1970).

64. Benita Roth, *Separate Roads to Feminism: Black, Chicana, and White Feminist Movements in America's Second Wave* (Cambridge: Cambridge University Press, 2004).

65. Hartmann, *From Mainstream to Margin*, pp. 148–9.

66. Pamela Johnston Conover and Virginia Gray, *Feminism and the New Right: Conflict over the American Family* (New York: Praeger, 1983); Jane Mansbridge, *Why We Lost the Equal Rights Amendment* (Chicago: University of Chicago Press, 1986).

67. Kristen Luker, *Abortion and the Politics of Motherhood* (Berkeley: University of California Press, 1984).

68. John Gray, *Men Are From Mars, Women Are From Venus* (New York: Harper-Collins, 1992).

69. Rebecca E. Klatch, *Women of the New Right* (Philadelphia: Temple University Press, 1987).

70. www.ncsl.org/statefed/hr3734.htm. 2004 National Conference of State Legislatures, "The Personal Responsibility and Work Opportunity Reconciliation Act of 1996."

71. US Department of Labor, Bureau of Labor Statistics.

72. *Ibid.*

73. *Ibid.*

74. Suzanne O'Dea Schenken, *From Suffrage to the Senate: An Encyclopedia of American Women in Politics*, vol. 1 (Santa Barbara, CA: ABC-CLIO, 1999), pp. 229–30.

FURTHER READING

Nancy Cott, *The Grounding of Modern Feminism*, New Haven: Yale University Press, 1987.

Flora Davis, *Moving the Mountain: The Women's Movement in America since 1960*, Urbana: University of Illinois Press, 1999.

Evelyn Nakano Glass, *Unequal Freedom: How Race and Gender Shaped American Citizenship and Labor*, Cambridge, MA: Harvard University Press, 2004.

Sharon Hays, *Flat Broke with Children: Women in the Age of Welfare Reform*, Oxford: Oxford University Press, 2004.

Jacqueline Jones, *Labor of Love, Labor of Sorrow: Black Women, Work, and the Family from Slavery to the Present*, New York: Basic Books, 1985.

Alice Kessler-Harris, *In Pursuit of Equity: Women, Men and the Quest for Economic Citizenship in 20th Century America*, New York: Oxford University Press, 2001.

S. J. Kleinberg, *Widows and Orphans First: The Family Economy and Social Welfare Policy, 1880–1939*, Urbana: University of Illinois Press, 2005.

Barbara Ryan (ed.), *Identity Politics in the Women's Movement*, New York: New York University Press, 2001.

Vicki L. Ruiz, *From Out of the Shadows: Mexican Women in Twentieth-Century America*, New York: Oxford University Press, 1998.

Leila Rupp and Verta Taylor, *Survival in the Doldrums: The American Women's Rights Movement, 1945 to the 1960s*, Columbus: Ohio State University Press, 1990.

11

ROBERT MCRUER

Queer America

In *A Queer Mother for the Nation* (2002), Licia Fiol-Matta looks critically at the political and literary career of Chilean Nobel laureate Gabriela Mistral. Fiol-Matta analyzes, in particular, the "queer" aspects of Mistral's life: a series of affairs with women, a non-normative gender presentation perhaps best described as "female masculinity," and a spectacularly non-reproductive maternal identity. Mistral's career as internationally renowned educator and poet depended upon her paradoxically maternal but celibate role as "Schoolteacher of America." Fiol-Matta's study considers how these non-normative features of Mistral's life were deployed to abet state-sanctioned heteronormativity, patriarchy, and a racialized nationalism. Dominant understandings of gender, sexuality, race, and nation were consolidated – in Chile and across Latin America – not in spite of but through Mistral's demonstrable queerness.[1]

From the perspective of the late 1980s, perhaps, one could make the case that in the United States, such a queer consolidation of dominant discourses was unthinkable. Queerness, in the United States, seemed at the time to mark the very limits of citizenship. Largely in response to the HIV/AIDS crisis, new forms of public dissent and civil disobedience had emerged, increasingly understood as "queer activism." In the academy, likewise, new forms of critical analysis developed, called – from the early 1990s on – "queer theory" or "queer studies." These projects, along with queer work in the arts, were oppositional, not hegemonic in any apparent way; they were often concerned with excavating how stigmatized queer desires and bodies materialized only beyond the boundaries of imagined communities such as the nation. Virulent homophobia, at the time, was fueled in large part by beliefs that AIDS was a "gay disease" that threatened to impact the "general population"; the conflation of AIDS with homosexuality and homosexuality's abject position in relation to the nation led some commentators on the right to suggest that the acronym stood for "America's Ideal Death Sentence."[2]

Yet what a difference a decade can make. In September 2002, a biography was released honoring Mark Bingham, who died on September 11, 2001, on United Airlines Flight 93, which crashed into a field in Pennsylvania. In the year following the attacks on the World Trade Center and the Pentagon, Americans had learned the legend of Flight 93 well. Although it can never be clear exactly what happened, many Americans believed that the diverse group of passengers banded together against the hijackers and brought the plane down to keep it from reaching the United States Capitol or some other symbolic national target. One of the participants in that effort was Bingham, a businessman and rugby player who – as liberal parlance would have it – "just happened to be gay." Republican Senator John McCain, who eulogized Bingham at a September 2001 service, was only one of many insisting that Americans owed Bingham and the other passengers an enormous debt of gratitude; McCain, in fact, believed that Bingham – who supported McCain's 2000 presidential bid – quite possibly saved his life. Collectively, the stories constructed Bingham, as the title of the 2002 biography would have it, as *Hero of Flight 93*.[3] From so-called "carriers" of America's Ideal Death Sentence to Queer Martyr for the Nation: the dead gay body in either scenario is indispensable (in that national identity is apparently inconceivable without it), but clearly, between the late 1980s and 2002, something had shifted.

This chapter will return to the contradictions legible in the United States at the turn of the twenty-first century, but I begin a century earlier, considering how queerness was similarly central to that period, fueling cultural anxieties about the proper meanings of gender, race, nation, and domesticity. I then consider the second third of the century, a period generally understood – especially after World War II – as one of American productivity, prosperity, and conformity; perhaps inevitably, queerness in this section more often appears as wedded to subversion or pathology, despite efforts to counter such seemingly natural linkages. The section that follows my consideration of the United States at mid-century will focus on liberation and normalization, respectively, effectively bringing the chapter back to the paradoxes with which I began. "Queer America," I hope to demonstrate, can be read through this overview as always both a paradox and a redundancy, as both a promise and a multifaceted problem.

Modern queers

In one of the most memorable scenes in Willa Cather's *My Ántonia* (1918), a bride and groom are thrown to the wolves. As the Russian immigrant Pavel lies dying, he tells his story to Mr. Shimerda, Ántonia's father.

Ántonia, in turn, overhears the story and translates it for the novel's narrator, Jim Burden. Pavel and his brother Peter, so the story goes, had been at the front of a wedding party; the horse-drawn cart they guided carried the bride and groom, while the carts behind them carried members of the wedding party and the couple's families. As the group speeds forward through the dark Russian woods, the carts are overtaken by packs of wolves, and Pavel and Peter hear screams behind them. As the wolves come closer to the lead cart, the brothers demand that the groom push the bride out to lighten the load; when the groom refuses, he too is thrown over the side in the ensuing struggle. Pavel and Peter escape with their lives but are ostracized by the community and emigrate to America.

Judith Fetterley identifies the embedded narrative of Pavel and Peter as an "anti-story" in Cather's novel. If the trajectory of My Ántonia, like so many American stories, is toward marriage and reproduction, traces of resistance to that trajectory are nonetheless evident. My Ántonia, in particular, moves readers toward Jim's rediscovery of Ántonia late in life, when she is living – as a sort of Earth Mother – on the Nebraska prairie with her husband and numerous children. The violent anti-stories that pepper the novel, however, reflect a more ambivalent – even hateful – stance on reproductive heterosexuality and the contained place of women in the domestic sphere.[4]

Such ambivalence was widespread at the turn of the twentieth century, as reaction to the first wave of feminism in the United States generated a retrenchment or reinvention of patriarchal conceptions of domesticity. Eve Kosofsky Sedgwick, looking at this transitional period in her landmark Epistemology of the Closet (1990), argues that it was marked by "a chronic, now endemic crisis of homo/heterosexual definition, indicatively male, dating from the end of the nineteenth century."[5] Although Sedgwick's analysis of homoeroticism or homo/heterosexual definition in such writers as Henry James lends credence to her thesis, there are ways in which the crisis she pinpoints might be as effectively understood as indicatively female. The "New Woman," at the end of the nineteenth century, had demanded access to educational, political, and professional venues from which she had been systematically excluded. Both the enfranchisement of this figure and the possibility of increased African American political and economic power (a possibility at least partially realized during the Reconstruction period that followed the Civil War) led to stricter understandings of, and controls upon, both the public and domestic spheres. The (often violent) reinforcement of white, male power led to undeniable suffering and marginalization for non-white and female subjects. The newly consolidated white, patriarchal home, however (or consequently), was always haunted by the specter of queerness, just as surely as the story of happy, reproductive domesticity narrated in *My Ántonia* is haunted by anti-stories of disintegration.

Lisa Duggan, examining what she terms the "lesbian love murder narra-tive," makes explicit these linkages and demonstrates that the specter of queerness haunting the early twentieth-century family was, as often as not, gendered female. In *Sapphic Slashers: Sex, Violence, and American Modernity* (2000), Duggan examines judicial, medical, and popular press accounts of the story of Alice Mitchell and Freda Ward, two women living in Memphis in the late nineteenth century. Until their families interve-ned, Mitchell and Ward had shaped a relationship involving passionate declarations of love, plans for an elopement and marriage, and gender transgression (Mitchell was to pass as a man in order to find employment). Distraught by the intervention of familial authority, Mitchell sought out Ward one day on the streets of Memphis and slit her throat. Duggan's project considers not only the representation of this tragic event in a variety of institutional venues but also the ways in which it was taken up by a larger cultural narrative emphasizing threats to the stability of the modern home and family life.

The Mitchell–Ward story and other sensational tales of female friendship, passion, and gender transgression often involved a love triangle (a proper relationship between a man and a woman threatened by the possibility of an improper relationship with another woman), plans to establish an alterna-tive domesticity through the "marriage" of two women, the intervention of female domestic and institutionalized male authority, and a violent conclu-sion. Whether the violent conclusion was real or mythologized, the wide-spread public awareness of such cases served both to secure patriarchy and to make patriarchy perpetually insecure, tenuous, or fractured.[6] By the 1920s, the disruptive potential of the "mythic mannish lesbian," a minor-itized figure supposedly external to the home but nonetheless always capable of threatening the family, was well established in the American cultural imagination.[7]

Duggan locates the lesbian love murder narrative alongside contempor-aneous accounts of lynching. Thousands of African Americans, mostly men, faced violence and death during this period because of fabricated charges of rape. While not parallel to the lesbian love murder narrative, given that lynchings were much more common, the "lynching narrative," according to Duggan, has components that are worth considering in conjunction with components of the lesbian love murder narrative: an imagined triangle included both proper (white male and female) and improper (black male and white female) alliances; a white and male power structure consistently

intervened to forestall the possibility of alternative domesticities and economies (African American economic and domestic autonomy); violence and
death ensued; the threat to patriarchal domesticity was again established as
supposedly external; and yet the white home remained haunted by a woman
who might desire differently, a woman who might refuse the constraints
placed upon her.[8]

Contradictory queer fantasies – representing simultaneously a threat to be
policed and contained and the promise of something different – were, of
course, generated in relation to men as well, as Sedgwick's study emphasizes. And male queer fantasies, likewise, sustained a complex connection to
racialized fears and desires. European writers such as John Addington
Symonds had, in the nineteenth century, appealed to a classical Greek
tradition in an attempt to ennoble same-sex love; this tradition slowly
crossed the Atlantic and – together with a more indigenous Whitmanian
celebration of passionate comradeship – allowed for vocabularies
defending, however tentatively, erotic connections between men.[9] What
was noble when the bodies in question were European or European
American, however, became more suspect when the bodies in question
were non-white.

Gregory Tomso identifies Charles Warren Stoddard's *The Lepers of
Molokai* (1885) as a text that lays bare these tensions. *The Lepers* details
Stoddard's visit to Hawaii, where an outbreak of leprosy had raised
concerns about the contact with racial difference inevitably brought about
by America's imperialistic forays into the Pacific. According to Tomso,
Stoddard's understanding of leprosy in Hawaii conflated the disease with
same-sex love; although he was clearly erotically drawn to what he perceived as "barbarism," Stoddard nonetheless could not comprehend
Hawaiians except by conflating their perceived racial difference, suscepti-
bility to leprosy, and homosexuality. "Barbarism," in Tomso's reading,
was the flip side of the contemporaneous classicism, propounded by
Symonds and others, that would associate noble homosexuality with
ancient Greece. Both attempts to understand male–male desire depended
upon essential racial difference; homosexuality was either symptomic of
"barbaric" cultures and degeneration or a peculiar distinction of genera-
tive western cultures at their supposed height. Regardless of which ex-
planatory frame was dominant, the nineteenth-century legacy ensured
that racial hierarchies, and anxieties about those hierarchies, would
remain central to comprehensions of queerness.[10] If, as W. E. B. DuBois
would have it, "the problem of the Twentieth Century" was to be "the
problem of the color line," that line was always crossed and recrossed by
queerness.[11]

These stigmatizing conflations, not surprisingly, generated resistance. That resistance, at least in some locations and perhaps most notably during the New Negro Renaissance of the 1920s and 1930s, in turn generated vibrant cultural forms. Not only could homoerotic and bisexual themes be discerned, sometimes faintly and sometimes more openly, in the work of writers and artists (such as Langston Hughes, Nella Larsen, Alain Locke, Claude McKay, Bruce Nugent, Wallace Thurman, and others), but enormous multiracial drag balls were a regular feature of Harlem life. The annual Hamilton Lodge Ball, for instance, was attended by thousands; it and other drag balls were not marginal but widely acknowledged cultural events, reported on by New York newspapers.[12] George Chauncey makes clear that, for gay New York City in the first third of the century, the appropriate metaphor was not "the closet" but "the gay world." "Coming out," at the time, still carried the connotation of a debutante's arrival, not necessarily the connotation of a deep secret suddenly revealed.[13]

This is not to suggest that many middle-class African Americans did not labor assiduously to avoid the stigma of queerness and to critique the exoticizing "primitivism" many white and some black visitors or residents associated with spaces like Harlem. On the contrary, some middle-class African Americans worked hard to gain access to the respectable domesticity and gender conformity analyzed by Duggan and to avoid the taint of barbarism analyzed by Tomso. Nella Larsen's *Passing* (1929), in particular, has been read as representing middle-class African American anxieties about queerness. While passing for white at a Chicago hotel, the main character, Irene Redfield, encounters an old acquaintance, Clare Kendry, who is not passing temporarily; Clare, Irene discovers, is married to a racist white man and passing as white in all facets of her life. Over the course of the novel, Clare returns to New York (where Irene lives) and re-enters African American life, enjoying the cultural scene in Harlem while regularly crossing back to life with her husband. Despite the fact that she herself passes when it is convenient, Irene is deeply troubled by Clare's supposed transgressions. Increasingly and perhaps inevitably, however, her judgment *of* Clare and the categorical disruptions she seems to represent is wrapped up in desire *for* Clare and those categorical disruptions. Despite an unhappy marriage and a husband who is at times openly hostile, Irene is firmly committed to her position in middle-class African American society, to a respectable and heterosexual domesticity. Her growing obsession with Clare, then, can be interpreted as a queer desire for mobility beyond the boundaries of that respectability. Clare's suspicious death, at the end of the novel, arguably represents (or participates in) a middle-class need to repudiate such desires.[14]

During the period, however, whether in the drag balls and cabarets; the blues performances of Bessie Smith, Ma Rainey, and others; the drawings or paintings of Bruce Nugent; the novels of Carl Van Vechten or Blair Niles; or the satirical remembrances of Wallace Thurman's *Infants of the Spring* (1932); queer possibilities were coming out all over. If modern queerness was, in many ways, made unthinkable in dominant discourses of home, family, race, and respectability, the modern queers brought into existence by those exclusionary discourses nonetheless produced a vital cultural legacy in spaces apart from them.

In and out, mid-century

According to Chauncey, the 1930s brought about a systematic backlash against public cultures of queerness; if contained but undeniably public expressions of queer sexuality and gender crossing were a part of the experimentation of the 1920s, the trauma of the Depression helped to generate a crackdown. Legal restrictions, bar raids, and other forms of authoritative control were so pronounced that Chauncey describes the net effect as nothing less than "a powerful campaign to render gay men and lesbians invisible."[15] LGBT (lesbian, gay, bisexual, and transgender) historians have long understood World War II as something of "a nationwide coming out experience"; Chauncey's study of gay New York provides evidence that before queers came out mid-century, they had actually been forced in.[16]

Representations of isolated individuals and shadowy experiences that might be interpreted as "closeted" are relatively common in the mid-twentieth century. "How he longed to tell them exactly what he was!" the narrator of Gore Vidal's *The City and the Pillar* (1948) says of the novel's main character, Jim Willard: "He wondered suddenly what would happen if every man like himself were to be natural and honest. Life would certainly be better for everyone in a world where sex was thought of as something natural and not fearsome, and men could love men naturally, in the way they were meant to."[17] A similar hope for open expression coupled with an awareness of how regularly such hopes were dashed can be read in the work of writers as diverse as Tennessee Williams, Carson McCullers, Allen Ginsberg, James Baldwin, and even Jack Kerouac or Ralph Ellison.

In *Aberrations in Black: Toward a Queer of Color Critique* (2004), Roderick A. Ferguson studies a chapter of Ellison's *Invisible Man* (1952) that was literally disappeared, expunged from the version of the novel that became canonical. Ferguson reads the removal of the chapter, which includes an open representation of a black queer character, through ongoing struggles over the meaning of family, domesticity, and labor. According to Ferguson, segregation and economic injustice for African Americans were unlikely to be understood, by sociologists or the culture at large, as systemic inequities and more likely to be understood as signs that non-normativity and pathology were somehow endemic to African American family life. Although *Invisible Man* at times purports to critique the demand for normative behavior and integration into the peculiar disciplines of liberal capitalism (disciplines that were and are peculiar in the sense that the demand for unmarked, abstract labor actually generated difference, marking whole populations as unfit, pathological, or undesirable), the closeting of the black queer chapter attests to the power of those normalizing demands.[18] The published version of *Invisible Man*, significantly, represents a closeted white character, the young Mr. Emerson, but his inclusion only emphasizes the importance of disavowing queerness, since the young man is clearly positioned as a figure for the narrator of *Invisible Man* to avoid.

Despite the closet's mid-century power, LGBT people began to shape or claim alternatives. If in fact World War II was a national coming-out experience, this was due in large part to a postwar refusal, by both men and women who had discovered or forged same-sex desires in the non-familial and often gender-segregated spaces of the war, to return to hometowns, families, and other sites now readable as closeted. John D'Emilio, Nan Alamilla Boyd, and others write of San Francisco's postwar emergence as a queer capital, a location where discharged military personnel remained or where large numbers of isolated individuals from other locations migrated.[19] Marc Stein, similarly, narrates the story of Philadelphia's emergence as what he labels the "city of sisterly and brotherly loves" and Elizabeth Lapovsky Kennedy and Madeline D. Davis tell the story of Buffalo, New York's lesbian community.[20] Kennedy and Davis explain how bar cultures and house parties flourished for white and black lesbians, and how women shaped defiant butch and femme identities that allowed for recognition, survival, and community in the conformist 1950s.

Leslie Feinberg's novel *Stone Butch Blues* (1993) and Audre Lorde's "biomythography" *Zami: A New Spelling of My Name* (1982), which both look back to the challenges faced by lesbians in the 1950s and 1960s, suggest that even working-class factory life provided spaces where women might find each other and shape queer identities. Factory life encourages, in Feinberg's character Jess Goldberg, the development of a radical labor consciousness; this consciousness even culminates, for a time, in union organizing that brings out of the closet the butch, femme, and transgender presence on the shop floor. In contrast to Feinberg, Lorde's representation of the period – implicitly suggesting that every open and safe space claimed at the time was matched by the construction of new closets – describes how women of color were often fired before they could even join the union. Some of the erotic connections Lorde describes in *Zami* arise as both black and white women negotiate the insecurities and fluctuations of a sexist and racist labor market.[21]

On the west coast in the early 1950s, a small group of Marxists and leftists led by Harry Hay founded one of the first organizations explicitly concerned with homosexual rights. The Mattachine Society developed a "minority thesis" that attempted to explain how the family pushed men and women into rigid roles. Because of the power of these roles, homosexuals were constructed as a deviant minority group. Simple education aimed at changing minds would not bring about societal transformation, Hay and his comrades believed, because the familial and economic systems of the culture would continue to conjure up "deviant" individuals. Systemic, institutional critique and solidarity with other oppressed groups were thus fundamental commitments for the early Mattachine Society. The decade of the 1950s, however, saw a pattern on the west coast not unlike the one Lorde recalls on the east, with a new closet constructed for each one exited. By the mid-1950s, and as Joseph McCarthy's campaign against "subversive" elements in American culture escalated, the more radical analysis put forward by the founders of the early Mattachine Society was supplanted by anxious desires for assimilation into the culture as it already existed. A new generation of leaders, eager to position lesbians and gay men as patriotic and non-confrontational and to curry favor with professionals (doctors, psychiatrists, and clergymen), dismissed both the institutional critique and solidarity with other minorities that the early Mattachine Society had emphasized.[22]

The late Mattachine Society's quest for respectability remains ironic given how ubiquitous mid-century queerness was. Alfred Kinsey's *Sexual Behavior in the Human Male* (1948) and *Sexual Behavior in the Human Female* (1953) made clear that homoerotic and bisexual desires and fantasies, as well as activity, were far more pervasive than many had believed. Lesbian "pulp" novels, moreover, with titles such as *Women's Barracks* (1950) and *Stranger on Lesbos* (1960), were widely available. Although often consumed by men, such books were also read by lesbians eager for representations of their own lives. In contrast to the pulp novels, books such as Claire Morgan's *The Price of Salt* (1952) and Jane Rule's *Desert of the Heart* (1964) seemed more sympathetically written with actual lesbian communities in mind. Despite the construction and fortification of the closet, the middle decades of the twentieth century can be read as years of queer cultural productivity. Other kinds of productivity, however, were simply more dominant: along with the oft-remarked – and vastly overstated – economic prosperity of mid-century came, for many Americans, a newly consolidated conformity.

Yet, as the 1950s gave way to the more apparently turbulent 1960s, signs of change were definitely on the horizon. It may not be entirely accurate (in terms of numbers) to say that for every Gladys Bentley there was a José Sarria, but the two performers nonetheless serve as useful illustrations of two competing mid-century paradigms. Bentley, during the 1920s, had been one of the most famous blues performers: openly lesbian and almost always performing in drag, Bentley had even married her white female lover in a butch/femme ceremony in 1928. In 1952, Bentley published an autobiographical retrospective on her life in *Ebony* magazine, titled "I Am a Woman Again." The retrospective detailed the miracle of hormone treatment, which supposedly allowed Bentley to reclaim what she perceived as her true identity.[23] David Serlin analyzes this reinvention of Bentley's life and concludes that "in remaking her own body [Bentley] was able to imagine simultaneously a new identity that was heterosexual, feminine, and Christian, made possible by a body that materialized her desire to enter . . . a respectable socio-economic niche recognized by the black middle-class mainstream." "I Am a Woman Again" alluded to a heterosexual marriage that was later denied by the man in question, but Bentley did in fact marry a year later. In contrast to 1928, she did not, this time, wear a tuxedo and her marriage – to a man – was legally recognized. A few years later, it was legally terminated through divorce.[24]

As Bentley's career waned, Sarria's waxed. Both may have been wearing dresses in the 1950s, but Sarria was doing so for the purposes of queer resistance. A drag performer at the Black Cat in San Francisco, Sarria appeared before packed audiences throughout the decade and into the 1960s. If for Bentley at the time, everyone was naturally heterosexual, for Sarria everyone was gay, at least once they entered the Black Cat. This included increasing numbers of heterosexual tourists who came to see Sarria's performances: "I told everyone," Sarria recalled years later, "that once you came in here your reputation was lost."[25] Sarria's act included camp interpretations of Carmen (as homosexual and running from the vice police) but ended with an open call for rights and solidarity; the audience was urged to link arms and join in a rendition of "God Save Us Nelly Queens." A full decade and a half before Harvey Milk became the first openly gay man to sit on the San Francisco Board of Supervisors, Sarria mounted a campaign, garnering 6,000 votes in 1961. Sarria did not come close to winning, but the campaign did allow queer (and Latino/a) communities to imagine new and public possibilities.[26] If Bentley's 1950s career symbolizes the pressures of conformity and the closet and puts forward a compulsory reinterpretation of the queer past, Sarria's career stands for the possibility of liberation, and sets its sights on an emergent queer (and non-white) future.

Liberation, Inc.

Heady with exhilaration from their participation in the Stonewall Riots in June 1969, the anonymous narrator of Edmund White's *The Beautiful Room Is Empty* (1988) and his friend Lou find it impossible to rest: "We hugged each other in bed like brothers, but we were too excited to sleep. We rushed down to buy the morning papers to see how the Stonewall Uprising had been described . . . But we couldn't find a single mention of the turning point of our lives."[27]

White's novel may end with the bittersweet implication that queer America, as the last third of the century began, remained invisible and marginal, but the implication is not borne out by the facts. The Stonewall Riots – when patrons of a Greenwich Village bar fought back during what was supposed to be a routine police raid – were reported in all the New York papers, and the *Daily News* put the story on the front page.[28] However aesthetically useful the myth of invisibility might be for White, 1969 was a year of increased LGBT visibility. Of course, the Mattachine Society, lesbian pulp novels, drag or transgender performers like Sarria, and countless other mid-century cultural forces suggest that invisibility never wholly comprehends queer America. LGBT activists, themselves, nonetheless, still understood 1969 as a turning-point, and their most famous slogan from the period – "out of the closets and into the streets" – suggests that they were in fact daring to imagine new kinds of visibility and new public cultures. These imaginative possibilities had germinated in other movements that LGBT people had participated in throughout the 1960s: the New Left, the women's and civil rights movements, student movements, campaigns in opposition to the Vietnam war, the counterculture. The Stonewall Riots seemed to authorize an insistence that these world-transforming movements also take into account a newly dubbed "gay liberation."[29]

The Gay Liberation Front (GLF) formed in the wake of the Stonewall Riots and, by the end of the year, chapters had sprung up in major cities and on college campuses around the country. The GLF put forward a unique combination of radical political analysis and countercultural values, a combination that is well documented in the anthology *Out of the Closets: Voices of Gay Liberation* (1972). In the introduction to that collection, Karla Jay insists, "We perceive our oppression as a class struggle and our oppressor as white, middle-class, male-dominated heterosexual society."[30] Many other gay liberationists, in *Out of the Closets* and in other documents, shared and developed Jay's critique of oppression and of exploitative systems like capitalism. Like the early Mattachine Society, gay liberationists were committed to coalition and to a structural critique of American society.

Tensions similar to those that divided the Mattachine Society plagued the GLF, however. Disgruntled members of the group almost immediately formed the Gay Activists Alliance (GAA), which was less interested than the GLF in alliances with other oppressed groups and less committed to sustained critiques of capitalism, patriarchy, racism, and war. It was through the GAA's efforts that homosexuality was removed from the American Psychiatric Association's list of mental disorders, but that achievement should not obscure the ways in which the GAA redirected or reoriented the movement. Whereas the GLF encouraged people to move *out*, the GAA, desiring integration into mainstream society and a place at the table, encouraged people to move *in*.[31]

The GLF and GAA both nonetheless contributed to building cultural institutions that mark the most enduring legacy of the LGBT 1970s. Even in mid-size cities, gay men could patronize discos, bars, and bathhouses – and such institutions were, increasingly, in recognizably gay neighborhoods. Gay male writers began to come out more explicitly in their work: 1978, for instance, saw the publication of openly gay novels like Larry Kramer's *Faggots* and Andrew Holleran's *Dancer from the Dance*. As the 1970s drew to a close, Holleran, White, and several others – to nurture this emergent literary work – formed the Violet Quill club in New York City.[32] Gay male readers avidly consumed the novels written by the Violet Quill, along with a range of other stories, some of them – such as Armistead Maupin's *Tales of the City* (1976), about gay life in San Francisco, and John Preston's *Mr. Benson* (1979), about a dominant gay master and his submissive slave – serialized in periodicals. *Mr. Benson* appeared in *Drummer* magazine (a periodical aimed at sadomasochistic [s/m] subcultures), and legend has it that men lined up at newsstands in gay neighborhoods to purchase each new installment. *Mr. Benson* represented fictionally an s/m subculture that was thriving in cities like New York and San Francisco. Michel Foucault is only the most famous participant in a scene that involved thousands – not all of them necessarily looking for a Mr. Benson of their own, but still inventing a variety of sexual pleasures and non-normative relations.[33]

The disco culture represented fictionally in *Dancer from the Dance* was likewise thriving in reality, due in large part to the artistry of performers such as Donna Summer, Thelma Houston, the Village People, and Sylvester. Disco was eventually superceded by other musical forms (due in part to a homophobic and masculinist campaign intent on declaring "Disco Sucks"), but the dance floor, throughout the last third of the twentieth century, continued to be a site where queer alliances, identifications, and disidentifications could emerge. Particularly for queers of color, both Marlon Riggs's film *Tongues Untied* (1989) and Jennie Livingston's *Paris Is Burning* (1991), for example, in part document the emergence of vogueing at Latino/a and black dance venues. Vogueing was a highly stylized and competitive dance form that commented on (often critically or subversively) the performances of gender, race, and class documented in fashion magazines such as *Vogue*.[34]

Although women participated in (or, in the case of disco divas or leather dykes, helped to build) all of these subcultures, the autonomous cultural spaces women established in the 1970s were also world-transformative. The Michigan Womyn's Music Festival, for instance, was founded in 1975 and initially drew about 2,000 women; the annual event provided a unique space for women's community. The festival was part of what came to be known more generally as "Lesbian Nation" – a world of coffeehouses, bookstores, softball teams, consciousness-raising groups, communes. In 1972, Judy Dlugacz and others formed Olivia Records, which employed women as producers and artists and distributed women's music throughout burgeoning feminist networks. In 1973, along with Parke Bowman, June Arnold founded Daughters, Inc., a small publishing house dedicated exclusively to women's writing. Daughters, Inc. would go on to publish numerous lesbian and feminist novels, including Arnold's own stylistically experimental *The Cook and the Carpenter* (1973) and *Sister Gin* (1975). Like other small feminist presses, such as the Women's Press Collective or Kitchen Table: Women of Color Press, Daughters, Inc. had trouble surviving financially and eventually shut down. Collectively, however, these small ventures helped spread a wide range of feminist ideas throughout the culture.[35]

The lesbian feminism of the mid and late 1970s has been critiqued for being merely cultural or separatist, cut off from the more radical analyses put forward by feminists a decade earlier.[36] Saralyn Chesnut and Amanda C. Gable, however, suggest that such critiques downplay the role of women's bookstores and community centers throughout the decade and into the 1980s. According to Chesnut and Gable, sites like Charis Books and More in Atlanta were important for putting feminist ideas into circulation and keeping them there. Directly or indirectly, autonomous women's spaces nurtured the emergence, in the 1970s and 1980s, of academic programs in women's studies.[37] This is not to suggest that the separatist ethos put forward by some members of Lesbian Nation should not be critiqued:

transgender women have consistently – and wrongly – been excluded from the Michigan festival. As Linda Garber demonstrates well in *Identity Poetics: Race, Class, and the Lesbian–Feminist Roots of Queer Theory* (2001), however, the lesbian feminist ideas of the period should not be dismissed so easily.[38] The writings of feminists of color, in particular (writers like Lorde, Gloria Anzaldúa, Cherríe Moraga, and others), put forward ideas that would later ground queer theory, even when their foundational role was not acknowledged. "We are the queer groups," Anzaldúa wrote in the ground-breaking anthology *This Bridge Called My Back: Writings by Radical Women of Color* (1981), "the people that don't belong anywhere . . . and because we do not fit *we are a threat*." Anzaldúa's suggestion that "the queer groups" might "live together and transform the planet" implies that, even if such theories were nurtured within Lesbian Nation, feminists of color, like their queer descendants, were already thinking beyond the nation in the late 1970s.[39]

In a television interview following his election to the San Francisco Board of Supervisors, Harvey Milk linked the New Left emphasis on coalition and participatory democracy and the countercultural desire for harmony: "There's tremendous harmony developing . . . I think it's vital that the minorities, the traditional ethnic minorities, and the gays, and the feminists, link together."[40] Over the course of the late 1970s and early 1980s, with the rise of the New Right in the United States, many forces converged both to threaten the harmony Milk perceived and make even more urgent his call for coalition. In 1977, Christian singer Anita Bryant waged a campaign in Florida called "Save Our Children." Wielding rhetoric that cast LGBT people, especially teachers, as predatory, in search of children to "recruit," Bryant convinced Florida voters to repeal a civil rights ordinance that existed in Dade County and that protected lesbians and gay men from discrimination. In California, Milk himself came to national prominence partially through the successful campaign against the Briggs Initiative, a proposal introduced by Senator John Briggs in 1978 that would have prohibited openly gay and lesbian people from teaching in California's schools.

Although the fight against the Briggs Initiative was successful, these two late 1970s campaigns were only the beginning: for the next two decades, anti-gay initiatives were repeatedly put before voters; these initiatives called for the repeal of existing LGBT civil rights laws or for a prohibition on the formation of new ones. The Supreme Court, in Romer v. Evans (1996), declared some initiatives of this sort unconstitutional, arguing that prohibiting the implementation of civil rights ordinances unfairly excluded an entire class of people from participation in political processes. As the century ended, however, anti-gay initiatives shifted their focus – and in fact escalated. Dozens of state legislative bodies declared that same-sex marriage would be forever prohibited within their borders, or that marriage would be defined only as the union of one man and one woman. When the question of prohibiting same-sex marriage was put directly to the voters of twelve states in the 2004 elections, it passed by overwhelming margins.

In November 1978, Harvey Milk, along with George Moscone, the mayor of San Francisco, was assassinated by Dan White, another member of the Board of Supervisors. At the time, thousands of Milk's supporters took to the streets in a peaceful candlelight vigil in his honor. The protests turned to riots, however, when a court verdict later declared that White was guilty only of manslaughter. The lawyers who successfully argued for this lessened charge, in a strategy that became known as "the Twinkie defense," convinced jurors that White assassinated Moscone and Milk in part because he ate too much junk food.

In the wake of the Milk assassination and White verdict, "we die, they do nothing" could have been a mantra for queer America as early as 1978. A decade later, in cities and towns across the country (and indeed, around the world), activists took to the streets to put forward precisely that claim. By 1990, more than 100,000 people in the United States had died from complications due to AIDS and hundreds of thousands more were infected with the human immunodeficiency virus (HIV). If the early 1970s marked a moment when gay liberationists came together with other oppressed minorities to put forward a systemic analysis of American political, economic, and cultural institutions, the late 1980s marked a similar moment. This time, however – declaring "We Die, They Do Nothing," and "Act Up! Fight Back! Fight AIDS!" – activists were actually calling themselves queer.

The cultural form that most captured the resistance this time was video. According to Alexandra Juhasz and others, independent video (often originally produced on handheld camcorders) worked to put forward representations of the crisis that stood in stark contrast to those put forward by mainstream media. The Testing the Limits Collective and Damned Interfering Video Activists (DIVA TV) documented the activities of the AIDS Coalition to Unleash Power (ACT UP), a direct-action group formed in 1987 to protest what they perceived as the government's criminal neglect of people living with AIDS. Some of ACT UP's most famous actions include disrupting traffic on Wall Street, storming the National Institutes of Health, and disrupting mass at St. Patrick's Cathedral in New York City.[41] Other independent film and video makers who sought to intervene in the ways in which the AIDS crisis was understood in the United States (and throughout the world) include John Greyson, Jean Carlomusto, Gregg Bordowitz, Isaac Julien, and Pratibha Parmar.[42]

For much of the 1980s, LGBT or queer activists developed a strong, experiential awareness of the exclusions and limitations imposed by the state, and not only in relation to HIV/AIDS. The case of Sharon Kowalski and Karen Thompson is a good example of both queer exclusions and the critical, coalitional consciousness such exclusions could sometimes generate. Kowalski and Thompson were living together as a closeted couple in St. Cloud, Minnesota, when a drunk driver crashed into the car Kowalski was driving, killing Kowalski's niece, mildly injuring Kowalski's nephew, and seriously injuring Kowalski herself. Kowalski's parents refused to recognize the relationship between Kowalski and Thompson and, over the course of seven years, Minnesota courts consistently granted custody to Donald Kowalski, despite Sharon's repeated requests to go "home" with Thompson. Donald Kowalski not only refused to acknowledge that his daughter and Thompson were lovers and that his daughter's stated preference (through various bodily signs) was to live with Thompson, but even that his daughter could have any preferences at all. LGBT, feminist, and disability groups rallied to support the couple; "Free Sharon Kowalski" cells popped up around the country. Only in 1991, however, after Thompson and Kowalski had been separated for several years, did Minnesota courts finally declare that they could again live together. Thompson herself was often called, during and after this period, to speak to various groups about her experiences. As she encountered lesbian, gay, feminist, and disability activists around the country, she developed a critical consciousness about not just her own but others' oppression, speaking eloquently about gender oppression more generally, AIDS, homelessness, and the exploitation endemic to transnational capitalism.[43]

If queerness could generate a systemic critique of oppression, however, it could also – as I suggested at the beginning of this chapter – be contained and partially incorporated into the systems it ostensibly opposed. As neoliberalism in the final decade of the twentieth century implicitly encouraged minority groups to "commodify their dissent," the desire for assimilation, respectability, and consumption supplanted more radical calls for social change.[44] Ellen Degeneres came out on a television sitcom (*The Ellen Show*) in 1993, a year that was also dubbed by fashion magazines as the year of "lesbian chic." For LGBT people with money, a worldwide travel industry flourished, and gay pride merchandise (clothing, jewelry, rainbow flags) was increasingly available in gay neighborhoods. If Gay Pride celebrations themselves had formerly staked a defiant claim to the public space of the streets, they were more and more sanctioned by major cities as official (consumer) events. Feminists and gay liberationists had critiqued marriage and the military, but many LGBT people in the 1990s simply wanted to be included in these institutions. Even if the 2004 election and turn-of-the-century anti-gay initiatives against same-sex marriage slowed the LGBT rush down the wedding aisle, they could not keep a multimillion-dollar marriage industry from recognizing a lucrative market. Whether or not queer America is fairly described, at the beginning of the twenty-first century, as bought and sold, it is definitely, in many locations, being acknowledged and catered to.

The controversial April 30, 2000 Millennium March on Washington (MMOW) for lesbian, gay, bisexual, and transgender rights is a good concluding example not only of these processes of queer incorporation, but of the queer possibility that something more democratic and hopeful might still exist just beyond the boundaries of respectability. In 1998, leaders of the Human Rights Campaign (HRC) and the Metropolitan Community Church (MCC) called for the march. From the beginning, leadership for the march was top-down, with the HRC and MCC alone defining which issues would be central to the event. Grassroots organizers around the country were critical of the fact that they were not consulted, of the consistent lack of attention to anything more than token diversity throughout the planning process, and of the monolithic focus by march leaders on normalizing issues such as marriage rights as opposed to more sweeping calls for social justice and for a critique of the multiple systems of power (including corporate capitalism) that sustain injustice. Far from critiquing corporate capitalism, HRC was understood by many critics as craving corporate sponsorship (and, in fact, corporate logos were ubiquitous at the march). Queerness, to judge by the MMOW, had become a normal part of the American cultural, political, and economic tapestry.

Yet fractures could nonetheless be traced in the early twenty-first-century queer consensus. A local group called Freaks Are Family, formed by members of the D. C. Radical Faeries and Bi Insurgence, decided to protest the homogenization of both the movement and the MMOW. Despite being small in number (about fifty protesters gathered on the day of the march), the Freaks Are Family event – like Gay Shame Days organized in other locations to protest the corporate takeover of queer culture – was much more diverse than the MMOW more generally, including clearly identifiable members of transgender, leather, bisexual, faerie, and bear communities ("bears" are hirsute and usually large men). Perverse erotic proclivities (decidedly not the homogenous and domesticated married identity sought after by the MMOW), multiple genders, and various disabilities were also represented – and these could be read both on protesters' bodies and through the homemade signs that they carried (which differed sharply from mass-produced signs displaying HRC's blue and gold equals sign).[45] For Freaks Are Family, and groups like them, "Queer America" is not necessarily desirable, if such a concept marks the dilution of more capacious understandings of community and desire and the incorporation of LGBT people into a docile consumerism. Queer America, instead, is always something to move outside of or beyond, even if the democratic, just, and freaky world beyond its borders can still only be discerned faintly on the horizon.

NOTES

1. Licia Fiol-Matta, *A Queer Mother for the Nation: The State and Gabriela Mistral* (Minneapolis: University of Minnesota Press, 2002). On the more subversive possibilities of "female masculinity," see Judith Halberstam, *Female Masculinity* (Durham, NC: Duke University Press, 1998).
2. See Paula A. Treichler, *How to Have Theory in an Epidemic: Cultural Chronicles of AIDS* (Durham, NC: Duke University Press, 1999), p. 13. On terms like "general population" and "carriers," see Jan Zita Grover, "AIDS: Keywords," in Douglas Crimp (ed.), *AIDS: Cultural Analysis/Cultural Activism* (Cambridge, MA: MIT Press, 1988), pp. 17–30.
3. Jon Barrett, *Hero of Flight 93: Mark Bingham* (Los Angeles: Advocate, 2002).
4. Judith Fetterley, "*My Ántonia*, Jim Burden, and the Dilemma of the Lesbian Writer," in Karla Jay and Joanne Glasgow (eds.), *Lesbian Texts and Contexts: Radical Revisions* (New York: New York University Press, 1990), pp. 150–1.
5. Eve Kosofsky Sedgwick, *Epistemology of the Closet* (Berkeley: University of California Press, 1990), p. 1.
6. Lisa Duggan, *Sapphic Slashers: Sex, Violence, and American Modernity* (Durham, NC: Duke University Press, 2000).
7. See Esther Newton, "The Mythic Mannish Lesbian: Radclyffe Hall and the New Woman," in Martin Duberman, Martha Vicinus, and George Chauncey, Jr. (eds.), *Hidden from History: Reclaiming the Gay and Lesbian Past* (New York: Meridian, 1989), pp. 281–93.
8. Duggan, *Sapphic Slashers*, pp. 29–31, 40–2.
9. See Didier Eribon, *Insult and the Making of the Gay Self*, trans. Michael Lucey (Durham, NC: Duke University Press, 2004), pp. 190–205.
10. Gregory Tomso, "The Queer History of Leprosy and Same-Sex Love," *American Literary History*, 14,4 (Winter 2002): 747–75.
11. W. E. B. DuBois, *The Souls of Black Folk* (New York: Signet Classics, 1969), p. xi.
12. George Chauncey, *Gay New York: Gender, Urban Culture, and the Making of the Gay Male World, 1890–1940* (New York: Basic Books, 1994) pp. 332–5, 325–9.
13. *Ibid.*, pp. 6–8.
14. See Deborah E. McDowell, Introduction to *Quicksand and Passing* by Nella Larsen, ed. Deborah E. McDowell (New Brunswick, NJ: Rutgers University Press, 1986), pp. xxiii–xxxi; Hazel Carby, "It Jus Be's Dat Way Sometime: The

Sexual Politics of Women's Blues," in Ellen Carol DuBois and Vicki Ruiz (eds.), *Unequal Sisters: A Multicultural Reader in U. S. Women's History* (New York: Routledge, 1990), pp. 238–49.

15. Chauncey, *Gay New York*, p. 331.

16. John D'Emilio, *Sexual Politics, Sexual Communities: The Making of a Homosexual Minority in the United States, 1940–1970* (Chicago: University of Chicago Press, 1983), p. 24; Chauncey, *Gay New York*, pp. 10–12.

17. Gore Vidal, *The City and the Pillar*, rev. ed. (New York: Ballantine, 1965), p. 179.

18. Roderick A. Ferguson, *Aberrations in Black: Toward a Queer of Color Critique* (Minneapolis: University of Minnesota Press, 2004), pp. 54–81.

19. John D'Emilio, "Gay Politics, Gay Community: San Francisco's Experience," *Making Trouble: Essays on Gay History, Politics, and the University* (New York: Routledge, 1992), pp. 74–95; Nan Alamilla Boyd, *Wide Open Town: A History of Queer San Francisco to 1965* (Berkeley: University of California Press, 2003).

20. Marc Stein, *City of Sisterly and Brotherly Loves* (Chicago: University of Chicago Press, 2000); Elizabeth Lapovsky Kennedy and Madeline D. Davis, *Boots of Leather, Slippers of Gold: The History of a Lesbian Community* (New York: Routledge, 1993).

21. Leslie Feinberg, *Stone Butch Blues* (Ithaca, NY: Firebrand, 1993); Audre Lorde, *Zami: A New Spelling of My Name* (Trumansburg, NY: Crossing Press, 1982).

22. D'Emilio, *Sexual Politics*, pp. 64–5, 122–5.

23. David Serlin, *Replaceable You: Engineering the Body in Postwar America* (Chicago: University of Chicago Press, 2004), pp. 111–58.

24. *Ibid.*, pp. 156, 151.

25. Boyd, *Wide Open Town*, p. 58.

26. *Ibid.*, pp. 57–62; D'Emilio, "Gay Politics," pp. 82–3.

27. Edmund White, *The Beautiful Room Is Empty* (New York: Knopf, 1988), pp. 227–8.

28. Martin Duberman, *Stonewall* (New York: Dutton, 1993), p. 202.

29. D'Emilio, "After Stonewall," *Making Trouble*, pp. 241–3.

30. Karla Jay, Introduction to the first edition, Karla Jay and Allen Young (eds.), *Out of the Closets: Voices of Gay Liberation* (New York: New York University Press, 1992) p. lxi.

31. D'Emilio, "After Stonewall," p. 247–9.

32. See David Bergman, *The Violet Hour: The Violet Quill and the Making of Gay Culture* (New York: Columbia University Press, 2004).

33. See David M. Halperin, *Saint Foucault: Towards a Gay Hagiography* (New York: Oxford University Press), pp. 85–99.

34. See Marcos Becquer, "Snap!thology and Other Discursive Practices in Tongues Untied," *Wide Angle*, 13,2 (1991): 11–16.

35. See Lillian Faderman, *Odd Girls and Twilight Lovers: A History of Lesbian Life in Twentieth-Century America* (New York: Penguin, 1991), pp. 215–45.

36. See Alice Echols, *Daring to Be Bad: Radical Feminism in America, 1967–1975* (Minneapolis: University of Minnesota Press, 1989), pp. 243–86.

37. Saralyn Chesnut and Amanda C. Gable, "'Women Ran It': Charis Books and More and Atlanta's Lesbian Feminist Community, 1971–1981," in John

Howard (ed.), *Carryin' On in the Lesbian and Gay South* (New York: New York University Press, 1997), pp. 241–84.

38. Linda Garber, *Identity Poetics: Race, Class, and the Lesbian–Feminist Roots of Queer Theory* (New York: Columbia University Press, 2001).

39. Gloria Anzaldúa, "La Prieta," in Cherríe Moraga and Gloria Anzaldúa (eds.), *This Bridge Called My Back: Writings by Radical Women of Color* (Latham, NY: Kitchen Table: Women of Color Press, 1981), p. 209.

40. The interview is included in Robert Epstein and Richard Schmiechen, producers, *The Times of Harvey Milk* (Black Sand Productions, 1984).

41. Douglas Crimp, with Adam Rolston, *AIDS DemoGraphics* (Seattle: Bay Press, 1990).

42. Alexandra Juhasz, *AIDS TV: Identity, Community, and Alternative Video* (Durham, NC: Duke University Press, 1995).

43. Karen Thompson and Julie Andrzejewski, *Why Can't Sharon Kowalski Come Home?* (San Francisco: Spinsters/Aunt Lute, 1988).

44. See Thomas Frank, *Commodify Your Dissent: Salvos from the Baffler* (New York: Norton, 1997).

45. The preceding two paragraphs on the MMOW are adapted, with permission, from Robert McRuer, "Composing Bodies; or, DeComposition: Queer Theory, Disability Studies, and Alternative Corporealities," *JAC: A Quarterly Journal for the Interdisciplinary Study of Rhetoric, Culture, Literacy, and Politics*, 24,1 (2004): 63–6.

FURTHER READING

Henry Abelove, Michèle Aina Barale, and David M. Halperin (eds.), *The Lesbian and Gay Studies Reader*, New York: Routledge, 1993.

Deborah Carlin and Jennifer DiGrazia (eds.), *Queer Cultures*, Upper Saddle River, NJ: Pearson-Prentice Hall, 2004.

José Esteban Muñoz, *Disidentifications: Queers of Color and the Performance of Politics*, Minneapolis: University of Minnesota Press, 1999.

David Román, *Acts of Intervention: Performance, Gay Culture, and AIDS*, Bloomington: Indiana University Press, 1998.

Eve Kosofsky Sedgwick, *Tendencies*, Durham, NC: Duke University Press, 1993.

Siobhan B. Somerville, *Queering the Color Line: Race and the Invention of Homosexuality in American Culture*, Durham, NC: Duke University Press, 2000.

Susan Stryker, and Stephen Whittle (eds.), *The Transgender Reader*, New York: Routledge, 2003.

Michael Warner, *The Trouble with Normal: Sex, Politics, and the Ethics of Queer Life*, New York: Free Press, 1999.

KENNETH P. O'BRIEN

The United States, war, and the twentieth century

No major advanced industrial nation has suffered less or profited more from its twentieth-century wars than the United States. Nor has any nation dispatched its troops to as many places across the globe in the late twentieth century to defend and extend its national interest. At the end of the nineteenth century, the United States possessed one of the smallest armies in the industrial world; a century later its armed forces spanned the globe, bristling with deadly hardware and sophisticated technology, a military power without peer. To a large extent, this remarkable transformation had resulted from participation in two European wars, which had necessitated a reorganization of society and the establishment of new controls over its citizens.

The Spanish-American and Philippine-American Wars

By the 1890s, many influential Americans believed their economy required access to foreign markets to avoid future depressions. Incorporating this notion into a broader ideological framework, influential policymakers sought to establish an indirect control of large areas of the Caribbean and the Pacific. These ideas, informed by notions of racial hierarchy and articulated through a gendered vocabulary, provided the larger context for the war of 1898, as two presidents faced a growing Cuban insurrection against Spanish rule.[1]

Between 1895 and 1897, American diplomats had pressured Spain to resolve the crisis on the island, with little result, and by late 1897 many Americans believed Spanish rule in the Caribbean must end. In February 1898 two events – the de Lome letter and an explosion aboard the battleship *Maine* while in Havana that killed 266 US sailors – triggered the final movement toward war. To President McKinley's rambling war message the Congress attached the Teller Amendment, specifically denying US territorial interests in Cuba. With great fanfare and public enthusiasm, the United States went to war against a country that threatened neither its "security" nor its "vital interests."[2]

The Army, with only 28,000 trained troops, little equipment, and no supporting bureaucracy, was completely unprepared for the fight. Even after a tenfold increase in size, it remained ineffective and ill equipped, as demonstrated by the Army's near disaster in the hills surrounding Santiago. The Navy, having been modernized over the previous decades, fared much better, easily defeating the Spanish fleets in Manila Bay and Santiago harbor. Spain received $20 million for the Philippines, which McKinley finally decided to keep, and ceded its colonies in the Caribbean to the United States. By asserting control over Cuban treaties and the right to intervene in domestic Cuban disputes, the American government violated the spirit, if not the letter, of its earlier promise and earned the disdain of the Cubans who had fought against the Spanish.[3]

The struggle for an American empire in the Pacific, however, was just beginning with the war's end. The imperialists in the Senate faced strong opposition from opponents who questioned the effect of far-flung colonies on democratic government. Most anti-imperialists believed the acquisition of the Philippines was against the nation's interests and a violation of its Constitution. In addition, a number also thought the Filipinos were simply too inferior to be incorporated into American society. After a long debate, the Senate failed by a single vote to set the Philippines free.

Another, and ultimately equally ineffective, opposition developed in the Philippines themselves. On February 4, 1899, Philippine nationalist forces attacked American positions around Manila. The resulting Philippine-American War cost $400 million and 4,200 American lives, making it much more expensive than the war with Spain.[4] Between 1899 and 1902, the United States sent a total of 125,000 troops to wage a vicious counter-insurgency war. While the popular press reported atrocities by both sides, special emphasis was given to brutal American tactics, including torture, and a rural reconcentration policy that left thousands dead.[5] During the war, approximately 20,000 Philippine soldiers lost their lives, while several hundred thousand civilians perished from the war's dislocations.

The occupation that followed illustrated the complexity of American colonial rule, as Governor General William Howard Taft quickly restored civil authority, built schools, and improved sanitation systems.[6] As progressives, Americans assumed a community of interest with the colonial peoples that never actually existed. They believed their national democratic experiment was exportable, without regard for geographical boundaries and cultural traditions. This idea of a distinct American mission had deep historical roots, and as it became "the keystone of US foreign policy ideology," the United States "succumbed to the temptations of an assertively nationalist foreign policy."[7]

In truth, the wars growing out of the Cuban insurrection were neither "splendid" nor "little," to use John Hay's famous claim, but they were important, bequeathing both a larger modernized Army with an international presence and a more powerful presidency. In the following decade, McKinley dispatched 2,500 US troops to China without congressional authorization, and Theodore Roosevelt, his successor, grabbed the rights for an isthmusian canal by assisting Panama's separation from Columbia.

The Great War

In the first decades of the new century, the United States achieved a regional hegemony in the Caribbean as it claimed the right to intervene throughout the region, a right it frequently exercised. Hardly "wars," these military interventions reveal the arrogance behind US relations with its southern neighbors, as detachments of Marines landed throughout Central America more than thirty times in seventeen years. As a consequence, people died, including the 65 Americans and 500 Mexicans who perished in the 1914 attack on Veracruz, which was undertaken to foster regime change in Mexico.

In time, America's attention turned to Europe and the Great War that had erupted in 1914. In April 1917, after years of disputing the marine rights of neutral nations, Woodrow Wilson finally committed the United States to active participation in the brutal war. He asked Congress to join the Allies in "the most terrible and disastrous of all wars," with "civilization itself" hanging "in the balance." From his opening rhetorical salvo to his somber conclusion, Wilson defined the issues in the starkest moral terms, a conflict between democrats and autocrats, a war that was necessary to create a world "made safe for democracy."[8]

Declaring war was one matter, fighting it another. "Good Lord," cried a shocked Senator after hearing testimony about the need for a vastly expanded Army, "You're not going to send soldiers over there, are you?"[9] Indeed they did; within eighteen months 2 million "Doughboys" had landed in France. To wage war, the government mobilized manpower, industry, and public opinion, in effect, permanently expanding the range and power of the American state. In early 1917 the Army numbered 127,588 regular troops, with another 80,446 in organized National Guard units. Early in the conflict, Congress passed the Selective Service Act, under which 24 million men were registered, 2.7 million of whom were inducted through the work of thousands of local draft boards. In all, 5 million men served between 1917 and 1919.

Yet, not all who were called served. Over 300,000 draft registrants failed to appear for induction, while another 3 million who were eligible failed to register, leading authorities to conduct armed "slacker raids" for draft evaders. In some areas of the rural South, draft opposition was so strong that three governors requested federal troops to hunt down armed deserters.[10]

The 5 million who did serve needed to be housed, clothed, trained, and equipped. In 1917, the Army undertook the largest construction program in its history, while the Quartermaster Corps, with a prewar annual budget of $186.3 million, struggled to spend forty times that amount in the nineteen-month war. Yet, supply failures continued to plague the Army, as its troops often trained without equipment at home and then fought in France with Allied tanks, airplanes, and guns.[11]

The Army's supply difficulties reflected some of the larger problems of the war economy. Federal agencies expanded dramatically, in both number and size, with federal civilian employment doubling. The new agencies, staffed by men who had worked in the industries they were now overseeing, preferred cooperation to coercion, as they coordinated the production and distribution of armaments and other war goods. Herbert Hoover's Food Administration, for example, advertised widely to gain voluntary compliance with its "meatless" and "wheatless" days and advocated increasing private vegetable gardens for food production.

When persuasion proved ineffective, however, the government quickly placed critical industries in effective receivership for the duration.[12] In late December 1917, for example, after fuel and transportation problems temporarily paralyzed the economy, Wilson seized the railroads and subsequently granted extraordinary authority to the War Industries Board and its chairman, financier Bernard Baruch to coordinate the war economy. The Overman Act (1918) gave the President extraordinary discretionary powers to reshape government agencies without congressional oversight. The system that finally emerged in early 1918 placed supervisory authority in government-business boards, which reported to the WIB, while the military procurement offices retained much of their traditional power.[13] Although Baruch eventually made the system work, the WIB was hardly an unqualified success. Even "cost plus" contracts that guaranteed profits to industrial firms, for example, failed to maintain industrial production when millions of former workers donned military uniforms.

For industrial workers, the war proved to be a particular boon. Samuel Gompers and the American Federation of Labor used the war emergency to obtain labor seats on both the War Industries Board and the National War Labor Board, which then supported many union demands, including an eight-hour day. Consequently, the Board issued hundreds of rulings that relied on voluntary compliance by companies to recognize unions, grant fairer wages, and improve working conditions.[14] The mainstream unions proved particularly adept at expropriating the language of war, as when they referred to recalcitrant employers as "Junkers." In short, the war offered organized labor a state-sponsored legitimacy that unions parlayed into dramatically increased membership.

Not all unions, however, welcomed the new conditions. The more radical unions, particularly the IWW, were shattered by the emerging "War Welfare State," through assaults by local vigilantes and federal indictments under the Espionage Act, which provided the legal basis for more than a thousand wartime indictments. Among those convicted were Eugene Debs, the perennial Socialist Party presidential candidate, and Robert Goldstein, a film producer who violated orders from wartime censors by re-inserting scenes of rampaging Redcoats attacking defenseless colonialists during the American Revolution into his film, *The Spirit of '76*. For this crime, Goldstein received a ten-year sentence, which was later commuted to three.[15]

To monitor the home front, the Bureau of Investigation expanded to more than five times its 1917 size. In addition, at least six other federal agencies fielded a domestic spy unit, making this the era when "American political intelligence had come of age."[16] State and local governments moved in concert with their federal counterparts and quasi-governmental groups, creating "a cooperative relationship between federal and state power and a decentralized, voluntarist, nonbureaucratic mode of public administration."[17] For example, to support wartime conformity, the 250,000 volunteers of the American Protective League gathered rumors and reported suspicions about their neighbors. Characterized as "amateur sleuths and loyalty enforcers," they "bugged, burglarized, slandered, and illegally arrested other Americans."[18]

Official repression and vigilantism, which occasionally proved lethal, paralleled the extraordinary efforts of the Committee on Public Information. Characterized by its progressive chair, George Creel, as "the world's greatest adventure in advertising," the new agency employed 150,000 people in twenty-one divisions.[19] Using modern media, the CPI broadcast its messages widely, consistently defining Germans as barbaric "Huns" and "curs," who were ruled by a despot in the thrall of "Kultur." The Committee's assault on all things German rapidly spread across the country, resulting in bans on German language instruction in several states, even making "sauerkraut" into "liberty cabbage." Books were burned and men tarred and feathered. The Committee organized 75,000 "Four Minute Men," leading citizens who took their name from the four-minute scripted speeches they presented to more than 300 million fellow citizens in theaters, meeting halls, and churches during the war.[20] In addition, the Committee worked with the Post Office and the Censorship Board to deny access to the mails for publications that criticized the war effort.

The experience of the Great War, then, narrowed the scope of reform, disappointing Progressives like John Dewey who had vainly hoped that greater "social possibilities" might emerge from the slaughter. The war period, however, proved to be an especially congenial time for "social control" reforms. For example, after their intelligence had been measured by new I.Q. tests, the soldiers' virtue was jealously guarded by the Commission on Training Camp Activities. The Commission attacked both venereal disease and prostitution, with an educational campaign against the first and a campaign to establish prostitute-free "moral zones" surrounding military camps against the other. As a result, more than a hundred "red light" districts were closed and 15,000 prostitutes imprisoned.[21] The purity campaign even followed the Doughboys to France, where the crusaders dramatically cut the venereal disease rates among enlisted men, but not among either their officers or the MPs assigned to police the brothels.[22]

In 1919 reformers used the war's implicit call for greater social controls to finally gain the ratification of the Eighteenth Amendment, which prohibited the manufacture and sale of alcoholic beverages. The war also aided the passage of the Nineteenth Amendment, which guaranteed women's suffrage in national elections, but only after the National Women's Suffrage Association traded its support for the war for President Wilson's reluctant endorsement. In addition, Congress passed the War Risk Insurance Act that provided more than a half billion dollars between 1917 and 1919 to families whose men were in the armed forces. Between the soldiers' allotments and WRIA money, many families' incomes exceeded prewar levels, allowing working women to become much more selective about employment.[23] While the total number of employed women changed little, the war induced significant job-shifting, with many women leaving domestic work for better pay in war industries.

With 5 million men in uniform, war industry drew millions of migrants, including African Americans, to cities in the North and South. The migrants, who often followed prewar kinship trails, met segregation, hostility, and constant disputes over social services and housing.[24] East St. Louis, Illinois, for example, erupted in a race riot in July 1917 that left scores dead, almost all of whom were black. The riot dramatically underscored the dilemma facing African Americans, who struggled with the issue of supporting a government that failed to deliver even a semblance of colorblind justice at home. The Army was still segregated and rife with racial conflict.

Despite his acute understanding of the white majority's underlying racist attitudes, W. E. B. Du Bois called upon people of color to "forget [their] special grievances and close ranks" with their fellow Americans, a wartime accommodation for which he was roundly criticized.[25]

The peace that descended on November 11, 1918 was accompanied by new social struggles, in both the United States and war-shattered Europe. During the next year, inflation accelerated and labor unrest increased, making 1919 the most strike-ridden year in American history. Racial riots erupted in several major cities, including Washington, DC, where six died, and Chicago, with a toll six times greater, signaling an end to African American hopes for a better life. Toward the end of the year, Attorney General A. Mitchell Palmer, reacting to a string of anarchist bombings, initiated the "Red Scare," during which thousands were arrested and hundreds deported with scant regard for legal due process. In time, labor unrest, racial violence, and the Red Scare all abated, leaving in their wake an anti-radical residue that was expressed in both the restrictive National Origins Acts of 1921 and 1924 and the explosive growth of groups such as the American Legion and the KKK. The nation was as divided at the war's end as it had been while it was being fought.

Even though war agencies were quickly disbanded in 1919, some changes brought to government, society, and culture by the war remained. The postwar federal government remained significantly larger than it had been in 1916, while the Army doubled its prewar size. War tax policy, which relied more on personal and corporate income taxes, became a permanent fixture in the postwar state, as did much of the security apparatus that had been created. And, the Great War again reinforced the power and prestige of the presidency.

Yet, even presidential power had limits. On January 8, 1918 President Wilson delivered his "Fourteen Points," the last of which called for a "general association of nations" to provide "mutual guarantees of political independence and territorial integrity to great and small nations alike."[26] Wilson took the idea to Paris, where it survived the internecine negotiations to emerge as Article Ten of the Treaty of Versailles, but in the Senate the combination of a fiercely fought and well-led opposition and Wilson's refusal to accept modest reservations to Article Ten, doomed American ratification and with it, membership in the new League of Nations.

World War II

Throughout the 1920s European affairs engaged American diplomats, who served on League of Nations commissions, worked to isolate the Russian

Revolution, facilitated capital transfers among Western nations, and sought reductions in armaments among industrialized nations. After the onset of the Great Depression, however, American leaders turned to more nationalist solutions to the nation's growing economic problems, as suspicions of all European entanglements, including World War I, grew.

Once war in Europe erupted on September 1939 the Roosevelt administration pressured legislators to modify the trade restrictions embedded in the Neutrality Acts of the 1930s and began supplying Great Britain with arms and war materiel. In August 1941, Roosevelt and Churchill met and announced the Atlantic Charter, which amounted to a joint declaration of war aims that promised national self-determination, free trade, and freedom of the seas. Despite the serious, often acrimonious, debate about the direction of American policy that accompanied each step toward war, by October 1941 the Roosevelt administration had extended America's defensive perimeter well into the North Atlantic, where the Navy became embroiled in an undeclared shooting war against German submarines. At the same time, the rift with the Japanese over their invasion of China, which had been renewed in 1937, widened. After two years of increasing economic pressure, the Japanese believed they had to choose between war with the United States and their ambitions in East Asia. They chose war, launching their attack on Pearl Harbor that naturally ended all debate and unified outraged Americans.

For America, World War II would be both a "two-front" war and much longer than the Great War, which meant that social reorganization would be much more thorough. Even though the administration had used the years between the German attack on Poland and the Japanese assault on Pearl Harbor to dramatically accelerate the military build-up begun in the 1930s, the nation was still largely unprepared for war. Unlike the Great War, World War II became a "total" war on the home front, at least as far as one could be waged by a corporate capitalist economy with a democratic political culture leavened by a strong strain of local autonomy.

Beginning in 1940, millions of men registered for the draft, a million of whom were inducted before Pearl Harbor. The new conscript army roughly reflected the make-up of the larger society, giving a degree of credibility to Hollywood's "All American platoon" that melded young men from all ethnicities (save African Americans) and backgrounds into a single combat unit. Through its 6,433 local volunteer boards, the draft worked well, providing the men needed to expand the armed services to more than 11 million by 1943.[27]

To support them, federal civilian employment almost quadrupled, with the new agencies constituting a second coming of the New Deal's "alphabet soup," as the war's OEM, NDAC, SPAB, OPACS, OPA, OPM, and WPB replaced the PWA, WPA, NYA, and CCC. Ironically, nonmilitary governmental offices grew even faster during the war than they had during the New Deal.[28] Despite this rapid expansion of government agencies, effective coordination of industrial production remained elusive. Some consumer industries, for example, actively resisted converting to war production, especially given the improving economic conditions of the early 1940s. Even after the conversion process, industrial coordination remained messy.

Yet, the "Arsenal for Democracy's" output was astonishing. For example, synthetic rubber, which became a critical commodity after the Japanese seizure of Southeast Asia, flowed from government-owned factories, with output increasing from 8,383 long tons to 753,111 by 1944.[29] Other production "miracles" included Ford's huge plant outside Detroit that belched forth almost 9,000 bombers and the Kaiser shipyards that cut the production cycle of a Liberty ship from 355 days to four.[30] By 1944, the United States was out-producing all the Axis powers combined by a factor of two. Certainly, not all US weapons were well designed. The under-armored, under-gunned Sherman tank, for one, disgusted their crews, who nervously called them "Purple Heart Boxes."[31]

As in World War I, government spending directed by thousands of "dollar-a-year" men from corporations especially benefited the largest firms; over one-half of the $175 billion awarded in prime war contracts went to the thirty-three largest US firms while the smallest 90 percent received less than 10 percent of war spending. Expressed differently, the largest 100 corporations produced 30 percent of all goods in 1940, a figure that more than doubled by 1943![32] Secretary of War Henry Stimson noted, "If you are going to try to go to war. . .in a capitalist country, you have to let business make money out of the process or business won't work."[33] American corporations made money in this war, lots of it, doubling their after-tax profits between 1940 and 1943.

As employment in war industries grew, so did union membership, which increased by more than 50 percent between 1940 and 1945. The New Deal's Wagner Act had certainly altered the pattern of industrial relations by making government the final arbiter of labor unrest, creating a system that valued "industrial democracy" and spoke to the "democratic promise of American life."[34] During World War II the War Labor Board struck a somewhat different balance, promising corporations labor stability and unions modest wage increases in exchange for profits and production. Through wage and price controls, the government contained the cost of living, in the process making collective bargaining less important. This highly politicized system effectively reduced organized labor to "a ward of the state."[35] In 1943, for example, after the United Mine Workers walked out, breaking the CIO's 1942 "no strike" pledge, congressional conservatives took their revenge by passing the Smith–Connolly War Labor Disputes Act, which limited the right to strike, over Roosevelt's veto.

By mid-1942 businesses needed more workers if they were to continue to expand war production, and with government support, they began to recruiting women actively. During the conflict, more than 6 million women went to work outside their homes, increasing their percentage in the labor force by 50 percent. Since most of these new workers were married, many with children, local businesses and their bureaucratic allies pressed for federal childcare funding, which was provided by the Lanham Act.[36] Women who entered war factories were reassured by extensive ad campaigns that they did not risk their femininity by such labor. Moreover, the war jobs were understood to be temporary, "for the duration" only, which meant that at the end of the war, millions of "Rosies" were to stop riveting and return to their homes. They did, many voluntarily, many not. Consequently, the extraordinary changes witnessed in publicly authorized gender roles during the war did not survive the peace.

Since war work was concentrated in specific cities, 13 million civilians changed their counties of residence during the war. The population explosions in numerous cities brought with them overcrowded housing, inadequate social services, and increased fears of youth delinquency. For example, after the population of Mobile, Alabama doubled in three years, the Federal Housing Authority built 11,000 residential units, which were hardly sufficient. In addition, the local agencies faced constant problems, such as finding qualified teachers who were willing to work split shifts and classrooms where they could meet students.[37]

The different levels of government – federal, state, and local – could each affect local community life. Behind the encouragement offered by the Office of War Information to conserve and save precious materials, lay the demands of rationing, which were administered through local War Councils in cities and states. These same councils organized civilian protection down to the block level, providing an unprecedented intrusion of government agents into neighborhoods. Wages and prices were to a large extent directly controlled, as were manpower, profits, and rents. Even so, the organization of the home front more often relied on voluntarism and coordination than coercion, with that phrase "for the duration" hinting at the limits of governmental control over American businesses, communities, and families.[38]

Since American soldiers said "home" was what they were fighting for, the Office of War Information defined the war as necessary to protect the "American Way of Life." It worked through the Bureau of Motion Pictures to shape the content of Hollywood films and the Advertising Council to mobilize home front support for war bond drives, scrap drives, and Victory Gardens. While wartime information control and censorship of the media were pervasive, the OWI used discreet guidance rather than fiat, in effect censoring with a velvet glove. It was censorship, nonetheless, with tight control maintained over the millions of images shot by commercial and military photographers.[39] The agency's frank acknowledgment of some of America's social problems, such as racism, outraged congressional conservatives, who saw OWI bureaucrats as a collection of liberals dedicated to the re-election of the President. Southern Democrats, in particular, took offense, and in 1943, they seized an opportunity to cut the agency's budget drastically.[40]

The patterns of American race relations remained largely unchanged during the war. The armed forces were thoroughly segregated, and the location of basic training camps throughout the South proved especially nettlesome to African Americans in uniform.[41] Many leaders within the African American community, struggling with the same issues they had faced twenty-five years earlier, adopted the symbolic "Double V," with two distinct victories to be won, one against totalitarianism abroad and the other against racial injustice at home. This conception joined the ideological implications of the war against militant tyranny with the African American domestic struggle and its refusal to accept the prevailing patterns of racial discrimination.[42]

African Americans often faced terrible employment and housing prospects despite the unprecedented establishment of the Fair Employment Practices Committee by Executive Order 8802 in June 1941. The Committee had few staff, little authority, and less stature. When African Americans were hired, they often suffered abuse from white workers, such as in Baltimore in 1942, where white unionists protested the admission of two African Americans to a welding school, and in Philadelphia the next year, where unionized white transit workers waged a war of their own against nondiscriminatory hiring practices.[43] In the summer of 1943 race riots erupted in Detroit and New York City, leaving behind scores of dead and a tattered image of American democracy. In both cases competition for residences and jobs provided tinder for racial conflict. In that same summer, groups of off-duty sailors roamed the streets of Los Angeles, first attacking Hispanic youths wearing the popular, jazz-inspired "Zoot Suit" and later anyone who appeared Hispanic. The rioting, which lasted for a week, highlighted the emergence of a new minority, one that, according to the final report issued by the study commission, faced an old problem: racism.

The administration's response to racial and ethnic conflict attempted to both ameliorate the underlying causes of social unrest and institute tighter means of social control. President Roosevelt sadly noted that in "some communities employers dislike to hire women," while in others "they are reluctant to hire Negroes." "We can no longer," he concluded, "afford to indulge such prejudice."[44] The theme of tolerance and inclusion that he sounded was one of the most pervasive of the war. But, at the same time, he ordered the FBI to gather intelligence and more closely monitor American citizens of every stripe, especially those who raised questions about the war. Consequently, the government's wartime international and domestic intelligence operations expanded dramatically, with much of the domestic effort aimed at monitoring fellow citizens. To meet its new responsibilities, the FBI increased both its number of agents and its budget fivefold.[45]

At times intelligence mattered little. The story of the decision behind Executive Order 9066, which authorized the removal of those of Japanese descent from the west coast, is by now familiar, but the fact that three intelligence services thought the action unwarranted is not. As December 1941 turned into January 1942, political pressure – fomented by racism, rumor, envy, and calculation of political advantage – to do *something* about the 110,000 men, women, and children of Japanese descent began to mount, as west coast newspapers and politicians vied with one another to feed the frenzy, ably assisted by Lt. General John L DeWitt, the commander of the Western Defense Command.[46] The Internment constituted a marked disruption to Japanese-American family and community life, as well as an economic loss estimated in excess of $400 million. Interestingly, the military commander of the Hawaiian Islands, General Delos Emmons, refused to order large-scale evacuations and internments, since he believed they would simply damage the local economy and the war effort. Hence, only 1,400 were interned out of a population of 150,000.

Ironically, General Emmons's decision was consistent with the administration's general wartime civil liberties policy. Since the administration believed that maintaining wartime unity was crucially important, the OWI, unlike the CPI in the earlier war, carefully crafted its public messages to distinguish between enemy governments and their people. And, with the important exception of the Japanese-American internment cases, the Supreme Court's rulings "protected the First Amendment rights of religious dissenters, naturalized citizens, and political extremists and often did so in language that ringingly affirmed fundamental liberties."[47]

Although civil liberties were not lost for most groups, lives were. Three hundred and thirty thousand men died in combat, another 110,000 from other causes, while almost a million others suffered serious injuries. These losses, undisputedly tragic, paled in comparison to the experience of millions of European and Asian families. This most destructive of all wars – 60 million dead, over half civilians – ended with the Allied firebombing of German and Japanese cities in the spring of 1945 and the atomic bombs delivered to Hiroshima and Nagasaki in early August.

While the A-bombs rightly symbolize the barbarism to which this war descended in its last year, they also characterize two other aspects: the technologies available to reach distant targets, which now included civilian munitions makers, and the intersection of politics with pure and applied science. The first news of the atomic bombs on Hiroshima and Nagasaki became a "psychic event of unprecedented proportions," a shocking reminder of the reach of the destructive power now available to governments.[48] But the bombs also symbolized the war's other technological achievements, such as radar and penicillin, and were celebrated as resulting from an unprecedented effort that cost 2 billion dollars, employed more than the 120,000, and necessitated the construction of new cities, such as Los Alamos, New Mexico. The vast scale of this project was unimaginable four years before.

In retrospect, many of the home front war's most vivid memories – the bond drives, the campaigns to save metals and rubber, and the volunteer work of all kinds – fed into the subsequent myth of the "Good War."[49] With peace came a sort of "normalcy," as federally funded day-care centers ceased operations, 7,000 local War Councils disbanded, and the USO canteens and clubs turned off their lights. Post-World War II liberals, like their counterparts twenty-five years earlier, fought a rearguard action to preserve a large degree of government control over the economy lest the depression return, but Congress liquidated war agencies as quickly as it could. Even so, the postwar government employed twice as many civilians, while the American military, even after demobilization in 1946, was four times its prewar size.

Despite some similarities, such as dramatically increasing inflation followed by a long period of prosperity, the postwar experiences of the two world wars were quite dissimilar for Americans. First, there was a dramatic contrast in national power: at the end of World War II, with most industrial economies in ruins, the United States was producing 50 percent of the world's industrial goods, and while the nuclear monopoly would be short-lived, it nevertheless represented an unparalleled military capacity. As the war ended, the nation's foreign policy elite tried to use all available power to create a world where capital, commerce, and ideas would flow without hindrance, even establishing new agencies, such as the World Bank and the International Monetary Fund, to facilitate its development. And, among the war's ideological legacies was a renewed commitment to freedom, articulated in the Four Freedoms, which reinforced arguments against racism, and its patterns of prejudice and discrimination.

Another defining legacy of World War II was an avowal to avoid two "errors" of the preceding decades: the refusal to join the League of Nations and the capitulation to totalitarian demands in the 1930s. Following this war, American leadership committed their nation to active participation in an international organization that promised collective security and a willingness to confront totalitarian aggression. Consequently, long before the ink dried on the formal surrender, the Truman administration was focusing on the postwar threat posed by its wartime ally, the expansionist, autocratic, communist Soviet Union.

The Cold War and beyond

Within a year the Grand Alliance that had fought against the Axis was in shambles, as the United States committed itself to "containing" the Soviets everywhere across the globe. The conflict quickly became pointedly ideological, even as it moved from one specific issue to another, from the administration of postwar Germany to the 1947 crisis in Greece. In March 1947, President Harry S. Truman adopted Wilsonian rhetoric in his appeal to Congress for a $400 million aid package for Greece, making it, in effect, an American moral declaration of the Cold War. The United States, he said, must "support free peoples who are resisting attempted subjugation by armed minorities and by outside pressures." It was a choice between "free institutions, representative government, free elections" and "terror and oppression."[50]

To engage the Soviets, the postwar demobilization was reversed. The National Security Act (1947) created the Department of Defense to unite all the military services into a single command and supply structure, the Central Intelligence Agency to gather intelligence abroad and conduct covert operations, and the National Security Council to directly advise the President. A year later, Congress approved a new peacetime draft, increasing the size and strength of conventional forces. New language was adopted to reflect these new realities, with government spokesmen abandoning "national defense" in favor of "national security," a "cold-war term" that reflected "open-ended commitments and the capabilities of anticipating and responding to political and military changes anywhere in the world."[51]

Subsequently, the United States quickly moved to support the economic recovery of postwar Western Europe with the Marshall Plan (1948), and a year later, it both fostered and then joined the North Atlantic Treaty

Organization, the nation's first military alliance. By 1949, the United States had stationed substantial military forces in Europe and Asia, where they would remain for the foreseeable future, all of which was legitimized by "NSC-68," the report issued in 1950 just before the Korean War. It became the blueprint for battling the Soviets during the next four decades.[52] By the early 1950s the impact of the new policies was apparent, in the shooting war in Korea and in American support for every right-wing militarist who proclaimed himself an anti-communist. This Cold War made permanent many of the features of World War II's warfare state: a technologically sophisticated military supported by a military-industrial-academic complex, large state intelligence agencies with both international and domestic responsibilities, a more powerful executive branch in general and presidency in particular, and a clearly defined enemy who possessed both the power and ideology to challenge an American vision of world order.

It reshaped American politics and society as well. Conservatives used the Cold War crisis to re-establish their political primacy by identifying New Deal liberals as part of an "un-American" leftist fringe. More than a bipartisan hunt for domestic spies serving foreign powers, the Republican inquisitors pursued their prey into the organized heart of American liberalism – unions, academia, and media – in their search for "fellow travelers." While the pogrom was short-lived, it had long-lasting effects, including its implicit and explicit calls for a perpetual national security state.[53]

The military industry, supported by government and academe, became even more deeply entrenched during the "long peace," especially after corporate suppliers learned to hold manufacturing jobs in far-flung congressional districts hostage to military budgets. By the Korean War, military expenditures were eating up 14 percent of the nation's GNP.[54] During the heady 1960s, for example, "Pentagon capitalism" consumed two-thirds of US tax dollars (which was one-half of the world's total military expenditures) and employed 10 percent of the labor force. But defense spending was unevenly spread across the landscape, moving jobs from the increasingly depressed North and midwest to the South and the West, enriching the Sun Belt at the expense of the Rust Belt. In fighting the Cold War, the United States invested more than 11 trillion dollars, distorting its political economy, while increasingly mortgaging its future.

Despite its power to reshape American policy and society, however, the Cold War was not a total war. In fact, to a significant degree, it was a stealth conflict, fought by proxies and money, as the American people enjoyed the satisfactions of their growing consumer culture. Consequently, the road leading from the end of World War II to the fall of the Berlin Wall in 1989 would be twisted, long, and very expensive. Even though US military planners came to rely on machines and technology as substitutes for men in uniform, there were times when Americans were asked to fight. Twice during that period, the United States initiated land wars in Asia that even with limited goals cost almost 100,000 American lives. Millions of Asians, of course, perished as well. Even after the losses in Vietnam ended the political support for the draft – an example of democracy in action – the military force structure remained at 2 million for the rest of the century. In fact, in the mid-1990s, the United States maintained more than 700 military installations in more than thirty countries around the world, staffed by almost a half million uniformed and civilian personnel.[55] And, by the end of the twentieth century, the United States was spending more on its military than the next fifteen nations combined.[56]

The fall of the Soviet Union had necessitated a re-evaluation of American policy, but before the promised peace dividend could be tallied, much less paid, the nation in 1991 became embroiled in a short war against Iraq, which had invaded Kuwait and threatened oil-rich Saudi Arabia. President George H. W. Bush, who pulled together an international coalition to help fight and finance the war, celebrated the victory by declaring, without conscious irony, "By God, we've kicked the Vietnam Syndrome once and for all."[57] In the wake of the 1991 war, with thousands of US troops remaining in Saudi Arabia and the Gulf to provide continued security while monitoring Iraq, the United States became the target of radical Muslims. One group attacked the World Trade Center in New York City in 1993, and subsequently others blew up the US embassies in Kenya and Tanzania in 1998 and the destroyer USS *Cole* in Yemen two years later. On September 11, 2001 al-Qaeda launched its infamous assaults on the Pentagon and the World Trade Center, killing more than 3,000 on American soil.

In his address to Congress nine days later, President George W. Bush, in tones reminiscent of Wilson and Truman, labeled the terrorists "heirs of all the murderous ideologies of the twentieth century." They posed, he said, a threat to the United States, indeed all civilization. They "hate our freedoms," he proclaimed, "our freedom of religion, our freedom of speech, our freedom to vote and assemble and disagree with one another."[58] However odd an assertion, it served by absolving the United States of any responsibility for the conflict while identifying the struggle with one of the nation's most deeply held core values, freedom. With the approval of Congress and the international community, American forces attacked Afghanistan, destroyed the al-Qaeda training camps, and overturned the Taliban regime. But Osama bin Laden and the al-Qaeda leadership eluded them.

Congress quickly passed the administration's Patriot Act, which signaled the impact this "war on terrorism" would have on domestic society, while President Bush charged Saddam Hussein's Iraqi regime with possessing weapons of mass destruction, close ties to terrorist networks, and a willingness to supply the networks with the weapons. None of this proved to be true. The subsequent war split the United States from its European allies, quickly soured world opinion, and became a central issue in the 2004 presidential race.

In the aftermath of September 11, the influence of a neoconservative group within the government, commonly referred to as the Vulcans, grew. The National Security Strategy, released in September 2002, revived ideas that had appeared, only to be repudiated, in the 1992 Defense Planning Guidance document that sought to prevent "the rise of any challenging power."[59] The 2002 NSS again insisted upon American dominance over any and all potential military rivals, while further asserting the right to use force "preemptively" whenever necessary. This last statement undermined the longstanding US efforts to create meaningful mechanisms of collective security. While the rhetoric and the larger goal of remaking the world were consistent with Wilson's moral strain, the chosen means were not. With the second Iraq War, the thread of collective security was finally shredded by the administration's willingness to act alone.

In looking back over the century, each major war extended the American state, creating a stronger military, a larger bureaucracy, a more powerful presidency, and new restrictions on speech, expression, and action. To wage the world wars, state power, which was enhanced for greater efficiencies in social and economic organization, often accelerated social movements and processes already under way, such as the concentration of industrial giants. Ironically, because of the need for national unity, it also fostered the inclusion of long-outcast ethnic groups, such as African Americans. After each conflict Americans looked beyond their borders and became more engaged in the world through formal and informal international organizations, all the while listening to US statesmen who conflated their "narrow national self-interest with global good."[60]

A century that began with a fiercely argued debate about the nature of the emerging American empire ended, according to many, with the creation of another. While surface similarities between these American empires are intriguing, their differences are much more profound. At the dawn of the twentieth century the United States was a regional power, a growing economic giant seeking a more secure future, while at its end, Americans possessed an economy and culture with global reach and a military that had assumed the mantle of the new Rome. "Never in history," wrote one observer, "had any single power possessed such military advantage, qualitative as quantitative, over any or all other nations, and never had the likelihood of another nation catching up seemed more remote."[61] In short, in fighting its wars during the "American Century," and ultimately defining its role as *the* world's liberal power, the United States had profoundly transformed both its society and its relation to the rest of the world.

NOTES

1. Matthew Frye Jacobson, *Barbarian Virtues: The United States Encounters Foreign Peoples at Home and Abroad, 1876–1917* (New York: Hill and Wang, 2000), pp. 247–52.
2. Frank Ninkovich, *The United States and Imperialism* (Malden, MA: Blackwell Publishers, 2001), p. 15.
3. Louis A. Pérez, Jr., *Cuba: Between Reform and Revolution* (New York and Oxford: Oxford University Press, 1995), pp. 168–88.
4. Anthony James Joes, *America and Guerilla Warfare* (Lexington: University Press of Kentucky, 2000), p. 120.
5. H. W. Brands, *Bound to Empire: The United States and the Philippines* (New York and Oxford: Oxford University Press, 1992), pp. 55–7.
6. Brian McAllister Linn, *The Philippine War, 1899–1902* (Lawrence: University Press of Kansas, 2000), pp. 326–28.
7. Michael Hunt, *Ideology and U.S. Foreign Policy* (New Haven and London: Yale University Press, 1987), p. 41.
8. Thomas J. Knock, *To End All Wars: Woodrow Wilson and the Quest for a New World Order* (Princeton: Princeton University Press, 1992), p. 121.
9. Robert H. Zieger, *America's Great War: World War I and the American Experience* (Lanham, MD: Rowman & Littlefield, 2000), p. 58.
10. Jeanette Keith, "The Politics of Southern Draft Resistance, 1917–1918: Class, Race, and Conscription in the Rural South," *Journal of American History*, 87, 4 (2001): 1336–7.
11. John Keegan, *The First World War* (New York: Alfred A. Knopf, 1999), pp. 373–4.
12. Paul A. C. Koistinen, *Mobilizing for Modern War: The Political Economy of American Warfare, 1865–1919* (Lawrence: University Press of Kansas, 1997), pp. 198–244.
13. Robert Cuff, *The War Industries Board: Business–Government Relations during World War I* (Baltimore: Johns Hopkins University Press, 1973), pp. 77–9 and 163–8.
14. Valerie Jean Conner, *The National Labor War Board: Stability, Social Justice, and the Voluntary State in World War I* (Chapel Hill: University of North Carolina Press, 1983), pp. ix–x.
15. Ronald Schaffer, *America in the Great War: The Rise of the War Welfare State* (New York and Oxford: Oxford University Press, 1991), pp. 15–16.
16. Theodore Kornweibel, *"Investigate Everything": Federal Efforts to Compel Black Loyalty during World War I* (Bloomington and Indianapolis: Indiana University Press, 2002), pp. 10–36.

17. William J. Breen, *Uncle Sam at Home: Civilian Mobilization, Wartime Federalism, and the Council of National Defense, 1917–1919* (Westport, CT: Greenwood Press, 1984), p. 201.

18. David M. Kennedy, *Over Here: The First World War and American Society* (New York and Oxford: Oxford University Press, 1980), pp. 81–2.

19. As quoted in Leslie Midkiff DeBauche, *Reel Patriotism: The Movies and World War I* (Madison: University of Wisconsin Press, 1997), p. 108.

20. Alfred E. Cornebise, *War as Advertised: The Four Minute Men and America's Crusade, 1917–1918* (Philadelphia: American Philosophical Society, 1984), p 158.

21. Nancy K. Bristow, *Making Men Moral: Social Engineering during the Great War* (New York: New York University Press, 1996), pp. 54–136.

22. Byron Farwell, *Over There: The United States in the Great War, 1917–1918* (New York: W. W. Norton and Co., 1999), pp. 141–7.

23. K. Walter Hickel, "War, Region, and Social Welfare: Federal Aid to Servicemen's Dependents in the South, 1917–1921," *Journal of American History*, 87, 4 (March 2001): 1362–91.

24. Peter Gottlieb, "Rethinking the Great Migration," in Joe William Trotter (ed.), *The Great Migration in Historical Perspective: New Dimensions of Race, Class, and Gender* (Bloomington: University of Indiana Press, 1991), pp. 70–76.

25. William Jordan, "'That Damnable Dilemma': African-American Accommodation and Protest during World War I," *Journal of American History*, 81, 4 (March 1995): 1562–83.

26. Knock, *To End All Wars*, pp. 111–13 and 144.

27. George Q. Flynn, *The Draft, 1940–1973* (Lawrence: University Press of Kansas, 1993), pp. 9–87.

28. Bruce D. Porter, *War and the Rise of the State: the Military Foundations of Modern Politics* (New York: The Free Press, 1994), p. 280.

29. Harold G. Vatter, *The U.S. Economy in World War II* (New York: Columbia University Press, 1985), p. 29.

30. David M. Kennedy, *Freedom from Fear: The American People in Depression and War, 1929–1945* (New York and Oxford: Oxford University Press, 1999), p. 650.

31. *Ibid.*, p. 583.

32. Gerald D. Nash, *World War II and the West: Reshaping the Economy* (Lincoln and London: University of Nebraska Press, 1990), p. 8.

33. As quoted in Allan M. Winkler, *Homefront U.S.A.: America during World War II*, rev. ed. (Wheeling, IL: Harlan Davidson, 2000), p. 14.

34. Nelson Lichtenstein, *State of the Union: A Century of American Labor* (Princeton and Oxford: Princeton University Press, 2002), p. 30.

35. Alan Brinkley, *The End of Reform: New Deal Liberalism in Depression and War* (New York: Knopf, 1995), p. 212.

36. Susan M. Hartmann, *The Home Front and Beyond: American Women in the 1940s* (Boston: Twayne, 1982), pp. 18–21.

37. Allen Cronenberg, *Forth to the Mighty Conflict: Alabama and World War II* (Tuscaloosa and London: University of Alabama Press, 1995), pp. 74–8.

38. William O'Neill, *A Democracy at War:America's Fight at Home and Abroad in World War II* (Cambridge, MA: Harvard University Press, 1995), pp. 129–142.

39. George H. Roeder, Jr., *The Censored War: American Visual Experience During World War Two* (New Haven and London, Yale University Press, 1993), pp. 1–25.

40. Winkler, *Homefront U.S.A.*, p. 67.

41. Catherine Lutz, *Homefront: A Military City and the American Twentieth Century* (Boston: Beacon Press, 2001), pp. 64–75.

42. Ronald Takaki, *Double Victory: A Multicultural History of America in World War II* (Boston, New York, and London: Little, Brown and Company, 2000), pp. 20–1.

43. Neil A. Wynn, *The Afro-American and the Second World War* (New York: Holmes & Meier, 1976), pp. 50–3.

44. As quoted in Michael S. Sherry, *In the Shadow of War: The United States Since the 1930s* (New Haven and London: Yale University Press, 1995), p. 101.

45. Daniel Kryder, *Divided Arsenal: Race and the American State During World War II* (Cambridge and New York: Cambridge University Press, 2000), pp. 225–42.

46. Roger Daniels, *Prisoners Without Trial: Japanese Americans in World War II* (New York: Hill and Wang, 1993), pp. 30–47.

47. Richard Polenberg, "World War II and the Bill of Rights," in Kenneth Paul O'Brien and Lynn Hudson Parsons (eds.), *The Home-Front War: World War II and American Society* (Westport, CT and London: Greenwood Press, 1995), p. 22.

48. Paul S. Boyer, *By the Bomb's Early Light: American Thought and Culture at the Dawn of the Atomic Age* (New York: Pantheon Books, 1985), pp. 21–6.

49. See especially Michael C. C. Adams, *The Best War Ever: America and World War II* (Baltimore: Johns Hopkins University Press, 1994), pp. 1–20.

50. As quoted in H. W. Brands, *The Devil We Knew: America and the Cold War* (New York and Oxford: Oxford University Press, 1993), p. 21.

51. Edward Pessen, *Losing Our Souls: The American Experience in the Cold War* (Chicago: Ivan R. Dee, 1993), p. 221.

52. Michael S. Sherry, *In the Shadow of War*, p. 125.

53. Ellen Schrecker, *Many Are the Crimes: McCarthyism in America* (Boston: Little, Brown and Company, 1998), pp. 373–413.

54. Robert Kaplan, *Imperial Grunts: The American Military on the Ground* (New York: Random House, 2005), p. 7.

55. Chalmers Johnson, *The Sorrows of Empire: Militarism, Secrecy, and the End of the Republic* (New York: Henry Holt and Company, 2004), pp. 154–5.

56. Benjamin R. Barber, *Fear's Empire: War, Terrorism, and Democracy* (New York: W. W. Norton, 2004), p. 20.

57. As quoted in Tom Engelhardt, *The End of Victory Culture: Cold War America and the Disillusioning of a Generation* (New York: HarperCollins Books, 1995), p. 299.

58. Ivo H. Daalder and James M. Livesay, *America Unbound: The Bush Revolution in Foreign Policy* (Washington DC: Brookings Institution Press, 2003), pp. 82–3.

59. Clyde Prestowitz, *Rogue Nation: American Unilateralism and the Failure of Good Intentions* (New York: Basic Books, 2003), pp. 272–3.

60. Neil Smith, *American Empire: Roosevelt's Geographer and the Prelude to Globalization* (Berkeley: University of California Press, 2003), p. xii.

61. Jonathan Schell, *The Unconquerable World: Power, Nonviolence and The Will of the People* (New York: Henry Holt and Company, 2003), p. 321. While bookshelves are being filled with numerous studies of the New American "Empire," the conception has both definitional and practical problems, which suggest that even if American power, in all its forms, constitutes an empire, it will probably be short-lived.

FURTHER READING

Andrew J. Bacevich, *American Empire: The Realities and Consequences of U.S. Diplomacy*, Cambridge, MA and London: Harvard University Press, 2003.

Niall Ferguson, *Colossus: The Price of America's Empire*, New York: The Penguin Press, 2004.

Thomas Fleming, *The Illusion of Victory: America in World War I*, New York: Basic Books, 2003.

Aaron L. Friedberg, *In the Shadow of the Garrison State: America's Anti-Statism and its Cold War Grand Strategy*, Princeton: Princeton University Press, 2000.

Matthew Frye Jacobson, *Barbarian Virtues: The United States Encounters Foreign Peoples at Home and Abroad, 1876–1917*, New York: Hill and Wang, 2002.

John Jeffries, *Wartime America: The World War II Home Front*, Chicago: Ivan Dee, 1996.

Chalmers Johnson, *The Sorrows of Empire: Militarism, Secrecy, and the End of the Republic*, New York: Henry Holt and Company, 2004.

David M. Kennedy, *Over Here: The First World War and American Society*, New York: Oxford University Press, 1980.

Paul A. C. Koistinen, *Mobilizing for Modern War: The Political Economy of American Warfare, 1865–1919*, Lawrence: University Press of Kansas, 1997.

Daniel Kryder, *Divided Arsenal: Race and the American State During World War II*, Cambridge and New York: Cambridge University Press, 2000.

David Mayers, *Wars and Peace: The Future Americans Envisioned, 1861–1991*, New York: Macmillan 1998.

Frank Ninkovich, *The Wilsonian Century: U.S. Foreign Policy since 1900*, Chicago and London: University of Chicago Press, 1999.

Louis A. Pérez Jr., *The War of 1898: The United States and Cuba in History and Historiography*, Chapel Hill: University of North Carolina Press, 1998.

Bruce D. Porter, *War and the Rise of the State: the Military Foundations of Modern Politics*, New York: The Free Press, 1994.

George H. Roeder Jr., *The Censored War: American Visual Experience During World War Two*, New Haven and London, Yale University Press, 1993.

Michael S. Sherry, *In the Shadow of War: The United States Since the 1930s*, New Haven and London: Yale University Press, 1995.

Ronald Takaki, *Double Victory: A Multicultural History of America in World War II*, Boston, New York, and London: Little, Brown and Company, 2000.

Robert H. Zieger, *America's Great War: World War I and the American Experience*, Lanham, MD: Rowman & Littlefield, 2000.

13

STEPHEN J. WHITFIELD

The culture of the Cold War

When the French writer Simone de Beauvoir visited the United States in 1947, she was deeply saddened by the conformism that seemed so pervasive. "This country, once so passionate about individualism," she later recalled, "had itself become a nation of sheep; repressing originality, both in itself and in others; rejecting criticism, measuring value by success, it left open no road to freedom except that of anarchic revolt; this explains the corruption of its youth, their refuge in drug-taking and their imbecile outbreaks of violence." Beauvoir conceded that some books and films pointed to political resistance; and "a few literary magazines, a few almost secret political newsletters" also "dared oppose public opinion." But such artifacts could gain little traction against "the anti-communist fanaticism of the Americans," which "had never been more virulent. Purges, trials, inquisitions, witch-hunts – the very principles of democracy had been rejected." The air that she had breathed in the United States had become "polluted."[1]

The indictment that the Left Bank existentialist offered encapsulates a common understanding of the culture of postwar America, and her emphasis upon a cramped and repressive society was not misplaced. Serious domestic criticism was made to feel unwelcome in the United States, in the context of a geopolitical struggle against Stalinism – the term coined by the *New York Times*' correspondent in Moscow in the 1930s, Walter Duranty.[2] With its mass purges and mass murders, its slave labor camps, its obliteration of any semblance of civil liberty and its concentration of power in a single dictator whose cruelty was topped only by Adolf Hitler, Stalinism violated virtually every norm of decency; and the Soviet regime threatened to implant its political and social system elsewhere. Such a peril seemed to overshadow any effort in the United States to alter its existing arrangements; and therefore anti-communism put liberalism on the defensive. Radicalism was even more stigmatized, since it might only fortify the propaganda of Stalinism and its sympathizers.

The effect upon public culture was to reduce the options, to stifle intellectual independence, and thus to promote authority at the expense of liberty, stability at the expense of change, and order at the expense of reform. In the era from the end of the 1940s until the early 1960s, rebels were without causes, as though there was nothing warranting a legitimate opposition. Conflict was muffled for the sake of consensus; and historians have often noted the consequences: the suppression of dissent, the enfeeblement of the Bill of Rights, and the short-circuiting of the progressive struggles for racial and sexual equality and for the rights of labor. Such historians have tended to confirm the impressions of Simone de Beauvoir in associating the era with anxiety and terror, because Americans lived in the shadow of the dreadful either/or of being either Red or dead. At best the choice seemed to come down to Cold War or Armageddon. No wonder then that fear was the emotion that seemed to blanket a nation previously known for its can-do optimism. Though Ronald Reagan spent much of the 1950s jauntily promoting the cause of General Electric, which brandished the slogan "progress is our most important product," he packed a gun at the beginning of the decade; after all, communists in Los Angeles might try to ambush him.[3] When the President of the Screen Actors Guild has to be prepared to lock and load, vigilance has become manic.

The "tyranny of the majority" that Alexis de Tocqueville converted into the axial principle of democracy, after visiting Jacksonian America, was magnified when the progressive legacy of the New Deal and the Fair Deal seemed to go down to defeat in 1952. Conformism seemed to trump the controversy upon which civic debate was supposed to thrive. The theologian Reinhold Niebuhr had closely and anxiously followed the election returns that November, and told his young daughter while walking along Riverside Drive in New York City: "You poor girl, you've never lived under a Republican administration. You don't know how terrible this is going to be."[4]

The pressure of the Cold War called for a closing of ranks, and projected the ideal of homogeneity. The American Way of Life was understood to be singular. Unforeseen, still over the horizon, was the celebration of pluralism, the recognition that difference could be a source of strength rather than a dangerous divisiveness. Senator Joseph R. McCarthy (Republican Senator for Wisconsin) was the most notorious embodiment of the effort to impose anti-communist conformity. But McCarthyism itself was the political expression of the pieties and orthodoxies that were designed to constitute an embattled unity in the struggle against communism. The enforcers of that harmony were the legislative investigating committees – especially the House Un-American Activities Committee (HUAC) and the Senate Internal

Security Subcommittee. The Federal Bureau of Investigation (FBI) enlarged its scope beyond apprehending criminals who drove stolen vehicles across state lines, and became an official – if usually furtive and feckless – monitor of intellectual and cultural life.

The writ of institutions like the FBI and HUAC was stretched to include figures not normally considered threatening. No jurist was a more vigorous champion of freedom of expression than Supreme Court Justice Hugo M. Black. Such a stance vexed the FBI, especially in 1953, during the appeals process of the convicted atomic spies, Julius and Ethel Rosenberg. Agents were therefore stationed inside the Supreme Court, almost certainly due to the authorization of Chief Justice Fred Vinson, to keep Black under surveillance. To the music lover, Leonard Bernstein was a wondrously versatile and vibrant composer and conductor. To the FBI, he merited a paper trail of 666 pages (at taxpayers' expense). Bernstein was never a communist – unlike his longtime collaborator, the dancer and choreographer Jerome Robbins, a Party member from 1943 until 1947. When the Ford Motor Company, which sponsored Ed Sullivan's *Toast of the Town* on CBS, forced Robbins to cancel a scheduled appearance in 1950, he fled to Paris, just ahead of Sullivan's plea to HUAC to issue a subpoena. Though Robbins returned to New York the following year, in time to choreograph *The King and I*, that subpoena finally came in 1953. Fearful that his homosexuality would otherwise be exposed, Robbins named names before HUAC – one of whose Republican members, Ohio's Gordon H. Scherer, reassured the cooperative witness of plans "to see *The King and I* that very night and [I] would now appreciate it all the more."[5]

In 1960 a television viewer wrote the director of the FBI that "Groucho Marks [*sic*] be investigated as being a communist. Last night on his program [*You Bet Your Life*] both my husband and I understood him to pronounce 'the United States' as 'the United Snakes.'" J. Edgar Hoover complied, and eventually amassed 186 pages of surveillance, without discovering any political subversiveness more disturbing than the comedian's opposition to the dictatorship of Francisco Franco of Spain. To the art lover, Marc Chagall was responsible for paintings of shimmering enchantment. To Soviet authorities, he was not a socialist realist; and therefore his canvases were banned. Chagall had left his native Russia in 1922. But that was a full five years after the Bolshevik Revolution, which stirred the suspicion of the FBI, which kept a file on the painter while he found refuge in the United States (1941–7). From 1952 until 1958, Chagall could not get a visa to return to the United States. But surely the *reductio ad absurdum* of the fear of domestic communism was the refusal to spare even the blind and the deaf. Helen Keller had advocated abolition of HUAC itself in 1943, and thus came to the attention of the FBI, which opened a file on her. She had also supported communist-front organizations, and admired the Soviet Union. But the FBI did not conduct a formal investigation, in part because a woman who was both deaf and blind posed no threat to national security, in part because conventional wiretaps were useless when the subject under surveillance could not use a telephone, in part because the manual finger language with which Helen Keller communicated could not be effectively decoded.[6]

To be troubled by such interventions so far from the normal field of federal jurisdiction does not mean that the politics of an artist should never be noticed – or criticized. Nor is it true that political arguments against a work of art are inherently illegitimate, for they can uncover the intentions behind an object as well as its implications. But when such a standard becomes pervasive and intensive, and so potent in its effects that countless careers are ruined and the public cannot make its own choices in the marketplace of ideas, then the United States has come to resemble – rather uncomfortably – the sort of society to which it wishes to be contrasted. A society that imposes political standards upon its art, or demands of its artists certain sorts of citizenship tests (uncritical loyalty, abject repentance), is too much like totalitarianism. Creativity is unlikely to flourish where the tastes of officials matter.

The Cold War politicized American culture. The values and perceptions, the forms of expression, the symbolic patterns, the beliefs and myths which enabled Americans to make sense of reality – these constituents of culture were contaminated by an unseemly political interest in their roots and consequences. The struggle against domestic communism encouraged an entanglement of the two enterprises of politics and culture, resulting in a philistine inspection of artistic works not for their contents but for the politics of the creators, endorsing the boycott of films that censors had not seen, favoring the removal from library shelves of books that vigilantes had not read. The application of political tests was not systematic, though it was not entirely haphazard either. Sometimes the tests were imposed by agencies of the federal government, and were designed to intimidate other branches or the private sector. Sometimes the demands of hyper-patriotism reflected the efforts of private employers, sometimes of self-appointed monitors of political morality who acted with official complicity. Sometimes the private sphere was ahead of the government in such efforts at regulation and purification.

But the effect was the same: the suffocation of liberty and the debasement of culture itself. Even by the narrowest chauvinistic criteria of the Cold War, the United States thus diminished itself in the global effort to be seen as an attractive and just society. The politicization of culture might win the allegiance of those who cherished authority, but not of those who valued autonomy. The politicization of culture might appeal to reactionaries abroad, but not to foreigners who appreciated creativity or critical thought.

And though intimately involved in curbing liberty, the state acted with popular approval and acquiescence; the will of the majority was not thwarted. Citizens imposed a glum repression upon themselves, and without denying rights to minorities – or at least to certain political factions, anyway. Indeed, American Legionnaires and the Catholic War Veterans were exercising their First Amendment rights in seeking to block other Americans from attending particular films and plays. The opportunity to dissuade other citizens from patronizing an institution or an individual has long been included in the definition of a democracy, and the marketplace – including the marketplace of ideas – has accepted the notion that unpopularity is decisive. No company – neither a movie studio nor a television network – is obligated to keep on its payroll those from whom the public has explicitly withdrawn its favor. This was the argument that Reagan advanced in falsely claiming that "Hollywood in fact has *no blacklist*. Hollywood does have a list handed to it by millions of 'moviegoers' who have said: 'We don't want and will not pay to see pictures made by or with these people we consider traitors.'" He added that "poor box office" explained why "a film producer" might not be "hiring an artist" who claimed to be a victim of persecution.[7]

Reagan misspoke. When HUAC subpoenaed Dalton Trumbo in 1947, he was an A-list scenarist. As a member of the Hollywood 10 (those who refused to cooperate with the committee), he defied the Committee and went to jail. Though he used "fronts" to submit scripts (like *Roman Holiday*), and in 1956 even won an Oscar under a *nom de plume* (Robert Rich), not until 1960 did Trumbo's name reappear on the screen. Most other members of the Hollywood 10, plus others who could not find employment in the era, were not conspicuous enough for the public to threaten to boycott movies associated with these "traitors."

Reagan (himself an FBI "informant") conceded that errors might exist on the "list," but insisted that "any person who feels he is a victim of discrimination because of his political beliefs can avail himself of machinery to solve this problem."[8] Indeed, that is how he met the actress who became his second wife. They met "cute" – under the impact of the Cold War – because Nancy Davis (*Hellcats of the Navy*) had been confused with another actress whose politics had become suspect. The entertainment industry blacklist that Reagan pretended was non-existent has since become the subject of dozens of books, and can scarcely be considered an index of popular opposition to politically distasteful artists. The blacklist was a racket. Near the end of the 1950s, MGM's André Previn was summoned to the Burbank office of the publisher of a feared magazine aimed at exposing "Reds" in Hollywood. A composer and arranger who would be nominated for thirteen Oscars (and win four), Previn could not help noticing how much drinking his interrogator had already done that day. The challenge was direct, however: "I have certain information that you gave benefit concerts for the Abraham Lincoln Brigade during the Spanish Civil War. What do you have to say to that?" Previn's reply was simple: he was only nine years old when the Spanish Civil War ended, and was still trapped with his family in Nazi Germany. The publisher stood up and smiled as he shook the musician's hand and said: "No harm in trying, eh?" Sometime later this vigilant anti-communist went to prison for blackmail.[9]

Thus did private enterprise sometimes try to sit in judgment on political activity, while government agencies sometimes even got into the movie business. The confusion of public and private realms typified the era. The animated film *Animal Farm* (1954) was produced in England, and may well be the most original feature-length movie in this genre to be produced there until *Yellow Submarine* (1968). Pitched at adults, *Animal Farm* rather faithfully adapted what is the most powerful political fable written in the English language since Swift. Yet producer Louis de Rochement's cinematic achievement can be traced to Washington, where the Psychological Strategy Board endorsed the idea of using the late George Orwell to trash-talk East European communism, which claimed to have inherited the historic struggle for social justice. *Animal Farm* got produced because of funding from the Congress for Cultural Freedom, a CIA subsidiary. It got the movie rights to the fable partly because the author's widow, Sonia Blair, had hoped to meet Clark Gable. Her husband's other enduring work became a film which bore an even greater official input. *1984* (1956) benefited from a six-figure subsidy from the US Information Agency, which also exercised control over the script. For good measure the executive director of a CIA "asset," the American Committee for Cultural Freedom, Sol Stein, vetted the scenario before the cameras had even rolled.[10]

The FBI got into the movie business far more modestly: the Bureau secretly filmed the patrons of a left-wing book store, Four Continents, in New York. At the same time some representatives of Hollywood had to present their anti-communist credentials to Congressmen. Gary Cooper distanced himself from communism, but was vague when asked to explain how he recognized it: "From what I hear, I don't like it because it isn't on the level."[11] Director Leo McCarey, a devoted Roman Catholic, assured HUAC that films such as *Going My Way* and *The Bells of St. Mary's* fared badly with Soviet audiences because "I have a character in there that they do not like." A HUAC investigator took the bait and asked: "Bing Crosby?" "No," McCarey replied. "God." Journalist A. J. Liebling reported that "the announcement that the Deity was under contract to a movie company was perhaps to be expected."[12] During the Cold War, the right of officialdom to interfere in cultural affairs was taken for granted. As late as 1964, when Simone de Beauvoir's partner was still the most influential French philosopher of the postwar era, Hoover scribbled on an FBI routing slip: "Find out who [Jean-Paul] Sartre is."[13]

While legislators were interrogating musicians and actors about their political beliefs and affiliations, university administrators were using political instead of academic criteria to evaluate the fitness of teachers. "There will be no witch-hunts at Yale," its president, Charles Seymour, declared in 1949, "because there will be no witches. We do not intend to hire communists."[14] The Association of American Universities agreed that members of the communist Party were a priori unfit to teach. Junior faculty members were unprotected anyway. Tenured professors were fired if they took the Fifth Amendment, which was supposed to protect them against compulsory self-incrimination. Tenured professors were also fired if they did not cooperate with the peer review boards that interrogated them. Tenured professors were also fired if a university president – perhaps relying upon the whispers of anonymous informers – found the accused to be insufficiently candid.

Even when suspected communists enlisted the sympathy of university peers and presidents, trustees could step in and remove the tenured professors anyway. In 1954, after economist Lawrence Klein repudiated his communist ties in a meeting with HUAC, his prospects for promotion with tenure at the University of Michigan improved. But regents blocked his retention, because he admired Norwegian socialism.[15] (In 1980 Klein won a Nobel prize in economics.) Because M. I. Finley took the Fifth Amendment, as he was Constitutionally entitled to do, Rutgers University sacked him. (He expatriated himself to England, where his magisterial scholarship in ancient history earned him a knighthood.) Communists supposedly lacked intellectual independence. But that charge was contested by philosopher Stanley Moore, whom Reed College had fired: "Some communist teachers are professionally competent and some aren't. The incompetent get eliminated by their colleagues in the normal course of faculty selection, the competent get eliminated by their employers in the sudden frenzy of political persecution."[16]

The domestic Cold War exacted a penalty upon the very notion of citizenship, which has been a minimal one. The Cold War demanded that Americans take sides, and stand up in a certain way. They were expected to be combatants in the war against communism. Neutrality was suspect, and so was a lack of enthusiasm for anti-communism. In 1956, near the end of playwright Arthur Miller's testimony before HUAC, a Congressman urged him to enrich the literature of political engagement. "Why do you not direct some of that magnificent ability you have to fighting against well-known communist subversive conspiracies in our country and in the world?", Representative Clyde Doyle (Democrat of California) asked. "Why do you not direct your magnificent talents to that, in part? I mean more positively?"[17] To be a good citizen did not include detachment.

Nor did the definition entail mobilization to achieve full racial equality. (Indeed, whites who fervently supported civil rights were suspected of communism.) The Cold War definition of citizenship did not include championing the rights of labor, or a federal guarantee of medical care. Stephen Spingarn, an aide to President Truman, noted in 1949 that "the consuming fear of Communism has led many sincere persons into the belief that. . . change (be it civil rights or a compulsory national health program) is subversive and those who urge it are either communists or fellow travelers."[18] Citizenship was rendered as synonymous with patriotism, in the narrowest and even the most primitive sense. Citizenship was not defined in terms of examining carefully what the FBI or the CIA or other agencies were doing to ensure national security. The Cold War demanded a sort of civic enlistment that was uncritical. "Progressives" (often a euphemism for communists) survived, barely, at least enough to forge a link between the militancy of the 1930s and a New Left that worked for social and political change in the 1960s. But even Norman Thomas, the quadrennial presidential candidate of the Socialist Party, took subsidies from the CIA. (Its conduit, the Kaplan Fund, supported Thomas's Institute of International Labor Relations.) The communist Party itself was shattered; and its advocacy of the interests of a foreign, totalitarian power contaminated the cause of a serious criticism of systemic problems of the polity.

What made the era distinctive, however, was less the eclipse of the Left than the peculiar prestige attached to the act of informing. It is not normally allocated a high status in western society. The central human villain in the New Testament is, after all, the disciple who betrays Jesus for thirty pieces of silver. But the culture of the Cold War was distinctive for having punctured the abhorrence of informing, which "in our time. . . is a duty." Thus proclaimed the Soviet defector Walter Krivitsky, as quoted by the most famous informer of the era, Whittaker Chambers.[19] Harvey Matusow, a professional informer who fingered 180 Americans (his count) but later recanted his testimony, knew that he "was on the lowest rung of the ladder of life." Yet his views on communism were solicited by pillars of respectable society: the President of Queens College, the superintendent of the biggest school system in the country (New York's), and the commissioner of the New York police department. "They looked to me for counsel and advice," Matusow crowed.[20]

How far the presumption was undercut was revealed in a school text entitled *Exploring American History* (1955), which the Yale historian Ralph Henry Gabriel coauthored. After warning vaguely against "false news" and "dangerous propaganda," the text offered its young readers the following advice:

> The FBI urges Americans to report directly to its offices any suspicions they may have about communist activity on the part of their fellow Americans. The FBI is expertly trained to sift out the truth of such reports under the laws of our free nation. When Americans handle their suspicions in this way, rather than by gossip and publicity, they are acting in line with American traditions.

While *Exploring American History* seemed to make an oblique criticism of the excesses of the Congressional investigating committees, the authors failed to separate the categories of military, diplomatic, and industrial secrets – however remote from the purview of high school students – and the general responsibility of surveillance that citizens are supposed to undertake. Honoring young tattlers was a mark of totalitarian societies, but it took the Cold War to include informing among the inventory of "American traditions."[21]

That heritage also included the Fifth Amendment, and to assert the right against compulsory self-incrimination was one way to avoid naming names. No career in American culture was more affected by a decision to do so, however, than Elia Kazan's. As a member of the Group Theatre, he had joined the Party in 1934 and had quit it a year and a half later. By the time of his 1952 summons before the House Un-American Activities Committee, no director was more in demand. In 1947 he had won both a Tony (an Antoinette Perry Award) for directing *A Streetcar Named Desire* on Broadway and an Oscar for directing *Gentleman's Agreement* for Twentieth Century-Fox. His decision to cooperate with HUAC thus made the role of informer respectable, and his advertisement in the *Times* advised others to emulate him. Those who knew at first-hand about communism, he urged, should go "either to the public or to the appropriate Government agency." In his autobiography he recalls wondering "why had I taken so long to even consider telling the country – that's what it amounted to – everything I knew? Was it because of the moral injunction against 'informing,' which was respected only depending on which side you were on?" He speculates: "If the situation were reversed, wouldn't the 'comrades' protect themselves without hesitation and by any means? Including naming me." In giving HUAC the names of sixteen communists whom he knew, Kazan told himself that his friend, Arthur Miller, could write plays in a jail cell, but a movie director could not work there, because financing and organization and collaborators were needed to make films. Hence the pertinence of Kazan's concluding public statement designed to justify cooperation with HUAC: "The main pictures I have made and the plays I have chosen to direct represent my convictions. I expect to continue to make the same kind of pictures."[22]

One of them was perhaps the most brilliant American movie of the decade, and is itself an effort to vindicate the imperative of informing. *On the Waterfront* (1954) lacks an explicitly political theme. But though the subject is nominally labor union corruption, the movie vividly exemplifies the political ethos of the era. The scenarist was Budd Schulberg, who had given HUAC fifteen names in 1951, and who has Terry Malloy (Marlon Brando), the young dock worker who has incriminated the gangsters, exult to their corrupt boss: "I'm glad what I done – you hear me? – glad what I done!" Kazan explained the subtext: "That was me saying, with identical heat, that I was glad I'd testified as I had." And the subsequent scene of the "shape-up," in which Malloy's co-workers ostracize him – "that, too, was my story, now told to all the world." Kazan added: "When critics say that I put my story and my feelings on the screen, to justify my informing, they are right. That transference of emotion from my own experience to the screen is the merit of those scenes," for "in the mysterious way of art, I was preparing a film about myself."[23] Though Brando would win an Oscar for Best Actor, he had been reluctant to work with Kazan, who had directed him in both the stage and screen versions of *A Streetcar Named Desire*, because of the HUAC testimony. Thus an electrifying, sympathetic portrayal of a "stoolie" was created by a star who had resisted working with an informer.

Kazan himself guessed that the theme of informing gives the Academy Award-winning film its special power: "After all, Terry's act of self-redemption breaks the great childhood taboo: Don't snitch on your friends. . . . Our hero is a 'rat.'" Having set up his friend Joey Doyle to be pushed from the roof, Terry is a sinner who redeems himself through repentance, confessing first to Father Barry (Karl Malden), and then to the victim's sister, Edie Doyle (Eva Marie Saint). But only public confession – testimony before the Waterfront Crime Commission – can really bestow absolution of guilt. It does not detract from the compelling power of *On the Waterfront*, however, to recognize how heavily the moral scales are tipped in favor of Terry Malloy. Since the hoodlums have already slain two other stevedores who had spoken to the Crime Commission, audiences are probably as desperately eager for him to "snitch" as are Edie Doyle and the waterfront priest who awaken Terry's conscience.[24]

The brutal union boss Johnny Friendly (Lee J. Cobb) and his "pistoleros" are merely murderers, and to describe their turpitude to the police is not an act that any citizen is likely on principle to oppose. The names that Kazan and Schulberg (and Cobb himself, another cooperative witness) gave HUAC belonged to colleagues and acquaintances who had not committed any crimes – much less gangland slayings. By switching the issue of informing from the politics of entertainment to the underworld of the waterfront, Kazan and Schulberg oversimplified the moral dilemma that they themselves faced. Though the citizenry may despise the "canary" and Terry's own former gang of "Golden Warriors" may repudiate its founder, movie audiences had to respect the "guts" of this informer in trying to secure his "rights" on the waterfront. That climactic shape-up walk resembles Christ's final bearing of the weight of the cross at Calvary and the longshoreman's hook is like His cross, just as Terry's forehead is bloodied as though from a crown of thorns. The culture of the Cold War thus managed to convert a Judas figure into a Christ symbol.

But the very excesses of the tyranny of the majority ought to invite an historiographical question. If conformist pressures and square-jawed severity were so feverish in the 1950s, how could the domestic Cold War have produced a ceasefire? Such repressive rigidity did not prove to be an intractable feature of the democratic condition. Somehow the dynamic of change had to be operating underneath the surface, waiting to explode in the 1960s. To be sure, no one had foreseen the radical revival that would erupt in that decade. Indeed, the political sociologist Seymour Martin Lipset traced a "decline in the sources of serious political controversy." Only incremental change could be predicted, "without ideologies, without red flags, without May Day parades," he wrote in 1960,[25] the very year that both the Student Non-Violent Coordinating Committee and the National Liberation Front in Vietnam were formed. Who could have predicted the tumultuous mass movements, the urban riots, the spasms of violence that were so convulsive that a President of the United States shied away from his own party's nominating convention in 1968? College students in the 1950s were often accused of passivity, and a silent generation was blamed for its apolitical indifference to the *res publica*. Yet their younger brothers and sisters had veered so dramatically to the Left that a plurality of those polled in October, 1968, would not have cast their votes for the three major candidates that year (Vice-President Hubert H. Humphrey, former Vice-President Richard M. Nixon, former Governor George C. Wallace). Instead the first choice was the former President of the National Bank of Cuba, which issued banknotes signed only with "Che."[26]

Ernesto Guevara had helped bring the revolution to power in 1959, which is when Professor William Appleman Williams published a book that would markedly influence at least one generation of younger students of American foreign policy. *The Tragedy of American Diplomacy* recorded a regret that the United States had been so committed to supporting exploitative and cruel dictatorships, and described American statecraft as driven by the corporate pursuit of market opportunities. The argument that the University of Wisconsin historian advanced was reasonable; Williams presented a sensible set of claims that was expressed in a moderate tone.

The reaction of *The National Review*, however, was apoplectic, and marked how narrow the framework of debate remained. Contributing editor M. Stanton Evans doubted the very sanity of William Appleman Williams, since the very idea of a quest for overseas markets as animating US diplomacy was preposterous. "America is now confronted with a danger," Evans asserted in the April 25, 1959 issue, "that its reasoning class – the segment of the population that deals professionally in ideas – has given over the orderly employment of reason." How else to explain that Williams's advocacy of an "open door for revolutions" was pivotal to one of the most terrifying books that Evans had ever read. The reviewer concluded: "This kind of analysis, offered as sober counsel on foreign relations by an American professor, sends more chills through me than any vision of atomic holocaust, or the lurking menace of Soviet power. Other dangers may promise death in the future; this is death here and now."

The Tragedy of American Diplomacy revealed a fissure that would crack wide open in the coming decade, and shatter the unified fight against communism. The caliber of a reaction like Evans's can be measured by the praise that Williams (US Naval Academy '44) later bestowed on the prudential foreign policy of President Herbert Hoover. Two years later, Williams was summoned before HUAC, which even subpoenaed the galleys of *The Contours of American History*. When it was published, Harvard's Oscar Handlin suspected "an elaborate hoax," with the author "ingeniously pulling the legs of his colleagues." Handlin was baffled that this "fantasy" was classified in libraries as non-fiction.[27]

1959 was also the year that MGM released *North by Northwest*. Alfred Hitchcock's communists – at least those who spy for "the other side" – are certainly sinister; in that decade, Hollywood could not have imagined otherwise. Philip Vandamm (James Mason) is dapper, but dangerous enough to orchestrate cold-blooded murder. His "secretary" (Martin

Landau) is either epicene because he is malignant or malignant because he operates according to what he calls his "woman's intuition." But *North by Northwest* breaks with the tradition of films that most famously includes *Casablanca* (1943), in which Rick Blaine and Ilse Lund realize that romantic attachments must yield to the larger cause of embattled humanity. *Casablanca* shows how a guy who sticks his neck out for nobody must learn the value of political engagement. That is the lesson that wives and other women must learn. But in Hitchcock's film, Roger Thornhill (Cary Grant) is so in love with secret agent Eve Kendall (Eva Marie Saint) that he briefly becomes a conscientious objector to the Cold War, in demanding that she be exempt from its demands. "I don't like the games you play, Professor," he tells the American spymaster (Leo G. Carroll), who is running Kendall, the unmarried blonde whose assignment is to pretend to defect to "the other side." The CIA's "Professor" replies: "War is hell, Mr. Thornhill, even when it's a cold one." To which Thornhill rebuts: "If you fellows can't lick the Vandamms of this world" without using morally dubious methods of counterespionage, "perhaps you ought to start learning how to lose a few cold wars." But though Ernest Lehman's script gives the Professor the last word in this debate ("I'm afraid we're already doing that"), a mild dissent is thus recorded to what John F. Kennedy's Inaugural Address would call a "long twilight struggle." (He had wanted to be played by Cary Grant in *PT 109* [1963], the film about the exploits of Lt. Kennedy in World War II.) By then the rhetorical ground was already shifting, so that Kennedy once posed the following paradox: "Why can a communist eat at a lunch counter in Selma, Alabama, while a black American veteran cannot?"[28]

Two British novels transmitted early signals of geopolitical change that even some dissident Americans were reluctant to accept. By blurring the moral categorizations of East and West and by questioning the very desirability of a clear-cut triumph over communism, these books were the harbingers of thaw.

Greeneland was the *terra incognita* of the Cold War. Early in the postwar era, the Department of State had blocked novelist Graham Greene from entering the United States because (mostly for his own amusement) he had joined the Oxford University Communist Club for a month in 1923. In 1952 he finally got his visa for the United States. Three years later he got his revenge, with *The Quiet American*. It was a prescient – that is, an unheeded – exploration of the American determination to defeat communism with problematic means. Its protagonist is Alden Pyle, a CIA agent who is involved in counterterrorism that kills and maims innocent civilians. Greene's narrator, a British reporter, blames Pyle for his innocence, believing that good intentions warranted intervention in the affairs of others: "I never knew a man who had better motives for all the trouble he caused."[29] Pyle is a deceiver who ends up deceiving himself, which is what his country would do in the next decade on a far more massive and lethal scale in Vietnam.

The very sincerity of American motives, a status that was supposed to vindicate one side in the bipolar conflict, was depicted as conducive to evil results; and thus the novelist anticipated the tragedy to come. But the director-scenarist Joseph L. Mankiewicz was oblivious to the quagmire into which his country was about to step, and obtusely reversed the ending of Greene's novel in adapting it to the screen in 1958. The United Artists version switches Pyle from an intelligence operative to a gung-ho employee with a private US aid mission, the "Friends of a Free Asia." The protagonist (Audie Murphy) really was telling the truth about his desire to facilitate an indigenous toy industry in Vietnam. Mankiewicz turns Greene's anti-American ending – with the murderous Pyle getting what he deserved – into a anti-communist final reel instead, with Pyle as the martyred victim of the communists.

Banned in the Republic of South Vietnam, Greene's novel was vastly superior in literary merit and in political judgment to *The Ugly American* (1958), which was so inescapable a bestseller that even President Eisenhower read it on vacation. Authors William J. Lederer and Eugene Burdick made image-making and practical know-how so decisive in the struggle for the allegiance of neutral countries that they missed the ideological dangers lurking in the real Asian versions of Sarkhan. In *The Ugly American* the good guys get out into the field and show the natives how to make things work better; the bad guys are the bureaucrats who get in the way of hands-on economic development. The novel offered unexceptionable proposals for an improved Foreign Service (language training, knowledge of the writings of Asian communists, personal modesty). But the two authors did not consider the military priorities that governed foreign aid, and missed almost completely the intensity of nationalist feelings in igniting the political revolutions which the United States faced. Greene could imagine the dangers of CIA machinations in Vietnam, though he never knew (or had even heard of) the agency's chief operative in Vietnam, a former advertising executive named Colonel Edward Lansdale. He is portrayed heroically (as Colonel Edwin Barnum Hillindale) in *The Ugly American*. Thus its readers did not have to face the moral quagmire into which the CIA was then getting sucked in Indochina. Not long thereafter, for example, 700 American troops under CIA auspices were dropped into Laos, organizing an army of about 40,000 Meo tribesmen as mercenaries against the communist Pathet Lao, in exchange for Meo control of the opium traffic in Southeast Asia's "Golden

Triangle." These were among the nasty political choices that *The Ugly American* did not adumbrate, for the novel's tepid criticism of American statecraft remained imprisoned in orthodoxy. *The Quiet American* proved far more illuminating in its consideration of how high a price would be paid for the illusion that the nation was equipped to defeat communism in Vietnam.

In 1963 Graham Greene was pleased to announce "the best spy story I have ever read": John le Carré's *The Spy Who Came In from the Cold*. Published only two years after the Berlin Wall had been erected, this was the first "thriller" ever to outsell all other works of fiction in the United States: 230,000 copies of *The Spy Who Came In from the Cold* were sold in American bookstores in 1964. The next year over 2 million more were purchased in paperback. The novel was written in under five months by a junior diplomat in the British embassy in Bonn, who had earlier served in MI5 – the domestic security agency – by infiltrating radical groups and seeking to identify possible Soviet agents.

The tale that le Carré concocts is ingenious. A London librarian named Liz Gold, who makes no secret of her membership in the British Communist Party, is granted by her employer a brief leave to visit East Germany. There she will participate in a cultural exchange program ostensibly to promote peace. In East Germany her idealism and love for Alec Leamas, a British intelligence operative who pretends to have defected, embroil her in a convoluted plot that implies a kind of moral equivalency between East and West. In East Germany Leamas thinks that he is supposed to neutralize the brutal Hans-Dieter Mundt, an alumnus of Hitler Youth. But Mundt is actually on Her Majesty's payroll, and Leamas is only a pawn who is being manipulated to eliminate Jens Fiedler, the Jewish second-in-command in the East German *Abteilung*. Fiedler has correctly suspected Mundt of being a double agent. But at the end of the novel, an East German working for the British kills the innocent Liz Gold as she tries to climb over the Berlin Wall to safety in the West. Repelled by the corruption and treachery of his own side, Leamas has also decided to stick his neck out for somebody. He joins her fleetingly by going back over the eastern side of the Wall, where he too is shot.

Earlier in the novel, Leamas's chief in London (named Control) tells him that "our methods – ours and the opposition's – have become much the same. I mean you can't be less ruthless than the opposition simply because your government's *policy* is benevolent, can you now?" The West does "do disagreeable things," Control admits. "But we are *defensive*."[30]

The Spy Who Came In from the Cold is hardly pro-communist. The East bloc spooks stationed in London are bullies who disdain their underlings; and the East Germans treat Liz, a believer in the authority of "History," quite as cynically as the British spies who work for the Circus. But though life in the East is bleak and drab, the West may have its own spiritual hollowness and nagging conscience to confront. The gracious Fiedler does not understand how Leamas can disclaim any ideals or larger purposes, and is baffled by the amoral thoughtlessness of the operatives at the Circus: "They must have a philosophy." But they don't. Le Carré traced the novel's origins to his own "great and abiding bitterness about the East–West ideological deadlock";[31] and he wanted his Anglo-American readers to wonder how their side could continue to deploy methods that tainted the rectitude of their own institutions. For the unprecedented popularity of *The Spy Who Came In from the Cold* signified a dramatic downshift in the ideological intensity that defined the Cold War.

Anti-communist ardor ceased to be decisive to American culture by the mid-1960s; the abscess of suspicion had been lanced. Some of the victims of the Cold War – especially blacklistees – lived long enough to be rehabilitated. In the fall of 1960, the President-elect and his brother Robert, the future Attorney-General, crossed an American Legion picket line to see *Spartacus*. This epic had been written by Trumbo, an alumnus of the Hollywood 10, and was based on the 1951 novel by Howard Fast, a former communist who had won the Stalin Peace Prize only six years earlier. In crossing that picket line, the Kennedy brothers ignored the intimidation of the American Legion and enlarged the contours of the politically permissible. De Beauvoir had alluded to "a few almost secret political newsletters." Surely she had in mind *I. F. Stone's Weekly*, whose publisher, editor, and sole contributor defied the orthodoxies of the Cold War without being muzzled. The newsletter first appeared in 1953 and took a decade to achieve a circulation of 20,000. By the time Stone shut it down, in 1971, his experiment in radical journalism had become a bi-weekly; but its circulation had gone north of 70,000.[32] He reached even more readers through the antiwar *New York Review of Books*.

The historian can also draw the happy conclusion that the culture of the Cold War was by no means synonymous with the culture of the 1950s, and in that asymmetry one can distinguish a relatively free society from a political system with totalitarian tendencies. The drive to inhibit art and thought left much untouched, and what was exempt from the scorched-earth policy of the patriots remains among the ornaments of the nation's culture. Four novels of the era, for example, remain canonical: J. D. Salinger's *The Catcher in the Rye* (1951), Saul Bellow's *The Adventures of Augie March* (1953), Ralph Ellison's *Invisible Man* (1952), and Vladimir Nabokov's *Lolita* (1955). All sorts of mainstream movies – ranging from John Huston's *The Treasure of the Sierra Madre* (1948) to Billy Wilder's *Sunset Boulevard*

(1950) and *Some Like It Hot* (1959) and to John Ford's *The Searchers* (1956) – enjoy a similar status. The domestic Cold War had no effect on the poetry of Robert Frost, or Sylvia Plath, or Robert Lowell, or Wallace Stevens. The most admired literary critic of the era, Edmund Wilson of *The New Yorker*, tended to minimize differences between the United States and the Soviet Union, without obviously curtailing his influence upon informed taste. In noting the vibrancy and richness of the artistic legacy that the era has bequeathed, the cultural historian need not be defensive.

But a contrast can be proposed. In 1937, for example, only two dozen Soviet films were released – because Stalin wanted to screen everything in advance. He demanded, in effect, the right of final cut. Such extraordinary power exercised by one dictator was not only a reason to be anti-communist, but also resulted in a frightening rigidity that the American system even at its crudest managed to avoid. The worst lasted for about a decade and a half, and then some equilibrium was regained. The obsessions began to recede; the fevers somehow went down. But brevity should not be an alibi for scholarly neglect. The impact of the Cold War upon American culture – or even upon national identity – should not be depreciated. John Updike achieved early literary renown in that era; and in the last of his novels devoted to Harry "Rabbit" Angstrom, the protagonist muses: "Without the Cold War, what's the point of being an American?"[33]

NOTES

1. Simone de Beauvoir, *Force of Circumstance*, trans. Richard Howard (New York: G. P. Putnam's Sons, 1965), pp. 372–5.
2. Sally J. Taylor, *Stalin's Apologist: Walter Duranty, the New York Times's Man in Moscow* (New York: Oxford University Press, 1990), p. 167.
3. Michael Paul Rogin, *Ronald Reagan, the Movie and Other Episodes in Political Demonology* (Berkeley: University of California Press, 1987), p. 30.
4. Quoted in Elisabeth Sifton, *The Serenity Prayer: Faith and Politics in Times of Peace and War* (New York: W. W. Norton, 2003), p. 328.
5. Roger K. Newman, *Hugo Black: A Biography* (New York: Pantheon, 1994), pp. 422–3; Ralph Blumenthal, "FBI's Endless Bid to Peg Bernstein as 'Red,'" *International Herald Tribune*, July 30–1, 1994, p. 18; Deborah Jowitt, *Jerome Robbins: His Life, His Theater, His Dance* (New York: Simon and Schuster, 2004), pp. 176–7, 191, 194–5, 228–31; "Jerome Robbins, May 5, 1953," in Eric Bentley (ed.), *Thirty Years of Treason* (New York: Viking, 1971), p. 633.
6. Tom Kuntz, "The Non-communist Party of the First Part Was an Upstart," *New York Times*, September 20, 1998, IV, 7; Benjamin Harshav, *Marc Chagall and His Times: A Documentary Narrative* (Stanford, CA: Stanford University Press, 2004), pp. 518, 528–34; Dorothy Herrmann, *Helen Keller: A Life* (New York: Alfred A. Knopf, 1998), pp. 281–3.

7. Ronald Reagan to Hugh Hefner, July 4, 1960, in Kiron K. Skinner *et al.* (eds.), *Reagan: A Life in Letters* (New York: Free Press, 2003), pp. 148–9.
8. *Ibid.*
9. André Previn, *No Minor Chords: My Days in Hollywood* (New York: Doubleday, 1991), pp. 31–2.
10. Tony Shaw, *British Cinema and the Cold War: The State, Propaganda and Consensus* (London: I. B. Taurus, 2001), pp. 93–114.
11. "Gary Cooper, October 23, 1947," in Bentley, *Thirty Years of Treason*, p. 153.
12. Quoted in Stefan Kanfer, *A Journal of the Plague Years* (New York: Atheneum, 1973), pp. 56–7.
13. Athan G. Theoharis and John Stuart Cox, *The Boss: J. Edgar Hoover and the Great American Inquisition* (Philadelphia: Temple University Press, 1988), p. 37.
14. Quoted in Ellen W. Schrecker, *No Ivory Tower: McCarthyism and the Universities* (New York: Oxford University Press, 1986), p. 111.
15. David A. Hollinger, *Science, Jews, and Secular Culture* (Princeton: Princeton University Press, 1996), p. 132.
16. Quoted in Schrecker, *No Ivory Tower*, pp. 238–9.
17. "Arthur Miller, June 21, 1956," in Bentley, *Thirty Years of Treason* pp. 823–4.
18. Quoted in Alice L. George, *Awaiting Armageddon: How Americans Faced the Cuban Missile Crisis* (Chapel Hill: University of North Carolina Press, 2003), p. 8.
19. Whittaker Chambers, *Witness* (Chicago: Henry Regnery, 1952), p. 463.
20. Harvey Matusow, *False Witness* (New York: Cameron and Kahn, 1955), p. 96.
21. Quoted in Frances FitzGerald, *America Revised: History Schoolbooks in the Twentieth Century* (Boston: Little, Brown, 1979), pp. 120–1.
22. Elia Kazan, *A Life* (New York: Alfred A. Knopf, 1988), pp. 459–60, and "A Statement," in Victor S. Navasky, *Naming Names* (New York: Viking, 1980), p. 206.
23. Budd Schulberg, *On the Waterfront: A Screenplay* (Carbondale: Southern Illinois University Press, 1980), p. 132; Kazan, *A Life*, p. 500.
24. Kazan, *A Life*, p. 528; Navasky, *Naming Names*, pp. 199, 209–10.
25. Seymour Martin Lipset, *Political Man: The Social Bases of Politics* (Garden City, NY: Doubleday Anchor, 1963), pp. 443, 445.
26. Todd Gitlin, *The Sixties: Years of Hope, Days of Rage* (New York: Simon & Schuster, 1987), p. 344.
27. Quoted in David Green, *The Language of Politics in America* (Ithaca, NY: Cornell University Press, 1992), pp. 245–6; William Appleman Williams, in Henry Abelove, Betsy Blackmar *et al.* (eds.), *Visions of History: Interviews* (New York: Pantheon, 1983), pp. 132–5; Oscar Handlin, *Truth in History* (Cambridge, MA: Harvard University Press, 1979), pp. 145, 161.
28. Quoted in Thomas L. Friedman, "Cold War Without End," *New York Times Magazine*, August 30, 1993, p. 45.
29. Graham Greene, *The Quiet American* (New York: Penguin, 1977), p. 60.
30. John le Carré, *The Spy Who Came In From the Cold* (New York: Coward-McCann, 1963), pp. 23–4, 142–4.
31. John le Carré, "Spy Story," *New York Times Book Review*, March 12, 1978, p. 38.

32. Neil Middleton (ed.), Introduction to *The I. F. Stone's Weekly Reader* (New York: Random House, 1973), pp. xi–xii.
33. John Updike, *Rabbit at Rest* (New York: Alfred A. Knopf, 1990), pp. 442–3.

FURTHER READING

Eric Bentley (ed.), *Thirty Years of Treason*, New York: Viking, 1971.
Peter Biskind, *Seeing is Believing: How Hollywood Taught Us to Stop Worrying and Love the Fifties*, New York: Pantheon, 1983.
Thomas Doherty, *Cold War, Cool Medium: Television, McCarthyism, and American Culture*, New York: Columbia University Press, 2003.
Walter L. Hixson, *Parting the Curtain: Propaganda, Culture, and the Cold War, 1945–1961*, New York: St. Martin's Press, 1997.
Stefan Kanfer, *A Journal of the Plague Years*, New York: Atheneum, 1973.
Peter J. Kuznick, and James Gilbert (eds.), *Rethinking Cold War Culture*, Washington DC: Smithsonian Institution Press, 2001.
Lary May (ed.), *Recasting America: Culture and Politics in the Age of Cold War*, Chicago: University of Chicago Press, 1989.
Alan Nadel, *Containment Culture: American Narratives, Postmodernism, and the Atomic Age*, Durham, NC: Duke University Press, 1995.
Victor S. Navasky, *Naming Names*, New York: Viking, 1980.
Frances Stonor Saunders, *Who Paid the Piper?: The CIA and the Cultural Cold War*, London: Granta, 1999.
Ellen W. Schrecker, *No Ivory Tower: McCarthyism and the Universities*, New York: Oxford University Press, 1986.
Stephen J. Whitfield, *The Culture of the Cold War*, 2nd ed., Baltimore, MD: Johns Hopkins University Press, 1996.

14

HUGH WILFORD

Secret America: the CIA and American culture

Spying and writing have always gone together. In Britain, where the modern intelligence agency was born, intellectuals moved smoothly back and forth between secret government service and the literary life, some, like the journalist Malcolm Muggeridge, even spending the morning at the typewriter before consulting with MI6 after lunch.[1] Somerset Maugham, Compton Mackenzie, Graham Greene, Ian Fleming, John Le Carré: all placed their powers of observation and divination at the disposal of the British secret state while mining their experience of intelligence work in their fiction. It was not just a case of satisfying the reading public's apparently insatiable appetite for the espionage novel. There seemed to be some basic connection between the roles of writer and spy: both were iconic, even heroic figures in modern culture, necessarily detached from ordinary society, yet gifted – cursed, perhaps – with unique insight into the darkest realms of human existence. "I, from very early, lived a secret life, an inward life," Le Carré once told an interviewer. "I seemed to go about in disguise."[2]

In this respect, the spies of the Central Intelligence Agency (CIA) were no different from their British counterparts. Indeed, the "man of letters" was, if anything, even more conspicuous a figure in the upper echelons of the American secret service than in MI6. During World War II, Norman Holmes Pearson, a noted Yale professor of literature and editor, alongside W. H. Auden, of the five-volume Viking *Poets of the English Language*, ran "X-2," the London-based counterespionage branch of the Office of Strategic Services (OSS), the United States' wartime foreign intelligence agency. After the war, when the OSS was resurrected as the CIA in order to fight a new "totalitarian" menace, the Soviet Union, the task of counterintelligence, or protecting one's secrets from theft by rival agencies, was inherited by another "Yalie," James Jesus Angleton, whose obsession with hunting for "moles" later came to verge, so many of his Agency colleagues suspected, on paranoia. A founding editor of the influential "little magazine" *Furioso* and friend of Ezra Pound, Angleton (who inspired the "complex and convoluted" character of Hugh Montague in Norman Mailer's "CIA novel," *Harlot's Ghost*) was known, among his many other code and nicknames, as "the Poet."[3] One of Angleton's several protégés in the Agency, Cord Meyer, had edited the Yale *Lit* and published short stories in the *Atlantic Monthly* before becoming a spy.[4] He used his position as Deputy Director of Clandestine Services to recruit to the CIA a number of young critics and poets associated with John Crowe Ransom's *Kenyon Review*, house organ of the "New Criticism," a rigorously formalistic method of reading literary texts.[5]

Of course, once in the CIA, writing had to take second place to spying. Unless, like E. Howard Hunt (a long-serving CIA officer before he achieved notoriety as a leading player in the Watergate scandal), one was specifically tasked with improving the Agency's public image by penning flattering fictional portrayals of it (under the pen-name David St John, Hunt wrote several novels featuring Peter Ward, a would-be American James Bond), the challenge of fighting the international communist movement and all its devious stratagems was so demanding that it left little time for the literary life.[6] Besides, men like Tom Braden, who during the war had run missions for the OSS in occupied France, then after 1945 filled his time teaching English at Dartmouth College, were impatient to return to the fray, to abandon the contemplative life for the active. Moreover, even if there was little opportunity to write poetry in the heat of the Cold War, there was another, no less honorable part for these CIA officers to play in the process of artistic creation, one for which, by dint of their patrician backgrounds and educations, they were extremely well suited: that of cultural patron.

As well as being a political, economic, and (only occasionally, when other methods failed) military conflict, the confrontation between the United States and the Soviet Union was a clash of cultures. The communists were fond of pointing toward their cultural achievements as proof that they, not the western bourgeoisie, were the true heirs of the European Enlightenment – witness the excellence of Soviet cinema, theater, dance, art, music, and literature. The United States, in comparison, was a cultural wasteland, its few artists treated as mere ornaments by its capitalist class, and its workers cretinized by the idiotic products of its culture industries. Faced with these charges, which appeared to find a receptive audience among intellectuals in western Europe, Americans responded by accusing the Russians of disregarding the inherent value of culture, of subjugating art to the dreary dictates of a totalitarian political ideology. Not only that, the picture of the United States as a bastion of philistinism was, so they claimed, badly outdated. In fact, America was the seedbed of the most creative impulses in modern culture, as was shown by, for example, the influence of Ezra Pound and T. S. Eliot on modernist poetics. With Europe enfeebled by its recent political convulsions, and many of its artists seeking refuge over the Atlantic, it now fell to the United States to protect and nurture the best cultural traditions of western civilization.

Yet there were problems with this set of claims. American politicians were hardly known for their appreciation of modern art: indeed, one congressman, Representative George A. Dondero (Michigan), won himself considerable publicity by loudly denouncing the "horde of foreign art manglers" as a "pen-and-brush phalanx of the Communist conspiracy," while even the President himself, Harry Truman, once famously declared of a Yasuo Kuniyoshi semi-abstract, "if that's art, I'm a Hottentot."[7] This sort of philistinism seriously inhibited US government officials who wanted to counter communist propaganda by publicly displaying works of home-grown modern art. One traveling State Department exhibit, "Advancing American Art," which featured work by, among others, Adolph Gottlieb, Arshile Gorky, and Georgia O'Keefe, was the target of such vitriolic attack that it had to be canceled in mid-tour and its contents sold off as surplus government property (they fetched a mere $5,544).[8] Combined with the effects of this sort of "cultural vigilantism" was a fundamental contradiction. The whole point of American art was supposed to be that it was free, the unfettered expression of the individual consciousness: this is what distinguished it from the "agitprop" produced by the Soviet Union's "artists in uniform." How, then, could the US government openly mobilize American culture in the Cold War *kulturkampf*?

In these circumstances, it fell to the CIA to perform the role of official artistic patron, a kind of secret American ministry of culture. The Agency had already gained expertise in the covert funding of citizen groups who had a part to play in the superpower contest for "hearts and minds." In 1948 the Office of Policy Coordination (OPC), a newly created, semi-autonomous unit devoted to clandestine "political warfare" (there was some argument about whether the CIA itself, only established by the National Security Act of the previous year, was empowered to carry out covert operations), began passing money to trade union officials Jay Lovestone and Irving Brown to fund their anti-communist activities within foreign labor movements.[9] The following year saw the launch of the National Committee for a Free Europe, a New York-based organization which provided cover for OPC operations involving émigrés from the Eastern Bloc countries, such as Radio Free Europe, a radio station dedicated to broadcasting pro-American and anti-Soviet propaganda behind the Iron Curtain.[10] During the 1950s, when the OPC was folded into the CIA and its "front" operations inherited by the Agency's International Organizations Division (IOD), these covertly financed bodies were joined by numerous others, each intended to appeal to a particular citizen group, for example, students (the United States National Student Association), women (the Committee of Correspondence), and Catholics (the Family Rosary Crusade).[11] So extensive and diverse was this covert network that one senior intelligence officer, Frank Wisner, likened it to a "Mighty Wurlitzer" organ, capable of playing any tune the CIA deemed necessary.

The Agency's principal front organization in the "cultural Cold War" was the Congress for Cultural Freedom (CCF). Launched in 1950 at a rally of anti-communist intellectuals and artists in West Berlin, the CCF set up its permanent headquarters in Paris the following year, using massive CIA subsidies to fund an extraordinarily ambitious program of cultural activities, including literary prizes, art exhibits, and music festivals. Its location, in the citadel of western European Cold War neutralism, reflected the Agency's desire to carry "the battle for Picasso's mind" (as Tom Braden, first head of the IOD, later described it) to the communists. It also indicated that, ironically, anti-communist American literati stood to gain less from the CIA's new status as one of history's most generous artistic patrons than their uncommitted European fellows. The organization did have a New York-based affiliate, the American Committee for Cultural Freedom (ACCF), but this was only created to act as a conduit for CIA subsidies to its parent body, the international Congress, before the Agency began inventing fake "pass-through" charitable foundations instead (although, in the hands of the so-called "New York intellectuals," the ACCF did acquire an unruly life of its own, of which more below). Nonetheless, there were American writers and artists involved in the CCF's international program, as part of the CIA's efforts to "showcase" US high culture for the benefit of neutralist foreign intellectuals, with the result that Agency cultural patronage had domestic repercussions in America or, to use intelligence parlance, "blowback."

Combined with the prominence of many of the individuals concerned, this fact has ensured that, among the CIA's numerous front operations in the Cold War, the CCF has attracted the most attention from historians. For many years after the existence of the Agency's covert network was exposed by investigative journalists in 1967, scholarship about the cultural Cold War displayed a strong "revisionist" impulse. The CIA was credited with having exerted a heavily determining influence on high cultural production in the United States and its distribution abroad. In particular, the postwar preeminence of certain modernist cultural movements, such as Abstract Expressionism in painting, was ascribed, in part at least, to covert official sponsorship. The culmination of this school of thought was British researcher Frances Stonor Saunders's 1999 *Who Paid the Piper?* (or, to give it its less provocative American title, *The Cultural Cold War*), an enterprisingly researched and entertainingly written history of the CCF and allied CIA cultural activities.[12] Somewhat opposed to this interpretation, and more pronounced in writing about the cultural Cold War that has appeared since the publication of *Who Paid the Piper?*, is a tendency to express skepticism about the putative relationship between the CIA and modernism, and play down the Agency's control of the artists and intellectuals it secretly subsidized. The remainder of this chapter will attempt to present a summary of the main findings of both revisionist and "post-revisionist" historians of the cultural Cold War, exploring in particular the related questions of the CIA's aesthetic tastes, and the degree of control the Agency exerted over American high culture.

The CIA as cultural patron

"Suddenly, there were limousines, parties with lashings of smoked salmon, and so on," recalled Jason Epstein of the 1950s, when the Congress for Cultural Freedom appeared on the US literary scene. "People who couldn't normally afford the bus ticket to Newark were now flying first class to India for the summer."[13] American writers stood to benefit from the clandestine largesse of the CIA in several ways. First, there were travel expenses for attending international meetings of the CCF. The Agency wanted to show off the cream of American literary talent to European intellectuals, and thereby forge a sense of Atlantic cultural community. For their part, novelists, poets, and critics such as Mary McCarthy, Robert Lowell, and Dwight Macdonald were glad of the chance to travel in comfort to glamorous destinations (but often privately scornful of the quality of intellectual discourse at the Congress's meetings).[14] At a time when, thanks to rising rents and the decline of old bohemian neighborhoods, the existence of the freelance writer was becoming increasingly precarious, literary prizes and fellowships donated by such CIA pass-throughs as the Farfield Foundation made life that bit easier. Finally (and, when the *New York Times* published details of the Agency's covert cultural operations in 1967, most controversial of all), there were secret grants to literary magazines. Some of these, like the London-based, Anglo-American monthly *Encounter*, were creations of the CCF and, as such, received regular monthly subventions (in *Encounter's* case, from both the CIA and MI6). Others, whose existence predated that of the Congress, only received occasional injections of cash, usually to stave off the threat of imminent financial collapse. One such was *Partisan Review*, a title originally published in the early 1930s by the New York Communist Party, whose editors' fascination with literary modernism eventually caused them to break with their Stalinist sponsors and relaunch the magazine on an independent footing, after which it earned a reputation as one of the most important journals of intellectual opinion in the United States. It was precisely this combination of principled anti-Stalinism and cultural sophistication that would later put "*PR*" in line for CIA support in the cultural Cold War.[15]

The CIA displayed similar tastes in the realm of the visual arts. Here it is the so-called "Abstract Expressionists" – a movement whose guiding aesthetic principles received their fullest expression in the writings of New York art critic and *PR* editor, Clement Greenberg – who have featured most prominently in accounts of the cultural Cold War.[16] Again, many of the artists concerned had radical backgrounds – Jackson Pollock, for example, had worked in the studio of Marxist Mexican muralist David Alfaro Siquieros – yet had renounced communism in favor of a belief in art for its own sake.[17] Their painting, with its gestural expression of the individual artist's consciousness and total rejection of representation, constituted a massive rebuke both to the banal illusionism of the official style of Soviet art, Socialist Realism, and to the almost photographic mimesis of such "middlebrow" American painters as Norman Rockwell. Here was an artistic movement that, in all its formal difficulty and obscurity – attributes which help explain why professional explicators like Greenberg and Harold Rosenberg featured so prominently in its ranks – would surely appeal to even the most refined of European sensibilities. Yet, for all the high modernist aesthetics, it could also be claimed that there was something peculiarly *American* about Abstract Expressionism, with its giant canvases, its virile daubings of paint, its foregrounding of the *act* of artistic creation. Pollock – western-born, broodingly taciturn, hard-drinking – was the artist as cowboy, shooting paint from the hip, an incontrovertibly American culture hero.

Of course, the CIA was not the first patron to spot these qualities. A number of private American citizens had already begun collecting and exhibiting the Abstract Expressionists, emulating those European aristocrats whose patronage had earlier enabled the modernist avant-garde to evade the twin threats of totalitarianism and "kitsch". Foremost of these was Nelson Rockefeller, the fabulously wealthy President of the Museum of Modern Art and admirer of what he liked to call "free enterprise painting."[18] Another influential booster of the "new American painting" was John Hay Whitney, benefactor of New York's second great exhibitor of modern art after MoMA, the Whitney Museum. As well as commanding positions of immense power within the New York art world, these men were profoundly connected to the US intelligence community. Indeed, Rockefeller had pioneered many of the CIA's characteristic methods of "psychological warfare" while serving as Coordinator of Inter-American Affairs during World War II. He would later reprise this role when he took over from *Time–Life* executive C. D. Jackson as Dwight Eisenhower's Special Assistant for Foreign Affairs in 1954. Whitney, likewise, worked in Inter-American Affairs before joining the OSS. His secret service in the Cold War took the form of a berth on Harry Truman's "psy-war" planning unit, the Psychological Strategy Board. He also allowed the CIA to use the Whitney Trust as one of its pass-throughs. These and numerous other links between the worlds of intelligence and art – perhaps most telling of which was Tom Braden working as MoMA's executive secretary in the late 1940s – meant that the CIA did not always have to foot the bill in the Cold War promotion of American art. They also provided the Agency with a host of privately owned and internationally famous front institutions behind which it could conceal its interest in artistic patronage.

The typical CIA operation in this theater of the cultural Cold War, then, was a joint public–private venture, usually involving Rockefeller's Museum of Modern Art and the Agency's Congress for Cultural Freedom. In 1952, MoMA provided the art exhibit for the CCF's spectacular Masterpieces of the Twentieth Century festival in Paris, an event that established the Congress as a major presence in European cultural life and the Farfield Foundation as a credible front for the Agency. Although the new American painting was not on show at Paris – the exhibit took a mainly retrospective and Eurocentric view of modern art – the Cold War subtext was plain enough, with curator James Johnson Sweeney, an advisor to MoMA (and associate of *Partisan Review*), proudly proclaiming that the works he had chosen for display "could not have been created . . . by such totalitarian regimes as Nazi Germany or present-day Soviet Russia."[19] A second collaboration in 1954 resulted in a show of "Young Painters" consisting almost entirely of recent abstract works, with large cash prizes donated by the President of the Farfield Foundation, the Cincinnati gin millionaire and CIA's principal front-man in the cultural Cold War, Julius "Junkie" Fleischmann. It was presumably efforts such as these that August Heckscher of MoMA had in mind when he declared that the museum's work was "related to the central struggle of the age – the struggle of freedom against tyranny."[20] Then, in 1960, came the opening of the "Antagonismes" show at the Louvre, with the US participation chosen by MoMA, and the costs met by the Farfield and another CIA pass-through, the Hoblitzelle Foundation. Among the American artists represented were the Abstract Expressionists Pollock, Mark Rothko, and Frank Kline.

By no means were all of MoMA's exhibits sponsored by the CIA – the Rockefeller Brothers Fund remained the Museum's chief source of financial support throughout this period – nor were their organizers' tastes confined to Abstract Expressionism. Indeed, there was sufficient representational art featured in MoMA shows for one critic to complain that the Museum was dedicated less to the "art of our time" than the "art of our grandfathers' time."[21] In his encyclopedic 2003 history of the cultural Cold War, *The Dancer Defects*, David Caute accuses Frances Stonor Saunders of confusing the actual importance of Abstract Expressionism in the 1950s American art scene with the claims for its supremacy made by such critic-boosters as Clement Greenberg.[22] A number of art historians have similarly claimed that the "revisionist" school exaggerated MoMA's support for the new American painting in the early Cold War period, dating the beginning of the Museum's interest in promoting the Abstract Expressionists as a distinct avant-garde movement to as late as 1956.[23] Saunders has responded to such charges by arguing (not unpersuasively) that, while the Museum might have pandered to more conventional artistic tastes in many of its public exhibitions, its collection policies during the 1940s and 1950s were heavily slanted toward the acquisition of recent American abstraction. The evidence connecting Abstract Expressionism with MoMA – and, through MoMA, the CIA – remains, she insists, compelling.[24]

The "post-revisionist" argument that the CIA's aesthetic preference for modernism has been overstated seems most convincing when applied to the realm of music. Classical symphonies, Broadway musicals, even the jazz of Dizzy Gillespie, all were used by a large array of US government bodies (the postwar military government in Germany, the State Department, President Eisenhower's Emergency Fund for Art) in an attempt to persuade music-lovers around the world that America was no less hospitable to the aural arts than the literary and visual.[25] Yet, surprisingly, the CIA appeared reluctant to extend its patronage to America's musical avant-garde, experimental, "serialist" composers such as Milton Babbitt and John Cage, both of whom shared many of the same aesthetic ideas as and indeed often collaborated with the Abstract Expressionists.

Instead, the music program of the CCF, as it developed under the guiding hand of the organization's flamboyant General Secretary, émigré Russian composer and cultural Cold War impresario Nicolas Nabokov, seemed more concerned with presenting earlier European works that had either been banned or condemned as "formalist" by the Soviet authorities. The glittering 1952 Masterpieces festival opened with a performance of Igor Stravinsky's *The Rite of Spring*, with the composer himself sitting in the audience, flanked by the French President and his wife. Over the next thirty days nine separate orchestras performed works by over seventy composers dismissed by Communist commissars as "degenerate" and "sterile," among them Dmitri Shostakovich and Claude Debussy.[26] Here, indeed, were "the abundant riches which the mind of free man has created in the first half of our century" promised in the festival program, except that the emphasis clearly lay on the early 1900s, the Parisian "good old days," as one unimpressed spectator sniffily put it.[27]

If American avant-garde composers were overlooked by the CCF, American virtuoso musicians were very much in favor. The Paris performance of *The Rite of Spring* marked the first appearance in Europe by the Boston Symphony Orchestra (BSO). The huge expenses of transporting an orchestra across the Atlantic had been met by an IOD grant of $130,000, arranged by Tom Braden and BSO trustee C. D. Jackson (and recorded in the Congress accounts as a donation from "prominent individuals and associations").[28] "You know how much capital our enemies constantly make about the lack of culture in this country," Jackson explained to a colleague. "The Boston Symphony's music, played in Europe, with the attendant European publicity, would be a most startling and useful refutation of these charges."[29] Was the outlay worth it? Some observers reckoned not. "I thought [the festival] was trivial," recalled one of the CCF's founders, Melvin Lasky. "It's unimportant whether foreigners think Americans can play music or not."[30] Braden and Jackson, however, were delighted with the overwhelmingly positive responses of European audiences. "[T]he Boston Symphony Orchestra won more acclaim for the US in Paris," thought the former, "than John Foster Dulles or Dwight D. Eisenhower could have brought with a hundred speeches."[31] Thus was launched a collaboration that would continue throughout the cultural Cold War. "The juggernaut of American culture," writes Saunders, "the Boston Symphony became the CIA's answer to the agitprop trains of old."[32]

This is not to say that the CCF completely ignored American composers or the "New Music." Samuel Barber, Aaron Copland, and Virgil Thomson were all on the program of the 1952 festival (Thomson's adaptation of Gertrude Stein's *Four Saints in Three Acts* was sung by an "all-Negro" cast, pointing toward a subplot of the CIA's music program, the desire to feature African American performers wherever possible so as to dispel negative foreign perceptions of US race relations). Similarly, when two years later Nabokov arranged a follow-up event in Rome, a competition of twelve young composers with prize money adding up to $6,000 "donated" by Junkie Fleischmann, and the winners promised first American performances of their work by the Boston Symphony ("Now is that a prize or isn't it?," asked Nabokov), he included in the line-up several representatives of the atonal, "twelve-tone" school.[33]

However, Saunders's suggestion that the 1954 Rome competition marked the conversion of the CCF to the "serialist orthodoxy" is wide of the mark.[34] The twelve-tone school did not dominate the event, as she claims, and the likes of Babbitt and Cage continued to be ignored by the Congress. "As far as the New Music is concerned," writes Nicolas Nabokov's biographer, Ian Wellens, "there is no evidence to suggest that a 'hidden hand' was at work."[35] The reason for this state of affairs – a curious one, given the growing international stature of American experimentalists, Cage in particular, in this period – might simply be that Nabokov did not personally care for the new serial compositions, his tastes remaining rooted in the "tonal" tradition of Russian music. If so, then the situation can hardly have been helped by the spectacularly abusive response he received when he invited Pierre Boulez, one of the New Music's best-known exponents, to take part in the Rome competition. "What do you expect to resolve by these murky undertakings, by the concentration of numerous jumping-jacks in one single location, stuck there in a pit of liquid manure?," Boulez demanded to know. "They will undoubtedly learn to appreciate the quality of each other's sweat but they are unlikely to produce anything more fruitful."[36]

Nabokov's aesthetic prejudices notwithstanding, there is documentary evidence that the CIA's own tastes in the realm of the performing arts were far from high modernist. This exists in the form of a letter written in 1955 by Frank Wisner, who as Deputy Director of Plans oversaw the Agency's first campaigns in the cultural Cold War, in response to a request from Nelson Rockefeller for his reaction to a suggestion by Lincoln Kirstein that the New York City Ballet visit and perform in Moscow. This was not, Wisner felt, a good idea, because "it would place us at a comparative disadvantage in an area in which the Russians are most prominent." Former Director of Central Intelligence, Walter Bedell Smith, was of the same view, so Wisner reported, in a passage which is remarkable not only for its martial metaphors but also for the image it conjures of the DCI, a notoriously irascible and salty-mouthed army general, pondering the finer points of Cold War cultural diplomacy: "In fact, Bedell was opposed to governmental encouragement for American ballet to appear in Western Europe on the ground that it might well be met and challenged by a Soviet troup, and this would amount to our having elected to join battle with the opposition on grounds of his choosing and greatest strength."[37]

This attitude, combined perhaps with the fact that Nabokov was a composer rather than a choreographer, helps explain why dance did not feature prominently in the CCF's international program. Instead, American ballet tended to be promoted abroad by the overtly government-funded

President's Emergency Fund (which echoed the CCF's approach to music by neglecting avant-garde dancers such as Merce Cunningham in favor of more traditional fare).[38]

Wisner then goes on in his letter to Rockefeller – the only contemporaneous written record of the CIA's tastes in the early Cold War period available to researchers – to make several suggestions for future cultural exchange with the Soviet Union. Regarding music, "our initial presentations to Soviet audiences should aim for mass appeal" and be "expressive of our folklore or unmistakably typical of the US." Musical shows such as *Oklahoma, Carousel*, or *Kiss Me Kate* would suit this purpose; even *Ice Capades* might serve "as a good example of American showmanship in pageantry, skill, and precision." Another possibility, and a "pet theory of my own," Wisner professed, was to send "one of our top-flight 'name' jazz orchestras." It might be advisable to prepare the cultural ground in the Soviet Union by first exposing "their audiences to American symphonic organizations," such as, for example, the BSO. "A subsequent introduction of first-rate American jazz against this backdrop would serve to demonstrate the breadth and vitality of American musicianship in rather telling terms." Finally, having reasserted the desirability of using such productions to showcase the talents of "negro performers," in order to demonstrate simultaneously their "capacity" and "the opportunities they have in US artistic life," Wisner closed by pronouncing on the place of the visual arts in possible Soviet–American exchange. "In the realm of painting and sculpture, almost anything of quality that the US could exhibit is likely to surpass conventionalized Soviet efforts," he confidently told Rockefeller. "However, in initial displays, extreme modern or experimental forms should be avoided."[39]

Wisner's letter is concerned specifically with US cultural diplomacy in the Soviet Union, so should not necessarily be read as a definitive statement of CIA aesthetics in the cultural Cold War generally. There is still much good evidence to support the revisionist argument that there was a basic sympathy between many intelligence officers and modernist artists, based on such shared values as formalism, internationalism or "cosmopolitanism," and elitism.[40] That said, the letter, combined with other proof that "extreme modern or experimental forms" were not always privileged over the middlebrow or popular, cautions us that pragmatism was an equally, if indeed not more, decisive factor in shaping the CIA's cultural patronage. What mattered ultimately, the bottom line, as it were, was a cultural activity's effectiveness in helping the US cause in the Cold War. If an artist's work was considered unlikely to impress foreign opinion positively, then it would be ignored. One project, an international sculpture competition to design a monument to political prisoners, staged by the London Institute of Contemporary Arts and funded by the CIA via John Hay Whitney, was abandoned halfway through in the face of unfavorable British press attention.[41] Finally, there are two prosaic but nonetheless important considerations. First, because the CIA only patronized those cultural practices which needed financial subsidy, its patronage is bound in retrospect to appear highbrow. The Agency clearly was interested in such mass media as the Hollywood movie industry, but its influence over them was restricted by their economic self-sufficiency.[42] Second, it is possible that some intelligence officers, out of a desire to enhance their personal image and divert attention from some of their less benign covert activities in the Cold War, have since portrayed the CIA as a more "enlightened" cultural patron that it in fact was. In Agency legend, the cultural Cold War has come to perform something of a redemptive function.

Playing the CIA's tune?

If revisionism's account of the CIA's aesthetic preferences needs some nuancing, so too does its portrayal of the Agency's cultural influence. The implied claim of the British title of Saunders's book, that, by virtue of its cultural patronage, the American spy establishment called the tune of western intellectual life in the early Cold War, is problematic in several respects. To begin with, the CIA could not always predict or control the actions of the musicians, writers, and artists it secretly patronized. The history of the Congress for Cultural Freedom's involvement with America's avant-garde is littered with incidents of literary feuding, prima donna-ish tantrums, and various other forms of temperamental behavior, several of which are related by Saunders herself. A South American tour by Robert Lowell had to be curtailed when the poet threw away the pills prescribed for his manic depression, stripped naked, and mounted an equestrian statue in one of Buenos Aires' main squares, declaring himself to be "Caesar of Argentina" and his CCF minder one of his generals. Ad Reinhardt denounced his fellow Abstract Expressionists for "selling out," calling Rothko a "*Vogue* magazine cold-water-fauve," Pollock a "*Harpers Bazaar* bum," and Barnet Newman an "avant-garde huckster-handicraftsman." In 1957 Chicagoan novelist James T. Farrell resigned his chairmanship of the CCF's US affiliate, the American Committee for Cultural Freedom, at the end of a drunken evening in the course of which he had accused its members of failing to defend American civil liberties against McCarthyism and foreign intellectuals of believing that their best policy was "to flirt with Communists, insult us, and perhaps get more money out of us."[43]

Farrell's resignation points to two other, more serious problems with the revisionist thesis. One of these is that it presumes too much ideological unanimity among the American literary intellectuals involved in the CIA's cultural Cold War effort. The ACCF was badly divided over the McCarthy issue, with some members (mostly ex-communists) declaring that the Wisconsin Senator deserved their support in his crusade against domestic communism, and others (mostly liberals) dismissing him as a "political bum." The CIA was dismayed by this dispute: McCarthyism was the last issue it wanted to see being aired by one of its front organizations, partly because of the damage the "Red Scare" was doing to America's image abroad, and partly because some of the congressional witch-hunters were turning their attention to liberals within the Agency itself. Consequently, Michael Josselson, the CIA agent who administered the affairs of the Congress for Cultural Freedom from its headquarters in Paris, attempted repeatedly to discipline the Committee and, when this approach failed, resorted to trying to strangle it to death by cutting off its funding. Yet, surprisingly, the ACCF survived these attempts to repress it, limping on as a rump body of fanatically anti-communist New York intellectuals – and a source of nagging irritation to Josselson and his CIA superiors – until the end of the 1950s. In part, this situation was typical of the sort of difficulties that the Agency tended to experience with its front organizations, which often contained individuals whose Cold War zeal exceeded that of the professional spies (Jay Lovestone of the American Federation of Labor was another example). However, it is also tempting to discern a larger political significance in the clash between the ACCF and CIA, with the former embodying a kind of embryonic "neoconservative" consciousness that was at odds with the predominantly liberal anti-communist politics of the Agency officers housed in the International Organizations Division.[44] In any case, the history of the ACCF gives the lie to simplistic depictions of Cold War American intellectuals as so many ventriloquist's dummies and the CIA as their animating performer.

Farrell's remarks on his resignation from his ACCF point toward a second problem for the CIA: its inability to dictate how foreign intellectuals would respond to its cultural blandishments. While the Boston Symphony might have won plaudits for its performance in Paris, the most common response of French intellectuals to the Congress for Cultural Freedom's 1952 Masterpieces Festival – "cette fête américaine" – was one of haughty disdain. "Dear sirs, you have made a big mistake," Serge Lifar, head of the ballet troup at the Paris Opera, told the event's organizers (possibly piqued that his dancers had not been invited to perform). "From the point of view of spirit, civilization, and culture, France does not have to ask for anybody's opinion; she is the one that gives advice to others."[45] Inadvertently enflaming the cultural anti-Americanism of European elites was not the only trap awaiting the CIA. Forced to operate at one remove from the recipients of its patronage, the Agency often had to watch as foreign intellectuals spent CCF monies on pet projects that had little or nothing to do with the Cold War. This tendency was especially pronounced in Britain where, as the philosopher Isaiah Berlin observed, there was no shortage of "English intellectuals with outstretched hands making eyes at affluent American widows."[46] Sometimes this kind of local appropriation could be quite subtle, for example *Encounter*'s British editor Stephen Spender trying constantly to reduce American influence over the magazine and turn it into a vehicle for Bloomsbury literati such as himself. At other times, it was more crude, with officers of the CCF's British national affiliate taking friends out to lunch at expensive Soho restaurants and joking that American taxpayers were paying the bill.[47]

Like other patrons before it, the CIA discovered that, although it paid the piper, it did not necessarily call the tune. Resistance, appropriation, and unintended consequences all form important strands in the story of the cultural Cold War. However, they are not the main plot. In the final reckoning, the Agency's front operations in this field deserve to be judged, at least on their own terms, a success. In Britain, for instance, it did not really matter that Bloomsbury intellectuals used CIA patronage to buttress their dominance over the nation's literary life. They were modernists, after all, and therefore could be counted on broadly to support the CCF's cultural program. Moreover, a bit of local cultural camouflage could be a very useful thing. In the case of *Encounter*, it enabled the editors to overcome early suspicions that the magazine was a tool of American imperialism and pursue a consistently positive editorial line on US foreign policy without exciting too much local anti-Americanism. Some critics have contended that leading British intellectuals' generally acquiescent stance on such issues as the Vietnam war could be attributed, in part at least, to the influence of *Encounter* and other activities of the CCF. It is even arguable that some of the roots of recent British government support for the war in Iraq can be traced to clandestine American attempts during the early Cold War period to cultivate friendly contacts with the right wing of the Labour Party: Tony Blair and his followers are descended from the Gaitskellites, a group of "revisionist," pro-American Labour intellectuals who during the 1950s and 1960s participated extensively in CCF activities and regularly contributed to *Encounter*.[48]

What, though, about "blowback," the influence of CIA patronage on domestic American culture? In 1978 Allen Ginsberg wrote a sketch in which he imagined encountering T. S. Eliot on the fantail of a boat in Europe. "And yourself," the Beat poet asks the high priest of literary modernism. "What did you think of the domination of poetics by the CIA. After all, wasn't Angleton your friend? Didn't he tell you to revitalize the intellectual structure of the west against the so-to-speak Stalinists?" Eliot admits that he did know of Angleton's "literary conspiracies," but insists that they are "of no importance to Literature." Ginsberg disagrees.

> I thought they were of some importance since it secretly nourished the careers of too many square intellectuals, provided sustenance to thinkers in the Academy who influenced the intellectual tone of the West . . . And the Government through foundations was supporting a whole field of "Scholars of War". . . The subsidization of magazines like *Encounter* which held Eliotic style as a touchstone of sophistication and competence . . . failed to create an alternative free vital decentralized individualistic culture. Instead, we had the worst sort of Capitalist Imperialism.[49]

The picture is overdrawn, of course. In fact, when *Encounter* began appearing in 1950s London, Eliot had thought it so "obviously published under American auspices" that he kept his distance from it.[50] Similarly, in New York, several intellectuals refused to join the American Committee for Cultural Freedom – Columbia University art historian Meyer Schapiro, for example, turned down his invitation on the grounds that the ACCF was not "a 'Committee for Cultural Freedom', but an organization for fighting the world Communist movement"[51] – or quit when it took what they deemed to be too equivocal a line on McCarthyism. For that matter, even those who stayed behind failed to toe the CIA's line, pursuing a hardline anti-communist political agenda that had more to do with their peculiar ideological evolution from anti-Stalinist Marxists into neoconservatives than the needs of the national security state. Their example reminds us that political conviction mattered more than secret financial inducements in shaping the ideas of the cultural Cold War, that intellectuals as well as government officials were capable of determining political outcomes (as shown in the eventual triumph of neoconservatism over liberal anti-communism), and that Angletonian conspiracies did not always work.

We have also seen that modernism and CIA patronage did not necessarily go hand in hand. Indeed, where the performing arts were concerned, the Agency appears to have been aesthetically rather blinkered, giving a wide berth to the most experimental (and, with hindsight, we can now see, the most promising) work of the period. The evidence linking Abstract Expressionism and the American secret service is also more ambiguous than many revisionist accounts would have us believe. To give Ginsberg his due, it is in the realm of literature that the link between modernism and the CIA appears at its clearest, not only in the tastes of officers like Angleton (whose famous description of the spying business as a "wilderness of mirrors" was culled from Eliot's *Gerontion*)[52] but also in the covert subsidies to little magazines such as the *Partisan Review*. In the end, then, the most important blowback from the CIA's cultural operations abroad may well have been to shore up the authority of the old, *PR*-led literary avant-garde, at a time when it was being challenged by new movements who wanted to experiment with more traditional, "American" forms (such as Ginsberg's Beats). This is not to claim that the Agency can be credited with or blamed for the continuing dominance of modernism in American literary culture during the 1950s and 1960s. Still, it is worth wondering how writing might have developed in Cold War America without the "umbilical cord of gold" that united spy and artist.[53]

NOTES

1. See Malcolm Muggeridge, *Like It Was: The Diaries of Malcolm Muggeridge*, ed. John Bright-Holmes (London: Collins, 1981), p. 363.
2. Quoted in John L. Cobbs, *Understanding John Le Carré* (Columbia: University of South Carolina Press, 1998), p. 5.
3. Norman Mailer, *Harlot's Ghost* (New York: Random House, 1991), p. 1287. See the pen portraits of Pearson and Angleton in Robin W. Winks, *Cloak and Gown: Scholars in the Secret War, 1939–1961*, 2nd ed. (New Haven and London: Yale University Press, 1996), chs. 5 and 6.
4. Cord Meyer, *Facing Reality: From World Federalism to the CIA* (New York: Harper & Row, 1980), pp. 2–3.
5. Frances Stonor Saunders, *Who Paid the Piper? The CIA and the Cultural Cold War* (London: Granta, 1999), pp. 240–3.
6. Rhodri Jeffreys-Jones, *Cloak and Dollar: A History of American Secret Intelligence*, 2nd ed. (New Haven and London: Yale University Press, 2003), p. 162.
7. Quoted in David Caute, *The Dancer Defects: The Struggle for Cultural Supremacy during the Cold War* (Oxford and New York: Oxford University Press, 2003), pp. 545, 544.
8. *Ibid.*, p. 544.
9. See Anthony Carew, "The American Labor Movement in Fizzland: The Free Trade Union Committee and the CIA," *Labor History*, 39 (1998): 25–42.
10. See Eric Thomas Chester, *Covert Network: Progressives, the International Rescue Committee, and the CIA* (Armonk, NY, and London: M. E. Sharpe, 1995), ch. 4.
11. See Joel Kotek, *Students and the Cold War* (Basingstoke: Palgrave Macmillan, 1996), ch. 12; Helen Laville, *Cold War Women: The International Activities of American Women's Organizations* (Manchester and New York: Manchester

University Press, 2002), ch. 7; Richard Gribble, "Anti-Communism, Patrick Peyton, CSC, and the CIA," *Journal of Church and State*, 45 (2003): 535–58.

12. Saunders, *Piper*, published in the United States as *The Cultural Cold War: The CIA and the World of Arts and Letters* (New York: New Press, 2000). Three other important histories of the Congress for Cultural Freedom are Christopher Lasch, *The Agony of the American Left* (New York: Vintage, 1968), pp. 63–114 (the first and highly influential statement of the "revisionist" thesis); Peter Coleman, *The Liberal Conspiracy: The Congress for Cultural Freedom and the Struggle for the Mind of Postwar Europe* (New York: The Free Press, 1989) (a semi-official and laudatory account, which nonetheless remains useful); and Giles Scott-Smith, *The Politics of Apolitical Culture: The Congress for Cultural Freedom, the CIA and Post-War American Hegemony* (London: Routledge, 2002) (which illuminatingly employs the Gramscian concept of hegemony to theorize the Congress's impact on Western intellectual life).

13. Quoted in Saunders, *Piper*, p. 220.

14. Macdonald mischievously entitled a report on a 1955 CCF conference in Milan he had been commissioned to write for *Encounter*, "No Miracle in Milan." See Hugh Wilford, *The New York Intellectuals: From Vanguard to Institution* (Manchester and New York: Manchester University Press), p. 230.

15. See Saunders, *Piper*, pp. 335–40. *PR* was not the only journal associated with the "New York intellectuals" to receive covert subsidies from the CIA. See Hugh Wilford, "Playing the CIA's Tune? *The New Leader* and the Cultural Cold War," *Diplomatic History*, 27 (2003): 15–34.

16. For "revisionist" studies of links between Abstract Expressionism and the Cold War American state, see Francis Frascina (ed.), *Pollock and After: The Critical Debate* (London: Harper & Row, 1985), which contains essays by Max Kozloff, Eva Cockroft, and David and Cecile Shapiro; Serge Guilbaut, *How New York Stole the Idea of Modern Art: Abstract Expressionism, Freedom, and the Cold War*, trans. Arthur Goldhammer (Chicago: University of Chicago Press, 1983); and Saunders, *Piper*, ch. 16.

17. Caute, *Dancer Defects*, p. 547.

18. Quoted in Saunders, *Piper*, p. 258.

19. Quoted in *ibid.*, p. 268.

20. Quoted in *ibid.*, p. 272.

21. Clement Greenberg, quoted in *ibid.*, p. 267.

22. Caute, *Dancer Defects*, pp. 550–6.

23. See, for example, Michael Kimmelman, "Revisiting the Revisionists: The Modern, its Critics, and the Cold War," in *The Museum of Modern Art at Mid-Century: At Home and Abroad, Studies in Modern Art*, 4 (New York: MoMA, 1994). Nancy Jachec, *The Philosophy and Politics of Abstract Expressionism* (Cambridge: Cambridge University Press, 2000) makes much the same point about MoMA's exhibition policies but still argues that the US government deliberately promoted Abstract Expressionism because Marxist and Existentialist influences on the movement's aesthetics rendered it attractive to noncommunist left audiences in western Europe. Finally, see also Robin Burstow's excellent article, "The Limits of Modernist Art as a 'Weapon of the Cold War': Reassessing the Unknown Patron of the Monument to the Unknown Political Prisoner," *Oxford Art Journal*, 20 (1997): 68–80.

24. Saunders, *Piper*, pp. 264–75.
25. See Kris Russman, "The Coca-Colonization of Music: Cultural Strategies of the American State Department and the CIA Regarding the Performance of Music during the Cold War," D. Phil. dissertation, University of Cambridge, 2002.
26. See Saunders, *Piper*, ch. 8.
27. Congress for Cultural Freedom Festival Program, Congress for Cultural Freedom Papers, Joseph Regenstein Library, University of Chicago; Herbert Luethy, quoted in Ian Wellens, *Music on the Frontline: Nicolas Nabokov's Struggle against Communist and Middlebrow Culture* (Aldershot: Ashgate, 2002), p. 58.
28. Saunders, *Piper*, p. 117.
29. C. D. Jackson to Henry Cabot, August 14, 1951, C. D. Jackson Papers, Dwight D. Eisenhower Presidential Library, Abilene, Kansas.
30. Quoted in Saunders, *Piper*, p. 124.
31. Quoted in *ibid.*, p. 125.
32. *Ibid.*
33. Quoted in *ibid.*, p. 221.
34. *Ibid.*, p. 223.
35. Wellens, *Music on the Frontline*, p. 125.
36. See Russman, "Coca-Colonization of Music," appendix 5.
37. Frank Wisner to Nelson Rockefeller, "Cultural Exchange with the Soviet Union," September 14, 1955, Nelson A. Rockefeller Papers, Washington DC Files, Special Assistant to the President for Foreign Affairs, 1954–5, Rockefeller Archive Center, Tarrytown, New York.
38. See Naima Prevots, *Dance for Export: Cultural Diplomacy and the Cold War* (Middleton, CT: Wesleyan University Press, 1998).
39. Wisner to Rockefeller, September 14, 1955, Rockefeller Papers. It is interesting to note that Nelson Rockefeller's papers also contain correspondence suggesting that Wisner not only closely monitored the reception of Robert Breen's production of George Gershwin's opera *Porgy and Bess* when it toured Europe with State Department backing (a venture generally considered one of the United States' most successful attempts at Cold War cultural diplomacy), he might also have been behind the official decision to sponsor the tour in the first place. In a letter of April 1955, Rockefeller tells Wisner, "You rendered a great service to our country in getting this started." Rockefeller to Wisner, April 12, 1955, Rockefeller Papers.
40. For a highly suggestive analysis of the ideological homologies between modernism and Cold War American cultural power, see Alan Sinfield, *Literature, Politics and Culture in Postwar Britain* (Oxford: Blackwell, 1989).
41. See Burstow, "Limits of Modernist Art."
42. See Saunders, *Piper*, ch. 7. David Eldridge, "'Dear Owen': The CIA, Luigi Luraschi and Hollywood, 1953," *Historical Journal of Film, Radio and Television*, 20 (2000): 149–96, is an important corrective to Saunders's account of the CIA's activities in the US film industry, in particular her misidentification of Carleton Alsop as the Agency's "man in Hollywood."
43. Saunders, *Piper*, pp. 347–9, 277, 232–3.
44. See Hugh Wilford, "'The Permanent Revolution'? The New York Intellectuals, the CIA and the Cultural Cold War," in Helen Laville and Hugh Wilford (eds.),

The US Government, Citizen Groups and the Cold War: The State–Private Network (London: Routledge, 2006).

45. Quoted in Saunders, *Piper*, pp. 122–3.
46. Isaiah Berlin to Arthur Schlesinger, Jr., June 6, 1952, Arthur M. Schlesinger, Jr., Papers, John F. Kennedy Memorial Library, Boston.
47. See Hugh Wilford, *The CIA, the British Left and the Cold War: Calling the Tune?* (London: Frank Cass, 2003), chs. 6 and 8. There are a number of other recent studies of CCF activities in particular countries. See, for example, Pierre Grémion, *Intelligence De L'Anticommunisme: Le Congrès pour la liberté de la culture à Paris (1950–75)* (Paris: Fayard, 1995); Michael Hochgeschwender, *Freiheit in der Offensive? Der Kongress für kulturelle Beziehungen und die Deutschen* (Munich: Oldenbourg, 1998); John McLaren, *Writing in Hope and Fear: Literature as Politics in Postwar Australia* (Cambridge: Cambridge University Press, 1996); Ingeborg Philipsen, "Out of Tune: The Congress for Cultural Freedom in Denmark, 1953–1960," in Giles Scott-Smith and Hans Krabbendam (eds.), *The Cultural Cold War in Western Europe, 1945–1960* (London: Frank Cass, 2003), pp. 237–53; Margery Sabin, "The Politics of Cultural Freedom: India in the Nineteen Fifties," *Raritan*, 14 (1995), 45–65; and Tity de Vries, "The Absent Dutch: Dutch Intellectuals and the Congress for Cultural Freedom," in Scott-Smith and Krabbendam, *Cultural Cold War*, pp. 254–66.
48. See Hugh Wilford, "Literati Dine Out on the Cultural Cold War," *Times Higher Education Supplement*, July 4, 2003, 18.
49. Quoted in Saunders, *Piper*, pp. 248–9.
50. Stephen Spender to Michael Josselson, October 22, 1953, Congress for Cultural Freedom Papers
51. Meyer Schapiro to Irving Kristol, October 22, 1952, American Committee for Cultural Freedom Papers, Tamiment Institute Library, New York University.
52. Winks, *Cloak and Gown*, p. 327.
53. The phrase is Clement Greenberg's, quoted in Saunders, *Piper*, p. 259.

FURTHER READING

David Caute, *The Dancer Defects: The Struggle for Cultural Supremacy during the Cold War*, Oxford and New York: Oxford University Press, 2003.

Peter Coleman, *The Liberal Conspiracy: The Congress for Cultural Freedom and the Struggle for the Mind of Postwar Europe*, New York: The Free Press, 1989.

Burton Hersh, *The Old Boys: The American Elite and the Origins of the CIA*, New York: Scribner's, 1992.

Rhodri Jeffreys-Jones, *The CIA and American Democracy*, 3rd ed., New Haven and London: Yale University Press, 2003.

   Cloak and Dollar: A History of American Secret Intelligence, 2nd ed., New Haven and London: Yale University Press, 2003.

Christopher Lasch, *The Agony of the American Left*, New York: Vintage, 1968.

Frances Stonor Saunders, *Who Paid the Piper? The CIA and the Cultural Cold War*, London: Granta, 1999.

   The Cultural Cold War: The CIA and the World of Arts and Letters, US ed., New York: New Press, 2000.

Giles Scott-Smith, *The Politics of Apolitical Culture: The Congress for Cultural Freedom, the CIA and Post-War American Hegemony*, London and New York: Routledge, 2002.

Giles Scott-Smith and Hans Krabbendam (eds.), *The Cultural Cold War in Western Europe, 1945–1960*, London: Frank Cass, 2003.

Evan Thomas, *The Very Best Men: Four Who Dared: The Early Years of the CIA*, New York: Simon & Schuster, 1995.

Robin W. Winks, *Cloak and Gown: Scholars in the Secret War, 1939–1961*, 2nd ed., New Haven and London: Yale University Press, 1996.

15

JOHN HELLMANN

Vietnam and the 1960s

Kennedy's New Frontier

When he assumed the presidency in January 1961, the forty-three-year-old John F. Kennedy and his glamorous wife Jacqueline transformed the White House into an exciting and inspiring set of images. Television, still a young medium, was for the first time in virtually every household in America. Three broadcast networks controlled what was seen on the national screen. The news appeared at dinnertime for a fifteen-minute period, and would soon expand to a half-hour. This was followed by "prime-time" entertainment consisting mainly of Westerns and family situation comedies such as *Father Knows Best*. Heavily censored, these shows provided Americans with an idealized reflection of themselves. Kennedy and his family brought to the news the same telegenic good looks, knowledge of Hollywood and the media, and innate sense of drama and high style found in the nation's entertainment. Novelist Norman Mailer had predicted before the election that with Kennedy in the White House the American frontier myth would "emerge once more, because America's politics would now be also America's favorite movie, America's first soap opera, America's best-seller."[1]

In forming his cabinet and staff Kennedy had made a show of gathering around him the "best and brightest" from the nation's elite universities and major corporations. His Inaugural Address was full of elegantly balanced sentences ("Ask not what your country can do for you – ask what you can do for your country") that evoked orators of classical antiquity. He and his wife hosted Nobel prize winners and other eminences from the world of arts and letters at glittering White House dinners. Photographers were invited into the White House to capture scenes of the President conducting business as his little son John-John played under the desk in the Oval Office or daughter Caroline rode the pony Macaroni on the grounds. JFK established the Peace Corps to offer young volunteers an opportunity to give up the comforts of affluent America to go into the frontier of the developing world.

He associated himself with the Mercury astronauts, who early in his administration entered space in competition with the Russians. Where during the 1950s President Dwight Eisenhower had held press conferences that could be edited for later broadcast, Kennedy dazzled a live television audience with his wit and command of language.

Kennedy did not hesitate to put himself in the position of the hero struggling to meet challenges. He stumbled badly within the first months of his administration in the embarrassing debacle that became known as the Bay of Pigs, in which an American-sponsored invasion of Cuba by exiles seeking to topple the communist government of Fidel Castro ended in defeat. But JFK only increased his popularity by taking full responsibility. Turning to the space race with the Russians, he boldly committed the nation to setting foot on the moon by the end of the decade, and Congress increased the funding for the space program by a half.

Fulfilling his rhetorical definition of the 1960s as the "time of maximum danger," Kennedy responded to particularly intractable problems by shaping them into movie-like crises. These intense experiences were easily related to the image of the young hero wrestling with contending forces before resolving the situation with decisive action. This pattern is apparent in his confrontations with Soviet Premier Nikita Khrushchev over Berlin, the executives of the US Steel corporation over an inflationary rise in steel prices, and with southern governors over resistance to desegregation. The quintessential example was the Cuban Missile Crisis, the dramatic thirteen days during which the world watched as Kennedy demanded that the Soviet Union withdraw nuclear-armed missiles that they had secretly installed in Cuba ninety miles off the shore of Florida.

The White House was not the only setting for the new power of the televised image. The Civil Rights Movement had gathered force in the 1950s with legal challenges and demonstrations of civil disobedience, and the 1960 Presidential campaign was also the year of the first "sit-ins" by black students attempting to desegregate lunch counters in the South. Civil rights leader Martin Luther King, Jr. was particularly adept at using television to expose the violent racism that had been holding down African American citizens since the last union troops left the South at the end of Reconstruction. President Kennedy watched the news along with the mass of other white Americans, and like his fellow citizens was appalled at the spectacle of snarling police dogs, powerful water cannon, and club-wielding policemen in Birmingham, Alabama, and other southern cities attacking women and men peacefully attempting to assert their rights. After initial reluctance and caution, JFK used his role as what Mailer called "the leading man" of the new national movie to speak for and to Americans as the first

President to define the second-class citizenship of black Americans as a moral issue for every individual:

> We preach freedom around the world, and we mean it, and we cherish it here at home, but are we to say to the world, and much more importantly, to each other that this is the land of the free except for the Negroes; that we have no second-class citizens except Negroes, that we have no class or caste system, no ghettoes, no master race except with respect to Negroes?[2]

In 1958 Kennedy had responded enthusiastically to a best-selling book entitled *The Ugly American* by William Lederer and Eugene Burdick that claimed that America was losing the Cold War in Vietnam and other countries of Southeast Asia because too many Americans abroad were confining themselves behind the walls of embassy compounds, like European colonialists, keeping at a remove from darker-skinned native people to enjoy the affluence and security to which they had become accustomed in contemporary American society. The authors dramatized a few American heroes who emulated legendary frontier heroes in returning to wilderness conditions and learning the tactics of the communist enemy in order to defeat them. Kennedy took out an advertisement in the *New York Times* announcing that he had sent a copy of the book to every one of his colleagues in the United States Senate, and he entered the White House convinced that communist-led "wars of national liberation" in lands formerly colonized by European empires could best be met by the new theory of counterinsurgency. Kennedy ordered the Pentagon to redefine the US Special Forces from guerrilla to counterinsurgency warriors and to expand their number and training. Over objections from the Pentagon, he insisted that they be allowed to wear the green beret that was their special emblem and which he kept on his desk in the Oval Office.

Kennedy's idea that America was a young nation fulfilling its ideals in contrast to the imperialism of older European powers and the new form of empire he saw in international communism was especially publicized by his championing of the Green Berets. In a series of articles in the popular press during his administration, the Green Berets were turned into symbolic heroes as they were portrayed as virtual supermen who spoke multiple foreign languages, employed high-tech equipment, and knew how to live off the land by eating jungle fauna and snake meat. It was emphasized that they were highly skilled warriors who were equally adept at giving medical care, guiding construction projects, and organizing self-defense units among the indigenous peoples. In the men wearing the green berets Americans could see a romantic image of the combination of modern expertise and primitive self-reliance that had defined Americans' self-concept since the days of the Indian wars on the early American frontier and which Kennedy was seeking to revitalize in the 1960s.

The small Southeast Asian nation of Vietnam became the new frontier on which this symbolic warrior was dramatized as enacting JFK's vision. Historically, Americans thought of themselves as a former colonial nation sympathetic to any other people seeking to win their independence. During the Cold War, however, they found themselves competing with the communist Soviet Union and China for leadership of the developing nations of the Third World emerging from the period of European colonialism. The communist and nationalist Ho Chi Minh had led a war from 1946 to 1954 to free Vietnam from France. Perceiving Ho's Viet Minh as agent of an international communist conspiracy, the United States under both President Harry Truman and his successor Eisenhower had supported the French in their attempt to retain their colony, eventually paying 80 percent of the cost of the French Indochina War. After the Viet Minh defeated the French at Dien Bien Phu, the latter agreed as part of the international Geneva Accords to give up their colony and for Vietnam to be temporarily divided into North Vietnam, held by the communists, and South Vietnam, where the nationalist but French-educated and Catholic Ngo Dien Diem was installed with American support. The United States had not signed the Geneva Accords, and the Eisenhower administration subsequently refused to go along with the agreement to hold elections to form a unified government for Vietnam. Instead, the United States supported Diem's government in the South while Ho consolidated his control of the North.

By the time Kennedy assumed office in Washington, a communist-led insurrection by the National Liberation Front was underway in South Vietnam. With his recent humiliation at the Bay of Pigs and Soviet Premier Khrushchev's threats of war over the status of Berlin, Kennedy felt that it was especially important to show strength in Vietnam. He subscribed to Eisenhower's "domino theory," that if one Southeast Asian nation fell to the communists then neighboring countries would inevitably fall as well, leaving the United States increasingly isolated. A Democratic administration was also particularly sensitive to the political capital Republicans had made in the preceding decade with their attacks on the administration of President Harry Truman over who had "lost" China in 1949 when the communist revolution overthrew the American-supported Chiang Kai-Shek. More generally, American leaders during the Cold War subscribed to the "lesson" they had learned as a result of the failed appeasement policy of Great Britain in the 1930s. Adolph Hitler had been allowed to grow in power by annexing neighboring countries in an attempt to satisfy Germany's territorial demands, only to lead to Britain's having to fight World War II from a weakened position. Seeing international communism as a similar threat directed by the totalitarian power of the Soviet Union, American leaders felt that they could not afford to show "weakness" by allowing a single country to enter the communist orbit.

Kennedy responded to the growing insurgency in Vietnam by sending in increasing numbers of "advisers," including a detachment of Green Berets, until a presence of several hundred Americans was expanded into a commitment of over 16,000. Anxious to keep his options open, Kennedy carefully discouraged the impression that the United States was at war, but at the same time Americans were provided thrilling accounts in popular news magazines, with accompanying photos, which showed American men engaged in a wilderness adventure, and on occasion dying, as they helped innocent South Vietnamese learn to fight a savage enemy.

On June 11, 1963, an eerily horrific and alien image came on American television news screens that clashed with the appealing vision of Vietnam as a familiar American frontier. In protest against repression from the Catholic-dominated government in South Vietnam, a Buddhist monk sat down in the middle of a busy intersection in Saigon, the capital city, doused himself with gasoline, and lit a match to immolate himself. This televised image elicited strong emotions around the world, and it drew attention to the difficulties that the United States government knew that the Saigon government was having in winning the allegiance of its own people and in combating the communist insurgency.

On November 1 the South Vietnamese president Ngo Dinh Diem was overthrown by a military coup supported by the Kennedy administration. Kennedy hoped that the removal of the Diem government would produce leadership better able to win the support of the people and thus further the strategy of counterinsurgency, but he was shocked when the generals leading the coup simply shot Diem and his brother Nhu, Kennedy's fellow Catholics.

Three weeks later, on Friday November 22nd, while on a campaign trip to Texas with his wife Jacqueline, Kennedy himself was shot in the head as his motorcade slowly wound through the streets of Dallas. The nation was stunned. The widow arrived in Washington with her Chanel pink suit spattered with the stains of her husband's blood. During the subsequent weekend the nation sat in deep gloom before the living-room screen. For the first time in history, an entire nation collectively attended a funeral, which included such indelible images as a riderless black horse and an eternal flame at the grave site.

Meanwhile, the television also brought to Americans tawdry images from Dallas. On Sunday morning the accused assassin Lee Harvey

Oswald, a self-styled Marxist who had demanded "fair play" for Castro's Cuba, was himself murdered by strip-club owner Jack Ruby on live national television while in police custody. Kennedy's successor, Lyndon Johnson, quickly appointed a commission of eminent Americans led by Chief Justice of the Supreme Court Earl Warren to reassure the public that Oswald was an unstable personality who had acted alone. Polls showed that a majority of Americans were disbelieving, and conspiracy theories proliferated as Americans speculated on what unseen forces were behind this catastrophic turn of events.

Johnson's Great Society and Vietnam

The new President moved decisively to assure Americans that only the face on the national screen had changed. Kennedy had led them onto a "New Frontier," and now Johnson promised that they would build a "Great Society" at home and ensure American power and credibility abroad. Johnson lacked the charisma and charm of his predecessor. But his success in passing civil rights legislation was the greatest advance for black Americans since the Civil War. Enjoying a huge and unusually pliable Democratic majority after his landslide victory over his extreme right-wing Republican opponent Barry Goldwater in the 1964 election, he rushed a record number of bills through Congress, constituting a "War on Poverty." He appeared equally dominant in foreign affairs. Before his re-election, while he positioned himself against Goldwater as a peace candidate ("we are not about to send American boys 9 or 10,000 miles away from home to do what Asian boys ought to be doing for themselves"), he seized on the doubtful report of a second attack on American destroyers in the Gulf of Tonkin by North Vietnamese torpedo boats by ordering bombing attacks on naval facilities.[3] He then won overwhelming approval from Congress for the Gulf of Tonkin Resolution, which authorized him to take any actions necessary in Southeast Asia to protect American troops.

In early 1965 Johnson responded to the deteriorating situation in Vietnam by sending large-scale regular American combat units into the South while beginning a sustained bombing campaign in the North. These decisions transformed Kennedy's failed counterinsurgency policy symbolized by the Green Beret into a conventional war in which American forces relied on their overwhelming technological power. As the Saigon generals plotted against each other in a series of coups, American generals took command of the struggle against the communist-led insurgency and North Vietnamese regular units.

The central American tactic was "Search and Destroy," in which army or marine units would move in an arc through the countryside, seeking to lure North Vietnamese units to attack them so that overwhelming firepower from artillery, fighter-bombers, and airborne units could be rapidly employed. The goal was to kill as many of the enemy as possible in a strategy of attrition. Another tactic of the new strategy was to remove villagers from the countryside, so that they would not be in the way of American firepower and could not, whether willingly or through intimidation, support South Vietnamese guerrillas. To achieve this end, large areas of the countryside were designated free-fire zones, in which anyone not an American or South Vietnamese soldier would be considered an enemy combatant. To make the enemy visible and deprive him of food, the countryside was sprayed with chemical defoliants. During Operation Ranch Hand from 1965 until 1971, "17.6 million gallons of Agent Orange were sprayed over approximately 3.6 million acres of Vietnam."[4] Johnson hoped that this massive effort would convince the North Vietnamese leader Ho Chi Minh that resistance by his primitive little country was too costly. In a major address at Johns Hopkins University on April 7 he promised that if the enemy would end their efforts in the South the United States would supply economic aid and expertise that would modernize all of Southeast Asia, transforming the Mekong River Delta even as President Franklin Roosevelt's Tennessee River Valley Authority had improved a backward part of rural America during the 1930s as part of the New Deal. The Great Society would complete the liberal dream of a rationalized democratic progress abroad as well as at home.

Johnson and his advisers knew that the strategy depended wholly on the premise that an intimidated Vietnamese enemy would perceive that the only reasonable course left for them was to give up their "aggression." The North Vietnamese and their allies among the indigenous population in the South, the National Liberation Front (NLF), saw themselves neither as aggressors nor as without hope of victory. They had been engaged in a struggle to win independence from foreign domination for centuries, and from their point of view the American war was the final episode of a struggle that had once been waged against China and more recently France. As Johnson steadily increased the number of American troops, the North Vietnamese matched each escalation with the steady introduction of fresh combat troops and supplies through the infiltration route known as the Ho Chi Minh Road. While Johnson's policy also ostensibly involved winning the hearts and minds of the South Vietnamese populace through American largesse, the result of combined American violence and economic aid was to increase the allegiance of some South Vietnamese villagers to the National

Liberation Front, labeled by the South Vietnamese government and Americans as Viet Cong or VC (Vietnamese communists), while driving approximately one quarter of South Vietnam's population en masse into squalid slums in the towns and cities, where to survive they turned to begging, black-market activities, and prostitution.

Confronted with an unconventional war in which the imperative was to produce dead enemy while also seeking to win the hearts and minds of the people, American soldiers serving in regular American combat units found it difficult to distinguish the enemy from the "innocent natives" that they were supposedly protecting. Grunts, as they called themselves, began responding to the contradictions between their announced mission and their actual experiences with emotions of cynicism, outrage, and confusion. In such memoirs as Ron Kovic's *Born on the Fourth of July* (1976) and Philip Caputo's *A Rumor of War* (1977), they would testify to their experience of enlisting with dreams of answering the call of John F. Kennedy to do battle on a New Frontier only to find themselves committing acts against the native populace that they identified with such enemies in earlier American history as the British Redcoats and German Nazis. Servicemen involved in Operation Ranch Hand would play on the slogan of American conservation at home that "only you can prevent forest fires," boasting that "only we can prevent forests." The strategy of attrition left them with little sense of accomplishment as they fought repeatedly for the same ground they had previously won and given up, while the pressure to produce enemy dead and confusion regarding the sympathies of the native populace led to an unofficial policy of "if it's dead and it's yellow, it's VC." Serving on tours of 365 days, enduring a war often experienced as being the victims of ambushes and booby traps as they walked down jungle trails, soldiers counted the remaining days until they could leave "the bush" or "Indian country" to return to "the World" (the United States).

Americans at home, audience for the first television war, began seeing images that disturbingly turned upside down the dream of Vietnam as setting for the transformation of a New Frontier into a Great Society. The American mission in Vietnam became a nightmarish demonstration of the inability of Americans to fulfill the scenario of their national mythology. The wished-for Western or World War II film became a horror movie. One of the salient aspects of the 1960s became the disorienting experience of sitting at the evening dinner table while watching violent and shameful scenes that seemed to deny every aspect of the television Westerns and family sitcoms that formed an understanding of who Americans had been and were now.

In August 1965 CBS correspondent Morley Safer narrated a story in which American marines were shown using Zippo cigarette lighters to set aflame the thatched roofs of huts in the village of Cam Ne as distraught old men, women, and children stood by. This would be the earliest of a series of images that would impress themselves indelibly on Americans to create an image of Vietnam that functioned as a disturbing new landscape of American mythology, a cul-de-sac of their frontier myth, a no-exit inversion of their most cherished assumptions.

As the war dragged on, Americans learned week after week of the latest tally of the "body count," the ratio of slain enemy to slain American and ARVN (Army of the Republic of Vietnam) troops by which Secretary of Defense McNamara measured progress in the war of attrition. The audience became accustomed to scenes of body bags in which American dead were returned to the United States. At the same time, they saw images suggesting that the Vietnamese people the United States was supposed to be helping were instead being dragged down into a miserable parody of the American way of life. The news showed young Vietnamese women dressed up like American go-go girls selling their bodies to American servicemen and young Vietnamese boys begging or selling hoards of black-market American goods on the streets. In 1968, after three frustrating and increasingly disturbing years accompanied by promises from administration and military officials that progress was being made and that there was "light at the end of the tunnel," Americans watched nervously as North Vietnamese regular troops lay siege to a remote American base in the northern highlands of South Vietnam called Khe Sahn. The American military command reinforced the base in hope of luring the enemy into a decisive battle, confident that American air and firepower would produce the reverse of the French defeat at Dien Bien Phu in 1954. Instead, the National Liberation Front used the Tet holiday to infiltrate the major cities of Vietnam and stage an uprising at the centers of the American presence, including a suicide mission that reached the inside of the compound of the American embassy. After initial disarray, the American military regrouped and succeeded in defeating the Tet Offensive with overwhelming firepower, inflicting massive casualties on the enemy. The scale of the attack, however, as well as the ability of the enemy to infiltrate the cities in such numbers, crystallized the growing doubts among Americans back home about the trustworthiness of their leaders' representation of the situation in Vietnam. The press began speaking of a credibility gap, as the American people in increasing numbers expressed skepticism about their leaders' pronouncements.

Images from the Tet Offensive undermined Americans' most cherished images of themselves. With the enemy entrenched within the centers of the

Vietnamese cities, commanders called in artillery and air support to bring the buildings down on them. The idea that Americans were in Vietnam primarily for the good of the Vietnamese, and that Americans always acted as agents of progress, was vividly denied by the images of massive destruction of such ancient achievements of Asian culture as the citadel in Hue. The new perception of the absurdity of the announced American mission was immortalized by an army major who, in explaining the pulverizing of Ben Tre, said that "It became necessary to destroy the town in order to save it."[5] The claim that Americans were helping a beleaguered innocent ally against a savage enemy was similarly contradicted by the image, captured on both news photograph and television footage, of the captain of the Saigon police force using a pistol to blow out the brains of a bound Viet Cong captive. No amount of reporting of the missing context (the captive was said to have been a participant moments before in the slaying of a Vietnamese family) could drain the blood-spewing image of the larger meaning it seemed to convey, that Americans were embroiled in a vicious civil war in which savagery was to be found on both sides.

During the same year as the Tet Offensive, John Wayne, Hollywood icon since the 1940s of the American Western and combat film, starred on American movie screens in his Vietnam film *The Green Berets*. Even as they had been inspired by Kennedy's call to serve on a New Frontier, Vietnam veterans would recount in their memoirs and oral histories of being inspired as children by images of Wayne as Sgt. Stryker fighting the Japanese in *The Sands of Iwo Jima* (1949). With the images of the Tet Offensive on the news, Wayne's Vietnam movie was greeted with scathing reviews and even bomb threats. Despite its financial success, this projection of American myth spawned no imitations or sequels as Hollywood avoided the conflicting passions Vietnam was creating at home.

Instead, Hollywood began producing Vietnam Westerns, or anti-Westerns, in which disturbing images of Vietnam on the news were projected back onto a revised portrait of the old West. Movies such as *Little Big Man* and *Soldier Blue*, both released in 1970, showed an old West in which innocent Native Americans were massacred by merciless white Americans. Vietnam was displaced to the old West, causing many Americans to reconsider the nature of the frontier myth itself, the story by which they understood the national history and character. The nation's image of itself was cracking apart.

Black Power, antiwar movement, and counterculture

During the same years that the Vietnamese were proving unwilling to give themselves up to the designs of the New Frontier and Great Society, those elements at home who had historically been repressed or ignored began producing their own liberation movements and upheavals. Johnson's War on Poverty was inadequate to its announced aims, and the expectations it created led to discontent and impatience. In addition, the war in Vietnam began opening views of America that radically departed from the narrative of American history contained in the nation's cherished myths.

The great advances for civil rights that culminated in the 1964 passage of the Civil Rights bill were met by outrage over continuing economic inequality and even rejection of the liberal goal of integration and assimilation of black Americans into a white-dominated society. A series of violent uprisings, or riots as they were termed, in the black ghettos of the cities of the North began in 1964 and were repeated for several consecutive summers in the decade, peaking in 1967 and 1968. There was also a shift among younger black activists away from nonviolence and collaboration with white allies. The angry rejection of whites manifested itself in the exclusion of former allies from organizations such as the Student Non-Violent Coordinating Committee (SNCC) and the creation of the violent, Marxist, and highly theatrical Black Panthers. Led by Huey Newton and Eldridge Cleaver, the latter a confessed former rapist, the Panthers modeled themselves on Third World anti-colonial revolutionaries. They adopted black paramilitary uniforms, operated community programs of free breakfasts for children in black communities, and referred to police as "pigs." Black intellectuals began denigrating the goal of integration in favor of an emphasis on black pride, history, and culture summed up in the slogan "Black Power." Leroi Jones, who took the African name Amiri Baraka, wrote books and essays belittling the advantages of living with white people and celebrating a claimed black superiority in culture and the arts. Some blacks began wearing their hair in Afros, wearing African-inspired dress, and eating soul food in conscious rejection of the white-imposed norms of American society.

Black Americans also became increasingly unhappy with the Vietnam War. It was the first war to be fought by a completely integrated American military, and at first blacks served with enthusiasm. In 1965 there had been considerable publicity in national news magazines about the significance of the black soldier for the pride and advancement of his race. The military also made fair claim to being the most racially progressive institution in American life. Nevertheless, lingering problems in the military and the changing atmosphere in the larger society led to serious resentment, polarization, and conflict. Because they had formerly been relegated to menial positions in service and support roles, black males tended to gravitate toward elite combat units. This led to their suffering casualties in the early years of the war in numbers out of proportion to whites. Moreover, the impact of the draft was far greater on their community, where the loss of the positive roles these young men might have been filling at home became an issue of concern to black leaders. Because of his belief in nonviolence, his awareness of the effect on the black community, and his observation that the United States was aligning itself against people in the underdeveloped world, Martin Luther King had come out early in opposition to the war. Then Muhammad Ali, heavyweight boxing champion of the world, declared that no Viet Cong had ever called him nigger and claimed a deferment as a conscientious objector, citing his membership of the black Nation of Islam. When his claim was denied, he refused to be drafted, with the result that he was stripped of his title and sentenced to five years in prison (eventually overturned by the Supreme Court). His example, and those of other figures such as former Muslim Malcolm X, modeled a new, more militant concept of black manhood that affected those in and out of the military.

The growing movement against the Vietnam War among whites also had important roots in the Civil Rights Movement. Early student activists, styling themselves a New Left to distinguish themselves from the rigidities of the Old Left of the 1930s, had met in 1962 in Michigan to form Students for a Democratic Society (SDS) and issue the Port Huron Statement. The manifesto was vague in its goals, but offered a critique of American society for being remote, manipulative, and alienating in its institutions, calling instead for a "participatory democracy." It paid little attention to foreign policy, but with the escalations in Vietnam by the Johnson administration student radicals began to see in Vietnam a particularly visible expression of everything they were criticizing about American society at home. At the University of Berkeley in 1964 civil rights activists had been leaders in the Free Speech movement against paternalistic and restrictive policies of the university administration toward students. Early opposition to the Vietnam War, small at first, came from a diverse array of such student radicals, older foreign policy "realists," and religious pacifists. Beginning as "teach-ins," demonstrations were concentrated on university campuses, particularly those of such elite institutions as the Universities of Wisconsin, Michigan, Harvard, and Yale.

As the war dragged on, the size and intensity of these demonstrations grew. Soldiers were being conscripted from among young men aged eighteen through twenty-six by a complex selective service system, or draft, that had been designed in the Cold War era to ensure that youths were channeled into needed occupations of both military and civilian society. At the outset of the Vietnam War this meant that deferments could be had for attending college or graduate school, for being a high school teacher, for being married, and so on. There were also various medical deferments. If unable to obtain one of these deferments, one could avoid the passivity of the draft by enlisting, choosing to be an officer or a non-combat specialist at the price of a longer period of service. As the escalations required a deeper pool of potential draftees, these deferments were gradually reduced, though the undergraduate college deferment remained in place. With only a couple of exceptions, the Reserve and National Guard units were not mobilized to avoid disruption of communities, with feared political ramifications, and they became havens from the draft. One effect of the draft system was that a generation of young men had their life decisions dominated by the threat of being sent to Vietnam. Those in college spent the four years they were safe from the draft with an awareness that others were fighting the war and the possibility that they would be sent if they fell behind in their progress toward graduation or immediately after graduation. This atmosphere added to the intensity of the emotions about the war on the college campuses, where it became increasingly popular to oppose a society labeled the System and seen as manipulated by the Establishment. Some demonstrators burned their draft cards. In 1967 a massive March on the Pentagon brought the various factions of the antiwar movement to the nation's capital, where Secretary of Defense McNamara watched nervously from his office, an event chronicled by Norman Mailer in his classic work of literary journalism entitled *The Armies of the Night* (1968).

As the next year's presidential election neared, members of the antiwar movement persuaded Senator Eugene McCarthy to accept the quixotic task of challenging a sitting president of his own party. In the midst of the 1968 Tet Offensive, the esteemed anchor of the CBS evening news, Walter Cronkite, concluded at the end of his broadcast on February 27 that "It seems more certain than ever that the bloody experience of Vietnam is to end in stalemate."[6] McCarthy was proclaimed a moral victor when he came close to defeating Johnson in the New Hampshire primary. Senator Robert Kennedy, the brother and heir apparent of JFK, responded four days later by declaring his candidacy. Johnson soon shocked the nation by declaring in a televised speech on March 31 that he would not be a candidate for a second term, and while persisting in his policy turned down the March request of his generals to increase the American force of over 500,000 troops in Vietnam with an additional 260,000. The two peace candidates competed in the primaries until in June Kennedy was shot in the head moments after declaring his victory in the climactic California contest. The assassin was an Arab busboy at the convention hotel, angered over pro-Israel statements made by Kennedy. The spiraling violence (only two months before, King had been assassinated by a white racist drifter as he stood on a motel balcony) left the antiwar movement divided and frustrated as the certainty of the nomination at the convention in Chicago of Johnson's Vice-president Hubert Humphrey approached. The movement turned to protests at the convention. When some of the protesters were provocative in their behavior, Chicago police waded into the protesters in what a presidential commission would later term a "police riot." With passions over the war escalating, and with inflammatory images transmitted over the mass media, violence had become a contagion across the land.

During these years a counterculture developed that overlapped with the antiwar movement. The members of the counterculture were known in the media and thus to the general populace as "hippies," though in many regions they began referring to themselves as "heads" or "freaks." Hippies, male and female, wore their hair down to their shoulders or beyond, and often wore beads, sandals, and robes or granny dresses. The counterculture was an expression of disaffection with broad aspects of American life as its members had experienced it growing up in the 1950s and early 1960s. Rapidly centering on a twenty-five-block district named for the intersection of two streets, Haight-Ashbury had by June 1966 drawn an estimated 15,000 hippies, causing a social scientist to compare the area to "'the delta of a river,' where all the unrooted sediment of America was washing ashore."[7] Hallucinogenic drugs such as LSD and the far milder marijuana functioned as the communal sacrament, offering ways to transform inner consciousness and break through the "doors of perception," as novelist Aldous Huxley had suggested in his book about taking the hallucinogen found in peyote mushrooms. Hallucinogens were thus seen as opening an inner frontier experience to adventurers of consciousness.

Peyote was a sacramental food for certain Native American tribes, and many in the counterculture looked to the original victims on the old frontier of the society they were rejecting as a model for their new, alternative way of life. The nuclear family was often derided in favor of experimental styles of group living, sometimes in a house near a college campus and in many cases in autonomous communes out in rural or desert areas. Free love was an ideal. Opposition to the Vietnam War from the counterculture was part of a critique of a "sick society" that was hostile to nature, whether a raped Mother Earth or an unrestrained sexuality. Like the Black Power and antiwar movements, the actual percentage of youth who lived these life-styles was relatively small, but as with those other youth movements the influence through the media was immense. As the Great Society was creating a nightmare inversion of American "progress" in Vietnam, the counterculture was adopting trappings of the mythic American antagonist, the Native American, or "Indian," at home.

The Black Power, antiwar, and counterculture movements overlapped into a youth culture that was most importantly mirrored and led by the rock bands. Because these bands comprised youth writing and performing songs for youth, and had a relatively fast pace of creation and mass distribution, rock music proved far more immediate than either the novel or film in reflecting and influencing the massive numbers of teenagers born after World War II that were coming of age during the 1960s. Rock performers pushed the margins of censorship, underlining their politics, their racial and class roots, however at variance with the "reality" presented by Hollywood, the White House, and the news media. The British pop group the Beatles arrived on American shores in early 1964, only two months after the JFK assassination and funeral, playing their own version of 1950s American rock and roll. They were met by huge audiences of teenage women who would scream, faint, and defy police lines. The four "mop-tops" proved to be both astonishingly creative and uniquely open to influences from the disparate sources of the global village to which Marshall McLuhan was drawing attention in his popular theories about the epochal effects of the mass media. As the decade unfolded, the Beatles held onto their mass audience while bringing into their music elements of classical European music, Indian ragas from the East, and avant-garde collage. Lyrically, they moved from energetic professions of teenage crushes to the introspective poetry and subversive attitude they found in the folk and protest music of their American peer Bob Dylan, whose folk music combined elements of Woody Guthrie's 1930s left populism with the disaffected hipster poetry of Allen Ginsberg and other Beats of the 1950s. Dylan was in turn influenced by the Beatles to back himself with an electric band and create a new folk-rock. The Rolling Stones, a London band that came hard on the heels of the Beatles' and other Liverpool bands' success, based their music on the decidedly adult themes of black American blues stretching back to the Mississippi delta region of the 1930s. Their aggressively sexual and outlaw image was an early influence on the move toward challenging inhibitions and conventions that characterized the decade. They were soon influenced by Dylan, as well as by the Beatles, and they rapidly moved toward an aggressive pop sound that along with the lyrics conveyed their feelings and social convictions.

Dylan and the British invasion, as well as the centering of the drug culture in California, next spawned bands in San Francisco such as Jefferson Airplane, the Grateful Dead, and Big Brother and the Holding Company, joined in Los Angeles by the Doors. The hallucinogenic experience of "trips" on the drug LSD inspired their psychedelic music with its lyrical themes of journeys into new modes of consciousness. They too entered the stew of mutual influence among the Beatles, Dylan, and the Stones. Psychedelia, pop, poetry, and blues combined in the introduction to the new culture of the black guitarist, singer, and songwriter Jimi Hendrix at the Monterey Pop Festival in 1967 during the period the media had dubbed the Summer of Love. In August 1969 his thundering, apocalyptic instrumental performance of the American national anthem the "Star Spangled Banner" at the huge outdoor festival at Woodstock would virtually define the various elements of the youth culture.

With a new President, Richard Nixon, elected to office pledging to achieve "peace with honor" in Vietnam, hundreds of thousands of young people journeyed to a four-day outdoor concert in upstate New York to hear a wide array of the most prominent rock performers. The audience openly used drugs, endured discomfort and rain without resort to violence, and shared food. Some took off their clothes, and a few made love in the open. As soldiers, mainly their working-class peers from small towns and inner-city ghettoes, struggled with the stalemated war in Vietnam, the gathering at Woodstock was celebrated and analyzed in the media as the apotheosis of the challenge presented by the new youth culture. Woodstock Nation had presented itself as a utopian, if spontaneously and vaguely achieved, alternative to the Great Society.

Polls showed that dislike of the Vietnam War was surpassed among the general populace by detestation of radicals and hippies. Richard Nixon had been elected President in 1968 in a three-way race against Hubert Humphrey and George Wallace. Wallace, the notorious segregationist governor of Alabama, had run as the candidate of the American Independent Party, and his surprising strength in the North among working-class whites was based on his blunt condemnations not only of young radicals but also of the liberal "social engineers" who were the architects of Johnson's Great Society. Nixon had claimed during the campaign to have a secret plan for ending the war, and he echoed Wallace's appeal to the backlash against both radicals and liberals by calling for "law and order" while attacking Great Society programs as well as hippies and protesters. The plan to end the war turned out to be Vietnamization, the gradual turning of the war back over to a more thoroughly American-trained and American-armed South Vietnamese. To buy time for this strategy, he increased bombing while gradually withdrawing American troops, and moved to defuse discontent among the young by instituting a draft lottery with the eventual goal of a volunteer army. When the antiwar movement responded to the refusal to bring the war to a quick conclusion with renewed demonstrations, Nixon extolled the Silent Majority and denounced what his Vice-President Spiro Agnew called "radilibs."

A completely different backlash had meanwhile developed among women in the youth culture. When they attempted to assert their viewpoint in the civil rights and antiwar movements they found themselves ridiculed into silence. Stokely Carmichael allegedly said that the only position for a woman in SNCC was "prone."[8] At the 1968 Miss America contest, female protesters paraded a pig and burned bras. Even as Carmichael had excluded white activists from SNCC, the Women's Liberation Movement proceeded to exclude men from the meetings of their new organizations as they sought to raise consciousness by sharing stories of their oppression.

"Personal is political" became a slogan that questioned the foundations of the patriarchal home. Women were also beginning to take advantage of the 1964 Civil Rights law that had included sex in barring discrimination in hiring. Other identity movements inspired by the success of the Civil Rights Movement included that of Native Americans, a group of whom in 1969 seized the island of Alcatraz as reclaimed Indian land, and Gay Liberation, which marked its origin in the Stonewall Riots of the same year, when homosexuals in Greenwich Village refused to acquiesce in routine raids of gay bars and violently threw off stereotypes of passivity and cowardice.

As 1969, and with it the 1960s, drew to a close, the nation was intensely divided over the meaning of its past and its direction for the future. Back in July, Americans had paused to watch on television as the United States landed its first man on the moon, fulfilling the commitment of John F. Kennedy at the outset of the decade to this extraordinary extension of the American frontier. But back on earth the new frontier was a struggle over the definition of savagery and civilization. Nixon continued with his Vietnam policy, responding to a massive moratorium in October by peace demonstrators in the capital and in cities across the country by making it clear that he would not be moved from his prosecution of the war.

In December 1969, the final month of a decade without precedent in the United States, three images appeared on the national screen that signified the violence and turmoil that had overtaken the optimism of the vision of the New Frontier at the beginning of the decade.

In *Life* magazine full-color photographs displayed the victims of an American massacre of South Vietnamese. During an operation in 1968 a company of American infantry had gone on a rampage of rape, sodomy, and murder of old men, women, and little children. The exposure of the My Lai massacre forced the nation to confront yet more evidence that the American mission in Vietnam was in no way the simple rescue effort represented in the official versions and press reports.

That same December photographs from California were published that suggested that the countercultural dream of an alternative America somehow freely constituted of peace and love also belied reality. Americans discovered that gruesome killings at the Los Angeles homes of the movie star Sharon Tate and the wealthy business couple the LaBiancas earlier in the year had been committed by a group of hippie-looking young men and women. The head of their Family, Charles Manson, was a mentally ill exconvict who had set himself up as leader of a commune in which he enjoyed the free love of a number of runaway girls who had gravitated toward Haight-Ashbury during the 1967 Summer of Love.

December brought another shock to the counterculture. On the recommendation of the leader of the San Francisco band Grateful Dead, the Rolling Stones hired the notorious Hells Angels motorcycle gang to act as security at their planned Woodstock West concert at the Altamont speedway. When bad drug trips among the concertgoers and pushing near the stage provoked the Angels, they responded by beating people. This violence lasted throughout the day, climaxing in the Angels' knifing of a black man who pulled a gun during an altercation as the Stones performed "Under My Thumb."

The turmoil surrounding Vietnam and the 1960s would culminate in the next decade in the killings of four students at the Ohio campus of Kent State University by National Guardsmen called out to confront protesters demonstrating against the "incursion" of American troops from Vietnam into Cambodia, the triumphant re-election of Nixon over the antiwar candidate George McGovern, followed by his humiliating resignation amid the Watergate scandal, and the final defeat of the American mission in Vietnam with the departure of the last helicopter from the embassy in Saigon in April 1975 as North Vietnamese troops entered the city. During the 1970s the Black Power, antiwar, and counterculture movements would dissipate as their members turned to individual pursuits amid the demands of adulthood and the constraints of prolonged economic recession brought on by inflationary pressures from funding the Vietnam War. In the 1980s the reaction against the turmoil of the 1960s would gain ascendancy with the election of conservative Ronald Reagan to the presidency. But the stalemated and conflicted nature of the American nation in the last month of 1969 would continue beyond the end of the Cold War.

NOTES

1. Norman Mailer, *Some Honorable Men: Political Conventions 1960–1972* (Boston: Little, Brown, 1976), p. 21.

2. Quoted in Terry H. Anderson, *The Sixties*, 2nd ed. (New York: Longman, 2004), p. 37.
3. Lyndon B. Johnson, *Public Papers of the Presidents 1963–64*, vol. II (Washington: Government Printing Office, 1965), p. 1391.
4. Robert D. Schulzinger, *A Time for War: The United States and Vietnam, 1941–1975* (New York: Oxford University Press, 1997), p. 193.
5. Quoted in Peter Braestrup, *Big Story: How the American Press and Television Reported and Interpreted the Crisis of Tet 1968 in Vietnam and Washington* (rpt. New Haven: Yale University Press, 1978), p. 177.
6. Quoted in James T. Patterson, *Grand Expectations: The United States, 1945–1974* (New York: Oxford University Press, 1996), p. 680.
7. Quoted in Jay Stevens, "The Counterculture," in Peter Stine (ed.), *The Sixties* (Detroit: Wayne State University Press, 1996), p. 132.
8. Quoted in Todd Gitlin, *The Sixties: Years of Hope, Days of Rage* (New York and Toronto: Bantam, 1989), p. 388.

FURTHER READING

Michael Anderegg (ed.), *Inventing Vietnam: The War in Film and Television*, Philadelphia: Temple University Press, 1991.

Lawrence M. Baskir and William A. Strauss, *Chance and Circumstance: The Draft, The War and the Vietnam Generation*, New York: Vintage, 1978.

Milton J. Bates, *The Wars We Took to Vietnam: Cultural Conflict and Storytelling*, Berkeley: University of California Press, 1996.

Morris Dickstein, *Gates of Eden: American Culture in the Sixties*, New York: Basic Books, 1977.

H. Bruce Franklin, *M.I.A. or Mythmaking in America*, New Brunswick, NJ: Rutgers University Press, 1992.

Todd Gitlin, *The Sixties: Years of Hope, Days of Rage*, New York and Toronto: Bantam, 1987.

Daniel C. Hallin, *The "Uncensored War": The Media and Vietnam*, New York: Oxford University Press, 1986.

John Hellmann, *American Myth and the Legacy of Vietnam*, New York: Columbia University Press, 1986.
  The Kennedy Obsession: The American Myth of JFK, New York: Columbia University Press, 1997.

John Carlos Rowe and Rick Berg (eds.), *The Vietnam War and American Culture*, New York: Columbia University Press, 1991.

Robert D. Schulzinger, *A Time for War: The United States and Vietnam, 1941–1975*, New York: Oxford University Press, 1997.

James E. Westheider, *Fighting on Two Fronts: African Americans and the Vietnam War*, New York: New York University Press, 1997.

16

ERIC HOMBERGER

New York City and the struggle of the modern

Throughout the twentieth century, New York City was the supreme American example of the two powers exerted by cities – the "hard" power of finance – the world of "big men, big deals, big money, and big ideas" celebrated in *Business Week* – and the often intangible "soft" power of cultural and social influence.[1] The Wall Street banker J. P. Morgan, and succeeding generations of the city's wealthy merchants, corporate moguls, bankers, and financiers, epitomized the domineering influence of finance upon the affairs of the city, and the extension of the city's influence across the globe as American wealth reached into every continent and every market. The city's cultural producers, its opinion-makers, editors, writers, and artists, an important component of the city's role as a producer and consumer of culture, played a decisive role in shaping something as intangible, and as influential as twentieth-century taste. At the heart of the city's influence lay in its success in projecting an idea or image of the city itself. The city was the home to some of the nation's most influential cultural icons. The more we learn about the creation of the Statue of Liberty, the Brooklyn Bridge, and the elegant, assertive skyscrapers which created the Manhattan skyline (from the Flatiron, to the Woolworth, Chrysler, Empire State Buildings, and the World Trade Center), the clearer it is that when it came to projecting *ideas* of the city through selected icons, no place in America came close to the success enjoyed by New York. In popular songs, photographs, paintings – in the multiple forms of representation – these icons defined the city and its urgent modernism. This "soft" power was rooted in the city's traditional role as an entrepôt of European ideas and a place where symbols of urbanity, pleasure, status, luxury, ethnicity, and moral strenuousness achieved a highly skilled manipulation and projection through both popular culture and elite institutions. No small part of what New York stood for in the postwar world was the idea of liberty, progress and modernity itself. "The masterword in the critical discourse of the era," wrote Thomas Bender, "was freedom."[2]

In terms of taste and opinion, the city's self-confidence was a wondrous thing. The assumption was that a performance at the Metropolitan Opera, concerts at Carnegie Hall and Lincoln Center, exhibitions at MoMA, the Guggenheim, or the Whitney, the rich variety of jazz clubs, Off-Broadway performances and the art scene in SoHo, had no serious rivals in America. It followed that what the *New York Times* said about a play, movie, book, exhibition, or performance mattered a great deal more than any other American daily newspaper – however unjustified. New York enjoyed a cultural leadership that worked through example, cool effrontery, and money; it had a strutting, catwalk culture, well-suited for display. New York was a place that set trends, and passed judgment upon the trendsetters. It was a process heavily laden with contradictions and ambiguities.

But there is another New York, and it is curious that it has attracted less historical analysis. The "other" is a conservative community marked by cultural caution, moralism, censoriousness, and self-righteousness, and which may be prophetic of trends in the larger cultural life of the present century. In this other New York the conservatives have been aggressively supported by the city's tabloids and its campaigns have often enjoyed the considerable benefits of being well funded. Moneyed New Yorkers have by no means universally admired "radical chic." On many occasions the city's conservative social leaders have been more than a match for the forces of innovation and creativity Greenwich Village won some of its celebrated battles with Park Avenue and the Upper East Side, but social leadership and influence remained with the rich. From Theodore Roosevelt to Rudolph Giuliani, Republican politicians have run for office on "values," and found a ready audience, especially in the city's large Catholic population, for morality reform. Self-professed "gatekeepers," seeking to repress unwholesome social behavior and manifestations of perverted taste, have long sought the authority to enforce moral values. For substantial periods of time they have pursued their campaigns with only intermittent resistance.[3]

The attempt by Mayor Giuliani to create a "decency commission" (as the Cultural Affairs Advisory Commission was popularly known) was a response to the highly controversial 1999 "Sensation" exhibit at the Brooklyn Museum. There was in Giuliani's plan a little echo of the mechanism of censorship created in Ireland in the 1920s. The twin pillars of the censorship were the interestingly-named Committee on Evil Literature, founded in the mid 1920s, and the Censorship Board, established in 1929, which banned 12,000 works of literature over the remainder of the twentieth century. The role of the Catholic Church in New York, which seemed so formidable in the city, was by comparison a pale echo of the aggressive, insular, anti-modern, and deeply conservative church in Ireland which banned novels by

Huxley, Wells, Faulkner, Hesse, and Greene. That kind of cultural reaction was inconceivable in New York in the past two decades, but at stake was the pre-9/11 cultural affairs budget of nearly $140 million, which included $110.5 million earmarked for the city's major art institutions. Culture was a substantial contributor, at $13 billion, to the city's gross product, but funding for culture – a classic "liberal" area of discretionary public expenditure – remained vulnerable at the hands of sanctimonious politicians and "community leaders." The public funding of the arts was an easy target for "culture" warriors on the right, and Mayor Giuliani and his allies proposed to punish the Brooklyn Museum, and other art institutions, for offering willful insult to public morals. Events, principally 9/11, changed perception of the mayor; those same events ended, at least for a year or two, public interest in attacks on artist and museum curators – except on grounds of their lack of patriotism and unwillingness to support the invasion of Iraq. Giuliani's departure from office, and his replacement by Michael Bloomberg, someone with a more Upper East side view of cultural things, made such a "culture wars" tactic less likely. But, once tossed in the air, possibilities lingered.

The complex struggle between artists, cultural institutions, tabloid newspapers, conservative politicians, and the Catholic archdiocese has been a regular fixture of the cultural battlefield in New York for well over a century. An example from the early stages of the struggle suggests how little the arguments have changed. The reception of Thomas Eakins's *The Gross Clinic* in the mid-1870s suggests the long history of struggle between rebel artists and cultural gatekeepers. A deeper reason for considering events from that era is that the consequences of the rejection of Eakins's masterpiece endured well into the twentieth century. The fate of *The Gross Clinic* reminds us of the depth of the cultural divisions in New York. So often thought of as the quintessential "liberal" metropolis, New York City was equally home to powerful and deeply conservative groups seeking to resist the new, and who rejected the rebels and artistic innovators whose restless demands for innovation gave the cultural meaning of New York its paradoxical edge.

Thomas Eakins was "discovered" in the two decades after his death in 1916. Against the barren landscape of American art in the nineteenth century, critics in the interwar years portrayed Eakins as a model of artistic seriousness and integrity. Lewis Mumford was a central figure in the campaign to celebrate a painter who had been on the right side of the culture wars in Victorian America.[4] Mumford stressed the Philadelphia painter's deep regard for modern science, his sharp hostility to bourgeois taste, and his determination to rescue American painting from the compromises and sentimentality of contemporary taste. Eakins showed American artists that there was a "usable past."[5] He was thus an ideal model for young American painters, though his early admirers did not dwell on how much the painter had learned from French academic art during his period studying in Paris in the 1860s. Eakins was a powerful realist, who made painting "face the rough and brutal and ugly facts of our civilization, determined that its values should grow out of these things, and should not look for its themes to the historic symbols of Europe."[6] A similar line was taken in the first monograph on the painter, Lloyd Goodrich's *Thomas Eakins: His Life and Work* (1933). Critics of Mumford's generation saw Eakins as an independent spirit, a cultural original like Melville or Emily Dickinson, "individual souls who had gone their own way and found their own heaven, no matter how solitary the path or unfashionable the destination. . ."[7]

The painting which exemplified the isolated integrity of Eakins was *The Gross Clinic*, an object of humiliating abuse from its early commentators in the 1870s. Its "frankly explicit subject" (a leading Philadelphia surgeon demonstrating a technique to medical pupils and colleagues at Jefferson Medical College), and its "bold realism" stretched conventional taste to the breaking point. The bright red blood on Dr. Gross's hand, not held aloft melodramatically to illustrate a point to his students but largely without dramatic emphasis, shook contemporaries.[8] It was the understatement of the gesture, its everydayness, which was so disturbing. Eakins offered *The Gross Clinic* and other paintings to the Committee of Selection for the 1876 Centennial Exposition to be held in Philadelphia. Its rejection was one of the touchstone moments in the history, and also the mythology, of modern art in America. The refusal of *The Gross Clinic* told critics in the interwar years that a serious artist could only stand in open hostility to contemporary taste.

What is perhaps less well known is the role played by leading figures in the New York art establishment in the rejection of Eakins's masterpiece. The selection panel for the Exposition included two Philadelphians, but was dominated by heavyweight establishment figures from New York: Daniel Huntington, President of the National Academy of Design, and the sculptors Henry Kirke Brown and his pupil John Quincy Adams Ward. Brown's celebrated equestrian statue of Washington in Union Square portrayed a triumphant military commander with an extended right arm, symbolic of authority. The magnificent raised leg of the horse give Brown's statue an energy and authority unique in the city's public statuary. J. Q. A. Ward's bronze statue of Washington, which stands on the steps of the Sub-Treasury (now the Federal Hall National Memorial) on Wall Street, was a similarly bold assertion of national character and destiny. Huntington, Brown, and

Ward were men of considerable reputation and striking success in securing important public commissions. Their negative judgment on Eakins entrenched the idea that *The Gross Clinic* was a critical "failure," and did much to blight Eakins's career. There was sharp criticism in Philadelphia of the painter's bohemianism, and his insistence on nude modeling in his studio. He was forced to resign from a teaching position at the Pennsylvania Academy of Fine Arts. To his critics in the 1920s, Eakins was both an heroic rebel and something of a sexual renegade.

When *The Gross Clinic* was exhibited in New York at the Society of American Artists in March 1879, critics were openly abusive. (It was Eakins's "Sensation" moment.) Pictures from that exhibition were sent to Philadelphia for an exhibit at the Pennsylvania Academy of Fine Arts, where Eakins taught, but *The Gross Clinic* was excluded. It was only in 1917, when a memorial exhibition of Eakins's work was held at the Metropolitan Museum in New York, that the balance of opinion decisively turned. Twelve years later, following his widow Susan's substantial gift of his work to the Philadelphia Museum of Art, the city made amends for its rejection of Eakins.[9] His reception tells us a great deal about the role of New York as a cultural arbiter. The panel of artists who dismissed his most powerful and original work in the 1870s was in effect countermanded by a younger generation of critics and enterprising cultural bureaucrats in the 1920s who endorsed Eakins's place in the pantheon of the modern movement. The confidently asserted opinion of New York was decisive on both occasions.[10]

With its considerable reputation for vice and immorality, it is not surprising that New York City has an equally long history of campaigns to suppress immoral behavior.[11] Everywhere one looked in the nineteenth-century city, there were campaigns waged and reforms urged. The enforcement of strict sabbatarian laws was regarded by campaigners as a crucial ingredient in the moral reform of urban life. Similar campaigns against saloons, aggressive campaigns against homosexuality, blasphemy, obscenity, abortion (strongly supported by physicians), prostitution, birth control, and pornography suggest the extent of social concerns. At the same time, complex problems of urban life, like the overcrowded and decayed tenements and the recurrent public health crises led experts, many trained in the organized methods of the Sanitary Commission in the Civil War, to focus upon the need for sanitary reform. In housing reform, and in such areas as child welfare and cruelty to animals, New York had a powerful influence upon national attitudes. But it was the problem of corruption in public life, culminating in the campaign to rid the city of the Tweed Ring in 1871, which confirmed the city's reputation as at once the most corrupt and vice-ridden, while being the home of the most energetic reformers.[12] In the twentieth century the reformers attacked aspects of popular culture, such as immorality and lewdness in the cinema, while maintaining a high level of vigilance toward the burlesque houses and nightclubs. There was an on-going attempt to rid the city of its illegal gambling and police corruption. New York City gave morality reformers an unending array of wickedness to attack.

At the heart of the diverse reform enterprises of the nineteenth century was an onslaught on deviance in its many shades and flavors. But that simplistic narrative broke down in the twentieth century. Largely due to the debacle of unenforceable prohibition legislation but also due to changing social mores and active resistance, the old "sunlight" and "shadow" reform story about the city lost its narrative coherence.[13] Moral-ity crusaders enjoyed the support of wealthy, socially visible New Yorkers, with Evangelicals especially prominent. Ten of the seventeen founders of the New York Society for the Suppression of Vice appear in the *Social Register.* One third of the founding supporters were millionaires. Among them was J. P. Morgan.[14] But there was also a small liberal strata within the elite, prepared to support resistance and defend personal liberty against the state. The story of moral reform in New York City draws on a complex range of social motivations, from evangelical benevolence to a paternalis-tic desire to save young men and women from the temptations of vice. The impact of those campaigns, not in this instance on the young prostitutes, the patrons of ghetto saloons, the readers of pornography, or women seeking abortions, but upon the city's liberal high culture, upon its writers and cultural commentators, suggests the terrain of the cultural struggle.

Anti-obscenity laws, ostensibly aimed at pornographers, had an ongoing impact upon writers and artists. Given the heavy concentration of publish-ers and magazines in New York, wherever censorship cases arose across the nation, they inevitably became New York issues. The federal anti-obscenity statute, the "Comstock Law" (1873), was the creation of Anthony Comstock, the industrious full-time secretary and agent of the New York Society for the Suppression of Vice from 1873 until his death in 1915.[15] The leadership of the NYSSV, and similar bodies across the nation, was drawn from the white, Protestant middle class, and drew upon the support of a broad swathe of wealthy New Yorkers, the city's press and churches. Wealth and social connections, and a powerful phalanx of churchmen, gave cru-saders like Comstock ready access to political leaders. Empowered as a special agent of the Post Office Department in 1873, Comstock boasted of having arrested more than 3,600 people for using the mail to circulate information about contraception and abortion, or for selling pornography and obscene objects. Private organizations with law-enforcement responsibilities like the NYSSV and the Society for the Prevention of Cruelty to Children, empowered by the New York Attorney General and the city District Attorney to act as the city's and state's representative in child abuse cases, were a response, somewhat short of vigilantism, to the weakness of legal and governmental power in the city. They were in effect rivals to the police force, and their distrust of the police reflected a widespread perception of the inefficiency and corruption of the force.[16]

Comstock recognized that successful reform campaigns depended upon getting headline-grabbing publicity for his case, and he had a kind of New York genius at inserting himself into the heart of moral reform issues. Early in his career he invited a reporter of the *Tribune* to accompany him on a raid on Sabbath-breaking saloons. His publicity stunts did not always come off, but he was seldom bested in the publicity firestorms which he initiated. When he raided the Knoedler art gallery in 1887, seizing 117 photographs of paintings, he met with fiery opposition led by a resolution passed by the Society of American Artists. Joseph Pulitzer's New York *World* doubted the wisdom of the raid. Comstock was defiant, correctly identifying the class content of his attack on a fashionable gallery: "Fifth Avenue has no more rights in this respect than Centre Street or the Bowery."[17] But he tended to confine his subsequent raids upon less well-defended targets. It was when Comstock flew off the handle and attacked the "wrong" targets that he attracted the sharpest criticism. In his later years the perception grew that he was increasingly erratic. His successors sought ways, with mixed success, to avoid his errors.

There was nothing in New York like the "quiet little arrangement" which made Boston proverbial among all enthusiasts for banning and prohibiting. When it was known that the Watch and Ward Society objected to certain passages in a book, and believed them to be in violation of the "little Comstock laws" which spread across the nation in the late nineteenth century, the members of the Boston Booksellers Committee refused to stock the book. There were eventually some one hundred titles on the Watch and Ward *Index Liberorum Prohibitorum*, including Hemingway's *The Sun Also Rises*, Van Vechten's *Nigger Heaven*, and Dos Passos's *Manhattan Transfer*. Actual prosecutions were somewhat less common than extra-legal banning, but this too befell Sinclair Lewis's *Elmer Gantry*, Upton Sinclair's *Oil*, and Theodore Dreiser's *An American Tragedy*.

Banning in the traditionally illiberal atmosphere of Boston did not mean that the same books were vulnerable to prosecution in New York. The chaotic state of the law, cultural and political differences between jurisdictions, as well as changing mores, acted as a restraint upon the NYSSV. But the reform movement drew upon the social status of some of its leading figures, which enabled reformers to circumvent some of the democratic resistances to reform. Commodore Elbridge Gerry, who brought charges against Wallack's, the Metropolitan Opera, and the Academy of Music, was a leading figure of the city's social elite. Gerry's extensive activities as a reformer suggest one of the ways that a conservative elite functioned in a raucous democracy.[18]

Comstock left an ambiguous legacy of repression in New York, though in his later years he no longer enjoyed the sympathetic support of the press. A barrage of mockery from Greenwich Village wits sought to destroy Comstock's image as a man of high morals. In Robert Minor's cartoons in *The Masses* he was seen as a repressed, sex-obsessed fanatic. The sharp pen of H. L. Mencken in *The American Mercury*, and the emergence of organized opposition to "comstockery" with the formation of the Free Speech League in 1920, made that decade a period of frustration for the NYSSV and its officers. The leaders of the Free Speech movement (who included the radical journalist Lincoln Steffens, the birth control advocate Margaret Sanger, and Emma Goldman, who had regularly been targeted by the police in attempts to suppress her trouble-making speeches) were absolutists, admitting no permissible government role in restricting the written or spoken word. Hostility to the activities of vice societies deepened as New Yorkers encountered the reality of Prohibition. They confronted Comstock's successors with wit and indignation, and carried a swathe of liberal opinion with them. Comstock's excesses, pomposity, and humorless self-righteousness made him an easy target for ridicule.

Under the activist leadership of John Sumner after Comstock's death, the NYSSV continued to make high-profile censorship raids.[19] Agents for the society, often responding to the anonymous complaints of the public, acted against suggestive theatrical posters, objectionable motion pictures, and lewdness in burlesque and ballet. As a result, posters were withdrawn, scenes dropped, language cleaned up. It must have seemed to Sumner that the NYSSV was a lone defender of morality in a community under siege from suggestiveness. It was when the society turned to the widespread problem of "dirty books" that Sumner encountered highly visible public resistance and sharp criticism on the grounds that the NYSSV lacked a proper democratic mandate. Among his first targets was Theodore Dreiser. In 1916 Sumner received a complaint from the Western Society for the Prevention of Vice. A Baptist minister in Cincinnati had found seventy-five "lewd" and seventeen "profane" passages in Dreiser's autobiographical novel, *The "Genius."* A temporary cessation-of-circulation order was made by the Post Office Department. The novel was in effect banned across the country. Sumner submitted a list of offensive and lewd passages to the publisher, John Lane, and warned that prosecution would follow unless the book was withdrawn. It was the mere threat of prosecution which was Sumner's most potent weapon. Lane withdrew the book, and urged Dreiser to seek an advisory judgment in the Appellate Court. The case was heard in 1918, but was dismissed (the court did not issue advisory judgments). The "banned" novel remained in Lane's warehouse until 1923, when Liveright reissued the novel. Sumner did not attempt a prosecution.[20]

Sumner was an industrious bully, and in 1919 he made a raid against Harpers, seizing copies of *Madeleine*, an autobiography of a French prostitute.[21] On a complaint by Sumner in 1920, James Branch Cabell's *Jurgen* was declared obscene and withdrawn from publication.[22] In February 1921 the editors of the *Little Review*, Margaret Anderson and Jane Heap, were found guilty of obscenity and fined $50 each in New York City.[23] Their offense: the publication of the "Nausicaa" section of Joyce's *Ulysses*. The publisher Ben Heubsch promptly abandoned the idea of publishing Joyce's novel. Sumner had less success when he tried to suppress a suggestive play, *The Demi-Virgin*, in 1921. The publicity resulting from his failed attempt to have the theatre's license revoked and the producer prosecuted kept public interest in the play at a fever-pitch.[24] Sumner filed a complaint against Thomas Seltzer in 1923 for publishing D. H. Lawrence's *Women in Love*, but without success.[25] E. E. Cummings's war memoir, *The Enormous Room*, published by Horace Liveright in 1922, attracted the attention of Sumner. At the point of mailing out review copies, Liveright was tipped off that Sumner planned a raid because the word "shit" appeared in the book. As a precaution, Liveright ordered a secretary to go through the entire edition, and ink out the word which gave such offense: "My father is dead! Shit. Oh, well. The war is over." When the second edition appeared in 1927, Cummings put Jean Le Nègre's remark into French. He now says, *"Mon père est mort! Merde! Eh b'en! La guerre est fini."* No more was heard from Sumner on this score. The record of the NYSSV in the 1920s was mixed, and when confronted with robust opposition (such as that provided by A. H. Woods, producer of *The Demi-Virgin*) the limits of Sumner's power became clear.[26]

The statute on which Sumner acted (Section 1141 of the Penal Law of New York State, concerning publishing and distributing an indecent and obscene book), was used by Detective John C. Pooler of the Vice Squad in New York to obtain a warrant for the seizure of all copies of *The Story of a Lover*, published anonymously in 1919 by Horace Liveright. The author of this book, perhaps the least erotic title ever to be prosecuted under section 1141, was Hutchins Hapgood, a Village stalwart, who had taken this opportunity to write candidly about his unhappy marriage with Neith Boyce. The publisher was cleared when a magistrate in the Jefferson Market Police Court dismissed the case. By insisting that the whole book be taken into account, and not simply isolated passages, judges in New York had begun to undermine the stern rigor of 1141. They were prepared to accept broader, exculpatory arguments about the moral import of the work taken as a whole. Nonetheless, it remained a lottery whether a prosecution would succeed. Edmund Wilson's *Memoirs of Hecate County*, published to considerable commercial success by Doubleday in 1946, was prosecuted in the Court of Special Sessions on an obscenity complaint by the NYSSV. Even expert testimony from Lionel Trilling could not save the book from a guilty verdict, which was upheld in the State Supreme Court and by the Supreme Court of the United States in 1948. W. H. Allen published a revised and corrected edition in London in 1951, claiming that it was "the only authentic and unexpurgated version of Edmund Wilson's famous book." When *Memoirs of Hecate County* was reprinted in America in 1959, the ban remained in effect in New York.[27]

The Comstock Act was used against *The Little Review*, *The New Masses*, and H. L. Mencken's *The American Mercury*. Over-zealous local Post Office officials in 1911 even banned the report of the Vice Commission of the City of Chicago. The broad discretion enjoyed by Post Office officials meant that any title which gave offense to a powerful local constituency might be placed on a nationwide list of prohibited books – in the company of Ovid's *Metamorphoses*, the *Decameron*, or *Mademoiselle de Maupin*. This wide-ranging cultural onslaught on writers and publishers coincided with attacks against radicals, trade unionists, anarchists, and foreigners.[28] The Mann Act of 1913, which forbid the transportation of women in inter-State commerce for immoral purposes, and Prohibition, which came into effect on January 16, 1920, gave the state greatly increased powers to interfere with private behavior. The norms of small-town America, and also the social anxieties of traditionalists meant that many were prepared to turn to the state to forbid behavior which was regarded as deviant.

"The Comstocks are in violent eruption," wrote Mencken. "Next month we are printing in the S[mart]. S[et]. A very good novelette by a new writer. But there are two hoors in it, and I fear we'll have to sit in jail for a few weeks. Well, I am reconciled to it. Every civilized American will spend a few weeks of every year in jail hereafter."[29] The wise-cracking irreverence which was directed at moralistic crusades in the 1920s lessened the capacity of the NYSSV to intimidate. The society's annual income from contributions fell from a high of $12,000 in 1929 to $5,000 in 1932.[30] But the cost of a prosecution was a serious matter, and publishers sought ways to evade

Sumner's threats. Sumner was not interested in limited editions, sold to wealthy private collectors of erotica. Like Comstock, he wanted publicity, and took trouble to make sure the press was informed when he went on a raid. To his opponents Sumner seemed to be a shake-down artist of a type familiar in the city's cultural life. Demagogic "community leaders" like the Rev. Bacon in Tom Wolfe's *The Bonfire of the Vanities* suggest the type. Enemies of censorship and critics of Puritanism and "Comstockery" grew bolder.

Liveright lobbied the state legislature in Albany against Sumner's "Clean Books Bill," which would have greatly strengthened moral censorship by allowing prosecutions for obscenity to be based exclusively upon a phrase or single sentence, and denying by judicial construction the ability of juries to consider the work as a whole. Despite the support of the Roman Catholic diocese, the Salvation Army, the YMCA, the NYSSV, and the Protestant Episcopal Church, in the face of a rip-roaring speech by Senator "Gentleman Jimmy" Walker (who remarked "I have never yet heard of a girl being ruined by a book") and some effective subcommittee testimony by the novelist Gertrude Atherton and Horace Liveright, the bill was defeated by a two to one majority. The danger of broad state censorship had passed, but the modern movement in literature defined itself largely in terms of the struggle against everything Comstock, Sumner, and the NYSSV stood for.[31]

Writers encountered other kinds of gatekeepers at every turn in their struggle to be published and find a readership. Theodore Dreiser's *Jennie Gerhardt*, a novel based upon his sister's sordid life, involved an illegitimate child and several extramarital relationships. The manuscript's raw force was much admired by Ripley Hitchcock, an editor at A. S. Barnes. Seeking to obtain a supportive reader's report, Hitchcock sent a copy of Dreiser's *Sister Carrie* to A. R. Cross, who complained that he had been deeply offended by the book, to the point where he tossed the novel into the fire rather than risk leaving it around his house. This ended the interest of A. S. Barnes in the work of Theodore Dreiser.

The stillborn publication of *Sister Carrie* in 1900 left Dreiser a notoriously "difficult" author to sell. But Hitchcock had a reputation as an editor who could take a controversial manuscript and make it acceptable to contemporary taste. He returned to the fray in 1911. His new employer, Harpers, were interested in *Jennie Gerhardt*, providing Dreiser agreed to allow the publishers to revise the text and cut "certain offensive material" from it. Dreiser reluctantly accepted the stipulation. Subsequent research on the manuscript and publishing history of the published novel revealed that 16,000 cuts had been made in the manuscript. Thousands of changes in wording transformed Dreiser's blunt, awkward style. Profanity was deleted, and Dreiser's slang was rewritten. References to sex were either dropped or muted. Much of the novel's social context was eliminated. Dreiser discovered, as he read the galleys, that he had written a conventional love story. Some of the cuts were eventually restored, but not all. An advance copy was sent to Hamilton Wright Mabie, one of the leading moral gatekeepers of the age. As associate editor of the popular Christian magazine *The Outlook*, Mabie published a "White List" of books which could be admitted into a Christian home. If Mabie objected, it was clear that Harpers had a problem. But his response was positive. Hitchcock's heavy attack on the text had been a success, and most reviewers approved of the novel. Sales were "rather disappointing" but Dreiser's career was rescued. The unexpurgated text of *Jennie Gerhardt* was not published until 1992.[32]

Writers learned to anticipate the moves of gatekeepers, the "invisible censors" memorably described by Francis Hackett in the *New Republic*:

> By the censor I do not mean that poor blinkered government official who decides on the facts that are worthy of popular acquaintance. I mean a still more secret creature of still more acute solicitude, who feels that social facts must be manicured and pedicured before they are fit to be seen. He is not concerned with the facts themselves but with their social currency. He is the supervisor of what we say we do, the watchman over our version and our theoretical estimate of ourselves. His object, as I suppose, is to keep up the good old institutions, to set their example before the world, to govern the imitative monkey in us. And to fulfil that object he continually revises and blue-pencils the human legend. He is constantly at the elbow of every man or woman who writes. An invisible, scarcely suspected of existing, he is much more active, much more solidly entrenched, than the legal censor whom liberals detest[33]

In the correspondence between authors and editors one can see, in a careful negotiating of permissible euphemisms, the limits set by the man with the blue pencil. With each of his early novels, John Dos Passos had problems with "bad language." Allen & Unwin, the London publishers of *1917 – One Man's Initiation*, demanded he remove "disrespectful references to Jesus." In return he managed to keep "several whores and one prophylaxis." The printers demanded further expurgations. Writing to a friend, he feared that "[t]he poor thing will be gelded for fair by the time it comes out."[34] *Three Soldiers* encountered the same kind of resistance in New York:

> If you people give me my *Jesuses*, *sonsofbitches*, etc., I'll give you some alleviation in other quarters. If you like some of the *Jesuses* can be spelled *Jez'* – but I don't want them cut out. I think its very important to put down the American lingo as it is, and I think people will bet accustomed to it very easily.[35]

Defending *Manhattan Transfer* in 1925, Dos Passos wrote that

> it took a great deal of aspirin to get me through smut talks with Harper and his brother. Did you know that Kerist? was not blasphemous, but that Christ! was? And when a chaste vaudeville lady spoke of "three a day," Harper and his brother, thought three men? I ask you. Still my next novel, after the battle with the gelding shears was found to be not quite castrated, perhaps half a testicle remained on the left side.[36]

When further resistance to the demands of censorship proved impossible, authors resorted to a calculated blurring of detail. Hemingway, who had a reputation as a prickly author, accepted the need for "artful vagueness" about the physical relations between Jake and Brett in *The Sun Also Rises*. A careful parsing of the text by Kenneth Lynn suggests that they enjoyed oral sex. The closer Hemingway got to trade publication, the more aggressive he found the editorial gatekeeping. Robert Bridges, editor of *Scribner's Magazine*, proposed to pay Hemingway $16,000 for pre-publication serialization rights for *A Farewell to Arms*. But he insisted upon eliminating terms likely to give offense (shit, fuck, son of a bitch, whore, whorehound, balls, cocksucker, Jesus Christ). Despite this, the June issue of *Scribners* was banned from newsstand sale in Boston. Some of these offending terms were restored in the published text of the novel, but Perkins drew the line at "c—s—r" for "cocksucker."[37]

Writers of patent seriousness nervously contemplated the prospect that they might be censored. To that extent, Sumner and the NYSSV had won their greatest victory. In the struggle for modernity and freedom of expression, such self-censorship made serious writing difficult, and sometimes impossible. Writing to Maxwell Perkins in early 1925, F. Scott Fitzgerald asked if the scene in *The Great Gatsby* in which Tom and Myrtle "disappear for a while" was "noticeably raw." "Does it stick out enough so that the censor might get it. It's the only place in the book I'm in doubt about on that score." Perkins was sure there would be no objection to the scene, and there was none.[38]

The Random House edition of Joyce's *Ulysses* (copyrighted Nora Joseph Joyce, 1942, 1946) contained a foreword by Morris L. Ernst, lawyer for the defendants in the most celebrated obscenity case of the century. The foreword, dated New York, December 11, 1933, began with a happy sentence: "The new deal in the law of letters is here." The verdict of the Hon. John M. Woolsey in the United States District Court for the Southern District of New York denied the government's motion for a decree for forfeiture. *Ulysses* was thus deemed not an "obscene book" under the meaning of that term in section 305 of the Tariff Act 1930, Title 19 United States Code,

Section 1305, and could legally be admitted into the United States. Judge Woolsey's decision was a landmark case: literary works, if of "artistic integrity," now had a legal defense. "Stately, plump Buck Mulligan" began his morning descent from the stairhead, bearing a bowl of lather, and Joyce was able to gain American copyright on his novel. The typesetters went to work on the Random House edition within ten minutes of Bennett Cerf learning the judge's verdict, so great was the fear of a pirated edition.

The issue of censorship had made a distinctive battlefield of New York City. The *Ulysses* decision shifted the struggle to the federal courts, and the opponents of censorship had won. The cause of censorship itself was weakened for a generation, though the "literary merit" argument was successful in only a small number of important cases, including that of Allen Ginsberg's *Howl*. In the eyes of conservative critics by the late 1950s, the actual consequences of the *Ulysses* decision for New York City were seen on 42nd Street in the proliferation of S & M bookstores, porno movies, curbside drug trade, and the strutting prostitutes on the "Minnesota Strip" on Eighth Avenue. Some two decades separated the *Ulysses* decision from the descent of 42nd Street into the lower depths, but in the view of the Manhattan Institute for Policy Research, the Op-Ed pages of the *New York Post* and *Wall Street Journal*, and in the pages of *The City Journal*, there was a direct connection. A series of legal decisions, much celebrated by liberal friends of high culture, facilitated an explosion of pornography in the city. The merchants on 42nd Street, famously responsive to changing commercial possibilities, saw their chances and took them. The city virtually lost control of the streets, and it took several decades, and the highly influential intervention of Michael Eisner's Disney Corporation, before a clean-up succeeded.[39]

The transformation of 42nd Street coincided in the 1980s with an overwhelming conservative attack on the National Endowment for the Arts, documented in Richard Bolton's invaluable *Culture Wars*.[40] In June 1989, the Corcoran Gallery of Art in Washington, fearing the defeat in Congress of legislation reauthorizing the National Endowment of the Arts, canceled an exhibition of the work of the photographer Robert Mapplethorpe. Dennis Barrie, director of the Contemporary Arts Center in Cincinnati, was charged in 1990 with "pandering blasphemy" for showing a traveling retrospective of Mapplethorpe. One of the wrinkles of that case was the Municipal Court decision to allow the prosecution to isolate an individual photograph for presentation to the jury, which in the case of Mapplethorpe dramatically increased the prosecution's chances of getting a conviction. Nonetheless, after two hours' deliberation, the jury acquitted the museum and its director on all charges.

The actions of the Post Office under the "Comstock Law" served to federalize decisions to ban individual works. As America has become more conservative, community values, which in the past sometimes blunted the sternness of censorship and obscenity laws, increasingly were used by interest groups to strengthen restrictions. From the 1973 *Miller v. California* decision in the Supreme Court, juries were allowed to rely upon state or even community values in obscenity decisions. The potential threat to artistic freedom seems likely to grow. What is so distinctive in the culture of New York and other large urban areas, is an irreverence and freewheeling openness – the very qualities which makes them increasingly isolated. Such cities are little bristling neighborhoods of free-thinking in a continental culture growing increasingly religious and increasingly intolerant of "Greenwich Villagism," wherever it might be found.

NOTES

1. "The City Whose Business is Bigness," *Business Week*, October 13, 1956, pp. 125–41, cited in Robert A. M. Stern *et al.*, *New York 1960: Architecture and Urbanism between the Second World War and the Bicentennial* (New York: Monacelli Press, 1955; new ed. Cologne: Benedikt Taschen Verlag, 1997), pp. 61–2.
2. Thomas Bender, *New York Intellect: A History of Intellectual Life in New York City from 1750 to the Beginning of Our Own Time* (New York: Alfred A. Knopf, 1987), p. 339.
3. Andrea Friedman, *Prurient Interests: Gender, Democracy, and Obscenity in New York City, 1909–1945* (New York: Columbia University Press, 2000).
4. Donald L. Miller, *Lewis Mumford: A Life* (New York: Weidenfeld & Nicolson, 1989); Thomas P. Hughes and Agatha Hughes (eds.), *Lewis Mumford: Public Intellectual* (New York: Oxford University Press, 1990).
5. Van Wyck Brooks, "On Creating a Usable Past," *The Dial*, 64 (April 11, 1918): 337–41.
6. Lewis Mumford, *The Brown Decades: A Study of the Arts in America 1865–1895* (New York: Dover, 1955), p. 215. First published 1931.
7. Lewis Mumford, *My Works and Days: A Personal Chronicle* (New York: Harcourt Brace Jovanovich, 1979), p. 244.
8. William Innes Homer, *Thomas Eakins: His Life and Art*, second ed. (New York: Abbeville Press, 2002), p. 81. First published 1992.
9. Carol Troyen, "Eakins in the Twentieth Century," in Darrel Sewell (ed.), *Thomas Eakins* (New Haven: Philadelphia Museum of Art in Association with Yale University Press, 2001), pp. 367–76.
10. In May 1930 the Museum of Modern Art staged a joint show of the work of Winslow Homer, Albert Pinkham Ryder, and Eakins, officially endorsing their realist work as a model for contemporary painting.
11. David J. Pivar, *Purity Crusade: Sexual Morality and Social Control, 1868–1900* (Westport, CT: Greenwood Press, 1973); Paul Boyer, *Urban Masses and Moral*

Order in America 1820–1920 (Cambridge, MA, and London: Harvard University Press, 1978).

12. Eric Homberger, *Scenes from the Life of a City: Corruption and Conscience in Old New York* (New Haven: Yale University Press, 1994), ch. 1 (tenement reform), ch. 2 (the attack on abortion), and ch. 3 (political corruption), seeks to draw some of these themes together, and place them in the context of New York in the midnineteenth century.

13. Among many examples, see Edward Crapsey, *The Nether Side of New York; or, The Vice, Crime and Poverty of the Great Metropolis* (New York: Sheldon & Co., 1876); Thomas de Witt Talmage, *The Night Side of New York Life* (Chicago: J. Fairbanks 1878); James D. McCabe, Jr., *New York by Sunlight and Gaslight* (New York: Union Publishing House, 1886).

14. Nicola Beisel, *Imperiled Innocents: Anthony Comstock and Family Reproduction in Victorian America* (Princeton: Princeton University Press, 1997), ch. 3.

15. The most detailed account of the "Comstock Law" is in Helen Lefkowitz Horowitz, *Rereading Sex: Battles Over Sexual Knowledge and Suppression in Nineteenth-Century America* (New York: Alfred A. Knopf, 2002), ch. 16. See Walker Gilmer, *Horace Liveright: Publisher of the Twenties* (New York: David Lewis, 1970), pp. 60–80, for a discussion of Comstock's successor, John Sumner, in the 1920s.

16. Timothy J. Gilfoyle, "The Moral Origins of Political Surveillance: The Preventive Society in New York City, 1867–1918," *American Quarterly*, 38 (1996): 637–52. The actual effectiveness of the Preventive Societies in reducing vice is unclear.

17. Haywood Broun and Margaret Leech, *Anthony Comstock: Roundsman of the Lord* (New York: Albert & Charles Boni, 1927), pp. 223–5.

18. Gerry's title came from his leading role in the New York Yacht Club. A perfect type of late nineteenth-century Protestant social reformer, he was grandson of a "Signer" of the Declaration of Independence, his mother was a Goelet, and he married a Livingston. Gerry was in the "400" and the *Social Register*. His role as founder of the American Society for the Prevention of Cruelty to Children was a lasting social legacy.

19. Sumner retired from the NYSSV in 1950, and lived to the age of 91. See his obituary in the *New York Times*, June 22, 1971, p. 38.

20. Dreiser's defense counsel, Joseph S. Auerbach, published his argument before the Appellate Division of the New York Supreme Court in *Essays and Miscellanies*, 3 vols. (New York: Harper & Brothers, 1922), vol. III, pp. 130–65. The story of the suppression of *The "Genius"* is well told in F. O. Matthiessen, *Theodore Dreiser* (New York: William Sloane Associates, 1951), pp. 166–70.

21. *Madeleine: An Autobiography*, with an Introduction by Ben B. Lindsey (New York: Harper, 1919). The publisher was fined $1,000 and denounced from the bench for publishing this book. See on this Mencken to Ernest Boyd, December 20, 1919, *Letters of H. L. Mencken* (New York: Knopf, 1961), 165, 175.

22. See *Jurgen and the Law: a statement, with exhibits, including the court's opinion, and the brief for the defendants on motion to direct an acquittal*, ed. Guy Holt (New York: R. M. McBride & Company, 1923).

23. See Margaret C. Anderson, "Ulysses in Court," *The Little Review* (January–March 1921): 22–5; Margaret C. Anderson, *My Thirty Years' War: an Auto-*

biography (New York: Alfred A. Knopf, 1930), pp. 214–27. John Quinn defended Anderson and Heap, but refused to mount a principled attack on censorship or its legal foundations. See B. L. Reid, *The Man From New York: John Quinn and His Friends* (New York: Oxford University Press, 1968), pp. 441–60.

24. Friedman, *Prurient Interests*, pp. 102–3. The failure to close *The Demi-Virgin* also shut down Sumner's strategy of using the city's license commissioner to enforce moral standards. The commissioner's powers to act in this manner were rejected in the Appellate Division.

25. The complaint against *Women in Love* was made by John Ford, a Justice in the New York Supreme Court. He formed an alliance with Sumner in 1923 to strengthen the state laws concerning obscenity. Out of their campaign the Clean Books League was founded. The story of Ford's campaign is told in Paul S. Boyer, *Purity in Print: The Vice-Society Movement and Book Censorship in America* (New York: Charles Scribner's Sons, 1968), ch. 5. "As for Justice Ford," wrote an angry Dos Passos, "I think he's got to be *fought* and I consider cutting out a word giving aid and comfort to the enemy. Freedom of the Press does not mean compromise. It means publishing what Tom, Dick and Harry damn please and letting people lump it if they don't like it" (quoted in Virginia Spencer Carr, *Dos Passos: A Life* (Garden City, NY: Doubleday & Co., 1984), p. 176.

26. Gilmer, *Horace Liveright*, pp. 35–6. The altered passage appears in Cummings, *The Enormous Room*, with an Introduction by the Author (Harmondsworth: Penguin Books, 1971), p. 222.

27. Louis Menand, "Edmund Wilson's Vanished World," *New York Review of Books*, 51, 14 (September 23, 2004): 86.

28. *Revolutionary Radicalism: Its History, Purpose and Tactics*. Report of the Joint Legislative Committee Investigating Seditious Activities, 8 vols. (Albany, New York: New York State Legislature, 1920); Julian Jaffe, *Crusade Against Radicalism: New York During the Red Scare, 1914–1925* (Port Washington, NY: Kennikat Press, 1972).

29. Mencken to Fielding Hudson Garrison, February 11, 1921, *Letters of H. L. Mencken*, 218.

30. See Stanley Coben, *Rebellion Against Victorianism: The Impetus for Cultural Change in 1920s America* (New York: Oxford University Press, 1991); NYSSV income in Boyer, *Purity in Print*, p. 138.

31. The defeat of the Clean Books Bill is described in Gilmer, *Horace Liveright*, pp. 69–80.

32. Theodore Dreiser, *Jennie Gerhardt*, ed. James L. West III (Philadelphia: University of Pennsylvania Press, 1992).

33. Francis Hackett, *The Invisible Censor* (New York: B. W. Heubsch, 1921), pp. 2–3.

34. Carr, *Dos Passos*, p. 171.

35. Dos Passos to Eugene F. Saxton, March 1921, Dos Passos Collection, Houghton Library, Harvard University, cited in Carr, *Dos Passos*, p. 176.

36. *The Fourteenth Chronicle: Letters and Diaries of John Dos Passos*, ed. Townsend Ludington (Boston: Gambit, 1973), p. 361.

37. Kenneth S. Lynn, *Hemingway* (London: Simon & Schuster, 1987), pp. 155, 270–1, 325, 382.

38. *Dear Scott/Dear Max: The Fitzgerald–Perkins Correspondence*, ed. John Kuehl and Jackson R. Bryer (New York: Scribner, 1971), pp. 91–2.

39. Marc Eliot, *Down 42nd Street: Sex, Money, Culture, and Politics at the Crossroad of the World* (New York: Warner Books, 2001).

40. Richard Bolton (ed.), *Culture Wars: Documents from the Recent Controversies in the Arts* (New York: The New Press, 1992).

FURTHER READING

Rick Beard and Leslie Cohen Berlowitz (eds.), *Greenwich Village: Culture and Counterculture*, New Brunswick, NJ: Published for the Museum of the City of New York by Rutgers University Press, 1993.

Richard Bolton (ed.), *Culture Wars: Documents from the Recent Controversies in the Arts*, New York: The New Press, 1992.

Paul S. Boyer, *Purity in Print: The Vice-Society Movement and Book Censorship in America*, New York: Charles Scribner's Sons, 1968.

Marc Eliot, *Down 42nd Street: Sex, Money, Culture, and Politics at the Crossroad of the World*, New York: Warner Books, 2001.

Andrea Friedman, *Prurient Interests: Gender, Democracy, and Obscenity in New York City, 1909–1945*, New York: Columbia University Press, 2000.

Walker Gilmer, *Horace Liveright: Publisher of the Twenties*, New York: David Lewis, 1970.

Martin Green, *New York 1913: The Armory Show and the Paterson Strike Pageant*, New York: Scribner's, 1988.

Helen Lefkowitz Horowitz, *Rereading Sex: Battles Over Sexual Knowledge and Suppression in Nineteenth-Century America*, New York: Alfred A. Knopf, 2002.

Andrew Kirtzman, *Rudy Giuliani: Emperor of the City*, New York: William Morrow, 2000.

Christine Stansell, *American Moderns: Bohemian New York and the Creation of a New Century*, New York: Metropolitan Books, 2000.

Robert A. M. Stern, *et al*, *New York 1960: Architecture and Urbanism between the Second World War and the Bicentennial*, New York: Monacelli Press, 1955; new ed. Cologne: Benedikt Taschen Verlag, 1997.

17

WILLIAM BROOKS

Music: sound: technology

An overview

America, Gertrude Stein declared, was "the oldest country in the world because . . . America created the twentieth century" – not through art or
literature, one infers, but through industry and invention.[1] Thus it was Thomas
Alva Edison, arguably, who inaugurated modernism in America. He electrified
the country, he changed night into day – and he transformed sound for ever.

Before Edison's phonograph, sound was ephemeral: something heard
could not be heard again. True, certain sounds – *music* – could be documented in written scores; but such artifacts merely traced experiences that
truly existed only in the moment. Recordings changed all that; and by
making sound permanent, they altered music's very nature. "Modern"
music, then, is in large part the story of sound technology, of its consequences, and of the responses by musicians and listeners.

In the beginning, recordings were mechanical. A reverse megaphone
focused sound waves onto a diaphragm to which was attached a stylus; this
etched an image of the sound onto a cylinder. To hear the recording, the
process was reversed. There was nothing electrical, nothing chemical: the
mechanism was wholly consistent with the technology for musical instruments, which took the relatively small sounds produced by an agitated
string, a reed, or buzzing lips, and rendered them audible over a substantial
distance. The gramophone differed only in that the sound source was a
diaphragm activated by a needle driven by grooves in wax.

So it was not its technology that set the gramophone apart. Rather it was
its neutrality: whereas previous instruments had been timbrally consistent,
stylistically preconditioned, the gramophone was featureless: one could
hear from it literally anything that could be recorded. The gramophone
was not an instrument but a transducer, mapping information in one
domain (sound) to and from another (object). It did for the whole of sound
what phonetic alphabets had done for speech uncounted centuries earlier.

What followed from this for the making of music? First, music's economic center shifted irrevocably away from the source domain (performance) and to the mapped domain (recording); modern music began when consumers could buy the possibility, rather than the experience, of hearing. Second, the responsibility for creating the sounded work expanded to include not only composers and performers but technicians, manufacturers, businessmen – all helped produce the object the listener would buy. Third, recordings became factors in the creative process: music was made for records, with full awareness of the possibilities and limitations, just as music previously had been made for piano, or violin, or contrabassoon. Fourth, the technology's complete neutrality concerning content also implied an aesthetic and social neutrality. Opportunity and privilege ceased to be constraints; anyone could listen to anything, at any time, for essentially the same price. The seeds of what would later be called a postmodern, appropriative music were already sown.

All these consequences, all these transformations, were enacted on an international scale; but Americans like Stein liked to think that Americans had got there first. In any case, certain implications of sound technology were surely reinforced by three persistent and pervasive aspects of American ideology.

The first was the dialectic between diversity and unity, summarized most succinctly in the national motto: *e pluribus unum* (from many, one). For three centuries, America had celebrated its polycultural origins; it claimed to welcome differences, to nurture exceptions. Yet at the same time it described itself as a great melting pot, a crucible in which would be formed a new, united people. Multiplicity would spawn not only variety and tolerance but also the vigour and originality of a truly hybrid species: the American would be "a new man."[2]

The workings of this dialectic, with the body politic sometimes in conflict, leaning sometimes this way, sometimes that, motivated much of modern American culture, its pathologies as well as its accomplishments. Sound technology perfectly suited the dialectic. On one hand, recordings manifested cultural and individual difference on a scale hitherto inconceivable; they captured music as it was actually practiced, in ways that notation never could. On the other, the neutrality, economy, and portability of the new media enabled cultures and individuals to interpenetrate as never before. Whereas previously it had taken time, money, and considerable effort to move beyond one's own musical environment, now it took immense discipline to preserve that environment; change, interaction, and innovation shaped musical cultures, rather than tradition and consistency.

A second aspect of American ideology followed in part from the first: equality of opportunity and rejection of privilege. In America, it was claimed, anyone could become President, or a millionaire, or a hero; futures were built on initiative, not birthright or endowment or an exclusive education. But the proof of this claim rested on highly public inequalities – of wealth, of influence. The resulting elites, even when newly created, struggled mightily to preserve their positions. Though the victims changed, deprivation and prejudice were necessary to the culture's self-description: without them there could be no success stories. For the underdogs, oppression was brutal indeed; few injustices exceed those perpetuated by slavery and its aftermath.

Again the new technology matched the ideology. Whereas previously musical opportunities had been circumscribed by economic status or cultural background, now music was available to anyone, anywhere, at any time. Whereas previously music's production had required performance, which in turn required specialized, expensive training and facilities, now music could be produced and disseminated by anyone: anyone might produce a record, create a hit. But there were, inevitably, oppressive consequences; underpaid, exploited performers and songwriters built the fortunes of stars and moguls. More broadly, success required an audience, and wealth and power flowed in one direction: stars and consumers stood on opposite sides of an economic gulf in exactly contrary positions to earlier musicians and patrons. Stardom – success – was both an object of desire and an establishment to overthrow.

A third component of American ideology attempted, in part, to rationalize such inequalities. Americans mistrusted judgments, especially judgments that rested on imprecise or arcane attributes. American philosophers were pragmatists; American science proved itself in applications. Ambiguously but persistently, Americans were anti-intellectual and anti-aesthetic, chary of ideas or artworks having uncertain material worth.

Music, with its mysterious notation, its ephemeral qualities, was especially suspect. In the nineteenth century, however, America had evolved a practical framework for measuring music's value: the sheet-music industry, subject to exactly the same commercial forces and economic tests as any other. In the twentieth, recording technology extended that industrial domain to include sound itself, bypassing matters of interpretation, of performance. As the technology evolved – in broadcasting, in copyright law – it was the commercial model that prevailed. European states used the new media to further national cultures; America demanded that everything be tested in the marketplace. Broadcasting must earn its way; aesthetic merit was no defense against lost profits; new music must prove its worth.

Sound technology evolved throughout the twentieth century, and its implications, though glimpsed very early, were not fully realized until quite late. Along the way musical culture underwent a series of transformations, and each of these was linked to changes in the inventions themselves, the devices with which modern music would be created. We must begin with a history of these.

Music technology: a brief history

In Edison's first design (1877), a needle etched grooves into tinfoil wrapped around a cylinder; and though less fragile substances soon replaced the foil, the design remained unchanged. It precisely suited the uses Edison envisioned: his device would provide single-purpose, one-time etchings that would allow sounds (primarily spoken) to be stored, moved, and retrieved in a different location at a different time. This gramophone was a kind of stenographer, a telegraph made physical; it was not a manufacturing device.

However, it quickly became apparent that recordings of celebrated voices had commercial value; willy-nilly, Edison had created a new industry. His technology, however, hindered mass production; each copy of a cylinder had to be etched by the same mechanical operation as the original. In the new century Edison's company fell behind the Victor Talking Machine Company, which had adopted a different format developed over a decade before by Emile Berliner in Germany: a flat disc with the etching and reproducing needles moving slowly along the axis, tracing a long spiral groove. Now manufacturing could be informed by the long history of printing: a negative was cut from the original, and this was used to press the grooves into as many blank discs as desired. Recordings could be mass-produced at very little cost, and attention shifted from preservation to dissemination.

The entire process was still mechanical, however, limited by the horns used to focus or amplify the sound. Even the largest recording horns could accommodate only a double handful of instrumentalists, and these had to crowd round the device as Renaissance singers had crowded around part-books. Reproduction was equally inadequate; amplifying horns had limited power, and they distorted recordings much as a megaphone distorts the voice. There was no competition between live and recorded music; records advertised live performances but did not replace them.

Then, in the mid-1920s, a series of inventions transformed the situation entirely. From a new industry, broadcasting, came microphones, which enabled the recording stylus to be driven electronically rather than mechanically; from cinematic experiments came the triode, a vacuum tube that amplified sound electronically. These and other innovations were soon adopted by the recording industry. On a 1925 Columbia disc, two thousand voices sang "*Adeste Fidelis*," a recording impossible with acoustic horns; electronic amplification of this generated an experience that, for the first time, approximated the effect of the event itself.[3]

The next major changes occurred a quarter-century later, in the decade following World War II. Magnetic tape replaced discs in making master recordings; and, although discs remained the format for dissemination, slower playback speeds permitted each "long-play" platter to contain more music – eventually nearly a half-hour per side. Shortly thereafter cooler, more portable amplifiers appeared, when transistors began to replace tubes in the early 1950s. Together these innovations created recordings and broadcasts having "high fidelity" but which could be radically displaced from their origins: the concert hall moved to the bedroom; the club, to the beach; a car contained many worlds. The tape cassette, introduced in 1963, further displaced the listening experience: soon thereafter devices such as "walkman" players enabled listeners to carry about their own sound-spaces, largely inaudible to others nearby. The balance between collective and individual experience, crucial to American culture, shifted irrecoverably toward the individual; the society of listeners – the audience – fragmented into an anarchy of isolated experiences.

In the final quarter of the century there occurred an even more radical transformation. Previous advances had concerned analogue transducers: microphones, cartridges, amplifiers, and other devices that mapped sound waves into or from analogous wave-forms on storage media. The new technology supplemented transducers with digital converters; now sound was recorded not as continuously fluctuating wave-forms but as strings of numbers. Everything changed: the CD replaced the LP; digital manipulation permitted unlimited editing; and recordings were disseminated as numerical data (over the Internet, for instance), rather than in physical form. These developments were continuous and interactive, currents in a sea rather than a series of watersheds; and they are ongoing. Storage devices will continue to shrink in the coming century, and it seems likely that biotechnology will eventually make possible the complete internalization, the literal embodiment, of sound reproduction.

Loosely speaking, then, the twentieth century included four generations of sound technology, at roughly quarter-century intervals. These became successively more diffuse, as did the products: from the clearly etched platter, introduced at a quite precise moment, to inscrutable binary coding that emerged gradually. And they successively traced certain trajectories with respect to performance, production, and distribution.

At the outset, before the microphone, performers were solely responsible for the actual music; others merely operated the recorders, manufactured the copies, and distributed them to consumers. After 1925, however, performers yielded some authority to sound engineers, who could adjust the balance and apparent acoustic either electronically or by repositioning equipment. The product could be broadcast as well as purchased, and manufacturers' attention shifted in part to reception and away from recording. Consumers' options increased substantially, and new listening experiences could be had at little or no cost simply by adjusting a dial.

Magnetic tape gave still more authority to engineers and editors; indeed, sometimes performers simply supplied raw material from which a product was fashioned. And tape cassettes began to shift that authority to consumers, who now could select excerpts from products and recopy them in new, personally created, continuities. Manufacturers, gradually losing control of the recorded object, shifted focus once again, building empires of artists or genres (the names attached to products) rather than the products themselves.

Finally, digital sound, together with personal computers, the Internet, and user-friendly software, gave consumers potential authority over all aspects of the musical object. Dissemination, reproduction, and manipulation could all be accomplished by a single device; material could be downloaded, edited, processed, and played in a single operation which dissolved distinctions between performance, reproduction, and reception. Manufacturers were in a sense product-less, and they directed their efforts instead toward controlling modes of distribution, concentrating on software, copyright, and law.

Again it must be emphasized that all these developments were international; but equally it can be said that many found particular resonances in America. Entrepreneurial egalitarianism evoked many associations: the frontier, "Yankee ingenuity," individualism, self-sufficiency. Each innovation placed music-making more directly in the hands of the listener; each reduced the need for specialized training; each undermined the privilege formerly associated with "art." And in retrospect, it seems that each phase, each quarter-century, was marked at the time. In concert music, the defiant "modernism" of the 1920s was succeeded by the defensive "avant-garde" of the 1950s, which yielded to the more neutral "new music" of the 1980s. In jazz, "Dixieland" was followed by "swing," then by "bop" and "free" jazz, and finally by "fusion."

Clearly, it is simplistic to attribute these and similar transformations in American musical traditions only to the effects of a changing technology. Each quarter-century was marked by a devastating war; the economy surged and spluttered; developments in education, medicine, and consumer goods radically altered social mores and gender relations. All of these, and many other factors, affected the whole of American culture; but in the domain of music, the impact of sound technology was distinctive, pervasive, and precise. In the remainder of this chapter we shall consider this impact in four broad areas: use, understanding, performance, and composition.

Use

Even the most primitive technology had one immediate and extraordinary effect: the physical and temporal displacement of reception from performance. Music was produced at one place and time and heard in another. Listeners acquired the ability to call up music at will, first in the home and later virtually anywhere; for the first time they could, in effect, compose the sonic continuities of their lives. To some extent they also (re)composed the recorded material itself; at the very least they determined its amplitude (volume), and later in the century they could also alter balance (left/right) and equalization (treble/bass). Received music was quite radically altered as a result: a Strauss tone poem played softly on a home stereo differed utterly from the same work heard in a concert hall; broadcasts from dance halls were heard by outsiders, not participants. In such circumstances, the music was often used for purposes quite removed from those associated with the original context. Technological displacement thus extended beyond time and place to include matters of attention and function.

At least three significant developments followed. First, to choose a music was also to choose a badge, a mark of identity, an article of sonic clothing that was both fashion and statement. This phenomenon peaked with the technology that most suited it: battery-powered transistor radios (later, "boom-boxes" or "ghetto-blasters") that made music both portable and public. After mid-century, battles to control sonic environments became a narrative cliché, as groups of youths used amplified sound to mark territories on beaches, parks, and streets. Indeed, the much-vaunted "youth culture" in modern America distinguished itself, to a large extent, through music: it was rock and roll (before it, jazz; afterwards, rap) that separated the young from their elders, defining and enlivening generational boundaries. In fact, even the elders used music that way; in the twentieth century, more than ever before, it became plausible to sense something of a person's personality and social position simply by asking "What do you listen to?". And when in the era of "walkman" players musical choices became less public, music served more as a private narrative, constituting a personal soundtrack over which unfolded the story of one's life.

A second consequence was the adaptation or creation of new musical products to suit new environments. Car radios, for example, required music that occupied a rather narrow dynamic range, so that levels could be set and left while driving. Traditional art music, with extreme dynamic and timbral contrasts, was highly unsuitable, and even much jazz was problematic. Amplified pop music, on the other hand, was relatively constant, and its rise corresponded almost exactly to the rise of the car radio. For those who preferred a less driving pulse, there was equally uniform "easy listening"; and toward the end of the century, even art music embraced a compressed dynamic range, notably but not exclusively in the "minimalism" of, say, Philip Glass.

Third, sonic displacement made it possible to create musical backgrounds that were imposed independent of the listener, usually to manipulate behaviors or emotions. This phenomenon was not new; court musicians, folk fiddlers, hotel orchestras all had facilitated certain activities: conversation, dancing, courtship. But amplifiers and loudspeakers, cheap and indefatigable, could offer music anywhere, any time: in elevators, in grocery stores, in factories. Music technology intersected with behaviorism (that quintessentially American psychosocial theory) in the 1930s to produce a new industry, of which the Muzak Corporation became the symbol, devoted to increasing production or contentment among workers, shoppers, and other captive groups simply by manipulating the soundscape that surrounded them.

It was in the cinema, however, that background music was most obvious. Silent film was accompanied by live musicians who, like their nineteenth-century theatrical counterparts, played excerpts evoking particular affects: love, anger, confusion, and so forth. As the medium developed, however, both composers and directors sought more precise control over emotional import; newly composed, continuous scores supported the narrative with art-music techniques that ranged from leitmotiv to illustrative percussion. In the 1920s there finally emerged a technology that stored sound as well as images on the projected film, thereby altering the function, attributes, and economics of background music and, indeed, many aspects of America's musical life.

Even before sound-on-film, film scores were deliberately manipulative; in this, the cinema continued a long tradition of "affective" music reaching back to the Baroque. But the new technology allowed scores to be far more precise and far less constrained by practicalities. Musical events could correspond exactly to the narrative, and since the score would be played live only once it was possible to employ extraordinary forces or to fuse music with sound effects. Film composers also developed remarkable skills in balancing convention with innovation. On one hand, a kind of doctrine of affect required the use of techniques and qualities that listeners already associated with certain emotional states; on the other, strategic innovations enhanced emotional impact and encouraged critical acclaim.

Film therefore became a medium through which musically unsophisticated listeners could encounter new musical idioms. In film scores listeners tolerated and even enjoyed a level of dissonance that they might not have accepted at home or in the concert hall; they welcomed ethnic instruments, electronic effects, sheer noise into musical continuities; they embraced extreme juxtapositions of style, of sources. Even in its early years, film scoring anticipated the polycultural mélange of the century's end; film music was postmodern from the start. And as the genre evolved, its pluralism became more explicit. Narrative underscoring was replaced by musical commentary that sometimes verged on the ironic, and after mid-century film scores were increasingly compiled from existing material rather than created anew. The "compilation score" relied on listeners' memories of older material or on associations formed when excerpts were marketed; it was the cinematic equivalent of the personal soundtracks listeners were already creating for themselves.

Sound-on-film also changed the musical economy. Employment for instrumentalists – pianists, organists, theatre musicians – was curtailed drastically and abruptly; to continue working, these had to join the music industry in Los Angeles, New York, eventually Nashville. In smaller communities such musicians had often formed the core of musical life; they taught privately or in schools, played in churches, offered chamber music to subscribers, underpinned community orchestras. When technology compelled them to leave, retire, or take up other trades, their disappearance strongly reinforced the shift away from diverse, regional cultures to a more uniform, national one – from music-making to music-buying.

But if technology removed the musical core from communities, it also provided replacements. Social dancing, for example, continued much as it always had; but now the music came from loudspeakers, not live performers. A formerly marginal figure – the M.C. or compère – became the only personality physically present. Transformed into a "disc jockey" – the person who physically played the recordings – he became the de facto mediator between the product and the listener.

In vaudeville, revues and early broadcasting, the master of ceremonies served primarily to introduce, to provide transitions, humor, or commentary; decisions about programming were made by others. But now the disc jockey selected records, compiled playlists, and commented on new releases. An increasingly public and glamorous figure, he presided at dance venues ranging from small-town gymnasia to national broadcasts, serving both *in loco parentis* and as a spokesman for youth. And on radio he emerged as a creative force, using multiple turntables to produce new continuities in which singles were overlapped and blended. As an arbiter of taste, the deejay both reflected and influenced the new measure of success: the industry's popularity "charts" of "top-forty" hits. He was meant to mediate between popular and corporate interests; and when the payola scandals of the late 1950s impugned his impartiality, the public outrage was a measure of the betrayal.

By the 1970s the record hop and its broadcast equivalents had ended. Their place was filled in part by clubs dedicated to dancing, always to recordings. New inflections of popular genres – notably "disco" – arose, and the deejay's role became still more active: by improvising a mix of discrete releases, adjusting tempo as well as timbre and amplitude, he ensured that the dance never stopped. He was more creator than promoter, and his allegiance shifted from producers (the record companies) to users (dancers and listeners).

From this it was a small step to treating recordings essentially as raw material. As CDs replaced LPs, the discarded media became, in effect, sonic junk for the deejay to sculpt into new forms, often with interjected commentary. Scratching, dub, and related practices elevated him to performer: an improviser and poet who created, on behalf of listeners, a soundtrack and commentary for their lives. His techniques were easily adapted to the emerging digital technology, in particular to the practice of sampling: storing in digital form small fragments of pre-recorded material to be played at will. Samples were initially limited to highly stylized fragments – a singer's scream, a burst of percussion – but as computer memory increased, they came to include drum tracks, bass lines, even complete recordings. The manipulation of these became both simpler and richer as successive artist-performers toyed with recognition, commentary, and parody. Eventually, "downloadable" music converted listeners themselves into artists, blurring irrevocably the boundaries between song and sample, reception and re-composition.

The recording industry responded to each of these transformations with new products that captured the practices of deejays (or listeners). Thus, for example, the early continuities created from singles were mirrored in LP "concept albums" offering similar continuities of mood or function. Similarly, the mixes made by disco deejays were captured not only in albums containing continuous dance music but by the "extended play" single: a hybrid form, long enough to exhaust itself (and the listener) but short enough to remain a discrete product. Even more strikingly, the reuse of

LPs by dub or hip-hop artists was itself recorded and sold, a recording of recordings being played; and by separating commentary from turntablism, the industry regained more conventional control of the genre thus created: rap.

Thus mediation has evolved cyclically. Each new product both mirrors and motivates the use of the previous technology in what are, in effect, sonic sculptures. Within each cycle the mediator – the sculptor – becomes ever more obvious, until he himself becomes objectified, becomes a product; around this new mediators appear, and the cycle repeats. In general, over the century, technology has evolved in ways that shift the entire process slowly toward the listener, the amateur, and away from professionals: the technician gives way to the turntablist, the composer to the compiler. The struggle to maintain economic and material control of the product – indeed, to redefine the law so that notions of product still apply – has been the fundamental undertaking of the music business for at least half a century, and there is every reason to think it will continue in the century to come.

Understanding

Technology, then, changed the nature of musical products and their mediation (by performers, deejays, listeners themselves). But it also profoundly affected how those products were understood. Throughout history, in most cultures, certain music had been deemed beneficial to individuals or societies; other music had been condemned as demeaning or subversive. In America as in Europe, notation served, in part, to select and preserve good music; a cultured citizenry, Americans assumed, would be musically literate, versed in an art-music canon of proven worth, established by musicians and critics of great probity.

At the same time, music's demonic aspect – its ability to arouse undesirable emotions, unwanted behaviors – was the subject of constant vigilance. Sound technology raised the stakes. Whereas notation required specialist mediators (performers, teachers, cultivated amateurs) who decided what would be heard, recordings provided both good and evil in unmediated form. Listeners' choices could no longer be guided; indeed, as technology allowed for more and more privacy, their choices became invisible, unknowable.

These developments again resonated with particular force in the United States. America had been founded in part to model for the world the virtues – and economic benefits – of a certain kind of morality; its constitution, grounded in notions of natural law and eternal truths, negotiated a complex balance between public morality and private belief, between social regulation and individual initiative. Music, like much of American life, was constantly reviewed with this balance in mind; if new developments seemed to upset it, they were challenged, condemned, even censored.

Hence the twentieth century saw a steady stream of attacks on and defenses of America's evolving music. Interestingly, the peaks of criticism coincided roughly with periods of great technological change. Thus the introduction of realistic, electronic recordings helped characterize the "jazz age," whose music was debated morally as well as aesthetically, often by individuals whose agendas concerned racial purity or racial equality. Some argued that the seductive power of the beat made the innocent licentious, plunging them into savagery and, quite literally, blackness; others championed the new music, declaring its energy and inventiveness to be signs of a new, hybrid cultural vigor.

Similarly, postwar innovations fueled the rock and roll revolution of the mid-1950s, which was likewise accompanied by fulminations against the degradation of the country's youth. This controversy, too, was entangled with deeply rooted prejudices; the new music impregnated traditional pop music with elements from black and country traditions, thereby threatening to undermine the cultural purity, the rectitude, of white, middle-class America.

Then again, the Vietnam era included "walkman" players, which made music totally private, and massive amplification systems, which made it totally public. Like its music, the youthful "counterculture," driven by protests against the war and enriched by sexual and pharmacological experiments, was viewed as both a covert threat and a public outrage.

And the final revolution, precipitated by digital sampling, attacked ownership itself; it *was* the communist takeover (at least in the domain of popular music) that the political right had so long feared. This music too was assailed, often by the very people who sought to profit from it; and the polarization both produced and reflected extreme socio-musical genres like gangsta rap. As the Internet permitted music to be exchanged ever more freely, public debate shifted to the courtroom rather than the music itself, which entered a shadowy realm in which vice and virtue intermingled.

Each of these transformations was paralleled by changes in how music is learned, how musical understanding is acquired. It was evident from the start that the new technology could capture musical details that transcriptions could not; wire recorders were early ethnographic tools used to preserve the music of Native Americans and other folk populations. By the 1920s recording had become, in effect, an alternate form of notation for genres like jazz, blues, and what was then called "hillbilly" music (a white genre that derived especially from Appalachian folk traditions).

343

Performers learned by listening, and recordings allowed them to listen at a distance; a player in New York could copy something from Kansas City as easily as something played in the room. Moreover, whereas oral-tradition mentors had generally used inherited sets of exercises and pieces, recordings made it possible for pupils to skip about at will, intermingling styles and sources with little regard for traditions or conventional techniques.

This phenomenon furthered innovation in jazz and popular styles, but its most radical effects were on folk musics. These often became entirely displaced from their sources; indeed, some styles persisted only because persons outside the tradition had learned them from recordings. In the 1930s and 1940s the collector, the performer, and the scholar were conflated into single individuals, or families of individuals – the Lomaxes, the Seegers – who championed and preserved music that was in no sense theirs, making field recordings and promoting these as models from which listeners could learn.

And they did. By the 1960s a white guitarist from Brooklyn (Dave Van Ronk) could become a leading exponent of the Mississippi delta blues style. More famously, a Jewish Minnesotan (Robert Zimmerman) could recreate himself as "Bob Dylan," carrying forward an agrarian, populist, largely Protestant tradition. And Joan Baez, native New Yorker, part Hispanic-American, sang traditional Appalachian ballads wholly removed from her place and time. These and others together became catalysts for a "folk revival" that was altogether unprecedented: a genre that preserved and reproduced the sounds of various traditions entirely outside of their cultural frameworks. Thereafter it grew increasingly difficult to predict the actual ethnic or geographic origins of "folk" musicians: that Klezmer clarinetist may have been born a Catholic cowboy.

Technology affected oral traditions everywhere; but again, American culture was particularly responsive. Originally constituted from immigrant communities, Americans had always debated their place: was the country to be a mosaic, a patchwork of subcultures, or was it to be an alloy fused in the new world? Recordings complicated matters, for musical "cultures" thereafter were no longer united by genetic, historical, or geographical factors. Ethnic identities became performative, not hereditary: whether elements in a crucible or cards in a deck, Americans created their new musical communities by acts of self-construction.

Recording affected art-music education as well. In the nineteenth century music could be cultivated only in performance; to hear a Schubert symphony one had either to attend a concert or to read or play from score. Hence music "appreciation" was confined to illustrated lectures on the chautauqua and lyceum circuits; few universities offered music curricula, and secondary schools concentrated on music literacy, taught primarily through simplified versions of "great works."

As technology evolved, however, music was increasingly "appreciated" through recordings; performance skills like score-reading atrophied. With high-fidelity LPs the canonic repertoire became universally available in unsimplified form, and it became possible to "teach" music in large classes, virtually anywhere, without recourse to performers. Not coincidentally, mid-century saw an astonishing growth in university music curricula. Higher education became the employer of first resort for art musicians of all types – musicologists and theorists first, then composers, and eventually even performers.

Primary and secondary schools carried practice-based education forward until the 1970s; but in the century's final decades, confronted with diminishing funds and children who played recordings rather than instruments, music education slowly collapsed. Although it was still possible to learn the piano or sing in a choir, such skills were no longer deemed necessary. It now sufficed to be a skilled consumer of musical products; the mark of culture was the CD collection, the display of taste. And tastes could and did vary; increasingly, self-education in self-selected specializations made notions of a high-art canon less and less relevant.

With changes in education came changes in public music-making. Amateur institutes, singing societies, music clubs all diminished in importance or disappeared altogether. Music gradually faded from political or protest movements; except for black Americans, the International Workers of the World (the "wobblies"), active before World War I, was the last protest group to use collective song effectively. By the 1930s protest was articulated primarily by single voices (Woody Guthrie, for instance); after World War II performers like The Weavers balanced precariously between social activism and commercial success; and in the 1960s protest songs became products for purchase. By the end of the century, self-defined audiences – warring groups of fans – had almost entirely replaced the socially or economically defined classes associated with musical genres in earlier years.

Similar transformations occurred in the Protestant church. In American sects, music had been sung either collectively (in hymns, at revival meetings, on all-day "singings") or by designated representatives (the church choir); a personalized experience, participatory if possible, was deemed essential to spiritual enlightenment. Recordings encroached on that experience, and even today many churches resist using recorded music in services.

Amplification, however, was different. In the 1930s the Hammond organ, a kind of proto-synthesizer, was rapidly adopted by poorer congregations. With this emerged a tradition of amplified gospel singing, especially in black churches. Thereafter, the boundaries between secular and sacred were quickly blurred; and when "gospel" was transmuted into "soul" in the postwar decades, an entire religious tradition merged, in effect, with commercial music.

In white churches the merger occurred much later, spurred as much by the folk revival as by gospel music. And many white congregations, shrinking and aging as the century progressed, created parallel services rather than accepting amplified music into traditional worship. But the balance had shifted irrecoverably; by the end of the century the long-established industry devoted to church anthem and congregational hymns had been largely supplanted by broadcasting and recording conglomerates whose battles to control "contemporary Christian" music rivaled those over audiences in the entertainment industry.

Performance

Technology, then, transformed the use and understanding of music; it also affected judgments about music's qualities – about what and how to perform. Indeed, the arbiters themselves changed; musicians and critics were joined by engineers, editors, producers, and executives to shape and assess "records" that both depended on and differed from "performances." The influence of these new collaborators expanded as technology evolved, from choosing among alternate takes on discs to constructing continuities on magnetic tape to creating products directly in digital environments.

The received repertory of art-music was increasingly heard on recordings and broadcasts rather than in concerts; and as a result, many listeners came to expect performances to re-create recordings. The previous century had prized personality, spontaneity, and improvisation; now approbation depended on precision and fidelity to the score. After mid-century there was no excuse for error, for unconsidered impulse; the musicians simply made a new, preferred take and their collaborators edited the continuity.

Responses differed widely. The Canadian pianist Glen Gould famously abandoned public performance, devoting himself solely to carefully constructed recordings and broadcasts.[4] Others defied the emerging commodification of performance: one interesting ploy was the "direct-to-disk" movement of the 1960s, which promoted certain recordings in part because they had *not* been edited. It was the flaws that were to be cherished, just as slight imperfections in hand-made chairs made them preferable to factory furniture.[5]

Technology affected concert music throughout all Western societies; more distinctively American was its effect on other genres. Three of these –

popular music, musical theatre, and jazz – were altered in striking and related ways. Space precludes a discussion of music theatre, and some aspects of jazz are discussed in chapter 18. What follows is a brief overview of the interaction of technology with popular music.

For a start, microphones instantly transformed popular singing. Certain early performers actually flaunted their dependence on the new technology; "Whispering" Jack Smith was, as his name implied, inaudible without amplification. "Torch" singers (Helen Morgan, Ruth Etting) exploited the intimacy of microphonic recording, setting themselves apart from blues belters like Bessie Smith and variety stars like Fanny Brice. A new singing style – "crooning" – inverted the attributes of nineteenth-century *bel canto*, which had stressed projection, precision, and enunciation. The new virtues – soft-spoken delivery, creative phrasing, and a relaxed displacement of accent – epitomized all that was modern, all that amplification implied.

But they also motivated new departures. Instrumental technology at first mirrored vocal effects; Lester Young's half-breathed saxophone wordlessly echoed Billie Holiday's speech-like song. By the 1950s, however, electrification of the guitar, which at first merely made a very soft instrument more audible, had become so pervasive and sophisticated that, in effect, a new instrument was created. Experiments by musician-inventors like Les Paul led to new "solid-body" designs, in which sound processing was "played" as much as the strings. Volume, timbre, and articulation quickly became expressive parameters.

Rock and roll followed, and vocal performance changed accordingly; louder environments induced a delivery that was virtually shouted, heavily accented, with rhythm counting far more than diction. Elvis Presley bridged the genres with a voice capable of crooning (in "Love Me Tender") but also of rhythmic and dynamic drive ("Hound Dog"). Sound processing quickly moved beyond amplification to encompass reverberation, phase-shifting, and other effects. A new generation of instrumentalists, as much inventors as performers, developed skills with devices that they themselves designed or modified. Results that conservative musicians and engineers rejected – distortion, feedback, interference – became stylistic assets. By the mid-1960s successful innovation in popular music depended heavily on a *lack* of conventional training; musicians had to learn in the new environment, plugged in and turned on.

The digital era further redefined useful skills: creating and applying software for sound-files had almost nothing in common with performing on the piano or even the electric guitar. Nor was it necessary to sing: vocal music now was dominated by rhythmicized speech ("rap"), with melodic fragments (quite possibly sampled) used only as counterpoint or background.

By century's end software and hardware were cheap and powerful; the average adolescent could afford and apply technology that had been restricted to professionals even five years earlier.

Twentieth-century popular music, then, traced a clear trajectory from traditional training to self-instruction, from projected melody to amplified speech, from tone to noise. "Modern" performers, throughout the twentieth century, gradually moved away from melody, away from song – arguably, away from music. Modernism, in that sense and in that context, gradually disassembled the techniques and values with which the century began, replacing these with new devices and procedures developed by amateurs working in a technological environment. In American culture, especially, all this seems very familiar, both sympathetic and threatening: twentieth-century musicians became the modern equivalents of nineteenth-century pioneers and outlaws.

Composition

Throughout the twentieth century, recordings served the popular music industry as a new source of profit; in jazz, they built communities of players and devotees. For proponents of art-music, at their most democratic, recordings served to disseminate culture, to elevate society, in part by severing art from privilege. At the same time, however, recordings undermined what Walter Benjamin called a work's "aura": the enhanced experience associated with a unique, irreproducible work of art.[6]

Before recordings, each performance of an art-music score would be different, and each could be recaptured only in the unreliable simulacrum created by memory. This was both a blessing and a tragedy: it elevated performance to an art in itself, with its own "aura," and it required from listeners full engagement; but it made it impossible to share an experience, to directly pass on a musical inheritance. Recordings enabled music to be heard again, passed directly to associates or descendants; but they also devalued the acts of listening, of performance. Only an unrecordable music carried an aura of uniqueness.

Art music also differed from commercial music in that its composers were part of a long-running debate between Americanists and Europhiles. This in turn was entangled with musical education: ought an American composer study in a European cultural centre, or ought that composer be self-taught? The latter seemed more appropriate to the "new" world; the former seemed necessary to an esoteric, historically self-aware discipline like art music.

Thus individualism and conformity waged a particularly vicious battle in the hearts of art-music composers; and although the latter predominated during the progressive era before World War I, it was individualism that dominated for the remainder of the century. The interaction of the two was captured most pithily in the oxymoron that came to be applied to several generations of composers: the American "experimental tradition."

The start of that tradition, arguably, was the protean figure of Charles Ives, whose paradoxical aesthetic is mirrored in his social position: patron and artist, outsider and establishment, visionary and businessman. Ives's own training was thorough but unconventional. He valued far more the memories of his childhood – village bands, camp meetings, barn dances – than the formal, European schooling he received at Yale. His own experience, shaped by utopian thought of the previous century (notably but not exclusively New England Transcendentalism), led him to a radically egalitarian position: anyone could make music; everyone was a composer. "The day will come," he wrote, "when every man while digging his potatoes will breathe his own epics, his own symphonies (operas, if he likes it) . . ."[7]

Egalitarianism led Ives to two aspects of what subsequently became "experimental" music. First, he accepted sounds that had been rejected as "unmusical" or "ugly": noises, mistakes, new tunings, pluralist cacophonies. And second, he subjected both these new sounds and more conventional ones to systematic procedures: schemes newly invented to regulate the overlay or evolution of rhythms, pitches, dynamics.

Both of these positions represented composerly applications of certain aspects of mechanical reproduction. Like the gramophone, Ives aspired to aesthetic neutrality: anything could be recorded; anything could be used. Like later technology, Ives applied a kind of processing to sound, creating continuities that were logical but quite possibly inconsistent with conventional aesthetic values.

At the same time, Ives rejected the fixedness of recordings and even the fixedness of the score. Many of his pieces invite spontaneous decisions, even improvisation, by the players; many will be heard very differently in different performances in different spaces. The score, for Ives, offered a sketch of an idea rather than a set of instructions; his music, he hoped, would continue to evolve even after his death, as future generations contributed their own ideas and interpretations.

The paradoxes of this position were carried forward by Henry Cowell, Ives's close associate and the catalyst for uncounted experimental initiatives. Cowell was to some extent an ethnomusicologist, very interested in recording and preserving music from non-Western cultures. Like Ives, he invented complex schemes to regulate certain aspects of composition; and he created works ("mosaics") that changed from performance to performance, works that could never be correctly represented by a single recorded continuity.

Cowell's thinking influenced John Cage, whose application of chance techniques allowed him to explore systematically the dialectic between fixedness and change. On the one hand, chance procedures could be completely transparent, used to generate scores as easily by a machine as by a person. On the other, chance could also be applied in performance itself, so that the order or the overlay of events was unpredictable. The results would differ – sometimes hugely – from performance to performance, and a recording of a single performance had no particular authenticity; the music resisted recording, even though its performance might include electronic technology. In some of the *Variations* created in the 1960s, Cage wrote scores that describe only processes for composition and that he himself realized using complex circuitry that was beyond any one person's control.

Indeed, control was the axis around which American postwar art music polarized. The same technology that Cage employed to circumvent control was used by others to affirm composerly authority. A series of synthesizers devised and built in the Columbia–Princeton studios promised complete control over pitch, timbre, time, and intensity: in effect, they converted composers into sculptors of recorded sound rather than collaborators with performers. Synthesized music was created only once, by the composer directly, in a single "correct" version destined solely for recording.

Recorded compositions (of any sort) were also indefinitely repeatable, whereas works presented live might well never be heard again. Thus new music tended to be heard on recordings rather than in concert halls, which instead served to validate selected compositions by associating them with canonical works whose value had been affirmed by critics, historians, and patrons.

Confronting indefinite repetition, composers adopted three strategies. The first was to rely upon recordings, upon repetition, to make comprehensible, perhaps even familiar, works whose construction was so arcane or complex that they could not possibly be grasped in a single hearing. Music of this sort stood quite self-consciously apart from nineteenth-century ancestors, which had to be quickly grasped since quite possibly there would be no second chance. In America it was primarily associated with academia, bolstered by journals, associations, conferences, and other appurtenances of a "research" domain.

A second strategy was to defy repetition, to make music that could be properly experienced only live. For highly individualized performances associated with chance or improvisatory scores, or for music wedded to theatre, performance art, or dance, recordings served as documentation only. To play them again and again was to mis-represent, not illuminate, the true nature of the work.

A final strategy was to make repetition the actual subject of composition. In Steve Reich's *It's Gonna Rain* (1965), a section of magnetic tape was spliced to form a loop that would play endlessly; a second loop, on a different machine, was overlaid to create a relationship that would vary systematically over a long period of time. Reich and others moved on to apply similar procedures in "minimalist" music for instruments, providing players with small units of material that were played again and again in slowly changing patterns. Minimalism quickly blended with commercial music and other traditions to produce hybrids that were linked to popular or ethnic styles as much as to technology. Even when intended for live performance, much of this music spoke most clearly on recordings, suited better to the diffuse listening of a home environment than the focused attention of a concert hall.

In some ways, then, minimalism revived the populist experimentalism that had animated earlier experimental music. Minimalist techniques were transparent, requiring little specialized training for either application or comprehension. With the advent of the PC, music was, in effect, constructed rather than composed, and anyone with the right software could make the attempt. Composition in America was pried away from academia and returned to the general public. Even more esoteric composers adapted; by century's end promoting a score rested far more on the distribution of "realizations" (usually synthesized) than on the score itself; the recording, in effect, preceded the performance.

Envoi

In certain domains (architecture, dance, perhaps literature), it can be argued that modernism is relatively well defined; and though the details may be disputed, the rise of a "postmodern" aesthetic is largely accepted. In music the picture is much less clear. If sound technology enabled a new, "modern" approach – in art music and traditional genres, as well as in popular music – it also carried the potential to undermine, even destroy, this approach. Technology created a new industry; but as it evolved it problematized the very notion of "product," so that each corporate consolidation precipitated a populist incursion. Technology made possible the preservation of repertories; but it also redistributed these, engendering hybrids that both expanded and corrupted their sources. Technology gave composers absolute authority over their work; but it also undercut their traditional status by enabling untrained individuals to apply, idiosyncratically, new compositional tools.

In no sense, I say again, did these developments occur only in America. But a combination of circumstances and ideology has highlighted them in the United States to a greater extent than elsewhere. The interaction of corporate domination and individual enterprise is central to American politics, and it has been played out almost mythically in the recording industry. The cultural dialectic between difference and interpenetration remains crucial to America's identity; and this has been manifested in the interaction of various recorded musical traditions.

In music, then "modernism" may not be a period at all, but rather an erratic journey from the ephemeral to the persistent, the rare to the commonplace. And as American ideology continues to impose itself forcibly on the remainder of the world, as America's dialectics are thrust willy-nilly into global consciousness, music can remain a useful, if complex, guide to changing social and economic circumstances.

NOTES

1. Gertrude Stein, *The Autobiography of Alice B. Toklas*, in *Selected Writings of Gertrude Stein*, ed. Carl Van Vechten (New York: The Modern Library, 1962), p. 73.
2. As early as 1782, J. Hector St. John de Crèvecoeur wrote: "What, then, is the American, this new man? He is neither an European nor the descendant of an European; hence that strange mixture of blood, which you will find in no other country." Crèvecoeur, *Letters from an American Farmer* (New York: New American Library, 1963), p. 63.
3. The recording, by the Associated Glee Clubs of America, appeared as a 12-inch disc released as Columbia 50013-D.
4. For Gould's own views, see especially "Music and Technology," in Tim Page (ed.), *The Glenn Gould Reader* (New York: Knopf, 1984), pp. 353–68.
5. Direct-to-disk recordings also minimized tape noise, furthering the impression of actually being present at a live event.
6. See Walter Benjamin, "The Work of Art in the Age of Mechanical Reproduction," in *Illuminations*, ed. Hannah Arendt, trans. Harry Zohn (New York: Harcourt Brace and World, 1968), pp. 219–53.
7. Charles Ives, "Postface to *114 Songs*," in Howard Boatwright (ed.), *Essays Before a Sonata, The Majority, and Other Writings* (New York: W. W. Norton, 1970), p. 128.

FURTHER READING

Michael Chanan, *Repeated Takes: A Short History of Recording and Its Effects on Music*, London: Verso, 1995.

Ruth Schwartz Cowan, *A Social History of American Technology*, Oxford: Oxford University Press, 1997.

Richard Crawford, *America's Musical Life: A History*, New York: W. W. Norton, 2001.

Timothy Day, *A Century of Recorded Music: Listening to Musical History*, New Haven: Yale University Press, 2000.

Evan Eisenberg, *The Recording Angel: Explorations in Phonography*, New York: McGraw-Hill, 1987.

Charles Hamm, *Yesterdays: Popular Song in America*, New York: W. W. Norton, 1979.

H. Wiley Hitchcock, (ed.), *The Phonograph and Our Musical Life*, Brooklyn: Institute for Studies in American Music, 1980.

Mark Katz, *Capturing Sound: How Technology Has Changed Music*, Berkeley: University of California Press, 2004.

William Howland Kenney, *Recorded Music in American Life: The Phonograph and Popular Memory, 1890–1945*, Oxford: Oxford University Press, 1999.

James P. Kraft, *Stage to Studio: Musicians and the Sound Revolution, 1890–1950*, Baltimore: Johns Hopkins University Press, 1996.

Andre Millard, *America on Record: A History of Recorded Sound*, Cambridge: Cambridge University Press, 1995.

Robert Philip, *Performing Music in the Age of Recording*, New Haven: Yale University Press, 2004.

Timothy D. Taylor, *Strange Sounds: Music, Technology, and Culture*, New York: Routledge, 2001.

Paul Théberge, *Any Sound You Can Imagine: Making Music/Consuming Technology*, Hanover, NH and London: Wesleyan University Press, 1997.

18

PAUL OLIVER

African American music of the twentieth century

Introduction

Recognition of the role of blacks in American arts and particularly in twentieth-century music, raises fundamental questions concerning their contribution to the formal, white, and largely Euro-American based traditions. The works of the violinist and composer Clarence Cameron White, the performances of the piano prodigy Blind Tom Bethune, and the compositions of William Grant Still are essentially within the western concert tradition, written or performed by African American musicians. To argue otherwise is to imply that their music merits separate consideration purely on the grounds of color. This raises issues of authenticity in black music traditions, and the recognition or disregard of them, including matters of racial identity related to music production and performance. In this chapter what are variously considered as the "folk," "vernacular," or "popular" traditions are discussed, being those created and performed by blacks for themselves and, initially, for their own communities.

By definition African American music is not African, nor is it purely American, but a synthesis of both. An overview of both the African and the Euro-American cultural traditions reveals behavioral, linguistic, structural, melodic, and rhythmic features, among many others, which are embodied in the musical forms of African Americans in the twentieth century. This also applies to black cultures in Latin America, for example Brazil or Colombia, and the Caribbean, such as Trinidad and Martinique. Each is different and has created a distinct music tradition, expressive of the uniqueness of the acculturation of British, Portuguese, Spanish, and French elements with the traditions of black cultures from various regions in West Africa. Though essential to consider in a comprehensive review of black music in the Americas as a whole, the focus here is on their presence in the United States.

A factor of major importance in a discussion of black music in the twentieth century relates to access to recordings of black artists which were issued only after 1920. Consequently, writing on the early years must be based on inferences drawn from limited contemporary documentation and historically late recordings. It is a characteristic of African American music that great importance is placed on self-expression, personal techniques, and improvisation; hence the artists are generally cited in large numbers. Some particularization is therefore necessary, and the names and recordings of certain orchestras, bands, musicians, vocal groups, and individual singers are cited. Although their distinctive qualities may be summarized in this outline of African American music, necessarily they are brief and representative only.

The nineteenth-century background

While the span covered is that of the past century, African American music of the period is largely based on its inheritance of music from the nineteenth century, and even earlier. There is no doubt as to the significance of slavery in the generation of black culture, based in part on the origins of the slaves in Africa and of their being brought to the Americas to provide labor. While this was not conducive to music-making, early reports confirm that musical aptitude was far from uncommon and often encouraged by plantation-owners.

Worship and communication was in English and black song traditions were partly shaped by the influence of ballads and songs, particularly of Anglo-Scots and Irish origin. African and Western scales and approaches to singing were synthesized, and even when black orchestral music was unknown, fife and drum bands of military origin were comparatively widespread.

With a large proportion of the black population illiterate or inadequately educated, music was the expressive art that was most naturally developed and one which had persisted throughout the slavery period. Song was used to set the pace of labor and with gang leaders calling lines to which the members of the work groups responded collectively. Such "call-and-response," of African origin, continued to accompany labor where collective work was involved, whether it be the felling and logging of timber or the laying and straightening of railroad lines. It persisted in the singing in churches, the playing of instrumental music, and in the structure of solo blues. With virtually no written music, folk traditions developed of instrumental performance which were used for the entertainment of plantation owners and farmers, and of their black workers during and after the slavery period. Traditions of improvising musical instruments from gourds and cigar boxes, where conventional instruments were unavailable, led to techniques of playing to produce sounds that paralleled those of the field workers. Such "vocalized tones" became an essential part of jazz, in which improvization was fundamental, in both solo and collective performance.

The influence of the church on African American religious music was considerable. Baptist and Methodist churches predominated and the influence of John and Charles Wesley and of Dr. Watts on the evolution of Spirituals is evident. The "spirituals," or sacred songs, of the slave period reportedly declined following Emancipation. Nevertheless, there was a measure of survival of the slave traditions in song, line shouts, and ring-shouts, which persisted in the South to the 1930s.

While the Civil War (1860–5) had resulted in freedom for the former slaves, the disharmony and disruption created by the period of Reconstruction (1865–75) and the subsequent struggle on the part of the dominant white population to regain power ultimately led to discriminatory legislation in the southern states. Segregation was to last for over sixty years, during which time the black communities developed their distinct patterns of behavior, religious sects, and arts, most notably the music forms here summarized. Although many spirituals were collected and transcribed following the Civil War, there is a lack of documentation of early secular black music and song. Drum and string traditions of regions in West Africa may have influenced much North American black music, including the origins of the American banjo. Parody and stereotyping of black dancing and entertainment on banjos, fiddles, and homemade instruments was the main feature of minstrelsy from the mid-1830s, with white musicians performing in "blackface" – burnt cork make-up.

The tours of the Fisk Jubilee Singers gained world-wide appreciation, but the spirituals were adapted for concert performance, which led to their subsequent inclusion in the formal western repertoire. It was in the South that the Jubilee songs that followed Emancipation first appeared. With the rise of black churches of many denominations, instrumental music played an increasingly important part in their services, as did the dramatic delivery of the sermons by the new preachers. This new gospel music was largely an urban phenomenon. It may be seen as a reaction against the strictures of the formal Methodist and Baptist churches and as a response to the dilution of the power of the spirituals caused by their interpretation for white concert audiences.

New music in a new century: 1900–1930

At the close of the nineteenth century "Jim Crow" segregation legally separated the white and black communities, but blacks expressed their detachment from the white populace in a remarkable resurgence of creative music, both sacred and secular, which was to last throughout the new century.

Off-shoots of the Methodist Church, the African Methodist Episcopal Church and the National Baptist Convention were claiming large numbers by the beginning of the twentieth century. Smaller Holiness churches had also been founded, often by individual preachers with local congregations. The rise of the Sanctified and Pentecostal Churches and the founding of the Church of God in Christ were marked by the use of musical instruments in the services as the worshipers made "a joyful noise unto the Lord." The Jubilee songs which had celebrated Emancipation contributed to the rise of gospel songs, which often took sixteen-bar forms and which were readily accompanied by piano, drums, and stringed instruments. Members of the congregation joined in with choruses, responses, hand-clapping, calls, and "holy dancing," as recorded by such preachers as Reverend D. C. Rice and Elder J. E. Burch. In the northern cities, to which many southern blacks migrated, empty premises were converted into "store-front churches," under the direction of city pastors, many of whom were self-appointed but driven by their convictions.

On street corners, "jack-leg" evangelists were often powerful preachers and strong singers, like Blind Willie Johnson and Blind Joel Taggart, who played their own guitar accompaniments. The visual handicap which denied them work in the fields or factories accounted for the number of "blind" singers. Often they had "lead boys" to guide them, some of whom became guitar evangelists themselves, like the young Josh White. A "crossover" of influences can be traced in the relationship of gospel to the secular music forms of the close of the nineteenth century. Of these, ragtime was among the first and most prominent, and its influence on church musicians, or even of church music on ragtime, was to be heard in the playing of Arizona Dranes, a blind woman pianist from Texas.

A number of black minstrel troupes existed and toured extensively in the late nineteenth century at a time when black songwriters and composers, including James Bland and Ernest Hogan, were among the first to have their popular songs published as sheet music. "Blackface" minstrel shows, although they parodied black culture, may have contained some elements indicative of black music of the period, especially banjo-playing styles and repertoire. Banjo "rags," largely extemporized with accented off-beats, were current late in the century when plantation dances were nostalgically recalled. Most popular was the competitive cakewalk dance. Banjo rags and cakewalks influenced the syncopated piano compositions of ragtime, played by black pianists in the nightclubs of Sedalia and St. Louis, Missouri.

Prominent was Scott Joplin, composer of the *Maple Leaf Rag* of 1897. James Scott and Artie Matthews worked in the new idiom, some of their piano rags bearing the legend "banjo imitation," although their syncopated structure was considerably advanced.

Ragtime pianists recorded on cylinder and made piano rolls in New York, where the music spread quickly, influencing the new music of dance orchestras. With his Society Orchestra, James Reese Europe recorded items such as "Down Home Rag" in 1913. Pianists in New York and the developing black sector of Harlem responded with their own version of ragtime, known as "stride." More free in form and permitting extemporization, it was developed by such pianists as James P. Johnson, Willie "The Lion" Smith and their prodigy, Thomas "Fats" Waller, composers for the stage shows that were a strong feature of New York entertainment in the first quarter of the century.

With the success in 1898 of *"Clorindy": The Origin of the Cakewalk*, by Will Marion Cook, musical shows became popular. The first all-black show on Broadway was Bert Williams and George Walker's 1903 "African" production *In Dahomey*. Ragtime pianist Eubie Blake and songwriter Noble Sissle scored a hit with *Shuffle Along* in 1921 and Flournoy E. Miller and Aubrey Lyles's *Runnin' Wild* popularized the Charleston dance. Singers Adelaide Hall and Ethel Waters, and dancer Bill Robinson, attracted the crowds to the *Blackbirds* companies which played successive years in London. The coming of "talkies," or motion pictures with sound, brought such black musical shows to an end, the last being the celebrated *Porgy and Bess* of 1935, with music by the white composer George Gershwin.

Jazz in New Orleans and Chicago

With the publication of sheet music, ragtime had spread rapidly. In New Orleans, Louisiana, the *Red Book of Rags* extended the repertoire of the black musicians. The city had long been noted for the musical creativity of its black population; urban slaves gathered in "Congo Square" to dance to African rhythms up to the mid-nineteenth century, while sophisticated and musically trained black freedmen performed in symphony orchestras. Others played in brass bands for parades and public functions, while string bands were popular for social dancing. After Reconstruction, black musicians played for African American functions, including funerals and Mardi Gras parades. A number learned to play instruments on the Louisiana plantations which shipped cotton from New Orleans, some owners encouraging brass bands among their employees.

By the turn of the century a new form of New Orleans music was developing, shared by brass and string bands. Many chose to play "by ear" and improvize on their instruments. A marked feature was collective improvization, with musicians responding to each others' playing and performing in harmony. A band structure developed in which the trumpet took the lead, a clarinettist played an obligato, and a trombonist provided a lower counterpoint, this "front line" playing against the rhythm patterns of banjo or guitar, string or brass bass, percussion, and later, piano. Collective jazz improvization did not mean that each instrumentalist extemporized freely, but within the ensemble, improvising on the melodic line or the chord sequence of the tune performed.

A distinction is sometimes made between the more forceful and sometimes coarser-toned "uptown" music of players in the poorer districts and from the plantations, and the smoother "downtown" music of the trained Creole musicians. Though the originators of the music are to some extent unknown, the uptown cornet player Buddy Bolden is widely recognized as one of the principal innovators of ragtime, which was to become known as "jazz." His contemporaries, Willie "Bunk" Johnson, and Joe Oliver, whose playing earned him the accolade of "King," helped instruct the next generation. Inspired soloists and band leaders, pianist Ferdinand "Jelly Roll" Morton, trumpet-player Louis Armstrong, and the soprano saxophonist Sidney Bechet, left the city to spread the new jazz abroad; Bechet was playing in Europe and Russia by 1919. The clarinet-playing Tio brothers and Alphonse Picou, the cornet and trumpet-playing Freddie Keppard and Sam Morgan, and trombonists Kid Ory and Honore Dutray, among many others, became celebrated front-line musicians.

Young whites rapidly acquired the jazz techniques and a white group, the Original Dixieland Jass Band, popularized the name "jazz" for the new music. With the closing in 1917 of "Storyville," the licentious district which provided employment for numerous black bands, trios or solo pianists, many musicians moved north, particularly to the black ghetto on the South Side of Chicago, where King Oliver's Creole Jazz Band proved a sensation. Many other locations hosted New Orleans bands, to whose music were danced the turkey trot, the shimmy and subsequently, the quickstep, foxtrot, and lindy hop.

Bars and clubs featured late night "slow drags," the close dancing and improvization being associated with the blues more than with ragtime. Blues has often been considered a progenitor of jazz, but as no pre-jazz blues has been identified it may have been assimilated later. Indubitably, blues expression became a significant aspect of jazz, the traditional twelve-bar form used by blues singers being adopted by jazz musicians. They also developed a "vocalized" style of playing, with moans and growls made by using mutes, thrust into or covering the horn of a brass instrument.

Folk song and blues

Black secular traditions, including the ballads and folksongs of the "songsters" were seldom noted until a few books of collected songs were published in the 1920s. Collecting African American folksong had been undertaken from the beginning of the century. The first was by a black academic, Thomas Talley, whose *Negro Folk Rhymes* of 1922 was an important documentation of nineteenth-century song. Early collectors included Howard Odum and Charles Johnson, whose *Negro Workaday Songs* were collected in Mississippi and the Carolinas, a rich body of folksongs and ballads, many being recorded later by "songsters," including Papa Charlie Jackson of New Orleans, Peg Leg Howell from Atlanta, Frank Stokes from Memphis, and the Texan, Henry Thomas.

Black ballads, such as "John Henry," often in the sixteen-bar, four-line form, followed the Anglo-Scots tradition. But some, like "Stack o' Lee" and "Frankie and Albert," had a couplet and refrain, three-line structure, which may have merged with the free-form improvized plantation "field hollers" to create the blues. Blues was heard by Gertrude "Ma" Rainey in 1902, but it was William C. Handy, band-leader and composer, who first heard it in Mississippi in 1903. Handy's "Memphis Blues" (1912) established the genre and its form.

Blues was commonly in a twelve-bar, three-chord, and three-line form, the first line being repeated with a third rhyming line added, a structure which facilitated improvization. Rejecting the banjo, early blues singers replaced it with the more expressive guitar, developing techniques such as cross-note tunings and playing with a bottleneck slide on the strings. Diminished thirds and sevenths, known as "blue notes," were used frequently in blues and in jazz.

Blues was both a musical idiom and a state of mind, becoming a vehicle for self-expression through song and instrument. Ma Rainey was one of its most powerful exponents and mentor to Bessie Smith, whose blues was delivered on the vaudeville stage with unrivaled power and feeling. Lucille Hegamin, Ida Cox, and Clara Smith were among the many singers who performed in tent shows or on the stages of the Theater Owners Booking Agency (TOBA), operated by black businessmen. Their circuit included theatres in Atlanta, Memphis, New Orleans, and Dallas as well as the northern cities.

Professional singers on vaudeville shows helped spread the blues to all regions, but the majority of blacks in the South heard the new idiom in the medicine show. Vendors of patent medicines and panaceas sold cure-alls on street corners, attracting purchasers with black and white entertainers and Native American "medicine men." White country singer Jimmie Rodgers, and black songster Frank Stokes were among the many entertainers who brought blues to the medicine shows.

By the mid-1920s, regional folk blues traditions became evident in the South, from the lean and poetic work of Blind Lemon Jefferson from Texas, to the growling and instrumentally complex performance of Charley Patton, in Mississippi. As strongly influential were Blind Blake, Blind Willie McTell, and Barbecue Bob in the Southeast. Many played on the streets or in the "juke joints" that served rural black communities as drinking parlors. The social context of the blues was conveyed in its lyrics, with such themes as work, unemployment, migration, railroads, drinking and gambling, crime and punishment, disasters and war. Love, sex, and separation, were prominent, performed by solo singers with guitar, or at the piano.

Blues piano playing emerged from the Southern work camps where black labor was employed in timber and turpentine industries. Pianists entertained in "barrelhouses," crude recreation facilities linked with the work camps. To achieve the favored blue notes they employed "crushing" techniques, the almost simultaneous playing of adjacent keys. Barrelhouses gave their name to the piano style which employed ragtime and blues elements in a powerful combination, pianists such as Will Ezell and Speckled Red (Perryman) making recordings of this tradition.

Recording in the studio and the field

The importance of the recording of individual, group, and regional approaches to a number of idioms, both secular and sacred, cannot be overstated. Musical transcriptions fail to convey the expressive qualities of tone that are characteristic of jazz and blues of different styles, periods, and individual performance. Only recordings can capture the brilliance of Louis Armstrong's opening cadenza on "West End Blues" (1925), or the deep, textured voice of Charlie Patton on "Mississippi High Water Blues" (1930). Although the formative two decades of jazz were not recorded, we are fortunate that phonograph recording preserved the sounds of African American music thereafter. Black music on seventy-eight rpm (revolutions per minute), ten-inch discs commenced in 1920.

Jazz was first recorded by the white Original Dixieland Jazz Band in New York, in 1917, black jazz band leader Freddie Keppard having rejected the offer to record. Black jazz was recorded in New Orleans by a few bands, notably those of Sam Morgan, Papa Celestin, and Joseph Robichaux; "hot," exciting jazz developed rapidly in Chicago, where King Oliver, Louis Armstrong, and Jelly Roll Morton all recorded. New York hosted the Harlem and city bands of Clarence Williams, Fletcher Henderson, and Duke Ellington in the late 1920s. Other regional traditions were largely unrepresented, but field unit recordings of the "Territory" (Midwest) bands indicate their distinctive musical characters. Black jazz influenced northern white musicians, among them the Austin High School Gang. Exceptional in tone and improvization, the young trumpet-player Leon Bix Beiderbecke recorded, and was a featured soloist with the so-called "King of Jazz," Paul Whiteman, whose orchestra anticipated the rise of "big bands."

Seventy-eight rpm recordings were first made and marketed to blacks as "Race Records." Following the success of "Crazy Blues," made by Mamie Smith in 1920, records by female blues singers were very popular on the Okeh and Paramount labels. Motivated by their success, record "scouts" sought new artists, some companies, including Columbia and Victor, employing field units to record southern artists. Regional styles were identifiable in rural areas but recording often took place in the cities. Male artists dominated the rural blues. Among their number were Texas Alexander, Tommy Johnson, and Furry Lewis (vocals with guitar accompaniment), from Texas and Mississippi. Pianists, including Little Brother Montgomery and Roosevelt Sykes, were recorded solo in Chicago, where Hersal Thomas made his "Suitcase Blues" and Clarence "Pine Top" Smith his "Pinetop's Boogie Woogie," shortly before his death in a barroom brawl in 1928.

"Boogie woogie," a development of southern barrelhouse piano, featured eight beats to the bar bass rhythms and right-hand improvizations. With many variants the boogie idiom flourished until the 1950s in the playing of Jimmy Yancey, Cripple Clarence Lofton, and Big Maceo. A few folk bands were recorded, including the Dallas String Band and the Mississippi Sheiks, although groups like Cannon's Jug Stompers and the Memphis Jug Band, using improvized instruments such as jug or washboard, and featuring harmonicas, proved more popular. Recording of black sacred music was rapidly introduced after the secular successes, including harmonizing gospel groups and quartets, such as the Fairview, Golden Leaf, and Selah Jubilee singers. A few also sang secular songs. One such group was the Norfolk Sacred Quartet, which also recorded as the Norfolk Jazz Quartet. Preachers such as Reverend Gates and Reverend Nix, with their congregations, proved very popular. Several Evangelists recorded, including Washington Phillips from Texas, who played dulceola. Regrettably, the limitations of the standard ten-inch record meant that three minutes were rarely exceeded, most titles being of lesser duration, tailoring or curtailing many jazz performances.

Awareness of the origins and richness of African American folk music was stimulated by recordings made for the Library of Congress Archive of American Folk Song by John A. Lomax and his son Alan in the 1930s. Several were made in southern penitentiaries, including Parchman Farm, Mississippi. In Sugarland, Texas, Iron Head Baker was featured with a convict work gang, while at Burkeville, Texas, a railroad gang sang collective responses to the lead of Henry Truvillon. The great songster Leadbelly (Huddie Leadbetter), unrivaled for his wide repertoire, powerful voice, and playing of the twelve-string guitar, was discovered in the Angola Penitentiary, Louisiana, and brought to New York to perform and record for folk music enthusiasts. The reminiscences of the New Orleans pianist Jelly Roll Morton, and the boogie piano of Albert Ammons were also recorded for the Library of Congress.

The Lomaxes had been helped by African American writers Zora Neale Hurston and John Work, among others, and in 1941 a survey of northern Mississippi blues with John Work led to the recording of the guitarist "Son" House and the first to be made by Muddy Waters. Other important field recordings were made independently by Harold Courlander and Frederick Ramsey Jr. in Alabama and Mississippi. Subsequently, in the 1950s, Alan Lomax embarked on his "southern journey," bringing attention to surviving rural singers such as the powerful guitarist Mississippi Fred McDowell. While the roots of the blues were being uncovered the music was taking new turns.

Black music at mid-century (1930–1960)

With the increasing demands of northern industries and the desire to escape racial segregation, blacks migrated to northern cities, notably to the black ghettos of Chicago's South Side and New York's Harlem. Though racially distinct in domestic terms, black clubs and theatres attracted white clienteles and audiences in the 1920s, the music of the southern blacks becoming diffused through much of the United States. The Depression saw the virtual end of vaudeville blues, ragtime, and stride piano, though during Prohibition illicit clubs and speakeasies provided live music. Only a few new preachers appeared on record, but there were even fewer recordings by street evangelists. New store-front churches had opened and unaccompanied harmonizing quartets, including the Heavenly Gospel and Golden Eagle Singers flourished. Concert spiritual singers, especially Paul Robeson, were popular, while the long-standing Fisk, Nashville, and Tuskegee University Jubilee choirs made a few records during the 1930s.

From the 1920s, larger bands, such as those under the direction of pianist Fletcher Henderson and the diminutive drummer Chick Webb, were major attractions in the clubs and dance-halls of Harlem. The Depression was followed by a new wave of orchestral jazz, with Duke Ellington's Orchestra being the best-known. Ellington was regarded, then and now, as the greatest jazz composer. A strong measure of humor was introduced in jazz by the multi-instrumentalist Wilber Sweatman and the entertainer and band leader Cab Calloway. Bands became larger, using "sections" of front-line brass and wind instruments, with supporting strings, percussion, and rhythm instruments, although usually with only one piano.

These aggregations needed arrangers to organize the performance and the passages that sections might play. The new trends featured saxophone virtuosi, like Coleman Hawkins, Lester Young, and Charlie Parker. "Big band jazz" received a powerful input from Count Basie, a pianist formerly with Bennie Moten's band in Kansas City, who injected a strong measure of blues into the jazz idiom. Blues vocalists with the big bands included the powerfully voiced Joe Turner and Jimmy Rushing. They were all from Kansas City, as were the exceptional boogie-woogie players, Albert Ammons, Pete Johnson, and Meade Lux Lewis. They were featured in the "Spirituals to Swing" concerts, held at the Carnegie Hall in 1938.

A principal purpose of the concerts was to demonstrate the musical range and skills of the new "swing" orchestras, of whom many were white. Their form of arranged jazz appealed to a more popular, dance-orientated audience. Using musical scores, the featured improvising soloists were often the band leaders, among them trumpet player Harry James, trombonist Tommy Dorsey, and the clarinettists Artie Shaw and Benny Goodman, all of whom were white. Swing bands were prominent in musical films and helped raise the spirits of servicemen in World War II, during which the popular band leader Glenn Miller was lost in a plane accident. For over twenty years, with the exception of the peak of the Depression, recording of jazz, swing, and blues continued until 1943, when shellac rationing was introduced and the large companies were obliged to suspend operations.

Combining blues and jazz was often achieved with humor. In the band context there was often little room for blues of social significance, the emphasis being placed on entertainment. A witty combination of popular song, blues, and jazz was evident in the singing and sax playing of Louis Jordan with his Tympany Five. A new wave of expressive women singers became prominent with the bands, notably Ella Fitzgerald with her own orchestra, and later, Dinah Washington and Lil Green. But the most moving singer to bring blues expression to jazz of the late 1930s and early 1940s was Billie Holiday.

Recording of rural blues singers recommenced after the worst years of the Depression had past. A few songsters remained, Blind Willie McTell from Georgia being a notable survivor, while jug bands continued. Earlier styles of blues playing and singing persisted in the bottleneck guitar style of Kokomo Arnold and Bukka White. Some singers used steel-bodied "Dobro" guitars to achieve greater volume, while Big Joe Williams from Mississippi, Sleepy John Estes of rural Tennessee, and Blind Boy Fuller from the Carolinas ensured the continuity of rural local traditions. But the bass figures and guitar slide technique of the young Mississippi singer Robert Johnson, famous for his "Crossroads Blues," anticipated future trends.

Women blues singers of the non-vaudeville type now recorded in greater numbers, guitar-playing Memphis Minnie and pianist Georgia White among them. Some, like Lil Johnson, joined the experienced singers who adapted to northern urban life, including Big Bill Broonzy, Tampa Red on guitars, and Georgia Tom Dorsey on piano, to develop the humorous "hokum blues". Augmented with the boogie or blues piano of, among others, Big Maceo Merriweather, the harmonica playing of John Lee "Sonny Boy" Williamson, and the rhythms of Washboard Sam, these musicians created a forceful, urban blues genre in Chicago and Detroit. More contemplative was a "cool" form of blues with a near-crooning vocal style developed in the wake of Leroy Carr's records, sung to piano accompaniment by Walter Davis. Georgia Tom, however, took another direction, becoming a major composer of gospel songs under his name of Thomas A. Dorsey.

Trad, bebop, cool and modern Jazz

Critical and historical writing on jazz was initiated mainly by Europeans, but, in the late 1930s, studies in United States by such writers as Frederick Ramsey Jr., Bill Russell, and Rudi Blesh, led to the publishing of jazz histories in books and magazines. Their efforts had resulted in the rediscovery of veteran New Orleans musicians Willie "Bunk" Johnson, Avery "Kid" Howard (trumpets), and George Lewis (clarinet) among many others. A "revival" of the traditional "hot" New Orleans style was encouraged and recorded on location in that city or, in the case of Kid Ory and his Creole Jazz Band, in San Francisco. This was the home of the revivalist white Yerba Buena Jazz Band led by Lu Watters. The world-wide popularity of "Dixieland" reflected the more brash, "good time" approach of the Original Dixieland Jazz Band. There had been interest in jazz in Europe in the prewar years, and it proved to be very popular in the postwar era in France, England and Australia, and soon after in Germany. Some black musicians chose to live in Europe, including Sidney Bechet in France.

While nostalgia and the desire to perpetuate traditions inspired the "trad boom," major innovations were made by a number of musicians who had a big band or swing background. These were the innovators of what was often termed "bebop" but which was more accurately described as "cool jazz." The fiery intensity of "hot jazz" was opposed by those who sought to "play cool." Among them were the innovative saxophone players, Lester Young and Charlie Parker. Dizzy Gillespie challenged the hot trumpet players with his inventive improvizations, using original chord sequences and jumping keys. Charlie Christian was among the first to use an amplified guitar, and the pianist Thelonious Monk played against the drums of Max Roach to introduce new concepts of harmony and rhythm. Among the foremost performers was the Modern Jazz Quartet led by the pianist John Lewis.

Duke Ellington maintained his eminence in composition and in his experiments with orchestral jazz. Generally the big bands declined as the potential of bebop was explored. Much cool jazz was white, but "hard bop" was essentially black. Developed in the 1950s and 1960s, largely in Detroit and Philadelphia, the latter used gospel harmonies and soul inflections, as in the playing of Art Blakey and Horace Silver. Free jazz, which became prominent in the 1960s, was based on modal harmonies and was developed in the 1960s by such singular and inventive musicians as the reflective trumpet player Miles Davis and the saxophonists John Coltrane and Archie Shepp. From this emerged the extemporized, free form jazz of Ornette Coleman, and the jazz-rock combination of Charles Correa and Herbie Hancock which continued to the early 1970s.

The many forms of modern jazz saw the increasing use of mixed black and white bands. Following the end of a Musicians' Union ban, with the wide availability of long-playing recordings, jazz had become an international and cross-cultural musical language. Japanese, Russian, and other European and Asian jazz musicians were now numerous, and continued to enrich the idioms.

Rhythm and blues

Most major record companies resumed production after the war, but in the late 1940s a number of "independent" concerns sprang up with access to black blues and both traditional and modern jazz bands. They also used other means to promote new singers and new trends, among them juke boxes and radio, with its "disc jockeys" and featured artists. Generally, the records were marketed under the overall label of "rhythm and blues." Seventy-eight rpm ten-inch discs continued to be produced until the mid-1950s, when the first microgroove long-playing records were introduced, which enabled whole sessions to be on one record and permitted items of varied length, free of the former three-minute limit. While musicians were less restricted, advances in recording technology made the use of electrically amplified instruments wholly acceptable.

Blues became increasingly a band music for entertainment, with appearances of singers and bands in urban nightclubs, which often led to "residences," or periods of continuous employment. Now less personal and contemplative, such blues featured loud singing against band settings. The influence of Joe Turner from Kansas City was evident in the vocals by blues shouter Wynonie Harris with Lucky Millinder Orch, and in Roy Brown's vocals with Tiny Bradshaw. Musicians from Texas, including the pianist Charles Brown, migrated to California to join the West Coast blues scene which had developed. In New Orleans the veteran singer of the "classic" tradition, Lizzie Miles, was still active with revivalist jazz groups.

In spite of the changes that were taking place, the "lowdown," "downhome" blues of an essentially rural nature, even though many of the singers had moved to the cities, was still popular in the southern states. Big Joe Williams, who played a unique nine-string guitar, was prominent in Mississippi, while in Texas the guitarists Smoky Hogg and, most significantly, Lightnin' Hopkins, maintained the tradition, but in highly personal terms. A cluster of singers in the Baton Rouge area of Louisiana developed a regional style, "swamp blues," which was extensively recorded in the 1950s.

During the postwar years hundreds of thousands of black Americans migrated from the South to northern cities, many singers and instrumentalists among them. Boogie pianists, including Clarence Lofton and Charlie Spand, continued to entertain in the Chicago rent-parties. Another party-pianist, Jimmy Yancey, used Afro-Cuban *habanera* bass figures related to the tango in his accompaniments to his blues-singing wife, Estelle "Mama" Yancey. Then, in the 1950s, a major revolution in Chicago blues was created by migrants of the generation born in the second decade of the century.

Blues guitar-playing was profoundly redirected by Aaron T-Bone Walker, who pioneered electrically amplified guitar. B. B. King was one of the first to follow his lead, but others soon took up electric instruments. Among them was John Lee Hooker, who had left Memphis in 1943 to settle in Detroit, where he eventually recorded his hit, "Boogie Chillen." At the same time Muddy Waters (Morganfield) moved from Mississippi. His advancement of the Chicago blues band with the adoption of amplified and electric instruments was followed rapidly by the powerful harmonica and guitar player Howling Wolf (Burnett), and by guitarist Elmore James, who was influenced by Robert Johnson. All these singers had migrated from Mississippi. With Little Walter (Jacobs) and James Cotton on amplified harmonicas their bands generated an energy and volume of sound in the clubs of the South and West Sides unprecedented in the blues. Taylor and J. B. Hutto were among the many other band leaders, to be followed by younger blues musicians, who included guitarist J. B. Lenoir.

Extrovert artists with electric instruments and backing groups, and using contemporary lyrics, were the inspiration of rock music, including the skillful and witty guitarists Bo Diddley (Ellas McDaniel) from Mississippi and Chuck Berry, born in California. The eccentric Little Richard (Penniman), the forceful Ray Charles, both from Georgia, and Fats Domino from New Orleans, based their music on boogie and blues, with a considerable measure of gospel delivery. Boadly, the extrovert playing and singing of all these artists was termed "rock and roll." Their influence on white singers, including guitarist Elvis Presley and the Memphis pianist Jerry Lee Lewis, inspired the "rock revolution," to which the Beatles, the Rolling Stones, the Who and other British bands brought new dimensions.

From the sixties to the year of the blues

Innovative African American music in the 1950s was often created by southern-born artists who made their reputations after moving to the cities. Yet there were still musical forms that appeared in the South, among them being zydeco. A black version of Louisiana Cajun (Acadian) music, with some of the vocals in French, zydeco was played on accordions and guitars, with washboard percussion. Prominent among the zydeco performers was accordionist Clifton Chenier, while Clarence Garlow popularized the music at a local level in Louisiana and East Texas.

Gospel music as sung by quintets and sextets had remained popular. Frequently, unaccompanied groups like the Five Blind Boys from Alabama and the Five Blind Boys of Mississippi, demonstrated their vocal versatility without compromising their religious message. The Spirits of Memphis, Sensational Nightingales, Fairfield Four, and the Staple Singers were among other vocal groups. Among the prime singers in the gospel field was Mahalia Jackson from New Orleans, a soloist with a soaring voice who had been influenced by the recordings of Bessie Smith. Another was Rosetta Tharpe, sometime singer with the Lucky Millinder Orchestra in the 1940s, who played guitar, and as Sister Rosetta Tharpe, recorded fine duets with another gospel artist, Marie Knight. Choral groups were still appreciated, the Clara Ward Singers being among the most admired. Many preachers were to be heard in store-front churches but far fewer were recorded; those that were revealed the continuity of the tradition of topical sermons dramatically expressed. They included Reverend Kelsey and Reverend C. J. Franklin, father of the gospel-influenced soul singer Aretha Franklin.

Musicians from Britain were subject to a ban on their playing in the United States, but although there was a reciprocal Musicians' Union ban on visiting US performers except as "variety" or intermission artists, there was a growing awareness of blues in Europe. Visits in the early 1950s by Lonnie Johnson, Josh White, and Big Bill Broonzy, were augmented by tours as intermission artists for Chris Barber's Jazz Band by Champion Jack Dupree, Sonny Terry, and Brownie McGhee, among others. Little had been published on blues until the late 1950s and early 1960s, when the first histories and analyses appeared. As had been the case with jazz, a number of these were by European authors. No African American authors wrote on jazz or blues until Leroi Jones (Amiri Baraka) and Ralph Ellison. Again, blues history matched that of jazz, in that numerous blues singers were discovered and recorded, or "rediscovered," having recorded in earlier years.

The rapid growth of European interest was accelerated by the annual Folk Blues Festivals which toured throughout Europe in the 1960s, arranged by the German promoters Horst Lippman and Fritz Rau, with bass player Willie Dixon acting as their Chicago agent. Traditional and rediscovered or newly discovered artists, such as Son House, Sleepy John Estes, Lightnin' Hopkins, and J. B. Lenoir, played to large audiences, and so Europeans had the opportunity to hear more blues singers than had most Americans. With the end of the reciprocal ban on visiting artists in Europe, following the success of the Beatles in the United States, solo tours by Alec "Sonny Boy" Williamson and Little Walter Jacobs on harmonicas, and guitarists such as B. B. King and Johnny Shines among many others were arranged in the 1960s and 1970s, with several European countries promoting annual blues festivals. Many were interviewed for specialist publications and some also appeared on radio and television. Appreciative of their reception, several blues singers chose to reside in Europe.

Throughout the 1960s and 1970s considerable changes took place in urban blues, with greater emphasis on new structures, vocal expression, and artist/audience relationships. Guitarist B. B. ("Blues Boy") King and vocalist Bobby Bland were among the many who developed "blues with soul." The increasing number of black radio stations and the general expansion of promotional activities led to the greater popularization of soul music, with Aretha Franklin, and Ray Charles reflecting different aspects of its development. Of particular importance was the crossover of gospel harmonies and techniques of vocal expression to secular music. In the "disco" era of largely improvized dance, James Brown, dubbed the "godfather of soul," and Stevie Wonder developed "funk," an earthier form of soul, with socially committed lyrics. Quartets and quintets were formed and extensively recorded, singing "doo-wop" harmonies and fronting electric bands. This period witnessed the rise of such groups as Diana Ross and the Supremes, and the male Temptations group formed in Alabama. With solo artists, including Sam Cooke, Aretha Franklin, and Mary Wells, these singers reached a larger popular audience and, through their recordings on Motown and other labels, exercised a measure of influence on the Beatles and other early rock groups.

By the 1980s much of jazz, blues, and soul music had become international and was largely abandoned by African American singers and musicians, but the rise of "rap" and "hiphop," with their rhythmic emphasis and often spectacular break-dancing, indicated that their creative drive was still present. Rap is a form of narrative which probably derives from the earlier "toasts," with its verbal rhythms and emphasis on rapid use of language. Melody as such is not employed, while the words and phrases used are direct and not screened or encoded as in the blues. Kurtis Blow, Mr. Magic, Grandmaster Flash, Whodini, the Beastie Boys, and Ice-T were among major rap artists of the 1980s and 1990s, some like the Public Enemy duo using the violent form of "gangsta rap."

Meanwhile, gospel music continued to have its following, with soloists Inez Andrews, preacher Solomon Burke, and vocal groups such as the Pilgrim Travelers conveying their messages through tours and recordings. By the mid-1980s gospel music declined on record but remained a strong element in both Baptist and Pentecostal Churches. Music had been customary in the Holiness Churches and the Church of God in Christ, but the 1980s and 1990s witnessed the rise of the versatile proponents of the "sacred steel" movement in the House of God Churches, with the Campbell Brothers and Willie Eason among the players of the pedal-steel and lap-steel electric guitars. With their slide techniques, their reflective solos, and vigorous fast pieces, their playing has synthesized many characteristics and qualities of the African American traditions.

The end of the century led many enthusiasts to reflect upon the birth of the remarkable family of African American music forms which had developed since 1900, and which had shaped the growth of popular music genres throughout the world. With regret for the passing of some idioms as new forms arose, all have had their nostalgic following. Jazz had been profoundly influential on the development of all forms of popular music in the first half of the twentieth century; blues has been the major influence on popular music subsequently, giving musical form and instrumental expression to rhythm and blues, rock and roll, and, with the influence of gospel, to much of soul. The year 2003 was officially declared by the United States Congress as "The Year of the Blues," as it marked the centenary of W. C. Handy first hearing the blues played in Mississippi, which was the inspiration of his compositions.

The heritage of black music

Although blues, ragtime, jazz, and gospel song were essentially of black and southern origin, they were widely diffused. Whether their sources were folk traditions or more sophisticated and urban origins they were influential on music and culture in many ways.

The arrival of ragtime and jazz in New York coincided with the growth of Harlem, which became the home of many black artists and writers. Although certain members of the Harlem Renaissance, notably Alain Locke, acknowledged the vigor of jazz they desired more refinement in its composition and execution. Some artists found inspiration in the new music, like the mural painter Aaron Douglas, whose murals for the Schomburg library carried Symbolist associations, or Archibald Motley, a few of whose paintings depicted jazz musicians.

Other writers and artists of the Renaissance were profoundly moved by the blues, Langston Hughes producing his anthology of poems *The Weary Blues* in 1923. Later poets, and writers who included Sterling Brown, Richard Wright, and Ralph Ellison, drew on both blues and jazz, the significance of the latter reflected even in the post Second World War writing of Tony Morrison. Visual artists such as Jacob Lawrence and later, Romare Bearden, drew upon blues for inspiration, some writers identifying a "blues aesthetic" underlying the spontaneity and structuring of their works. Jazz and blues, and to a considerable extent, gospel song, had introduced western music and art in new or forgotten modes of expression to music. Many Western composers and musicians, such as Frederick Delius, Darius Milhaud, Kurt Weill, Igor Stravinsky, Aaron Copeland, and George Gershwin among others, welcomed the new music and assimilated aspects of it, rhythmically, tonally, and structurally in their compositions.

Nevertheless, the black idioms retained their special characteristics, improvization, both solo and collective, acting as vehicles for highly individual and personal expression. The a-a-b form of the blues permitted the invention of a new and rhyming line to extend the theme or "answer" the proposition of the repeated first line. Many blues, such as those by Robert Pete Williams, guitarist from Louisiana, were totally original and improvized on the spot; others used "floating" phrases, or standard lines, with new rhyming ones, imparting fresh meaning to the original. Additionally, the responsorial character of black song was represented in the blues by each two-bar phrase within the vocal being answered by a two-bar instrumental phrase, whether through self-accompaniment or by the accompaniment of other musicians. The structure enabled musicians of new acquaintance to work together, whether in a blues duo or trio or in a New Orleans band, or with "head arrangements" in the complex big bands of Duke Ellington and others.

All this meant that the composer and the performer were essentially one and the same, the performers not gaining credit for their faithful interpretation of a composer's musical concepts but essentially expressing their own. Every jazz or blues performer is therefore unique, though some may be inspired to heights of improvization or meaningful expression that others might not attain. In consequence, the creativity of much, indeed most, essentially African American musical forms is embodied in the collective unity of performing groups and the essential creativity of its individual players, whose identities and reputations are fundamental to the understanding of the respective genres and subgenres. It follows that any discussion of black music in the twentieth century must involve not only the identification of many genres, both sacred and secular, but also the names of some of their principal exponents, however obscure they may be.

In a review of black music one is obliged to consider the many changes in the idioms that have often been brought about after relatively short periods of time. These may be attributed to the freedom of singers and musicians to innovate and create without the need to accord with specific norms. All forms of black music may be perceived as statements of identity, both solo and collective. It is evident that African American singers and musicians in creating new styles and directions in music also tend to withdraw from them when they are adopted by white performers.

Both jazz and blues in their various genres have become international and in so being, to a considerable degree they have lost their black audiences. Formerly, this was true of ragtime piano, to orchestral ragtime, to New Orleans jazz, to musical shows, and to swing music. In the more recent or longer-lasting idioms it is true of rural and urban blues, to rhythm and blues and rock and roll, and to soul music, as these were imitated and exploited by white bands and individuals, not merely in the United States but in Europe and, by the end of the twentieth century, all over the world. Their successors in the forms of hip-hop and rap have been rapidly diffused through advances in the media, and are either taken to extreme forms by black performers or are being discarded by them.

Whether the African American genius for musical creativity will be expressed in a new idiom cannot be predicted. But whatever the future may offer in the way of new music the musical revolution that was created by Black Americans in the twentieth century will undoubtedly be lasting in its influence.

FURTHER READING

A substantial literature exists on all aspects of black music. The following works are comprehensive overviews of aspects of the subject. All contain bibliographies.

Rudi Blesh and Harriet Janis, *They All Played Ragtime*, London: Cassell, 1958.

Paul Friedlander, *Rock and Roll. A Social History*, Boulder, CO: Westview Press, 1996.

Nelson George, *The Death of Rhythm and Blues*, London: Omnibus Press, 1988.

Michael Haralambos, *Right On: From Blues to Soul in Black America*, London: Causeway Press, 1994.

Anthony Heilbut, *The Gospel Sound. Good News and Bad Times*, New York: Limelight Editions, 1985.

Leroi Jones (Amiri Baraka), *Blues People: Negro Music in White America*, London: MacGibbon and Kee, 1965.

Charles Keil, *Urban Blues*, Chicago: University of Chicago Press, 1966.

Neil Leonard, *Jazz and the White Americans*, Chicago: University of Chicago Press, 1962.

Lawrence Levine, *Black Culture and Black Consciousness*, Oxford: Oxford University Press, 1977.

Alan Lomax, *The Land Where the Blues Began*, London: Methuen, 1993.

Albert McCarthy, *Big Band Jazz*, London: Barrie and Jenkins, 1974.

Albert Murray, *Stomping the Blues*, New York: McGraw-Hill Book Co., 1976.

Paul Oliver, *Songsters and Saints: Vocal Traditions on Race Records*, Cambridge: Cambridge University Press, 1984.

The Story of the Blues, London: Pimlico (Random House), 1990.

Arnold Shaw, *Black Popular Music in America*, London: Collier-Mcmillan, 1986.

Alyn Shipton, *A New History of Jazz*, London: Continuum, 2001.

Eileen Southern, *The Music of Black Americans. A History*, New York: W.W. Norton, 1983.

Michael Tisserand, *The Kingdom of Zydeco*, New York: Avon Books, 1999.

Allen Woll, *Black Musical Theater: From Coon Town to Dream Girls*, Baton Rouge: Louisiana State University Press, 1989.

19

WALTER METZ

Hollywood cinema

Hollywood, soon to become the United States' national film industry, was founded in the early teens of the twentieth century by a group of film companies which came to Los Angeles at first to escape the winter conditions of their New York- and Chicago-based production locations. However, the advantages of production in southern California – particularly the varied landscapes in the region crucial for exterior, on-location photography – soon made Hollywood the dominant film production center in the country.[1]

Hollywood, of course, is not synonymous with filmmaking in the United States. Before the early 1910s, American filmmaking was mostly New York-based, and specialized in the production of short films (c. 1909, a one-reel short, or approximately ten minutes). At the time, French film companies dominated global film distribution, and it was more likely that one would see a French film in the United States than an American-produced one. However, by 1917, the effects of World War I on global film distribution – severely limiting French companies' abilities to release films world-wide yet having little effect on the global demand for new films – would allow the Hollywood film industry to expand and stabilize.

The story of the formation of Hollywood also involves a set of filmmakers leaving New York and traveling to Los Angeles. On the business side, an independent producer, Carl Laemmle, fought the major New York-based filmmaking enterprise of the latter half of the first decade of the twentieth century, the Motion Picture Patents Corporation (MPPC), over their attempt to monopolize filmmaking in the city. Despite winning a major court ruling against the MPPC's monopolistic practices, Laemmle left for California to establish Universal studios in Hollywood in 1915. Similarly, the producer Thomas Ince built Inceville, a large studio that by 1916 was producing epic features like *Civilization* (1916), a pacifist critique of World War I.

On the creative side, the career of D. W. Griffith traces the move from New York to Hollywood. Between 1909 and 1913, Griffith was the major director at the Biograph Company, a New York-based producer of shorts for whom Griffith made hundreds of intricately edited last-minute rescue films (such as 1909's *The Lonely Villa*). When Biograph, heavily invested in the two-reel short, refused to allow Griffith to make a feature-length film, he left the company and financed his own film, the epic *The Birth of a Nation* (1914). Coupled with *Intolerance* (1915), his even more intricately edited masterpiece, Griffith's feature-length films offer an extreme exemplar of the formation of the Hollywood cinema. *Intolerance*, in particular, is a Hollywood film par excellence. It is a sweeping epic whose failed quest for grandeur began Griffith's fall. Its connection to Los Angeles is legendary: the massive Babylonian set was erected in the city, and when Griffith went bankrupt, it remained a tourist attraction for many years because no one had the money to dismantle it. It was finally taken down during the Depression, thanks to the New Deal's WPA program.[2]

By 1917, the classical Hollywood cinema was organized around a studio system. The industry evolved into an oligopoly, the control of an industry by a small number of companies. By the 1930s, the hierarchy of these companies had become firmly established. The major players in the studio system, referred to by film historians as the "big five," were: Paramount, MGM, 20th Century Fox, Warner Bros., and RKO. These studios were fully vertically integrated, meaning they controlled large holdings in all three areas of the film industry: production, distribution, and exhibition. One step down the ladder were the "little three," so-called because they had less investment in exhibition real estate. The little three were: Universal, Columbia, and United Artists. Sometimes, this hierarchy is split differently because RKO was less well positioned in exhibition than the so-called "bigger four." On the fringe of the studio system were Republic and Monogram, even smaller production outfits whose specialty was the making of cheap genre films, such as Westerns.

The Hollywood studio system was a well-oiled machine for the generation of huge profits. With vertical integration comes the ability to maximize profits by assuring that each layer of the industry is forced to conform to the same efficiency practices. For example, production and exhibition are naturally two sectors of the film industry that are at odds. To make large profits, the producers of movies want them to be made cheaply. The exhibitors of movies, on the other hand, want the movies to be of high quality so as to generate public interest in the product they are offering. So, the studio system colluded between these two sectors of the industry. Under practices like blind buying and block booking, the studio would require its exhibitors to purchase a set of films, sight unseen, rather than just the big budget film they might ordinarily want in isolation because it featured big stars and was guaranteed to generate audience interest. Under this system, a studio could ensure continuous profits, generated not only by the few quality films it might happen to have made in a given year, but instead via all of the films – good or not – that its factory line churned out.

Despite the extremely limited artistic component of the studio system economic model, this organization resulted in a great many wonderful films, as varied as *The Wizard of Oz* (MGM, Victor Fleming, 1939) and *Citizen Kane* (RKO, Orson Welles, 1941). This is largely because such a system demands aesthetic differentiation of product to accompany economic practices of standardization.[3] That is to say, what the production wing of the studio system wants is a factory model in which the same product is churned out with reliability and quality. However, while this system can work unfettered in the shoe industry, where it is perfectly possible to want to buy the same shoe over and over again because it pleases one's foot, the same cannot be said for movies. It is unlikely that one is going to keep buying tickets for the same movie over and over again. Instead, the Hollywood studio system relies on standardization (of production methods and of content) alongside product differentiation.

No category of Hollywood filmmaking is more driven by standardization and differentiation than is the genre system. Hollywood cinema's genres allow the efficient production of many films that are designed to seem different from one another. Thus, while no one would go to see the horror film *Dracula* tens of times a year, Universal studios in the 1930s could use the same sets and talent to make a cycle of horror films that were mostly like *Dracula*, but with narrative and aesthetic differences. Thus, during the 1930s, Universal made horror films about Frankenstein, the Invisible Man, the Wolfman, as well as sequels and intertextual permutations which combined them together, such as *Frankenstein Meets the Wolf Man* (1943).

This economic system of film production allowed the Hollywood film industry to weather the Depression and World War II. In the immediate postwar period, Hollywood's economic stranglehold on American national cinema reached its apex, with the years 1946–7 representing the largest per capita movie attendance in American history. However, by the late 1930s, forces emerged which would change the economic structure of Hollywood. In 1938, an antitrust case was filed against the Hollywood studio system that would come to be known as the Paramount case. Because of the intervening Second World War, the case was not fully adjudicated until 1948, at which time the Hollywood studios signed a consent decree with the Justice Department admitting to oligopolistic collusion.

However, rather than crippling the studio system, the tenets of the Paramount decree in the long run ended up preserving the Hollywood system.

The Paramount decree forced the studios to cleave off one facet of their vertically integrated system, exhibition. Due to the forces of postwar suburbanization, by the early 1970s the studios' expensive real estate holdings in downtown urban centers would be deserted, becoming spaces for the exhibition of international art cinema and pornography. Of the three parts of the business of moviemaking, the least capital intensive, yet most profitable, is distribution, over which, to this day, the former Hollywood studios continue to exert a stranglehold.

The selling off of their exhibition infrastructure, nonetheless, did radically change the Hollywood industry. By 1960, the classical Hollywood studio system was gone, replaced by what has come to be known as "the New Hollywood." There are three major periods of the New Hollywood: the 1960s period, which responded to the full effects of the Paramount decree; the "Hollywood Renaissance" (1967–72), in which these economic changes allowed briefly for an unprecedented level of experimentation in mainstream American filmmaking; and a return to the "blockbuster" mode of moviemaking with the spectacular summer release of *Jaws* in 1975. The quest after huge profits generated out of a relatively small number of major studio-distributed films continues unabated in contemporary Hollywood to this day.

The first period of the New Hollywood, roughly 1960–8, is marked by a precipitous decline in studio prestige. A number of films from this period could be used to mark the transformation in Hollywood, but *Psycho* (1960) is the iconic one. The late 1950s films of Alfred Hitchcock were widescreen, high gloss color spectaculars featuring major Hollywood stars; *North by Northwest* (1959), starring Cary Grant is a good example. Some of these films, like *Vertigo* (1958), were financial disasters. *Psycho*, on the other hand, was made for Universal with Hitchcock's television crew, in black and white on a small budget. The film featured no "A" list stars, instead relying on the eclectic casting of Anthony Perkins and Janet Leigh. The success of *Psycho* dovetailed with an industry shifting toward the pursuit of genre-bound formulas of sensation that would appeal to a rising postwar youth culture.

The use of a television crew to shoot a Hollywood film offers a useful metaphor for the role of television in Hollywood's transformation. While traditional film historians sometimes reduce the story to one of blind studio heads ignoring the rising importance of the new medium of television, in fact the story of Hollywood's response to television is quite complicated. For one, the studio heads tried desperately to subsume the burgeoning television industry, but were stalled by a number of forces, not the least of which was the fear of government regulation, given that the Hollywood industry was a known antitrust violator. For example, Hollywood tried to create television systems which people could watch in movie theatres, but these systems failed for reasons related to government regulation and failed technological innovation.[4] Television gained popularity throughout the 1950s, and began to compete with the cinema as America's top choice for audio-visual entertainment. Hollywood engaged in a number of technological innovations related to the presentation of movies – quadraphonic stereo sound, anamorphically produced widescreen images, and three-dimensional images, among them – in order to lure viewers away from television screens and back into seats at movie theatres. It was a losing battle.

The remarkable growth of the television industry and the precipitous decline of the film industry in the 1950s are perhaps best captured by the story of television producer Desi Arnaz and RKO studios. In 1950, band leader Desi Arnaz and his wife, "B" level film star Lucille Ball, sold their idea for a sitcom, *I Love Lucy*, to the CBS television network. Shooting the show on film to protect middle-aged Lucy's beauty image allowed for the sale of the then un-appreciated syndication rights. Desi and Lucy formed a television production company, Desilu, and convinced CBS to allow them control over these syndication rights. The enormous profitability of *I Love Lucy* in syndication – it has shown every day in Los Angeles since 1951, and countless times and places around the world – put Desilu in the position of expanding its position in the industry.

In the meantime, RKO was being run into the ground by Howard Hughes, who was using the studio as a place to turn his girlfriend into a movie star. In 1956, Arnaz used the syndication profits of *I Love Lucy* to buy the production venues of RKO. These became the Desilu Studios, where a large percentage of 1960s American television, as varied as *Star Trek* and *The Brady Bunch*, was produced. Over the years, the industrial distinction between film and television has gradually faded, such that Hollywood is now the location for the production of both theatrically released films and major narrative television shows, both of which are produced interchangeably in what used to be the location of the classical Hollywood studio system. All major Hollywood studios now have wings devoted to the production of shows meant for airing on prime-time television, both network and basic cable.

The story of Desilu buying RKO is one example of how the late 1950s can be seen as the last days of the classical Hollywood studio system. However, there are other examples, among which was Fritz Lang's last American film, *Beyond a Reasonable Doubt*. Made in the death throes of RKO in 1956, the film fundamentally altered the narrative terms of the classical Hollywood studio film. For most of its story, Hollywood had relied on Aristotelian principles of narrative construction, largely inherited from the nineteenth-century well-made play. By 1917, popular American screenwriting manuals were codifying these narrative devices into what we now know as "three-act structure."[5]

The effects of the Paramount decree immediately seemed to do greater damage to the Hollywood system. Lang's *Beyond a Reasonable Doubt*, released by RKO in 1956, violated the basic principles of the three-act structure film. The film concerns a man, Tom Garrett (Dana Andrews), an author who begins the film in conversation with a powerful liberal news-paper publisher, Austin Spencer. The publisher recoils against the preening of the city's district attorney, jubilant that he has sent another man to his execution. Tom and Austin scheme to plant evidence in a murder case that seems to implicate Tom. Their plan is to let Tom go to trial, and be convicted in the capital murder case. Then, at the last minute, Austin will arrive with the damning evidence against the death penalty.

All goes as planned until Austin, on his way to the courtroom to exoner-ate Tom, dies in a freak, melodramatic car crash. Tom is sentenced to death, but Austin's daughter, Susan (Joan Fontaine) fights desperately to clear her boyfriend. She works throughout the second act to secure a gubernatorial pardon. In the third act, just as she is about to succeed, Tom lets slip a key piece of evidence that actually implicates himself in the murder. Susan, realizing he is really guilty, informs the governor of this fact. The film ends with Tom being led off to the gas chamber.

Beyond a Reasonable Doubt thus offers a complete subversion of the three-act structure, classical Hollywood narrative. It encourages our invest-ment in Tom's innocence, only to produce a second ending in which our belief in him turns out to be completely wrong. It is thus, in effect, a film with two second turning points, each one of which contradicts the other. *Beyond a Reasonable Doubt* thus serves to demonstrate the collapse of the narrative efficiency of the studio system of filmmaking. At a dying studio, the German modernist filmmaker, Fritz Lang, was able to import alternative narrative forms into the Hollywood system.[6]

The first New Hollywood period (1960–7) is partially characterized by these sorts of disruptions in the studio system. A good example of this sort of disruption lies in the production of gothic horror films in the early 1960s. While *Psycho* (1960) is typically positioned as an iconic marker for the shift between the "old" and New Hollywoods, Alfred Hitchcock was a major filmmaker in Hollywood during a huge portion of its history. A better example is the case of William Castle. An exploitation filmmaker during the 1950s, Castle specialized in making films for the matinée audience, inventing gimmicks to make his horror films seem scarier than they actually were. Castle would take out insurance policies on the spectators, in case they died of fright while watching his film, for example. In 1964, Castle secured a deal with Columbia Pictures for a horror film, *Strait-Jacket*, starring Joan Crawford. The film begins with a young girl witnessing her mother (Crawford) murdering her father with an axe. This flashback scene is followed by the main plot of the film, in which the adult daughter is seemingly reconciled with her mother, newly released from a mental institution. New axe murders begin occurring in the small town where they live, and everyone looks toward Crawford's character as the obvious suspect. However, in the film's Act III climax, Crawford struggles with the axe murderer, who turns out to be her daughter wearing a Joan Crawford mask!

Strait-Jacket represents the shift in the New Hollywood from character dramas (1943's *Casablanca*) toward exploitation spectacle (axe murder horror films). In fact, one could suggest that what in the classical Hollywood period represented the fringes of Hollywood (low budget genre films at the exploitation level) would become the main "A" films of the New Hollywood (slasher films and gross-out comedies and the like). In addition, no films from the first New Hollywood period better illustrates the loss of studio prestige. The last image of the film features Lady Columbia with her head at her feet, the victim of William Castle's axe. Given how seriously corporations take their brand logo, this mutilation of Lady Columbia is remarkable.

More notable, however, is what the first New Hollywood period films did to the star system of classical Hollywood. The iconic films in this vein are those featuring aging female "A" level stars from classical Hollywood melodramas. *Whatever Happened to Baby Jane?* (Robert Aldrich, 1962) is the key film here because it weaves its gothic horror around the two key women stars in this tradition, both John Crawford and Bette Davis. These stars' last decades in the New Hollywood were filled with such low budget horror appearances, in which the female aged body came to signify horror, and not the beauty that their young bodies represented in such classical Hollywood films as *Dark Victory* (1939) or *Mildred Pierce* (1945).

Such is not the case, significantly, for male stars. A good example here is the case of MGM's 1966 film, *Hot Rods to Hell*. A classical mainstream first New Hollywood exploitation film, this features Dana Andrews as a middle-aged salesman, who, because of a car accident, is forced to move across country with his family. During the road trip, the family is accosted by psychotic teenagers, juvenile delinquents intent on running them off the road. At the end of the film, Andrews's character has had enough, and stages an Act III climax in which he places his car on the highway in the dead of the night. Thinking he is playing chicken with them, the teenagers attempt to ram his car. They discover the car is abandoned too late, and smash their own car on the desolate highway. Andrews stands over their wounded bodies, smashing their already destroyed car with a crow bar. Thus, he ends the film triumphantly, secure in his generically formed Hollywood masculinity. While Davis and Crawford are forced to shift genres, from glamorous melodrama to exploitation horror, Andrews is allowed to age gracefully, secure in his ability to defeat the villains, just as he was able to do in his classical Hollywood films, as in the film noir, *Laura* (Otto Preminger, 1944).

While there are many films, like *Strait-Jacket* and *Beyond a Reasonable Doubt*, which point to major shifts between the classical and New Hollywoods, in general Hollywood continued to produce films that would appeal to a mass audience and make large profits. As Tom Schatz points out in his essay, "The New Hollywood," the film industry was intent on continuing the big budget, high profit mode of filmmaking into the 1960s.[7] Thus, when *The Sound of Music* generated blockbuster profits on its release in 1965, all the other Hollywood studios followed suit, trying to replicate its success. Most of the studios almost went bankrupt in trying to do so, and the wave of late 1960s musicals proved disastrous. Films like *Doctor Doolittle* (1967) lost most of the money heaped into their super spectacular productions. The most embarrassing story to come out of this experience was *Oliver!* (1968), a big budget musical based on the work of Charles Dickens. Its disastrous release was counterbalanced by Academy Award nominations, the Oscar voting reflecting not so much the quality of the films as the amount of money invested. Thus the critically maligned musical won the best picture statuette, in the process beating *2001* (MGM, Stanley Kubrick, 1968), one of the most inventive of Hollywood films.

As a result of the collapsing finances of the Hollywood studios, they became easy targets for takeovers. The result was, that by the end of the 1960s, Hollywood studios were largely tax loss write-offs for larger conglomerates. Gulf and Western, an oil company, for example, bought Paramount Pictures in 1966. In this new business climate, where Hollywood film companies were run by people who made little distinction between the various commodities their different divisions made, and thus had little interest in the production of art, a more relaxed mode of production for Hollywood films resulted. One result was that a number of film school graduates were allowed into the Hollywood system; the first time directors did not have to work their way up through the union craft system to helm Hollywood films. In addition, less money was available overall for film production, and so smaller budgets were assigned to each film. To address this, the films were niche marketed toward smaller potential audiences, the idea being that smaller budget films did not have to appeal to a mass audience in order to make a small profit.

This period, from 1967 to 1975, has been described as the "Hollywood Renaissance," a second period of the New Hollywood in which a number of near experimental films were made within the studio system. The contrasting business and artistic environment of Hollywood during this period means that the films are largely conflicted, and need to be discussed as such. For example, Columbia Pictures released *Easy Rider* in 1968, a film directed by two young men, Peter Fonda and Dennis Hopper, who had been present in Hollywood as children in the 1950s, Fonda because of his famous actor father, Henry, and Hopper because he was a teenage actor appearing on numerous television shows throughout the 1950s.

On the one hand, *Easy Rider* is a remarkable film, importing modernist aesthetics into the Hollywood cinema. While modernism had appeared in the classical Hollywood studios films in fits and starts (Orson Welles' *Citizen Kane* and numerous postwar films noirs, for example), the Hollywood Renaissance films repeatedly used an aggressive, non-classical style. The beginning of *Easy Rider* features non-continuity editing (scenes are begun in close-up without an establishing shot to identify the location and content of individual shots) and narrative events which reference the thematics of modernism. As Captain America (Fonda) rides his motorcycle off into the American Southwest to discover himself anew, he throws his watch into the sand, breaking it. This image of a broken watch signifying the end of traditional life was, of course, central to Quentin's narration in the second chapter of William Faulkner's *The Sound and the Fury* (1929), one of the iconic works of American modernist literature.

On the other hand, the economics of the Hollywood Renaissance films were driven by a niche marketing that was not necessarily tied to radical politics. Thus, *Easy Rider* could be marketed toward the counterculture without actually endorsing countercultural values. The first place the two motorcycle riders stop in their epic quest eastward (generically, against the grain of the American Western, traveling, as they do, on motorcycles rather than horses and going east rather than west) is at a countercultural commune. Hopper's character observes that the young men and women have no idea what they are doing, planting seeds in fallow sand, without water. As our heroes leave the commune, it is quite clear that their rebellion against mainstream America is doomed to failure. The end of the film reiterates this failure, when both of our heroes are murdered by rednecks after leaving New Orleans, their final destination. The Hollywood Renaissance films were thus aesthetically innovative but thematically similar to their 1950s and early 1960s classical counterparts, vilifying the idea of social protest while rejecting conventional lifestyles.

This is the point of Steve Neale's essay, "New Hollywood Cinema," which asks the provocative question, "What's 'new' about the New Hollywood?"[8] Neale's answer is the one that my analysis of *Easy Rider* has led to: aesthetic newness tempered by ideological continuity with Hollywood conservatism. This formulation can be repeated across many of the masterpieces of the Hollywood Renaissance. Formally, it is hard to find a more visually aggressive Hollywood film than *The Graduate* (Mike Nichols, 1967). A niche-marketed film attempting to appeal to the youth culture, the film features Benjamin Braddock (Dustin Hoffman), who returns to his upper-middle-class parents in Los Angeles, having succeeded in a fine, East Coast university. He arrives completely alienated, uncertain what he wants to make of his life. With nothing else to do, he lashes out against his parents' generation by sleeping with his parents' friend, Mrs. Robinson (Anne Bancroft).

The film's first act, devoted to this affair, is filled with formal innovations. Benjamin's alienation is represented by shooting him through the fish tank in his room, associating him with the imprisoned fish in the tank. At the first turning point of the film, Benjamin is forced to tell his new girlfriend, Elaine (Katharine Ross), of his now-ended affair with her mother. A beautiful focus pull allows Elaine's face gradually to come into focus as she realizes that the older woman with whom Ben confessed to having an affair was not just any woman, but in fact her own mother. As Elaine kicks Benjamin out of her bedroom, a zoom shot with a wide angle lens mounted on the camera produces an exquisite shot of alienation. As Mrs. Robinson says goodbye to Benjamin, we are presented with one of the oddest over-the-shoulder two-shots in Hollywood history. The space between Benjamin and Mrs. Robinson is grossly exaggerated by the remarkable use of the wide angle lens.

However, for all of its stylistic aggressiveness, *The Graduate* remains a relatively conventional Hollywood melodrama. The application of three-act structure to the love story is as simple as it gets: boy meets girl, boy loses girl, and boy gets girl back. This is the basic structure of *The Graduate*, and indeed any Hollywood romance. In these terms, the ending of the film, in which Ben rescues Elaine from marrying Carl, a fraternity boy chosen by her parents because he is not Ben, is remarkably conventional. Ben and Elaine run from the church and board a bus headed for parts unknown. As they sit in the back row, they are presented in two-shot, staring directly ahead. The film presents this moment ironically, getting us to question the happy ending. The shot lasts too long, almost two minutes, and we gradually see the smiles on their faces drain away as they realize they have nothing to say to one another. Then, the soundtrack presents "The Sound of Silence," the Simon and Garfunkel song that during the first act of the film was associated with the depravity and alienation of the Mrs. Robinson affair. The film thus suggests that there is no hope of Benjamin rebelling against his parents' generation, that his choice of Elaine has in fact sealed his fate, doomed to live a life exactly like his parents'. Here, as in *Easy Rider*, the possibility of the radical reinvention of the American experience is teasingly presented, but then viciously and conservatively denied.

More importantly, the basic visual structure of *The Graduate* produces this moment as inevitable closure. The first shot of the film is a zoom out from Ben's head resting against a white pillow on his airplane ride home to California. In the next sequence, he crowds the right-hand side of the widescreen image as he rides the people mover at the airport on his way to collect his luggage. This leaves room for the credits on the left-hand side of the image, but also forms the thematic motif of the film: what will fill the other half of the space Ben inhabits? The last shot of the film answers this ideological and structural question: Elaine will. In no uncertain terms, *The Graduate*, for all of its visual inventiveness, closes back upon itself with the most basic, conservative gesture: boy will be man when girl becomes woman, and they will live their lives together.

While one could focus on any number of niche market sectors of the Hollywood Renaissance, perhaps the most distinctive is the blaxploitation film of the early 1970s. With the release of *The Learning Tree* (Gordon Parks, Sr., 1969), Hollywood, after almost a century of direct discrimination against African Americans, finally allowed a major studio film directed by a black man. In the wake of this, a cycle of films intended to appeal to urban audiences developed. The most interesting, *Shaft* (Gordon Parks, Sr., 1971) and *Superfly* (Gordon Parks, Jr., 1972), represented a reinvestment in the thematics of the film noir, redirected toward black Americans. This was both a crass marketing ploy (*Shaft* could be interpreted as merely 1941's *The Maltese Falcon* with a black private detective), and a means of providing for a more radical critique of the Hollywood representational tradition. *Blacula* (William Crain, 1972), for example, begins with a wonderful scene sequence in which vampirism is associated with the traumatic global history of slavery: a white slave trader dines with an African prince, but then lusts after the prince's wife. As he is betrayed by the white slaver, and entombed and left to die, the black man vows to avenge the evils of slavery across time. He does so by coming back to 1970s America as a vampire. However, the rest of *Blacula* features a straightforward and uninteresting telling of the Dracula mythology, ending with a standard exploitation scene in which Blacula's face is rotted by the rays of the sun, his eye sockets filled with maggots.

It would rest with filmmakers outside of the Hollywood system to make truly radical genre films. In contrast with *Blacula*, Bill Gunn's vampire film, *Ganja and Hess* (1973), is a radical story of an upper-class black man whose vampirism requires him to prey upon the black underclass in Harlem. Gunn had secured the money from Kelly and Jordan, a fringe Hollywood production company, on the promise of delivering a blaxploitation film. In fact he delivered a radical, modernist critique of the vampire genre. Kelly and Jordan recut the film and released it as *Blood Couple* to the drive-in movie market. However, Gunn kept an unbutchered print of *Ganja and Hess*, and deposited it in the Museum of Modern Art's film library, assuring that the film would continue to be available in its original form.

No filmmaker's story better expresses the ideological shortcomings of the Hollywood Renaissance than that of Melvin Van Peebles. Trained in the theatre, Van Peebles fled America in the 1960s, training as a filmmaker in France, releasing a highly regarded, French New Wave-influenced, character drama, *Story of a Three Day Pass* (1968). He was lured back to Hollywood by Columbia Pictures, to make a race comedy, *Watermelon Man* (1970). The film turned out to be too radical, and Van Peebles was restrained from doing what he wanted with his film, about a white man played in whiteface by a black actor, Godfrey Cambridge, who, at the film's first turning point, is turned black by the comic malfunctioning of his tanning bed. In the first act of the film, Jeff is indifferent to the Civil Rights Movement. However, after he turns black, he is confronted with the tangible effects of racism, finally losing his job as an insurance salesman because he discovers the company is bilking black people, and ending the film as a comic black militant, training as a revolutionary who uses a mop as a spear.

Discouraged by the Hollywood production process, Van Peebles decided to make his next film, a deconstruction of the Hollywood Western, *Sweet Sweetback's Baaadasssss Song* (1971), with independent financing. In this way, Van Peebles succeeded in producing the cinematic equivalent of such radical black literature as Ishmael Reed's *Yellow Back Radio Broke Down*. Despite the influx of African American talent into Hollywood during the Hollywood Renaissance, the truly radical work continued to be made outside the confines of the mainstream American film industry located in Hollywood.

Whatever the failures of the Hollywood Renaissance, a new idiom in American cinema had developed in the last half of the 1960s and the early 1970s. A new generation of filmmakers were making films critical of the traditional Hollywood generic view of America. Revisionist films were produced across the genres: Sam Peckinpah's *The Wild Bunch* (1968) asked questions about the nature of violence by placing the gunfight at the beginning of the film while *Little Big Man* (Arthur Penn, 1970) questioned classical Hollywood's depictions of Native Americans. By 1973, the force of the Hollywood Renaissance began to shift. *The Exorcist* (1973) was partly a meditation on the nature of religion in America, and partly a spectacular horror film in which a little girl projectile-vomited and twisted her head around in astonishing images. *The Godfather* (1974) also offered a conventional return to the gangster film, yet on an epic scale.

However, it was not until the summer 1975 release of *Jaws* that it became clear that the Hollywood Renaissance was dead. A film that came in frighteningly over-budget for minor studio Universal, *Jaws* made over $100 million during its first release. This huge profit placed Universal among the most profitable of the Hollywood film studios, and as a result of a long-term deal with blockbuster filmmaker Steven Spielberg, is now among the biggest and most financially stable studios in the New Hollywood.

Jaws, while wonderfully constructed, both narratively and aesthetically, represented a sea change in the films of the Hollywood Renaissance period. While a clear Watergate allegory – Chief Brody keeps the beaches open after the mayor claims that the island's economy will collapse, resulting in the needless death of a little boy – the film's pessimism is contained in its first act. The resulting two acts of the film are about Chief Brody recovering from his mistake and getting the job done. As Saigon was falling to the Viet Cong in the summer of 1975, Chief Brody caused millions of young people to return to the movie theatre and watch him eliminate the threat to the American ship of state.

The resulting films, the third period of the New Hollywood, would be taken over by filmmakers from the same generation as those of the Hollywood Renaissance, but Spielberg and George Lucas would rebel against the cultural critique of the earlier films. The summer success of Lucas's *Star Wars: A New Hope* (1977) is the crucial example. While a film like *Annie Hall* (Woody Allen, 1977) suggests the impossibility of intimate contact between two people, *Star Wars* builds an allegory about American values triumphing over the evil Empire. Lucas's film skips back across the Hollywood Renaissance and the social turbulence of the 1960s to classical Hollywood itself. *Star Wars* is based on the films of Lucas's youth, from an America which saw itself as morally just and able to believe in its heroes. Thus, simplistic movie serials (*Flash Gordon* and *Buck Rogers*, in particular) are emphasized, and the morally ambiguous Hollywood films (1956's

The Searchers) that it references are stripped of their content and used merely for plot points: the first turning point of *The Searchers*, when Martin discovers his aunt massacred, is replicated when Luke discovers his aunt and uncle massacred.

The success of *Star Wars* fundamentally changed Hollywood filmmaking at the aesthetic and narrative level but, in terms of the industry, merely returned the business toward the production of big-budget, mass audience blockbusters. While minor political shifts – the difference between Reaganite conservatism and Clintonite centrism – are of some importance, what is more crucial is the basic return of the industry to a blockbuster mode. Spielberg and Lucas would collaborate on the Indiana Jones movies throughout the 1980s, producing another trilogy of blockbusters based on the simplistic movie serials of their youth. Their protégés would follow suit, one example being Robert Zemeckis' successful trilogy at Universal, the *Back to the Future* series.

Back to the Future (1985) is an important film for establishing the clear Reaganite values of 1980s cinema as expressed in Hollywood's return to mass-market blockbusters. The film concerns Marty McFly (Michael J. Fox), a teenager living in a lower-middle-class household in suburbia. His father is a wimp, bullied around by his boss. Marty enters a time machine, which takes him back to 1955, to witness his parents' courtship. At the film's first turning point, he accidentally prevents his parents meeting and thus endangers his future existence. He spends the rest of the film fixing this, finally succeeding at the "Enchantment Under the Sea" dance which forms the climax of Act III. There, he plays rock and roll music on his guitar while, out on the dance floor, his future mother and father kiss and fall in love. With Marty's help, his father learns to stand up to his future boss. When Marty returns to 1985, his family now lives in Reaganite, yuppie opulence, far from the drudgery he left at the beginning of the film. The "there's no place like home" ideology of classical Hollywood, particularly *The Wizard of Oz*, is hereby given a remarkable, bootstraps Reaganite twist.

To add insult to injury, the music Marty plays is the classic rock from the 1950s. While out on stage, Chuck Berry's cousin hears Marty playing, and calls his cousin on the phone, telling him that he has found the new sound they need. In an absurd redefinition of the racial history of American popular music, Marty the white kid teaches Chuck Berry how to make blues-influenced black rock and roll music! The story of Elvis making radical black music palatable for white America is thus turned on its ear in a white supremacist fantasy of creativity. In this way, contemporary Hollywood blockbusters provide ideological fantasy resolutions of real-world complex problems.

Contemporary Hollywood cinema is the heir to what Robin Wood calls "the Lucas–Spielberg Syndrome."[9] While Spielberg has graduated into a more mature filmmaker interested in social trauma – *Schindler's List* (1993) and *Amistad* (1997) – much of contemporary Hollywood cinema is released in the summer with the expectation that things blowing up will reassure a troubled nation. Every summer, films are released by each studio with the intention of making over $100 million and thus keeping the studio in business for another year. A good number of these films succeed in this goal because they resonate with enough people: *Independence Day* (Roland Emmerich, 1996), *Spider-Man* (Sam Raimi, 2002), and the new *Star Wars* trilogy are three cases in point.

Some blockbusters vary the reductive formula in remarkable ways. When James Cameron needed the resources of not one major Hollywood studio but two to realize his epic retelling of the Titanic tragedy, his film's $200 million budget was ridiculed as unreasonable. Yet Cameron's gamble paid off. *Titanic* (1997) is a remarkable blockbuster, reliant not on the male *bildungsroman* motif of almost all other blockbusters (*Star Wars*, 1988's *Batman*, etc.), but instead on the building of a young girl's adulthood. While films like *Rocky* (1977) and *Star Wars* were famous for their thousands of repeat male teenage viewers, *Titanic* was a sensation among teenage girls. No blockbuster has followed in this tradition, but the phenomenal success of *Titanic* indicates that the third New Hollywood formula is generic, but not completely predictable.

The other principle effect of Lucas's consolidation of the New Hollywood blockbuster period lies in the development of special effects research, innovation, and diffusion. When Lucas made *Star Wars* at 20th Century Fox, special effects work had not appreciably advanced since the 1950s. Much of the work on the film was like George Pal movies in the 1950s, and *2001* in the late 1960s was based on miniature model work, Claymation, and other standard practices. In an astonishingly bad business deal, 20th Century Fox signed over the toy merchandizing rights for *Star Wars* to Lucas himself. The phenomenal, unprecedented success of *Star Wars* merchandizing made Lucas one of the major financial players in Hollywood, and indeed intensified Hollywood's overall financial interest in "franchise" movies, capable of supporting multi-industry advertising campaigns, ranging from book and music tie-ins, to toys, all the way to fast food meals, fabrics, and theme park rides.

With the toy profits, Lucas built a special effects house, Industrial Light and Magic (ILM), which became the state of the art facility for making special effects part of standard practice in the creating of high budget Hollywood films. While other such houses have sprouted around the world over the past twenty years, many of them started and/or staffed by Lucas alumni, ILM continues to be a major player in special effects work in Hollywood.

The resulting technology, particularly CGI (computer generated images), has provided one of the most important technological shifts in the history of Hollywood since the coming of sound. Computers now allow for the quick and cheap production of epic crowd scenes (like those in 2000's *Gladiator*, for example) that in the days of classical Hollywood (for example, 1959's *Ben-Hur*) would have required thousands of extras. Hollywood films have become so reliant on computer technology that entire films can be produced without actors, as can be seen in a film like *Final Fantasy: The Spirits Within* (2001).

The most profitable effect of CGI technology has been in the field of animation. Walt Disney in the 1930s classical Hollywood studio system was an anomaly: he ran a production-only studio which released its animated features through RKO. The Disney Corporation re-emerged in the early 1990s as a major player in Hollywood because of its expertise in feature-length animation, largely as a result of the success of *Beauty and the Beast* (1991). Because these films blended a deft mix of material of interest to young children and their parents, Disney became among the most financially profitable studios in contemporary Hollywood. This is a long way from their classical Hollywood status as a production-only studio.

CGI, however, by the late 1990s, became a technology that effectively rendered obsolete the hand-drawn animated feature. Pioneered by a small California company, Pixar, computer animation is now the standard practice for the generation of these highly profitable animated features. Most major studios have a feature animation unit, Fox, for example, producing the successful film, *Ice Age* (Chris Wedge, 2002). Disney, seeing the writing on the wall, bought up Pixar, and even though it has recently dissolved that merger, has also shifted exclusively to computer-generated animation.

Disney's ability to buy up Pixar leads to another observation about the long-term history of the Hollywood film industry. Under the weight of Reaganite deregulation, the major effect of the Paramount decree – the divorce of production–distribution from exhibition – has largely been eroded. Most major Hollywood studios today are both vertically and horizontally integrated, part of large international conglomerates that have synergistic control over many facets of the media business, ranging from video games and films to books and music. Disney is part of Capital Cities/ABC, thus having vertically integrated control to produce, distribute, and exhibit media content.

The great success story regarding this facet of the industry is the conglomerate now called Time-Warner/AOL. This is the parent company of Home Box Office, a pay-cable television channel begun in 1971. Under the lax restrictions associated with Reaganite deregulation, HBO was able to become a major financier of Hollywood films, having a ready-made exhibition venue that is its base pay-cable service. For a while, Fox chair Rupert Murdoch worried that HBO would swallow Hollywood whole. Cameron needed $200 million to produce *Titanic*, a burden that was too large for one studio to shoulder, but HBO generates about $300 million in cash each month (30 million subscribers paying roughly $10 per month). HBO now not only has its hands in much Hollywood film financing, it also produces financially successful and critically acclaimed original television programming (shows like *The Sopranos* and *Sex and the City*).

In short, for all its historical variability over its almost 100-year history, Hollywood has proven remarkably resistant to threatening change. Continuity editing and three-act structure narrative serve as the base of American media content, the prime producer of which is a small artists' colony in southern California. The global reach of Hollywood's distribution network is breathtaking. Action film blockbusters tend to earn even more in international markets than in North America. Thus, the future of Hollywood as America's premier export seems assured, which means that the ideological shortcomings of the system will be with us for quite some time.

NOTES

1. Kristin Thompson and David Bordwell, *Film History: An Introduction*, 2nd ed. (Boston: McGraw-Hill, 2003), p. 42.
2. David A. Cook, *A History of Narrative Film*, 4th ed. (New York and London: W. W. Norton, 2004), p. 78.
3. Janet Staiger, "Standardization and Differentiation: The Reinforcement and Dispersion of Hollywood's Practices," in David Bordwell, Janet Staiger, and Kristin Thompson, *The Classical Hollywood Cinema: Film Style and Mode of Production to 1960* (New York: Columbia University Press, 1985), pp. 96–112.
4. Douglas Gomery, "Failed Opportunities: The Integration of the U.S. Motion Picture and Television Industries," *Quarterly Review of Film Studies* (Summer 1984): 219–28.
5. Linda Seger, *Making a Good Script Great* (Hollywood: Samuel French, 1987).
6. Catherine Russell, *Narrative Mortality: Death, Closure, and New Wave Cinemas* (Minneapolis and London: University of Minnesota Press, 1995).
7. Thomas Schatz, "The New Hollywood," in Jim Collins, Hilary Radner, and Ava Preacher Collins (eds.), *Film Theory Goes to the Movies* (New York: Routledge, 1993), pp. 8–36.

8. Steve Neale, "New Hollywood Cinema," *Screen*, 17,2 (Summer 1976): 117–22.
9. Robin Wood, "Papering the Cracks: Fantasy and Ideology in the Reagan Era," *Hollywood From Vietnam to Reagan* (New York: Columbia University Press, 1986), p. 162.

FUTHER READING

Tino Balio (ed.), *Hollywood in the Age of Television*, Boston: Unwin Hyman, 1990.

Donald Bogle, *Toms, Coons, Mulattoes, Mammies, and Bucks: An Interpretive History of Blacks in American Films*, rev. ed., New York: Continuum, 1989.

Alexander Doty, *Flaming Classics: Queering the Film Canon*, New York and London: Routledge, 2000.

Thomas Elsaesser and Warren Buckland, *Studying Contemporary American Film: A Guide to Movie Analysis*, London: Arnold, 2002.

Douglas Gomery, *The Hollywood Studio System*, New York: St. Martin's Press, 1986.

Shared Pleasures: A History of Movie Presentation in the United States, Madison: University of Wisconsin Press, 1992.

John E. O'Connor and Martin A. Jackson (eds.), *American History/American Film: Interpreting the Hollywood Image*, New York: Continuum, 1988.

Andrew Sarris, *The American Cinema: Directors and Directions, 1929–1968*, Chicago: University of Chicago Press, 1968.

Robert Sklar, *Movie-Made America: A Cultural History of American Movies*, rev. ed., New York: Vintage, 1994.

Janet Staiger, *Interpreting Films: Studies in the Historical Reception of American Cinema*, Princeton: Princeton University Press, 1992.

Janet Wasko, *Hollywood in the Information Age*, Austin: University of Texas Press, 1994.

20

PAUL BUHLE

Popular culture

Deep background

The origins of American popular culture can be traced back to a centuries' old hybridization with deeply racist overtones made clearest in the minstrel show, and a socially constructed "frontier" consisting of pioneers, wild Indians, bad men, and two-fisted (or two-gun) heroes. The innovative center of modern American popular culture emerged, most significantly, during the last two decades of the nineteenth century. Extensive immigration and urbanization, along with technological and market breakthroughs, suddenly prompted a multifaceted mass culture where tens of thousands and then hundreds of thousands and more could simultaneously enjoy the same newly minted music (definitely including dance), literature, vaudeville, and then film; likewise assorted items packaged for the emerging consumer, from California fruit to bicycles and even "vacations."

Key newer sources of popular culture were rooted in the cultures of those who used English as a second language, and for good reasons. Among Jews especially, but also other groups, the most secular and socialistic-minded segment of the respective populations abjured the raw prejudices of older white America, on race issues in particular. Locked out of most existing business opportunities, newer immigrants by the thousands also rushed to embrace the burgeoning culture industry. There, within the evolving tastes and markets that the outsiders studied and learned how to shape, lay both the entepreneurial genius and the performative talent of impresarios, musicians, actors, athletes, and so on.

The breakthroughs in commercial literature's "pulp" paperback and periodical had come earlier and from more traditional American (or Yankee) sources. The detective novel and the Western had grown up alongside the weekly "story" tabloid and encouraged a commercial lithography that gave the magazine of the late nineteenth century a vibrancy as well as a circulation previously lacking. It also gave steady work to the growing ranks of popular artists no longer reliant upon selling their oil portraits of nature scenes and prominent individuals.

If the "foreigner" of popular literature tended to be the source of a dark conspiracy, the readership of the emerging yellow press, especially of the comic strip first appearing in 1896, was overwhelmingly immigrant. As with silent film, the need to convey meaning without much use of English (or any other language) began here, in a corner of the mainstream, and then spread rapidly with technological and market possibilities.

The German-American tavern, so unlike the American bar, had fostered an atmosphere during the 1860s–90s in which families would gather to hear all manner of entertainment. Its patrons could not compare to the crowds at vaudeville theaters, but these ethnic spaces made a unique and enduring contribution. Here, audiences listened, over beer and a generalized *gemutlicheit*, to social criticisms aimed not, as in vaudeville, at ethnic stereotypes, but at "American" cultural backwardness and myopia. This was, in a sense, the avant-garde set within styles of modernizing popular culture, with its "freethinkers" and radicals looking ahead to a different possible future.

Yiddish language culture and the underlying heritage of *Yiddishkayt* (diasporic Jewishness), contributed vastly more. Yiddish itself was conglomerate (its Jewish critics called it "mongrel") middle high German with admixtures of Hebrew, French, Slavic, and, increasingly, English. Its speakers and its readers (for centuries most of the latter were women, since Hebrew was the proper text of religious intellectuals), in the midst of the collapsing social infrastructure of the mid-nineteenth century, offered a perfect milieu for adaptation. Not by accident were traveling "gypsy" orchestras for the most part Jewish, while most of the leading producers of Hollywood film by the 1930s had been born within a few hundred miles of each other in the East European Jewish Pale.

Impoverished Jews from the Pale, landing in New York in large numbers during the 1890s, were preceded by smaller waves of German Jews, creating an important contrast and rivalry. Successful German-Jewish merchants, devoted to high culture, founded the Julliard School as well as the Ethical Culture Society, and swiftly acquired the *New York Times*, a flagship of propriety. Scornful of their eastern European cousins as uneducated and uncouth, they could not easily appreciate that the absence of a background of high culture disguised a vast potential strength of folk culture.

Here lay the sources of multiple innovations. Within the Yiddish world proper, a new kind of short fiction about city life was rapidly invented, no longer typified by sentimental clichés of seduced virgins but characterized by near-realist depictions of tenement life borrowed, in no small part, from the sophisticated European model of Zola. Rebellious dramas about gender, even Ibsen productions set down in the United States for the first time, were seen in Yiddish versions decades before uptown English-language versions. Lower East Side audiences who knew little English meanwhile watched early films, some of them shown on sheets draped over clotheslines in courtyards, humble precursors of the movie palaces to follow.

Eastern European Jews raced into vernacular zones that German Jews had inadvertently prepared for them, most obviously in music. The German-American Witmark family had been in the United States for several generations, but succeeded spectacularly with the sheet music business burgeoning in the 1880s–90s. Gus Kahn, arriving in Chicago in 1892, became Al Jolson's favorite lyricist, devising vaudeville standards like "Yes, Sir, That's My Baby," "Carolina in the Morning," and, later, the score for Eddie Cantor's show *Whoopee*. Immigrant Jewish lyricists and music vendors were also perfectly capable of goyishe (Gentile) nostalgia pieces like "Waitin' for the Robert E. Lee" or "School Days" (or the official Indiana state song, "By the Banks of the Wabash, Far Away").

Their contribution might also be seen as preparing an early approach to vernacular modernism. The Witmarks had turned out demeaning minstrel melodies but responded quickly to the first of the black popular composers reaching Tin Pan Alley. They introduce the Cakewalk to audiences growing weary of "mother" songs. More importantly, they helped introduce the music exciting the big city adolescent of the new century in the dance steps that held the promise of liberated or at least more overt heterosexuality.

The subsequent "dance craze" might be contrasted usefully to the bicycle craze of the previous decade. The latter, rooted in the largely middle-class ownership of early models and (at least in printed images) the streets of small towns and country lanes rather than big city traffic, signaled among other things the "New Woman" and the new mass culture of organized leisure. The bicycle was a possession in ways that the automobile would become for its first two decades of mass production. It offered evidence of worldly success for more or less ordinary people in ways that commoners in the rest of the world could only envy. The dancer, by contrast, owned nothing but her (and his) own body. The new intimate dancing, associated in the popular mind with urban saloons, hinted strongly at a sexualized physical contact that had previously stigmatized the sinning man and fallen woman.

The dance hall, like jazz, was unquestionably associated closely with the "liquor interests." By 1901, four-fifths of such halls stood next to saloons, and the financial basis of their success was inevitably the sale of alcohol, with dance space and music, free or at low cost, the lure that made profit possible. Ethnic social clubs, lodges of long-standing, and even labor union headquarters took on new functions, so great was the demand. By the

1910s, large commercial halls sprang up, elaborate dance palaces preparing the way for the movie palaces of the 1920s. Here, for a few hours at least, the masses of young working people enjoyed a certain splendor, however vicarious, escaping the reality of office boredom, factory drudgery, and the inevitable trials of domestic life ahead.

Heterosocial advance, race, and class

Behavior within and outside the halls fostered manners and morals crucial to the evolution of modern popular culture. Women and men meeting without chaperones and often for the first time, smoking cigarettes, hugging, "stealing" kisses while squeezing each other on and off the dance floor, even exchanging ribald phrases, made a mockery of the waltz culture of the previous generation. An exaggerated propriety was replaced by an exaggerated intimacy. Dances were accompanied by shouting, singing along, dipping, and shaking. To win male attention, women dressed themselves provocatively and sometimes outlandishly (as in male attire), drank liquor, and readied themselves for other activities.

The contrast between the public park behavior of the middle classes and working classes, widely noted by historians, held special significance. Created as an urban pastoral (at least an imitation pastoral) by the gentility, intended to preserve nature and promote healthy exercise, the parks were seized upon by working people as sites to play sports, take picnics – and have sexual encounters. Living at home, the young had few alternatives. "Petting in the Park," visually realized as a dance number in Busby Berkeley's musical spectacular *Golddiggers of 1933*, was by that time a generation established. The rules for the dance hall also held for the spectacular entertainment zones, above all Coney Island, where the chance meeting, the ride on the Ferris wheel or tunnel of love, had a similar framing and possible conclusion.

As the emerging commercial mass culture blurred the distinctions between reality and the fantasy of romance, traditional boundaries of various kinds were eroded. Like their middle-class counterparts, young working adults born into the families of the urban poor advanced, not necessarily to happier or more democratic futures, but definitely to more heterosocial ones. Despite financial constraints, there was evidence of a new measure of personal freedom.

The displacement of African American culture, both symbolic and real, played an undeniable role in the process. Not until the middle 1910s at the earliest would sufficient concentration of black Americans outside the South – in Harlem – make a leap into modernity possible. Suddenly, the neighborhood

named for the city's vanished ethnic origins would become the black metropolis for the black population, from Africa to the Caribbean. As minstrelsy fell
away (or seemed to fall away, for the white pleasure at commercial black
buffoonery would never vanish), new and more complicated forms of interracial cultural connections emerged. Bert Williams, Afro-Caribbean, born in
the tiny Antigua, starred in his own creations on Broadway, toured Europe to
sing and dance for royalty, triumphed in the Ziegfeld Follies (itself a gaudy
imitation of risqué Parisian "follies"), made several films, and died almost
literally on stage in 1922. His signature song, "Nobody" (later performed on
film by a white singer, with a black one behind him, mimicking gesture for
gesture), might be said to have explored the real shadow behind large phases
of modern American culture.

It would be impossible, of course, to exaggerate the role of jazz in this
process. The influence of New Orleans, an urban version of the plantation
society stretching southward into the Caribbean and Latin America with
distinctly different tastes and mores from the rest of North America, was
fundamental. Here, the crucial mixture of races and cultures developed into
a musical form which came north and made possible the breakthrough
jazz records mostly, if by no means entirely, by white imitators. Louis
Armstrong, a counterpart to Bert Williams but successful in managing and
surviving in his own realm, pioneered the solo and thus made possible so
many other soloists.

It would also be difficult to exaggerate related matters, enormously
positive for popular culture at large if also negative in certain respects.
The bitter disillusionment in American society following the First World
War, along with the disappearance of the popular mass-based radical causes
of the 1910s such as socialism, feminism, and industrial unionism, gave the
Jazz Age the underlying rationale for its rebellious, anti-Puritanical tem-
perament. Not until the 1970s would society see its like again, and for
similar reasons: official society had been discredited, but alternatives vanished; only personal life remained, with restraints ripe to be overthrown.
The illegal liquor industry – with the demimonde of colorful characters,
charismatic brutes, swinging singles (including prostitutes both amateur
and professional), now swelled with bootleggers and the syndicated pro-
fessionalization of organized crime – naturally became a major driving
force in musical entertainment and public culture of all kinds, from sports
to politics.

Large numbers of listeners to the phonograph and radio, populations
growing wildly during the 1920s, could take in the ambience while experiencing only the vicarious sensation of danger, violence, and interracial
contact. Bandleader Paul Whiteman famously promised to "make jazz into

a lady," stripping off its disreputable past. A decade later, swing, less an appropriation than a conglomerate form, brought newer dance styles and promoted a growing mutual sympathy among young people across racial lines. The rise of African American bandleaders like Count Basie and Duke Ellington hinted at the rapid changes further ahead. Still, any advance remained uncertain so long as the underlying race rules informally limiting personal contact between the sexes (while legally outlawing intermarriage) remained in effect.

Some of the most dire implications of American racism were on display in the admired cinema of the age, from *Birth of a Nation* and *The Jazz Singer* to *Gone With the Wind*, those phenomenally popular films that reinforced popular views of African Americans as childlike creatures whose culture could best be interpreted through the fake-sentimental mocking white gestures of an Al Jolson in blackface, but whose patent non-rationality remained somehow a danger to civilization. *Rhapsody in Blue*, a 1945 Hollywood "biopic" about composer George Gershwin, was typical of the kinder gestures. It managed to make black music "acceptable" by accommodating it to European forms. Therein lay, as well, the greatest weakness of American film in its early golden ages, silent or sound. It could not (and thanks to censorship, was not permitted to) breach the racial barrier meaningfully until the later 1940s when the boldest advocates of African American dignity on film were soon to be blacklisted for left-wing political beliefs or past personal associations.

Still, film was in many respects the most democratic of arts as well as the most engaging. More than any other, first foreshadowing network radio and then television, it was a genuinely new form of entertainment culture, distinct from theatre, the novel, religious or secular painting, and sport, but in some sense a combination of all these. Reproduced with great technical skill for an audience watching in a dreamlike state of near-total immersion, Hollywood's products could not help making a deep impression upon popular culture, and not only in the United States. Washington and the vast economic machine, reinforced by military forces, actually ruled; but for the peoples of the world, Hollywood *was* America.

Here again, the Jewish influence proved crucial, even when acknowledged only under duress. Jews, working in dozens of ways behind the camera unintentionally reinforced the anti-Semitic impression of political conservatives that the corrupting influence of Hollywood upon American youth was a result of some special Jewish taint. This charge was somewhat true in a different sense, for the influential writers and directors who came west from New York brought with them both sexual sophistication and a liberal or left-wing leaning, the latter reinforced as studio employees struggled to build unions and as the situation of European Jewry dramatically worsened. To the limited degree that controversial themes were permitted in films, the Jewish artist/intellectual had made possible a breakthrough toward a humane cinema.

Women, of course, were virtually nowhere in control of film production, even their relatively high numbers as "titlists" of silent films being reduced to near zero with the arrival of sound films and detailed scripts. Yet, from the first blossoming of Hollywood, they possessed a unique on-screen presence, and not only because of male viewers' projected fantasies. Women went to films in large numbers and were the prinicipal readers of film magazines. They responded in particular to romances. "Kiss me like in the movies" became a popular phrase of the 1920s, and on-screen kisses were liable to prompt off-screen ones. Censorship boards, established early, before 1920, and mostly at the behest of conservative Catholic and Protestant critics, managed intermittently to suppress overt sexual expression and language, inevitably encouraging the subtle sexual suggestiveness that became a fine cinematic art. The suppression of crime and violence, never so vigorous, merely prevented on-screen bloodshed.

Yet women's themes, not only physical desirability and material comfort but also a personal struggle for self-definition, were more overt than in any other sector of American (and perhaps global) culture. For every Joan Crawford or Katharine Hepburn there were scores of dumb blondes (or brunettes), clothes-horse fashion models and (especially before 1934) sluttish girls-gone-bad. But the presence of formidable role models, from sophisticated comedy (by and large, the closest Hollywood films were to come to high culture, by way of adaptations from Broadway hits) to crime to costume drama, had a significant impact.

Nor were women the only outsiders to be placed at center stage. The gangster film so popular in the early 1930s offered a case in point, almost an on-screen revenge for the damage done by official society to the lives of ordinary people. The horror film, with émigré technicians adapting Weimar cinematic weirdness to Hollywood scale, featured characters like Boris Karloff's "Frankenstein" monster, created from human parts, despised and attacked by an uncomprehending and unforgiving mob; or his constant counterpart of the 1930s, Bela Lugosi, the vampire with the saddest eyes in the cinema. Perhaps it was fated that those other outsiders, proletarians like Abbott and Costello, should in a decade's time satirize the monster film so effectively, re-enacting in comic form the public fears that had suddenly grown insignificant in the face of global horror.

The social effects of the Depression and then war also gave the ordinary guy (less often girl) a significance that cinematic populism exalted. New

Dealish sentiments were evinced and extended leftward, with Paul Muni, Gary Cooper, or James Stewart as heroic exemplars of outraged decency at the social effects of unemployment and, however belatedly, the threat of fascism. Whatever their personal beliefs, Muni was seen as the man on the run (*I Am a Fugitive from a Chain Gang*), Cooper the naïf (in *Meet John Doe*) who learns he has been duped by American fascists, Stewart the savings bank manager (in *It's a Wonderful Life*) who will give up everything to save his little town from the clutches of the mighty. Even Humphrey Bogart, the apparently hardened existentialist, gave up romance in *Casablanca* in the name of the global anti-fascist cause; or led his racially integrated tank-crew of *Sahara* across the African desert, heroically determined to save the day.

Something else important had taken place, almost unseen east of Los Angeles. Hollywood had through the war years retained an oligopoly from the production angle, but an unsteady one. Important studios barely survived the early Depression; "Poverty Row" small production facilities briefly flourished – but often went under just as quickly. The dream of production by independent minded producers and prestigious stars actually grew, and efforts at autonomous production (or semi-autonomous units within studios) produced a few brilliant moments such as *Citizen Kane* (1940), along with genre box office successes in family films and Westerns. Visions of "workers control" (rarely described as such), the nearest that socialistic ideas ever approached American workplace culture, seemed to take hold in the glory years of industrial unionism and even within the film capital as film moguls appeared more and more the useless appendages of eastern bankers. Mob elements, the only permitted union leaders of Hollywood until the 1940s, kept the industry workforce in line, but against increased resistance. To the optimistically inclined, anything could happen, even something as seemingly unlikely as a commercial genre of documentaries, where social rebels made themselves particularly prominent working in various capacities on widely hailed films like *The Spanish Earth, The Plow That Broke the Plains, The River* and *The City.*

Network radio, in stark contrast, quickly became a near-complete oligopoly transmitting homogeneous programming. The networks swamped local stations in audience reach, and the advertisers (operating through agencies) thereafter effectively decided upon content. Sports and, later, the Second World War offered the potential for high points of effective and popular news coverage. Light comedy borrowed from vaudeville, "white" jazz, radio versions of popular films and drama series, such as *Cavalcade of America* and *Theater Guild of the Air*, meanwhile held top spots along with crime-action series for young and old alike. The radio precursor of what would become the television situation comedy ("sitcom") may have been a unique contribution of American radio, because of the marshalling of writing and acting talent, effectively drawing upon ethnic talent (*The Goldbergs* featuring Gertude Berg) or exhibiting the particular strengths of distinctly American characters (the single working woman of schoolteacher *Our Miss Brooks*), or exhibiting the wisecracking comedian as social commentator (Jack Benny, Fred Allen, and George Burns). In this world, African Americans like other racial minorities, remained invisible or worse, the butt of ridicule, as most evidently in the top-rated *Amos 'n Andy*.

The blandness dominant across radio genres, and their painfully bad treatment of race, were echoed in the sorry decline of the daily comic strips as art and as commentary. After promising beginnings of much antic humor, the vivacity of early newspaper strips faded by the late 1920s, displaced by quasi-realistically drawn strips with dubious narratives. Tarzan, Terry and the Pirates, and others introduced new stereotypes as baneful as the old ones, but now often closely related the US global role. People of dusky hues either assisted or plotted against the Aryan heroes in locations from Africa to the Middle East, Asia and the Pacific, while a feline "Dragon Lady" successfully confused the issues. Meanwhile, domesticity reigned on the home front, with former flapper Blondie ruling the household, and a super-human Mammy Yokum in charge of hopeless fellow rednecks. Comic books, rising rapidly into a major publishing industry at the end of the 1930s, caught the publishing industry by surprise with sometimes well-crafted and even humorous art appealing ("all in color for a dime") to a juvenile audience. Sales, however, centered on the superhero – Superman, Batman, and dozens more created by 1940 – as drawn by overwhelmingly Jewish youngsters in sweatshop studios of Greater New York.

The war and after

Wartime, for all its grimness, boosted the role of American popular culture in countless ways. It effectively brought the "teenager" of malt shop fame into existence, as the narrative protagonist of films and radio drama on the home front. It moved rural populations with little money into urban loca-tions with real money, forming the customer base for the small record companies that recorded the likes of Hank Williams and Muddy Waters. It provided both need to escape and means to escape, resulting in the highest levels of film production ever seen, rising steadily from the Depression years to a peak, in 1946, of tickets sold and studio profits. Likewise, it bestowed upon children a vastly enlarged realm of comic book possibilities. Western and war action abounded, along with multitudes of funny animals, notably updated young women's role models, and even "good girls" of science fiction adventures clad only in skimpy shorts and metallic brassieres or in mysterious "jungle cloth," either perpetually threatened by monsters or perfectly capable of defending themselves (and suspiciously weak males) from danger.

Wartime transformed Hollywood, if only temporarily, into a grandly patriotic town in which left-leaning writers could be paid previously unimaginable salaries for turning out action films, achieve heights of artistry with Broadway adaptations, find or create the "conscience" audience for liberal messages, and even thread together black musicals which treated African American performers with dignity. Features like *Sahara* and *Woman of the Year* cast icons like Humphrey Bogart and Katharine Hepburn in a new light, moody exemplars of subtle emotion, while the plebeian taste for Abbott and Costello or even Hopalong Cassidy offered screenwriters rich opportunities to attack the wealthy and redeem the impoverished (even the non-white impoverished). The "Termite Terrace" of Warner Brothers' animators did not invent Rosie the Riveter, but made her a nighttime sex bomb – between shifts of patriotic but also highly skilled war production.

When armed conflict ended, war and its consequences could be seen more realistically in important films like *The Story of G. I. Joe* and *A Walk in the Sun*. Working-class dramas almost never made in the 1930s could now be made portraying film noir existentialists in *Cornered, Act of Violence, The Strange Love of Martha Ivers*, or *Force of Evil*. John Garfield, Alan Ladd, Robert Ryan, or Robert Mitchum were icons of a bleak moment for American culture, even as film revenues dropped sharply. Many younger talented writers, directors, and actors fled Hollywood for New York and live television drama. Experiments in independent film like *The Lawless* (about Chicano teens in a small California town) or *Give Us This Day* (from the foremost Italian-American novel, *Christ in Concrete*), politically and artistically innovative, meanwhile fell victim to a combination of political attack and the collapse of independent production companies.

By this time, network radio, comic books, and much of Depression era and wartime culture had entered a final golden age. Producer Norman Corwin, who made his name during the war with "We Hold These Truths," broadcast across national radio on the 150th anniversary of the Bill of Rights (a mere eight days before the bombing of Pearl Harbor), emerged a giant of audio culture, winner of the prestigious "One World" Award for his role on United Nations Radio. The world of animation, meanwhile, saw the invention of all manner of new characters, many of them – like the mice or bird against cat or dog, Bugs Bunny against hunter Elmer Fudd – posing the cleverness of the weak against the blundering strength of the giant. A new creative force within animation, artists and technicians who had abandoned Disney Studios after the calamitous 1941 strike, formed UPA, adding a variant of abstract expressionism with a political punch, climaxing in an unprecedented Museum of Modern Art showing and the first of network television's prime-time animated features, *Gerald McBoing Boing*.

Jobs in comics and animation, however, ceased to exist within a decade. Corwin, himself no communist, was bitterly attacked for "communistic associations" and exiled from the medium that he had uplifted. UPA Studios, pursued by the FBI, collapsed after losing their controversial artists (Jay Ward went on to make *Rocky and His Friends*, the notoriously acerbic animated feature of 1960s television; meanwhile, John Hubley and his collaborator Faith Hubley would create the films that persuaded the Academy to shift award designations from "Best Cartoon" to "Best Animated Feature").

After a postwar burst of creative energy including bebop, folk music, and early Beat literature, a cultural blandness settled in, along with the ubiquitous quest for "security." If the 1920s skilled worker had been world-famous for his new Model T (or even Model-A) Ford purchased on installments, and the Depression and wartime worker renowned in smaller ways for the omnipresent rebuilt jalopy, the worker of the late 1940s had a newer automobile fresh from the production line, whether Chevrolet, Ford, Plymouth, or tiny Crosley, if not the substance of upward mobility. The determined war veteran, whose experiences and mythos dominated so many areas of popular culture for years, managed to go to college on the GI Bill and came out with a job or profession that could facilitate home ownership and a car, on monthly payments. Old neighborhood and ethnic connections seemed to dissolve overnight when massive highway and building subsidies, home-mortgage tax benefits, and a rush of advertising produced heterogeneous (if generally all-white) neighborhoods. But the real desire to begin anew, in a family-owned homestead after generations of apartment living, was as palpable in the lower-middle class as the proliferating mink coats among the new rich.

The first years of network television radiated the uncertainty of the age with its expansive, polyglot, and, at least in some ways, democratized public culture. The marginal economic importance of early network television, with affiliated stations (i.e., audiences) clustered in eastern cities and producers carried over from New Deal years, provoked a remarkable spell of creative freedom. Along with a vaudevillian variety-show atmosphere grew up a 1930s-style theatrical drama that, despite warnings and purges, lasted almost until 1960. Dramatic themes shifted from the complexities of social "problems" (the poor or disoriented) to the dangers of psychotics or career criminals (to be neutralized by the likes of *Dragnet*'s policemen) and the process of "normalization" (the protagonist of *Marty* leaves ethnic neighborhood life behind, to marry and presumably suburbanize). The race controversy in the headlines even emerged on the small screen.

At first, simply to own a television set (rather than watching it in a neighborhood tavern) had offered evidence of personal progress. But to the next generation of teens at "passion-pit" drive-ins, and to young males armed with "muscle cars," not to mention assorted minorities and their variously transformed vehicles – rebuilt Caddies to Low-Riders – the automobile came to occupy ever more space in life and fantasy. From *The Wild One* (a motorcycle drama) and *Rebel Without a Cause* (with its notorious cars-over-a-cliff "chicken run"), rebellion itself was associated with the internal combustion engine.

But cultural perspectives, in other respects, had meanwhile badly narrowed. The Cold War had a severe effect, for instance, on the folksong revival that had been quietly building since the first Manhattan concerts of the later 1930s, taking flight with Woody Guthrie, Leadbelly, and Paul Robeson during the war years, and racing ahead with a galaxy of new stars into the early 1950s. Then suddenly the Weavers, with two recent songs on the Top Ten, could not get a regular booking. Be-bop, which placed Dizzy Gillespie on a 1949 cover of *Life* magazine surrounded by adoring black and white teenagers, was (like the Beat literature that began to emerge) seen to be part of a subterranean, outlaw existence, scarred by drugs and a sense of anomie within a staid America. EC Comics, renowned for its painfully realistic war comics and socially oriented horror line, responded to an approaching congressional investigation (for the purported corruption of youth) first with *Mad Comics*, a slashing satire of commercialism, and then, in 1955, with *Mad* magazine, evading the "Comics Code" by leaving the format of "comics" entirely for a black-and-white non-comic format. *Mad* magazine became the most popular satirical publication in global history, but at a considerable cost.

Meanwhile, Hollywood saw its revenue and cultural impact greatly reduced. Although relying on technological breakthroughs (Cinemascope, Cinerama, and Three-D), and biblical spectaculars, it lost customers not only to television but to sophisticated "foreign" films as studios sold off more and more of their assets. Salvation lay, ironically but logically, in reselling old products and in producing new shows for the same deadly competitor on the small screen.

Redemptive rebellion

Recovery of popular culture's dynamism was to come from the margins, as nearly always. That a cross-dressing thirteen-year-old running away from his southern home could become Little Richard; or that part-Native American Johnny Cash would become the bearer of somber messages for downbeat Middle American audiences; or that Richie Valens would introduce versions of Mexican standards into the patois of what rapidly became rock and roll – this was something that industry barometers like *Variety*, or the giant record companies with their talent scouts, had not remotely anticipated. Thanks to trans-racial teen enthusiasm, and a handful of shrewd showmen from small-label record companies to stage and radio, America saw an astonishing growth in record sales and enthusiasm for live music almost overnight. Out of a corner of banished "folk" performers and their protégés, meanwhile, came talents like Joan Baez and Bob Dylan, suddenly popular on campuses and in urban clubs for the young and self-consciously hip.

Powered by a combination of shrewd promotion and a sense of widespread generational alienation, those seemingly at the margins moved into the mainstream. Decades before "Gangsta Rap," singer-spokesmen like Doors, Country Joe and the Fish, the MC5, and Neil Young, joined by British imports Donovan, the Rolling Stones, the Animals, and even, sometimes, the Beatles, introduced anguish and protest along with youthful exuberance in successful entertainment. Motown, black capitalism at its most creative, turned out supercharged hits, while Aretha Franklin became the Queen of Soul. Among the most intense local environments, Bill Graham and San Francisco's Fillmore Theater seemed to radiate a wider meaning for music: a statement of a generation.

Meanwhile, antiwar sentiment urged rebellion against the draft and the military. In this context, "peace and love," the mantra of a generation that also employed the birth control pill and marijuana (less often LSD) to enlarge or escape the roles expected of them, seemed altogether subversive.

If the sit-down strike in factories had been a real-life drama for a few hundred thousand Americans in the later 1930s, and the sit-in at southern lunch counters by a few thousand brave participants an act with huge symbolic significance around 1960, the "be-in" was in many ways a media creation built upon youth enthusiasm. Like the antiwar demonstrators who rushed home to watch themselves on television, the much-derided hippies often shaped themselves by what they learned about youth culture on television and in popular magazines, or simply from street-talk and musical lyrics. San Francisco's Haight-Ashbury district, inundated with runaways, occupied a space in young people's imagination that it could not possibly realize in a drug-scarred real life.

Yet, in acting as they did, millions of the young rejected the former consensual goals and widely held social values of military mobilization, patriotic anti-communism, premarital chastity (for women in particular), racial and gender role certainties. A print culture of "underground" newspapers, created for and mostly by the young, produced the most dramatic development in American journalism for generations, as much in layout and in their muckraking coverage of local university officials, politicians, and businessmen as in their coverage of the war and the demonstrators. Outspoken radical magazines, led by the Catholic-based *Ramparts*, shocked the mainstream into covering what had been so effectively covered up: the participation of leading American intellectuals and artists, not excluding popular culture's most severe critics, in a Central Intelligence Agency-funded operation, the Congress for Cultural Freedom.

The rebellious moment affected the most heavily commercialized sectors of popular culture in complex ways. The most prosperous youth generation in American history would naturally become tomorrow's consumers, moving on from tie-dyed T-shirts to marriage, home mortgages, and consumer durables. For these market reasons, and the resistance of film- and television-makers to drastic change, the media "culture of the 1960s" emerged belatedly, at the verge of 1970 or slightly later.

The "social sitcom" associated with television's *M*A*S*H* (eventually to become the most frequently repeated in media history) and with the daring shows of producer Norman Lear (*All in the Family, The Jeffersons, Maude and Mary Hartman, Mary Hartman* among others) had been premised on the youthful viewers' disdain of racism, war, and the occupant of the White House. Furious battles with network censors brought victories never subsequently reversed – even if the most noticeable result, over the long run, would not be social commentary as often as risqué banter and heavily sexualized musical performance.

An exceptionally dark, naturalistic view of American life meanwhile opened to audiences with *Midnight Cowboy*, the 1969 Hollywood classic that broke through the barriers of the X rating to a mass audience. (Three years later, *Deep Throat* hit the cinemas and steadily became one of the most lucrative features in film history, the film that brought "adult" cinema out of the shadows.) The *Godfather* dramas, *Blue Collar, Silkwood, Taxi Driver, Dog Day Afternoon*, and many others patently lacked happy endings or a heroic protagonist. Films about the courage of ordinary people, like *Norma Rae*, about a textile worker who led a union organizing campaign in a southern town, returned to 1930–40s style Hollywood melodrama but also revealed dark corners of the American business world. Even lighthearted films like Mel Brooks's mega-hit *Blazing Saddles* seemed to ridicule collective myths (in this case the "winning of the West" by white heroes and pure-hearted women) long important to the American psyche.

There were many other important indications that the combination of the US defeat in Vietnam, the energy crisis, and Watergate cast a spell over popular culture. An Age of Aquarius (named by a Broadway musical) predicted for the 1970s, with long hair, social harmony, and understanding, seemed to take root in surviving corners of the counterculture, in urban villages such as Madison, Wisconsin; Eugene, Oregon; or Burlington, Vermont; and large stretches of San Francisco and Berkeley. But even in these cheerful hold-outs, the dominant musical culture – where not the disco of an openly and proudly gay culture, or the affirmative feminists sounds of "I Am Woman" and its many imitations – was certain to be the musically rendered dissolution of the "Woodstock Nation" in favor of a grimmer reality.

Bruce Springsteen's blue-collar New Jersey, where industrial work had vanished and the latest generation of sons returned from Vietnam, drugged and troubled, became emblematic of a larger complaint, echoed in many corners of popular culture. Youthful dreams of freedom, community, and love survived, if anywhere, in the notes of hope about the power of music to heal wounds. A sense of betrayal and bitter disappointment ran deeper, along with a growing, almost overwhelming nostalgia. Perhaps inevitably, the very early 1970s gave birth to a rapid proliferation of "Oldies" radio shows and live musical performances. Music from the birth of rock and roll to the later 1960s marked a "past" of happier, more innocent days. Don McLean's 1971 hit "Bye, Bye, Miss American Pie" seemed to many listeners to say it all, about the "day the music died" and the pleasure of looking backward. Robin Williams's brilliant portrayal of space alien/flower child Mork, in the television hit "Mork and Mindy" wonderfully demonstrated that the sixties had never ended – it had only been exiled to an alternative reality.

The dark side of rebellious culture was palpable by the middle 1970s. "Outlaw" country (male) musicians, like the latest, sequined versions of transgressive or "glitter" rock, were now posturing and not especially rebellious. Indeed, according to the musical indications and clothes fashions, the familiar hippie uniform of long hair and practice of smoking marijuana spread from a utopian-minded middle class to an embittered working and sub-working class during the 1970s. "Free love," become promiscuity made possible by the birth control pill and loss of religious-based personal guilt, yielded to sexually transmitted diseases and an end to the best promises of a liberated sexuality, especially among the careless young. Now, as in earlier decades, the beautiful bodies on the film and television screens, the delirious pleasures described in popular songs, stood at an increasing distance from reality. Perhaps only the veritable collapse of jazz from mass involvement to precious art form demonstrated clearly how the old creative energies and their link with a sort of mass bohemianism had faded.

Repression's uneven return

The new moment might be identified, before Ronald Reagan's 1980 election, in *Star Wars* (1979) as readily as in the Iran disaster of US foreign policy – even if the genre of the scifi megadrama had been launched by the original *Planet of the Apes*, a satirical treatment of McCarthyism and America's self-destructive impulses. The frontier as image, commercial and personal, seemed to beckon once more, the great vision of conquest imaginatively realized in President Reagan's carefully constructed version of "morning in America." Not for the first time, reality (at least politics and the infinite power of dedicated corporate resources) seemed to imitate art. But now the imitation reached an apex when a president recalled his movie moments as real World War II experiences. The larger-than-life had become life itself.

The racial dynamics of popular culture, moving in an egalitarian direction since the 1940s with an arguable high point in the 1976 showing of *Roots* (still the most popular television mini-series ever), now veered backward. Ideas of minorities' collective advance were rapidly replaced by narratives of individual advance, away from the dark shadow of the ghetto and a shameful past. The individual black, Asian, or Latino actor appeared more frequently, to be sure, but mainly as the selfless assistant, gun-toting supporter of the film hero, the fear-provoking thug, or minstrel-like joker.

If the changes of the immigration law in 1965 assured whites a minority status in future America, the cultural retreat of the 1980s helped to create or perpetuate a new, rapidly growing class of outsiders. African Americans seemed, from this perspective, to enjoy a near-insider status, with a galaxy of athletic stars including golf hero Tiger Woods and tennis champions, the Williams sisters; entertainment headliners like Michael Jackson; and a handful of intellectual or institutional celebrities along with their high-powered boosters, like Oprah Winfrey. The black rage expressed in the Los Angeles riots of 1992 and the white rage at the O. J. Simpson trial offered a contrasting lesson reflected in tabloid coverage and in the rhetoric of radio talk shows. For the poor, nothing had been gained in popular culture that could not be lost again.

Ronald Reagan, the actor-as-President, seemed to play to his Evangelical audience, declaring the proximity of nuclear Armageddon. At other times, all was apparently well, at least within the United States. The ecological dangers referenced so frequently in films and television since the original Earth Day of 1970 had become mere figments of an overactive liberal imagination and of government bureaucrats craving control of Americans' personal lives and their business opportunities.

So many other symbols of cultural change now steadily became their opposites. As critic Thomas Franks would point out, the notion of rebellion was to re-emerge, but now attached to expensive, ecologically wasteful off-road vehicles and ultimately the sports utility vehicle, promising "freedom" from all manner of bothersome restraints. The aerobic "me generation" of the 1970s, abandoning old routines to take care of mind and body according to new rules, gave way to increasingly overweight generations eating fast food on the run. A private life of home ownership and consumerism had come to dominate culture as never before; not even the 1950s, with its memory of the Second World War and the battlefield deaths of Korea, could compare.

Perhaps it should have been no surprise that the fall of the Iron Curtain, the largest political event in a half-century, scarcely seemed as significant as the reinvention of American private lives through electronic culture. The Internet, created to be a failsafe communication method during and after a nuclear holocaust, was (unlike similarly based technologies) no mere nightmare machine of terror. Inspired as early radio had been, by the imaginations of hobbyists, college dropouts and "nerds" (a word that took on surprisingly new meaning) took the field, this time actually keeping control of some of their grandest efforts. At the moment when the military intelligence services backed away from the emerging Internet in the late 1980s, servers moved forward and the first "search engines" appeared. The World Wide Web appeared in 1989. Host computers using the Net rose from a mere 80,000 in 1989 to more than 50 million by the turn of the century, a figure projected to continue with no end in sight.

It would be a mistake to see this development apart from CDs and the downloading of music from the Internet, cable television, and DVDs, because all together they comprised a new phase of interactive popular culture, unthinkable only a decade earlier. They signaled the expansion of capitalism as much, perhaps, as the nineteenth-century railroad and the twentieth-century automobile. Was this to mark the vast democratization of the culture with new technological possibilities at the fingertips of millions of ordinary consumers, or evidence of a further loss of community contact?

The question was important because it returned to the familiar debate about the significance of popular culture, now on very different ground. There was greater reason to fear conformity than there had been in the

1950s as the media came under monopoly control. National "shock Jocks" and bland musical selections increasingly drowned out local radio because so few stations continued to be owned in their home regions. Federal Communications Commission decisions permitted ever greater crossovers from the print world to television and films, allowing one baron (Rupert Murdoch) far more concentrated power than the Moguls of old.

But this ominous development could not be accurately measured as a victory for anything like the culture of traditional, Protestant-based American conservatism. Something of the "Vietnam syndrome," the anxiety of US troops occupying a nation far from home, remained alive within popular culture, among Republicans almost as much as Democrats, notwithstanding the defeat of presidential candidate John Kerry in 2004, personal symbol of the Vietnam veteran. Likewise, abortion rarely followed pregnancy in film or television and "gay marriage" was disdained in large parts of the nation – perhaps the most potent spectre unleashed by Republican advertisements during the 2004 elections. But the specter of a "Big Brother" checking library cards and bedrooms was dreaded even by many conservatives and even in the midst of supposed terrorist threats. Most remarkably, within the seemingly endless refurbishing of war themes for popular treatment, the Second World War and its "greatest generation" remained the only war, the only warring generation, to be successfully celebrated. So much of fundamental importance was unresolved.

The impact of the newer immigrant groups upon popular culture remained, above all, very much in doubt. Latinos, the most rapidly increasing sector of the population, had already changed the musical culture of large cities by the 1990s. The small-scale capitalization required of music clubs and CDs, which had earlier facilitated the emergence of hip-hop, would now doubtless do the same for "world pop" in what was an increasingly diverse culture. Not since the 1890s–1910s had technological and demographic changes created such a potential for cultural transformations, even as those very changes prompted anxieties in those resistant to the very idea of diversity.

The very idea of modern culture, it seemed to critic Harold Rosenberg in 1949, lay in the resistance to definition. The working class (Rosenberg was at the time under the spell of Rosa Luxemburg's texts warning against Marxist elitism) meanwhile, would define itself only in terms of its potential, not its restrictive and restricted present reality. It, like modernity itself, was about to change. Rosenberg's thesis ill-suited the postwar blue-collar generation of bowling alleys and tract houses, although it captured some of the disappointment and despair of a Bruce Springsteen speaking for the rock-and-roller become Vietnam vet and looking out at a darkened future.

The cultural critic was, for all her/his weakness, better equipped than the optimists of "morning in America" and their successors to go to the heart of popular cultural innovation in a society where fantasy was nonstop and retailed space constantly expanded, but where deep feelings of solitariness and uncertainty remained omnipresent.

FURTHER READING

Paul Buhle, *From The Lower East Side to Hollywood: Jews in American Popular Culture*, London and New York: Verso, 2004.

Paul Buhle (ed.), *Popular Culture in America*, Minneapolis: University of Minnesota Press, 1987.

Paul Buhle and Dave Wagner, *Radical Hollywood*, New York: The New Press, 2002.

Jim Cullen, *The Art of Democracy: a Concise History of Popular Culture in the United States*, New York: Monthly Review Press, 1996.

Thomas P. Frank, *Conquest of Cool: Business Culture, Counter Culture and the Rise of Hip Consumerism*, Chicago: University of Chicago Press, 1997.

Fred Goodman, *The Mansion on the Hill: Dylan, Young, Geffen, Springsteen and the Head-On Collision of Rock and Commerce*, London: Jonathan Cape, 1997.

Ron Goulart, *Comic Book Culture: an Illustrated History*, Portland, ME: Collector's Press, 2000.

Charles Harpole, general ed., *History of the American Cinema*, 10 vols, Berkeley and Los Angeles: University of California Press, 1990 to present.

Jeff Kisseloff, *The Box: an Oral History of Television*, New York: Penguin, 1995.

David Marc, *Demographic Vistas: Television in American Culture*, Philadelphia: University of Pennsylvania Press, 1984.

Kathy Peiss, *Cheap Amusements: Working Women and Leisure Time in Turn of the Century New York*, Philadelphia: Temple University Press, 1986.

Tom Pendergast and Sara Pendergast (eds.), *The St. James Encyclopedia of Popular Culture*, 6 vols, Detroit: St. James Press, 2000.

Roy Rosenzweig, *Eight Hours for What We Will: Workers and Leisure in an Industrial City, 1870–1920*, Cambridge: Cambridge University Press, 1983.

Jerry Wexler and David Ritz, *Rhythm and the Blues: a Life in American Music*, New York: Knopf, 1995.

BRENDA MURPHY

Theatre

At the beginning of the twentieth century, the American theatre was for the most part a medium of mass entertainment. In the cities, the theatre meant popular melodrama in enormous theatres like the Bowery in New York as well as the likes of Sarah Bernhardt from France touring in plays by Rostand and Racine and Ellen Terry and Henry Irving from England playing in Shakespeare and Shaw. American stars E. H. Sothern, Julia Marlowe, and Richard Mansfield acted in Shakespeare, and Ethel, Lionel, and John Barrymore starred in contemporary plays by American and English writers. The theatre also meant numerous American companies touring in old American standards like the ubiquitous *Uncle Tom's Cabin* and James O'Neill's thirty-year vehicle, *Monte Cristo*. Increasingly risqué revues like the Ziegfeld Follies played alongside minstrel shows and the wholesome family entertainment of vaudeville. To the early twentieth-century public, the theatre included burlesque, circus, and "extravaganza," as well as the Yiddish theatre, the settlement house theatre, and the puppet theatre.

Not very well represented on the theatre scene before World War I was literary drama by Americans. Because there was no international copyright treaty before 1891, it had traditionally been more profitable for a theatre manager to pirate a British play or have a European play translated, than to pay royalties on a play by an American. Bronson Howard, said to be the first American to make his living solely by writing plays, was a real anomaly in the 1870s and 1880s. American playwrights like David Belasco, Edward Harrigan, Augustin Daly, and James A. Herne managed to get their plays on the stage by producing them themselves, and often acting in them. After the copyright law was passed, however, managers became more interested in producing plays by Americans. A new generation of literary playwrights emerged at the turn of the twentieth century, better educated men and women who thought of themselves as professional playwrights, and wanted to write plays that were of the same literary quality as the new work by such playwrights as Ibsen, Shaw, Sudermann, Hauptmann, and Rostand that was coming from Europe. Among them were Clyde Fitch, Augustus Thomas, Edward Sheldon, William Vaughn Moody, Rachel Crothers, Langdon Mitchell, Percy Mackay, and Stephen Phillips. Although their work is no longer produced and seldom read, even in universities, it was vitally important in its time, establishing an American drama that was worthy not only of production but of publication, a drama that must be seen as literature.

The modern American theatre is usually regarded as beginning in the second decade of the twentieth century, with several companies that grew out of the Little Theatre movement associated with Maurice Browne and his wife Ellen van Volkenburg in Chicago. These included the Chicago Little Theatre, Boston's Toy Theatre, and the Wisconsin Dramatic Society as well as the best known of them, the Washington Square Players and the Provincetown Players in New York's Greenwich Village. All of these groups were influenced by the Art Theatre movement in Europe, particularly by the ideas of Edward Gordon Craig and Max Reinhardt, who insisted that the theatre was a "synthetic art," which required the harmonious blending of all its elements – writing, acting, scene design, lighting, music, and even the audience's place in the theatrical space – in order to achieve its full effect. Many of their members were also impressed by the simple, natural acting of Dublin's Abbey Players in the literary "folk" drama of J. M. Synge, Lady Gregory, Lennox Robinson, and William Boyle when they toured the United States in 1911 and 1913. The Provincetown Players, also known as The Playwrights Theater, established as its major goal the production of new plays of literary quality by Americans. In its short life, from 1915 to 1922, it produced ninety-three plays by forty-seven American playwrights, almost none of whom had had plays produced before. Among the writers whose plays premiered at the Provincetown were Eugene O'Neill, Susan Glaspell, Edna St. Vincent Millay, Wallace Stevens, Djuna Barnes, Theodore Dreiser, and Sherwood Anderson. Central, along with Alfred Stieglitz's Photo-Secession Gallery (known as 291) and *The Masses* magazine, to New York's discovery of modernism in art and thought, known as the Little Renaissance, the work at the Provincetown's tiny Playhouse had a great impact on American theatre in the period around World War I. Although its members liked to think of themselves as the avant garde of the American theatre, the Provincetown was actually a fair microcosm of literary playwriting during this period. The plays that it produced tended to be of two general types, socially oriented or lightly satirical realist plays and non-representational, experimental plays meant for the art theatre.

The Provincetown's realist plays were the culmination of a small movement in the American theatre dating back to the 1880s, when literary critics like William Dean Howells and Hamlin Garland began to praise the elements of literary realism they saw in the work of American playwrights William Gillette, Edward Harrigan, and especially James A. Herne, as, if not the equivalent of Ibsen, Shaw, and Sudermann, at least evidence that literary realism was possible on the American stage. In the early twentieth century, realism, both literary and theatrical, became a conscious aesthetic with younger playwrights like Fitch, Crothers, Mitchell, and Sheldon, who saw that the conventional forms of melodrama and the "well-made play" no longer reflected the perceived reality of the average American audience at any level, and sought through a conscious realism to represent "life as it is," whether in the middle-class comedies of Fitch, the Shavian discussion plays of Crothers, or the straightforward representations of women caught in urban poverty by Sheldon and Mitchell. Fortunately for them, the technical development of American scenic art was ahead of the writers who strove to create an illusion of reality on the stage. As early as the 1880s, David Belasco and Steele Mackaye, who saw the stage as a realistic environment, took a great interest in creating a photographic image of reality in their sets, as well as a beautiful stage picture. They and the designers who emulated them were happy to serve playwrights who aimed at an illusion of reality on the stage. On the other hand, Howells set the literary goal in calling for plays that emphasized the psychologically believable representation of character over plot and integrated moral and social dilemmas into the action. He affirmed what Shaw called the "drama of discussion," in which the argument over the issue becomes the action of the play and dramatic closure is achieved through the resolution of the argument, a form that was used effectively by Rachel Crothers in *A Man's World* (1910) and *He and She* (1912) and Augustus Thomas in *As a Man Thinks* (1911). In order to achieve the audience's identification with the characters and the society they represented, the realist playwrights took an interest in staging that went beyond the pictorial, insisting on living-room sets whose decoration expressed the personalities of the characters who lived in them and urban environments that suggested the circumstances in which poor people actually lived.

Because realism came late to the American stage, it could still be seen as experimental in the teens, as it was when the Provincetown Players produced Neith Boyce's *Winter's Night* (1916) and Susan Glaspell's *Trifles* (1916), in which carefully designed kitchen sets helped to establish the inner lives of the women characters who are the subjects of the plays, and Eugene O'Neill's plays about sailors, such as *Bound East for Cardiff* (1916) and the *Moon of the Caribbees* (1918), in which, as critics said, "nothing happened," except that the audience came to understand some of the characters. Juxtaposed with these plays on the Provincetown programs were works that were perceived as wildly experimental, displaying the influence of modernist thinking through their break with the representational aesthetic goals of realism and their aim to produce "presentational" drama instead. Early works along these lines often took their aesthetics from fantasy, allegory, fairy tale, or, in the case of Edna St. Vincent Millay's antiwar play *Aria da Capo* (1919), the Harlequinade. Others, such as Alfred Kreymborg's *Lima Beans* (1916), a "scherzo in three acts" written in free verse, in which the actors moved like marionettes and the lines were intoned with a musical rhythm, aimed at a completely new modernist theatrical idiom.

Most significant for the future of American modernist drama was O'Neill's growing interest in dramatizing the subjective reality of a character on the stage rather than the supposed objective reality that realism aimed to capture. This was done rather clumsily in *Where the Cross is Made* (1918), in which O'Neill tried to make the audience "go mad" along with the characters by bringing hallucinations onto the stage, and much more effectively in *The Emperor Jones* (1920), in which the audience is gradually drawn into the terror that Brutus Jones experiences in his Jungian journey into his own memory and the collective unconscious. By 1921, when he wrote *The Hairy Ape*, O'Neill had become acquainted with German expressionism, and this play is much more like the German plays than his earlier experiments with dramatizing subjective reality. But it is characteristically American in being an eclectic mix of realism and expressionism.

In the same year, the Provincetown Players produced Susan Glaspell's *The Verge*, a dramatization of the Nietzschean quest of a female artist in horticulture to get beyond "the edge of life" and create a truly new form of life. Her play begins in the realism of society comedy, but shifts to an expressionist mode that reflects the character's Dionysian ecstasy as she moves beyond good and evil at the end of the play, killing the man who would keep her from pushing the boundaries of life and creativity even further.

O'Neill's attempt to understand the "soul of man" and his spiritual quest for meaning was to fuel nearly two decades of experimental playwriting which established him as the United States's most significant modernist playwright. O'Neill was appalled by the loss of faith in a sustaining religious myth and the lack of connection with the past in modern American culture. His plays of the 1920s and 1930s reflect his own unsuccessful quest for what he called "God replacements" in plays such as his experiment in "total theatre," the Nietzschean tragedy *Lazarus Laughed* (1928), and the expressionistic *Dynamo* (1929) and *Days without End* (1934). His larger project, however, was an attempt to overcome the loss of faith by remaking myth and mythicizing history. He used the classical Greek myth of Phaedra and Hyppolytus in *Desire under the Elms* (1924) and the historical figures of Marco Polo, the thirteenth-century Venetian merchant who traveled to China, and Ponce de Leon, the Spanish explorer who searched for the Fountain of Youth in Florida, in *Marco Millions* and *The Fountain*, to represent what he saw as the divided soul of the modern American, the pragmatic man of action who is troubled by the need for romantic love and spiritual fulfillment. This conflict is most fully developed in *Strange Interlude* (1928), a struggle among business, science, high culture, romantic myth, and traditional religion for the soul of America. It was to be developed further in the 1930s, in O'Neill's most ambitious project, a cycle of plays entitled *A Tale of Possessors, Self-dispossessed*, which he destroyed before they could be produced. Only two plays remain to indicate his critique of American values in the cycle, *A Touch of the Poet* and the reconstructed *More Stately Mansions*.

During this period, O'Neill experimented extensively with non-representational theatrical techniques, particularly masks. In *All God's Chillun Got Wings* (1923), the pathology of racism is externalized as a white character focuses the racism that undermines her love for her black husband onto an African mask, which she eventually stabs. *Lazarus Laughed* has the most elaborate system of masks in all of O'Neill's work. In each of its scenes, the Crowd wears forty-nine different masks, representing O'Neill's versions of the seven ages of human beings and seven general character types. As the scene in the biblical story shifts from Bethany to Athens to Rome, all forty-nine masks exhibit different ethnic characteristics. In *The Great God Brown* (1926), masks serve the function of psychological masking and unmasking, as the characters wear masks that carry the image they want to have before the world, while their faces, revealed in private, convey the ravages of their personal experience. Beyond this obvious use, however, the masks take on a power that O'Neill found in his study of African masks. When Bill Brown steals Dion Anthony's mask after he kills him, he takes possession of his identity and his soul as well.

O'Neill experimented with other ways of dramatizing subjective experience, notably the dialogic technique he developed for *Strange Interlude*, in which the action in the "objective reality" of the realistic play freezes as a character delivers his or her thoughts to the audience in a stylized aside. It is *Mourning Becomes Electra* (1931) that most fully integrates O'Neill's modern world view with his modernist aesthetic for the theatre, however. In this play, he used a technique he called "unreal realism," moving away from the anti-realist techniques of the earlier experiments in favor of a realistic theatrical idiom that merely suggests the subjective rather than emphasizing it. Although it pushes the boundaries, the play never breaks with the representational aesthetics of realism. Rather than wearing masks, the Mannon family have mask-like faces that indicate the artificiality of their public personae. The dialogue is literary and symbolic, but it remains within the realistic frame. Myth and history are joined in this three-play cycle which re-enacts the classic Greek myth of Electra, the antithesis of family values, in the context of the American Civil War, the historical proof of the failures of American democracy.

During the 1920s, the modernist experimentation that emerged from the art theatre had some effect on what its practitioners referred to as the "commercial" theatre emanating from Broadway to the rest of the nation. Expressionism in particular took hold, but in a characteristically American way. A few plays, like Sophie Treadwell's *Machinal* (1928), based on the notorious Ruth Snyder murder trial, emulated the desperate intensity of the Germans and the O'Neill plays. The most successful American expressionist plays, however, were comedies, plays that used the techniques of expressionism to parody the world view of its practitioners as well as satirizing American attitudes and values. Elmer Rice's *The Adding Machine* (1923) and George S. Kaufman and Marc Connelly's *Beggar on Horseback* (1924) make fun of both American business culture and the "highbrow" culture associated with modernism. The overwhelming majority of literary American plays in the middle part of the twentieth century, however, were realistic, the American version of Europe's bourgeois realism.

In the 1920s, the Broadway theatre was the primary source from which theatrical entertainment of high quality proceeded. The New York theatre reached the peak of its productivity in the 1925–6 season, when there were 255 new productions in the Broadway theatre. This might be compared with 115 in 1915–16 or 41 in 2003–4. The Broadway audience was middle class, and it was interested in plays that represented middle class concerns. The middle-class realism that pervaded the American theatre in the 1920s and 1930s embraced a wide spectrum of American life, from the urban, high-society comedy of Philip Barry, S. N. Behrman, and Rachel Crothers, to the character studies of small-town America by George Kelly, Sidney Howard, Lewis Beach, and Zona Gale. This rich body of literature constitutes a *comédie humaine* for the American middle class between the two world wars, a revealing representation of values, conflicts, desires, and forces.

During the 1930s, a more earnest form of social melodrama came to the fore in answer to the threatening economic conditions at home and the threat of fascism in Europe. In plays like *The Children's Hour* (1934), *The Little Foxes* (1939), and *Watch on the Rhine* (1941), Lillian Hellman used the deep structure of melodrama, which represents social reality as a battle between easily recognizable forces of good and evil, to address the cultural anxiety around sexual identity, the effects of unbridled capitalism on American society, and the dangers posed by European fascism. Hellman, and other playwrights like Sidney Kingsley and Robert Sherwood, kept their plays within the mode of realism with realistic settings, believable if rather sensational situations, and psychologically complex characters, thus implying that the struggle between good and evil was the underlying dynamic of human social order.

The thirties was also a period of experimentation with non-representational political drama, particularly in the leftist labor theatre, which adapted the agitation-propaganda, or agit-prop, techniques that were imported from Europe into a straightforward, confrontational leftist aesthetic. The agit-prop theater used simple situations, type characters or recognizable caricatures of political figures, songs, slogans, and direct challenges to the audience to incite involvement in the cause. A portable theatre, it needed little in the way of props and sets, and could be put on in union halls and other public venues. The techniques of agit-prop were used in the Living Newspapers of the short-lived Federal Theatre Project (1935–9), the only federally subsidized theater in American history. Its director, Hallie Flanagan, who had produced Living Newspapers at Vassar College, commissioned productions on the housing shortage (*One Third of a Nation*, 1938), the farm crisis (*Triple A Plowed Under*, 1936), and public ownership of utilities (*Power*, 1937). It was partly because of these productions that the Federal Theatre Project was shut down by Congress in 1939, many of the politicians considering it too left wing for government subsidy. The techniques of agit-prop even reached Broadway in The Group Theatre's production of Clifford Odets's *Waiting for Lefty* (1935), a play occasioned by a New York taxi-drivers' strike. Odets juxtaposed agit-prop techniques with traditional realistic scenes that dramatized the difficulties of the workers' lives within a theatrical idiom that was familiar to the audience, gaining its sympathy for the strike through its identification with the characters before the play's ending, when an actor rose from the audience and led it in a chant of "Strike! Strike! Strike!"

At the end of the decade, Eugene O'Neill took a break from his experimental play cycle to write three realistic plays that were based on his family and his life as a young man in 1911 and 1912. *The Iceman Cometh* (1946), *Long Day's Journey Into Night* (1940, produced 1956), and *A Moon for the Misbegotten* (1947) have come to be viewed as his best work and the greatest achievements of American realism. Their intense focus on the individual in the context of the psychological dynamics of the family suggested the direction the American theatre was to take in the 1940s and 1950s.

In the years after World War II, the realistic and the experimental lines of development in the American theatre came together in what was to be the most distinctive and influential American theatrical development of the twentieth century. Playwrights Tennessee Williams and Arthur Miller, in collaboration with director Elia Kazan and designer Jo Mielziner, created a form of total theatre that remained within the boundaries of dramatic realism while it dramatized the subjective reality of one of the characters. These productions synthesized dialogue, acting, scenery, lighting, and music into an integrated theatrical idiom that quickly became known worldwide as "the American style."

The first play of this group was Tennessee Williams's *The Glass Menagerie* (1945). Williams called this a "memory play," defining an aesthetics that was not expressionism, but made use of expressionist techniques. In the first scene, Tom Wingfield addresses the audience directly, shattering the illusion of the invisible fourth wall that characterizes realism and establishing the presentational mode of the play. Tom directs the audience's attention to the dramatization of his memories, which plague him with a sense of guilt, although he has tried to free himself from his family by taking to the road, as his father had done before him. In Mielziner's set, the brick wall next to Tom became transparent, as the light behind it slowly brightened, allowing the spectators to see his mother and sister in their apartment. When Tom joined them in the apartment, the wall ascended, leaving the spectators with an invisible fourth wall and a dramatization of Tom's memories that was not overtly distorted by his subjective view of them as in expressionism, but a seemingly objective representation of the past. In the final scene, Williams and Mielziner reminded the spectators once again that the play was memory, and thus Tom's subjective version of events, as he once again addressed the audience and the light slowly dimmed behind the brick wall.

In their collaboration with Elia Kazan on *A Streetcar Named Desire* (1947), *Cat on a Hot Tin Roof* (1955), and *Sweet Bird of Youth* (1959), Williams and Mielziner experimented further with the aesthetic of subjective realism. In *Streetcar*, they used more expressionist effects as Blanche Du Bois's mental condition deteriorated from "hysteria" and "neurasthenia" to psychosis, and she became increasingly more desperate and was finally raped by Stanley Kowalski. In *Sweet Bird of Youth*, the lighting, such as bright follow spots on the two characters who view their lives primarily as performances, constantly reminded the spectators that they were in a theatre. Both plays, however, remain within the bounds of representational theatre and the goal is the audience's sympathetic identification with the characters, not their alienation from them. Kazan's Method-trained actors, many of whom were his students at the Actors Studio, were devoted to the ideal of authenticity in performance, an emotional truth that came from the depths of the actor's experience within the "given circumstances" of the play. Subjective realism is at its most complex in *Death of a Salesman* (1949), in which Arthur Miller collaborated with Kazan and Mielziner to dramatize the juxtaposition of a putative reality in the "present" time on stage with the memories of events seventeen years earlier that are running like a film in Willy Loman's mind. Miller insisted that Willy has reached the point where the events in his mind are as real to him as the events that are happening around him. To dramatize this, Mielziner used lights and transparencies as he had in the Williams plays to show a seamless progression between Willy in the present interacting with the people in his environment and Willy in his memory interacting with people as he imagines them to have been in the past. This scenic idiom gave the audience a greater sympathy for the "real" Willy by drawing them into an understanding of his inner life. The result is a production whose audience feels that it understands Willy Loman far better than any of the characters in the play do, enabling a full appreciation of his tragedy

The possibilities of subjective realism for dramatizing the subjective reality of the characters without the audience's losing touch with the illusion of objectivity were so great that plays using this theatrical idiom were everywhere in the 1950s. Arthur Miller complained that the American theatre had entered an "era of gauze," turning inward and ignoring the social and political life of the American as citizen. He tried to counter this with *The Crucible* (1953), a dramatization of the Salem witch trials that served as a historical analogy for McCarthyism and the Congressional investigations into the political beliefs of individual citizens, including Miller, which had resulted in blacklisting and other forms of political persecution. Several playwrights, such as Lillian Hellman, Maxwell Anderson, Saul Levitt, and Barrie Stavis, followed Miller's lead in writing historical dramas with a clear analogy to current political events, and Miller would write increasingly overt political plays in *Incident at Vichy* (1964) and *The Archbishop's Ceiling* (1977). For the most part, however, the American theatre in the 1950s steered clear of politics. The plays that were produced on Broadway and sent forth to the rest of the country in innumerable touring companies were most often musical comedies, family dramas, and romantic comedies. Besides Williams, Miller, and O'Neill, the major literary playwrights of the fifties were William Inge, Robert Anderson, Lillian Hellman, with her family dramas *Toys in the Attic*

(1951) and *The Autumn Garden* (1960), and Lorraine Hansberry, with the first Broadway play by a black woman, the family drama *A Raisin in the Sun* (1959). The five longest-running plays during the decade were four musicals, *My Fair Lady* (1956), *The Music Man* (1957), *The King and I* (1951), and *Guys and Dolls* (1950), and George Axelrod's comedy about sexual frustration and temptation, *The Seven Year Itch* (1952).

By 1959, a younger generation of playwrights had arisen for whom the Broadway theatre seemed empty and increasingly irrelevant to the significant concerns of Americans, a purely commercial venture that catered to businessmen on expense accounts and suburban housewives. Like the generation of the Little Renaissance before them, these playwrights found an outlet for their ground-breaking theatrical experiments in smaller theatres located a distance from Broadway. The Off-Broadway theatre first established itself through its fresh and imaginative approaches to existing plays, such as José Quintero's productions of Williams's *Summer and Smoke* (1952) and O'Neill's *The Iceman Cometh* (1956) at the Circle in the Square in Greenwich Village and the Martinique's production of *The Crucible*, all of which were considered better than the Broadway originals. The watershed production for Off-Broadway, however, was the Living Theatre's staging of Jack Gelber's *The Connection* in 1959. This play, a theatricalization of the Beat aesthetic, had all the elements of an avant-garde theatre for the early 1960s. Its subject matter was too daring for Broadway. The main action consists of a group of drug addicts waiting for their dealer to make a delivery. The Living Theatre's improvisational approach to the production, in which the whole company collaborated on a performance complete with jazz accompaniment, was perfect for the intimate Off-Broadway theatre (because of union regulations, Off-Broadway theatres can have no more than 299 seats).

The Off-Broadway theatre quickly drew the most avant-garde of the new generation of playwrights, who were influenced by a new theatrical idiom which the British critic Martin Esslin named the Theatre of the Absurd. It was informed by the new philosophy of Existentialism and made use of a broad range of performance techniques from vaudeville and silent films to highly poetic monologue. In this form of presentational theatre, traditional realism was rejected in favor of what the playwrights felt was a deeper form of representation, that of the existential truth behind surface reality. The typical absurdist play is a metaphor for some aspect of human existence. In Samuel Becket's *Waiting for Godot*, for example, two characters while away the time with nonsense while they wait for Godot to come and give meaning to their lives, but of course Godot never arrives. The most significant American playwright in the absurdist tradition is Edward Albee, whose early works, *The Sandbox* (1960), and *The American Dream* (1961), are now considered classic examples of this kind of play. In *The Sandbox*, a family consigns its dying grandmother to a sandbox, where she literally begins to bury herself. *The American Dream* takes the myth of the happy American family, which was re-emphasized weekly on popular television shows such as *Leave It to Beaver* and *The Adventures of Ozzie and Harriet*, to absurd extremes. These plays led audiences to question their beliefs about themselves and American culture. *The Zoo Story* moved in a slightly different direction, proposing the possibility of redemption and meaning as Jerry tentatively makes human contact with the seemingly bland and passive Peter, who has retreated from the tensions of daily life to an isolated bench in a park.

Albee's career is a good illustration of the effect that Off-Broadway had on the American theatre, and especially on American playwriting, in the second half of the twentieth century. After the success of his one-act absurdist plays, Albee was considered something of an *enfant terrible* in the American theatre, and Broadway welcomed his first full-length play, *Who's Afraid of Virginia Woolf?* (1962), a tightly constructed one-set play which remains claustrophobically within the bounds of middle-class "living room" realism, while the "games" that George and Martha play and Albee's brilliantly literary and funny dialogue introduce the element of the absurd into this world. *Virginia Woolf* ran for 664 performances to great critical acclaim, assuring Albee of entrée to Broadway for his next few plays.

Although *A Delicate Balance* (1966) won the Pulitzer Prize and, like *Virginia Woolf*, was made into a film, some of these, such as *Tiny Alice* (1964), *Seascape* (1975), and *The Lady from Dubuque* (1980), were difficult literary plays, quite bewildering to audiences. Although *Tiny Alice* was a qualified commercial success, several commercial failures made it increasingly hard for Albee to get produced on Broadway. As he had in his youth, Albee in his fifties turned to alternatives, like regional, foreign, and university theatre, for his productions. In his seventies, he again achieved unexpected critical and commercial success in New York, with the Off-Broadway production of *Three Tall Women* in 1994. As it had in 1962, Off-Broadway success again opened the Broadway stage to Albee, and he has had two revivals and a successful new play, *The Goat, or Who Is Sylvia?* (2002), on Broadway since then.

Albee's career illustrates a general trend in the second half of the twentieth century, in which the economic and artistic dominance of Broadway over the American theatre has broken down, and the demarcation between "art" theatre and "commercial" theatre has blurred considerably. Consequently, the younger playwrights who grew up with Off-Broadway as an experimental stage have moved freely between the two, finding different venues as they chose to work in various theatrical idioms. This is more natural to them than to older playwrights like Williams and Miller, who struggled during the 1970s and 1980s to get their more experimental work produced and became increasingly frustrated with the Broadway theatre and with theatre critics who expected them to go on writing for ever in the way they had written for the theatre of the late 1940s. For Williams, whose work was affected by diminished craftsmanship because of drug and alcohol abuse, this was a particularly bad period. Although most of his plays from the sixties and seventies are weak on structure and coherence, they exhibit a powerfully imaginative playwright experimenting with the new theatrical idioms that had become available to him, particularly the existential metaphors of absurdism, as in *The Red Devil Battery Sign* (1975), and the grotesque and arresting visual images which had always appealed to him, but that he could use now without worrying about staying within a realistic framework, as in *The Gnädiges Fräulein* (1966). Williams's last Broadway play, *Clothes for a Summer Hotel* (1980), which is based on Scott and Zelda Fitzgerald, uses startling visual images and poetic dialogue to make Williams's final theatrical statement about his perennial theme, the unconquerable soul of the artist surviving despite the most adverse of circumstances.

Arthur Miller had two Broadway commercial successes in the 1960s, his controversial experiment with the representation of the individual psyche in *After the Fall* (1964), with its autobiographical allusions to his marriage with Marilyn Monroe, and his less publicly autobiographical *The Price* (1968). They were followed by two commercial failures on Broadway, both experimental in form, *The Creation of the World and Other Business* (1972) and *The American Clock* (1980). After these, Miller did not have a Broadway production of a new play until *Broken Glass* in 1994. He continued his writing undeterred, including his experimentation with dramatizing the American psyche in several one-act plays. And he did not back away from his exploration of the moral issues related to the contemporary social and political order. *The American Clock* (1980) and the television adaptation of *Playing for Time* (1980) followed *Incident at Vichy* and *The Archbishop's Ceiling* in taking well-thought-out and sometimes controversial stands on contemporary issues. Miller's insistence in *Playing for Time* on holding the victims of the Holocaust morally responsible for their actions within the Nazi concentration camps was particularly controversial. His late plays, *The Last Yankee* (1991), *Broken Glass* (1994), and *Resurrection Blues* (2002), have continued to premiere in regional theatres such as New Haven's Long Wharf and Minneapolis's

Guthrie, and in London, where Miller was considered the United States' most important living playwright until his death in 2004.

In the last quarter of the twentieth century, yet another generation of playwrights and theatre artists were looking for new spaces in which to experiment with alternatives to the "safe" theatre of Broadway, and the Off-Broadway theatre that they perceived as becoming just a smaller version of Broadway with its commercial values. They found them in tiny, alternative spaces like coffeehouses, churches, warehouses, and garages. Originally, the term Off-Off Broadway referred only to non-profit theatres with fewer than 100 seats and productions with unsalaried actors, but it has come to be applied to all kinds of alternative theatre that rejects representational drama, integrated characterization, and linear plot-lines in favor of heightened or shocking visual images, shifting, "transformational" characters, and disrupted or non-linear narratives. There is a great deal of the postmodern sensibility in many of the plays, but the Off-Off Broadway theatre cannot be defined by postmodernism. Its chief characteristic is its constant experimentation, its flexibility, its direct response to contemporary culture. This phenomenon is not restricted to New York, as many cities throughout the United States have their equivalents to Off and Off-Off Broadway. The older regional theatres, self-designated as "resident nonprofit professional theatres," like the Guthrie in Minneapolis, Hartford Stage, Chicago's Goodman, Houston's Alley, New Haven's Long Wharf, Washington's Arena, Louisville's Actors, and San Francisco's American Conservatory, became more established and more "safe" as the century wore on. They came to rely on large subscription lists of an aging and mainly middle-class and middlebrow audience, and began to count their greatest successes as the productions that moved on to Broadway from their theatres. In fact these theatres now often cooperate in groups of two or three on productions that are beyond their financial means individually with the hope of going on to New York after playing at the regional theatres. Growing up around these theatres are smaller venues and theatre groups that correspond to Off-Off Broadway, and offer venues for experimental and non-commercial work. Established regional theatres often have smaller performance spaces for experiments as well.

As Arthur Miller noted, the impetus of American theatre was essentially reversed in the second half of the twentieth century. He told a reporter in 2002, "Broadway doesn't originate anything anymore. It used to be the opposite."[1] With the exception of prohibitively expensive musical extravaganzas like *The Lion King*, produced by Walt Disney Theatrical Productions, very few plays now originate on Broadway. Most plays are developed through a series of workshops and see production in a regional or university theatre before they see Broadway, if they ever do. And not making it to Broadway is no great detriment to a play or playwright in the twenty-first century.

The generation that grew up in the Off-Off Broadway theatre and its regional equivalent has a different attitude toward the New York theatre than previous generations had. The two best-known playwrights of their generation illustrate this well. Sam Shepard, who had his first plays produced in Off-Off Broadway venues like Theatre Genesis and La MaMa in the mid-1960s, became a world-famous playwright without ever having a premiere on Broadway. From the outset his plays bore the marks of his aesthetic gifts, with their startling visual images, their integrated rock music, and their highly evocative poetic language. Shepard's earliest works centered on the culture heroes of his Southern California youth, the cowboy, the rock star, the gangster, and the movie mogul. They were perfect vehicles for the Off-Off Broadway theatre. As he matured, Shepard began to focus on an admittedly autobiographical dysfunctional family with his trilogy, the *Curse of the Starving Class* (1977), *Buried Child* (1978), and *True West* (1980). Shepard won the Pulitzer Prize for *Buried Child* in 1979, without its being produced on Broadway, and he has not sought productions in the Broadway theatre. Beginning with his association with Joseph Chaikin's Open Theatre, he has worked most effectively in collaborative settings. His plays have originated in such theatres as the Royal Court in London, the Magic in San Francisco, and the Public in New York. His original theatre idiom has been called "hyper-realism" by some critics, paralleling the movement in the visual arts. Through detailed realism in some aspects of the sets, costumes, and colloquial dialogue, he is able to write plays that contain abstract scenic elements, long poetic monologues, highly symbolic allusions, and hallucinatory episodes without sacrificing the audience's belief in the reality of the characters on stage in plays such as *Fool for Love* (1983), *Simpatico* (1994), and *The Late Henry Moss* (2000). With his highly allusive, imagistic, and evocative language, he was America's most poetic playwright in the latter part of the twentieth century. A gifted actor and director with a successful film career, Shepard also has an extraordinary artistic versatility that is the goal of many in his generation.

Shepard's versatility is exceeded, perhaps, only by that of his contemporary, David Mamet, who has been an actor and acting teacher, a respected director of both theatre and film, and a writer of fiction, essays, and film scripts as well as plays. Mamet's playwriting career began in Chicago with the thirty-scene comedy about the urban single life, *Sexual Perversity in Chicago* (1974), a then startlingly frank and irreverent look at sexual mores.

His plays, indeed, often opened in regional theatre and in the case of *Glengarry Glen Ross* (1984) and *The Cryptogram* (1994), in England.

As a playwright, Mamet is concerned with many of the moral issues that preoccupied Arthur Miller, and his best-known play, *Glengarry Glen Ross*, is often seen as an updating of *Death of a Salesman*. Like Miller, he seems to relish unexpected stands on controversial issues, and he received a great deal of criticism for what many critics considered his biased view of sexual harassment in *Oleanna*. Aesthetically, his great contribution is in the writing of dialogue that combines a consciousness of the power dynamics involved in the speech act with a highly artistic sense of the poetics of plain speech, profanity, and silences. Like Shepard, he became more interested in exploring the dynamics of the family as he entered middle age, with a dark view of the contemporary American family in *The Cryptogram* and a positive view of the Victorian family in his film, *The Winslow Boy* (1999).

The alternative theatre, Off-Off Broadway theatre and its analogs throughout the nation, was by far the richest source for new drama and theatre in the last three decades of the twentieth century. Within the alternative theatre were several movements with clearly defined aesthetic and socio-political agendas. Among the earliest were two African American groups. The Black Arts Repertory Theatre, whose guiding spirit was Amiri Baraka (LeRoi Jones), expressed a revolutionary political agenda that rejected white liberalism and promoted black separatism. The less political Negro Ensemble Company was established with a grant from the Ford Foundation to help address the lack of venues for plays about African American life. The first inspired young playwrights such as Ed Bullins and August Wilson. The second provided a theatrical group for such playwrights as Alice Childress, Samm-Art Williams, and Charles Fuller. The alternative theatre was also an important cultural site for the women's movement in the last third of the twentieth century. Building on their collective experience in groups such as the Living Theatre and the Open Theatre, and making use of techniques adapted from agit-prop and the guerrilla street theatre of the antiwar movement, theater companies with a feminist agenda, such as Megan Terry's Omaha Magic Theatre, the lesbian theatre ensemble Split Britches, and At the Foot of the Mountain Theatre in Minneapolis, developed a feminist theatrical aesthetic. The feminist theatre is collaborative and anti-hierarchical in nature. It pays particular attention to issues of power in relation to gender and ethnicity, and rejects the linear plot, integrated characterization, and traditional realism as phallocentric. Instead, plays like Terry's *Calm Down, Mother* (1965), and Maria Irene Fornés's *Fefu and Her Friends* (1976) explored techniques such as transformational gender-crossing characterization and multi-sequential scenes to produce a drama that expressed their feminist vision. The gifted poet Ntozake Shange's *For Colored Girls Who Have Considered Suicide When the Rainbow is Enuf* (1976) was one of the few feminist plays to make it to Broadway. An unplotted "choreopoem" with minimalist staging, which combines music, dance, and dialogue spoken by characters individuated only by color, and was brought into being through a long process of collaboration among the artists, Shange's play is a prime example of feminist theatrical techniques.

In contrast with the feminist playwrights, August Wilson, whose interest in playwriting began with the Black Arts Movement, has been embraced by the commercial Broadway theatre as well as the critical world. Profiting from the workshop process at the Eugene O'Neill Theatre Centre National Playwrights Conference and his long collaboration with director Lloyd Richards at Yale Repertory Theatre, Wilson had eight plays produced on Broadway, six of which were nominated for the Pulitzer Prize, two of them winning. His ambitious plan was to write a cycle of ten plays, each of which represents the experience of a typical group of African Americans in one decade of the twentieth century. His theatrical aesthetic is analogous to the "spiritual realism" of fiction writers like Toni Morrison. Its theatrical idiom suggests a stage reality in which the spectator is meant to believe, but it is one which is occasionally invaded by the supernatural, as when an angel appears in *Fences* (1986) and a familial ghost in *The Piano Lesson* (1988). Thus Wilson conveys the fact that the supernatural is very much a part of his characters' reality. His drama is infused with music, through which he marks the history of black culture in America. In the play that brought him to national attention, *Ma Rainey's Black Bottom* (1984), a generational conflict is enacted through the older blues musicians and a young trumpet player who wants to play jazz. Wilson has fulfilled W. E. B. DuBois's injunction to produce a theatre for, by, and about black people. A white character seldom enters the universe of his plays, and he has insisted that his plays never be acted by white actors. Although the family and the dynamics within the black community are his central concerns, he records the effects that larger economic, social, and political forces, particularly racism, have had on the black community in each of the decades he writes about.

Many lines of alternative theatre joined to make the American theatre what it was in the last third of the twentieth century. Besides the groups who identified themselves through ethnicity and gender identity, there were activist theatres such as El Teatro Campesino, which was organized in conjunction with the farm workers movement in California, and was the starting point for a prolific Latino theatre movement that has served as a focal point for such playwrights as Luis Valdez, Eduardo Machado, and Maria Irene Fornés. More aesthetically oriented, less political alternative theatre, such as that of New York's Wooster Group and San Francisco's Mabou Mines, succeeded that of the political activists. Charles Ludlum's Ridiculous Theatre, the experiments of Robert Wilson and Richard Foreman, and solo performance artists like Karen Finley, Laurie Anderson, and John Leguizamo are all examples of alternative theatre. Toward the end of the twentieth century, one of the most important sources for American theatre and drama was the universities. A new generation of playwrights and theatre artists who were trained to create theatre in academic theater programs set the tone for the literary theatre of the 1980s and 1990s. David Henry Hwang's M. *Butterfly* (1988), with its postmodern deconstruction of gender, ethnic, and imperialist cultural stereotypes, shows evidence of his education at Stanford and the Yale School of Drama, where these issues were major concerns of the 1980s. Hwang's play was one of the few in the 1980s to originate on Broadway, and, winning a Tony Award and Pulitzer Prize as well as being a major commercial success, it brought these issues, and the postmodern approach to them, into the mainstream.

Two years earlier, Hwang's Yale colleague George C. Wolfe had had his *The Colored Museum*, a postmodern parodic treatment of the cultural forces and images that forge the identity of a young black man, produced in New York. Wolfe went on to become the producer of the prestigious New York Shakespeare Festival, which had been founded by Joseph Papp in 1954 and grown into a major producer of literary and experimental theatre at the Public Theatre in Greenwich Village. There he produced not only Hwang's *Golden Child* (1998), but several other influential plays: *Twilight: Los Angeles, 1992* (1994) by Anna Deavere Smith, who has taught at Yale, Stanford, and New York University, *Topdog/Underdog* by Suzan-Lori Parks, a graduate of the Yale School of Drama, and the play that perhaps best defines the American theatre at the end of the twentieth century, *Angels in America* (1993), by Tony Kushner, who has a graduate degree from NYU.

All of these plays share a focus on identity politics, raising issues of gender, ethnicity, and sexual identity. They all exhibit an awareness of the postmodern aesthetics of the eighties and nineties, although all of them have integrated characters with whom the audience can sympathize and identify rather than the shifting, transformational characters associated with the alternative theatre. Each of them is also trying to grasp an important truth about the United States of America. From the parodic figure of Lincoln in Parks's play to the millennial angel in Kushner's, all of these playwrights are creating images for the United States' identity and addressing its conduct in the world. Theirs is an educated theatre, meant, like the presentational theatre of the thirties, to confront audiences with the issues of the day, but with a perhaps exaggerated consciousness of the aesthetic issues of the later twentieth century. The American theatre that entered the twenty-first century was far from the theatre that entered the twentieth. No longer the entertainment behemoth that has room for all forms of performance, it is enlivened by a dynamic but uneasy dialectic between the popular, "commercial" theatre dominated by the lavishly produced musical and an elite "art theatre" with a small but dedicated audience spread throughout the country.

NOTES

1. Quoted by Jeff Barnen, "Arthur Miller Debuts New Play," July 15, 2002. www. theage.com.

FURTHER READING

Thomas P. Adler, *American Drama, 1940–1960: A Critical History*, New York: Twayne, 1994.

C. W. E. Bigsby, *A Critical Introduction to Twentieth-Century American Drama*, 3 vols. Vol. I, *1900–1940*. Vol. II, *Tennessee Williams, Arthur Miller, Edward Albee*; Vol. III, *Beyond Broadway*, Cambridge: Cambridge University Press, 1982–5.

   Contemporary American Playwrights, Cambridge: Cambridge University Press, 1999.

   Modern American Drama, 1945–2000, Cambridge: Cambridge University Press, 2000.

Gerald Bordman, *American Theatre: A Chronicle of Comedy and Drama, 1865–1914*, New York: Oxford University Press, 1994.

   American Theatre: A Chronicle of Comedy and Drama, 1914–1930, New York: Oxford University Press, 1995.

   American Theatre: A Chronicle of Comedy and Drama, 1930–1969, New York: Oxford University Press, 1996.

Sally Burke, *American Feminist Playwrights: A Critical History*, New York: Twayne, 1996.

Malcolm Goldstein, *The Political Stage: American Drama and Theater of the Great Depression*, New York: Oxford University Press, 1974.

Errol G. Hill and James V. Hatch, *A History of African American Theatre*, Cambridge: Cambridge University Press, 2003.

Thomas S. Hischak, *American Theatre: A Chronicle of Comedy and Drama, 1969–2000*, New York: Oxford University Press, 2001.

John Houchin, *Censorship of the American Theatre in the Twentieth Century*, Cambridge: Cambridge University Press, 2003.

Brenda Murphy, *American Realism and American Drama, 1880–1940*, Cambridge: Cambridge University Press, 1987.

Congressional Theatre: Dramatizing McCarthyism on Stage, Film, and Television, Cambridge: Cambridge University Press, 1999.

The Provincetown Players and the Culture of Modernity, Cambridge: Cambridge University Press, 2005.

Jack Poggi, *Theater in America: The Impact of Economic Forces, 1870–1967,* Ithaca, NY: Cornell University Press, 1968.

Matthew C. Roudané, *American Drama since 1960: A Critical History,* New York: Twayne, 1996.

Richard G. Scharine, *From Class to Caste in American Drama: Political and Social Themes since the 1930s,* Westport, CT: Greenwood, 1991.

Yvonne Shafer, *American Women Playwrights, 1900–1950,* New York: Peter Lang, 1995.

Susan Harris Smith, *American Drama: The Bastard Art,* Cambridge: Cambridge University Press, 1997.

Ronald H. Wainscott, *The Emergence of the Modern American Theater, 1914–1929,* New Haven: Yale University Press, 1997.

Don B. Wilmeth and Christopher Bigsby (eds.), *The Cambridge History of American Theatre,* 3 vols. Vol. I, *Beginnings to 1870*; vol. II, *1870–1945*; vol. III, *Post-World War II to the 1990s,* Cambridge: Cambridge University Press, 1998–2000.

EMORY ELLIOTT

Society and the novel in twentieth-century America

In his *Maps of the Imagination: The Writer as Cartographer* (2004), novelist Peter Turchi suggests that there are important links between maps, stories, and the mind, including the fact that the study of all three seem to have begun at about the same point in history: Turchi states: "Alphabetic texts, the earliest extant geographical maps, and the earliest extant map of the human brain" date back to around 3000 BC, thereby suggesting a close association among them. He says, "To ask for a map is to say, 'Tell me a story.'" Noting the similarities between maps and stories, Turchi quotes Emerson: "The Writer is an explorer: Every step is an advance into new land." Turchi himself asserts that "artistic creation is a voyage into the unknown. In our own eyes, we are off the map."[1] He compares finding one's way in an unknown land or in the mind itself to the experience of writing: discovering the subject, through trial and error, failed attempts, and wrong paths taken, finally to find new knowledge of the world and the self which then enables the writer to guide others to make their own discoveries.

Beginning in the late nineteenth century and continuing to the present, novels have provided American readers with maps for living in a rapidly expanding and evolving country. As the population grew and moved across the landscape, new and established Americans read stories that depicted the opportunities, values, and challenges that the complexity of being or becoming American presented to individuals. While peoples in all times and places have needed maps and narratives, this need has been especially compelling in the vast immigrant nation of the United States in the last two centuries. Between 1880 and 2000, over eighty million people left their countries, cultures, languages, and loved ones to travel extraordinary distances to a country about which they knew little or nothing and typically had many misconceptions but where they hoped to make a new life and prosper.[2] Every individual and family who underwent this passage had their particular stories of struggle, failure, or success. Even for those born on American soil, it was often necessary to travel to create a better life.

Dreiser's *Sister Carrie* (1900), opens with eighteen-year old Carrie boarding a train in her farming community of Columbia, Indiana, to seek work in the factories of Chicago, a very different world in which she must learn to survive. The narrator says of her "the threads which bound her so lightly to girlhood and home were irretrievably broken."[3] As a result of luck, looks, talent, and willingness to make compromises, Carrie becomes a success in the growing entertainment business in Chicago and then New York. Still, throughout her experiences, she feels insecure, confused, and dissatisfied about what is expected of her and what behavior is acceptable. Hundreds of thousands of women and men have embarked upon lives in America without roadmaps or role models and have had to invent ways to chart their paths through a complex and often hostile society. In 1906, Upton Sinclair's *The Jungle* presents the innocent and determined Lithuanian immigrants, Jurgis and Ona Rudkus, who try through hard work and sacrifice to pursue their American dream but who instead are forced to endure brutal living and working conditions, criminality, exploitation, and humiliation in the meat-packing slums of Chicago only to lose their home, self-respect, and finally their lives.

What these two stories, one of conditional success and one of complete failure, have in common are characters who are bewildered most of the time because they lack guidance and knowledge of the society and culture in which they are living. In spite of their wide variety of forms, subjects, and narrative methods and styles, the novels of the United States in the twentieth century nearly always have had a degree of pedagogical intent, providing readers with insights into the nature of the time and place in which their American characters find themselves and how those conditions play crucial roles in their lives. Most of these novels teach readers much about the American physical settings, history, politics, economics, and social conditions that are the contexts for the characters' experiences. In this chapter, I examine the relation of American fictions to the human conditions in which they have been written and which they have attempted to represent.

1900–1945

By the end of the nineteenth century, the American novel had certainly come of age. Mark Twain and Henry James were major international figures while many others, including the "realists" Edith Wharton, Willa Cather, William Dean Howells, Harold Frederick, Sarah Orne Jewett, Hamlin Garland, Kate Chopin, Charlotte Perkins Gilman, Edward Bellamy, Henry Adams, George Washington Cable, and Rebecca Harding Davis, were also widely read and admired. In the 1890s, an important and influential group of novelists emerged on the scene that included the African Americans Charles Chesnutt, Francis Harper, Paul Lawrence Dunbar, and Pauline Hopkins, the Jewish immigrant Abraham Cahan, and the Norwegian H. H. Boyesen, who were soon joined by the "naturalists": Theodore Dreiser, Stephen Crane, Frank Norris, Jack London, and Upton Sinclair. Many of these writers continued to be productive during the early decades of the new century.

Cather's *My Ántonia* (1918) is an example of a novel that focuses upon places, especially the farming town of Black Hawk, Nebraska, and the lives of recent Russian and eastern European immigrants as viewed through the eyes of Jim Burden, first seen as the American-born boy and then as an adult. As he grows up with his immigrant friends, Jim comes to admire these people, but he leaves them behind to go to Harvard and then to practice law in New York. After twenty years, Jim visits Black Hawk to see his best childhood friend, Antonia. He recalls the joys of growing up with Antonia, who had stayed and raised a family while the other girls left Nebraska to become business women. In their youth a few of these women had been drawn sexually to Jim but he shied away from them. Years later, in a loveless marriage and routine career, Jim clings to his precious memories of those women, the prairie, and the struggles and triumphs of people whose strengths and desires cause his present life to feel diminished and empty. Cather's novel conveys insights into the formation of individual identity in the West and the role of occupations, economics, cultural heritage, sexuality, and class in the formation of a person's economic and social gains and psychological and spiritual losses.

When World War I began in Europe in 1914, the United States remained neutral until 1918. Many Europeans and a significant percentage of Americans viewed such isolationism as evidence of American provincialism. When Germany sank five American ships heading to France and England, President Wilson declared war. American forces made a crucial difference and enabled the Allies to attain victory in 1918, and America emerged from the war as a more powerful global military and economic power. American patriotic pride was then at a high point, but a national yearning to cling nostalgically to a nineteenth-century agrarian and rural past and to traditional Protestant religious and cultural values resulted in powerful resistance to the changes brought on by the modernist movement.

By refusing to join the newly created League of Nations, the United States government discouraged and alienated many artists. During the 1920s and 1930s, many American novelists moved to Paris as expatriates or spent long periods there. Many Americans shared the anxious vision of the twentieth century that appeared to be supported by the thought and writing of

Nietzsche, Darwin, Freud, and Marx. Their theories raised questions about the legitimacy of religious beliefs, the viability of democracy, the possibility for fair economic conditions, and the existence of a personal God. T. S. Eliot's *The Waste Land* (1922) expressed this sense of alienation with a vision of a collapsing modern world where religious values were seen as mere myths and where the events of everyday life had become futile and meaningless.

When the stock market crashed in October 1929, the nation entered the decade of the Great Depression during which millions of Americans were reduced to poverty. With his *The Grapes of Wrath*, John Steinbeck and others began to produce novels that directly addressed the widespread unemployment, hopelessness, and suffering. Labor unions and political activists, some of whom joined socialist organizations or the Community Party, sought more sweeping reforms. John Dos Passos's *The Big Money* and James T. Farrell's *Studs Lonigan* trilogy were among the "proletarian fictions" that addressed contemporary social problems.

Although it is commonplace that the international movement of modernism began in Europe and moved to America in the 1920s and 1930s, Quentin Anderson and others have argued that the intellectual roots of modernism can be found in the works of Ralph Waldo Emerson, Edgar Allan Poe, Walt Whitman, Emily Dickinson, and in the writings and music of African American artists. In their fictions, modernist authors engaged controversial subjects like sex, race, ethnicity, class, addiction, and psychological problems that had previously been viewed as unsuitable for serious fiction. Such books also focused on characters who would have been deemed unacceptable in earlier works: criminals, the impoverished, the mentally disturbed, the physically impaired, and those with unconventional moral attitudes. Using stark realism as well as the bizarre and grotesque, modernist works shocked readers in order to awaken them.

Often considered the first American modernist novel, *The Great Gatsby* captures so much of the spirit and style of the 1920s. In tune with the new money, fast lives, and the youthful desire to escape family ties and social conventions, F. Scott Fitzgerald's novel exposes an American world of wealthy men, impressive cars, ostentatious parties, and soaring ambitions. A poor boy in the Midwest, James Gatz fell in love with the beautiful and rich Daisy Fay but was rejected by her because of his lower social status. Believing in the unlimited possibilities of America, he changed his name and reinvented himself in order to become wealthy at whatever cost. In the meantime, she somewhat reluctantly married the wealthy Tom Buchanan, and the newly rich Gatsby buys a mansion near theirs. The narrative describes the process by which Gatsby's dream leads to his involvement in the bootlegging business, his association with criminals, his distress when Daisy rejects him again, and his humiliation before Nick Carraway and Daisy's friend Jordan Baker when Tom Buchanan insults him as "Mr. Nobody from Nowhere."[4] Finally, Gatsby is murdered by the misguided George Wilson, who believes that Gatsby has killed his wife Myrtle, when it was Daisy who killed her in a hit-and-run accident. The novel reveals Gatsby's American dream to be a romantic self-delusion that leads to an American nightmare.

A book full of geography and detailed descriptions of places, like the area of Long Island on which Gatsby lives, Fitzgerald's novel warns those who might wish to leave the security of their southern or midwestern towns to seek their destiny in the urban East. Near the end, Nick says: "I see now that this has been a story of the West, after all – Tom, and Gatsby, Daisy and Jordan and I, were all Westerners, and perhaps we possessed some deficiency in common which made us subtly unadaptable to Eastern life." In the face of the enormous optimism, growing wealth, and national pride of the 1920s, *Gatsby* ends with Nick's jeremiad about the folly of believing in a better future: "I became aware of the old island here that flowered once for Dutch sailors' eyes – a fresh green breast of the new world . . . [it was] the last and greatest of all human dreams." [5]

Although a very different kind of person, Ernest Hemingway also emerged in the early 1920s to become a celebrated American novelist. With his lean prose style that drove a wedge between the novels of the previous generations and the prose fiction of emerging modernism, Hemingway created a new cool and measured narrative voice characterized by ironic detachment, understatement, cynical bemusement, and an anticipation of hurt, loss, and failure that permeated even moments of pleasure and joy. Hemingway's novels captured the deep ambivalences of the period when celebration of recent military victory and a booming economy poised against a pervasive fear that some unforeseen iceberg, such as awaited the Titanic, may lie ahead for the western world. In the spirit of Emerson, Hemingway's works taught Americans not to place their hopes in dreams but to know themselves and trust in their inner voice. The Hemingway code does not depend on religion or the judgments of others but upon each individual's personal and situational ethic. In *The Sun Also Rises*, arguably his most famous novel, Hemingway draws attention to the expatriate movement of many writers by placing his story in France and Spain. Linking geographical maps to his narrative, he has his main character and narrator Jake Barnes describe the streets and neighborhoods of Paris in precise detail and sketches for readers the mountains and villages of the Basque country of France and Spain.

Many modernist writers also employed new literary techniques to challenge readers to be more aware and attentive because they believed that serious literature should deepen a reader's experience of life and convey valuable lessons. Adapting some of James Joyce's methods in *Ulysses*, William Faulkner often employed the stream of consciousness technique of taking the reader inside a character's mind to observe the illogical and erratic flow of perceptions, images, and ideas, thus requiring the reader to discover or create coherence and meaning from the apparent jumble of disconnected thoughts. He also used multiple narrators, four in *The Sound and the Fury* and fourteen in *As I Lay Dying*, to suggest that there are many different ways that people will perceive and interpret the same events and thereby to challenge the reader to formulate his or her own view from all of the various perspectives.

At the center of Faulkner's *As I Lay Dying* lies Addie Bundren, mother of five and wife of Anse, on her deathbed. The narrative follows the Bundrens' nine-day journey to Jefferson to bury Addie near her people. In keeping with the connections between maps and stories, Jefferson is on the map of the imaginary Yoknapatawpha County, Mississippi, Faulkner's "own little postage stamp of native soil,"[6] as he called it. Remarkably, Faulkner represents these poor uneducated people in ways that enable readers to understand their thoughts, which they are unable to express themselves. He gives voices to the inarticulate so that their feelings and psychological problems are accessible to us. The most intelligent of the children is the second son, Darl, who is devoted to Addie in spite of her seeming rejection of him and her favoritism toward his younger brother Jewel, who is actually the child that resulted from Addie's affair with the minister, Reverend Whitfield. While Darl suspects that Jewel is illegitimate, he is never sure. Faulkner associates Darl with Hamlet because as brilliant as he is, he is unable to act. When Addie's body attracts vultures, Darl finally takes action, setting fire to a barn where they parked the wagon, but Jewel saves the coffin. The family commits Darl over to an asylum.

In the long section in which Addie actually speaks, the reader discovers that Darl inherited his intelligence from her. Addie had been a teacher but hated her students, and her father had been cynical and taught her that "the reason for living was to get ready to stay dead a long time." She says that "the only way I could get ready to stay dead [was to] hate my father for having ever planted me." Suffering sado-masochistic disorder, cultural impoverishment, and depression, Addie marries Anse to escape the schoolhouse, but never expecting to find happiness. When she becomes pregnant with her first son, Cash, she feels violated and wishes to have no other children, so that when she becomes pregnant with Darl she says: "I believed that I would kill Anse" and "my revenge would be that he would never know that I was taking revenge." In plain language, Addie explains complex philosophical positions she develops to justify her actions. She seduces Reverend Whitfield because corrupting a man of God is the worst sin she can imagine and because she wants a child of her choosing to cancel out Darl, whom she did not want. Then, she reasons: "I gave Anse Dewey Dell to negative Jewel. Then I gave him Vardaman to replace the child I had robbed him of [by getting pregnant with Jewel]."[7]

Brilliant and nearly mad, Darl and Addie represent millions of people trapped in poverty in America in the 1930s, limited by forces they cannot control and full of desperation and rage. By making a woman central in the narrative, Faulkner draws attention to the stifling conditions of the lives of the great majority of women even after the Nineteenth Amendment and the decade of the flapper. While marriage and the family are held in high regard as the foundation of American society, this novel shows that the nuclear family can also be dysfunctional and destructive. Yet, it is easy for society to ignore such situations and dismiss them as anomalies because the suffering are often poor and silent.

An important development in the modernist movement for both public culture and for the development of literature and the arts in America was the acknowledgment of the ethnic and gender pluralism of American culture. In many ways, the most consequential social achievement of modernism in America was the Harlem Renaissance, or to use more inclusive terms, the New (or the Modern) Negro Renaissance. Just as jazz and the blues moved to the center of American culture in the modern period and came to be recognized as the most original American music, so too did writing by African Americans become a powerful presence in American literature in the 1920s and 1930s. With the intellectual leadership of W. E. B. Du Bois, who inspired assertiveness, a host of black writers, many based in New York City, published important fiction, essays, and poetry, and gave public readings and lectures. The novelists include Langston Hughes, Claude McKay, Jean Toomer, Zora Neal Hurston, Nella Larsen, Ida B. Wells, Jessie Fauset, James Weldon Johnson, Sterling Brown, Wallace Thurman, Carl Van Vechten, George Schuyler, Arna Bontemps, Rudolph Fisher, Lillian Smith, and Walter White, among others. These writers explored themes related to the lives of African Americans and wrote experimental stories and novels using non-traditional narrative techniques and examining provocative subjects. Upon close and extensive examination of the many black writers of this period, critics have recognized that many of the components of modernism were already present in the nineteenth-century writings of African Americans.[8]

Cultural anthropologist and author Zora Neal Hurston was a highly controversial figure because many believed her literary works to be degrading to African Americans in their frank representation of poverty, violence, and sexuality. In writing in this way, however, Hurston was very much a figure of the modernist movement. Although raised in poverty by her grandmother, Hurston graduated from Howard University and then studied with the famed anthropologist Franz Boas at Barnard College. Her research and creative work display a deep awareness of the importance of place and landscape in a person's life and writing. Throughout her career, she produced several anthropological studies and a wide range of literary works. Defying the male dominant society, Hurston challenged assumptions about what was proper for a woman writer to depict.

Her most powerful and recognized novel is *Their Eyes Were Watching God*. This is an autobiographical *Bildungsroman* that traces the life of Janie Crawford Killicks Starks Woods, who, like Hurston, was conceived when her mother was raped, and raised by her grandmother. In the novel, Janie's first marriage is arranged by her grandmother, but she soon discovers that she is unable to love her husband. When she meets young Joe Starke, whom she calls Jody, they run off, get married, and open a general store in the black community of Eatonville, Florida, where Joe soon becomes the richest man and the mayor.

In her youth, Janie is an insecure young woman who accepts Jody's verbal and physical abuse as the price of being a woman. Over the years, such behavior wears her down, but she finds a deeper spirit of resistance within her and frees herself from Jody's control. In the most famous scene of the text, Janie and Jody are having one of their usual angry, public arguments on the porch of the store. Since she is now about forty years old, Jody has begun to berate her for her old age and unappealing figure even though she remains quite youthful. She recognizes that it is Jody who is feeling old and insecure, and waits until his insults go too far: "God almighty! A woman stay round uh store till she get old as Methusalem . . .! Don't stand dere rolli' yo' pop eyes wid yo'rump hangin' nearly to you' knees!"[9]

Sensing that she has the community on her side, Janie "took to the middle of the floor to talk right into Jody's face, and that was something that hadn't been done before." Drawing upon the African folk tradition of trading insults, or "playing the dozens," Janie counters more barbs by saying that she looks her age and is "uh woman every inch of me," and then launches what proves to be literally a deadly blow: "Humph! Talkin' bout *me* lookin' old! When you pull down yo' britches, you look lak de change uh life." The narrator says that "Janie had robbed him of his illusion of irresistible maleness that all men cherish." The other men "laughed, and would keep on laughing." Through the power of words, Janie has repaid Jody for all the years of physical and verbal abuse by humiliating him and rendering him powerless: "For what can excuse a man in the eyes of other men for lack of strength?"[10] In shame, Jody falls ill with kidney disease, quickly weakens, and dies. She soon meets the much younger Tea Cake, and they have a tumultuous but loving marriage until he is bitten by a rabid dog and in his madness tries to kill Janie, who shoots him in self-defense. In her murder trial, she is found not guilty, and the story ends with Janie telling her life story.

Their Eyes has been important for the development of African American literature and women's writing in the latter part of the twentieth century. Her work has influenced Alice Walker, Toni Morrison, Paule Marshall, and Maya Angelou, and her use of dialect and frank dialogue, as well as her lyrical descriptions of nature, the tropics, and human passions infused literary realism with new vigor and sensuality and informed and inspired many works of the Black Arts movement of the 1960s and beyond.

1945–1975

After the 1941 attack on Pearl Harbor, the war commanded the attention of the American people. Hollywood produced a steady stream of patriotic films, and some novelists, Fitzgerald and Faulkner among them, moved to Hollywood to write screenplays. Meanwhile, Saul Bellow, Norman Mailer, Karl Shapiro, and John Cheever joined the armed services, and Hemingway went to the front as a war correspondent. During the war, American writers continued to publish in the traditions of modernism and realism, but the postwar period brought about a period of reflection upon the massive destruction and death caused by war and the Holocaust. After 1945, the war itself became the material for many fictional works, the most notable being John Hersey's *Hiroshima*, Norman Mailer's *The Naked and the Dead*, James Jones's *From Here to Eternity*, Herman Wouk's *The Caine Mutiny*, and Joseph Heller's *Catch-22*.

While intellectuals and artists pondered the implications of the war for the future of humanity, most Americans emerged from World War II with a sense of national pride in their victory. Leaders proclaimed that the United States was the most powerful country in the world and that its mission was to spread the model of individual freedom and democracy that could bring peace and prosperity to all nations. However, the invention of the atomic bomb and President Harry Truman's use of it to destroy the Japanese cities of Hiroshima and Nagasaki in 1945 opened "the atomic age" that would be characterized by the constant threat of nuclear war. Between 1950 and 1989, Americans lived in fear that the Soviet Union might launch a surprise attack that could destroy the United States in minutes. Intellectually, the postwar period was powerfully influenced by existentialism, whose key figures had been Søren Kierkegaard, Martin Heidegger, and Gabriel Marcel, but whose most significant voice in the 1950s and 1960s was that of Jean-Paul Sartre. The existentialists proposed that each individual must accept responsibility for his or her own moral decisions and the larger consequences.

As a result, the individual self became a central focus of many postwar novels. A generation of American novelists that included Robert Penn Warren, Vladimir Nabokov, J. D. Salinger, Walker Percy, Harper Lee, John Hawkes, Richard Wright, Ralph Ellison, James Baldwin, Eudora Welty, Carson McCullers, Paul Bowles, Jack Kerouac, Ken Kesey, Harper Lee, Isaac Bashevis Singer, Truman Capote, Gore Vidal, Saul Bellow, Flannery O'Connor, John Rechy, John Cheever, Hubert Selby, William Styron, John Updike, Bernard Malamud, Joan Didion, and Kurt Vonnegut wrote fiction that explored the search for spiritual meaning and moral values in a nuclear age. They often employed detached narrators who use irony, understatement, and sardonic humor as they explore the burdens of modern life and the torments of the soul. Avoiding sentimentalism and romanticism, they depicted the psychological trauma and strange sense of unreality and the uncanny that individuals experience in the face of human cruelty, brutality, and incomprehensible evil.

Malamud's novels depict the lives of displaced individuals, either people who have relocated from one culture to another or those who seek a sense of belonging in a world that they feel is alien. His characters are often lonely losers inhabiting gritty Jewish neighborhoods, searching for love or following a dream in situations sometimes productive of bitter results but sometimes of miraculous redemptions.

The works of southern women writers Eudora Welty and Flannery explore aspects of gender and regional differences that shape their characters. Their stories are about the power of love and family, the problems of communication and understanding, and the suffering of loneliness and loss. Their tales are not grim and depressing, however, but are provocative, symbolic, perplexing, and sometimes violent.

Perhaps the greatest turmoil in America in the period between 1950 and 1965 was generated by the Civil Rights Movement. President Truman ended racial discrimination in the armed forces while the 1954 Supreme Court case of *Brown v. Board of Education* declared segregation in schools and other public places to be unconstitutional. In Montgomery, Alabama, Rosa Parks tested this ruling and was arrested for refusing to give up her seat to a white person on a public bus. The Reverend Martin Luther King, Jr. joined the black community in supporting Parks and powerfully addressed the issues of injustice, gaining national attention and launching the Civil Rights Movement that he led until his assassination in 1968.

During the 1950s, there were also dramatic changes in the lifestyles of the nation. Many women who had worked in factories and offices during the war lost their jobs or stepped aside so that male war veterans could find employment. Television became affordable even for working families, and situation comedies like *Ozzie and Harriet* both reflected and shaped the lives of millions. Lives of white middle-class Americans seemed to have become so standardized and routine that novelists and sociologists began to write about the problems of the conformity, blandness, and anonymity of the new society. Among the works to reflect this were Sloan Wilson's novel, *The Man in the Gray Flannel Suit*, David Riesman's *The Lonely Crowd*, William H. Whyte's *The Organization Man*, C. Wright Mill's *The Power Elite*, and Paul Goodman's *The Lonely Crowd*.

While the great writers of color other than African Americans did not emerge until the late 1960s, there were several Asian American authors whose work was being recognized in the 1950s. These included Louis Chu, whose *Eat a Bowl of Tea* is notable, and Sylvia Chang, whose *Frontiers of Love* was an important contribution. Latino/a authors emerging in the 1950s include Jose Antonio Villarreal (*Poco*); Raymund Barrio (*The Plum Pickers*); Ron Arias (*The Road to Tamazanchale*); and Tomas Rivera (*And The Earth Did Not Devour Him*). Among Native Americans were Mourning Dove (Christine Quintasket or Humishu-ma), John Joseph Mathews, D'Arcy McNickle, John Milton Oskison, Ella Deloria, S. Alice Callahan, Zitkala-Sa (Gertrude Simmons Bonnin), and John Rollins Ridge.

Although the place of African American literature in the canon of American literature was still not well established in the 1940s, several events and many works published in the 1950s and 1960s by black writers resulted in African American texts becoming central to the teaching of American literature by the 1970s. The African American writers of prose fiction whose works became best known in the postwar years were Richard Wright, Ralph Ellison, James Baldwin, Chester Himes, Ann Petry, and Paule Marshall. While all of these authors explored the conditions of life for African Americans in the United States, each also addressed universal human themes that went beyond race relations in America, and each employed very different styles and narrative methods. The three who had the largest impact on American literature are Wright, Ellison and Baldwin.

Their novels take the reader inside the minds of such isolated characters as Wright's Bigger Thomas in *Native Son* to discover how they struggle with racism, poverty, and violence. When *Native Son* appeared in 1940, it shocked both white and black readers by presenting an unapologetic depiction of the brutal life in a Chicago ghetto and a main character, Bigger Thomas, who starts out as vulnerable and confused and becomes defiant and threatening. *Native Son* opened American literature to a new kind of writing by African Americans. In 1952, Ralph Ellison published *Invisible Man*, a complex *Bildungsroman* that traces the life of an unnamed black man who moves from the South to the North, from rural poverty to the center of culture and politics in New York. Ellison blended several complicated techniques of modernist narrative, including stream of consciousness, an elaborate symbolic structure, a wide range of myths and literary allusions, and elements from popular culture and from African folklore and folk culture. In 1952, James Baldwin, published his first novel, *Go Tell It On The Mountain*. In his lyrical and passionate prose style, Baldwin told an autobiographically based story of the epiphany of self-realization that comes to John Grimes on his fourteenth birthday in Harlem. Baldwin weaves into the novel the narratives of several other family members to create a mini-history of African Americans from slavery times to the 1940s.

By taking leadership of the United Nations in 1949, the United States found itself in a dominant position in the non-communist world. Between 1947 and 1989, US foreign policies were formulated in relation to the actions of the Soviet Union. The 1962 Cuban Missile Crisis, President John F. Kennedy's successful opposition to the siting of Soviet missiles on the island, followed by his assassination in November 1963, changed the United States. The many conspiracy theories surrounding the assassination shattered national confidence and a profound gloom prevailed in the late 1960s and early 1970s. As the war in Vietnam escalated in the late 1960s, opposition to the war led to riots and demonstrations against the war and more generally the racial and gender injustices in society.

1975–2005

Once American military forces were out of Vietnam, the nation entered a period of reflection and apparent calm. Tim O'Brien (*If I Die in A Combat Zone*) and Phil Caputo (*A Rumor of War*) are among the many writers who examined the effects of the war while filmmakers depicted aspects of the war in films like Michael Cimino's *The Deer Hunter*, Francis Ford Coppola's *Apocalypse Now*, and Stanley Kubrick's *Full Metal Jacket*. Most Americans wanted to turn their backs on this painful history and seek a new beginning.

During the 1960s, many American writers joined political movements and made social issues subjects of their writing at the same time as several

European philosophers formulated ideas that would launch a major theoretical revolution. Challenging long-accepted assumptions about the nature of knowledge and critical judgments, Michel Foucault, Jacques Derrida, and others dramatically changed the ways that intellectuals and artists thought about society and power. Among many novelists who were influenced by such new thinking, whether directly or indirectly, was Norman Mailer. Mailer's participation in the protest at the Pentagon in 1968 was the subject of his novel *The Armies of the Night: History as a Novel, The Novel as History*. His subtitle raises the question of whether personal or historical accounts of events are any more truthful or factual than fictional or imagined accounts. Because the war and the Watergate scandal of the early 1970s generated suspicion of all authority, many writers were open to new theories of perception, knowledge, and interpretation. This in part explains the enthusiasm for "deconstruction" and "post-structuralism," new theories which questioned everything and inspired new themes and methods in literature and art.

For literature, one result was a serious rethinking of the official canons of books and authors studied in the schools and universities. As more scholars and teachers began to acknowledge the contributions of women and writers of color to American literature, textbooks and course outlines that had been limited mainly to white male authors became more diversified. The Civil Rights Movement and new immigration from different parts of the world led to a recognition of the cultural diversity of America. While many would embrace the new postmodernism, both before and afterwards there were those drawn to realism because of the compelling immediacy and relevance of their stories to the social changes in America. Among them are Joyce Carol Oates, Robert Stone, Richard Ford, Russell Banks, Larry McMurtry, Philip Roth, Truman Capote, Jerzy Kosinski, George Chambers, Max Apple, John Gardner, Tobias Wolff, Bobbie Ann Mason, Raymond Carver, Ann Beattie, Alice Adams, Bret Ellis, Tom Wolfe, John Irving, Mary Robinson, Jay McInerney, Mary McCarthy, and Susan Straight.

Philip Roth's first novella, *Goodbye, Columbus* (1959), won the National Book Award, but he achieved international fame with his third novel, *Portnoy's Complaint* (1969). In *The Breast* (1972), Roth draws upon Kafka's short story "Metamorphosis" to create the character of David Kepesh, who finds himself transformed into a giant breast and who appears again in *The Professor of Desire* (1977) and *The Dying Animal* (2001). Another recurring character in Roth's work is Nathan Zucherman, who appeared first in *My Life as a Man* (1975) and more recently in *I Married a Communist* (1998), and *The Human Stain* (2000), among others. Drawing upon his Jewish heritage, Roth has often written with sharp wit and satire about his Jewish characters. In the 1980s, Roth's work seemed to move onto a higher plane with his novel *The Counterlife* (1986), for which he received the National Book Critics Circle Award, which he won again in 1991 for *Patrimony*. Since then he has won the PEN/Faulkner Award for *Operation Shylock* (1993) and *The Human Stain*, the National Book Award for *Sabbath's Theater* (1995), and the Pulitzer Prize for *American Pastoral* (1997).

In 2004, he published *The Plot Against America*, which many critics regarded as his best novel yet. In this he proposes an alternative America in which the aviation hero Charles Lindberg, whom many claim was an isolationist and Nazi-sympathizer, wins the Presidency in 1940. Roth creates a highly plausible narrative in which Lindberg and his fellow American fascists enact anti-Semitic policies that limit religious freedom and relocate Jewish families from their neighborhoods into towns across the United States where they will be the only Jewish people in their communities. While Roth has used some of his works in the past to critique problems in the government, *The Plot Against America* may be even more controversial for it depicts conditions that are similar to those of the present in which the administration is using the terrorist attacks of 2001 to justify the illegal invasion of Iraq, the imprisonment of people without charges or legal council, and the limitation of the freedoms of American citizens.

While African American literature was well-established by 1970, important new black writers came upon the scene in the concluding decades of the twentieth century, including Alice Walker, Toni Morrison, Ernest Gaines, Walter Mosley, Paule Marshall, Octavia Butler, Terry McMillian, Alex Haley, Gordon Parks, David Bradley, Gloria Naylor, Ntozake Shange, John Edgar Wideman, Shirley Anne Williams, Ishmael Reed, Nathaniel Mackey, Clarence Major, Toni Cade Bambara, Samuel Delany, August Wilson, and Patricia Gaines. Asian American fiction writers who had a significant impact on American literature in the later part of the century include Frank Chin, Amy Tan, Laurence Yep, Kyoko Mori, Shawn Hsu Wong, Maxine Hong Kingston, John Okada, Toshi Mori, Hisaye Yamamoto, Theresa Hak Kyung Cha, Jessica Tarahata Hagedorn, Tran Van Dinh, Chang-rae Lee, Gish Jen, Lois-Ann Yamanaka, Chitra Divakaruni, Bharati Mukerjee, Ruth Ozeki, Nina Revoyr, and Susan Choi among others. Latino/a novelists who have been highly successful in recent years include Rolando Hinojosa-Smith, Rudolfo Anaya, Richard Rodriguez, Oscar Zeta Acosta, Sandra Cisneros, Alicia Gaspar de Alba, Richard Vasquez, Cherrie Moraga, Helena Maria Viramontes, Julia Alvarez, Ana Castillo, Denise Chavez, Cristina Garcia, Oscar Hijuelos, Piri Thomas, Sergio Troncoso, Sandra Benitez, Abraham Rodriguez, Junot Diaz, Achy Obejas, Carla Trujillo, and Elizabeth

Nunez. Leading Native American fiction writers include N. Scott Momaday, Paula Gunn Allen, Michael Dorris, Louis Erdrich, Simon Ortiz, James Welch, Leslie Marmon Silko, Gerald Vizenor, Greg Sarris, William Least-Heat Moon, Sherman Alexie, Leanne Howe, Susan Power, Henry Gordon Jr., Betty Louise Bell, David Treuer, Louis Owens, Robert J. Conley, Janet Campbell Hale, Linda Hogan, Diane Glancy, and Adrian C. Louis.

One of the most widely read and influential works of contemporary social realism is Alice Walker's *The Color Purple*. Born into a sharecropper family in Georgia in 1944, Walker was fortunate enough to attend Spelman College, and was being recognized as an important new voice by 1972. *The Color Purple* won the Pulitzer Prize in 1983 and the American Book Award and became a commercially successful film.

Constructed in the epistolary form, the novel tells the story of Celie, a young black woman growing up in the South who at fourteen is raped by a man she believes to be her father. After she has two children with him, her mother dies, and "Pa" gives her children to a minister in town and marries her off to a man she knows only as "Mr." She is forced to raise Mr.'s children from a previous marriage and endure his verbal and physical abuse. Her younger sister Nettie runs off and joins missionaries going to Africa. Soon, Mr.'s former lover, Shug Avery, a woman of the world, returns to visit him. Shug enables Celie to discover that she prefers sex with women, and then she becomes her lover. For years, Celie writes letters to Nettie but never receives replies, but she discovers that Mr. has been stealing Nettie's letters. Shug and Celie go to live in Memphis, where Celie starts a successful business. When Shug goes off with a young man, Celie is heartbroken, but then Nettie returns with Celie's now adult children. With Celie's new wealth, the family is prosperous and joyful. While *The Color Purple* is primarily a work of social and psychological realism about the brutality of racism and sexism, the later chapters take on a postmodern playful quality. Many readers were initially troubled by the series of rather magical events that produce the happy ending, but others came to recognize that Walker was using self-reflexivity, narrative incongruity, and playfulness, elements more often found in postmodern fiction, to suggest that, for once, African Americans can triumph in the end.

In 1967 in *The Atlantic*, John Barth published an essay, "The Literature of Exhaustion," in which he declared that realism and modernism were no longer producing vibrant and engaging literary forms and that writers needed to invent new modes of expression for new postmodern realities. As Barth recognized, change had already begun with the publication of William Burroughs's *Naked Lunch* in 1959 and in works of the 1960s by

Flannery O'Connor, John Hawkes, Kurt Vonnegut, Ishmael Reed, and Thomas Pynchon, but his essay signaled the beginning of a new era.

The two most distinguishing features of postmodernist writing are self-reflexivity and narrative fragmentation. Frequently, the writer stresses that he or she is the creator of an artificial world and that the narrator is a character whom the author invented. Sometimes "the author" is also a character who keeps reminding the reader about the artificiality and fictionality of the novel. Verbal playfulness, self-reflexivity and self-mocking underscore the point that a novel is not life and that no real lives or people are at stake. In accord with insistence on destabilizing the reader's sense of the "reality" of fiction, such novels seldom follow a linear timeline, but rather they frequently present events in fragments that are out of linear sequence, thereby leaving the reader disoriented, even temporarily bewildered. Such fictions demand the reader's total concentration and intense engagement. In some ways, fiction writers borrowed some of these narrative techniques from the cinematic styles of movies and television dramas like *Hill Street Blues*, yet at the same time, movies of the late 1980s and the 1990s like *Pulp Fiction, Get Shorty, Short Cuts,* and *Fargo,* also learned techniques from postmodern prose fiction. Many works of postmodern fiction, as, for example, Don DeLillo's *White Noise,* and Pynchon's *The Crying of Lot 49* and *Vineland,* are extremely funny books as well as being intellectually complex and challenging. Also, Robert Coover's *The Public Burning* and Toni Morrison's *Beloved, Jazz, Paradise,* and *Love* are passionate, excoriating critiques of injustice and inhumanity. What they have in common is that they challenge readers to question everything: their society, themselves, and the texts they are reading.

In recent decades, numerous writers have embraced the new forms and techniques that would characterize what came to be called self-reflective, experimental, or postmodern fiction. These include Walter Abish, Paul Auster, Steven Katz, Gilbert Sorrentino, Madeline Gins, Clarence Major, Richard Brautigan, William Gass, Donald Bartheleme, Ronald Sukenick, Raymond Federman, Don DeLillo, Joseph McElroy, Guy Davenport, Jonathan Baumbach, William Gaddis, William Kennedy, Rachel Ingalls, Richard Kostelanetz, Ron Silliman, Harold Jaffe, June Arnold, Kathy Acker, and William Gibson.

In the middle of a highly successful career in which she had produced four novels that critics perceived to be a blend of social and magical realisms, including the remarkable *Song of Solomon,* which is full of allusions to Ralph Ellison's *Invisible Man,* creating a kind of conversation, or black signifying, with Ellison, Toni Morrison took an artistic risk in the mid-1980s when she composed her 1987 novel *Beloved.* Abandoning the linear plot line of her early works, she employed a fragmented structure, using time shifts and flashbacks to reveal different aspects of the history and the lives of the characters at different moments in the past, often repeating scenes with new pieces of information revealed each time. The power and importance of individual and collective memory is a central theme of the narrative, and the style and structure of the novel are designed to operate the way human memory does with recollections operating like pieces of a large puzzle being put into place. Through her powerful language and images and penetrating psychological revelations, Morrison takes the reader deep inside the process whereby slavery and its psychic devastation continues to affect the thoughts and feelings of those who have been permanently scarred by its cruelty and horror. *Beloved* won the Pulitzer Prize, and certainly led to her receiving the Nobel Prize for Literature in 1993.

In 1989, the Cold War ended when the financially weakened Soviet Union succumbed to peaceful uprisings in many of the countries and republics that it had controlled. In August 1989, East and West Germans joined together to tear down the Berlin Wall that had been constructed around the city of West Berlin in 1961 by the Soviets to prevent people from escaping communist control. Most Americans celebrated the destruction of the wall as an American victory of democracy and capitalism over communism. With the Soviet Union no longer an apparent threat to the security of the United States, Americans turned their attention inward again during the 1990s. However, beginning in 1979, when the religious revolutionaries in Iran had held Americans hostage, a series of violent attacks by radical Muslim regimes and terrorist groups directly or indirectly against American interests indicated an increasing hostility toward the United States in much of the Middle East and the Asian Pacific. On September 11, 2001, the attack on the World Trade Center and the Pentagon dramatically altered American society and culture in ways few would have predicted. After forty years of thinking that only those nations with nuclear weapons posed a serious threat, the country now had to recognize the need to remain attentive to all global partners and enemies. Since the United States emerged as a global power at the beginning of what has been called "The American Century," the tendency of the nation to adhere to isolationist principles had been questioned by many writers at home and abroad. That now changed but not necessarily for the better. Certainly, American literature in the twenty-first century will be influenced by the events of that terrible day and by the ways that the United States government responded. American culture has already begun to move beyond postmodernism to new forms and subjects still to be discovered.

It is likely now that the "maps of the imagination" that novelists construct will be increasingly international as the United States appears no longer able or inclined to withdraw into isolation. The pre-9/11 novels by Don DeLillo, *Mao II* (1991) and *Underworld* (1997), seem to have been prophetic. In *Mao II*, DeLillo's reclusive novelist Bill Gray is assassinated by Arab terrorists in Lebanon, and in *Underworld*, which has a photo of the World Trade Center towers on the dust jacket, he explores the national paranoia that led to the massive build-up of nuclear weapons and spy networks after the Soviets tested a nuclear bomb in 1953. In his post 9/11 novel, *Cosmopolis*, the protagonist Eric Packer is a billionaire executive with a global network of companies, surrounded by bodyguards as he works in his office in an armored limo. Day and night, he is in contact with his offices around the globe and tracks his profits on electronic screens, but his limo remains stuck in New York traffic for an entire afternoon. On the relationship between literature and terrorism, DeLillo has said:

> In a repressive society, a writer can be deeply influential, but in a society that's filled with glut and endless consumption, the act of terror may be the only meaningful act. People who are in power make their arrangements in secret, largely as a way of maintaining and furthering that power. People who are powerless make an open theater of violence. True terror is a language and a vision. There is a deep narrative structure to terrorist acts, and they infiltrate and alter consciousness in ways that writers used to aspire to.[11]

The connections between minds, maps, and stories will surely remain in American fiction, but the troubling question is whether the truths of American novels about the problems of our society and culture will ever penetrate the public consciousness effectively. In the meantime, the United States continues to be trapped within the destructive seventeenth-century Puritan extreme binary thinking of God versus Satan, Good versus Evil, Success versus Failure, and Us versus Them. Can our writers ever enable the United States to construct a map that charts a middle way?

NOTES

1. Peter Turchi, *Maps of the Imagination: The Writer as Cartographer* (San Antonio, Texas: Trinity University Press, 2004), p. 11.
2. *Immigration: The Demographic and Economic Facts: The Quantities of Immigrants in the United States*, Cato Institute and the National Immigration Forum. http://www.cato. org/pubs/policy_report/pr-imquant.html
3. Theodore Dreiser, *Sister Carrie* (New York: The New American Library, 1961), p. 7; see also Quentin Anderson, "The Emergence of Modernism," in Emory Elliott (ed.), *The Columbia Literary History of the United States* (New York: Columbia University Press, 1988), pp. 695–714.
4. F. Scott Fitzgerald, *The Great Gatsby* (New York: Charles Scribner's Sons, 1925), p. 130.

5. *Ibid.*, pp. 177, 182.
6. William Faulkner, from an interview with Jean Stein in the *Paris Review* in 1956, reprinted in James B. Meriwether and Michael Millgate (eds.), *Lion in the Garden: Interviews with William Faulkner, 1926–1962* (New York: Random House, 1968), p. 255. Faulkner said: "Beginning with Sartoris I discovered that my own little postage stamp of native soil was worth writing about and that I would never live long enough to exhaust it, and by sublimating the actual into the apocryphal I would have complete liberty to use whatever talent I might have to its absolute top."
7. William Faulkner, *As I Lay Dying* (New York: Random House, 1930), pp. 161, 164, 168.
8. See Houston Baker, A. Jr., *Modernism and the Harlem Renaissance* (Chicago: University of Chicago Press, 1987).
9. Zora Neal Hurston, *Their Eyes Were Watching God* (New York: J. B. Lippincott Co., 1937), p. 121.
10. *Ibid.*, pp. 122, 123.
11. Vince Passaro, "Dangerous Don DeLillo," *New York Times Magazine*, May 19, 1991, p. 144.

FURTHER READING

Houston A. Baker, Jr., *Blues, Ideology, and Afro-American Literature: A Vernacular Theory*, Chicago: University of Chicago Press, 1984.
 Modernism and the Harlem Renaissance, Chicago: University of Chicago Press, 1987.
Tony Bennett (ed.), *Popular Fiction: Technology, Ideology, Production, Reading*, New York and London: Routledge, 1990.
Richard Chase, *The American Novel and Its Tradition*, New York: Doubleday, 1957.
Henry Louis Gates, Jr. (ed.), *"Race," Writing, and Difference*, Chicago: University of Chicago Press, 1986.
Ihab Hassan, *Radical Innocence: Studies in the Contemporary American Novel*, Princeton: Princeton University Press, 1961.
Linda Hutcheon, *A Poetics of Postmodernism: History, Theory, Fiction*, New York and London: Routledge, 1988.
Elaine H. Kim, *Asian American Literature: An Introduction to the Writings and Their Social Context*, Philadelphia: Temple University Press, 1982.
Brian McHale, *Postmodernist Fiction*, New York and London: Methuen, 1987.
Marcienne Rocard, *The Children of the Sun: Mexican-Americans in the Literature of the United States*, trans. Edward G. Brown, Jr., Tucson: University of Arizona Press, 1989.
Ramón Saldivar, *Chicano Narrative: The Dialectics of Difference*, Madison: University of Wisconsin Press, 1990.
Warren I. Susman, *Culture as History: The Transformation of American Society in the Twentieth Century*, New York: Pantheon, 2984.
Tony Tanner, *City of Words: American Fiction, 1950–1970*, New York: Harper & Row, 1971.

James Vinson (ed.), *Twentieth-Century Western Writers*, Detroit: Gale, 1982.

Linda Wagner-Martin, *The Modern American Novel 1914–1945: A Critical History*, Boston: Twayne, 1990.

James L. W. West, *American Authors and the Literary Marketplace Since 1900*, Philadelphia: University of Pennsylvania Press, 1988.

Alan Wilde, *Middle Grounds: Studies in Contemporary American Fiction*, Philadelphia: University of Pennsylvania Press, 1987.

23

TIM WOODS

"Preferring the wrong way": mapping the ethical diversity of US twentieth-century poetry

In the nineteenth century, poets like Whitman and Dickinson seemed to thrive on the impulse to push at boundaries and to seek out new idioms for an American vernacular poetics. In reaction to the weary genteel romanticism of much poetry at the turn of the nineteenth century, this transgressive impulse became more pronounced with the innovations generated by modernist poets such as William Carlos Williams, T. S. Eliot, and especially Ezra Pound, whose mantra "make it new" encapsulates this energetic thrust. While modern American poetry is indeed a broad, disparate field, embracing a range of practices and styles, nevertheless, no study of American poetry in the twentieth century can legitimately ignore the signal contributions of the modernists T. S. Eliot, Ezra Pound, William Carlos Williams, Robert Frost, and Wallace Stevens. Many of the driving formulations and elaborations of contemporary poetics owe themselves to Pound's intervention in what he saw as the dilapidated and dead-end poetics of late-nineteenth-century romanticism. His development of Imagism was a formative thrust in the energy of modernist poetics, summed up in the three Imagist dicta:

1. Direct treatment of the "thing," whether subjective or objective.
2. To use absolutely no word that did not contribute to the presentation.
3. As regarding rhythm: to compose in sequence of the musical phrase, not in sequence of a metronome.[1]

These tenets were put forward in an attempt to check what Pound saw as the vague use of language and the interference of the ego in contemporaneous poetry. He sought a language of absolute efficiency, which led to attempts to rid language of those facets that reveal the materiality of discourse. The image was an attempt to capture the "primary form" of "every concept, every emotion [which] presents itself to the vivid consciousness."[2] *The Cantos* (1916–69) and a host of smaller poems, exemplified Pound's Imagist techniques, although as he became more ensnared in fascistic ideology and authoritarian pronouncements about what passed muster as adequate poetry, Pound's influence caused increasing angst among his left-wing poetic admirers, during a period of sharply divided political affiliations in the 1930s and 1940s.

To Ezra Pound's Scylla, T. S. Eliot was the Charybdis of American modernist poetics. Heavily indebted to the aesthetic ideologies of Pound, Eliot's gloomy disaffection with the masses, in such poems as *The Waste Land* (1922) and *Four Quartets* (1935–44), together with his careful protection of a mandarin cultural tradition, his interest in French symbolism and ancient literary narratives, implicitly indicate a modernism that was a rejection of consumer culture. Although obsessively marking his distinction from Eliot, William Carlos Williams also focused upon modernism as an exhilarating opportunity for cultural renewal, although in his case, without recourse to the dead-end European classical culture. In such works as *Spring and All* (1923), *The Desert Music* (1954), and *Paterson* (1946–63), Williams's modernism manifested itself in an American idiom combined with European aesthetic experiments such as surrealism and cubism, to form a new attention to the elemental locality of the American nation and its vernacular. Famously advocating that there is "no ideas but in things," Williams produced a poetics of collage that sought to make poetry a consequence of a shared community and democracy. Wallace Stevens, another large influence in American modernist poetics, espoused a poetics more closely akin to symbolism. In works like *Harmonium* (1923) and *Ideas of Order* (1935), Stevens focused on "philosophical" preoccupations, although he was also a highly visual poet with lush word patterns and evocative images. Elsewhere Robert Frost turned his back on the fragmented and fractured poetic technique and a manifestly political content, and sought to reinvigorate a deliberately unsophisticated, egalitarian poetry that could be read for aesthetic enjoyment as much as being explored for its more somber preoccupations. In this respect, his *Complete Poems* (1942) shows him to be the heir of the romantic individualism of the Transcendentalists like Emerson and Thoreau. Yet others, like E. E. Cummings, arguably the most technically innovative modernist poet, experimented extensively with grammar, typography, spelling, and word invention. As can be seen in his *Complete Poems* (1972), he put in place a challenging, subversive "disjunctive poetics" that was sufficiently defamiliarizing and eccentric to be simultaneously extolled for its daring originality, and marginalised as a technical novelty that is clever yet ultimately hollow. Hart Crane's *The Bridge* (1930), centered upon the symbol of Brooklyn Bridge, produced a poetics that traversed American history with its exploration of myths of America's origins and its rhetoric of legitimation. Yet such modernist impulses also produced their conservative repercussions. Robinson Jeffers published poetry in such numerous collections as *Flagons and Apples* (1912) and *Roan Stallion, Tamar and Other Poems* (1925) that sounded anxieties about the destruction of nature by human interference. The southern Fugitive Poets (including John Crowe Ransom, Allen Tate, and Robert Penn Warren), gave vent to their anti-industrial agrarian ideology with its feelings of southern despair, historical defeat, alienation from the nation, and efforts to cling to an idealized version of poetry that echoes an earlier genteel tradition, in *The Fugitive* (1922–5) and consolidated in *Fugitives: An Anthology of Verse* (1928). These poets reinforced their poetic practice with the New Criticism, with its stress on ahistorical literary analysis and its focus on the text as an aesthetic object uncluttered by social influence.

Somewhat overshadowed by these male giants, modernism embraced a wide range of practices by poets who are often overlooked but are increasingly being repositioned as central figures. For example, Gertrude Stein's experimentations with words in *Tender Buttons* (1914), and her interrogations of long-established definitions of syntax and grammar, have had a long and varied impact upon a large number of successive writers. Other poets' engagements with the versatility and lability of language have equally gone largely unrecognized: Mina Loy's *Last Lunar Baedeker* (1982) and her interests in Futurism and feminism; H.D.'s (Hilda Doolittle's) treatment of feminism and psychoanalysis in a carefully constructed structure of mythical references in works like *Helen in Egypt* (1961) and *Trilogy, 1944–1946* (1973); Marianne Moore's unending and rigorous ambivalence toward language in her meticulously patterned verse in *Poems* (1921) and *Observations* (1924); the many volumes by Edna St. Vincent Millay with her celebrated sonnet form; Louise Bogan's rich metaphysical poetry in collections such as *Body of This Death* (1923) and *The Sleeping Fury* (1937) that charts a woman's experience in a changing culture; and other contributions from poets such as Amy Lowell with her praised volume *Sword Blades and Poppy Seed* (1914), and Laura Riding's extraordinary pressured language, which in some ways defies the categories of experimental modernism.

Another modernist figure, Louis Zukofsky, emerged as a leading intellectual who bound together a loose affiliation of poets who surfaced in New York during the early 1930s. Sharing common socialist political views and a Judaic heritage, the Objectivists initially comprised Zukofsky, George Oppen, Charles Reznikoff, with William Carlos Williams working on the side, although they later came to include Lorine Niedecker and Carl Rakosi. Zukofsky's seminal 1931 essay, in which he describes "Objectivist" poetics as a combination of "Sincerity and Objectification," adopted a deliberately provocative stance, challenging the prevailing poetics of reason with a new ethical language. For example, Zukofsky speaks about love as a "truer" basis for knowledge than reason in many of his writings, but most notably in the long poem "A." This "new" ethical concern was sustained by the Beats and the San Francisco Renaissance and the Black Mountain School poets, and more recently, it has been evident in the work of the "Language" poets and some of their immediate forebears, such as Larry Eigner, Theodor Enslin, Robert Creeley, Robert Duncan, and Jerome Rothenberg. The Objectivist ethical terms, "love" and "sincerity," appear, in the light of the rhetoric of antihumanism in modernist literary and cultural theory, to be strangely sentimental and naïve. The apparent naïveté rests in the odd juxtapositioning of ethical terms ("sincerity" and "love") with epistemological terms ("objectification" and "reason"). Yet as Roland Barthes has argued, the discourse of feeling was constructed as a transgressive, "unwarranted discourse" within the context of modernism's increasing concern with erotic desire rather than love.[3] The Objectivist lexicon consequently jars uncomfortably with the "epistemological" language of many modernists.

What this Objectivist poetics calls for, on the one hand, is a phenomenological concentration in its insistence that poetry must get at the object, at the thing itself, while on the other hand, it must remain "true" to the object without any interference from the imperialist ego, dismissing any essentialism and calling for the "wisdom" of love or sincerity. The first approach leads to an epistemological and occasionally ontological poetics with a focus on the "being" of the object; while the second approach recognizes the limits of this representation and instead sets up a stance to the world that situates the subject/reader in an ethical relation to the world. Yet it is not simply a case of one discursive pole supplanting and ousting the other. Rather the Objectivist coalition created the conditions for a new ethical poetics to emerge. The Objectivist critical lexicon and poetic practice produced a space wherein the discourse of ethics was gradually recognized as a significant *supplement* to the modernist poetic lexicon of subjectivity, self-identity, and being.

Thus, modernism in the United States produced an exhilarating period for American poetry, in which modernism and politics expanded in a number of directions. Many critics have sought to characterize the development of American poetry as a process of "making it new," following Ezra Pound's time-honored definition of what ought to keep poetry alive. Consequently, a great deal of critical effort has gone into investigating the linguistic play in American twentieth-century poetics. Yet this interest in formalism arguably excludes an equally important preoccupation within modernist poetics – a discourse of responsibility. The linguistic experiments and "games" are not simply formalist in concern but are engaged in a more serious concern with ethics, with rethinking the relationship between language and ethics. Much has been written about the politics of form in American poetry, but little has been specifically written about the ethics of form. The following questions have been central to these poets: In what ways can formal experiments with language be said to have an ethical dimension? What are the ethical responsibilities of a "language"-centered poetry? Of what does an ethical poetry for the late twentieth century consist? I have characterized Objectivist poetics as a "poetics of the limit," which is a proposition that Objectivist poetics developed a powerful utopian and ethical vision, a poetics of the "beyond," of openness to unimagined possibilities and hence a call for a radical transformation of the present.[4] Objectivist poetics disrupts totality as a way of presenting us with a glimpse of what things in their interrelatedness might become if they were allowed to rest in their affinity rather than forever being stuffed into a new system of identification or stifled by an imposed social totality.

Consequently, American modernist poetics was deeply concerned with the problem of how ethics manifests itself as linguistic representation in poetic form. The Objectivist lineage has been first and foremost an indigenous redefinition of American poetic modernism. As David Antin has argued, this poetic lineage has shifted poetics from questions of personal expression to matters of construction and composition; it has reinvented the techniques of collage central to European modernism; and it has adopted at the same time, as Charles Olson says, the example of Williams's and Pound's incorporation of "non-poetic" narrative materials in the making of poetry.[5] This chapter is therefore partly focused upon the more overtly politicized consciousness in American poetry, following the Objectivist tradition, and considers the legacy of the "ethical narrative" to the work of the "Language" poets, as it manifests itself in a distinctive minimalist treatment of words as things in themselves. It is this trajectory of American twentieth-century poetry that provides its most energetic writing. Broadly speaking, this strand of American poetics in the twentieth century has been marked by a particularly vibrant engagement with international and national poetic movements whose concerns have been to reconceive the ways in which we think and operate as human beings. Such efforts include the following broad-spectrum emphases, articulated most cogently by Jerome Rothenberg and Pierre Joris in their introduction to their two-volume anthology, *Poems for the Millennium*:

- a conviction that this century's poetry has been characterized by an overall investigation of new forms of language, consciousness, and social/biological relationships

- a breakdown of the conventional boundaries between poetry, art and politics, leading to reinvigorated poetic practices in which there is an increasing realization of the politics of the referent
- experiments with the unconscious and altered forms of perception (driven by the work of Surrealists in the 1920s, the psychedelic experiments in the 1960s, and the meditative experiments in the 1970s)
- a return to the belief in poetry as a performance, from Futurist and Dadaist innovations, sound-poems, simultaneities, to the "new orality" and the expanded textsound and performances of post-Second World War decades
- language experiments, including sound and performance innovations, as well as experiments with visual and typographical forms, efforts to devise a nonsyntactical (abstract) poetry, and explorations of new languages and those (dialects, creoles, pidgins) that had found themselves on the fringes of accepted literature
- ethnopoetics and related reassessments of the past and of alternative poetics in the present; a widespread attack on the dominance of European "high culture," which has led to an increasing number of movements exploring poetic practices with gender, class or ethnicity at their center[6]

In exploring these emphases, I am concerned with plotting the energy and dynamism that these new trajectories have provided twentieth-century poetry. One should discuss the various trajectories within the development of American poetry, in which different groups of poets demonstrate affiliated interests and stylistic preoccupations, in the full realization that these trajectories should *not* be construed as discrete paths that have no connection with each other. On the contrary, many of these trajectories collide with each other tangentially or more fully, so that, for example, a poet clearly engaged with the poetics of formal innovation may also be regarded as a poet concerned with environmental matters; or a poet who might be preoccupied with issues of epistemology might also clearly be regarded as a neo-romanticist.

Consequently, one finds movements and periods that sit astride each other, often consisting of hybrid interests and crossed paths. For example, by the early 1920s, a series of literary discussions in lower Manhattan (Greenwich Village) and upper Manhattan (Harlem), sections of New York City, was beginning to manifest itself as an African American cultural movement known as the Harlem Renaissance. It was the cultural manifestation in the 1920s of a massive social movement with roots in the broken promises of the post-Civil War Reconstruction period. More than a literary movement and more than a social revolt against racism, the

Harlem Renaissance exalted the unique culture of African Americans and redefined African American expression. African Americans were encouraged to celebrate their heritage and to become "The New Negro," a term coined in 1925 by sociologist and critic Alain LeRoy Locke. The Harlem Renaissance brought the black experience clearly within general American cultural history and its cultural impact was profound. Pursuing an art directly tied to the fortunes of a political agenda and centered upon such common themes as alienation, marginality, the use of folk material, the use of the blues tradition, and the problems of writing for an elite audience, the Renaissance saw a wide variety of work emerge, from Claude McKay's sonnets, Countee Cullen's lyrics, the work of Sterling Brown and James Weldon Johnson, to Langston Hughes's experiments with twelve-bar blues mode. Arguably one of the boldest projects of the period emerges in Jean Toomer's *Cane* (1923), a text that explodes the generic boundaries in a strongly innovative fashion. Defying simple categorization as poetry, prose, or drama, the piece encompasses all three in synthesis of light/dark, North/South, black/white, urban/countryside, narrative closure/fragmentation; this brooding text anticipates modernist and other later twentieth-century developments in creative writing.

Langston Hughes, one of the most significant African American writers of the Harlem Renaissance, was "discovered" working as a hotel bellhop in New York. He keyed into a wide variety of intellectuals, musicians, and black politicians in the 1930s, and went on to become one of the most influential African American writers of the twentieth century. Proud of his folk heritage and steeped in the language and music of the people of Harlem, Hughes often adopted the rhythms and shapes of blues and jazz music in his poetry, foreshadowing the work of people like Amiri Baraka in the 1950s and 1960s. He also used his poetry and other writing to "explain and illuminate the Negro condition in America," fighting for human rights despite his subjection to discrimination. In "The Same," he allies himself with the racial oppressed and exploited around the world, demonstrating an intimate connection between capitalist exploitation and racial prejudice. A poem such as "Negro" celebrates the African American's blackness, showing the early stages of the "Black is Beautiful" campaign launched in the 1960s during the era of civil rights demonstrations. Furthermore, there is the strategy of re-correcting the white perspectives of America, questioning who has a right to America and its literary heritage. So, in "I, Too," he says "I, too, sing America," echoing the famous poems of Walt Whitman in *Leaves of Grass*, in which Hughes offers a critical supplement to Whitman's inevitably white vision of what America meant to the individual. Writing alongside Hughes was Claude McKay. Composing sonnets about black experiences, poems like "If We must Die" or "The Lynching" often demonstrate a clear political edge. "America" demonstrates how there is a love–hate relationship between the African American poet and America: it continues to "feed me bread of bitterness," and "sinks into my throat her tiger's tooth,"[7] but nevertheless, the poet finds himself loving the place, since the worse America treats him, the stronger and more resolute he is to confront its inequalities. There is a Romantic revolutionary urge to stand up against oppression and the poems seek to raise consciousness about injustice, oppression, inequality, and the perpetuation of modern slavery.

An important period of self-awareness and the celebration of African American cultural heritage, the Harlem Renaissance augmented a clear period of politics in poetry, yet one that was clearly oriented by an ethical vision of the United States. In addition to the Objectivists and the poets of the Harlem Renaissance, other poetries were similarly engaged in an overt energetic espousal of ethics and politics in the 1930s and 1940s. The relation of social and political issues to poetry was hotly debated in such journals as *The Masses, Liberator, The New Masses, Dynamo, Morada, The Anvil,* and *Partisan Review,* and in much of the poetry of the period, either directly or indirectly. Michael Gold wrote manifestos exhorting a proletarian poetry; John Wheelwright produced a hybrid poetry of Christianity and Marxism; Muriel Rukeyser produced a strongly committed first book of poetry entitled *Theory of Flight* (1935); and this is not to mention work by poets as diverse as Genevieve Taggard, Edna St. Vincent Millay, E. E. Cummings, Richard Wright, Edgar Lee Masters, Edwin Markham, William Vaughn Moody, Lola Ridge, Gwendolyn Brooks, and Carl Sandburg, all of whom contributed to the range of socially engaged poetry marked "political" in the period.

The inheritance of modernism passed on in the late 1940s and 1950s to several groups of poets, among whom were a middle generation of American poets: John Berryman, Elizabeth Bishop, Randall Jarrell, Robert Lowell, Theodore Roethke, Karl Shapiro, and Delmore Schwartz. With the edifices and monuments of traditionalism well and truly undermined by the first wave of modernism, these poets were not involved in the same wholesale aesthetic sabotage of Pound or Carlos Williams. Nonetheless, despite this ease of acceptance – some, like Lowell and Jarrell, achieved considerable literary reputations – their poetics did not break formal molds and in many ways, their poetry can be seen as a literary counterpart to the social conformity and bourgeois respectability of Cold War America. Theirs was a poetry shorn of the ethical poignancy of a poetics striving for a new language and form to deal with the pressures of postwar consciousness. This contentment and complacency are also evident in the next generation of poets, often termed the "New Formalists," such as James Merrill, W. S. Merwin, and Richard Wilbur, whose poetry was reminiscent of pre-modernist meters and forms, with more than a whiff of nostalgia about it. Arguably, it was Lowell and Berryman alone of these poets who carved out a more transgressive poetics, gradually breaking with the confines of traditional metrical verse. The so-called Confessional poets of the 1950s, who included poets like Lowell and Berryman, but also Anne Sexton, Sylvia Plath, and W. D. Snodgrass, sought to define the creative act as a process of raw self-exposure, an unmediated expression of inner, urgent emotion stirred up by personal, and often acute, experiences. In this, they managed to create "permission" for poets to utilize intense emotion and autobiographical subjects, exploring as they did such personal experiences as madness, hatred, drugs, and the proclivity to suicide. Less a movement than poets working in a like-minded manner, Lowell's autobiographical *Life Studies* (1959) had paved the way, followed by Sexton's *To Bedlam and Part Way Back* (1960), Plath's *Ariel* (1965), and Berryman's *Dream Songs* (1964–9). In other areas, A. R. Ammons developed a meticulous meditative poetics interested in particularity and the general; while moving in feminist directions, Adrienne Rich developed a poetics of complexity, irony, and intense structural patterns alongside these poets in the 1950s and 1960s. Her poetry became increasingly political and less private: her concerns were sexual politics, the Vietnam war, and issues of language and representation, evident in widely acclaimed volumes like *Diving into the Wreck* (1973) and *The Dream of a Common Language* (1978).

For all the permissiveness of the Confessional poets, the lineage of Objectivist poetics with its ethical strand and disruptive activity in poetics was more properly inherited by the development of Projectivist or Black Mountain poetics, which emerged under the dominant leadership of Charles Olson at Black Mountain College in North Carolina in the 1950s. A leading alternative college of its day, it was home to a wide variety of major figures, including painters, composers, and dancers, and poets such as Robert Creeley, Ed Dorn, Hilda Morley, John Wieners, Robert Duncan, and Denise Levertov were associated with it in various ways. The founding rationale for Black Mountain poetics occurred primarily in the teachings and writings of Olson, particularly in his essay "Projective Verse" (1950). In that essay, Olson puts the case for what he calls an "open" poetry, in which "FIELD COMPOSITION" substitutes for the "closed form" of previous poetics. Olson quotes Robert Creeley's statement that "FORM IS NEVER MORE THAN AN EXTENSION OF CONTENT" and insists on the compositional pressure of poetry in his addition that "always one perception must must must MOVE, INSTANTER, ON ANOTHER."[8] Attention to the line as a unit of breath is a major principle of Black Mountain poetics, although this was a flexible and non-prescriptive formulation. This style was reflected in the typography of the poems themselves, as the length of each line and the line-breaks indicated the unit or measure of utterance. Such a reaching for new representations, at every moment in writing, necessitates the practice of a new ethic of perception, an "ALTERNATIVE TO THE EGO-POSITION" as Olson put it.[9] Language cannot be rigidly codified, regulated, or programmatically structured as Pound for example thought, since it is in a state of perpetual movement. This diminishes the importance of the dominant, co-ordinating subject, "the lyrical interference of the individual as ego,"[10] which in turn opens the way for the reader to participate in the performance of the writing. The concern of Black Mountain College writers for maintaining the "breath of the word" in their writing, the physical performative dimension of discursive practice, is part of their attempt to reintegrate language with the dynamics of social context. Olson's attempt to return language to the sphere of dialectical movement is evident in such works as his huge epic *The Maximus Poems* (1960–8) and shorter works like "The Kingfishers" (1950); and these poems and Olson's intellectual rationalizations of his poetics, formed one of the major trajectories for subsequent developments in post-Second World War developments in American poetry.

Another frequent touchstone for discussions about the development of American poetry in the post Second World War decades was the appearance of two influential poetry anthologies in the 1960s. Donald Hall's *New Poets of England and America* (1962) and Donald Allen's *The New American Poetry: 1945–1960* (1960). Hall's anthology presented a collection of poets who adhered to a notion of traditional craftsmanship and subject matter, and believed that poems should be well-made objects to be evaluated independently of the author's intentions or private experiences. Allen's anthology, by contrast, set out to celebrate the irrational and spontaneous instead of the decorous and elegant. Reaching back to the likes of Whitman and Carlos Williams, Allen's poets saw themselves as accentuating the American idiom and landscape. Although mostly male, many were from the "new" ethnic backgrounds: Jewish, Irish, Italian, black, and gay – and they lived in New York or San Francisco, engaging closely with other arts such as jazz and painting. The most celebrated of this new group of poets was the Beat movement led by Allen Ginsberg and Jack Kerouac, including poets like Gregory Corso, Gary Snyder, Lawrence Ferlinghetti, Kenneth Rexroth, Michael McClure, Lew Welsh, William Everson, Philip Whalen, and Philip Lamantia. Five years before Allen's anthology saw the light of day, the San

Francisco Renaissance and the Beat movement was "born" at a fêted reading event at the Six Gallery in San Francisco in autumn 1955, described by Kerouac in *The Dharma Bums*.[11] The word "Beat," first used by Kerouac, implied exhausted, beatitude, and the jazz improvization that inspired so many Beat writers. In many respects, the social impact of the Beats is incalculable – many of the things we take for granted today stemmed directly or indirectly from their impact, not only in terms of lifestyle but also in terms of civil liberties, such as the relaxation of censorship. Though their work has been understandably attacked by feminist critics, they were not entirely oblivious to gender issues and one can see in aspects of their work the formation of a nascent gay sensibility. They undoubtedly widened the expressive potential of literature, breaking the back of the elitism of the New Criticism and opening literature up to an unending series of collaborations with other forms of expression, particularly in the field of music. Yet Beat writing contained a range of different ethical engagements: in Snyder's work such as *Myths and Texts* (1960) and *Turtle Island* (1974), one gets a spare, meditative, Zen-like poetics that presages much of the current interest in ecocriticism; in McClure's works like *Hymn to Saint Geryon* (1959), one gets a poetics that is closely associated with the physical body and primitivism; in Ginsberg's poetry, one gets an angry social prophet in a poetics that is vivid, direct, declamatory, and provocative, and in collections like *Howl and Other Poems* (1956), one can detect the influence of jazz improvization and sense of measure in its spontaneous style and free deviation. Despite these varieties, Beat writing was ecstatic, oral, and incantatory – offering irreverent perspectives on contemporary social circumstances and aiming to enlarge public consciousness about the pressures of conformity in the 1950s.

Poets centrally associated with the New York School, such as John Ashbery, Frank O'Hara, Kenneth Koch, Barbara Guest, and James Schuyler, were not entirely oblivious to the influence of the Beats, although their principal influences stemmed from French experimentalism, especially the fictional work of Raymond Roussel. Although eschewing a programmatic ideology, a good outline of their aesthetic ideas and stance is to be found in O'Hara's essay "Personism: A Manifesto," something of a caricature of Olson's essay "Projective Verse." According to O'Hara, personist poetry is driven by the immediacy and uninterrupted impact of everyday experience, and his notion that "You just go on your nerve"[12] clearly echoes the spontaneity and anti-formalism of the Beats. Yet other poets such as Ashbery and Koch did not entirely adhere to this approach, since their use of such forms as the sestina, sonnet, and ottava rima suggests a hybrid style of the traditional with the innovative. Several of these poets are attracted to parody and pop culture (see for example, Ashbery's references to Popeye in "Farm Implements and Rutabagas in a Landscape"), and contest clear distinctions between high and low culture. In many respects, form emerges as an essential preoccupation for these poets, not least since a few of them were active art curators and critics. Of this group, Ashbery surfaces as a principal figure in American poetry, especially after the publication of *The Tennis Court Oath* (1962) and *Self-Portrait in a Convex Mirror* (1975). His poetry manifests one of the defining terms of postmodernism – indeterminacy, or the conditionality of truth – as his poetry becomes a form of representing the unpresentable in its obliqueness and allusional tactics. Characteristic of an age in which forms of authority and legitimacy are increasingly suspected as the covert imposition of hegemonic ideologies, Ashbery's compositional techniques steer away from closure and finality, leaving the text in a series of unstable and unfixed quandaries, such as the play of the words "I," "you," and "poem" in "Paradoxes and Oxymorons." As this poem indicates, Ashbery is less concerned with the definition of a poem, and more with the mind processes of thinking with things as the poem emerges. There followed in the late 1960s a second generation of the New York School, including Ted Berrigan, Ron Padgett, Anne Waldman, Tom Clark, Bernadette Mayer, and Amiri Baraka. A pulsating and audacious poetry scene firmly rooted in a culture of publicly performed poetry, it was located in New York's Lower East Side at such venues as Les Deux Mégots, Le Metro, and the Poetry Project at St. Mark's Church (which has proved to be a seminal forum for poets to this day). The import for literary history of this loosely defined community of writers lies partially in its reclamation of an orally centered poetic tradition, modified to develop the possibilities for an aesthetically bold, mischievous poetics and a libidinal politics of resistance.

Further developments in the period from the 1950s and to the mid-1970s include the significant impact of Jerome Rothenberg's study of ethnopoetics and multiculturalism, performance poetry, and the emergence of the term "deep image." Inspired by the Spanish Andalusian "deep song," and the surrealist-influenced work of Lorca, "deep image" poetics sought to capture the essence of a perception in a moment of near mystical enlightenment. Resonant, stylized, and heroic in tone, "deep image" poems tend to be structured as a series of self-sufficient images, and although there were some serious exponents of this technique such as Diane Wakoski, Clayton Eshleman, and Robert Kelly, it was a short-lived and unsystematic approach that could not really be described as a school or movement in its own right. Robert Bly, a key figure in this group, who perceived Anglo-American modernism as a cul-de-sac, sought to separate the interior from the social. In *Silence in the Snowy Fields* (1962), one gets a poetics in which the poet abandons the social world to perform a spiritual voyage toward self-transcendence. Often producing a poetry akin to the Beats in their visionary mystical insights, Bly opened a path for poets like Galway Kinnell, W. S. Merwin, Louis Simpson, and James Wright, all of whom found in the unconscious a basis for ethical values, which can in turn be used to assess contemporary political realities like the iniquitous effects of industrial capitalism or the Vietnam War. Another significant approach is the development of aleatorical or chance procedures, most notably in the work of John Cage and Jackson Mac Low. For example, Cage's compositions frequently depend upon non-intentional methods, such as mesostics and the use of *I Ching* casting operations to free language from the confines of syntax and to defamiliarize it. Echoing some of the activities of Dada, Mac Low uses similar procedures for the production of randomly generated statements; and although aleatory poetry was not widely practiced, it nevertheless re-emphasized the preoccupations of indeterminacy and performativity that so characterized postmodern poetics.

In the 1970s and 1980s, a number of poets sought to rescue a poetry of meter and coherent discursive narrative destroyed by the modernists in the 1920s and their subsequent emulators. Distrustful of the forms and styles of the 1960s radicals, volumes like Robert Pinsky's *An Explanation of America* (1979) and C. K. Williams's *I Am the Bitter Name* (1972) contained stinging political critique, yet in measured, discursive lines that steered clear of challenges to poetic convention and its experiments in style and composition. A poetic ally of Pinsky, Robert Haas has garnered equal public acclaim for his less traditional metrical and more fragmented verse, in volumes like *Praise* (1979) and *Human Wishes* (1989). Other poets of this generation include Frank Bidart, Sharon Olds, Louise Glück, Jorie Graham, Carolyn Forché, and Philip Levine, poets who are not necessarily affiliated with one another but whose poetics engage with ordinary everyday events and subjects and often show traits of the Confessional poets in the range and intensity of emotion represented in their poems.

1978 saw the launch of a small, New York-based magazine called L=A=N=G=U=A=G=E, which was to be something of a landmark for an emerging tendency within American avant-garde writing, the so-called "Language" poets. These writers were particularly interested in redefining the unit of linguistic awareness from the line to the word, but also more broadly in the relation of aesthetics to politics, in challenging the reification of language. Poets such as Lyn Hejinian, Barrett Watten, Bob Perelman, Bruce Andrews, Charles Bernstein, Ron Silliman, Carla

Harryman, Rae Armantrout, Leslie Scalapino, Diane Ward, Susan Howe, and Robert Grenier, found their precursors in the poetic "lineage" that includes the Objectivists, the European avant-garde, and aspects of the Beats and the Black Mountain poets. Writing, publishing, and reviewing their own poetry and theoretical essays in self-established small journals and "manifesto" magazines like L=A=N=G=U=A=G=E, *This, Tottel's, Poetics Journal, Hills,* and *The Difficulties,* the "Language" poets practiced a strategic engagement with contemporary theories of language, subjectivity, and aesthetics, to challenge the orthodoxies of canonical and normative poetries, showing how this becomes a means of combating reification in modern society, which is itself motivated by deep ethical concerns.

The eruption of "Language" poetry in the 1980s – with the important anthology by Ron Silliman entitled *In The American Tree* (1986), and the books on poetics such as the compilation edited by Bruce Andrews and Charles Bernstein entitled *The L=A=N=G=U=A=G=E Book* (1984), Barrett Watten's *Total Syntax* (1985), Steve McCaffrey's *North of Intention* (1986), Ron Silliman's *The New Sentence* (1987), Charles Bernstein's *The Politics of Poetic Form* (1990) and *A Poetics* (1992) – belies the fact that many of these writers had been active since the late 1960s and early 1970s. In fact, if it is not too early to write its history, "Language" poetry appears to have had at least two phases to its development so far. Earlier works, for example Silliman's *Crow* (1971) and *Mohawk* (1973); Andrews's *Vowels* (1976), *Praxis* (1978), and *Jeopardy* (1980); and David Melnick's *Pcoet* (1975), often show experiments with single letters, words, or signifiers. For instance, *Crow* explores the phonemic associations and combinations between and in words by splitting syllables across lines:

> ma
> chines
> shines.[13]

Mohawk explores similar patternings of words, repeating in various grids and designs a "core" set of words. Each page works like a template for the succeeding page, albeit a template for variation.

The aesthetic ideology underpinning this early poetic practice of "Language" poetry appears to have been partly motivated by a desire to wipe the linguistic slate clean, refocusing attention on how words operate without the conventional clutter of grammatical apparatus. Rather than continuity, the emphasis falls on discontinuities, interruptions, and disjunctions; and it is clear that linearity is only one means of effecting significance, not the sole means. Meaning arises from the juxtaposition of words, phrases, syllables.

This self-reflexive arrangement of language – language writing itself – raises the question of what happens when images cease to register for the reader and yet the writing goes on being produced. The poem suggests by this "listing" procedure that units of meaning integrate into wholes as a basic process of reading. The signifying chain can begin with any word, at any point, and a narrative can be "constructed." Yet, as Andrews has written on another occasion, "Think don't narrate": it is precisely such "narrativizing," formalizing impulses that the poem interrupts, as any imposition of form becomes a hypostatization.

There are limits to this exploration through the single-unit focus, ignoring as it does the operations of ideology at work in larger organizational units of form, grammar, and narrative production. "Language" poets appear to have recognized such limitations around the early 1980s, when they began to examine and experiment with larger forms, moving into a second phase, in works like Barrett Watten's *Complete Thought* (1982), Ron Silliman's *Tjanting* (1986), Lyn Hejinian's *My Life* (1980), and Charles Bernstein's *The Sophist* (1987). An increasing interest in how forms shape, reinforce, or interfere with language systems and their structures of significance also begins to become apparent. These take a whole variety of shapes: for instance, experiments with typography, as in Bruce Andrews's *Love Songs* (1982); the interaction of different modes of signification, like the juxtaposition of visual images with text, or the juxtaposition of different texts superimposed upon one another, as in the collaborative poem *LEGEND* (1980); or the substitution of syllables or letters to produce unexpectedly different signifiers in familiar phrasal constructions ('Would you do me the flavor of buying that sty?'), as in Bernstein's poem 'Outrigger' in *The Sophist*.[14]

It might be argued that Charles Bernstein and many of the "Language" poets sought to release an "alternative" Other that has been systematically and repeatedly suppressed by the structures of writing. Yet that "Other" finds itself everywhere in the contemporary United States. One astonishing piece of information is that twenty years ago, there were simply no acknowledged, much less published, Native American "poets" in America, albeit a handful of exceptions which proved the rule, and went unheralded as American writers. A renaissance occurred in the 1960s partly driven by such new anthologies as Jerome Rothenberg's *Shaking the Pumpkin* (1972). Nowadays, developments in contemporary American poetry could not ignore poets such as James Welch, Joy Harjo, Wendy Rose, and Simon Ortiz. The Native American is, of course, heavy with romantic representation in narratives about American westward expansion, from Puritan narratives to contemporary Hollywood films. However, the onetime frontier that separated the forces of "civilization" and the "savages" i[s] easily distinguishable. Joy Harjo, a member of the Creek tribe[,] lished several collections of poetry, amongst which are *She H[e] Horses* (1983) and *In Mad Love and War* (1989). Harjo's work e[,] issues of hybrid ethnicity and interrogates myths of American identity, [s] working by repetition (reminiscent of the steady beat of the ceremo[nial] drum), and her poems often depict the mesa-strewn territory of the South[,] west, with a rich lushness of feel for the landscape. The function of memory in writing the past crops up time and again, especially as it functions as a source of the forgotten, marginalized, obscured past. In "Remember," Harjo speaks of identity formed by the relation with the earth and the landscape. Memory's power lies in forming the history, identity, and present consciousness of people. The implication of the poems is that to forget is an abandonment of self-identity, a self-crippling, a surrender to the dominant culture which is in effect an alienation. Lines from "New Orleans" speak of memory that "swims deep in blood, / a delta in the skin," and in an interview, Harjo is asked about this line:

Int: You said once, memory is like "a delta in the skin", so you are "memory alive," your poetry stems from memory always at work.
Harjo: It is Creek, and touches on the larger tribal continental memory and the larger human memory, global. It's not something I consciously chose; I mean, I am not a full-blood, but it was something that chose me, that lives in me, and I cannot deny it. Sometimes I wish I could disappear into the crowds of the city and lose this responsibility, because it is a responsibility. But I can't. I also see memory as not just associated with past history, past events, past stories, but nonlinear, as in future and ongoing history, events, and stories. And it changes.[15]

Harjo's work, like that of so many Native American poets, is about survival, the perpetuation and longevity of Native American traditions and cultures: in this, she speaks for the dispossessed, the lost of rural, urban, and reservation America. Her poetry is a constant celebration of the struggle to survive against all the odds; and in this respect, she seeks to reclaim a language, culture, and ways of telling.

Engaged in much the same reclamation and rewriting of an ignored culture as the Native American poets, is Chicano/Chicana writing, a development in ethnic poetry of major significance in recent decades. When one thinks of literature of the American West, it is generally not that of the Latino/Latina peoples that springs to mind. Instead, Mexican populations in films seem to be either the bandits or outlaws, or the silent and passive victims of American individualism and entrepreneurship gone awry, as in the film *The*

Seven. However, recent scholarship and writing are attempting
. and restore the American Hispanic contribution to American
e. The uniquely "Wild West" of the untamed American frontier, a
of unlimited opportunity, has been transformed into an academic
ourse about borders, where multiple intersecting cultures engage in
mplex interactions of resistance and accommodation, conflict and assimi-
ation, most notably in Gloria Anzaldua's work entitled Borderlands/La
Frontera. Both literal and metaphorical relationships with the land play an
important role in questions about race and gender. Just as the history of the
West has a past longer than the United States of America and its Puritan roots,
so does the literature of the area. Marked by the Nuyorican Café poets,
Jimmy Santiago Baca, Pedro Pietri, Victor Hernandez Cruz, Gary Soto, Tato
Laviera, Lorna Cervantes, and Pat Mora, the 1990s witnessed an explosion of Latino/Latina writing, and not just in various and diverse forms,
but also in the distinctions which compose the Latin-American population, such as Mexicano/Chicano, Cuban, and Puerto Rican. Key issues
that find their way into the poetry of these writers are representations of
the West rewritten as a site of resistance and border tension; the ways in
which intersecting cultures result in syncretic mixtures, racial and cultural
mestizaje (the mixing of cultures and races); and the use of the land as
both a literal and metaphorical reflection of ethnic identity. Representing
persistent suffering from racial prejudice, the poetry often takes the form
of cultural instruction, to Chicanos as well as white Americans, as in
Abelardo Delgardo's poem "Stupid America," which laments the waste of
aesthetic talents through the ignorance of the American population. Concentrating upon the hand as an instrument of creation or destruction, it
questions whether the Chicano hand will be allowed to contribute to
America or be forced to destroy it. Albeit with regard to a different
ethnic context, similar questions about identity, origins, and belonging,
are asked by Asian American poets like Li-Young Lee, Garrett Hongo,
Kimiko Hahn, and Cathy Song.

Many critics have written about the so-called "linguistic turn" apparent
in the work of the "Language" poets and in other recent contemporary
poetry. Yet if the "linguistic turn" was the realization of the dependence of
consciousness on language, a major factor in the discrediting of subjectivity
as a principle of modernity, then the "ethical turn" of the late 1980s and
early 1990s was a reinstatement of the responsibilities of subjectivity. However, this reinstated subject is not a sovereign, founding subject but one that
is shaped by models of existence which look to aesthetic experience and its
forms as ways of understanding aspects of subjectivity that are not reducible
to the cognitive or the rational. Hence, music becomes important in art as a

model that is most distant from representation. This goes hand-in-hand with ideas of the subversion of self-consciousness based on language as the representation of the ideas of the subject. Bruce Andrews confirms this ethical stance in his introduction to the anthology *Floating Capital: New Poets from London*: "Reading? The reader builds *in relation to* (every possible phenomenology and ethnomethodology is a sourcebook) embodiments of next as Other, as activity of Facework. The *I* departure is the multiplication of I."[16] Language attesting to the word of the Other in sound becomes the basis for an ethical poetics. All the efforts of the post-Beat poets to introduce a new spoken poetry, of writing seeking the performance of the tongue and intersubjective communication, enacts this ethical attestation to the Other. As Charles Bernstein has said of his poetic practice, "I prefer the wrong way – anything better than the well-wrought epiphany of predictable measure – for at least the cracks and flaws and awkwardnesses show signs of real life."[17] Lying in these cracks and fissures, is a sort of "negative identity," where the reader gets glimmers of another social structure, another sexual ideology, another life-world, through the current language of the day. To this degree, this writing is a "situated ethics," one that poses an alternative to a coercive moral absolutism on one hand and to an inchoate postmodernist relativism on the other. Poetic activity of this sort becomes an ethical poetry, a "poetics of the limit," that becomes a poetics of interruption. This "ethical turn" is part of an attempt to preserve the role of the subject in view, while respecting the difference of the (other) object, and forms a principal characteristic of the diversity of practice in the different trajectories of American twentieth-century poetry.

NOTES

1. Ezra Pound, "A Retrospect," in *The Literary Essays of Ezra Pound*, ed. T. S. Eliot (London: Faber, 1954), p. 3.
2. Ezra Pound, "Vorticism," *Fortnightly Review* (September 1914): 573.
3. Roland Barthes, *A Lover's Discourse, Fragments* (1977; Harmondsworth: Penguin, 1990).
4. Tim Woods, *The Poetics of the Limit: Ethics and Politics in Modern and Contemporary American Poetry* (New York and Basingstoke: Palgrave Macmillan, 2002).
5. David Antin, "Modernism and Postmodernism: Approaching the Present in American Poetry," *boundary* 2, 1 (Fall 1972): 98–133.
6. Jerome Rothenberg and Pierre Joris (eds.), *Poems for the Millennium* (Berkeley: University of California Press), pp. 2–3.
7. *The Poems of Claude McKay* (New York: Harcourt, Brace and Company, 1922), poem 3.

8. Charles Olson, "Projective Verse," in *Charles Olson: Selected Writings* (New York: New Directions, 1966), p. 16.
9. Charles Olson, *Mayan Letters* (London: Jonathan Cape, 1968), p. 29.
10. Olson, "Projective Verse," p. 24.
11. Jack Kerouac, *The Dharma Bums* (1958; London: Grafton, 1972), p. 14.
12. Charles Bernstein, "Outrigger," *The Sophist* (Los Angeles: Sun and Moon, 1987), pp. 27–30.
13. Ron Silliman, *Crow* (Ithaca, NY: Ithaca House, 1971), p. 10.
14. Charles Bernstein, "Outrigger" *The Sophist* (Los Angeles: Sun and Moon, 1987), pp. 27–30.
15. Joy Harjo, interview in Laura Coltelli (ed.), *Winged Words: American Indian Writers Speak* (Lincoln: University of Nebraska Press, 1990), p. 57.
16. Bruce Andrews's introduction to Adrian Clarke and Robert Sheppard (eds.), *Floating Capital: New Poets from London* (Elmwood, CT: Potes and Poets Press, 1991), p. iv.
17. Charles Bernstein, *A Poetics* (Cambridge, MA: Harvard University Press 1992), p. 2.

FUTHER READING

Michael Davidson, *The San Francisco Renaissance: Poetics and Community at Mid-century*, Cambridge: Cambridge University Press, 1989.

Elisabeth A. Frost, *The Feminist Avant-garde in American Poetry*, Iowa City: University of Iowa Press, 2003.

Richard Gray, *American Poetry of the Twentieth Century*, London, Longman, 1990.

Robert von Hallberg, *American Poetry and Culture, 1945–1980*, Cambridge, MA: Harvard University Press, 1985.

James de Jongh, *Vicious Modernism: Black Harlem and the Literary Imagination*, Cambridge: Cambridge University Press, 1990.

James Longenbach, *Modern Poetry after Modernism*, New York: Oxford University Press, 1997.

Marjorie Perloff, *The Poetics of Indeterminacy*, Evanston, IL: Northwestern University Press, 1981.

Radical Artifice: Writing Poetry in the Age of Media, Chicago: University of Chicago Press, 1991.

Peter Quartermain, *Disjunctive Poetics*, Cambridge: Cambridge University Press, 1992.

Andrew Ross, *The Failure of Modernism: Symptoms of American Poetry*, New York: Columbia University Press, 1986.

Geoff Ward, *Statutes of Liberty: The New York School of Poets*, London: Macmillan, 1993.

Tim Woods, *The Poetics of the Limit: Ethics and Politics in Modern and Contemporary American Poetry*, New York and Basingstoke: Palgrave Macmillan, 2002.

INDEX

CAMBRIDGE COMPANIONS TO LITERATURE

The Cambridge Companion to William Blake edited by Morris Eaves

The Cambridge Companion to Wordsworth edited by Stephen Gill

The Cambridge Companion to Coleridge edited by Lucy Newlyn

The Cambridge Companion to Byron edited by Drummond Bone

The Cambridge Companion to Keats edited by Susan J. Wolfson

The Cambridge Companion to Shelley edited by Timothy Morton

The Cambridge Companion to Mary Shelley edited by Esther Schor

The Cambridge Companion to Jane Austen edited by Edward Copeland and Juliet McMaster

The Cambridge Companion to the Brontës edited by Heather Glen

The Cambridge Companion to Charles Dickens edited by John O. Jordan

The Cambridge Companion to George Eliot edited by George Levine

The Cambridge Companion to Thomas Hardy edited by Dale Kramer

The Cambridge Companion to Oscar Wilde edited by Peter Raby

The Cambridge Companion to George Bernard Shaw edited by Christopher Innes

The Cambridge Companion to W. B. Yeats edited by Marjorie Howes and John Kelly

The Cambridge Companion to Joseph Conrad edited by J. H. Stape

The Cambridge Companion to D. H. Lawrence edited by Anne Fernihough

The Cambridge Companion to Virginia Woolf edited by Sue Roe and Susan Sellers

The Cambridge Companion to James Joyce, second edition edited by Derek Attridge

The Cambridge Companion to T. S. Eliot edited by A. David Moody

The Cambridge Companion to Ezra Pound edited by Ira B. Nadel

The Cambridge Companion to W. H. Auden edited by Stan Smith

The Cambridge Companion to Beckett edited by John Pilling

The Cambridge Companion to Harold Pinter edited by Peter Raby

The Cambridge Companion to Tom Stoppard edited by Katherine E. Kelly

The Cambridge Companion to Herman Melville edited by Robert S. Levine

The Cambridge Companion to Nathaniel Hawthorne edited by Richard Millington

The Cambridge Companion to Harriet Beecher Stowe edited by Cindy Weinstein

The Cambridge Companion to Theodore Dreiser edited by Leonard Cassuto and Claire Virginia Eby

The Cambridge Companion to Willa Cather edited by Marilee Lindemann

The Cambridge Companion to Edith Wharton edited by Millicent Bell

The Cambridge Companion to Henry James edited by Jonathan Freedman

The Cambridge Companion to Walt Whitman edited by Ezra Greenspan

The Cambridge Companion to Ralph Waldo Emerson edited by Joel Porte and Saundra Morris

The Cambridge Companion to Henry David Thoreau edited by Joel Myerson

The Cambridge Companion to Mark Twain edited by Forrest G. Robinson

The Cambridge Companion to Edgar Allan Poe edited by Kevin J. Hayes

The Cambridge Companion to Emily Dickinson edited by Wendy Martin

The Cambridge Companion to William Faulkner edited by Philip M. Weinstein

The Cambridge Companion to Ernest Hemingway edited by Scott Donaldson

The Cambridge Companion to F. Scott Fitzgerald edited by Ruth Prigozy

The Cambridge Companion to Robert Frost edited by Robert Faggen

The Cambridge Companion to Sylvia Plath edited by Jo Gill

The Cambridge Companion to Ralph Ellison edited by Ross Posnock

The Cambridge Companion to Eugene O'Neill edited by Michael Manheim

The Cambridge Companion to Tennessee Williams edited by Matthew C. Roudané

The Cambridge Companion to Arthur Miller edited by Christopher Bigsby

The Cambridge Companion to David Mamet edited by Christopher Bigsby

The Cambridge Companion to Sam Shepard edited by Matthew C. Roudané

The Cambridge Companion to Edward Albee edited by Stephen J. Bottoms

CAMBRIDGE COMPANIONS TO CULTURE